THE XOO BOOK
a guide to exozoology

edited by Michael Joseph Halm
with contributions by Lemcia Mal

"Until Heaven and Earth pass away ...
until it all comes true." (Mt 5:18)

© 2017 by Hierogamous Enterprises
Cincinnati, Ohio

OTHER TITLES FROM   HIEROGAMOUS ENTERPRISES

- *Cross Words with Jesus*
- *Proverbials: Proverbs in Verse*
- *Psalms, Hymns and Inspired Songs: self-hate to Love through the Scriptures*
- *Reignbeau's Riddles and Rhymes*
- *Sherlock Holmes and the Mad Doctor*
- *The   Wizard   Who Couldn't and Other Basilian Tales*

and coming soon: *How to Ger High*

'ell-'ound: [headless hell-hound] see heath-hound

'i'iwi: [*National Geographic Encyclopedia of Animals*] nectar, insect and invertebrate-eating songbird from Hawaii, Terra (alpha Zodiaci III)

á baoa qu: [*The Book of Imaginary Beings* by Luis Borges] peach-fuzzy, eyeless, tentacled transparent cephalopodan

a-kao-ut: [*Space Pirate* by Jack Vance] swift flyer from Pherasic

A. C.: [astral cat acronym, Monster Galaxy] turquoise lynx-like felinoid with star on forehead

a'kweth: [Star Trek] sandworm from T'Khasi, Nevasa (40 Eridani) system

aa: [stirianaa mondegreen,] genengineering bacteria from Stiria, Stir system

aad: [i-less aiad] cave dragonfly from Friatica, Friaticalida system, Galaxiki galaxy

aalaus: [German aal-laus portmanteau] louse-like insectoid pest infesting eels from Germa system

aalth: [Ba-Golik] small pet from T'Khasi, Nevasa (40 Eridani) system

aan: [devaaan mondegreen] swarming insectoid from Deva system

aant: [*St. Nia's Saints*: "St. Naa's Aants"] 2-headed ant-like insectoid from Naa's star system

aapaard: [Dutch aap-paard portmanteau, palindrome] centauroid with ape-like upper body and horse-like lower body from Draapa binary system

aapep: pleated "moon serpent" from Egypt, Terra (alpha Zodiaci III)

aard: [aardvark, aardwolf backformation] burrowing ancestor of aardvarks, aardsharks and aardwolves

aardshark: [aardvark-shark portmanteau] large, voracious, hairy amphibian with large ears, long tubular snout and both claws and fins

aariov: ["The Giants of Pigell" by Wim Vandemaan] fist-sized, ochre yellow ichthyoid from Pigell (Vega (alpha Lyrae) VIII)

aasfesser: ["scavenger", "World of Primordial Soup" by Arndt Ellmer] crab-like pest from Camouflage, Jamondi cluster

aatxe: ultradimensional bovine from Spain, Terra (alpha Zodiaci III)

aatxegorri: red steer from Spain, Terra (alpha Zodiaci III)

aazab: [bazaar aazab palindrome dark rose ornithoid from Baza binary system

aazgont: ["Manhunt on Lepso" by Dirk Hess] 8-legged crocodililan with blue-red scales used for recording infrared images from Hakain IV

ab: [bananivore ananymondegreen] bipedal, green carnivore with bushy tail and collar from Erovina stsem; [bananaeater ananymonde-green] nector-eating anteater-like creature from Retaetna system

aba: [Space Patrol: "Husky Becomes Invisible"] ornithoid whose eggs cure "the floats" from Mars (alpha Zodiaci IV)

abac: monster from Lake Llyon Llion, Wales, Terra (alpha Zodiaci III)

abada: [*Dell Crossword Puzzle Dictionary*] rhinoceras; [Mythical Creatures List] Congo unicorn, aka abath

abaia: large, deep lake eel from Melanesia, Terra (alpha Zodiaci III)

aballin: [Forgotten Realms] ooze like stagnant water but acidic

abannic: [cinnabar abannic palindrome, (*The World of Synnabarr* by Raymond C. S. McCracken] red-orange ornithoid from Mars (fka alpha Zodiaci IV))

abath: see abada

abay: [yabanarisi ananymondegreen] wasp-like insectoid from Isira system

abbagouchie: [museumofhoaxes.com by Alex Boese] creature like owl, fox and deer from Puerto Rico, Terra (alpha Zodiaci III) [Jim Wilson at Webster Echo] aka "dryland piranha"

ābbe-i-chahār-sar: [beheaded dābbe-i-chahār-sar] 3-headed, winged creature

abma: [abma yamba palindrome] yamba-like amphisbæna

abnauayu: alma-like pongoid from Caucasus mts., Terra (alpha Zodiaci III)

aboma: [*Dell Crossword Puzzle Dictionary*] snake from S. America, Terra (alpha Zodiaci III)

abomzo: [Outernauts] mature chumzo with large forelegs and back spikes

aborpmi: [improbable elb aborpmi palindrome] rare variety of elb-like spheroid, see isualpmi

abraxan: [*Fantastic Beasts and Where to Find Them* by Newton Artemis Fido Scamander] giant, palomino pegasus

abs: ["The Hypno-ball" by Kurt Brand] roo-like carnivore with 2-fingered "hands" from Lovely

abtu: [*Book of the Dead* by Budge] ultradimensional creature

aburra: [kookaburra mondegreen] ornitoid ancestor of cuckoo and kookaburra

Abydonian lizard: ["Stargate: The Movie"] feast food animal with exoskeleton, said to taste like chicken from Abydon

ac: [ranac mondegreen] yellow ornithoid from Ra system; [canard ananymondegreen] duck-like ornithoid from Dra system; [canavar ananymondegreen] beagle-headed rabbit-like burrower from Rava system

acacia: [*Dell Crossword Puzzle Dictionary*] locust, see cicada, cicala

acari: [*Dell Crossword Puzzle Dictionary*] monkey from S. America, Terra (alpha Zodiaci III)

acari(d): [*Dell Crossword Puzzle Dictionary*] mite, parasitic insect, see atomy, accarus

accarus: [*Dell Crossword Puzzle Dictionary*] mite, see acari(d), atomy

acervus: [tsounkranacervus mondegreen] antlerless deer-like ruminant from Tsounkra system

achalerai: [*Monster Manual* by Skip William, etal.] large flightless ornithoid with 4 stilt-like legs, shaggy vestigial blue-green wings, parrot-like head

achanch: [Armenian dziachanch mondegreen] pegasoid with horsefly-like head and wings and horse-like torso

achteg: [nachteg elision] leg-less, murre-like nocturnal dracoid

achtegator: [achteg alligator portmanteau] alligator-like predator whose bite morphs victim into achteg

achtengaal: [Afrikaans nachtengaal elision] nightingale-like ornithoid from Afrika binary system

achtvlinder: [Dutch nachtvlinder elision] moth-like insectoid noted for achtvlinding from Netherlander system

achuur: ["Battle of the Neptune Moon" by H. G. Ewers] giant nocturnal predatory dinosauroid from Alyra system

acid snake: [*Star Trek annual #2*: "The Final Voyage"] serpentine creature that emits acid from belly from Carnel

acidophile: extremophile resistant to extreme acid

acixem: [Mexican acixam palindrome] purplish pink ornithoid from Mexica system

ack: [moonack mondegreen] woodchuck-like creature from Luna (alpha Zodiaci IIIb)

acklay: ["Attack of the Clones"] praying mantis-like crustacean with a protective crest, three eyes, six legs each with a scythe-like claw from Vendaxa, Jedi galaxy

aco: [guanaco mondegreen] llama-like desert ruminant from Gua system

acoip: ["at times emit tapioca" palindrome] creature that produces tapioca-like secretion

acolet: [beheaded pacolet] swift gan ceann

acromatula: [*Fantastic Beasts and Where to Find Them* by Newton Artemis Fido Scamander] hairy, black 4.5-meter arachnoid from Borneo, Terra (alpha Zodiaci III)

actornis: [onactornis mondegreen, onactornis in Rotcano palindrome] off-white flightless ornithoid

acuot: [toucanary ananymondegreen] yello, long-necked ornithoid from Yra system

acupa: [*Dell Crossword Puzzle Dictionary*] weakfish

ad: [Estonian kanad mondegreen,] diurnal ornithoid from Eston, Ka system; [Azerbaijani Agcaqanad mondegreen] mosquitoid from Azerbaija system, related to hgin; [danax ananymondegreen] gray ornithoid from Xa system

adak: [hanadak mondegreen] grizzly-headed baboon-like creature from Ha system

adanda: ["Dead Diver" by Wim Vandermaan] insect from Lepso (Firing II)

Adarna eagle: [Filipino] eagle whose song lulls to sleep and whose dropping petrify from Philippines

addee: [adder backformation] adder prey

äddry: ["Dead Diver" by Wim Vandermaan] slim, smoldering metallic red, carnivorous octoped

adna: [adna manda palindrome] manda-like amphisbæna

ado igdaigh: ["mirror of the soul", "The Mountains of The Gods" by H. G. Ewers] aka urgho falat, pigeon-sized, shimmering blue song ornithoid with short, dark red beak from Toulminth (Ovenden IV)

adon: [iguanadon mondegreen] toothless, beaked herbivorous dinosauroid from Igua system

adonster: [adon monster portmanteau] monstrous, carnivorous beaked dinosauroid

adu: [Sudan adus palindrome reddish yellow ornithoid from Suda system

adyh: ["The Sentinel of Foppon" by Hans Kneifel] large, colorful, predatory ornithoid

ae: [seal aes palindrome] pale "red" (yellow-orange) sirenian with dark brown extremities

aeco: [ocean aeco, Socean aecos palindromes] hippopotamus-seahorse, seahorse-like sea creature with hippoid head related to evir from Socea, Soce system

aegospotamimus: [aegospotamus backformation] mouse-like hippopotamus

aegospotamus: [Lat. mondegreen] hippoid-mouse from Aegopotamia, Aegopotam system

aehw: [wheat aehw palindrome] pale brownish yellow ornithoid from Whea, Whe system

aelurec: [cerulean aelurec palindrome, *Edgeworld Chronicles* by Paul Stewart and Chris Riddell frosty blue creature from Edgeworld, Cerulea system

aem: [Crayola meat aem palindrome] brownish yellow ornithoid from Crayol A system

aempersaendeu: [Kor. &] 2-D das-like creature

aep: [pear aep palindrome chartreuse yellow ornithoid

aepycamel: [*After the Dinosaurs* by Donald R. Prothero] 6-meter giraffe-like camel from Miocene

aepyornis: [*After the Dinosaurs* by Donald R. Prothero] aka elephant bird, large, flightless bird from Madagascar, Terra (alpha Zodiaci III)

aerc: [cream aerc palindrome] very pale reddish ornithoid, see gnim

aerd: [dreaded aerd palindrome] frightening predator

aerg: [great aerg palindrome] essel-like creature in large and smaller varieties

aergator: [aerg alligator portmanteau] alligator-like predator whose bite morphs victim into aerg

aerob: [boreal aerob palindrome gnat-like insectoid from arctic Borea, Bore system

aerobster: [aero lobster portmanteau] lobster-like giffinoid

aerovore: [*Orion's Arm edition Encyclopedia Galactica*] aka gray dust, bionano goo responsible for Nanodisaster, Conver Wars, Sagittarius Frontier Wars, Zeon

aet: [teal aet palindrome bluish green ornithoid from Tea, Te system

aethonon: [*Fantastic Beasts and Where to Find Them* by Newton Artemis Fido Scamander] chestnut-colored pegasus

aetrot: [torteau aetrot palindrome] equinoid with red spots, flaming mouth and ears

af: [koanaf mondegreen] shellfish from Koa, Ko system; [tanamin-pitoloha ananymondegreen] 7-headed hydra-like creature from Ahiolotipnima system

afanc: [*The Big Bad Book of Beasts* by Michael Largo] crocodilian with humanoid face, beaver-like tail-fin from Wales

Afghant hound: [Afghan-ant portmanteau] large, slender, sextipedal caninoid with long, thick hair, pointed muzzle, drooping ears, compound eyes and antennae

Afpran bear: ["Phantoms in Terrania" by Ernst Vlcek] Janus-headed ursinoid from Afpra

afrak: ["FthinraKathi" by Dale Murphy] creature from T'Khasi, Nevasa (40 Eridani) system

afrotheria: [*After the Dinosaurs* by Donald R. Prothero] large family of animals all originating in Africa, including elephantines, sirenians, hyraxes, tenres, golden moles, aardvarks, elephant shrews

ag: [jag mondegreen] jay-landshark triphibian; [gananoid ananynymondegreen] long-necked quadruped from Diona system

aga: [Indonesian/Malay naga elision] hibernating dracoid from Wintria, Pfetea system, Galaxiki galaxy

agama: [*Dell Crossword Puzzle Dictionary*] starred lizard from tropics, see hardim

agator: [ag alligator portmanteau] alligator-like predator whose bite morphs victim into ag or aga

agenbite: [Peter Macinnis]: carrion-eating toothless snake, except on Little Ugly where it's herbivorous

ager: [an onager mondegreen] off-white ass-like equinoid; ager: [tanager mondegreen] forest ornithoid from Ta system

aggedor: ["The Monster of Peladon" by Terrance Dicks, "Curse of Peladon" by Brian Hayles] one-horned, fanged, pig-faced bipedal quest beast of Peladon's trisilicate mines

aggedoor: [aggedor door portmanteau] bipedal, pig-like unicorn able to travel through portals

aggee: [backformation] prey of aggers from Segga system

agger: [Lat. "mound"] mound-like invertebrate

aghag: [Maltese naghag elision] sheep-like ruminant

aghagator: [aghag alligator portmanteau] alligator-like predator whose bite morphs victim into aghag

aghta: [naghta elision] cathgan-like amphisbæna

agi: [unagi backformation,] mock seaserpent

agali: [nagali elision] 2-D das-like creature

agon: [dragon spoonerisms] dracoid from Dralfzar, Drasta or Drice systems

agony: see venom

agouti: [*Dell Crossword Puzzle Dictionary*] rodent from S. America, Terra (alpha Zodiaci III), see cavy, degu, paca, coypu

agreno: [Perry Rhodan] light brown, 6-legged mount with large mandibles, mid-body notch, sharp, sour odor used by Skaharans from Luuhr

agriothere: [*After the Dinosaurs* by Douglas R. Prothero] huge bear from Pliocene

agua: [*Dell Crossword Puzzle Dictionary*] huge toad

agumi: [Dell Crossword Puzzle Dictionary] pigeon-like trumpeter

ah: ["ah at times emit taha" palindrome, argah mondegreen] gray weaverbird gestalt

aha: sphecid wasp, related to aha ha or 200-kg perch from Nile River, Egypt, Terra (alpha Zodiaci III)

ahcuotnu: [untouchable elb ahcuotnu palindrome] electric variety of elb-like spheroid, see ignatni

ahgum: [mughal ahgum palindrome greenish ornithoid from Mugha system

ahik: ["Invasion of the Shadow" by H. G. Ewers] from Fireplace (aka Hephaestus), Boscyks system

ahla: [Maltese nahla elision] bee-like insectoid

ahlh: [*The Romulan Way* by Terisa Halekala-LoBrotto, *The Disinherited* by Diane Duane and Peter Morwood] aka slime devil

ahoai: [ahoai diaoha palindrome] diaoha-like amphisbæna

ahr: [nahr elision] bat-mouse, ancestral to mouse and bat

aht: [thanator ananymondegreen] predator from Tota system

ahuizotl: [*Fiend Folio* by Eric Cagle, etal.. "five-armed dog"] simian with dog-like head, glossy brown fur and white underbelly and clawed hand on prehensile tail, especially fond of eyes, teeth and fingernails [*Here Be Monsters* almanac] from Meso-America, Terra (alpha Zodiaci III)

ahuizotlope: [ahuizotl antelope portmanteau] ahuizo

ahulph: [*The Anome* by Jack Vance] domesticated anthropoid from Durdane that communicates by odor

ahvaal: [Estonian ahv-vaal portmanteau ape-whale, large ichthanthropoid from Eston

ahvaalope: [ahvaal antelope portmanteau] ahvaal with antlers

ahwin: ["ahwin at times emit taniwha" palindrome] seamonster gestalt

ai: [janais mondegreen] pet from Ja system

aiad: [naiad elision dragonfly-like insectoid from Sdaia, Sda system

aibad: [Debian aibad palindrome red ornithoid from Debia, Deb system

aico: [social aicos palindrome] insectoid gestalt

ailen: [carnelian ailen rac palindrome] pale to deep red or red-brown rac from Oita system

ailon: [magnolia ailongam palindrome] whitish gam

ailuht: [Thulian ailuht palindrome pink ornithoid from Thulia, Thul system

aine: ["aine at times emit taenia" palindrome] tapeworm gestalt

air-whale: [*On the Storm Planet* by Cordwainer Smith] aerial cetacean from Henriada, see skywhale, six-legged air-whale

airit: [stirianaa ananymondegreen] geneered bacterium from Aa rogue planet, see airyt

airyt: [tyrian airyt palindrome purple ornithoid, related to flightless yt, from Tyria, Tyr system, see vuam, nedom, airit

aishravas: [beheaded haishravas] 4-headed wingless pegasoid

aiwa: [*Creatures of the Galaxy* by Phil Brucato, Bill Smith, Rick D. Stuart, Chuck Truett] 10-meter sea and air steed from Naboo, Jedi galaxy

aj: [janais ananymondegreen] pet from Sia rogue planet

aja-ekapad: ["lightning goat", *The Big Bad Book of Beasts* by Michael Largo] one-legged goat with spiral horns able to to produce sparks with its hooves from India

ajada: [buaja darat mondegreen] large, lavender rat-like dracoid

ajar: [rajah ajar palindrome deep, bright saffron ornithoid from Ra-Ja system

ajyrrebzzaj: [Crayola jazzberry jam ajyrrebzzaj palindrome] dark red-violet ornithoid from Crayol A

ak: [Turkish karabatak backformation] ornithoid ancestral to kara bat and cormorant, see daq; [kanaliha ananymondegreen] chicken-like ornithoid from Ahila system; [kananésgi ananym] arachnoid from Éna, Ig system; [kanatsisdatsi ananym] wasp-like insectoid from Ista, Istad system; [beheaded sak] headless bovinoid; akak nasna; [kanair ananymondegreen] yellow ornithoid from Ria system; [kananésgi ananymondegreen] arachnoid from Igsena system; [kanatsisdatsi ananymondegreen] wasp-like insectoid from Istadsistan

akak: [danakak mondegreen] mouth parasite from Da system

akateko: [Japanese] small red hand-like arboreal animal from Japan, see handbird

Akhaar medusa: [Perry Rhodan] huge methane-breather from Akhaar, Tryco-Simm system

akhlut: [*Monster Spotter's Guide to North America* by Scott Francis] man-eating amphibious wolf (or dirus) from Bering Sea

akibah: ["Dreams from a Foreign Dimension" by H. G. Ewers] wild Arkonide cattle

akin: [manakin mondegreen] fruit-eating ornithoid from Ma system

akinom: ["Death in the Turquoise Sea" by Andreas Findig] little, turquoise ornithoid from Auroch-Maxo-55, Segafredo galaxy

akk: [*Creatures of the Galaxy* by Phil Brucato, Bill Smith, Rick D. Stuart, Chuck Truett] Jedi companion lizard with lightsabre-resistant hide from Jedi galaxy

akman: ["In the Walls from Eryx" by Howard Phillips Lovecraft and Kenneth Sterling] wringling, slimy creature

ako: [ako yoka palindrome] yoka-like amphisbæna

akola: ["The Steel Swing of Orxh" by Peter Terrid] dangerous sea creature from Xoaixo, Llaga-del-Armgh system

aku: [*Dell Crossword Puzzle Dictionary*] victor fish

akui: [akui ziuka palindrome] ziuka-like amphisbæna

akuni: ["The Gentlemen of the Blue Crystals" by H. G. Francis] predatory felinoid with 4 slit eyes, green scales and vulture-like beak from Takota's world

akvaryum: [Turkish akvaryum baligi backformation] ichthyoid ancestral to fisk and goldfish

al-mi'raj: [*Fabulous Beasts and Demons* by Heinz Mode] yellow hare with one black horn from Arabia, Terra (alpha Zodiaci III), see jackalope

al: ["al at times emit tala" palindrome] parasitic cave macropod gestalt

al'diiz: ["Death in the Turquoise Sea" by Andreas Findig] paumyr worm that stimulates budding of plant-island from Auroch-Maxo-55, Segafrendo galaxy

al'diz: [one-i al'diiz] cyclops worm

Alaam's bass: [Balaam's ass spoonerism] singing ichthyoid from Alaam system

alabaster golem: golem of alabaster

alaifer: [alaifer drefiala palindrome] drefiala-like amphisbæna

alama: [Hauma *] 2-D pentapus or hexapus

alan: [*Dell Crossword Puzzle Dictionary*] hunting wolfhound

alazb: [Star Trek] arachnoid from T'Khasi, Nevasa (40 Eridani) system

albatross: [*QPB Encyclopedia of Word and Phrase* Origins by Robert Hendrickson] aka mollyhawk, goony bird, Cape Hope sheep

albertosaur: [*Feathered Dinosaurs: The Origin of Birds* by John Long and Peter Schuten] gorgosaur-like tyrannosaurid from Alberta, Terra (alpha Zodiaci III)

albino ant: ["13 Against Arkon" by Andreas Findig] white ant-like insectoid from Ertus (Kreit III)

albinoid: [Resident Evil: Code Veronica] T-virus infected salamander with electric shock, matures in just 10 hrs.

albinowl: [albino-owl portmanteau] predatory polar ornithoid

Alborak: [Koran] silver horse able to travel at hundreds of kilometers per second from Arabia, Terra (alpha Zodiaci III)

alca: [*Dell Crossword Puzzle Dictionary*] razor-billed auk, see murr(e)

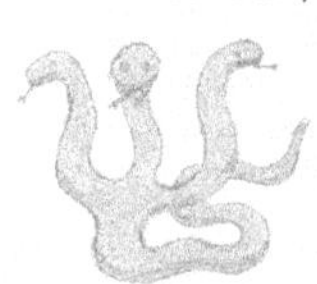

Aldebaran serpent: ["Hide and Q" by C. J. Holland] 3-headed, leg-less reptilian from Aldebaran (alpha Tauri) system

alectrosaur: ["unmarried lizard", *Feathered Dinosaurs: The Origin of Birds* by John Long and Peter Schuten] 5-meter tyrannosaurid from late Cretaceous

alectrotaur: [alectrosaur minotaur portmanteau] variety of tyrannotaur

alejandro: [Monster Galaxy] creature from Monster galaxy, see alyx

alf: [flax alf palindrome] pale brownish yellow ornithoid

Alfzarian dragon: ["Honorable Enemies" by Poul Anderson] dracoid from Borthudian mts., Alfzar, Betelgeuse (alpha Orionis) system

Algolian dung beetle: ["Shakedown: Return of the Sontarans" by Terrence Dicks] dung beetle-like insectoid from Algol (beta Persei) system

āli: [tsulisdanāli mondegreen] catfish-like ornithoid from Da, Tsuli system

aligerbil: [aliger gerbil portmanteau] gerbil-like pegasoid

aliha: [Estonian kanaliha mondegreen] chicken-like ornithoid from Ka system

alil: [lilac alil palindrome] pale silvery gray ornithoid

alināga: [beheaded kalināga] 999-headed snake

alināgator: [alināga alligator portmanteau] alligator-like predator whose bite morphs victim into kalināga

alioramimus: [aliormus backformation] herbivorous tyrannosaur mimic

alioramus: [*Feathered Dinosaurs: The Origin of Birds* by John Long and Peter Schuten] 6-meter tyrannosaurid with sharp cones on snout

aliped: [*Dell Crossword Puzzle Dictionary*] wing-footed creature

alit: [The Elder Scrolls III: "Morrowind"] tail-less, short-legged, bipedal predator from Vvardenfell grasslands, Morrowind, related to guar and kagouti

Aljew eagle: ["Departure into Space" by William Voltz] eagle-like ornithoid from Conyers, moon of Firmer, Sapa system

alkaliphile: extremophile resistant to extreme alkali

allan: [*Dell Crossword Puzzle Dictionary*] gull or hawk from Scotland, see skua, jaeger

allegory: [Piers Anthony] green reptile with long toothy snout from Xanth

allesfressee: [backformation] allesfesser prey

allesfresser: ["omnivore", "The Experimental Criminals" by Ernst Vlcek] black, armored, wildcat-like, felinoid predator with 3 green slit eyes, 4 rows of teeth and long hook-tipped tail from Roulawan, Argnos system

allet: [stellar alletts palindrome] plasmoid adapted to living within star, see sretni

allghoi khorkoi: ["death worm"] desert worm that spits yellow acidic saliva, able to generate bio-electrical shock from Mongolia, Terra (alpha Zodiaci III)

allicanto: metallic-colored desert lizard from Atacama desert, Chile, Terra (alpha Zodiaci III)

allig: [alligator backformation] slug-like alligator prey

alligator: crocodillian from New World; [alligator mondegreen] alligator-like predator whose bite morphs victim into allig

alligoator: [alligator-goat portmanteau] scaly omnivorous ruminant with short legs, long tail and backward curved horns

allistinker: [Terra Monster] gray swamp-dweller with bushy white-striped tail, backplates, yellow underbelly, see fouligator from Terrarium

allocamelus: [ass-camel] donkey-headed camel

allognathosuch: [*After the Dinosaurs* by Donald R. Prothero] small crocodillian with both sharp and shell-crushing knobby teeth from Paleocene

allosaur: ["donkey-lizard", *The Mistaken Extinction* by Lowell Dingus and Timothy Rowe] large theropod dinosaur

allotaur: [allosaur minotaur portmanteau] donkey-headed bovinoid

allsnouter: [*The Snouters* by Harald Stümpke] slender notochord with no limbs, including enterorrinus, wholesnouters

alma(sti): 1.5-meter, reddish brown pongoid from Altai mts., Mongolia, and Tien Shan mts, China, Terra (alpha Zodiaci III)

Alman medusa: [Perry Rhodan] sea creature from Alma

aloe: [*Speculum Orbis Terrae* by Cornelis de Jode] leg-less murre-like goose with 4 fins, and fish-like tail

alopex: [*Fabulous Beasts and Demons* by Heinz Mode] huge boy-eating fox from Thebes

aloze: [Continuum] 1-meter, 30-kg carrion-eating cave lizard from Dark Hook Peak, Dornique, Andromede

alpaca: [*Dell Crossword Puzzle Dictionary*] llama-like creature from S. America, Terra (alpha Zodiaci III)

alpacat: [alpaca-cat portmanteau, palindrome] wooly, long-necked felinoid

alpacatastrophe: [Godville] very explosive alpaca

alssarg: [nalssarg elision, grassland nalssarg palindrome] ruminant from Sla, Gra system

alssargator: [alssarg alligator portmanteau] alligator-like predator whose bite morphs victim into alssarg

alt: [althorn backformation] ruminant with upright horns

altama: [altamah-ha mondegreen] ATM-like egg-layer, see money ha-ha, golden goose

altamaha-ha: [*Monster Spotter's Guide to North America* by Scott Francis] large, dark, humped basilosauroid from Altamaha River, Georgia, Terra (alpha Zodiaci III)

aludio: [Ken's aludio noidülasnek palindrome] noidülasnek-like amphisbæna from Ken's system

aluk: [Yeht-Golik] ichthyoid from T'Khasi, Nevasa (40 Eridani) system

alusn: [Armenian havalusn backformation] pelican-chicken, ornithoid ancestral to a chicken and pelican

alutnar: ["alutnar at times emit tarantula" palindrome] tarantula gestalt

alvarezsaur: [*The Mistaken Extinction* by Lowell Dingus and Timothy Rowe] terapod related to mononykus

alvone: ["The City of Puppets" by H. G. Ewers] man-sized scavenger arthropod

alxasaur: [*Feathered Dinosaurs: The Origin of Birds* by John Long and Peter Schuten] 3.8-meter therizinosaur with small head with leaf-shaped teeth, long arms and large claws, short tail

alxataur: [alxasaur minotaur portmanteau] bovinoid with small head, long arms and large claws, short tail

alyx: [Monster Galaxy] creature from Monster galaxy, see alejandro

alzia: [Hildegard of Bingen's Lingua Ignota] magpie-like ornithoid from Hildegrad's world

am: [small ams palindrome] gnat-like insectoid;]manatee ananymondegreen] manatee-like sea creature from Eeta system

äm: [liäm mondegreen] lamb-like caninoid

amakihi: [*National Geographic Encyclopedia of Animals*] seed and insect-eating songbird from Hawaii

Amara snake: [Amara lab balarāma palindrome] geneered amphisbæna from Amara laboratory

amarillo: [Final Fantasy] yellow flan-thick ooze

amarok: [Inuit, *Monster Spotter's Guide to North America* by Scott Francis] giant, nocturnal warg-like caninoid, possibly same as waheela, from N. E. Pacific coast, Terra (alpha Zodiaci III)

amatanooroch: [beheaded and curtailed yamata-no-orochi] 7-headed, 7-tailed, very large dracoid with red eyes and mossy, forested back

amazu: [namazu elision] giant catfish

amber pencil: ["The Worm Turns" by Gregory Benford] long cylindroid propelled by blue burning gas from HD209458 system

ambiortus: [T*he Mistaken Extinction* by Lowell Dingus and Timothy Rowe] earliest flightless carinate from early Cretaceous, ancestral to ichthyornis and birds

ambulocetus: ["walking whale", *After the Dinosaurs* by Donald R. Prothero] sea lion-sized whale ancestor with vestigial hooves related to pakicetus and dalanistes from Eocene

amdok: [*Warrior of Llarn, Theif of Llarn* by Gardner F. Fox] scaly, Shetland pony-sized megapodan with 3 eyes, large powerful jaw, whip-like tail used as steed from Llarn

amebalea: [Basque ameba-balea portmanteau, amoeba-whale, cetacean with only vestigial skeleton, from Bema, Aela system

amhuluk: [*Monster Spotter's Guide to North America* by Scott Francis] 30-meter horned lake snake from Forkend Mt. lakes, Ore., Terra (alpha Zodiaci III)

amikuk: [*Monster Spotter's Guide to North America* by Scott Francis, Mythical Creatures List] amphibious, man-eating dracoid with slimy pelt (illustrated by Ben Patrick as with triple jaws like tu-long and 4 eyes) with 4 humanoid arms from Bering Sea

amin: [fanamin-pitoloha mondegreen] hydra from Fa (iota Orionis) system

ammonia mouse: ["The Deadly Invension" by William Voltz] ammonia-breathing mouse-like rodentoid that exhales hydrogen from Makrabasen

amob: [amob aboma palindrome, a mob mondegreen] aboma-like amphisbæna gestalt

amou: [tin amou backformation] large flightless (female) or blood-sucking (male) ornithoid

amp-eater: ["L'il Abner" by Al Capp, ampmeter elision] electovore from Lower Slobbovia, Terra (alpha Zodiaci III)

amperor: [Terra Monster] winged quadruped with pincher-tipped tail, from Terrarium

ampersa: [Port. &] 2-D das-like creature

amphi: ["Lord of the Lost World" by Harvey Patton] dolphin-like amphibian with smooth, scaleless, greenish skin, white underbelly, pointed snout, 4-finger-like extensions on 6 leg-fins, both gills and lungs, communicate with whistling, croaking and chirping from Ysath'Thor

amphicyon: [*After the Dinosaurs* by Donald R. Prothero] aka beardog from Eocene

amphisbæna: [*Natural History* by Pliny the Elder] serpent with false head on tail, said to protect in pregnancy when alive and cure rheumatism when dead

amphivena: [*The Big Bad Book of Beasts* by Michael Largo] lizard-bird with feathered wings, scaly body and tail-head

amphorae: [*Worlds Apart: Nat. Hist. of Furaha and Earth* by Souren Nyoroge] bottle-like bottom-dwellers from Furaha (alpha Phoenicis IV)

ampint: [Terra Monsters] small, black-and-blue pongid with large front paws, see gorillamp, from Terrarium

amplituda: [Tajil &] 2-D das-like creature

amreg: [German sherherd] sheepdog-like caninoid

amregator: [amreg alligator portmanteau] alligator-like predator whose bite morphs victim into amreg

amselch: [German Amsel-Elch portmanteau] blackbird-elk, black griffinoid with antlers from Germa system

amurraupe: ["Escape from Thantur-Lok" by Susan Schwartz] source of shiny, opalescent silk

amynodont: [*After the Dinosaurs* by Donald R. Prothero] aquatic hippoid from Priabonian age (late Eocene)

amzia: [Hildegard of Bingen's Lingua Ignota] wasp-like insectoid from Ignota, Hildegard's system

amzzar: [Crayola razzmatazz at-amzzar palindrome] crimson-rose ornithoid from Crayol A system, see at

anab: [Crayola, Banana Mania Inaman anab palindrome] yellow ornithoid from Inama, Crayol A system; nector-eating songbird-like ornithoid from Tiuga system

anacus: [After the *Dinosaurs* by Donald R. Prothero] gompothere with 4.3-meter straight tusks from Miocene

anæbsihpma: [amphisbæna ananym] serpent with tail-like head

anagalid: [*After the Dinosaurs* by Donald R. Prothero] rabbit and rodent ancestor from Danian age (early Paleocene), ancestral to uintathere

anai: [*Dell Crossword Puzzle Dictionary*] termite from Philippines, aka anay

ananymouse: [ananym mouse mondegreen] surreal rodentoid that reverses creature names and palindromizes

anaquit: [bananaquit mondegreen] short-necked relative of ban

anasa: [*Dell Crossword Puzzle Dictionary*] squash bug

anay: see anai

anbel: ["The Crown of Roewis" by Michael Marcus Thuraer] worm-like symbiot of Gurraks that removes blemishes and plaque, and closes small wounds from Roewis (Grosnor III), Nubecula Major

anca: [bianca mondegreen] cockerel-like ancestor of ptarmigan and partridge

anchorwhip: [*After Man* by Dougal Dixon] venomous snake with anchor-like tail; [*Star of Astarte* by Hans Kneifel] prey of flugskerne from Venus (alpha Zodiaci II)

ancoracephalus: ["anchor-head", *The New Dinosaurs* by Dougal Dixon] lambeosaur with anchor-shaped crest, related to sprintosaur

andelgalornis: [*After the Dinosaurs* by Donald R. Prothero] large flightless bird from Miocene

andrewsarchus: [*After the Dinosaurs* by Donald R. Prothero] largest predatory land mammal, 2-meter shoulder height (twice the size of Kodiak)

ane: [nane elision] anthropoid with large, softly glowing eyes, no nose, small mouth, white skin, flexible (because boneless); [ane tena palindrome] tena-like amphisbæna

ang: [siamang mondegreen] pongoid with throat sac from Siam, Terra (alpha Zodiaci III)

angator: [siamangator] alligator-like predator whose bite morphs victim into ang from Siam, Terra (alpha Zodiaci III)

angbut: [*City of the Chasch* by Jack Vance] food ichthyoid of the Green Chasch from Nion

angelfish: [Xanth series by Piers Anthony] aka xangelfish, very nice ichthyopteryx with gauzy wings and halo from Xanth or [Xanthian mondegreen] Xa, Thia system

angghav: [Armenian anggh-hav portmanteau] vulture-chicken

anglewhale: [rightwhale extrapolation] cetacean that turns in angles, not in curves, see cutewhate, obtusewhale and rightwhale

angleworm: [Xanth series by Piers Anthony] worm that turns in angles, not in curve, from Xanth, see cuteworm, obtuseworm and rightworm

angorat: [angora-rat portmanteau] wooly rodentoid from Woolarra III, Galaxiki galaxy

angraur: [Outernauts] mature angrin with large, brown ears, bushy tail, blue body and teeth

angrin: [Outernauts] creature with large, brown ears, bushy tail, blue body, see angroo, angraur

angroo: [Outernauts] immature angrin with large, brown ears, bushy tail, blue body

angurusaur: ["Godzilla Raids Again" aka "Gigantis, the Fire Monster" by Shigeru Kayama] 120-meter tall biped with nearly useless forearms, back plates, outward-pointing fangs, small ears, multiple brains, breaths hellfire

anhangüera: [*O Desafio das Bandeirantes* ed. by Carlos Eduardo Klimmick Pereira, Flávio Maurice de Anbrade, Luiz Eduardo Ricon de Freitas] hellfire-breathing animals from Brazil, Terra (alpha Zodiaci III)

anid: [cardinal anid rac palindrome] dark to vivid red rac from Oita system

anigōli: [Cherokee Tsalagi] perch-like ichthoid from Tsalagia, Tsalagi system

anihc: [China pink nip anihc palindrome] reddish pink nip or sor from Chin system

anilo: [Carolina anilo rac palidrome] blue variety of rac

animadvert: [*Encyclopedia Galactica*] geneered animal that displays, secretes or excretes advertisements

anka: [beheaded yanka] 2-headed hydra-like dracoid

ankheg: ["The Ecology of the Ankheg" by Mark Feil] 3-meter, yellowish-brown, six-legged burrowing, acid-spitting arthropod with black compound eyes, mandibles, antennae

ankhegator: [ankheg alligator portmanteau] alligator-like predator whose bite morphs victim into ankheg

ankistpocervus: [candiacervus extrapolation] deer with hook-like antlers

ankylosaur: armored dinosaur with short legs, club-like tail and spiked torso from Cretaceous

annava: [savannah annavas portmanteau] ruminant from tropical grasslands

annei: [sienna anneis palindrome] reddish or yellowish brown ornithoid

Annian seaserpent: [beheaded Rannian seaserpent] 2-headed seaserpent

annippus: [nannippus elision] gan ceann from Za, Clea system

anoa: [*Dell Crossword Puzzle Dictionary*] forest ox

anole/i: [*Dell Crossword Puzzle Dictionary*] lizard from Americas, Terra (alpha Zodiaci III)

anoo: [beheaded and curtailed tanoor] 3-headed, 3-tailed, very large dracoid with red eyes and mossy, forested back

anooba: [*Creatures of the Galaxy* by Phil Brucato, Bill Smith, Rick D. Stuart, Chuck Truett] hyena-like caninoid from Tatooine, Jedi galaxy

anouar: ["The Wandering Soul" by Hans Kneifel] nocturnal, pack predator with whitish fur with huge, red eyes, long tail, long claws preying on rodsamon from Haghjameite

anqä: [Al-Mas'udi] aka simurgh, huge humanoid-faced bird

anqutan: [Azerbaijani anqut qutan portmanteau] mallard-pelikan ornithoid

ansan: [nasna ananym] right-to-left half-creature, see nasna

ant cow: aka aphid or plant louse

ant-bear: [*Land of Terror* by Edgar Rice Burroughs] six-legged ursinoid as large as an elephant from Azar

ant-cow: [ant cow mondegreen] ant-like insectoid that secretes nourishing liquid

ant-lion: [*The Big Bad Book of Beasts* by Michael Largo] dog-sized crustacean with ant-like body and lion-like head, males carnivorous, see antlion

ant-lizard: see formisaur

ant-panther: [bezant panther mondegreen] ant-headed panther-like felinoid from Bez system

antaconda: [ant-anaconda portmanteau] long, 6-legged dracoid with antennae

antelopeater: [antelope-eater portmanteau] monstrous carnivore able to suck up antelopes like an anteater does ants, see bokeneter

antennalope: [Nextel, museumofhoaxes.com by Alex Boese] antelope with antennae rather than antlers

antgora: [angora-ant portmanteau] 6-legged insectoid with long, silky hair

anthillbilly: [anthill-hillbilly portmanteau] mountain goat-like insectoid

antholops: [*Physiologus*] bovine with large saw-like horns

anthracothere: [*After the Dinosaurs* by Donald R. Prothero] pig-like artiodactyl from Priabonian age (late Eocene)

antic: [Cyclopedia of Worlds] 4.6-meter sea predator with 2 pairs of steering fins behind head, delta-shaped tail, narrow jaws from Dakka, Neptune system

Antivillian leafhopper: ["Growlers" by Larry England] insectoid from Antivill

antlion: [Piers Anthony] lion-headed ant with stingers from Xanth, see ant-lion

Antosian phoenix: [*High Stakes* by David Peters] phoenix-like ornithoid from Antos

antukai: [*Monster Spotter's Guide to North America* by Scott Francis] grizzly-sized otter from Forkend Mt. lakes, Ore., Terra (alpha Zodiaci III)

anura: [*Dell Crossword Puzzle Dictionary*] toad

ao: [omao mondegreen] greenish or pale lavender thrush-like [beheaded iao] ornithoid of ill omen, ao ao nasna

ao ao: [Guarani] voracious, man-eating fanged sheep-like peccary, so called by its cry

ao-inu: [Jap. "blue dog"] wing-less ha-inu from Japan, Terra (alpha Zodiaci III)

aoa: [*Planar Handbook* by Bruce Cordell, etal.] silvery, magic-reflecting spheroid surrounded by "droplets" related to xag-yas and xeg-yis

aobonati: [aobonati titanoboa palindrome] titanoboa-like amphisbæna

aobrehtae: [oabrehtae feather boa palindrome] feather boa-like amphisbæna

aoc: [coal aoc palindrome] black variety of rokh-like rahc

aosagíbí: [*Mujara 5* by Shigeru Mízuki] glowing blue heron from Japan

aoudad: [*Dell Crossword Puzzle Dictionary*] wild sheep with large horns from Africa, see arui, argali, udad

ap: [apish backformation] pongoid

apapanu: [*The Howling Stones* by Alan Dean Foster] large rock-like water-spouting creature from Parramat archipelago, Senisran

apatemyid: [*After the Dinosaurs* by Donald R. Prothero] insectivorous mammal with long front teeth, scissor-like premolars and long fingers from Paleocene

apatosaur: brontosaur relative

apatotaur: [apatosaur minotaur mondegreen] brontotaur relative

ape-bear: ["At the Zoo" by Rick Shelley] 1-meter, 33-kg gold to chocolate brown marsupial from Dilrgao, see arctopithicus

aphelops: [*After the Dinosaurs* by Donald R. Prothero] acerathere with short proboscis and prehensile lip, long legs from Miocene

apmahc: [champagne eng apmahc palindrome] buff-cream (slightly pale to very pale reddish) bison-like eng

apodis: [apus, piscium extrapolation] bird of paradise-like ornithoid

aporad: [*Warrior of Llarn* by Gardner Fox] large horned felinoid of Llarn

Aporis spider: ["Phantoms in Terrania" by Ernest Vlcek] arachnoid able to spin 100-meter net between trees from Aporis

apot: [topaz apot palindrome] yellow-brown ornithoid

appaken: ["Alarm-alpha" by H. G. Francis] voracious predator of whale-like prey from Ertus (Kreit III)

appalachiosaur: [*Feathered Dinosaurs: The Origin of Birds* by John Long and Peter Schuten] tyrannosaurid from island-continent Appalachia, Terra (alpha Zodiaci III)

appamoosa: [appaloosa-moose portmanteau] equinoid with moose-like antlers and spotted rump

apple jelly: [jelly extrapolation] greenish jelly-thick ooze

aps: [feldspar aps dlef palindrome] tan dlef, see arg

apt: [*The Warlord of Mars* by Edgar Rice Burroughs] 2-meter white pongoid with 2 arms, 4 legs, hippo-like mouth with 2 large slightly curving tusks, large multi-lidded compound eyes from Mars (alpha Zodiaci IV)

aptaleon: see Babylonian calopus

aptera: [*Dell Crossword Puzzle Dictionary*] wingless creature

apusaur: [Apodian] leg-less, murre-like flying dracoid from Apus constellation

aq: [buraq mondegreen] ruby red pegasus

aqen: [Albanian peshkaqen backformation] land-shark shark ancestor from Alban system

aquilae: [aquila, piscium extrapolation] eagle-like ornithoid

aqua-bat: [*Gobber's Compendium of Common Oceanic Species*] long-tailed, pointy-eared, gargoyle-faced wyvern-like dracoid from Ganymede (alpha Zodiaci Vc)

aquaeonius: small, extinct sea creature from Manticore (Manticorea V), Galaxiki galaxy

aquanine: [Terra Monster] dark blue pack-hunting aquatic fox, see niptune and carnivice from Terrarium

aquarin: [Terra Monster] hooved, 3-horned dracoid from Terrarium

aquariusaur: seaserpent-like dinosaur from Aquarius constellation

aquatasnap: shark-like ichthyoid from Deepsea (Phoenix IV), Galaxiki galaxy

aquavirius maggot: [*Fantastic Beasts and Where to Find Them* by Newton Artemis Fido Scamander] hydrokinetic brain-like worm

aquit: [bananaquit mondegreen] nectar-eating songbird from Baba system

ar: [Croatian zecar backformation] beagle-rabbit, lop-eared lapoid ancestral to rabbit and beagle; [renar mondegreen] reindeer-fox, antlered, bushy-tailed ruminant; [ranac ananymondegreen] yellow ornithoid from Ca system

âr: [Romanian catâr backformation] cat-mule ancestor to cat and mule, equinine with claws and whiskers

ara: [Ararat mondegreen] mountain-dwelling rodent from Ara constellation, see arara; [aranahippus ananymondegreen] equinoid from Suppiha system
ara hoot: [*Planiverse* by Alexander Dewdney] 2-D sea animal from Arde, Shems system
araba: [*Dell Crossword Puzzle Dictionary*] howling monkey, see mono
araka: [araka makara palindrome] makara-like amphisbæna
ara(ra): [*Dell Crossword Puzzle Dictionary*] macaw, parrot from Brazil
arabe: [*Le Mammouth Bleu* by Luc Alberny] milk mammal from Grande Euscarie
arachnenguine: penguin-like aquatic ornithoid with long, tiger-striped mandible-like beak
arachnoid: spider-like creature
aradik: ["Mysterious Zyrph" by H. G. Francis] poisonous giant, spider-scorpion with orange and black stripes, black horn from Zyrph, Manam Turu galaxy
arahatliq: [Azerbaijani narahatliq elision] crab-like crustacean from Azerbaija system
aramari: ["The Galactic Syndicate" by K. H. Scheer] chlorine-breathing, poisonous snake
āranka: [beheaded hāranka] ornithoid gan ceann
arany: [Hungarian aranyhal backformation] ichthyoid ancestor from Hungaria, Hungar system
arapai: ["The Santa Claus Planet" by Frank M. Robinson] alleycat-like fur and food animal
arapaima: [*River Monsters* by Jeremy Wade] 3.3-meter, 230-kg fish from Amazon, Terra (alpha Zodiaci III)
arberiverim: [*The World of Synnabarr* by Raymond C. S. McCracken] ratking gestalt from Mars (fka alpha Zodiaci IV)
arbilu: [arbilu culibra palindrome] culibra-like amphisbæna
arbocila: [arbocila calicobra palindrome] calicobra-like amphisbæna
arbrosaur: [*The New Dinosaurs* by Dougal Dixon] aka tree-lizard, dinosaur adapted to trees

abrotaur: [abrosaur minotaur portmanteau] aka tree-bull, arboreal bovinoid
arcane ooze: [*Monster Manual* by Skip Williams, etal.] primordial ooze
arcaneo: [Terra Monster] monster from Terrarium
archaeohippo: [archaeohippus hippo portmanteau] hippoid from Archae system
archaeohippus: [*After the Dinosaurs* by Donald R. Prothero] leaf-eating horse from Miocene
archæopteryx: [Herman von Meyer] aka reptile-bird, tinshemet, reptilian ornithoid with teeth and wing-claws
archæoraptor: aka dino-bird, missing link between dinosaurs and archæopteryx with bird-like head and dromæosaur body
archæothere: [*After the Dinosaurs* by Donald R. Prothero] giant swine from Rupelian age (early Oligocene)
archelon: [*The Big Bad Book of Beasts* by Michael Largo] 4-meter sea turtle
archosaur: [*The Mistaken Extinction* by Lowell Dingus and Timothy Rowe] ancestor to both birds and crocodiles and croc-like griffinoid
archtocyon: ["bear-dog", *After the Dinosaurs* by Donald R. Prothero] bear-sized arctocynoid
arckee: [backformation] archer prey from Zeut
arcker: ["Beasts of Zeut" by William Voltz] 90-cm, deadly beavers with round black head, back pouch, symbiotic with croccisor and spicoulo, rarely violet from Zeut [aka Taimon, Dschadoq]
arctodus: [*After the Dinosaurs* by Donald R. Prothero] 3/4-tonne, short-faced, black bear [*The Museum of Hoaxes* by Alex Boese] from Siberia, Terra (alpha Zodiaci III)
arctopithicus: ["bear-ape", *Historie of Foure-Footed Beastes* by Edward Topsell] bear-like quadruped with ape-like head
Arcturian ape: ["Dawnstar Rising" by Paul Levitz] pongoid from Arcturus (alpha Boötis) system
ard: [French canard mondegreen, drab ard palindrome] drab duck-like ornithoid from Ca system

ardipithecus: [*After the Dinosaurs* by Donald R. Prothero] walking ape

arenahippo: [arenahippus hippo portmanteau] hippoid from Arena system

arenahippus: [*After the Dinosaurs* by Donald R. Prothero] horse from Danian age (early Eocene)

aresil: [Liseran aresil palindrome] purple ornithoid

Arethian flu virus: ["Eye of the Needle"] virus producing flu-like symptoms from Areth

arg: [gray arg palindrome] pale black dlef, see aps

argah: [*Legacy* by Michael Jan Friedman] egg-layer

argali: [*Dell Crossword Puzzle Dictionary*] wild sheep from Asia, see rasse

argas: [*Dell Crossword Puzzle Dictionary*] tick, see acarid

argator: [arg alligator portmanteau] alligator-like predator whose bite morphs victim into arg

argea: [*The Cry of the Onlies* by Judy Klass] 6-legged arboreal creature from Boaco VI

argemop: [pomegranate ananymondegreen] red jelly-thick ooze from Eta system

argen: [negra argen palindrome] black creature from Spain, Terra (alpha Zodiaci III), see arg

argentosaur: ["silver lizard", *The Big Bad Book of Beasts* by Michael Largo] 39-meter herbivorous dinosaur from Argentina, Terra (alpha Zodiaci III)

argentotaur: [argentosaur minotaur portmanteau] silver-colored bovinoid

arghooler: [trumpeter swan backformation] variant of oboe swan with mating call with droning component

argidram: [mardi gras argidram palindrome] purplish ornithoid

arglatch: [narglatch elision] fierce hunter

argle: [nargle elision] packrat-like pest

argmid: [dim gray argmid palindrome] dim gray ornithoid

argopelter: [*Monster Spotter's Guide to North America* by Scott Francis] reclusive creature that argopelts (hurls splinters and branches at passerby from tree hollow)

argumzio: [Hildegard of Bingen's Lingua Ignota] gryphon from Ignota, Hildegard's system

argus: [Xanth series by Piers Anthony] lungfish with boar-like head with tusks and 3 eyes in chevron along torso from Xanth

arietis: [aries, piscium extrapolation] egg-laying ram-like quadruped

arimäer: [*Laire* by William Voltz] aka relationship bird, ornithoid from Bostell, moon of Välgerspäre, Torgnish system or Algstogermaht aka Tschuschik

aris: [ookaris mondegreen] blue simian pet

arisi: [Turkish yabanarisi backformation] wasp-like insectoid from Yaba system

ariz: [Hildegard of Bingen's Lingua Ignota] butterfly-like insectoid from Ignota, Hildegard's system

Arkarian waterfowl: ["Starship Mine" by Morgan Grendel] ornithoid noted for mating habits from Arkar

arkliukas: [Lithuanian juru arkliukas backformation] ancestor to juru and seahorse from Lithuan system

arknoust: [tsuonkracervus ananymondegreen] bovinoid from Suvreca system

arlzak: [narlzak elision] large mealworm-like burrower

armadillo bear: [Avatar: The Last Airbender: "City of Walls and Secrets"] armored ursoid

armadillo wolf: [Avatar: The Last Airbender] armored wolf-like caninoid

armored mantis: [*The World of Synnabarr* by Raymond C. S. McCracken] bright green, 2.1-meter, 180-kg mantis with metallic blue wings from Mars (fka alpha Zodiaci IV)

arn: [barn owl spoonerism] large ruminant dependant on symbiot for digestion

arna: [*Dell Crossword Puzzle Dictionary*] aka arni, arnee, water buffalo from India

arnee: see arna

arner: [arnee backformation] water buffalo predator

arni: see arna

arnokh: [gaarnokh mondegreen] gray-green horned creature

arnu: [sunray arnus palindrome] orange ornithoid

aro: [aro lora palindrome] lora-like amphisbæna

aroc: [coral aroc palindrome] pink ornithoid, see roc

arok: long seaworm with fins and gills from Relegooturnia (Phoenix IV), Galaxiki galaxy

aroll: ["Speculation of Death" by H. G. Francis] green-furred, chupacabra-like felinoid with suction-cupped tail from Akkantho

arollope: [aroll antelope portmanteau] aroll with antlers

arrasti: [Basque narrasti elision] reptilian

arrau: [*Dell Crossword Puzzle Dictionary*] turtle from Amazon

arsinothere: [*After the Dinosaurs* by Donald R. Prothero] fka embrithopod, elephant-sized hyrax with two bony nose-horns from Eocene Turkey or Paleocene China, Terra (alpha Zodiaci III)

ärter: [Perry Rhodan] 4-legged mount dinosaur from Nagath (Cepor II), Erendyra galaxy

arthrobacter: extremophilic bacterium resistant to extreme alkaline, see vibio, psychrobacter

artie: [Perry Rhodan] flocking creature noted for mass shedding at sunset from Arptot, Take Rischen empire, Greulfin galaxy

artiu: [artiu duitra palindrome] duitra-like amphisbæna

arui: [*Dell Crossword Puzzle Dictionary*] wild sheep from N. Africa, Terra (alpha Zodiaci III), see (ao)udad

arwhal: [narwhal mondegreen] spotted, tusked cetacean

arwhalope: [arwhal antelope portmanteau] arwhal with antlers

Arxisto hawk: ["Wastetime" by H. G. Francis] 2-meter hawk-like flightless ornithoid hunted for neck scent gland from Arxisto (Arx II), Hercules cluster (M13)

ary: [toucanary mondegreen] yellow, long-beaked ornithoid from Touca system

arzazl: ["The Arena Fighters" by H. G. Wers] 20-cm penguin-like ornithoid with shiny, snow-white hairy feathers with black back stripe, short legs, yellow webbed feet, blue scaly five-fingered hands from Chiume

arzazling: [backformation] immature arzazl, hand-sized tadpole-like creature from Chiume

arzazlingator: [arzazling alligator portmanteau] alligator-like predator whose bite morphs victim into arzazling

arzazlope: [arzazl antelope portmanteau] arzazl with antlers

as: [argas mondegreen] grey tick

asakku: [Assyrian] animal-headed anthropoid

asaur: [genasaur backformation] goose-reptilian griffinoid

ascarid: [*Dell Crossword Puzzle Dictionary*] pinworm

ascon: [*Dell Crossword Puzzle Dictionary*] small sponge

asep: [pesanat ananymondegreen] light brown, nocturnal nimravid from Ta system

asgurd: [Perry Rhodan] predatory mount from Weir Misty, Häturinssan (Zaytgraver VI), Sombrero galaxy

ashi-magari: ["leg-turner"] soft, cottony dust-bunny-like nocturnal tripper

ashtah: [nashtah elision] 6-legged, bloodthirsty, green, sleek-sinned sauroid with triple row of teeth, diamond-hard claws, long barbed tail

asi: [Turkish denizanasi backformation] jellyfish-like sea creature from Deniza; [*Dell Crossword Puzzle Dictionary*] mollusk from Samoa, Terra (alpha Zodiaci III)

asiatosuchus: [*After the Dinosaurs* by Donald R. Prothero] 4-meter crocodilian from Paleocene

askhan: [*Prophet of the Stars* by Hans Kneifel] mount from Anubis

asno: [*Dell Crossword Puzzle Dictionary*] ass from Spain, Terra (alpha Zodiaci III)

aspara: [Islandia] scarlet-beaked white seagull with brown back, swift and agile as swallow from Doring marshes

aspidochelone: [*The Big Bad Book of Beasts* by Michael Largo] giant sea tortoise

aspis drone: ["The Ecology of the Aspis Drone" by Jonathan M. Richards] off-white insectoid with chitinous shell, 6 clawed legs, 2 multifaceted eyes, short blunt antennae and long proboscis

aspis: small, very musical dragon

assassin bug: [Piers Anthony] insect which kills other insects on contact from Xanth

assp: [ass-asp portmanteau] venomous equinoid with large ears, serpentine neck and head

Astran dragon: [*The Stars Are Ours* by Andre Norton] winged yellow-green 2.5-meter snake from Astra (Deutero-Sol II), with small flat head on a long neck, protruding belly, 25-centimeter claws, large webbed feet

astrapothere: [*After the Dinosaurs* by Donald R. Prothero] mastodon-like creature with trunk and enlarged tusks

astro-viper: serpentine with venom which causes Nagoid limb atrophy

astruca: [Corsican *] 2-D pentapus or hexapus

asu: [susanasus ananymondegreen] snouter from Susa system

asvinni: [Belarussian svinnia backformation] porpoise-pig amphibian ancestral to pig and porpoise from Belaruss system

asyendietha: [gaasyendietha mondegreen] gray-green dracoid

asyÿyriak: [*Creatures of the Galaxy* by Phil Brucato, Bill Smith, Rick D. Stuart, Chuck Truett] avian-eater with long brown and green hair, six legs with talons, long neck, hiberate in hollow trees, from Kashÿyÿk, Jedi galaxy

at: [pesanat mondegreen, tan at palindrome] light brown, noctunal nimravid from Pesa system; [Eng. @] 2-D shapeshifter, see chioccda, gi, golbangi, klammerraffer, miukumauka, papaki, shu; [tanager ananymondegreen] forest-dwelling ornithoid from Rega system; [tanam ananymondegreen] gray ornithoid from Ma system; [tanote ananymondegreen] wild caninoid from Eta system

atanodon: [Atanodon odonata palindrome] toothed dragonfly-like insectoid

atanooro: [beheaded and curtailed matanooroc] 5-headed, 5-tailed, very large dracoid with red eyes and mossy, forested back

ataur: [asaur minotaur portmanteau] goose-bovinold griffinoid

atazi: [Azerbaijani at-tazi portmanteau] horse-greyhound, large greyhound-like caninoid steed from Azerbaija system

atch: [natch elision] bushy-footed squirrel-like creature with large eyes, snout and crest

ate: [tanate mondegreen] wild dog from Ta system

atee: [megamanatee mondgreen] large sea mammal from Megama system

ateel: [manateel mondegreen] snake-like sea mammaloid from Ma system

ateles: [*Dell Crossword Puzzle Dictionary*] spider monkey, see quata, coaita

ateng: [Indonesian/Malay banateng backformation] bison-like beast, related to teng, from Ba system

atengator: [ateng alligator portmanteau] alligator-like predator whose bite morphs victim into ateng

athach: [*Monster Manual* by Skip Williams, Jonathan Tweet and Monte Cook] 3-armed, sickly-green pongoid with soft brown fur, pear-shaped face and black teeth

athair: [Irish nathair elision] green serpentoid from Snowi, Nejstea system, Galaxiki galaxy

athol: ["Ah-OOooool!", The Mysterious World] giant fish-eating chiropteran with flat, monkey-like face, small body and 3.6-meter wingspan and haunting howl and aversion to people

atholope: [athol antelope portmanteau] athol with antlers

atne: [magenta atne gam palindrome] purplish red gam, see elet

atomy: [*Dell Crossword Puzzle Dictionary*] mite, see acari(d), acarus

ator: [Ken's ator krotasnek palindrome] krotasnek-like amphisbæna from Ken's system

atrat: [tartan atrat palidrome] multicolored striped rodentoid

atrociraptor: ["cruel thief", Feathered Dinosaurs: The Origin of Birds by John Long and Peter Schuten] 80-cm dromaeosaur with short snout with backward-angled teeth

atrociraptor: ["cruel thief", *Feathered Dinosaurs: The Origin of Birds* by John Long and Peter Schuten] 80-cm dromaeosaur with short snout with backward-angled teeth

atsaldi: [Cherokee Tsalagi] ichthoid from Tsalgi system

atterjack: [natterjack elision] insectivorous toad-like batrachoid

attogurp: [centigurp extrapolation] pink furball able to bounce, roll, fond of spheres, and be in elghteenplex places at once, see gurp

Aubrey's dog: [Aubrey of Montdidier's dog, dragon] dracoid from Aubrey's world

aug: [guanaco ananymondegreen] llama-like desert animal from Oca system

auga: [nauga elision] animal hunted to extinction for its durable hide

augator: [auga alligator palindrome] alligator-like predator whose bite morphs victim into auga

augi: [iguanadon ananymondegreen] herbivorous dinosaur from Noda system; [iguanat ananymondegreen] 6-legged sauroid from Ta system

augrey: [*Fantastic Beasts and Where to Find Them* by Newton Artemis Fido Scamander] aka Irish phoenix, small, greenish-black vulture-like bird from Ireland, Terra (alpha Zodiaci III)

aukoala: [auk-koala portmanteau] amphibian with razor-bill, short wings, webbed feet, large ears, sharp claws, marsupial pouch

aura moose: ["The Deadly Test" by Hans Kneifel] huge quadruped from Pthor

aura: [*Worlds Apart: Nat. Hist. of Furaha and Earth* by Souren Nyoroge] honey producing insectoid from Lake l'Ambique, Furaha (alpha Phoenicis IV); [*Dell Crossword Puzzle Dictionary*] turkey buzzard or vulture, see urubu, condor

auroch: extict ox-like bovine, [*Unexplained!* by Jerome Clark] see rimi

aurok: [naurok elision] desert ornithoid

aus: [walaus mondegreen] green aquatic insectoid

aushfa: [Ili-Golik] creature from T'Khasi, Nevasa (40 Eridani) system

aut: [Icelandic naut elision, mondegreen] bovoid from Suliua system

autilus: [nautilus elision, palindrome] sea aut, chamber-shelled cephalopodan mollusc from Sulitua system

aux: [Perry Rhodan] acid-spraying, lizard-like predator from Curayo, Minzant system, Puydor galaxy

av: [*Unofficial Questarian Guide*] bee-like insectoid from Tev'Meck, MakTar system

ava: [*Dell Crossword Puzzle Dictionary*] hummingbird, see topaz, colibri; [nava elision] large ruminant

avalancher: [*Monster Manual III*] large, rock-like hexapod with one glowing orange eyestalk, toothed mouth

avant: [avant garde dog mondegreen] precognitive guarddog

avar: [Turkish canavar backformation] monstrous ar (beagle-rabbit) from Ca system

aved: [devanaan ananymondegreen] insectoidal helicopteryx from Naa system

aveilebnu: [unbelievable elb aveilebnu palindrome] fantastic variety of elb-like spheroid, see idercni, issopmi

aven: [unkindness of ravens spoonerism] raven-like gan ceann

avespa: [Galician ave-vespa portmanteau] bird-wasp from Galic system

avi: [OviPets] egg-laying ornithoid, see haliaeetus, psittaco, struthio

avimimus: ["bird-mimic", *Feathered Dinosaurs: The Origin of Birds* by John Long and Peter Schuten] 1.5-meter oviraptorosaur with partially fused arm bones, long legs

avoc: [avocet mondegreen] wading variety of et from Pia or Touca systems
avocet: [*Dell Crossword Puzzle Dictionary*] aka avoset, wading bird, see ibis, rail, crane, egret, heron, stilt, jacana, flamingo
avod: [cordovan avod roc palindrome] reddish brown roc
avolakia: [*Age of Worms Overlord* by Erik Mona] ghoulish wormspawn from Greyhawk
avoset: see avocet
avray: [*Brightness Falls from the Air* by James Tiptree, Jr., Daneii "horror, doom"] plum-colored decapodal arachnoid from Damiem, Yrrei system
aw: ["Tabu Sector Leron" by Arndt Ellmer] beast from Leron, Gulbert Leron system
awa: [*Dell Crossword Puzzle Dictionary*] milkfish, see sabalo
awiyusti: [Cherokee Tsalagi] antelope from Tsalagi system
awku: [awku nu-kwa palindrome] nu-kwa-like amphisbæna
awoo: ["Prince of Peril" by Otis Adelbert Kline] large, scaly, gray wolf-like creature with spiny ruff from Zarovia (alpha Zodiaci II)
axilim: ["The Iron Finger of God" by Gisbert Haefs] bovoid from Dyon's world (Dyon I)
axolotl: [*The Big Bad Book of Beasts* by Michael Largo] "walking fish", devolved salamander with larval gills
axolotlope: [axolotl antelope portmanteau] axolotl with antlers
ay: [beheaded bay] red gan ceann
aya: [*The Queen of Zamba*, etc. by L. Sprague de Camp] equinoid steed from Krishna, tau Ceti system
ayc: [cyan ayc palindrome] blue ornithoid
aye: aye-aye nasna
aye-aye: bushy-tailed monkey with chopstick-like mid-fingers from Madagascar
ayff: ["Spiders in the Desert" by Ernst Vlcek] giant ornithoid of prey
ayklisty: ["Mysterious Zyrph" by H. G. Francis] giant sauroid from Zyrph
ayoba: [ayoba daboya palindrome] daboya-like amphisbæna

ayu: [*Dell Crossword Puzzle Dictionary*] sweetfish
ayuk: [*King David's Spaceship* by Jerry Pourelle] moose-like creature with prehensile tail and semi-prehensile claws from Makassar
az: [xag-az mondegreen] ancestor of xag-az
azabache: [Final Fantasy] jet-black flan-thick ooze
azdyryth: [Pellucidar series by Edgar Rice Burroughs] small whale-like sea creature with gator-like head from Pellucidar
azeb: [nazeb elision] gold-spotted hellfire-breathing creature
azi: [atazi mondegreen] light brown horse-greyhound steed
azined [denizanasi ananymondegreen] jelly-fish-like creature from Isa rogue planet
azul: [Final Fantasy] blue flan-thick ooze
azzi: [azzi pizza palindrome] food porcoid which is also source of milk and cheese, related to egasua
azzip: [pizzazz azzip palindrome] magenta ornithoid
azzipede: [azzip centipede portmanteau] azzip larva
azzit: [stizza azzits palindrome] reddish brown ornithoid
b: [Piers Anthony] insect of any of many subspecies; bumble b, quilting b, sewing b from hives that b-devil, b-foul, b-lieve, b-seige, and b-wilder from Xanth, [banana b palindrome] yellow b
b'rd: [i-less bird] eye-less cave ornithoid noted for sonar, see ivore
ba: [Basque ganba backformation] prawn-like sea creature from Ga system
ba'albeast: ["Passages" by Joe Haldeman] noted for chittering mating challenge from Selva, Confederation space
baaboon: [baa baboon portmanteau] wooly baboon-like simian
Baakinese eagle: ["Hejji" by Theodore "Dr. Seuss" Geisel] eagle from Baako, only creature to travel over mountains surrounding Baako valley
bab: [baby bab palindrome] blue ancestor of floob-boober-bab-boober-bub

babelf: [babel fish backformation] non-telepathic babel fish mimic

babel fish: [*Hitchhiker's Guide to the Galaxy* by Doug Adams] small, telepathic ichthyoid able to translate sounds into thoughts when stuck in ear

babewyn: [*The Adventuress of Henrietta Street* by Lawrence Miles] savage, devilish pongoid, hunted on St. Belique, Caribbean Sea

babi: [babirusa mondegreen] deer-like ancestor of babirusa

babirusa: [*National Geographic Encyclopedia of Animals*] hippoid from Indonesia

babookaris: [*The Future Is Wild* by Dougal Dixon] grassland-dwelling simian descended from red-faced, non-prehensile-tailed uakari

bacillus: extremophilic bacterium resistant to extreme acid, see natronobacterium, clostridium

badger: [The Big Bad Book of Beasts by Michael Largo] burrower with black-and-white striped face "badge"

badgermole: [Avatar: The Last Airbender: "The Cave of Two Lovers"] brown badger-like burrower with one white and two black stripes, facemask and mole-like shovel-claws

badzi: [Armenian bad-dzi portmanteau] duck-horse pegasoid from Armen system

bag monkey: ["The Time Command" by Clark Darlton] deformed simian from Scimore

bagelope: [bagel antelope portmanteau, "The Ecology of the Bagelope" by Kel'anth] wheel-like creature eaten as "bagel" when beheaded

bagg: [baggy backformation] bag-like creature, see bagpuss

baggator: [bagg alligator portmanteau] alligator-like predator whose bite morphs victim into bagg

bagmonk: [bagpuss extrapolation] bag-like toy animal simian

bagorah: [*Ghostbusted*] bat-like monster from Korghan

bagpiper: [trumpeter swan backformation] swan-sandpiper-like ornithoid with bagpipe-like call

bagpuss: ["Bagpuss",] bag-like toy animal felinoid, see bagg

bai ze: [*Monsters almanac*, "white marsh"] shaggy quadruped from China

bail: [bevy of quails spoonerism] straw-colored cuboid

baja: ["The March Through the Underworld" by Ernst Vlcek] pongoid from Cronot, Heith system

bajda: [Maltese pernici bajda backformation] ptarmigan-partridge ornithoid ancestral to partridge and ptarmigan

bak: [fanback mondegreen] egg-laying sauroid from Fa (iota Orionis) system

bakabayo: [Filipino baka-kabayo portmanteau] cow-horse, milk equinoid

bakamaru: ["Seed of Reason" by Daniel Hatch] green, arboreal felinoid from Cham

baktee: [Fr. Johann Martin Schleyer's Volapük bakter "bacterium" backformation] host of Schleyer's bacterium

baktermit: [Albanian bakter-termit backformation] bacterium-termite symbiot from Alban system

baku: [Sankai Ibutsu] yellow and black tapir-like chimera with elephant's trunk, rhino's eyes, ox's tail, tiger's paws that eats bad dreams from Japan, Terra (alpha Zodiaci III)

balæna: island-sized fish with sabre-like dorsal fin

balarāma: [Mahabharata] monstrous snake

balaseli: ["Passage" by Joe Haldeman] flying creature both like manta and bat with 3.6-meter wingspan, 12 legs, glossy black back, white underside with hook-like cilia able to skin victim before eating alive, faced in rite of passage to adulthood from Obelobel

balat srar: [*Planiverse* by Alexander Dewdney] 2-D sea animal from Arde, Shems system

balaur: dracoid with 3 or more serpentine heads, fins from Romania

bald iggle: ["L'il Abner" by Al Capp] cute little wide-eyed, guileless creature hunted to extinction because it induces truthfulness, see iggle

bald mammoth: [Godville] elephant-like mammoth without hair

baldlab: [mynynym] hairless Labrador-like caninoid

baldnander: [*Here Be Monsters almanac*] creature that baldnands (shapeshifts)

baligi: [Turkish yilanbaligi backformation] eel-snake, amphibious serpentoid from Yila peninsula, Snowi, Nejstea system, Galaxiki galaxy

ball creature: [*Han Solo at Star's End* by Brian Daley] docile, nocturnal spheroidal herbivore that moves by bouncing from Duroon, Jedi galaxy

balloon animal: ["Beast of the Underworld" by Kurt Mahr] large spheroid with feeding tentacles from Afrot (Frua III)

balloon mouse: ["A Dark and Stormy Night" by Larry Blamire] tiny dustmite-like creature

balloonie: ["Superman under the Red Sun"] light blue batrachoid with 2 lidless eyes and 2 short antennae able to blow up into a lighter-than-air spheroid from Krypton, Rao system

balu: [*Dell Crossword Puzzle Dictionary*] wildcat, lynx from Sumatra, Terra (alpha Zodiaci III)(

baluchithere: aka paracerathere, largest land mammal, 5.5-meters at shoulder, long-legged rhinoid with longish neck and no nose horn

bambiraptor: [*A Field Guide to Dinosaurs* by Henry Gee and Luis V. Rey, *Feathered Dinosaurs: The Origin of Birds* by John Long and Peter Schuten] 70-cm bird-like dromaeosaur with relatively large brain

bamoda: [*Cyclopedia of Worlds*] 2.5-meter green-gray sea predator, similar to docile guchod, from Dakka, Neptune system

Bampire vat: large bloodthirsty pitcherplant-like planimal from Bampire Empire

bamsun: ["The Third Law" by Cathrin Hartmann] animal from Intrawelt, Dwingeloo galaxy

ban: [band of swans spoonerism, bananaquit mondegreen] long-necked relative of anaquit

bananaquit: [*National Geographic Encyclopedia of Animals*] nectar-eating songbird from Caribbean and S. America

bananivore: [Terra Monsters] bipedal, green carnivore with bushy tail and collar from Terrarium

bananteater: [Terra Monster] bushy-tailed ardvark-like nector-sucker, see bananivore, from Terrarium

bandara: [*Creatures of the Galaxy* by Phil Brucato, Bill Smith, Rick D. Stuart, Chuck Truett] sand-dwelling beetle-like insectoid with loud mating call from Devaron, Jedi galaxy

bandersnatch: [*Through the Looking Glass, and What Alice Found There* by Charles "Lewis Carroll" Dodgson] creature with extensible neck and frumious; ["Dear Mom" by Stephen C. Fisher] larger-than-man-sized woodwoose (blue-black lagardbird) from La Paz

bandicoot: [*Dell Crossword Puzzle Dictionary*] rat from Ceylon or India, Terra (alpha Zodiaci III)

bandito: [*The Ultimate Monster Guide* by Jaymond] green biped with 3-toed claws, fangs, 1 eye, large tail, and exoskeleton

banditry: ["The Great Silence" by Marianne Sydow] symbiotic nyzel, farrn and drohs

banefly: [Outernauts] non-flying, six-legged immature ruinfly

Banerian hawk: ["If Wishes Were Horses" by Nell McCue and William L. Crawford] hawk-like ornithoid from Baneria

banteng: [*Dell Crossword Puzzle Dictionary*] wild ox from Malaysia, Terra (alpha Zodiaci III)

bantengator: [banteng alligator portmanteau] alligator-like predator whose bite morphs victim into banteng

**banth**: [Barzoom series by Edgar Rice Burroughs] dog-like decapodal predator, 3.5-meters long, yellow-skinned, hairless except for great bristly mane, several rows of needle-like fangs, enormous green eyes and powerful tail from Mars (alpha Zodiaci IV)

bantha: ["Star Wars IV: A New Hope" by George Lucas, *Tatooine Manhunt* by Bill Slavicsek and Daniel Greenberg] large quadruped with long thick fur, (males) with long spiral horns, believed by Dim-U priests to hold key to a new golden age from Jedi galaxy

bar juchne: ["Xoology" by Kittenbaker] huge bird with 24-meter egg from Szurane

bara-gnu: ["The Robot Rebels" by Ernst Vlcek] long-horned gnu breed on Betabara II

baragon: [Godzilla series] 45-meter saurian with body back shell, large ears, curved forehead horn, ability to spit lightning bolts and leap great distances

barb: [*Dell Crossword Puzzle Dictionary*] horse from Barbary, pigeon or horse-pigeon pegasoid, see nun, dove, pouter, roller

barbet: [*National Geographic Encyclopedia of Animals*] woodpecker relative from S. America, see barb, et

barbourofelis: [*After the Dinosaurs* by Donald R. Prothero] sabre-toothed nimravid from Miocene

barbu: ["prickle-face", L'Isle inconnoe by Guillaume Grivel] creature larger than dog from coastal woods of L'Isle Inconnoe, Indian Ocean, Terra (Sol)

bardaj: [Perry Rhodan] 6-legged predator from Nubecula Major

bardelot: [*After Man* by Dougal Dixon] sabre-toothed predatory rat

bardicant: [*Araminta Station* by Jack Vance] large and voracious but lithe, slate-gray omnivore with skewer-like tail from Deucas

bardok: [*Yesterday's Son* by A. C. Crispin] white-furred creature from Sarpeidon, beta Niobe system

Barey slime worm: ["Exodus of Hearts" by Uwe Anton] dangerous slime worm from Barey IV

bargans: [Afrikaans barg-gans portmanteau] aka hogoose, griffinoid from Afrika binary system

bargump: [*Ghost-Walker* by Barbara Hambly] dominant predator from Midgwis (Elcidar Beta III)

baricou: [caribou spoonerism, baracuta] land baracuta-like amphibious polar ruminant

barking toad: [Warhammer 40,000] exploding toad-like batrachian from Catachan

barkslug: [*Edge Chronicles* by Paul Stewart and Chris Riddell] larval barkworm from Edgeworld, Cerulea system

barkslugator: [barkslug alligator portmanteau] alligator-like predator whose bite morphs victim into barkslug

barkworm: [*Midnight Over Santaphrax* by Paul Stewart and Chris Riddell] wild bookworm-like worm

barn beetle: see hessi

barnacle-goose: [*Herbal* by John Gerarda] goose-like ornithoid said to begin life in barnacle-like shell on seaside tree

Barnard cat: [*Cyclopedia of Worlds*] tail-less Haullshay cats adapted to Cathole (Barnard IV) with larger ribcage and eyes from Barnard's Star system

barnetta: [Monster Galaxy] insectoid with beehive hairdo from Monster galaxy

Barniter monkey: ["The Monster of Quinto Center" by H. G. Francis] piebald simian

barophile: extremophile resistant to extreme pressure

barr fly: ["Three Times Eternal Life" by Michael Nagula] insectoid

barracus: ["Humanity in the Twilight" by H. K. Scheer] 35-cm, blue-black ornithoid with 22-cm tail, metallic red underbelly, ochre yellow wings

barrel fish: [Godville] fish adapted to water barrels, usually dockside

barri: [*Creatures of the Galaxy* by Phil Brucato, Bill Smith, Rick D. Stuart, Chuck Truett] space-dwelling rock-eaters from Jedi galaxy

barylambda: [*After the Dinosaurs* by Donald R. Prothero] sheep-sized mammal from late Paleocene

barymu: [barylambda extrapolation] emu-like griffinoid

barythere: ["heavy beast", *After the Dinosaurs* by Donald R. Prothero] primitive mastodont with short tusks and no trunk from Priabonian (late Eocene)

basan: hellfire-breathing chicken from Iyo province, Japan, Terra (alpha Zodiaci III)

baseball bat: [Xanth series by Piers Anthony] long, thin leathery winged chiropteroid from Xanth

bashaw: [3-tailed Turkish hat] creature with three tails, see sanbi, umibouzu, vextail

basilisk: [*Fabulous Beasts and Demons* by Heinz Mode] aka cockatrice, dangerous creature with cock's body, iron claws and beak, triple snake's tail, whose stare is fatal enough to kill it by its own reflection

basilosaur: ["king-lizard", *Monster Spotter's Guide to North America* by Scott Francis] large sea serpent-like whale, which may have freshwater "lake snake" varieties, [*After the Dinosaurs* by Donald R. Prothero] related to gaviocetus and dorudon

basilotaur: basilosaur minotaur portmanteau] bull-headed lake snake

bask: [Xanth series by Piers Anthony] generic term for basilisk, cockatrice, henatrice, chickatrice, Land of Basks, Xanth

bassooner: [trumpeter swan backformation] swan-like ornithoid with bassoon-like call, see contrabassooner

Bast eel: [Bastille mondegreen] predatory eel-like ichthyoid that captures by swarming before beheading from Bast system

basto: [Amtor series by Edgar Rice Burroughs] large, wild blue boar-like creature with powerful tusks, elephantine-like hide from Amtor (alpha Zodiaci II)

bat-echidna: ["A Fact Sheet for the Marco Polo" and "The City and the Spaceship" by Hans Kneifel] bat-like echnida with red-black wings, long claws, fanged snout from Leffa, Mayselan system, Sombrero galaxy

bat-fish: ["Equinox" by Rick Berman, Brannon Braga and Joe Menosky] neucleogenic lifeform considered benevolent by Yankuri

bat-man: [batman mondegreen] bat-headed anthropoid

bat-snake: ["Hunters of the Sky Cave" bu Poul Anderson] 1-meter dracoid from Ardazir, Hatch nebula

batficli: [James Cooke Brown's Loglan batra ficli compound] butterfish-like ichthyoid from Logla, Brown's system

batflaki: [James Cooke Brown's Loglan batra flaki compound] butterfly-like insectoid from Logla, Brown's system

bathybius: [Thomas Huxley] gelatinous deep-sea organism

batonoid: [*After the Dinosaurs* by Donald R. Prothero] smallest known mammal, insectivore from Cenozoic

batrachopteryx: ["Exodus of Hearts" by Uwe Anton] flying batrachoid from Golundar

batsquatch: [bat-winged sasquatch, *Monster Spotter's Guide to North America* by Scott Francis] 1.8-meter simian-faced, dark purplish nape with bat-like wings from Mt. St. Helens/Mt. Rainier region, Terra (alpha Zodiaci III)

battering ram: [Xanth series by Piers Anthony] small, curly-horned, wooly sheep-like ruminant, related to hydraulic ram, from Xanth

bavarisaur: [*Feathered Dinosaurs: The Origin of Birds* by John Long and Peter Schuten] prey of compsognathus

bawk: [bol of hawks spoonerism] herbivorous hawk-like ornithoid

bay: [*Dell Crossword Puzzle Dictionary*] red horse, see roan

baya: [*Dell Crossword Puzzle Dictionary*] weaverbird, see maya, taha

baybear: [bayberry backformation] baybee honey-eating ursinoid

baybee: [bay, baby mondegreen] red bay-dwelling bee-like insectoid related to seabee

baybee bug: [babybuggy backformation] baybee-mimicking insectoid

baybee bugator: [baybee bug alligator portmanteau] alligator-like predator whose bite morphs victim into baybee bug

baykok: [*Here Be Monsters almanac*] liver-eating skeletal carnivore with glowing eyes

Bayov pig: [Bay of Pigs mondegreen] killer porcoid from Bayov's world

baz: [Polish bazant backformation] feathered insectoid from Pol system

baž: [Slovak bažant backformation] see baz

bazor: ["Bad Eggs" by Marti Noxon] parasite that hatches from egg as green and tentacled, becoming slimy and scorpion-like

be: [Navaho] deer-like creature from Diné system

be-i-chahār-sar: [doubly beheaded ābbe-i-chahār-sar] winged creature

bea: honey-collector from Habitat (Iestonian Spiral IV), Galaxiki galaxy

beach bear: [*After the Dinosaurs* by Donald R. Prothero] see kolponomos

bear belly: [bear beer belly portmanteau] furry spheroid

Bear Lake monster: [*Monster Spotter's Guide to North America* by Scott Francis] brown lake snake with ears, short flipper-like legs from Bear Lake, UT, Terra (alpha Zodiaci III)

bear-dog: [*Monster Spotter's Guide to North America* by Scott Francis] see waheela, amarok from N. Pacific coast, arctocyon

bear-lion: bear-headed lion-like felinoid, see cub

bear-dogator: [bear-dog alligator portmanteau] alligator-like predator whose bite morphs victim into bear-dog

bear-wolf: bear-headed wolf-like caninoid, see cub

bearcat: creature with both bear and cat characteristics from Stutz system; large, bug-eyed variety with double row of fangs from Fenris (zeta Lupi III)

beardale: [bear-airedale portmanteau] ursinoid with wiry tan hair with black markings from Skjoob, Bjosko system, Galaxiki galaxy

beardog: [*After the Dinosaurs* by Donald R. Prothero] aka amphicyon from Eocene

beardogator: [beardog alligator portmanteau] alligator-like predator whose bite morphs victim into beardog

beasant: [beasle-ant portmanteau, bouquet of pheasants spoonerism] wooglebug-ant-like insectoid

beasle: [boogle of weasles spoonerism] burrowing, predatory wooglebug-like insectoid

beast-were: [were-beast antonym] beastly anthropoid bimorph offspring of beast and were-beast, see subhu

beast-with-a-thousand-eyes: golem made from eyeballs

Beauty butterfly: [*Conscience Interplanetary* by Joseph Green] 40-kg parent-eating lepidopteran with gold-furry face

beavermine: [beaver-ermine portmanteau] burrowing rodentoid with short legs and flat, broad tail, valued for its fur

becard: [*National Geographic Encyclopedia of Animals*] insect, berry and seed-eating flycatcher bird from Meso-America, Terra (alpha Zodiaci III)

bedbug: [Xanth series by Piers Anthony] insect shaped like bed -- or with nests shaped like one -- from Xanth or [Xanthian mondegreen] Xa, Thia system

bedbugator: [bedbug alligator portmanteau] alligator-like predator whose bite morphs victim into bedbug

bedrat: [redbat spoonerism] bedbug-like rodentoid

bedsnake: ["Robot Hugs" by R. Hugs'] bedbug-like snake that preys on sleepers, see betserpi

bee hamster: ["Red Sun over Ruby" by Detlev G. Winter] palm-sized, hamster-like rodent with brownish-green fur, ranging sensors and transparent gossamer wings from Ruby (Omega II)

bee hemoth: [behemoth mondegreen] giant bee-like insectoid

bee urchin: [bee sea urchin portmanteau, beard of sea urchins spoonerism] bee-headed urchin-like triphibian

beebra: [bee-zebra portmanteau] black-and-white striped bee-like insectoid from Ahla, Ojikh system, Galaxiki galaxy

beefee: [Monster Galaxy] bovinoid from Taurus constellation

beefeel: [beefee eel portmanteau] eel-like seacow

beel: [bed of eels spoonerism, bee eel portmanteau] many-legged, many-winged, bee-eel-like triphibian

beer belly: [Reebok] meter-diameter spheroid with belly button

beerdvark: [Afrikaans portmanteau] boar-aardvark, tusked insectivore from Afrika binary system

beever: [beaver mondegreen] flying carpenter ant-bee-like insectoid

beez: honey-making gestalt from Gizmonian Steepes (Edonian cluster II), Galaxiki galaxy

bega: ["Persecuted and Outlaws" by Falk-Inglo Klee] shy, mountain goat-like ruminant from Aklund (Suuma II), Manam Turu galaxy

begator: [bega alligator portmanteau] alligator-like predator whose bite morphs victim into bega

behe: [behemoth mondegreen] mothra-like giant moth-like insectoid

behemoth: [Job 40:15-24] aka diplodocus, large swamp-dwelling ruminant with log-like tail ["The Movements of Her Eyes" by Scott Westerfeld]; ["Longshot" by Jack C. Haldeman] aquatic creature that leaves photo-active algae ballast behind from outside Local Cluster, 30-meter, tusked race animal like 3 elephants piled up with about as many legs, that eat volmer sprouts, lives to 85 yrs. from Dimian, Rigel system; [*New History of Ethiopia* by Hiob Ludolf] carnivorous hippoid; [*Imperial Moon* by Christopher Bulis] large, jungle game animal from Phiadora

behemothball: [behemoth mothball portmanteau] diplodocus-like dinosaur able to curl up like curl-up

behir: ["The Ecology of the Behir" by Eric Cagle] blue, 12-meter dracoid with 12 short legs, backspines, 2 headspines or smaller behir without lightning-breath from Halruaa

beholder: [The Infinite War] with conical body, one huge eye and 5 claws from Adum

Behrman's worm: ["The Treasure Divers" by Uwe Anton] delicacy on Pregaend

beipiaosaur: [*Feathered Dinosaurs: The Origin of Birds* by John Long and Peter Schuten] therizinosaur with hair-like forelimb and hip feathers from China, Terra (alpha Zodiaci III)

beipiaotaur: [beipiaosaur minotaur portmanteau] bovinoid with hair-like feathers

bekkar: ["The Heir Apparent" by H. G. Francis] rodentoid noted for carrying rabies-like disease, with calming purr and danger sense from Mehan'Ranton (Arkon II)

beldon: [*Creatures of the Galaxy* by Phil Brucato, Bill Smith, Rick D. Stuart, Chuck Truett] aerial creatures up to 10 km diameter from Bespin, Jedi galaxy

belemnite: cephalopod with large bullet-shaped shells from Cretaceous

Beletor parasite: [Buzz Lightyear: "Enemy without a Face" by Elizabeth Stonecipher] neck leech that induces aggression, stunned by cold

belgremer: [Laboris "hidden nest", "Fighter for Garbesh" by H. G. Ewers] nocturnal predator with scorpion-like stinger from Arpa Chai, Wahiet medionalis system

Bell spider: [David Bell in Game of Life] spacefaring arachnoid capable of c/5

Bell wasp: [David Bell in Game of Life] spacefaring insectoid capable of c/3

Bell waspider: [Bell wasp spider portmanteu] space-faring arachinsectoid capable of 8/15c

Belli's giant snake: ["Base Thunder God" by H. G. Francis] 30-meter long serpentoid

bellock: [Perry Rhodan] Celanese hunting animal

bellybreeder: ["The Island of the Lucky Ones" by Hans Kneifel] non-egglaying pterosauroid from Vetrahorn

beluga: [*Dell Crossword Puzzle Dictionary*] white whale, in upland and lowland varieties, see cet(e), orc, ork, grampus

belugator: [beluga alligator portmanteau] alligator-like predator whose bite morphs victim into beluga

BEM: [bug-eyed monster acronym] any monstrous creature with compound eyes

ben: [brood of hens spoonerism, BEM hen momndegreen] monstrous female chicken-like ornithoid with compound eyes, see bock

benddeer: [bender deer portmanteau mondegreen] many-legged deer-like creature able to bend around corners

bendee: [backformation] bender prey from Ugly Islands

bender: [Peter MavInnis] tough-to-kill 1.5-meter ichthyoid with many teeth, spines from Ugly Islands

benu: aka Egyptian phoenix, sacred eagle-like purple heron, see fêng-huang

beo: [Vietnamese con beo backformation] ancestor to con and panther from Disa

beped: mutant with two-thirds as many legs

ber: [Fr. Johann Martin Schleyer's Volapük "bear"] ferocious, polar mammal from Habitat (Iestonian Spiral IV), Galaxiki galaxy

bereglo: [*Languages of Pao* by Jack Vance] rodentoid from Pao

Berengarian dragon: ["This Side of Paradise" by D. C. Fontana] yellow-orange, crested, winged herbivorous 19-meter long dracoid with long tail, 700-year lifespan from Berengaria VI

bergriolet: ["Planet of the Zombies" by Dirk Hess] bergriol-like creature from Aramacs' world

bergruutf: [*Creatures of the Galaxy* by Phil Brucato, Bill Smith, Rick D. Stuart, Chuck Truett] 7-meter tall herbivore with armored frill from Teloc Ol-son, Jedi galaxy

berkomnair: ["Imperator of Arkon" by Rainier Castor] 3-meter elephantine from Iprasa (Arkon VI)

berol: ["The Stolen Space Fleet" by Clark Darlton] sparrow-sized, flying, beetle-like insectoid from Drorah (Akon V)

berret: [business or busyness of ferrets spoonerism, berkomnair-ferret portmanteau] elephantine ferret-like creature

berus: [doubly beheaded erberus] hellhound gan ceann, see heath hound

bervalni: [James Cooke Brown's Loglan berna valni compound] brain beast from Logla, Brown's system

bes sallur: [*Planiverse* by Alexander Dewdney] 2-D air animal from Arde, Shems system

besie: [Afrikaans skilpadbesie backformation] aka ladybug-tortoise, triphibian ancestor to tortoise and ladybug from Afrika binary system

bessie: [*Monster Spotter's Guide to North America* by Scott Francis] 12-meter lake snake from South Bay, Lake Erie or igopogoid from Beaverton, Ont., Terra (alpha Zodiaci III)

bètan: [Haitian bèt-tan portmanteau] beastly horsefly-like insectoid from Hait system

Betelguezean fungus: ["Swarm" by Bruce Sterling] anaerobic fungus edible by both Swarm and Humans from Betelgeuse (alpha Orionis) system

betserpi: [James Cooke Brown's Loglan betpu serpi compound] bedsnake from Logla, Brown's system

bexen: [*Stranger from the Stars* by Nancy Etchemendy] grass-dweller from Seldor, Sargas (theta Scorpii) system

bez: [bezant mondegreen] black ant-like insectoid with gold spots

bezant panther: [heraldry] monstrous felinoid with gold spots, flaming mouth and ears

bgregg: ["Leticron of the Superheavy" by William Voltz] animal sometimes fought the death for "sport"

bgreggator: [bgregg alligator portmanteau] alligator-like predator whose bite morphs victim into bgregg

bharal: [*Dell Crossword Puzzle Dictionary*] wild mountain sheep from Tibet, see sha, sna, rasse, urial, nahoor, oorial

bharalope: [bharal antelope portmanteau] bharal with antlers

bhāranka: [Hindi] 2-headed bird from India, Terra (alpha Zodiaci III)

bi: ["Confluence" by Brian Aldiss] cockerel whose crowing lasts over 20 yrs. from N. Myrin

bi-sodih: [Navaho] porcoid from Diné system

bianca: [Italian pernice bianca backformation] aka ptarmigan-partridge, ancestor to both partridge and ptarmigan

bibbling: [*Bibblings* by Barbara Paul] ornithoid necessary for the continued sanity of unmarried, fertile natives from Lodon-Kamaria

bibblingator: [bibbling alligator portmanteau] alligator-like predator whose bite morphs victim into bibbling

bicephalus: ["The Trap" by Finn Donovan] 2-headed serpentoid from Asidia's world
bicorn: man-eater with 2 horns, see man-eating cow
bident: [*Dell Crossword Puzzle Dictionary*] 2-year-old sheep, see teg(g)
bidporju: [James Cooke Brown's Loglan bidje porju compound] edgehog from Logla, Brown's system
bieu: [Fr. Johann Martin Schleyer's Volapük] bee-like insectoid from Schleyer's system
bifci: [James Cooke Brown's Loglan] bee from Logla, Brown's system
bifli: [James Cooke Brown's Loglan bifli clika (bee-like)] bee-like insectoid from Logla, Brown's system
big bird: [*Monster Spotter's Guide to North America* by Scott Francis] dark ornithoid with 4.5-meter wingspan, long tail, thin beak from S. Texas, and [*Unexplained!* by Jerome Clark] gorilla-like face, 3-toed feet
big brown thing: ["Deep Space" by Fred Olen-Ray and T. L. Lankford] large, space-dwelling, slimy, brown man-eater
big mast: [*Cyclopedia of Worlds*] aka fourth mast, 8-meter predator from Emeris, Sheel-Sen system
big pest: [The Tick: "Man-eating Cow"] bacterium causing gigantism in nematoid, stinking smut, and boll weevil
big red: ["Far Side" by Gary Larson] horse with spikes and mace-like tail, see knightmare
big red rock-eater: ["What's big, red and eats rocks?" answer] large, red saxiphage that eats any color rock
big red-rock-eater: [Lost in Space: "The Revolt of the Androids" by Bob and Wanda Duncan] large, white, hairy, saxiphagous anthropoid that feeds on rubies before hibernating
bigbi: ["Turning Point" by Josepha Sherman] long-legged, swamp-dwelling ornithoid from Thallon, Thallonian empire
bigeon: [trigeon backformation] bimorph in two of cigeon, kigeon, pigeon and wigeon forms
bigfoot: see sasquatch

bigg: [biggish backformation] sizeshifting creature, see larg
biggator: [bigg alligator portmanteau] alligator-like predator whose bite morphs victim into bigg
biglemin: [Haitian bigl-lemin portmanteau] beagle-lemming, large lemming-like mammal with long ears from Hait system
bikit: [Bulgarian/Croatian bik-kit portmanteau] bull-whale, horned, hoofed land cetacean
bikos: [Bulgarian bik-kos portmanteau] bull-blackbird, horned, hoofed, black pegasoid from Bulgar system
bilbear: [bilberry backformation] ursinoid from Bil, Whortle system, see whortlebear
bildad: [*Monster Spotter's Guide to North America* by Scott Francis] freshwater creature with kangaroo-like legs, webbed feet, hawk-like beak, beaver tail
Bilindian flu virus: [*Window on a Lost World* by V. E. Mitchell] virus that caused Bilindian influenza
billywig: [*Fantastic Beasts and Where to Find Them* by Newton Artemis Fido Scamander] 2.5-cm insect with sapphire-blue head-propeller wings, long thin stinger whose toxin induces levitation and giddiness from Australia
billywigator: [billywig alligator portmanteau] alligator-like predator whose bite morphs victim into billywig
bimbaccere: ["The Judgment of the Dragon Tree" by Marc C. Herren and Dennis Mathiak] giant, nocturnal lizard or "dragon" of Esero [El Hiero, Canary] island, Terra (alpha Zodiaci III)
bimm: [Perry Rhodan] 1-meter, 40-km flat sheet, warm-blooded with eye ring on stalk head from Tolimon, Revnur's system
bimorph: creature with two different forms like God-man pre- and post-incarnation
bingledip: [Winx Club] steed from Red Fountain stables
binjinph: [binjinphant mondegreen] arboreal ant-like insectoid
binjinphant: ["Droids" series] tesselated arboreal ferret-like macropoid from Tazzum-an, Jedi galaxy

bio: ["Transactions with Arkon-steel" by Kurt Brand] bred art of Ara, from Gom, Gonom system
bioparasite: [*Secret Satellite Troy* by K. H. Scheer] spacefaring amorphic parasite of Moby from Andro-Beta nebula

bippo-no-bungu: [*If I Ran the Zoo* by Theodore Geisel] large, floppy-crested ornithoid with long, striped neck, bulleye's belly and no beak from Hippo-no-Hungus, Dippo-no-Dungus or Nippo-no-Nungus jungles
bippopotamus: [bippo-no-bungu hippopotamus portmanteau, bloat of hippos spoonerism] hippopotamimus from Bippo-no-Bungus river valley
bird-dog: [birddog mondegree] bird-headed caninoid-like pegasoid
bird-man: [birdman mondegreen] bird-headed anthropoid
bird snake: [*After Man* by Dougal Dixon] whistling, predatory snake from Pacaus Islands
hiri: [Basque birigarro backformation] thrush-like ornithoid ancestral to garro and thrush
bishtar: [*The Queen of Zamba*, etc. by L. Sprague de Camp] elephantine cart-puller from Krishna, tau Ceti system
bisma: [James Cooke Brown's Loglan bisli manti] ice-ant from Logla, Brown's system
bisoo: [Outernauts] immature bizaur without tusks
bisse: [James Cooke Brown's Loglan bisli serpi] ice snake from Logla, Brown's system
bisva: [James Cooke Brown's Loglan bisli valni] icebeast from Logla, Brown's system
bit: [The Legend of Zelda: "The Adventure of Link"] red, gelatinous creature unable to jump, enemy of bots from Hyrule
bitingale: ["L'il Abner" by Al Capp] devil-bird whose bite burns for 24 years
bivare: [Outernauts] mature bizaur
bix: [Jerome Bixby mondegreen] bee-like insectoid from Jerome's system
biyelk: [Helliconia trilogy by Brian Aldiss, see yelk] from Helliconia, Batalix-Freyr system

bizaur: [Outernauts] gray creature with orange stripes and horns and tusks, see bisoo, bivare
blaab: bloob variety
blab: [blind crab portmanteau] see blind crab
black caiman: [*River Monsters* by Jeremy Wade] 6-meter broad-bellied crocodilian from Amazon, Terra (alpha Zodiaci III)
black hunter: [white hunter backformation] large, black, herding shark-like triphibian from Peggassa, Hippocrenea system, Galaxiki galaxy
black mercy: ["For the Man Who Has Everything" by Alan Moore] parasitic fungus feeding on bio-auro generated by heart's desire
black pudding: [*Monster Manual* by Skip Williams, etal.] 4.5-meter, 60-cm tall bubbling black pudding-thick ooze, elder variety up to 60 meters
Black River monster: [*Monster Spotter's Guide to North America* by Scott Francis] 6-meter, dark plesiosauroid with bulging eyes from Black River, NY, Terra (alpha Zodiaci III)
black thing: [*Monster Spotter's Guide to North America* by Scott Francis] aka Mulberry black thing, black bear or panther-like man-eater from Cumberland river valley, KY, Terra (alpha Zodiaci III)
blackdog: black hellhound in cat-headed, cow-headed and headless varieties
blackengale: [whitengale backformation] ornithoid which blackens cliffs with droppings
blackfish: [Syzygy by Michael G. Coney] shark-like predator, periodically telepathically controlled by breeding plankton from Arcadia
blade plage: [Resident Evil 4] plage with many tentacles, one bladed
blägböd: [Fr. Johann Martin Schleyer's Volapük] black ornithoid from Schleyer's system
blahb: bloob variety
blakasma: [James Crooke Brown's Loglan blanu kasma] blue bull from Logla, Brown's system
blakatma: [James Cooke Brown's Loglan blanu katma compound] blue cat from Logla, Brown's system

blamanti: [James Cooke Brown's Loglan blama/blanu manti compound] albino or blue ant from Logla, Brown's system
blanca: [Catalan perdiu blanca backformation] ptarmigan-partridge ancestor to partridge and ptarmigan
blanco: [Final Fantasy] white flan-thick ooze
Blandenboro beast: [*The Big Bad Book of Beasts* by Michael Largo] vampiric predator with cat-like head and forelimbs and snake-like body from N. Carolina, Terra (alpha Zodiaci III)
blanirda: [James Cooke Brown's Loglan blabi nirda (white bird) compound] white bird from Logla, Brown's system
blase tree goat: ["Ewoks" series] arboreal goat-like creature that hangs lethargically like sloth, from Endor's moon, Jedi galaxy
blastomeryx: [*After the Dinosaurs* by Donald R. Prothero] musk deer-like with large canines in males
blatigra: [James Cooke Brown's Loglan blanu tigra compound] blue tiger from Logla, Brown's system
blau: [Catalan ocell blau backformation] symbiot that causes bluing
bleachsucker: ["Finale for Snowman" by Hernamm Ritter] venomous centipede-like insectoid that stores prey in caves
bleater: [*Dell Crossword Puzzle Dictionary*] snipe from Europe, Terra (alpha Zodiaci III)
bledbird: [grue-bleen extrapolation] bluebird that turns red, not to be confused with bleenbird, blellowbird, blindigobird, blioletbird, bluebird, gebird, gredbird, redbird, reenbird, rellowbird, rindigobird, rioletbird, ruebird, vedbird or yedbird from Ora system
bleeb: [Cloudstone] orange variety of bloob
bleederfly: [Xanth series by Piers Anthony] blood-letting insect from Land of Flies, Xanth
bleenbird: [blue green portmanteau] blue bird that turns into green bird, not to be confused with bledbird, bleenbird, blellowbird, blindigobird, blioletbird, bluebird, gebird, gredbird, greenbird, grellowbird, grindigobird, grioletbird, gruebird, reenbird, ruebird,

veenbird, vuebird, yeenbird or yuebird from Ora system
blellowbird: [grue-bleen extrapolation] bluebird that turns yellow, not to be confused with bledbird, bleenbird, blindigobird, blioletbird, bluebird, gebird, grubird, ruebird, vuebird, yedbird, yeenbird, yellowbird, yindigobird, yioletbird or yuebird from Ora system
blend butterfly: ["Death in the Turquoise Sea" by Andreas Findig] butterfly-like insectoid from Auroch-Maxo-55, Segafredo galaxy
blender: ["The Galactic Physicians" by Susan Schwartz] hare-like creature from Ariga, Wartok system
bler: [shambler backformation] garbage pile gestalt mimicked by shambler
bligee: [bliger backformation] prey of blue tiger from Orlon system
bliger: see blue tiger
blightfly: [Outernauts] mature ruinfly
blind crab: ["Death in the Turquoise Sea" by Andreas Findig] from Auroch-Maxo-55, Segafredo galaxy
blind man: [*Cyclopedia of Worlds*] predator up to 4 meters with 10 to 16 cane-like legs to 18 meters, with rear mouth and shredding claws from Scanodon, Croft system
blindigobird: [grue-bleen extrapolation] bluebird that turns green, not to be confused with bledbird, bleenbird, blellowbird, blindigobird, blioletbird, bluebird, gebird, grindigobird, gruebird, indigobird, rindigobird, ruebird, vindigobird, vuebird, yindigobird or yuebird from Ora system
blindoe: ["Black Widow" spoonerism] deadly deer-mimicking arachnid from Wack system
blioletbird: [grue-bleen extrapolation] bluebird that turns violet, not to be confused with bledbird, bleenbird, blellowbird, blindigobird, blioletbird, bluebird, gebird, grioletbird, gruebird, rioletbird, ruebird, vedbird, veenbird, vindigobird, violetbird, vuebird, yioletbird, yuebird from Ora system
bliraffe: [portmanteau] see blue giraffe
blird: [black/bluebird spoonerisms] ornithoid parasite that cause blurred vision and bruise-

like markings in backblird, booblird, neckblird, armblird, legblird varieties

blister beetle: [Xanth series by Piers Anthony] insect whose sting raises painful blisters from Xanth

blistmok: [*Creatures of the Galaxy* by Phil Brucato, Bill Smith, Rick D. Stuart, Chuck Truett] dark red or teal sauroid from Mustafar, Jedi galaxy

blitzhorn: [Outernauts] white quadruped with red stripes, bluish antlers, see blitzy, blitzram

blitzram: [Outernauts] mature blitzhorn with white mane

blitzy: [Outernauts] large-eared, immature blitzhorn

blix: [Monster Galaxy] yellow and blue, pointy-eared felinoid with z-shaped tail that collects lightning charge, but drools from Gemini constellation

blizard: [blue lizard portmanteau, blizzard mondegreen] blue lizard

blob: ["The Blob" by Theodore Simonson and Kate Phillips] amorph that grows to 15 meters or more in diameter by absorbing flesh on contact, nearly impossible to kill; [*Creatures of the Galaxy* by Phil Brucato, Bill Smith, Rick D. Stuart, Chuck Truett] pink amorph used in races on Umgal, Jedi galaxy; [*Monster Manual* by Skip Williams, etal.] thickest ooze

blobb: bloob variation

blobster: [blob lobster portmanteau] claw-less lobster-like crustacean that absorbs prey with pseudopods

blok: [Code Lyoko] cubical burrowing hexapod with 4 eyes (brain-eye, red laser-eye, light blue freeze-eye, orange fire-eye), swiveling neck geneered by Xana

blood flea: ["The Nagus" by Ira Steven Behr] Ferengi food animal

blood maggot: [*Sandworld* by Richard A. Lupoff] food animal from Tyahn, Ptayeem system

blood-sucker: ["Exploration Team" by Murray Leinster] pale, vampiric flying, hairless simian that feeds after sucking from Loren II

blood-sucking monkey: [Monster Chiller Horror Theater: "Blood-sucking Monkeys from W. Mifflin, Pennsylvania"] vampire monkey from W. Mifflin, PA, Terra (alpha Zodiaci III)

blood-wasp: [Warhammer 40,000] jungle omnivorous wasp-like insectoid

bloodbeetle: [Power Lord series] 3-meter bloodhound-like beetle-like insectoid from Toran

bloodfish: pirhana-like ichthoid from Ekton

bloodhorn et: [bloodhornet mondegreen] blood-red et with horn-like call, see horn et

bloodhornet: ["The Headhunters" by Klaus Fischer] 25-cm, green-and-white hornet-like insect with steel-hard exoskeleton, large compound eyes, long antenna from Zamucc's world (Tziroom VI)

bloodworm: [*The Worlds of the Federation* by Shane Johnson] 2.4 to 5-cm translucent invertebrate with 4 bloodsucking tentacles from Arodi (Regulus A II and V)

bloomslang: [*National Geographic Encyclopedia of Animals*] bird and lizard-eating lizard from Africa, Terra (alpha Zodiaci III)

bloomslangator: [bloonslang alligator portmanteau] alligator-like predator whose bite morphs victim into bloomslangator

**bloob**: [Cloudstone] gelatinous blob usually with large, round eyes in many varieties, see bleeb, blobb, blahb, blaab, blub

bloobster: [bloob lobster portmanteau] bloob able to form lobster-claw-likw pseudopods

bloos: ["Departure of the Classic Car" by William Voltz] giant, acid-spitting spider from Horror (Dri'ir Trio I)

blope: ["Ewoks" series] hippoid swamp-dweller, Endor's moon, Jedi galaxy

blophor: ["Before the Final Battle" by Michael Marcus Thurner] small, heat-loving ichthyoid with long beards, that live in flocks, and secretes a Cypron euphoric from Tarquina, Tare Sharm galaxy

blowf: [blowfish backformation] blowfish mimic, see bigg

blowie: see blowfly

blowped: ["Minya's Astral Angels" by Jennifer Pelland] from waterworld Emerald

blu: [bluish backformation] blue shapeshifter
blub: underwater bloob variety
bludgersite: parasitic scavenger
blue ant: [Continuum] 5-cm ant-like insectoid from Lemur (aka Korina)
blue bottle fly: [Xanth series by Piers Anthony] insect with blue, bottle-shaped body from Xanth
blue bull: see nilgai
blue dog: see ao-inu
blue giraffe: ["The Blue Giraffe" by L. Sprague de Camp] aka bliraffe, Hickey's mutant giraffe
blue jellyfish: ["Spaceship of the Dead" by H. G. Ewers] blue jellyfish-like invertebrate from Olguchait
blue ox: [Paul Bunyan] rare blue-colored ox, not related to nilgai
blue salmon: blue, salmon-like ichthyoid hunted for skin from Refuge (Ubigeir VI)
blue tiger: ["Transplanetary: Gems of Orlon" by Cleo Kraft] aka bliger, blue tiger-like felinoid with black stripes on Orlon planetoid
blue-skinned grind: ["The Invisible Web" by H. G. Ewers] jungle-dwelling herd carnivore from Kasuir
blue-slug: ["Splinters of Glass" by Mary Rosenblum] thick, glutinous sulfurous water-dweller that continues to squirm and crawl even when cut from Europa (Jupiter (alpha Zodiaci V)b))
blue: furry with short "blue" (gray) hair, wedge-shaped head
bluebeak: ["The Soulless" by Kurt Mahr] ornithoid with blue beak from Roulawan (Argnos V)
bluebear: [blueberry backformation, "Star Colony Troy" and "The Secret of Gostack" by Kurt Mahr] blue, ursinoid food animal from Troy, Helena system or Gostack, Kellehrt system, see hucklebear
bluebird: [grue-bleen extrapolation] blue bird that remains blue, not to be confused with bledbird, bleenbird, blellowbird, blindigobird, blioletbird, gebird, gruebird, ruebird, vuebird, yuebird from Ora system

bluficli: [James Cooke Brown's Loglan bludi ficli compound] bloodfish-like ichthyoid from Logla, Brown's system
blunicorn: [blessing of unicorns spoonerism] blue unicorn with S-shaped horn
blurrg: [*Creatures of the Galaxy* by Phil Brucato, Bill Smith, Rick D. Stuart, Chuck Truett] saurian steed from Ryloth, Jedi galaxy
blurrgator: [blurrg alligator portmanteau] alligator-like predator whose bite morphs victim into blurrg
bly: [business of flies spoonerism, blyc and blychost fly portmanteaux] parasitic, diurnal fly-like insectoid
blyc: [blychost backformation] parasite
blychost: [Perry Rhodan] diurnal animal from Fossil, Mary system
blyf: [blyfish backformation] creature with bioluminescent lure
blyfish: see chelobis
bmola: see pamola
bo: [bubo mondegreen] lavender eagowl ancestors; bobo nasna
boa constructor: [boa constrictor malaprop] bower-bird-like feathered serpentoid that builds elaborate mudnests
boar: [*Dell Crossword Puzzle Dictionary*] wild pig with short legs, bristly hair and cartilaginous snout
boarca: [boar-orca portmanteau] killer amphibian with short legs, bristly hair and cartilaginous snout from Akyby, Rybyka system, Galaxiki galaxy
board: [boar-lizard/buzzard portmanteau] sterile worker boar-like lizard, see overboard (queen) and upboard (drone)
boarilla: [band of gorillas spoonerism, boar-gorilla portmanteau] boar-headed pongoid
boaring worm: [boring worm mondegreen] mutagenic worm that morphs host into boar
boarse: [boar-horse portmanteau] equinoid with short legs, bristly hair and cartilaginous snout
boax: [boa-ox portmanteau] bovinoid carnivore with large constricting tongue
bobbin: [bobbin' robin] red-breasted ornithoid that bobs its head pigeon-like

bobblack: [bobwhite antonym] small, brown ornithoid with black markings

bobbuck: [*Worlds Apart: Nat. Hist. of Furaha and Earth* by Souren Nyoroge] blue hexapod with large endsnout from Furaha (alpha Phoenicis IV)

bobby-dazzler: see gaudybird

bobo: [Outernauts] immature bobop

bobongo: [Outernauts] mature bobop with large forelimbs

bobop: [Outernauts] dark blue simian with yellow horn, see bobo, bobongo

bobrouk: [Czech bobr-brouk portmanteau] beaver-beetle, aquatic insectoid with broad tail and large mandibles

bock: [BEM cock portmanteau] monstrous male chicken-like ornithoid with compound eyes, see ben

bocodile: [bask of crocodiles spoonerism] amphibious predator with long snout and tail and shot legs

böd: [Fr. Johann Martin Schleyer's Volapük] ornithoid from Schleyer's system

bøffelg: [Danish bøffel-elg, buffel-eland portmanteaux] buffalo-elk/moose, elaborately antlered ruminant from Buffeland

bøffelgator: [bøffelg alligator portmanteau] alligator-like predator whose bite morphs victim into bøffelg

boga: [*Dell Crossword Puzzle Dictionary*] fish from W. Indies, see cero, testar

bogator: [boga alligator portmanteau] alligator-like predator whose bite morphs victim into boga

Bogadian horse: [Futurama: "The Lost Adventure"] blue steed with spots, yellow frog-like head with eyes on side, thin tail from Bogad

boghog: [*Mostly Harmless* by Douglas Adams] bog-adapted porcoid with valuable skin, but meat eaten only in desperation from NowWhat

boghogator: [boghog alligator portmanteau] alligator-like predator whose bite morphs victim into boghog

bogwing: ["The Gungan Frontier" by Chris McCubbin] leathery, web-footed, winged quadruped from Dagobah, Jedi galaxy

bogwingator: [bogwing alligator portmanteau] alligator-like predator whose bite morphs victim into bogwing

bohlinia: [*After the Dinosaurs* by Donald R. Prothero] giraffe ancestor

boisha: [*A Miracle of Rare Design* by Michael Resnick] food ruminant food from Artismo

boister: [bed of oysters spoonerism, boisterous backformation] loud, lice-like insectoid

boiz: [Hildegard of Bingen's Lingua Ignota] wingless locust from Ignota, Hildegard's system

bok: [kobe, kobi bok palindromes] dark red or light red-violet ornithoid

bokat: [Afrikaans portmanteau] goat-cat, felinoid with goatee and horns from Afrika bindary system

boke chee: [choke bee spoonerism] predatory pack insectoid that chokes its prey from Ahla, Ojikh system, Galaxiki galaxy

bokeneter: [Atrikaans] antelope-eater, see antelopeater

bokka: [Outernauts] immature bokkra

bokkra: [Outernauts] dog-fish with large mouth, see bokka, bokkrawr

bokkrawr: [Outernauts] mature bokkra

bokwus: [*Monster Spotter's Guide to North America* by Scott Francis] nape from British Columbia, Terra (alpha Zodiaci III)

bol kata: ["ball cutter", *River Monsters* by Jeremy Wade] nut-eating Amazonian pacu adapted to testicle-eating after invading New Guinea, Terra (alpha Zodiaci III), see candiru

bolbrawl: [Outernauts] plant-mimic with blossom-like crest lure and root-like tentacles

boleo: ["The Psi-fighter" by Achim Mehnert] ornithoid from Trilith Oct's world

bolla: [Albaniana] serpentine dracoid with 4 legs, small wings, faceted silver eyes, said to eat one person every twelfth St. George Day from Albania, Terra (alpha Zodiaci III)

bollog: ["Battle of Ferrol" by Michael Marcus Thurner] predator with clawed tentacles that attracts prey with strudel from Ferrol ((Vega (alpha Lyrae) VIII)

bollogator: [bollog alligator portmanteau] alligator-like predator whose bite morphs victim into bollog

bolly-bo: ["The School of Assassins" by William Voltz] 12-meter, purple, herbivorous duck-billed dinosauroid with marsupial belly pouch

bolognat: [bologna-gnat portmanteau] small biting insectoid with curved cylindrical worm-like body

bolognius: [Invader ZIM: "Bolognius Maximus" by Frank Conniff] mutagenic virus that morphs host into arm-less, leg-less, bone-less skin of meat

bolt: [*The Ultimate Monster Guide* by Jaymond] jet-powered, blue, omnivorous insectoid

bolty: ["Planet of a Thousand Delights" by William Voltz] giant, furry predator from Geegival, Virgo A galaxy

boma: [Knights of the Old Republic 2: "The Sith Lords] large, green quadruped from Dxun, Jedi galaxy

bomba: [*Edgeworld Chron*icles by Paul Stewart and Chris Riddell] 4-legged sauroid with nosehorns, fangs from Edgeworld, Cerulea system

bombat: [Peter Macinnis] bat noted for killing fish by dropping stones from Ugly Islands

Bombay runner: large cockroach from Indian Ocean, Terra (alpha Zodiaci III)

bombeetle: ["Space Bird" by James White] explosive beetle that powers migratory Spacebirdriders' space bird from Sector 9

bombwat: [wombat spoonerism] explosive marsupial

bomen: hive-minded creature in many different non-humanoid forms from Galaxiki galaxy

bon: bonbon nasna

bonbon: [*Monster Legends*] monstrous pongoid

bondegezou: ["man of the forest"] black and white, 1-meter tree kangaroo with short tail

bone eater: ["Bone Eater" by Jim Wynorski] golem made up of the bones of its victims, see gashdokuro

bonegnawer: ["Star Wars IV: A New Hope" by George Lucas] flying desert carnivore with tooth-filled jaws strong enough to crush rock, Jedi galaxy

bongar: [*Dell Crossword Puzzle Dictionary*] venomous snake from India, Terra (alpha Zodiaci III)

bongo: [*National Geographic Encyclopedia of Animals*] antelope relative from Africa, Terra (alpha Zodiaci III)

bongsird: [songbird spoonerism] ornithoid that makes an absurd gong-like sound

bonkey: [barrel of monkeys, bonobo monkey portmanteau] bonobo-headed simian

bonnacon: [Xanth series by Piers Anthony] large armored dracoid with bison-like horns, metalbone eyelids that uses droppings defense against pursuers from Xanth; [*The Big Bad Book of Beasts* by Michael Largo] bull-headed equinoid with combustible, sulphous flatulence from Greece, Terra (alpha Zodiaci III)

bonobo: [*National Geographic Encyclopedia of Animals*] non-aggressive, herbivorous pongoid from Congo, Terra (alpha Zodiaci III)

boobee: [booby backformation] large trapdoor bee-like insectoid that lures prey with startling cry into boobee trap

boober: boobee predator, see floob, floob-boober-bab-boober-bub

boobrie: white roaring loon from Scottish Highlands, Terra (alpha Zodiaci III)

booby: [*National Geographic Encyclopedia of Animals*] fish and squid-eating bird of tropics

boogen: ["The Boogens"] 60-centimeter centipede-like bloodsucker with whip-like tentacles

boogoleef: [Monster Galaxy] turquoise shelled molluscoid with red petal fringe from Gemini constellation

boojum: [*The Hunting of the Snark* by Lewis Carroll] pseudo-snark, able to make people suddenly vanish from Snark Island, Looking-glass world

booll: [boo-bull portmanteau] monstrous bovinoid

booly: [Monster Galaxy] red, bipedal bovinoid with floppy ears and large head from Taurus constellation

boomer: [*Dell Crossword Puzzle Dictionary*] male kangaroo

boomerangutan: [boomer, boomerang, orangutan portmanteau] kangaroo-orangutan marsupial

boomslang: [Dutch "treesnake", *Fantastic Beasts and Where to Find Them* by Newton Artemis Fido Scamander] green (male) or brown (female) snake from S. Africa, Terra (alpha Zodiaci III)

boomslangator: [boomslang alligator portmanteau] alligator-like predator whose bite morphs victim into boomslang

Boond ox: [boondocks mondegreen] wild, shabby ox-like bovine from Boond system

booroolong: [*National Geographic Encyclopedia of Animals*] arthropod-eating frog from Australia, Terra (alpha Zodiaci III)

booroolongator: [booroolong alligator portmanteau] alligator-like predator whose bite morphs victim into booroolong

bootesaur: big-footed dinosaur from Boötes constellation

bootfrat: [fruit bat spoonerism] boot-eating chiropteran

bootie: [*After Man* by Dougal Dixon] hawk-like crow

bootl: [bootleg backformation] creature noted for its addictive unfertilized eggs

bootlope: [bootl antelope portmanteau] bootl with antlers

boracu: [*Creatures of the Galaxy* by Phil Brucato, Bill Smith, Rick D. Stuart, Chuck Truett] 50-cm ubiquitous armored, quadrupedal scavenger from Jedi galaxy

boranglii: [*The Invasion of the Planet Wampetter* by Samuel H. Pillsbury] large, purple ornithoid from Wampetter

borcupine: [Avatar: The Last Airbender: "Appa's Last Days"] creature with cartilaginous snout and quills

bordok: ["Ewoks" series] medium-sized pony-like equinoid with erect mane and short, knobby horns used as beast of burden by Ewoks, Endor's moon, Jedi galaxy

borele: [*Dell Crossword Puzzle Dictionary*] black rhinoceras, see nasicorn

boreostracon: giant glyptodon from Pleistocene

borficli: [James Cooke Brown's Loglan borku ficli compound] bowfish-like ichthyoid from Logla, Brown's system

borhyaena: [*After the Dinosaurs* by Donald R. Prothero] hyena-like marsupial from Miocene

borhyaenid: [*After the Dinosaurs* by Donald R. Prothero] wolf/hyena-like marsupial predator from Paleocene

boring worm: ["Beyond Hope" by Herbert Haensel] parasite from Jamondi cluster

borogove: [*Through the Looking Glass* by Charles Ludwidge Lewis Carroll" Dodgeson] thin, shabby mop-like bird

borophage: [*After the Dinosaurs* by Donald R. Prothero, "borax-eater"] canine with bone-crushing teeth, see ringdocus, thylacine

boryx: [*Pawns and Symbols* by Majliss Larson] vicious, graceful, territorial, orange-furred predator from Tsorn, Rim, Klingon empire

Boschian monster: [*The Gardens of Delight* by Ian Watson] monster like those depicted by Hieronymus Bosch, found on 4H97801

boselaph: [*After the Dinosaurs* by Donald R. Prothero] 300-kg antelope from Miocene

bot: [The Legend of Zelda: "The Adventure of Link"] blue gelatinous creature that can combine into gestalt "giant bot", enemy of bits from Hyrule

bot(t): [*Dell Crossword Puzzle Dictionary*] fly larva

bothridon: amphibious porcoid

botik: ["In the Hand of the Executioner" by Clark Darlton] 1-meter, dark furry, flower-eating pongid with brown round eyes from Zercascholpek

bouncer: eye-less mammaloid with limited telepathy and green fur from Ruusan, Jedi galaxy

bourgeticrinus: sea lily weed (crinoid) from Cretaceous
bovalupus: wolf-like bovine
bovalupuss: [bovalupus puss portmanteau] wolf-cow-cat chimera
bovir: ["In the Light of Vega" by Christopher Montillon] bovoid from Fanta
bowfly: [Xanth series by Piers Anthony] stinger-shooting insect from Land of Flies, Xanth
bowlump: ["The Gungan Frontier" by Chris McCubbin] hairy mollusc with waterjet and spitting defense from Jedi galaxy
bowowl: [bow-wow-owl portmanteau] nocturnal, caninoid griffin with feathery hair, large head and eyes and hooked beak and talons
bowowlope: [bowowl antelope portmanteau] bowowl with antlers
bowtruckle: [*Fantastic Beasts and Where to Find Them* by Newton Artemis Fido Scamander] 20-cm arboreal walking-stick-like insectovore with long sharp claws that feeds on woodlice
box kite: [kite extrapolation] larger variety of kite, with many mouths, jellyfish-like tentacles and tether
boysen: [boysenberry backformation] dark red to near-black ursinoid
boyster: [bed of oysters spoonerism, boysen monster portmanteau] monstrous boysen
brabbe: ["Secret Conference of the Blues" by Arndt Ellmer] marine food animal from Roost (Simban II)
brachiopod: ["lampshell"] shelled invertebrate, ancestor of cyclostomes
brachiosaur: dinosaur from early Cretaceous
brachypothere: [*After the Dinosaurs* by Donald R. Prothero] last teleceratine rhino from Miocene
brahmathere: [*After the Dinosaurs* by Donald R. Prothero] huge giraffe with thick, short neck and moose-like horns from late Miocene

braidedhorn: [*Fossil Revolution* by Douglas Palmer] ox with horns curled together unicorn-like from Siberia, Terra (alpha Zodiaci III)
brain beast: ["Brain Beast"] beast created by Akalonians via brain energy, see id monster
brain sucker: [Resident Evil 2] 2-headed, brain-sucking insectoid with mandibles and many arms
brain: [*The Ultimate Monster Guide* by Jaymond] fast, sometimes invisible, purple hexapod
brain-eating insect: ["BrainDead" by Michelle and Robert King] insect that eats brains, particularly politicians'
braindeer: [brain reindeer portmanteau] brain-eating deer-like carnivore
brainsucker: [X-COM: Apocalypse] small, yellow quadruped used as weapons, which hatch from pods, attack and sometimes turn victim into drone before dying
brak: [Perry Rhodan] animal from Rolfth (Ontry-Melonzus IV); [Terra Monster] shaggy, green buffaloid, see bufflow, from Terrarium
bram: ["Manhunt on Hayok" by Hans Kneifel] giant blue and yellow tabby felinoid with silver eyes from Hayok cluster
branch-snake: [*This Moment of the Storm* by Roger Zelazny] non-walkingstick-like serpentoid from Tierra del Cygnus, 72 Cygni system
branchshedder: ["Star Bird Mystery" by Hans Kneifel] frightening colony animal
branirda [James Cooke Brown's Loglan brani nirda (brown bird) compound] brown ornithoid from Logla, Brown's system
braque: ["Keepsakes" by Mike Resnick] caninoid from Bednares V
braserpi: [James Cooke Brown's Loglan brani serpi compound] brown snake from Logla, Brown's system
braster: ["The Exiles of Pthor" by Hans Kneifel] yellow-furred ostrich-like ornithoid mount with knife-sharp claws and broad beak from Schleppe dimension
bratling: ["The Feme Singer" by Arndt Ellmer] flying livestock from Baikhal (Cain V)

bratlingator: [bratling alligator portmanteau] alligator-like predator whose bite morphs victim into bratling

brauz: [Hildegard of Bingen's Lingua Ignota] blackbird-like ornithoid from Ignota, Hildegard's system

bread-and-butter fly: [*Through the Looking-glass and What Alice Found There* by Charles Ludwidge "Lewis Carroll" Dodgeson] insect with wings like buttered bread slices and sugar-cube-like head from Looking-glass world

bread pudding: [pudding extrapolation] pudding-thick ooze

bream: [*Dell Crossword Puzzle Dictionary*] sunfish, see mola

bree: [cabree mondegreen] pronghorned griffinoid, see bret, brie, brit

breeza: [zebra spoonerism] fast white equine with black stripes and collapsible sail-like mane

bregit: ["Matter of Honor" by Burton Armus] Klingon food animal

brell: [buffalo, rhinoceras, elephant, lion, leopard acronym] ultimate big game, see llerb, rellb

breshkë: [Albanian breshkë pëllumb backformation] turtle dove-pigeon ornithoid ancestral to pigeon and turtledove from Alban system

bricken: [brood of chickens spoonerism] brick-colored flightless ornithoid

bricket: [*The New Dinosaurs* by Dougal Dixon] aka rubusaur, brown, lambeosaur with multicolored tail, triangular crest

briel: ["Enemy Alien Galaxy" by Clarke Darlton] color-shifting, fat, slow, lazy, food shellfish from Morka

briger: [brilliant tiger portmanteau, mondegreen] glowing tiger-like felinoid from Brillia, Brill system

brill: [Uplift series by David Brin] avian crayfish eaten toasted from Thennanin homeworld

brilliant tiger: ["Base Thunder God" by H. G. Francis] tiger-like predator with diamond-studded antlers and iridescent wing membranes between limbs from Akkantho

brint: ["Lost Sorceress of the Silent Citadel" by Michael Moorcock] alley-cat-like felinoid from Mars (alpha Zodiaci IV)

briper: [brood of vipers spoonerism, brite viper portmanteau] brown viper-like snake that turns white in winter

bristleback: [*The Elder Scrolls III: Morowind*] tusked boar-like porcoid of Solstheim, used as steed by Ricklings

bristlefish: ["Death in the Turquoise Sea" by Andreas Findig] ichthyoid with bristles from Auroch-Maxo-55, Segafrendo galaxy

brite beast: [brown-white portmanteau] brown creature that turns white in winter, see whown

britigra: [James Cooke Brown's Loglan brili tigra (brilliant tiger) compound] predator with antlers and wings from Logla, Brown's system

broadbeak: [*After Man* by Dougal Dixon] giant predatory songbird

broad-fronted deer: deer with 2-meter wide antlers from Pliocene

broad-fronted moose: 1.5-tonne moose with broad antlers

broc: [bask of crocs spoonerism] wine cellar-dwelling reptilian

bron-klyth: ["Fighter for Garbesh" by H. G. Ewers] gliding predator with black hairy body and two rows of long sharp teeth, two gold-colored eyes, four strong, but short legs, that retreat to mountains with age from Arpa Chai, Wahiet system

broncosaur: [bronco dinosaur portmanteau] wild horse-like dinosauroid steed

broncotaur: [bronco minotaur portmaneau] wild horse-bull

brondar: ["Attack against Earth" by William Voltz] heavily armored mount from Dashall

brontëosaur: ["The Infinormatics Laboratory" by Ian Stewart] sauroid with 2 spring-like legs from Ombilicus, see pogosaur

brontops: 4.2-meter Oligocene titanothere

brontornis: see thunderbird

brontosaur: ["thunder-lizard", *The Great Dinosaur Mystery and the Bible* by Paul S.

Taylor] apatosaur-diplodocus, dinosaur with apatosaur head and diplodocus body

brontotaur: [Far Side: "When Cows Ruled" by Gary Larson, brontosaur minotaur portmanteau] apatotaur-headed diplodocus

broodfiend: [Erik Mona in *Greyhawk Monstrous Compendium Appendix*] nearly headless worm-like creature with lizard, bat and ape-like features from Greyhawk

brookbu: ["The Flight of the Kelosker" by H. G. Ewers] large, cumbersome though fast predator with sharp teeth and claws

brost: [roast beast spoonerism] edible pea-soup-like fog from Rovarga, Gravor system, Galaxiki galaxy

browgoul: [Power Rangers] monstrous, metallovorous pe(s)t that hatches in corpse

brown pudding: [*Monster Manual* by Skip Williams, etal.] marsh-adapted pudding-thick ooze

brown snake: [Perry Rhodan] toxic, brown serpentoid from Lafayette (Collore IV)

brown trasher: [Xanth series by Piers Anthony] contentious brown bird that trashes things from Xanth

bruh: [*Dell Crossword Puzzle Dictionary*] macaque from India, see rhesus

brum: [Albanian brumbull backformation] large bugalo-like insectoid from Alban system

brunurupucis: [Latvian brunurupucis balodis backformation] turtle dove-pigeon ornithoid ancestral to pigeon and turtle dove from Latvi system

brut: [brutish backformation] desert predator

bu: [ube bu palindrome] lavender ornithoid

buaja darat: [*The Museum of Hoaxes* by Alex Boese] large, flightless dragon from Komodo Island

buajada: [buaja darat mondegreen] rodentoid

bub: ancestor of floob-boober-bab-boober-bub, see ugelb bub, elb bub

bubo: [*Dell Crossword Puzzle Dictionary*] eagle or horned owl, see katogle

buck: [badling of ducks spoonerism] aquatic ornithoid with duckbill

buckaroo: tamed buckeroo

buckeroo: [buckaroo mondegreen] cow-boy-like macropodan with antlers, see buckaroo

buckjumper: [Aussie] wild horse, see bronco

budger: [*Earth in Twilight* by Doris Piserchia] jungle-dwelling mutant

budgerigar: [*National Geographic Encyclopedia of Animals*] parrot from Australia, Terra (alpha Zodiaci III)

budong: [Farscape: "Green-Eyed Monster" bu Ben Browder] fish-like starship-eater from Farscape galaxy

budongator: [budong alligator portmanteau] alligator-like predator whose bite morphs victim into dubong

buffahi: [buffalo antonym] shaggy, long-horned, long-necked, long-legged giraffe-like bovinoid, see hi

buffalo-bear: [buffaloberry backformation] buffalo-headed ursinoid

buffalo-yak: [Avatar: The Last Airbender: "The Waterbending Master"] gray and white domesticated quadruped with backward-curving horns, furry hooved legs

buffant: [Monster Galaxy] turquoise elephantoid with red-tipped ears, trunk, tail and feet, fond of ferrying, ancestor of truffefant, from Virgo constellation

büffelch: [German Büffel-Elch portmanteau] buffalo-elk rumanant from Germa system

bufflow: [Terra Monster] large brak from Terrarium

bufo: [*Dell Crossword Puzzle Dictionary*] toad

bufod: [Fr. Johann Martin Schleyer's Volapük] toad-like amphibian from Schleyer's system, see rosip

bugalo: [Futurama series, bug-buffalo portmanteau] large milk-producing beetle-like insectoid, see zubrouk

bugator: [bug alligator portmanteau] alligator-like predator whose bite morphs victim into bug

bugbear: [Xanth series by Piers Anthony] ursinoid with multiple insectoid legs, feelers and compound eyes from Xanth or [Xanthian mondegreen] Xa, Thia system

bugblatter beast: [*Hitchhiker's Guide to the Galaxy* by Doug Adams] humanoid-eater from Traal

bugdog: [dugbog spoonerism] insect-headed caninoid

bugdogator: [bugdog alligator portmanteau] alligator-like predator whose bite morphs victim into bugdog

bugglum: [Cloudstone] 2-legged spheroid with antennae

bugh: [bug-ugh portmanteau] repulsively ugly insectoid

bugler: [trumpeter swan backformation] swan with bugle-like call

buglizard: [Ben 10: Omniverse: "The More Things Change" by Charlotte Fullerton] lizard-like predator that spews thick yellow fog vulnerable only to electricity from Lepidopterra

builder: ["Fungi from Yuggoth" by Howard Phillips Lovecraft] fractal-dimensional energy-eater like spiky lump that builds structures from dust, serving Yog-Sothoth

buitreraptor: ["vulture roost robber", *Feathered Dinosaurs: The Origin of Birds* by John Long and Peter Schuten] dromaeosaurid with slender snout with small, widely spaced teth, long arms and legs

bukavak: [Serbiana] 6-legged, nocturnal, water monster with gnarled horns from Serbia

bul: bulbul nasna

bulbul: [*Dell Crossword Puzzle Dictionary*] nightingale from Persia, Terra (alpha Zodiaci III)

buldoqu: [Azerbaijani buldoq-qu portmanteau] bulldog-swan, white-feathered triphibian with wrinkled face and long neck from Azerbaija system

bule: [barren of mules spoonerism, burro mule portmanteau] cross between a burro and a mule

bulette: ["Creature Features" by Gary Gugax] 3.5-meter armadillo/shark/snapping turtle-like monster with backcrest, related to gholbrorn, prefers Human to Elf or Dwarf meat

Bulgallian rat: ["Coming of Age" by Sandy Fries] frightening but not deadly rodentoid

bulganik: ["L'il Abner" by Al Capp] very rarely-seen bird

bull seal: [Xanth series by Piers Anthony] sharp-horned sirenoid from Xanth

bull-ant: large, horned insectoid, see bullet ant

bull-dog: [bulldog mondegreen] caninoid with bull-like horns and forehooves

bull-dogator: [bull-dog alligator portmanteau] alligator-like predator whose bite morphs victim into bull-dog

bull-dozer: parasitic mosquitoid that causes sleepiness in bulls

bull-finch: [bullfinch mondegreen] bull-headed horned finch-like ornithoid

bull-frog: creature with bull-like head and forelimbs with horns and hooves and batrachoid rear with jumping legs and webbed feet

bull-frogator: [bull-frog alligator portmanteau] alligator-like predator whose bite morphs victim into bull-frog

bulla: [*Dell Crossword Puzzle Dictionary*] seal from Vatican, Terra (alpha Zodiaci III)

bullar: bolla from S. Albania, Terra (alpha Zodiaci III)

bulldozer: [Xanth series by Piers Anthony] large rhinoceros beetle-like creature from Xanth

bullet ant: [You Might Be A Zombie and Other Bad News] 2.5-cm ant with most powerful arthropod sting that feels like a bullet from Central America, Terra (alpha Zodiaci III)

bullhorn: [Xanth series by Piers Anthony] rear-attacking bovine unicorn from Xanth

bulliv: [bull elephant portmanteau, mondegreen] large, clumsy insectoid

bullockornis: [*The Big Bad Book of Beasts* by Michael Largo] "demon duck", 2.4-meter webfooted flightless bird from Australia, Terra (alpha Zodiaci III)

bullsquid: [Half-Life] 1-meter slimy sandy brown, maroon or pale green biped from Xen dimension with dark spots, thick tail, slit-pupil side-eyes, red tooth-tipped feeding tentacles

bulreih: ["The Mutants of Erysgan" by H. G. Ewers] insect-cloud from Erysgan, Syveron system
bumblebee bat: [*The Big Bad Book of Beasts* by Michael Largo] tiny bat from Thailand, Terra (alpha Zodiaci III)
bumblebeetle: [The Future Is Wild by Dougal Dixon] imago stage of larval glimworm, insectoid with glide-forewings and propelling-hindwings, covered with sensory "hairs", flies up to 800 km/dy to find flish carcass to deposit eggs in
bumming herd: [humming bird spoonerism] moth-like insectoid gestalt that removes protective covering (clothes, fur, feathers) before finishing off prey
bundimun: [*Fantastic Beasts and Where to Find Them* by Newton Artemis Fido Scamander] green fungus-like dirt-eater with 2 eyes, spindly legs that secrets acid and reeks of decay
bunf: ["Warriors of Gazkar" by Susan Schwartz] Newfoundland dog-like canine from Lafayette (Collore IV)
bunnee: [bunner backformation] rabbitoid prey of bunner from Rombay system
bunner: [Bombay runner spoonerism] large cockroach-like insectoid predator from Rombay system
bunnyip: [bunny bunyip portmanteau] rabbit-bunyip portmanteau] burrowing land bunyip
bunny-hadger: [honey badger spoonerism] rabbit-headed burrowing porcoid
bunny-hee: [honey bee spoonerism] large burrowing insectoid
bunny-her: [bunny-hee backformation] unbunny-like bunny-hee predator
buntis: [Terra Monsters] large, pink-and-blue, bipedal yantis from Terrarium
bunyip: [*Journal of the Anthropological Institute*] swamp-dwelling man-eater from Australia, Terra (alpha Zodiaci III)
bunyipede: [bunyip centipede portmanteau] swamp-dwelling insectivorous bunyip larva
bur: [ruby bur palindrome] small, kiwi-like red ornithoid, see ebur, nibur

buraq: [Here Be Monsters almanac] pegasus from Middle East
burbot: [*National Geographic Encyclopedia of Animals*] fish-eating relative of cod from Northern Hemisphere
bureau thread: [thoroughbred spoonerism] bureau-dwelling thread-like dust mite gestalt, see nureau
burkoll: ["Son of the Gods" by Marianne Sydow] omnivorous, armored hyena-like nocturnal, reptilian pack predator from Pthor
burkollope: [burkoll antelope portmanteau] burkol with antlers
burman: short-haired, blue eyed, golden-fawn and blue-black furry with white feet (socks and gloves)
burmilla: silver, chinchilla (black-tipped white) and lilac (pale silvery gray) furry
burner: ["Morkheros Prophet" by Ernst Vlcek] 50-cm hopping pyrokinetic predator, strong enough to cripple a limb from Morbienne III
burnikki: ["Covenant of Dealer" by Rüdiger Schäfer] food animal from Intraworld, Dwingeloo galaxy
burra: [*The Courtship of Princess Leia* by Dave Wolverton] lungfish-like ichthyoid from Dathomir, Jedi galaxy
burrito: small, food burroid
burrog: ["The Death Machine" by H. G. Ewers] bovinoid from Xthor
burrogator: [burrog alligator portmanteau] alligator-like predator whose bite morphs victim into burrog
burro-wing: [burrowing mondegreen] small burro-like griffinoid with wingclaws adapted for burrowing
burro-wingator: [burro-wing alligator portmanteau] alligator-like predator whose bite morphs victim into burro-wing
burrodent: [burro-rodent portmanteau] long-eared, burro-like rodentoid
burtle: [bale of turtles, buru turtle portmanteau] blue and white chelonoid
buru: 4-meter blue and white crocodilian from swamps of India, Terra (alpha Zodiaci III)

bushar: ["The March through the Underworld" by Ernst Vlcek] predator from Cronot, Heith system
bush-antlered deer: deer with 2-meter wide bush-like antlers
bushcat: ["Seed of Reason" by Daniel Hatch] bush-dwelling felinoid from Chamal
bushmaster: [*National Geographic Encyclopedia of Animals*] small mammal-eating lizard from S. America, Terra (alpha Zodiaci III)
bushwackee: [wacky, bushwacker backformation] unpredictable, agile, bush-dwelling prey of bushwacking predator
bustard: [*If I Ran the Zoo* by Theodore Seuss Geissel] 1.5-meter, red and yellow, flightless bird with striped neck, large crest from Zomba-ma-tant Mts.
butch: [*Butch*] 50-cm thin, large-eyed anaerobic simian
butchee: [butcher backformation] food insectoid, prey of butcher, related to boke chee
butterfish: ["Uncharted Territory" by Connie Willis] perverse ichthyoid from Boohte
butterfly: [Xanth series by Piers Anthony] messy butter-oozing flying insect from Xanth or [Xanthian mondegreen] Xa, Thia system
butterfly-fish: [butterflyfish mondegreen] flying ichthyoid with colorful wing-fins
butterfly-ray: butterfly ray mondegreen] ray-like butterfly-fish relative
butterscotch pudding: [pudding extrapolation] pudding-thick ooze
button monster: [*Genus Loci* by Ben Aaronovitch] geneered button-like monster that hibernates in cocoons from Jaiwan
buzzard-wasp: [Avatar: The Last Airbender: "The Desert"] carrion-eating desert wasp that and rotten-meat-odored fluid ("honey")
by-est: [*Cyclopedia of Worlds*] pelagic nektonic that feeds on spapig from Shuttleworth, Amon Alpha system
byak: [buffalo-yak portmanteau] buffalo-headed yak-like ruminant

byakhee: ["The Festival" by H. P. Lovecraft] winged creatures like crows, buzzards, ants as well as winged buffalo, moles and zombies
byakher: [byakhee backformation] arial predator that byakhs (eats fliers)
byelpyo: [Kor. *] 2-D pentapus or hexapus
býkun: [Czech býk-kun portmanteau] bull-horse, see bicorn
byronosaur: [*Feathered Dinosaurs: The Origin of Birds* by John Long and Peter Schuten] 1.5-meter troodontid with long snout with many teeth, bird-like nasal airsac
byronotaur: [byronosaur minotaur portmanteau] bovinoid with long snout, many teeth and bird-like nasal airsac
ca: [bianca mondegreen] cockerel-like ornithoid from Bia system
cabalo: [*Dell Crossword Puzzle Dictionary*] horse from Latin America, Terra (alpha Zodiaci III)
cabbit: [colony of rabbits] rabbit-like furry gestalt
cabree: [*Dell Crossword Puzzle Dictionary*] pronghorn
cabret: see cabree
cabrie: see cabree
cabrit: see cabree
cacklebird: ornithoid that nests in nestbush
cackyll: [cackling jackyll portmanteau, Terra Monster] sneaky, black horned caninoid predator with razorback, see heckyll and grynn from Terrarium
cackyllope: [cackyll antelope portmanteau] cackyl with antlers
cacomistle: [National Geographic Encyclopedia of Animals] raccoon relative from Meso-America, Terra (alpha Zodiaci III)
cacteria: [colony of bacteria spoonerism] cactus-like coral
cactumimus: [cactumus backformation] herbivorous cactumus mimic
cactumus: [Outernauts] thorny, carnivorous plant mimic
cactus cat: [*Monster Spotter's Guide to North America* by Scott Francis] 60-cm, nocturnal, desert felinoid with branching tail, legspurs, see cactus-cat

cactus-cat: [Xanth series by Piers Anthony] green-and-brown striped felinoid with cactus-like needles and bony front leg blades from Xanth, see cactus cat

cadborosaur: [*Monster Spotter's Guide to North America* by Scott Francis] aka caddy, 12-meter eel-like creature with humps, horse- or camel-like head, flukes from Cadboro Bay, BC, possibly naitaka

caddy: see cadborosaur, golpher

cade: [*Dell Crossword Puzzle Dictionary*] pet lamb, see cosset

cadger: [cete of badgers spoonerism, caddy-badger portmanteau] aka cadbromimus, cadbrosaur-mimicking furry

caecilan: [*National Geographic Encyclopedia of Animals*] amphibian from Americas and Africa, Terra (alpha Zodiaci III)

caep: [peach caep palindrome] pale yellowish-pink, insectovorous ornithoid, see uph

cäf: [Fr. Johann Martin Schleyer's Volapük] beetle-like insectoid from Schleyer's system

cagit: [*Dell Crossword Puzzle Dictionary*] green parrot from Phillipines, Terra (alpha Zodiaci III)

cagon: [dragon spoonerisms] dracoid from Dromma, Drondor and Druckoo systems

caillie: see tapper caillie

cainothere: [*After the Dinosaurs* by Douglas R. Prothero] tiny chevrotain-like artiodactyl

cairn: [*Dell Crossword Puzzle Dictionary*] terrier, see skye

cairoka: [*The Courtship of Princess Leia* by Dave Wolverton] ornithoid from Alderaan, Jedi galaxy

çakalamar: [Turkish çakal-kalamar portmanteau] coyote-squid, amphibious predator with four legs and six tentacles, see sakalamar

cakfi: [James Cooke Brown's Loglan (ghastly)] slimy, venomous creature from Logla, Brown's system

caladrius: [*The Big Bad Book of Beasts* by Michael Largo] white "doctor bird" able to sense illness from Italy, Terra (alpha Zodiaci III)

calb: [black calb palindrome] black raven-like ornithoid, see looc

calcon: [cast of falcons spoonerism] thin, swift, predatory ornithoid

calconster: [calcon monster portmanteau] monstrous calcon

Caldorian eel: ["Unification" by Rick Berman and Michael Piller] 1.2-meter eel-like sea creature

calf: young cow, elephant, whale or any combination of any two or all three

calicobra: [calico-cobra portmanteau] venomous hooded serpentinoid with black, white and reddish markings from Snowi, Nejstea system, Galaxiki galaxy

calicothere: [*After the Dinosaurs* by Donald R. Prothero] knuckle-walking equinoid with long front and short back legs with claws

callicantzari: [Xanth series by Piers Anthony] carnivorous anthropoid with slit-eyes, bulbous nose, furry face, twisted tusks, a putrid stench and seemingly misplaced bones from caverns under Goblinland, Xanth

Calogar dog: ["Initiations" by Kenneth Billar] caninoid from Callogar, Delta Quadrant

Calonack elephant: [*Voiage de Sir John Maundebil*] elephantine creature from Calonack

calopus: aka Babylonian aptaleon, wolf-like creature with serrated horns, feline face, boar's snout, goatee, cloven forehooves, reptile's rear

calot: [Edgar Rice Burroughs] pony-sized decapod with frog-like head and 3 rows of razor-sharp teeth from Mars (alpha Zodiaci IV)

caltiki: ["Caltiki, the Immortal Monster" by Phillipe "Phillip Just" Sanjust] radioactive, flesh-eating, blood-sucking amoeboid worshiped by Mayans

camahueto: [*Here Be Monsters almanac*] seacow with narwhal-like horn from Chilean islands, Terra (alpha Zodiaci III)

camarosaur: dinosaur from late Cretaceous; lizard from Camar system

camelce: [R. B. Davenport of N. Y. *Herald*] see camelk
camelk: [camel-elk portmanteau] aka camelce, elk-like desert quadruped
camelopardalis: [piscium extrapolation] egg-laying giraffe-like quadruped
caminalcule: [Joseph H. Camin in *Systematic Zoology* by Robert R. Sokal] in 3-legged, spotted and fingered and 4-legged, unspotted and clawed varieties
camingo: [colony of flamingos spoonerism] pink ornithoid gestalt
camium: [camelopardalis, pscium exprapolation] egg-laying camel-like desert quadruped

 **cammel**: [camel extrapolation] [camel-like, desert beast of burden with four humps
cammelope: [cammel antelope portmanteau] cammel with antlers
camnel: [camel/cammel interpolation] camel-like beast of burden with three humps
camnelope: [camnel antelope portmanteau] camnel with antlers
camptosaur: [*The Mistaken Extinction* by Lowell Dingus and Timothy Rowe] ornithopod descendant
campus hippo: [hippocampus backformation] hippopotamus mascot from George Washington University
can-cell: ["The Clone Wars"] 1.5-meter dragonfly-like insectoid from Kashÿyÿk and Teth, Jedi galaxy
can't-eat-her: [c + anteater mondegreen] large toothless man-but-not-woman-eating carnivore with elongated snout, long, sticky tongue and shaggy tail, see chivalrous shark
canal shark: [Space: 1889] plesiosauroid predator, especially fond of Earthlings, from the canals of Mars (alpha Zodiaci IV)
cancri [piscium extrapolation] egg-laying crab-like crustaean
candiacervus: deer with spatula-like antlers, 40-cm at shoulder from Pleistocene
candiru: [*River Monsters* by Jeremy Wade] 13-cm flesh-eating or smaller blood-sucking fish attracted to waste from gills or penis, see bol kata
caniel: [Cocker spaniel spoonerism] caninoid with drooping ears, short legs and silky hair from Spocker system
canielope: [caniel antelope portmanteau] caniel with antlers
cannok: [*Creatures of the Galaxy* by Phil Brucato, Bill Smith, Rick D. Stuart, Chuck Truett] pesty metallomnivores from Dxun, Jedi galaxy
canoj: ["The Sentinel of Foppan" by Hans Kneifel] "guarddog" with square skull, 2 tusks from Foppan
cant: [colony of ants spoonerism] paralyzing ant-like insectoid gestalt, [bardicant mondegreen] in slate-gray bardi variety
cantaire: [Catalan ocell cantaire backformation] symbiot that causes singing
canthumeryx: [*After the Dinosaurs* by Donald R. Prothero] giraffe ancestor with straight horizontal horns
canx: [Manx cat spoonerism] tailless "flat cat" felinoid
canyon crawler: [Avatar: The Last Airbender: "The Great Divide"] large predator with 8 eyes on each side of head, forked tongue, sharp teeth, cephalothorax and abdomen, 4 skinny legs, many nostrils
canyon sailor: ["The End of the Crib" by H. G. Francis] predatory ornithoid from Alkordoon, Perseus arm
canzoo: [Josie and the Pussycats in Outer Space: "Anything You Can Zoo"] stinky animal
cāpcāun: creature with dog's headed and ogre's body from Romania, Terra (alpha Zodiaci III)
Cape Hope sheep: see albatross
capricorni: [piscium extrapolation] egg-laying horned goat-fish
capricornusaur: goat-fish-lizard chimera from Capricorn constellation
Caprochian parrot: ["The Last Days of the War, with Parrots" by James Alan Gardner] green and crimson mouse-sized lizard with brown blood that "parrots" negative thoughts

telepathically, eats uv-photosynthesizing Silk from Caproche

capromeryx: [*After the Dinosaurs* by Donald R. Prothero] pronghorn from Zanclean age (early Pliocene)

capybara: [*The Big Bad Book of Beasts* by Michael Largo] giant, tail-less rodent with webbed feet from S. Americas, Terra (alpha Zodiaci III)

cara: caracar nasna

carabuta: [baracuta spoonerism] dangerous herding amphibian with antlers

caracal: [*Dell Crossword Puzzle Dictionary*] lynx from Persia, Terra (alpha Zodiaci III)

caracalope: [caracal antelope portmanteau] caracal with antlers

caracara: [*National Geographic Encyclopedia of Animals*] predatory bird from S. and Meso-America, Terra (alpha Zodiaci III)

caracaracal: [caracara caracal portmanteau] flying lynx-like felinoid

caragling: [Outernauts] immature cragite

caraglingator: [caragling alligator portmanteau] alligator-like predator whose bite morphs victim into caragling

carakiller: [*The Future Is Wild* by Dougal Dixon] 2-meter flightless caracara with small, clawed vestigial wings and colorful head feathers for communicating warning or mating

carakrag: [Outernauts] mature carapusk with craggier carapace

carakragator: [carakrag alligator portmanteau] alligator-like predator whose bite morphs victim into carakrag

carapace: [*Monster Manual* by Skip Williams, Jonathan Tweet and Monte Cook] carapaced Illithid symbiot used as living armor, includes backwatcher, fastbreak, hardy, silent, slippery and strongarm varieties

carapato: [*Dell Crossword Puzzle Dictionary*] tick from S. America, Terra (alpha Zodiaci III)

carapatosaur: [carapato apatosaur portmanteau] tick-like dinosaur

carapini: [Outernauts] immature carapusk

carapusk: [Outernauts] brown chelonian, see carapini, carakrag

carata: ["Secret Circuit X" by W. W. Shols] vampiric tree-mimic with poisonous nettles from Venus (alpha Zodiaci II)

caratocious: 2-meter caterpillar from Betonia (Edonian cluster V), Galaxiki galaxy

card: [cardinal contraction] red ornithoid

cardiocaudate: ["heart-tail", "Escape from Thantur-Lok" by Susan Schwartz] creature from Ammh Riconab

carebat: [bearcat spoonerism] blood-sucking chiropteroid with wound-healing saliva

caret: [*Dell Crossword Puzzle Dictionary*] hawkbill turtle

careve: [Continuum] 2-meter insectoid with deadly mandibles from Igendal, Belverius Helenis system

cark: [cat-shark portmanteau] catfish-headed shark-like ichthyoid

carnage: [Spiderman mythos] psychic killer spawn of venom symbiot which in turn spawned toxin

Carnard bat: [Barnard cat spoonerism] prolific chiropteroid from Carnard system

carnivice: [Terra Monster] polar-adapted gray fox with white and turquoise markings, see niptune and aquanine from Terrarium

carnivorous mammoth: [Rembrandt Peale] with downward-curving tusk-like sabreteeth

carnotaur: [*The Mistaken Extinction* by Lowell Dingus and Timothy Rowe] ceratosaur descendant, see man-eating cow

carolig chew: [*Cyclopedia of Worlds*] long, furry, omnivore with two central mouths, colorless plates, 12 4-jointed legs with wire-brush-like feet, 3 to 6 antennae, up to 2.7 meters from Scanodon, Croft system

carpet-thing: ["A Walk in the Dark" by Arthur C. Clarke] aka tapetoid, shadowy creature that moves swiftly over rocks from Kralkor II

carpet-thingator: [carpet-thing alligator portmanteau] alligator-like predator whose bite morphs victim into carpet-thing

carreta: [*Dell Crossword Puzzle Dictionary*] marine turtle

carretine: [Susan Thorpe] clever red creature

carrion crawler: ["The Ecology of the Carriorn Crawler" by Jonathan M. Richards] 1-meter yellow and green worm-like creature with long stunning tentacles

carsellot: [Perry Rhodan] carnivorous thornbush mimic that moves by rolling from Cratcon (Felloy IV), Vayquost galaxy

cartwheel spider: spider that flees by doing eight-legged cartwheels from Namibia

cash-ok: ["The Silent Spaceship" by H. G. Francis] shaggy creature with felinoid head, long curved horn, and 6 legs that moves like chimp from Komouir (Tiffak II)

cassowary: [*National Geographic Encyclopedia of Animals*] rarite bird with bony crest (casque) and claws from New Guinea, Terra (alpha Zodiaci III)

castorocauda: ["beaver-tail", *The Big Bad Book of Beasts* by Michael Largo] 1-kg mammal with beaver-like tail

castoroid: giant Pleistocene beaver

cat o' nine tails: [Xanth series by Piers Anthony] 9-tailed cat from Xanth, see huli jing, kitsune and kuriho

cat owl: [Avatar: The Last Airbender: "City of Walls and Secrets"] cat-headed owl-like ornithoid with retractable claws, cat-like tail

cat-bird: [catbird mondegreen] ornithoid with cat-like head

cat-dog: cat-headed blackdog, see nimravid

cat-shark: [catshark mondegreen] amphibian predator with forelimbs with retractible claws, catfish-like whiskers and shark-like backfin

Catachan devil: [Warhammer 40,000] 40-meter scorpion-like jungle omnivore from Catachan

catapo: [Winx Club] small, sometimes red, insect

catapult: [Xanth series by Piers Anthony] sphinx-sized cat from Region of Cats, Xanth

catbird: [Xanth series by Piers Anthony] part bird, part cat from Region of Cats, Xanth, see cat-bird

catchee: [cat-chee, catcher backformation] easily caught tarchee-prey, chee with memorable swansong

catcus: [Continuum] cactus cat-like prey of grumphurr in silkat and kanitt varieties from Sotkaard, Galunis system, Firehorse constellation

catergator: [Avatar: The Last Airbender: "The Swamp"] large, green alligator-like reptile with barbell whiskers, wrap-around tailfin, kneefins

catfish: [Xanth series by Piers Anthony] part cat, part fish from Region of Cats, Xanth

catfly: [GreenSpace] four-winged cat-like scavenger

cathbwn: [Welsh bwncath "buzzard" backformation] cat-bittern griffinoid

cathgan: [Thongor series by Lin Carter] small but poisonous red snake from Lemuria

catlat: [*Galactic Patrol* by E. E. Smith] diminutive, but numerous, cephalopod with bulbous head, parrot-like beak and tentacles from Delgon (1127 II)

catoblepas: [Ethiopiana] monstrous bovine that feeds on poisonous herbs from Ethiopia; [Xanth series by Piers Anthony] scaly with snake-like hair, fatal gaze from Xanth

cattle shark: ["Far Side" by Gary Larson] land shark adapted to cattle herds

catus: [OviPets] egg-laying felinoid, sometimes with wings

catwalkingstick: [catwalk-walkingstick portmanteau] thin, multilegged felinoid able to camouflage in forest canopy

caudipteryx: ["wing-tail", *Feathered Dinosaurs: The Origin of Birds* by John Long and Peter Schuten] flying dinosaur with wings and tail joined

cavan: ["The Bandits of Terrania" by Ernst Vlcek] scavenger mount from Exota Alpha (Otinarm I), [*The Law of Glassbirds* by Hans Kneifel] Glynth and ["The Hidden Courtyard" by Christian Montillon] Mawego, Otensos system

cave-bear: [*La Citadelle des Glaces* by Paul Alperine] giant bear from Devil's Teeth, Erikraudebyg

cavout: [*Trullion: Alastor 2262* by Jack Vance] small food creature from Trullion

cavy: [*Dell Crossword Puzzle Dictionary*] pony or rodent from S. America, Terra (alpha Zodiaci III) or any stray animal

cawing wumpus: [Godville] beaked, mucus-secreting worm-like sizeshifter with retractable wings

cawk: [cast of hawks spoonerism, cawing hawk portmanteau] hawk-like ornithoid with cawing call, kawk

ce: [camelce mondegreen] elk-like camel relative

ceagle: [convocation of eagles spoonerism, ce eagle portmanteau] elk-eagle griffinoid with camel hump(s)

ceann: [gan ceann mondegreen] head-less equinoid from Ga system, see orse

ceasel: [colony of weasels] weasel gestalt

ceaver: [colony of beavers spoonerism] beaver gestalt

cebidae: [OviPets] egg-laying simian

cecil: [Motie series by Larry Niven] sea serpent

ceerc: [screech ceercs portmanteau, "The Secret Files of Dr. Drew", Rangers Comics #47] creature in screeching and stealthy varieties

celestail: [Terra Monsters] large-eared felinoid with 2 star-tipped tails, see staria, from Terrarium

celestailope: [celestail antelope portmanteau] celestail with antlers

celestoah: [Terra Monster] felinoid with 3 star-tipped tails and ears, see celestail, from Terrarium

cenguin: [colony or convent of penquins spoonerism] penguin-like ornithoid gestalt

centeroo: [nickleroo backformation] smaller nickleroo

centigurp: [Odd Squad: "The Trouble with Centigurps" by Guy Toubes] pink furball able to bounce, roll, fond of spheres, see gurp

centipede plage: [Resident Evil 4] head-eating centipede-like plage

centrodon: [dimetrodon backformation] small, short-legged dinosaur with sail

centurian: [Resident Evil 0] 10-meter T-virus infected mutant centipede

centycore: [Xanth series by Piers Anthony] carnivore with horse-like hooves, lion-like legs, elephantine ears, bear-like muzzle and branching 10-point antler from Xanth

cephalogade: [*After the Dinosaurs* by Donald R. Prothero] raccoon-like early bear from Chattian age (late Oligocene) that migrated to America in Miocene

cephalopodan: cephalopod-like creature, see glider squid, gring, poulp

cerastes: [*Dell Crossword Puzzle Dictionary*] horned viper

ceratis: [monoceratis mondegreen] one-horned monkey-centaur ancestor to mono and monoceratis

ceratosaur: face-horned dinosaur

ceratotaur: [ceratosaur minotaur portmanteau] face-horned bovinoid

ceratosuch: [*After the Dinosaurs* by Donald R. Prothero] horned crocodilian

ceratothere: ["horned beast", *After the Dinosaurs* by Donald R. Prothero] rhino ancestor from Miocene

cerberus: 3-headed hellhound from Hades, see trioskylos

ceretridon: ["Duel for a Dracowolf" by Wolf Read] "pet rock" with 5 legs, 4 beady eyes, 3-finger tail from Epona, Taranis (82 Eridanis) system

cero: [Dell Crossword Puzzle Dictionary] fish from W. Indies, see boga, testar

cerpedos: [*Memoires De Sir George Wollap* by Pierre Chevalier Duplessis] white-furred, red-eyed squirrel from Aprilis, New Britain Islands

cessirid: [*Monster Manual* by Skip Williams, Jonathan Tweet and Monte Cook] illithida variant

cetacea: [OviPets] egg-laying dolphin-like cetacean

cet(e): [*Dell Crossword Puzzle Dictionary*] whale, see orc, ork, beluga, grampus

ceti: [cetus, piscium extrapolation] egg-laying whale-like cetacean

Ceti eel: ["Wrath of Khan" by Harve Bennett and Jack B. Sowards] 35-cm 10-legged burrowing mollusk with large pinchers from Menkar (alpha Ceti) V

cetiosaur: ["whale-lizard"] dinosaur from early Cretaceous, see cetusaur

cetiotaur: [cetiosaur minotaur portmanteau] whale-like bovinoid

cetus: ["whale", Andromeda: "Belly of the Beast" by Matt Kiene and Joe Reinkemeyer] planet-eater that threatened Savion again after 6 millennia

cetusaur: large sea dinosaur from Cetus constellation, see cetiosaur

cey: [lancey mondegreen] ornithoid from La system

ch'i-lin: aka ssu ling, unicorn with deer-like body, ox's tail, hooves from W. China, Terra (alpha Zodiaci III)

ch'kariya: [*Surak's Soul* by J. M. Dillard] small, burrowing root-eater from T'Khasi, Nevasa (40 Eridani) system

cha-eh: [lha-cha-eh mondegreen] caninoid relative

chacalaca: [*National Geographic Encyclopedia of Animals*] chicken relative from Meso-America, Terra (alpha Zodiaci III)

chadre'kab: ["The Raven" by Bryan Fuller and Harry Kloor] Talaxian food animal from Delta Quadrant

chaf: [danchaf mondegreen] tree goblin from Da system

chahār: [dabbē-i-chahār-sar backformation] creature ancestral to dabbē-i, sar and dabbē-i-chahār-sar

chair creature: ["The Tomorrow People: War of the Empires"] chair-like creature

chaishravas: [beheaded uchaishravas] 6-headed wingless pegasoid

chaja: [*Dell Crossword Puzzle Dictionary*] screamer bird

chalmon: [chicken-salmon portmanteau] edible variety of hen

chama: [*Dell Crossword Puzzle Dictionary*] large mollusc

chamaeleontis: [piscium extrapolation] egg-laying chameleon-like lizard

chameleogoat: [Robot Hugs] goat with ability to camouflage itself by changing pigmentation

chameleon: [camel-lion] desert felinoid with with mane, hump

chameleot: [Outernauts] one-eyed, beach-dwelling lung-fish-like ichthoid, see chamopee, chamera

chamopee: [Outernauts] immature chameleot

chamora: [Outernauts] mature chameleot

champosaur: [*River Monsters* by Jeremy Wade] giant gator gar, [*After the Dinosaurs* by Donald R. Prothero] crocodile-like Mesozoic holdover

champotaur: [champosaur minotaur portmanteau] crocodile-like bovinoid, see byronotaur

changa: [*Dell Crossword Puzzle Dictionary*] mole cricket from S. America, Terra (alpha Zodiaci III)

changator: [changa alligator portmanteau] alligator-like predator whose bite morphs victim into changa

changchengornis: [*Feathered Dinosaurs: The Origin of Birds* by John Long and Peter Schuten] confusciusornis relative with smaller curved beak and long grasping toe, long two-feathered tail

chaos beast: [*Monster Manual* by Skip Williams, Jonathan Tweet and Monte Cook\ creature unable to maintain shape but able to temporarily assume fangs, claws, horns, pinchers, tentacles, etc. to attack, react by touch, [*Planar Handbook* by Bruce Cordell, etal.] hunted by Neraphim

chaousarou: [*Monster Spotter's Guide to North America* by Scott Francis, *Unexplained!* by Jerome Clark] aka champ, 9-meter, gray plesiosauroid from Lake Champlain, protected species in Vermont and Connecticut, Terra (alpha Zodiaci III)

chapin: [*Dell Crossword Puzzle Dictionary*] trunk fish

char: [*Dell Crossword Puzzle Dictionary*] brook trout

charaway: [*Cyclopedia of Worlds*] aka breen ale, animal from gas giant Chassana, Sheel-San system

chareptor: [Outernauts] mature charrputo

charger: [*Dell Crossword Puzzle Dictionary*] war horse

charlas: [*Memores De Sir George Wollap* by Pierre Chevalier Duplessis] tall hare with cat-like tail from Aprilis, New Britain Islands

Charles Mill Lake monster: [*Monster Spotter's Guide to North America* by Scott Francis] 2.1-meter green reptilian with webbed feet, green eyes from Charles Mill Lake, OH, Terra (alpha Zodiaci III)

chard: [pilchard, charred mondegreens\ black sardine-like eel

charling: [Outernauts] immature charrputo; [chattering of starlings, char backformation] immature char

charlingator: [charling alligator portmanteau] alligator-like predator whose bite morphs victim into charling

charrputo: [Outernauts] red, fiery, crablike creature

chasmoporthetes: [*After the Dinosaurs* by Douglas R. Prothero] cheetah-like hyena from Pliocene

chasmosaur: [*The Mistaken Extinction* by Lowell Dingus and Timothy Rowe] ceratops with both frill and horns

chasmotaur: [chasmosaur minotaur portmanteau] bovinoid with frill

chata(o)n: [French chat-taon, Haitian chat-tan portmanteau] cat-horsefly, nocturnal griffinoid with retractable claws, hooves, mane from Gérard's world

chati: [*Dell Crossword Puzzle Dictionary*] tiger cat from S. America

chatt: [chatty backformation] louse-like insectoid

Chatterb ox: [chatterbox mondegreen] noisy ox-like bovine from Chatterb system

chatterbox: ["The Return of the Kangaroo Rex" by Janet Kagan] pterodactyl-like blue, red, purple and yellow creature from Mirabile

chaus: [*Dell Crossword Puzzle Dictionary*] wildcat from Africa and India, Terra (alpha Zodiaci III)

chchrorl: ["The Enemy in the Dark" by Kurt Mahr] predator from waterworld Opghan (Ep-Hog II)

chchrorlope: [chchrorl antelope portmanteau] chchrorl with antlers

checkerboar: [checkerboard boar portmanteau] black and red wild porcoid

chee-choo: little green songbird

chee: [chimpanzee spoonerism mondegreen] polymorph from Zimpa system; [wol-la-chee mondegree] ant-like insectoid, see tarchee, boke chee, butchee, catchee

cheer: [*Dell Crossword Puzzle Dictionary*] see chir

cheese fly larva: [You Might Be A Zombie and Other Bad News] larva of fly found in casu marzu cheese

ceetah: [coalition of cheetahs spoonerism] fast felinoid predator

cheilostome: advanced bryozoan from Cretaceous

chelao: ["The Stranger" by H. G. Ewers] pale, silver-haired, humanoid-mimicking gestalt of ims, thread devils and membrillas

chelobis: [Cyclopedia of Worlds] aka bly bootman or blyfish, 2.5-meter underwater predator with long appendage with bio-luminescent bulb from Vorsor Vet, Sapain Saia Siriri system

chen: [chime of wrens spoonerism, *Dell Crossword Puzzle Dictionary*] snow goose

cher: [avalancher mondegreen] snow burrower from Avala system

cherfer: [*Creatures of the Galaxy* by Phil Brucato, Bill Smith, Rick D. Stuart, Chuck Truett] mnivorous herd quadruped, often aggressive (cherfing), from Elom, Jedi galaxy

chernogg: ["Colemayn's Search" by Hans Kneifel] predator from Pharst, Vogenmuker system, Manam Turu

chernoggator: [chernogg alligator portmanteau] alligator-like predator whose bite morphs victim into chernogg

cherofe: [i-less cheirofa] cave mollusk from Friatica, Friaticalida system, Galaxiki galaxy

cherry jelly: [jelly extrapolation] red jelly-thick ooze

cherry-ogg: [*Partridge's Concise Dictionary of Slang and Unconventional English*, rhyming slang] dog, aka cherry-hog

cherry-oggator: [cherry-ogg alligator portmanteau] alligator-like predator whose bite morphs victim into cherry-ogg
cherufe: [Araucanian] large, volcano-dwelling eater of young girls or [Mapuche] men from Chile, Terra (alpha Zodiaci III)
Cheshire bat: [Cheshire cat extrapolation] non-vampire bat able to become invisible except in mirrors
Cheshire cat: Alice in Wonderland by Charles Ludwidge "Lewis Carroll" Dodgeson] cat able to become invisible with its smile disappearing last
Cheshire rat: [Godville] rodent who drove out Cheshire cats and rendered Cheshire cheeseless
chessie: [*Monster Spotter's Guide to North America* by Scott Francis] 9-meter, dark, humped basilosauroid from impact-formed Chesapeake Bay
cheveh: [Star Trek] scavenger from T'Khasi, Nevasa (40 Eridani) system
chevrotain: [*National Geographic Encyclopedia of Animals*] omnivorous deer from Africa, Terra (alpha Zodiaci III)
chi: [beheaded ochi] large dracoid with red eyes green back and 5 heads; chi-chi nasna
chi-chi: [*Space Ark* by A. R. Lightner] simian from Shikai
chickaree: [*Dell Crossword Puzzle Dictionary*] red squirrel
chickasaurus: [Ruff and Reddy Show: "The Slick Chickasaurus Chick Trick"] large, bird-like dinosaur, see ornithomimosaur
chickmunk: [chicken-chipmunk portmanteau] small striped, arboreal ornithoid
chickpanzee: [chimpanzee-chicken portmanteau] chimp-like, egg-laying flying anthropoid
chickpanzer: [chickpanzee backformation] predator that panzers (squashes) chicks
chierofa: [*The Howling Stones* by Alan Dean Foster] molluscoid of outer reef, a delicacy when cured and heated from Parramat archepelago, Senisran
chiggee: [chigger backformation] minimite prey of mite larvae

chiggock: [*To The Slaughter* by Stephen Cole] geneered brainless, featherless turkey
chiilak: [*Creatures of the Galaxy* by Phil Brucato, Bill Smith, Rick D. Stuart, Chuck Truett] 2.2-meter furry, 6-limbed, amphibous biped from moon Misnor, Jedi galaxy
chikaru: [Anakana] creature from T'Khasi, Nevasa (40 Eridan) system
chikavac: long-beaked bird used as familiar to steal honey, milk, communicate with other animals from Serbia, Terra (alpha Zodiaci III)
chilak: [one-eyed chiilak] one-eyed furry octapod
chillbeak: [Terra Monster] flightless ornithoid with drill-like wings, horns and carapace, see pendril and turanon, from Terrarium
chilling fog: [*Monster Manual* by Skip Williams, etal.] thin cold, aerial ooze
chilling fogator: [chilling fog alligator portmanteau] alligator-like predator whose bite morphs victim into chilling fog
chim ung: [Vietnamese Disan chim ung mondegreen] hawk-like falcon from Disa system
chim. [Vietnamese chim cu, chim son ca, chim thiên nga, chim ung backformation] ornithoid ancestral to cu and cuckoo, with son ca songbird, with thiên nga swan and with ung falcon from Disa system
chimæra: [Homer] lion-headed, serpent-tailed goat from Homeria system, [Hesiod] 3-headed from Hesiodia system; any mixture of more than 2 animals
chimpanzebra: [chimpanzee-zebra portmanteau] centauroid with chimp head, arms and upper body on zebra's body
chin-chilla: [chinchilla mondegreen] hophead with soft pale gray fur from Thuban (alpha Draconis) system
chin: [Ili-Golik tshin] desert scavenger smaller than le'matya from T'Khasi, Nevasa (40 Eridani) system; chinchin nasna
china animal: [*The Wonderful Wizard of Oz* by L. Frank Baum] small, fragile, toy animal golem made china from China Country, Oz
chinaro: [tanchinaro backformation] silver-and-black ichthyoid from Ta system

chinch: [charm or chirm of finches spoonerism, chincha finch portmanteau] skunk finch-like pegasoid

chincha: [*Dell Crossword Puzzle Dictionary*] skunk, aka chinche

chinche: see chincha

chinchin: [Outernauts] yellow, fast kangaroo-rat-like rodentoid with bird-like tail, see chiraur, chiroo

ching huo tie: [Fringe] burrowing, parasitic, anaerobic metallophage arachnoid

chinpanzee: [chin chimpanzee portmanteau] arboreal, fruit-eating double-mouth from Thuban (alpha Draconis) system

chinpanzer: [chinpanzee backformation] chinpanzee predator

chinthe: leogryph from Burma, Terra (alpha Zodiaci III)

chintz: furry with top half colored and bottom white

chinzee: [Outernauts] immature, hornless chumzo with large ears

chinzu: ["Dorsai" by Gordon R. Dickson] food creature from the Hixabrod

chio: [Italian granchio backformation] crab-like crustacean form Gra system

chioccda: [Ital. @] 2-D snail-like at

chipmunk: [Xanth series by Piers Anthony] chipmunk with food psychokinetic ability from Xanth or [Xanthian mondegreen] Xa, Thia system

chipmunkey: [Terra Monster] brown simian with yellow stripes and gnawing beaver-like incisors from Terrarium

chir: [Dell Crossword Puzzle Dictionary] pheasant from Himalayas, see cheer

chiraur: [Outernauts] mature, rotund chinchin

chird: [chirping bird spoonerism] ornithoid that communicates with burps

chirit: [*After Man* by Dougal Dixon] inchworm-like squirrel

chiroo: [Outernauts] immature chinchin

chiropteroid: ["hand-wing"] bat-like creature

chiropy: [OviPets] egg-laying chiropteroid

chirostenotes: ["narrow-hand", *Feathered Dinosaurs: The Origin of Birds* by John Long and Peter Schuten] 2.5-meter toothless oviraptorosaur with short, powerful jaws

chiselhead: [*After Man* by Dougal Dixon] inchworm-like beaver

chiss: [*The Patchwork Girl of Oz* by L. Frank Baum] 10-bushel porcupine from Oz

chital: [*National Geographic Encyclopedia of Animals*] deer from India, Terra (alpha Zodiaci III)

chitalope: [chital antelope portmanteau] chital with antlers

chiton: [*Dell Crossword Puzzle Dictionary*] mollusc, clam

chivalrous shark: ["The Chivalous Shark"] man-eating shark that doesn't eat women, see can't-eat-her

chizpurfle: ["cheat-furtrim", *Fantastic Beasts and Where to Find Them* by Newton Artemis Fido Scamander] dustmite-like crustacean that feeds on electricity

chlak: [i-less chiilak] furry cave octapod, see chilak and chiilak

chloon: ["Time Bomb Cell Activator" by H. G. Ewers] giant, colorless teleporting amoeboid symbiot

cho: ["Imperator of Arkon" by Rainer Castor] beetle-like insectoid parasymbiot

chobee: [Xanth series by Piers Anthony] long-snouted reptile with wide nostrils, green corrugated skin, short legs in both soft-toothed and hard-toothed varieties from Xanth

chobeel: [chobee eel portmanteau] chobee-like eel

chober: [chobee backformation] chobee predator that chobs

chobolink: [chain of bobolinks spoonerism] pesky little ornithoid

chocol: ["chocol at times emit talocohc" palindrome] brown ornithoid gestalt

chocolate moose: [Xanth series by Piers Anthony] tasty ruminant, related to vanilla moose, from Xanth

chocolate pudding: [pudding extrapolation] brown pudding-thick ooze

chog: [chilling fog potmanteau] pea-soup-fog-like cloudcreature from Rovarga, Gravor system, Galaxiki galaxy

chogator: [chog alligator portmanteau] alligator-like predator whose bite morphs victim into chog

choke bee: [Xanth series by Piers Anthony] insectoid related to sneeze bee from Xanth

chokebear: [chokeberry backformation] ursinoid with forepaws able to choke its prey

choldfish: [charm of goldfish spoonerism, chollima goldfish portmanteau] pegasus-ichthyopteran-like triphibian

cholinhy: ["The Tribute Smiths" by H. G. Francis] 6-meter lizard with 2-meter saw-snout, bony tail from Tradom galaxy, HCG 87 cluster, Capricorn

chollima: wild pegasus from Korea, Terra (alpha Zodiaci III)

chomäl: ["The Curse of Ruby" by H. G. Francis] little, swamp-dwelling, yellow, predatory reptilian with poisonous "arrows" from Taumond, Kaokrat system

chomälope: [chomäl antelope portmanteau] chomäl with antlers

chomper: [Terra Monster] spiked, bulldog-like caninoid, see chompie, from Terrarium

chompie: [Terra Monster] bulldog-like caninoid, see chomper, from Terrarium

choose: [goose extrapolation, pl. cheese] ornithoid that secretes milk-like liquid

choodwuck: [woodchuck spoonerism] burrowing rodentoid

chopa: [*Dell Crossword Puzzle Dictionary*] rudder fish

chreean: [Perry Rhodan] scaly, chameleon-like, donkey-sized reptilian from Dorkh

chronimal: ["time-animal", *Decalogue of the Elements* by Ernst Vlcek] fat, black, scaly, 30-cm, 8-legged lizard that triggers timeshifts pastward or futureward from Negasphere

chroococcus: extremopilic bacterium resistant to extreme dryness

chshedder: [branchshreader mondegreen] frightening gestalt that chsheds from Bra system

chu'uathor: [*The Courtship of Princess Leia* by Dave Wolverton] ichthyoid from Dathomir, Jedi galaxy

chub: [*Dell Crossword Puzzle Dictionary*] squawfish

chuba: ["The Gungan Frontier" by Chris McCubbin] large-footed, very wide-mouthed batrachoid from Tatooine, Jedi galaxy

chubb: chubb-chubb nasna

chubb-chubb: ["The Chubb-chubbs Are Coming"] small, furry, purring creatures with food-blender mouths having many rotating rows of teeth

chubbee: [chubby backformation] spherical bee-like insectoid

chuchu: [The Legend of Zelda] gel from Hyrule

chuck: [*After Man* by Dougal Dixon] bird with large pinecone-cracking bill in red males and slender insect-and-carrion-eating bill in green females

chuckaboo: [*After Man* by Dougal Dixon] marsupial monkey

chuckwalla: [*National Geographic Encyclopedia of Animals*] lizard from W. U. S

chug: [*Rhialto* by Jack Vance] black-and-red striped serpentoid repellant to and in charge of sandestin

chugator: [chug alligator portmanteau] alligator-like predator whose bite morphs victim into chug

chugg: [*If I Ran the Zoo* by Theodore Seuss Geissel] insectivorous ornithoid with long thin neck and tubular snout, featherduster-like tail and two-toed feet

chuggator: [chugg alligator portmanteau] alligator-like predator whose bite morphs victim into chugg

chukar: [*National Geographic Encyclopedia of Animals*] chicken relative

chula: [terroranchula mondegreen] arachnoid from Terrora system

chummingbird: [charm of hummingbirds spoonerism] pack-hunting hummingbird-like predator

chumtoad: [Half-Life] bright, purple batrachoid with one red eye, backspikes, long blue tongue plays dead before leaving purple energy trail when teleporting back to Xen

chumzo: [Outernauts] pack-hunting simian with one horn, see chinzee, abomzo

chupacabra: [Span. "goat-sucker", *Monster Spotter's Guide to North America* by Scott Francis] 1.4-meter nocturnal, bipedal, bluish gray mottled therapod with large red eyes, 3-clawed hands, fangs, forked tongue, spine quills from Puerto Rico, Mexico and American Southwest; ["Chupacabra vs. the Alamo" by Peter Sullivan] vampiric pack caninoid, Terra (alpha Zodiaci III)

chuuchilla: [Monster Galaxy] sleepy, gold and orange creature

chuul: ["The Ecology of the Chuul" by Mike Mearls] large, pale yellow crustacean with pinchers and paralyzing tentacles that prefers sand to water

chuvvy: [*Partridge's Concise Dictionary of Slang and Unconventional English*] flea

chworkt: [*Pawn and Symbols* by Majlis Larson) white, furry creature with long digits and very long tail from Arcturus (alpha Boötis) system

ci: [ci mimic palindrome, Roman CI] uncentipede mimicked by pseudoci

cicada: [*Dell Crossword Puzzle Dictionary*] locust, see acacia, cicala

cicala: [*Dell Crossword Puzzle Dictionary*] locust, see acacia, cicada

cich: [one-i ciich] one-eyed creature

cigeon: [company of widgeons spoonerism, cyclops pigeon-wigeon portmanteau] one-eyed pigeon-like wigeon

cigar beetle: [cigarette beetle backformation] cigar-shaped beetle-like insectoid

cigarette beetle: [*The Big Bad Book of Beasts* by Michael Largo] tobacco-eating insect

cigau: bipedal lion-like felinoid from Sumatra, Terra (alpha Zodiaci III)

ciich: [Perry Rhodan] creature from Gys-Progher (Aggluth II)

cimi: [cimi mimic palindrome] predator mimicked by cimi mimic

cimzzar: [Crayola razzmic berry yrreb cimzzar palindrome] rose-purple yrreb from Crayol A

cingk: ["The Headhunter" by Klaus Fischer] toad-like amphibian from At-Cann

cingk killer: ["The Headhunter" by Klaus Fischer] 1-meter segmented, armored constrictor with wide, toothless mouth from At-Cann

cinnabunny: [Cloudstone, cinnamon bun/bunny portmanteau] cinnamon bun-like lapoid

cirb: [firebrick cirb erif palindrome] brownish red erif

Circassian cat: ["Violations" by Shari Goodhartz and T. Michael and Pamela Gray] funny-looking felinoid from Circassia

circulation bird: bird noted for flying in spiral until it flies up its rear and disappears leaving dropping droppings, see oozlum

ciremil: [Limerick palindrome] chartreuse ornithoid from Ireland, Terra (alpha Zodiaci III)

cirnimla: [James Cooke Brown's Loglan cirzi nimla compound] chair creature from Logla, Brown's system

cirocil: [licorice cirocil palindrome] black-bird-like ornithoid

cirrius: [Outernauts] cloudcreature with 2 eyes and mouth, see nimby, stratus

cisco: [*Dell Crossword Puzzle Dictionary*] whitefish

cish: [catfish spoonerism] fatty ichthyoid with feeding tentacles

citipati: [*Feathered Dinosaurs: The Origin of Birds* by John Long and Peter Schuten] 3-meter oviraptorosaur with facecrest, toothless beak

cla-gi-aih: [Navaho] turkey-like ornithoid from Diné system

clabb: [clabbert mondegreen] green monkey-like variety of ert from Troctopia, Qujhtba system, Galaxiki galaxy

clabbert: [*Fantastic Beasts and Where to Find Them* by Newton Artemis Fido Scamander] horned, hairless, mottled green monkey-like arboreal amphibian with webbed feet and hands, long limbs, and forehead pustule that glows and flashes at danger

clac: [i-less cilac] furry cave mammaloid from Friatica, Friaticalida system, Galaxiki galaxy

clack: [black cat spoonerism] dangerous chiropteran named for its sound

clackdaw: [clack jackdaw portmanteau, clattering of jackdaws spoonerism] jackdaw-like felinopteryx

cladosictis: [*After the Dinosaurs* by Donald R. Prothero] weasel-like marsupial from Miocene

cladpole: [cloud of tadpoles spooner] brightly-colored parasitic tree fungus which replaces trunk

clannfear: [*The Elder Scrolls III: Morrowind*] large lizard-like daedra like small bipedal triceratops

clarineter: [trumpeter swan backformation] swan-like ornithoid with clarinet-like call

classhopper: [cloud of grasshoppers spoonerism] grasshopper-like insectoid gestalt

clat: [cloud of bats or gnats, clowder of cats portmanteau] symtriot of bats, cats and gnats

clatta: [*After Man* by Dougal Dixon] sloth-like prosimian primate with armored tail

claw monster: ["Panther Girl of the Congo"] 4.5-meter crayfish

clawbird: [*Creatures of the Galaxy* by Phil Brucato, Bill Smith, Rick D. Stuart, Chuck Truett] black, carrion-eating ornithoid from Tatooine, Geonosis and Wayland, Jedi galaxy

clawed gargoyle: [Perry Rhodan] dangerous animal from Latura II

clawlossal: [Terra Monster] large, dangerous creature from Terrarium

clawlossalope: [clawlossal antelope portmanteau] clawlossal with antlers

clawster: [clawed monster portmanteau, Terra Monster] lobster-like creature from Terrarium

clawworm: ["Planet of Storms" by Michelle Stern] snail with iridescent green shell and claws from Thersunt

clay golem: golem from clay, originally anthropoid

clay pigeon: aka skeet, pigeon-like golem made from clay

cleft-back: [*After Man* by Dougal Dixon] antelope with warty back furrow for nesting tickbirds

clezmar: [*The Energy Riff* by Hans Kneifel] greenish-orange spherical sponge made edible with fermented antidote from Pembur, Draynare system, Valigo galaxy

clicken: [clutch of chickens] ornithoid that clicks

clickfly: [*A Door into Ocean* by Joan Slonczewsky] attendant to naked Sharers from Shora the Ocean Moon of Valedon

clider: [cluster or clutter of spiders spoonerism, click spider portmanteau] arachnoid predator of clickflies that clides (attracts with clinking)

cliffracer: [*The Elder Scrolls III: Morrowind*] leathery-winged, long-beaked creature with large vertical sail, flailing tail

climacoceras: ["ladder-horn", *After the Dinosaurs* by Donald R. Prothero] antelope with horizontal rung-like horn branches

climbing echidna: ["A Fact Sheet for the Marco Polo" and "The City and the Spaceship" by Hans Kneifel] teddybear-like echidna with 4 thick white paws with suction cups, large black eyes from Leffa, Mayselan system, Sombrero galaxy

clinger: [*Frostworld* and *Dreamfire* by John Morressy] beetle-like insectoid air-eater that glows when near body heat from Hraggellon (Dunuos II)

clingey: [*The Jesus Incident* by Frank Herbert and Bill Ransom] dangerous ground-dweller from Pandora

clivit: [V: "Breakout" by David Braff] sand monster

clivitro: [James Cooke Brown's Loglan clivi troku] living rock from Logla, Brown's system

clivolti: [James Crooke Brown's Loglan clife volti compound] leaf leaper from Logla, Brown's system

clizz: ["The Headhunter" by Klaus Fischer] very fast flying insectoid

cloak-cussed: [cloud of locusts spoonerism] tiny, invisible but loud, gnat-like insectoid

cloaker: [*Monstrous Compendium: Forgotten Realms Appendix* by William Conners, etal.] large manta-like flocking predator whose subsonic moan unnerves or nauseates prey

cloakfish: [*Worlds Apart: Nat. Hist. of Furaha and Earth* by Souren Nyoroge] blue ichthyoid with green spots, cloak-like tail from Furaha (alpha Phoenicis IV)

clobbee: [clobber backformation] tiny, easily smashed bee-like insectoid

clockbug: [*The Ark Sakura* by Kobo Abe] legless insect that feeds on fecal bacteria and rotates heliotropically using antennae

clockbugator: [clockbug alligator portmanteau] alligator-like predator whose bite morphs victim into clockbug

clod hopper: [clodhopper mondegreen] hopper golem made from clods

clodhopper: "The Gungan Frontier" by Chris McCubbin] grasshopper-like clawed, beaked, fast-breeding, water-hating biped with exoskeleton and spiked tail from Jedi galaxy

clostridium: extremophilic bacterium resistant to extreme acid, see natronobacterium, bacillus

clothes horse: ["I've Seen an Elephant Fly" by Frank Church and Oliver Wallace] horse-like clothes golem

clothesmoth: [clothes moth mondegreen] moth-like clothes golem

clothes mothorse: [clothes moth, clothes horse mondegreen] mothorse-like clothes golem

cloud bear: [cloudberry backformation] flying ursinoid, see cloud dropbear

cloud cat: [*Airborn* by Kenneth Oppel] cat-like flying creature

cloud dropbear: [cloud bear, dropbear portmanteau] cloud bear that preys on ground creatures

cloud viper: ["Doctor's Orders" by Chris Black] cloudeater from Draxxa

cloudeater: [*Edge Chronicles* by Paul Stewart and Chris Riddel] cloud-shrouded multicolored serpent from Edgeworld, Cerulea system, see rain sucker, uolc

cloudrop: [Cloudstone] cloud-like pet

cloud uolc: [mynynym] white to gray to black cloud viper

clough: [clattering of coughs] crow-like ornithoid

clout: flying disc-like game "bird", clay pigeon

clue bat: [blue cat spoonerism] bloodhound-like chiropteroid

cluster hive: [*The Dalek Factor* by Simon Clark] telepathic hive-mind able to mimic least threatening creature to prospective host from Pelt's world, Quadrille system

cmrlj: [Slovenian] bumblebee-like insectoid from Sloven system

cnednepedni: [independence cnednepedni palindrome] grayish blue ornithoid

co: [aico mondegreen] flea/tick-like insectoid pet pest

coaita: [*Dell Crossword Puzzle Dictionary*] spider monkey, aka quota

coal umbus: [columbus mondegreen] coal-black, nocturnal umbus

coati: [*Dell Crossword Puzzle Dictionary*] raccoon-like mammal

coatl: ["Snake Pit" by Connie Faddis] source of venom derivative from Vestalan

cob: [*Dell Crossword Puzzle Dictionary*] male swan

cobbat: [bobcat spoonerism] male swan-eating chiropteran

cobia: [*Dell Crossword Puzzle Dictionary*] sergeant fish

cobra-beast: [Book of Diabolu Legends: "Look What Happened To J'onn J'onzz"] cobra-like beast absorbs non-Humans

cobra-grande: [*River Monsters* by Jeremy Wade] see anaconda

cobrahma: [cobra-Brahma (bull)] bovinoid with hooded head, pendulous dewlap, long serpentine neck and shoulder hump

cobrozo: [Terra Monster] colorful cobra-like snake with rattle from Terrarium, see snozo and serpquin

cobster: [cob lobster portmanteau] lond-necked ornithoid with lobster-like craws, see elttobster

coc: [cocoa brown worb aococ palindrome] light brown cock-like ornithoid, see worb, ao

cock-horse: [cock horse mondegreen] cock-headed horse-like steed

cock-roach: [cockroach mondegreen] rooster-like amphibious insectoid

cock: [*Dell Crossword Puzzle Dictionary*] male chicken or salmon

cockagrice: creature with cock-like and pig-like characteristics, see pigasus

cockaroach: [cockatrice cockroach portmanteau, Mad Magazine: "Flesh Garden"] monstrous insectoid from Mong's world

cockatrice: [Jer. 8:17] snake-bird, see saurornithoid, tinshemet

cockfish: [Xanth series by Piers Anthony] fish that crows when sunlight lights its pool from Xanth

cockroach: [Xanth series by Piers Anthony] insect that crows like a rooster from Xanth or [Xanthian mondegreen] Xa, Thia system

cockyolly: dear little ornithoid

coconut pudding: [pudding extrapolation] pudding-thick ooze

coconut snake: [*The Cruise of the Kawa* by Walter E. Traprock (George Sheperd Crappel), museumofhoaxes.com by Alex Boese] snake that uses fangs to pierce cocoanuts and drink milk from Filbert Islands, Terra (alpha Zodiaci III)

cocquecigrue: [Francois Rabelais] creature embodying absolute absurdity whose coming is said will never be

Coe snail: [Tim Coe in Game of Life] spacefaring snail capable of c/5

coelantherid: ["In the Jungle of Kalamdayon" by Peter Terrid] 1-meter food ichthyoid from Travnor, Perlitton system

coelophysis: [*The Mistaken Extinction* by Lowell Dingus and Timothy Rowe] ceratosaur descendant

coelurosaur: [*The Mistaken Extinction* by Lowell Dingus and Timothy Rowe] tyrannosaur and ornithomimosaur ancestor

coelurotaur: [coelurosaur minotaur portmanteau] tyrannotaur and ornithomimotaur ancestor

coho: [*Dell Crossword Puzzle Dictionary*] silver salmon

cohomo: [Cole Hollow monster acronym, Monster Spotter's Guide to North America by Scott Francis] 2.4-meter, white, malodorous, 3-toed nape from Cole Hollow, IL, Terrab(alpha Zodiaci III)

colbi: ["Light of Oblivion" by Harvey Patton] ibex-like with shiny silver fur, males with long curved horns from Cherkaton, Hercules cluster

colibri: [Monster Galaxy] raging hummingbird-like ornithoid from Libra constellation, see ava, topaz

colin: [*Dell Crossword Puzzle Dictionary*] quail, see cower; [francolin mondegreen] chicken-like ornithoid from Fra system

collie: [*Dell Crossword Puzzle Dictionary*] sheep dog

colo claw fish: ["The Phantom Menace" by George Lucas] 40-meter eel-like, phosphorescent ichthyoid with flattened body, mouth-claws that sonically stuns prey from Naboo, Jedi galaxy

colobus: [*National Geographic Encyclopedia of Animals*] long-haired, arboreal simian from Africa, Terra (alpha Zodiaci III)

color cat: ["Superman under the Red Sun"] multicolor tiger-like felinoid

colour: ["The Colour Out of Space" by Howard Phillips Lovecraft] "dancing incandescence" or 8-cm soft, magnetic life-sucking "meteor" in solidified stste

colour-beast: [*Wonderland* by Mark Chadbourn] huge, telepathic creature able to change color so rapid it's invisible, source of blue moonbeam (invisibility maddening drug)

colugo: [*Dell Crossword Puzzle Dictionary*] flying lemur

columbae: [piscium extrapolation] dove-like ornithoid

coly: [*Dell Crossword Puzzle Dictionary*] see mousebird, shrike

comar: [*Ahandaba* by Uwe Anton] 1.5-tonne livestock from Nubecula Major

comb jelly: see ctenophore

comber: ["Fungi from Yuggoth" by Howard Phillips Lovecraft] fractal-dimensional like thin, filmy patch with internal filaments, minion of Yog-Sothoth

combustible tadpole: [Odd Squad: Sector 21] immature flaming frog

come-and-go animal: see noshingra
cometoid: ["The Comet Monster" by Robert Bernstein] comet-like monster
comistle: [cacomistle mondegreen] flying raccoon
commodius: creature with large, brain and 16 thin legs from Icarusopia system, Galaxiki galaxy
common dragon: [*A Hero's Guide to Deadly Dragons* by Hiccup Haddock III] aka garden dragon, green and yellow or brown dragon from Barbarian archipelago
compsognathus: ["slender jaw", *Feathered Dinosaurs: The Origin of Birds* by John Long and Peter Schuten] 1.4-meter bird-like dinosaur with long tail from Germany, Terra (alpha Zodiaci III)
con rit: [*On the Nature of Animals* by Aelian] aka sea-centipede, 45-meter many-finned sea serpent with lobster-like tail
con: [Vietnamese con beo, con dê, con huou, con kên kên, con la, con luon, con ong, con sâu, con thú, con tôm, con tran mondegreens] creature ancestral to bee, boa, eel, crayfish, grub, mule, panther, giraffe, goat, giraffe, panther and vulture from Disa
concrete golem: golem of concrete
con(e)y: [*Dell Crossword Puzzle Dictionary*] rabbit from Europe, Terra (alpha Zodiaci III)
conchoraptor: ["conch-thief", *Feathered Dinosaurs: The Origin of Birds* by John Long and Peter Schuten] 1.5-meter crestless oviraptorosaur with weakly curved claws, short, powerful jaws and nasal airsacs
condoor: [condor door portmanteau] condor-like ornithoid able to travel through portals
condoor dragon: [condoor condor dragon portmanteau] condoor-like dracoid able to travel through portals
condor dragon: [*Creatures of the Galaxy* by Phil Brucato, Bill Smith, Rick D. Stuart, Chuck Truett] 3-meter carnivorous, flying dracoid that prefers giant cave spiders from moon of Endor, Jedi galaxy
condor: [*Dell Crossword Puzzle Dictionary*] see vulture, aura, urubu

conduit worm: [*Creatures of the Galaxy* by Phil Brucato, Bill Smith, Rick D. Stuart, Chuck Truett] long, electrovorous worm from Coruscant, Jedi galaxy
condzoru: [James Cooke Brown's Loglan condu dzoru compound] handwalker from Logla, Brown's system
coneater: [*The New Dinosaurs* by Dougal Dixon] 3-meter hypsilophodont with 5 fingers, cone-cracking beak
conflagration ooze: [*Monster Manual* by Skip Williams, etal.] conflagration-triggering ooze
confuciusornis: ["Confuscius bird", *Feathered Dinosaurs: The Origin of Birds* by John Long and Peter Schuten] crow-sized toothless bird with short tailbone, see changchengornis
conkerbear: [conkerberry backformation] ursinoid that conks its prey
connirda: [James Cooke Brown's Loglan condu nirda compound] handbird from Logla, Brown's system
constrictosaur: ["Flash Gordon" series] constrictor reptilian from Mongo
constrictotaur: [constrictosaur minotaur portmanteau] constrictor vermitaur
contrabassooner: [trumpeter swan backformation] baboon-like bassoon swan predator
Conway wampus cat: large 6-legged cat from Arkansas, Terra (alpha Zodiaci III)
cookee: prey of hellfire-breathing creatures, like dragons that cook their prey before eating it
coon: [contraction] raccoon or [*Dell Crossword Puzzle Dictionary*] opossum, ["The Last Man of OSA Mariga" by Rainer Castor] sabre-toothed cephalopodan with suckered tentacles
coonigator: [*Monster Spotter's Guide to North America* by Scott Francis] raccoon-like scavenger with alligator-like jaws from Montpelier, VT, Terra (alpha Zodiaci III)
coot: [*Dell Crossword Puzzle Dictionary*] sea duck, see scaup, scoter, eider

cooter: [*National Geographic Encyclopedia of Animals*] turtle from E. U. S., Terra (alpha Zodiaci III)

copper cat: felinoid golem make from copper, see mishibizhiw

copper goose: [golden goose extrapolation] copper goose that lays copper eggs and resists being plucked

copy cat: [Xanth series by Piers Anthony] mimicking cat able to replicate a manuscript it sits on by extruding copy from its mouth from Xanth

coqui: [*National Geographic Encyclopedia of Animals*] small tree frog from Puerto Rico, Terra (alpha Zodiaci III)

cor: [rancor mondegreen] bipedal dinosauroid from Ra system; [*The Dirdir, The Pnume* by Jack Vance] rock-dweller, often red

coraknot: [*The First Kingdom* by Jack Katz] large, long-necked dracoid quadruped

coralhorn: [Terra Monsters] larger amphibious relative of coralpie from Terrarium

coralpie: [Terra Monster] turquoise sealamb, see coralhorn, from Terrarium

cordo: [*Attack of the Dinosaur* by Dirk Hess, "The March through the Underworld" by Ernst Vlcek] 13-meter blind, armored elephantine with 2 trunks, symbiot with Rockandos from Cronot, Heith system

corgi: [*Dell Crossword Puzzle Dictionary*] dog from Wales, Terra (alpha Zodiaci III)

corgodrill: [*Fortune's Light* by Michael Jan Friedman] small rainbow-colored pongoid from Imprima

corgodrillope: [corgodrill antelope portmanteau] corgodrill with antlers

corkscrew beetle: [*cortexclavus, The Wine of Violence* by James Morrow] insectoid from Carlotta, Malnovian belt, UW Canis Majoris system

corkscrew worm: ["Capt'n Virgil, Sportsman in Space" by David Brooks] very small, helical vermin from Arizant

corkscroo: [corkscrew mondegreen] macropodan that metamorphs from corkscrew worm-like larva

cormah: [shamrock cormahs palindrome] green ornithoid that mimics seaweed-covered rock

corneteer: ["Mortal Nature" by Stephen Dedman] sound-sensitive migratory herd animal from Northbergen

coro: ["Red Sun over Ruby" by Detlev G. Winter] antelope-like creature from Ruby (Omega II)

corpse-tearer: see nidhoggr

corru: [corru alligator backformation] woolyworm-like creature

corru gator: [corrugator mondegreen] alligator-like predator whose bite morphs victim into corru

corvi: [piscium extrapolation] crow-like ornithoid

corvusaur: black dracoid with feathery wings from Corvus constellation

coryphodon: [*After the Dinosaurs* by Donald R. Prothero] cow-sized pantodont that migrated across Bering Landbridge, related to rhino-sized hypercoryphodon

cosmic creature: ["The Cosmic Creature" by Jack Miller] long-lived shapeshifter

cosmic ray creature: ["The Creature That Couldn't Die" by John Broome] creature strengthened by cosmic rays

cosmido: corvid with small head, curved black beak, slightly protruding eyes from Dare Meron (Kargnickan II)

cosset: [*Dell Crossword Puzzle Dictionary*] small pet lamb, see cade

couch potato: ["Uncharted Territory" by Connie Willis] extraordinarily sedentary creature from Boohte

couerl: [Final Fantasy] aka cuar, cuahl, quirl, related to displace beast

couger: [cougar tiger portmanteau] cougar-headed tiger-like felinoid

couguar: [cougar jaguar portmanteau] cogar-headed jaguar-like felinoid

coumarq: [*Planet of Graves* by Clark Darlton] vermin insectoid from Arkon

coupari: long-haired cat with folded ears

courser: [*National Geographic Encyclopedia of Animals*] insect and seed-eating bird from Africa, erra (alpha Zodiaci III)
couse: [cover of grouse spoonerism, cow-grouse portmanteau] cow-headed grouse-like griffinoid
cow-beetle: [*Superior Beings* by Nick Walters] beetle-like insectoid the size of small cow attended by mobile gardener plants sticking out of bodies from Khorlthochloi's world
cow-bird: [cowbird mondegreen] ornithoid with horn-like crest that secretes milk-like liquid
cow-boy: [cowboy mondegreen] small cow-man, see buckeroo
cow-dog: cow-headed blackdog
cow-elephant: cow-headed elephant-like creature, see calf
cow-man: [cowman mondegreen] cow-headed anthropoid, see minotaur

cower: [*Dell Crossword Puzzle Dictionary*] quail, colin
cowhale: [cow whale portmanteau] cow-headed whale-like seacow, see calf
cowhalelephant: [cow, whale, elephant portmanteau] chimera like cow, whale and elephant, see calf
cowl: [cow-owl portmanteau] nocturnal 4-legged milk-producing ornithoid with hooked talons, short beak, and large forward-set eyes protected by hood-like facial skin
cowse: [cow-mouse portmanteau] bovinoid with large, round ears
coyotl: [Monster Galaxy] fox-like caninoid
coyotlope: [coyotl antelope portmanteau] coyotl with antlers
coypu: [*National Geographic Encyclopedia of Animals*] semi-aquatic rodent from S. America, Terra (alpha Zodiaci III), [*Dell Crossword Puzzle Dictionary*] see cavy, degu, paca, agouti
crab-bee: [crabby mondegreen] crab-like triphibious insectoid
crabatron: [*The Ultimate Monster Guide* by Jaymond] 4-legged crustacean with mandibles, eyestalks and eyes, pincers

crabbit: [crab-rabbit portmanteau] decapod with broad, flattened carapace, short antennae, 2 large pinchers, long ears and short tail, not cat-rabbit, see manx
crabdozer: [Ben 10: Omniverse: "The More Things Change" by Charlotte Fullerton] silicon-based armored predator with flame-retardant saliva
craboa: [crab-boa portmanteau, Monster Galaxy] creature from Cancer constellation
crabone: [Monster Galaxy] nutty-tasting arachnoid with skull-like body from Cancer constellation
crabug: [crab bug pormanteau] crab-like insectoid
crabugator: [crabug bug alligator portmanteau] alligator-like predator whose bite morphs victim into crabug
cradlefish: [Star Trek: Enterprise: "Vox Sola" by Fred Dekker] ichthyoid from Neethea
cragling: [Outernauts] immature craglite with just one eye, in red-eyed green "dark" variety
craglingator: [cragling alligator portmanteau] alligator-like predator whose bite morphs victim into cragling
craglite: [Outernauts] rock-like creature with two eyes, in red-eyed green "dark" variety, see cragling, cragzilla
cragon: [crown dragon portmanteau] lake snake that drowns prey
cragzilla: [Outernauts] mature craglite with three eyes
crahc: [charcoal aocrahc palindrome] dark gray thrush-like ornithoid, related to ao
crairtap: [patriarch crairtap palindrome] purple ornithoid
cranbear: [cranberry backformation] small, cranny-dwelling ursinoid
crane: [*Dell Crossword Puzzle Dictionary*] wading bird, see ibis, rail, egret, heron, stilt, avocet, avoset, jacana, flamingo; [Xanth series by Piers Anthony] thin, long-legged bird able to hoist rocks into trees from Xanth or [Xanthian mondegreen] Xa, Thia system
cranioceras: [*After the Dinosaurs* by Donald R. Prothero] dromomeryx with straight horns over eyes and behind ears

crat: [cat-rat portmanteau] cat-like rodentoid from Wintria, Pfetea system, Galaxiki galaxy
Crater Lake Monster: ["The Crater Lake Monster" by William R. Stromberg and Richard Cardella] lake monster from Crater Lake
crattler: [crat-rattler portmanteau] cat-like rodentoid with tail rattle, see crat
craulium: [Cyclopedia of Worlds] large animal on Palul (Lar Don), the Dinosaur Planet
craven: [Winx Club] crow/raven-like bird
crawfish-frog: [crawfish frog mondegreen] amphibian from Batrach system
crawfish-frogator: [crawfish-frog alligator portmanteau] alligator-like predator whose bite morphs victim into crawfish-frog
Crawfordsville monster: [*Unexplained!* by Jerome Clark] headless, 6-by-2.4-meter flying creature with fins sited over Crawfordsville, IN, Terra (alpha Zodiaci III), see rod
crawler: [Pern series by Ann McCaffrey] non-spinning arachnoid from Pern (Rukbat (alpha Sagittarii) III)
cray-spinner: [*Edge Chronicles* by Paul Stewart and Chris Riddell] small, translucent creature with diaphanous wings, eyestalks from Edgeworld, Cerulea system
crayfish-spider: see tuborg
creep: ["The Night of the Creeps" by Fred Drekker] black, slug-like brain-eating parasite
creepee: [creepy mondegreen, creeper backformation] rampant prey
creepeel: [creepy eel mondegreen] amphibiois eel-like ichthyoid
creeper: see rampant
creeping unknown: ["The Quatermass Experiment" by Nigel Kneale] space-borne spores in dormant state that grow into 6-meter tall amorphous parasite with long twining tentacles by consuming flesh, morphs host into fungus-like life-sucker carrying over memories and physical attributes to next victim
cremont: [*Earth in Twilight* by Doris Piserchia] jungle-dwelling mutant
creodont: bear-cat-like carnivore of Tertiary, see sarkastodon

cressi: [Cyclopedia of Worlds] needle-toothed snake-like nocturnal predator up to 8 meters from Scanodon, Croft system
cressie: [*Monster Spotter's Guide to North America* by Scott Francis] 6-meter eel-like lake snake from Crescent Lake, Newfoundland, Terra (alpha Zodiaci III)
cretahila: shrimp-like sea creature from Deepsea (Phoenix IV), Galaxiki galaxy
cretoxyrhina: [*The Big Bad Book of Beasts* by Michael Largo] "Ginsu shark", 6-meter shark with 8-cm teeth
cri: [cancri mondegreen] crab-like crustacean from Ca system
cri-tic: [Piers Anthony] loathsome blood-sucking insect from Mundania
cribrum: [*The New Dinosaurs* by Dougal Dixon] aka cribrusaur, 2-meter, pink flamingoid coelurosaur with sieve-like teeth, long neck and tail
cricket-bat: [cricket bat mondegreen] cricket-headed cheiropteroid
Crieff mosquito: ["The Star Bastard" by Robert Feldhoff] mosquito-like insectoid from Crieff
crimson tide: (*Bart Simpson's Treehouse of Horror Spine-tingling Spooktacular*) huge red sea monster, mascot of Harvard University
crinoceras: [crash of rhinos spoonerism, cri rhinoceras portmanteau] crab-like rhinoid
criosphinx: ram-headed lion
crippling: ["Bird-watchers' Slang" by Paul Beale] rare, colorful bird
crippingator: [crippler alligator portmanteau] alligator-like predator whose bite morphs victim into crippler
criptid: [*The Grey Prince* by Jack Vance] padfooted equinoid from Koryphon
croaker spaniel: [*Rainbeau's Riddles and Rhymes*] frog-spaniel
croator: [*Creatures of the Galaxy* by Phil Brucato, Bill Smith, Rick D. Stuart, Chuck Truett] asexual, flightless ornithoid with reflective plumage, very long proboscis that feeds on ichthyoids and insectoids from Wyndigal II, Jedi galaxy

crocababolone: [*Rainbeau's Riddles and Rhymes*] crocodile-abalone

crocadoodledoo: [*Rainbeau's Riddles and Rhymes*] crocodile-rooster

crocapoodledoo: [*Rainbeau's Riddles and Rhymes*] crocadoodledoo-poodle

croccisor: ["Beasts of Zeut" by William Voltz] 50-cm hemi-spheroid with 4 legs and extendable spines (some sensorium) from Zeut

croche: ["Beasts of Zeut" by William Voltz] carnivorous, forest-dwelling, 300-kg herd dracoid with reptilian jaw, brown scales, pungent odor, red-hot eyes, long tail and levitation organ from Crieff

crocodyllus: [*Perigrinationes ad Terram Sanctam* by Erhard Reuwich] 9-meter aquatic reptile with clawed feet from Egypt

crocosaur: ["Megashark vs. Crocosaurus" by Naomi L. Selfman, *Odin's Quest* by Cleon Jones] crocodilian dinosaur

crocotaur: [crocosaur minotaur portmanteau] crocodilian bovinoid

croizetoceras: ["lyre-horn", *After the Dinosaurs* by Donald R. Prothero] deer with lyre-shaped horns from Miocene

crooked lizard: see ankylosaur

crossbill: small red bird with twisted bill

crotalus: [*Dell Crossword Puzzle Dictionary*] rattlesnake or sidewinder

crotalusaur: [cotalus-saur portmanteau] dinosaur with rattle

crotalutaur: [crotalusaur minotaur portmanteau] bovinoid with rattle

crotcotta: [*Natural History* by Pliny] nocturnal dog-wolf with very strong teeth, instant digestion from Indo-Ethiopia

crow mite: [chromite mondgreen] mite that infests crows

crowdy: ["Sons of the Desert of Anoplur" by Ernst Vlcek] camel-like white mount with long neck, hooves, hump deformed into saddle from Anoplur (Notone II)

crown of thorns: [*Starcross* by Philip Reeve] giant land starfish with many barbed tentacles from Mars (alpha Zodiaci IV), extinct 100,000,000 BC

croydal: ["The Robot Man and the Mutant" by William Voltz] shy ursinoid from Birachy-chan (Tyk Ambazor IV)

croydalope: [croydal antelope portmanteau] croydal with antlers

cruiser bird: [frigate bird extrapolation] small frigate-like ornithpoid

cukka: [Teluga *] 2-D pentapus or hexapus

crum: [crumhorn backformation] tamable shabby creature noted for crumpled horn

crumm: [crummy backformation] louse-like insectoid

crup: [*Fantastic Beasts and Where to Find Them* by Newton Artemis Fido Scamander] omnivorous, ferocious fork-tailed terrier from S. E. England, Terra (alpha Zodiaci III)

crvuk: [Croatian crv-vuk portmanteau] worm-wolf, larval insectoid-caninoid symbiot, similar to pollop from Croat system

cryceptor: [Outernauts] mature crypeto

crypeto: [Outernauts] bluish scorpion-like creature, see crysling, cryceptor

cryptid: creature that remains mysterious, unphotographable, unverifiable, legendary

cryptile: [crypt reptile portmanteau, *The Future Is Wild* by Dougal Dixon] white desert agamid (frilled lizard) with mucusy, net-like frill for catching brine flies able to turn black when threatened

crysling: [Outernauts] immature crypeto

cryslingator: [crysling alligator portmanteau] alligator-like predator whose bite morphs victim into crysling

crystal bird: [Superman mythos] silicon-based ornithoid whose mass grave formed the Jewel mountains, Krypton, Rao system

crystal ooze: [*Monster Manual* by Skip Williams, etal.] crystallized ooze, see snowflake ooze

crystal spider: [*Edge Chronicles* by Paul Stewart and Chris Riddell] crystalline arachnoid from Garden of Light, Edgeworld, Cerulea system

crytophoca: [*After the Dinosaurs* by Donald R. Prothero] with praepusa, phocaponto-phoca, leptophoca, the first true seals from Miocene

ctenophore: [*The Big Bad Book of Beasts* by Michael Largo] aka comb jelly, spherical creature with comb-like cilia, some bioluminescent

cu: [Vietnamese chim cu mondegreen] chim-cuckoo-like ornithoid from Disa system

cua: [Vietnamese chim cu-cua portmanteau backformation] crustacean ancestral to chim and cuckoo-crab triphibian from Disa system;

cualg: [glaucous uo cualg palindrome] blue uo

cualgator: [cualg alligator portmanteau] alligator-like predator whose bite morphs victim into cualg

cuahl: see couer

cuail: [covy of quails spoonerism, cu-quail portmanteau] chim-cuckoo-quail-like ornithoid

cualg: [uocualg mondegreen] blue-black and brownish red furry

cualgator: [cualg alligator portmanteau] alligator-like predator whose bite morphs victim into cualg

cuar: see couerl

cub: young of bear, wolf, lion or combinations of any two or all three

cucina: [Latvian juras cucina mondegreen] rodentoid ancestral to juras and Guinea pig

cuckoo dragon: [*A Hero's Guide to Deadly Dragons* by Hiccup Haddock III] aquamarine or turquoise winged dragon that lays its eggs in bird's nests from Barbarian archipelago

cuckoo-bee: [cuckoo bee mondegreen] cuckoo-mimicking insectoid

cuckoo-dragon: [cuckoo dragon mondegreen] cuckoo-headed dracoid

cud lepus: [cuddlepus mondegreen] egg-laying rabbit-like ruminant

cudbear: [Cuthbert Gordon] purplish-red, cud-chewing ursinoid

cuddlepuff: [Outernauts] mature cuddlepus with lure stalk and 4 fins

cuddlepus: [Outernauts] mature cuddletee

cuddlepuss: cuddlepus puss portmanteau]

cuddletee: [Outernauts] pink cuttlefish-like sea creature, see cuddlish, cuddlepus

cuttleteel: [cuttletee eel portmanteau] pink cuttletee-like eel colony

cuddlish: [Outernauts] immature cuttle-fish-like cuddlepus

cuddopuff: [Outernauts] immature cuddotee

cuddopus: [Outernauts] mature cuddotee

cuddlepuss: [cuddlepus puss portmanteau] catfish-like ichthyoid with lure, whiskers and 4 fins

cuddotee: [Outernauts] ichthyoid with lure and 4 fins, see cuddopuff, cuddopus

cuddoteel: [cuddotee eel portmanteau] cuddotee-like eel colony

cuitlamiztli: [*Unexplained!* by Jerome Clark] see onza

cuk: [Fr. Johann Martin Schleyer's Volapük] donkey- or ass-like equinoid from Schleyer's system

cuka: [Latvian juras cuka mondegreen] cetacean ancestral to juras and porpoise

culibra: [*Dell Crossword Puzzle Dictionary*] snake from Spain, Terra (alpha Zodiaci III)

cupkatma: [James Cooke Brown's Loglan cupri katma compound] copper cat from Logla, Brown's system

curl-up: [M. C. Escher] aka wentelteefje, Krempeltierchen, roulenboule, 6-legged creature with sideward eyestalks that moves by curling and rolling

curlew: [National Geographic Encyclopedia of Animals] insect and invertebrate-eating bird from N. America, Terra (alpha Zodiaci III)

curra: [currassow mondegreen] chicken-pig-like pigasus

currant jelly: [jelly extrapolation] jelly-thick ooze

currassow: [*National Geographic Encyclopedia of Animals*] chicken relative from S. America, Terra (alpha Zodiaci III)

curset: [*Trullion: Alastor 2262* by Jack Vance] crab-like sea insectoid from Trullion

cus: cuscus nasna

cuscus: [National Geographic Encyclopedia of Animals] herbivorous mammal from S. Pacific, Terra (alpha Zodiaci III)

cutewhale: [acute anglewhale mondegreen] anglewhale that turns in less than right angles

cuteworm: [acute angleworm mondegreen] angleworm that turns in less than right angles

cutter: [roachcutter mondegreen] beetle-like insectoid prey of roachcutters from Ahla, Ojikh system, Galaxiki galaxy

cutthroat: ["At the Zoo" by Rick Shelley] raccoon-faced baboon-like creature from Albin

cuttlef: [cuttlefish backformation] small cephalopodan

cuttlefish: [Xanth series by Piers Anthony] white fish with knife-like tentacles from Xanth or [Xanthian mondegreen] Xa, Thia system

cuttless: [cutlass, cuttelf malopropisms] cephalopodan smaller than cuttlef

cw: [Welsh cwcw nasna] rabbit-cuckoo, long-eared burrowing griffinoid ancestral to both cuckoo and rabbit, and almost indistinguishable from ningen, from Pharr, Farpt system, Galaxiki galaxy

cwcwyddrywystrys: [Welsh cwcw-wydd-dryw-wystrys portmanteau] barnacle goose-like cross between cuckoo, goose, wren and oyster

cwcwystrys: [Welsh cwcw-wystrys portmanteau] cuckoo-oyster, barnacle goose-like ornithoid ancestral to cuckoo and oyster, with oyster and cuckoo

cwystrys: [Welsh cw-wystrys portmanteau] cw-oyster cross ancestral to cw (rabbit-cuckoo) and cwcwystrys

cy'een: [*Creatures of the Galaxy* by Phil Brucato, Bill Smith, Rick D. Stuart, Chuck Truett] long-necked ichthyosauroid from Chad, Jedi galaxy

cyanide-breathing butterflies: ["Dr. Pauli's Planet" by Carey Wilber] geneered butterflies that breathe cyanide

cyanocyne: [diehard Republican, "Huckleberry Hound"] aka huckleberry hound blue canine, see xanthocyne

cyban: [cybernetic animal contraction] animal that has been cybernetically augmented

cybhot: [Perry Rhodan] arachnoid flinging extremely toxic barbs from Boestris Zazoma

cycheep: [Outernauts] venomous, one-eyed, flying spheroid, see cycrow, cygon

cyclonine: [Terra Monster] wingtail adapted to stratosphere from Terrarium

cyclops bat: [Monster Buster: Hex Blast] one-eyed chiropteran that feeds on gingerbread men

cycrow: [Outernauts] venomous, one-eyed, winged, immature worm-like cycheep

cyena: [cackle of hyenas spoonerism] cackyll-hyena-like caninoid

cygi: [piscium extrapolation] swan-like ornithoid

Cygnonese dragon: [Josie and the Pussycats in Outer Space: "The Four-eyed Dragon of Cygnon"] dracoid with four eyes from Cygnon

cygnusaur: beautiful flying/swimming dracoid from Cygnus constellation

cygon: [Outernauts] marture cycheep with yellowish underbelly and pink butterfly wings

cynodont: [*The Mistaken Extinction* by Lowell Dingus and Timothy Rowe] thrinaxodon ancestor from Permian

cynr-cwcwyddrywystrys: [Welsh] barnacle goose-like griffinoid ancestral to chameleon and cwcwyddrywystrys

cypher: [*The Heir Apparent* by H. G. Francis] burgundy ornithoid from Arkon II

cypow: [Outernauts] mature cyror

cyroo: [Outernauts] immature cyror

cyror: [Outernauts] blue and orange caninoid, see cyroo, cypow

cza: [Polish szarancza, czasaltik mondegreens] locust-like insectoid from Szara, moon of Naslima, Slamina system, Galaxiki galaxy

czasaltik: [Perry Rhodan] swarming insectoid from Thorrin (Thorrtimer II), Whirlpool galaxy

D-bra: [dazzle of zebras spoonerism] colorful double-humped shellfish

da cova: [avocado dacova palindrome] avacado green insectoid

da: [adanda mondegreen] insectoid from Ada; [manda mondegreen] aquatic snake from Ma; [panda mondegreen] herbivorous ursinoid from Pa (eta Serpentis) system

daasvoël: [Afrikaans daas-aasvoël portmanteau] horsefly-vulture, small vulture-like ornithoid fond of horses

dābbe-i-chahār-sar: [Islam] 4-headed, winged creature in India Ocean, Terra (alpha Zodiaci III)

daboia: see daboya

daboya: [*Dell Crossword Puzzle Dictionary*] aka daboia, snake from India, see cobra, krite

dachshund pig: [*Thora's Escape* by Clark Darlton] dachshund-like food porcoid from Venus (alpha Zodiaci II)

dacjaw: [jackdaw spoonerism, dactillion jaw portmanteau] dacti relative with dactillion-like 2-part beak

dacti: [dactillion mondegreen] lion-like dracoid

dactillion: [*Creatures of the Galaxy* by Phil Brucato, Bill Smith, Rick D. Stuart, Chuck Truett] 4-legged, winged dracoid with 2-part beak from Utapau, Jedi galaxy

dadang: [*The Headhunter* by Klaus Fischer] tiny, cave flying insectoid that communicated via dance

dadangator: [dadang alligator portmanteau] alligator-like predator whose bite morphs victim into dadang

dadar: [*Hammer of Death* by H. G. Francis] hooved, dromedary-like desert equinoid from Pthor

daderyx: [momeryx backforation] deer relative with antlers, see momeryx

daeodon: [*After the Dinosaurs* by Donald R. Prothero] fka dinohyus, pig-like entelodon

dagg: [daggert mondegreen] small, pretty arboreal ichthoid from Troctopia, Qujhtba system, Galaxiki galaxy

daggator: [dagg alligator portmanteau] alligator-like predator whose bite morphs victim into dagg

daggert: ["The Gungan Frontier" by Chris McCubbin] small, pretty, fast-breeding, short-lived ichthyoid herbivore from Jedi galaxy

daggertooth: ["Hyperspace Nomads" by Arndt Ellmer] predator from Spectral empire

dagora: ["Dagora, the Space Monster" by Shinichi Sekizawa] 30-meter long lighter-than-air jelly-fish-like with 60-meter tentacles, crystalized by wasp venom

dagrug: [*Heretics of Tazolen* by Susan Schwartz] rodentoid pest from Tarkan branch universe

dagrugator: [dagrug alligator portmanteau] alligator-like predator whose bite morphs victim into dagrug

dagvna: [Cherokee] oyster-like creature from Tsalagi system

dah-nes: [dah-nes-tsa, tsa-e-donin-ee mondegreen] ram-fly relative

dah-nes-tsa: [Navaho] ram-like creature from Diné system

dahagmata: ["The Dream of the Navigator" by Rüdiger Schäfer] 20-meter, glittering yellow crystalline water-dwelling lump, source of deadly addictive euphoric "ulcers"

dahara: [Michael Kane series by "Edward Powys Bradbury" (Michael Moorcook)] pongoid the size of Shire horse with wide kangaroo-like tails and large hind legs used as steed on Kane's world

dahondra: ["Under the Crystal Lattice" by Arndt Ellmer] antelope-like ruminant from Arkon I

dahu: aka dairi, darou, darhut and tamarou, deer-like ruminant with two legs shorter than others from Europe, Terra (alpha Zodiaci III), like gyasutus

daiha: [kwandaioha mondegreen] cobra-like snake from Kwa

daioha: [kwandaioha mondegreen] cobra-like snake from Kwa

dairi: see dahu

daj: [jade daj palindrome] jade green ornithoid

dak: [Indonesian landak mondegreen] hedgehog-like burrower from La system

dake: [den of snakes spoonerism, dak snake portmanteau] hedgehog-snake with drill-like head

dakim: [Mikado dakim palindrome] yellowish ornithoid

Dakka shark: [Cyclopedia of Worlds] 11-meter carcharadon adapted to Dakka, Neptune system

daksi: [Cherokee] terrapin-like creature from Tsalagi system

dalam: [marmalade dalam ram palindrome] "red" (yellow-orange) ram-like ruminant

dalanistes: [*After the Dinosaurs* by Donald R. Prothero] whale ancestor with webbed hind feet, long snout and tail related to ambulocetus and rodhocetus from Eocene

Daley's bird: [X-1: "The Trap" by Finn O'Donovan] ornithoid with 4 wings

Daley's snake: [X-1: "The Trap" by Finn O'Donovan] 2-headed serpentoid

dalli: [red dalli kill-adder palindrome] red kill-adder-like amphisbæna

damaga: [Cherokee] horsefly-like insectoid from Tsalagi system

damagator: damaga alligator portmanteau] alligator-like predator whose bite morphs victim into damaga

damite: [pandamite mondegreen] heat-adapted ursinoid from Pa system

Damogran eagle: [Hitchhiker's Guide to the Galaxy series by Douglas Adams] frond-crested eagle-like desert ornithoid noted for paper mâché nests from Damogra

damruss: [Perry Rhodan] mount from Paricza, Punta-Pono system

damself: [damselfish bachformation] hong-haired beaver-like amphibian

dan: [devy of swans spoonerism, danax mondegreen] long-necked, gray ornithoid

danakak: ["A Star Is Born" by Jerry Oltion] mouth-dwelling scavenger symbiot of the Darefta

danax: [xanadu danax palindrome] gray ornithoid

dancer: ["Infernal Dance of the Giants" by William Voltz] thin, headless spacefaring giant with 7 legs from Pulsa, Whilor system

danchaf: [*Creatures of the Galaxy* by Phil Brucato, Bill Smith, Rick D. Stuart, Chuck Truett] aka tree goblin, 2-meter, ferocious, arboreal pack carnivore from Garban, Jedi galaxy

dandilion: [GreenSpace] dandelion-seedling-like aerial scavenger with puffy antennae and black eyes

dandy: [dandylion]

dandylion: [Terra Monster] felinoid with blossom-like tailtip, see purrpetal, from Terrarium

dang: [Filipino tandang backformation] rooster-like ornithoid from Ta system; [gnadnaf ananymondegreen] purplish ornithoid from Fa (iota Orionis) system

dangator: [dang alligator portmanteau] alligator-like predator whose bite morphs victim into dang

dangwhoodle: [wangdoodle spoonerism] centipede-like pest

danjitter: ["The Market of Xudon" by Hans Kneifel] trainable hawk-like ornithoid from Xodon (Xudomanyla IV), Black galaxy

dansa: [James Cooke Brown's Loglan (dancer)] giant headless heptapus from Logla, Brown's system

danta: [*Dell Crossword Puzzle Dictionary*] tapir from S. America, Terra (alpha Zodiaci III)

dap: [lap dog spoonerism] small, friendly caninoid with cylindrical body and very short legs

daphoenodon: [*After the Dinosaurs* by Donald R. Prothero] amphicyon or beardog that migrated to America in Miocene

dapwing: [deceit or desert of lapwings spoonerism] dap-like caninopteryx

daq: [Azerbaijani qarabatdaq backformation] aka ak, ornithoid ancestral to qara bat and cormorant, [Perry Rhodan] nocturnal pack predator from Titanic (aka Oharc)

daquir: [*Voyage Curieux dún Philadelphe dans des Pays nouvellement*] 3-horned bovinoid whose skin is used for belts on Waferdanos Island, N. Atlantic, Terra (alpha Zodiaci III)

dar: [vandar mondegreen] black lion from Va system

dara: [bandara mondegreen] beetle-like, sand-dwelling insectoid from Ba system

darasite: [Denarian, Denevan parasite spoonerisms] parasite that infests dara beetle from Ba system in Peneva and Penar systems

darasp: [Cyclopedia of Worlds] small animal from gas giant Chassana, Sheel-Sen system

darcan: ["Struggle for Exota Alpha" by Hans Kneifel] skiddish mount from Thargomindah, Exota Alpha

dardgog: [guarddog spoonerism] territorial caninoid

dardgogator: [dardgog alligator portmanteau] alligator-like predator whose bite morphs victim into dardgog

darelg: ["The Tryonic Alliance" by Susan Schwartz] domesticated livestock with red coat, broad chest, mane, back-turned horns, long ears, green eyes, beard, used for milk, meat and mount, from Ganroj, Thagg system, Stardust galaxy, Shapley supercluster

darelgator: [darelg alligator portmanteau] alligator-like predator whose bite morphs victim into darelg

darhut: see dahu

darjeel: ["Land of Forgetfulness" by Dirk Hess] mount from Akon

darjeelope: [darjeel antelope portmanteau] darjeel with antlers

dark tree: [Monsters of Faerün] cypress-like vampiric monster with fiendish face and two spindly arm-branches

darkmantle: ["The Ecology of the Darkmantle" by Jonathan M. Richards] dark brown, cave-dwelling cephalopodan with webbed tentacles, using echolocation and limited telekinesis to darken cave, related to piercer, roper and lou carcolh

Darkness: ["The Terror of the Darkness" by Joseph Lidster] space parasite that feeds on darkness in mind, turns minor annoyances into reasons to murder

daroon: [scandaroon mondegreen] carrier pigeon from Sca system

darou: see dahu

darr: [*Dell Crossword Puzzle Dictionary*] black tern

darsine: [sardine spoonerism] small, edible ichthyoid pegasoid from Peggassa, Hippocrenea system, Galaxiki galaxy

darso: ["The Puppets of Astera" by Hans Kneifel] large, swallow-like ornithoid from Astera (Muul II)

darter: [*Dell Crossword Puzzle Dictionary*] perch-like fish or snakebird, [*National Geographic Encyclopedia of Animals*] fish-eating bird of S. Asia, Terra (alpha Zodiaci III)

darthmunk: [Terra Monsters] creature from Terrarium

dary: [quandary mondegreen] sea creature from Qua system

das: [Lith. ampersandas mondegreen] 2-D creature with head, torso, one leg and tail from Ampera system

dasher: ["The Lazarus Effect" by Frank Herbert and Bill Ransom] large, deadly black water-walking beast from Pandora, see hooded dasher

dashta: [Star Trek] eel-like ichthoid with ability to use the Force from Ord Cetus, Jedi galaxy

daspletosaur: ["frightful, brawny lizard", *Feathered Dinosaurs: The Origin of Birds* by John Long and Peter Schuten] 9-meter, 2-tonne tyrannosaurid with characteristic postorbital bone

daspletotaur: [daspletosaur minotaur portmateau] bovinoid with postorbital bone

dat: [destruction of cats spoonerism] alpacatastrophe-like felinoid

datryma: [i-less diatryma] large, flightless cave ornithoid from Friatica, Friaticalida system, Galaxiki galaxy

datsi: [kanatsisdatsi mondegreen] wasp-like insectoid from Atsi, Ka system

daymare: [*The Right Hand of Dextra* by David J. Lake] ornithoid from Dextra

dbaluga: [upland baluga mondegreen] land-whale from Upla system

dbalugator: [dbaluga alligator portmanteau] alligator-like predator whose bite morphs victim into dbaluga

de: [gerde mondegreen] cormorant-dog pegasoid

dê: [Vietnamese con dê backformation] creature ancestral to con and goat from Disa system

dea: [dea head palindrome] worm-like food animal with regenerating head ancestral to dly and deadly spawn

deadly spawn: ["Deadly Spawn"] in immature state 8-cm worm; in mature state 2-meter, 1.5-tonne reddish creature with plant-like trunk, 3 heads each with large mouth, no eyes, 2 long tentacles with pinchers

deadpan: [Xanth series by Piers Anthony] ugly-faced creature fond of cooking fires from Xanth

deater: [sandeater mondegreen] desert creature from Sa, the Leech Planet

deathbeast: ["Dawnstar Rising" by Paul Levitz] deadly beast from Graan

deathgleaner: [*The Future Is Wild* by Dougal Dixon] diurnal predatory, scavenging cheropteran with 1.3-meter wingspan

deathwatch beetle: [*The Big Bad Book of Beasts* by Michael Largo] wood-eating, rapping insect

debaril: [*The New Dinosaurs* by Dougal Dixon] 60-cm, adaptable desert dinosaur with black beak

debarilope: [debaril antelope portmanteau] debaril with antlers

Debbie monster: [Odd Couple: "The Odd Candidate" by Lowell Ganz and Mark Rothman, "The Monster from the Planet Debbie"] monstrous creature from Debbie

debra: [donkey zebra portmanteau, dazzle of zebras spoonerism] donkey-headed zebra-like equinoid

decigurp: [centigurp extrapolation] pink furball able to bounce, roll, fond of spheres, and be in ten places at once, see gurp

declan: ["Avatar" by James Cameron] dracoid steed from Pandora, moon of Polyphemus, alpha Centauri system

dedramixxi: ["The Cell Activator" by Hans Kneifel] long-limbed, black and yellow furry tetramorph with long skull or short, web-footed, gilled, barbed-toothed or with wolf-like head, long tail with barbs and suckers or with gliding wings, thin tail from Cyrsic nr. Black galaxy

deel: [land eel mondegreen] serpentine from La system

deer pig: [Avatar: The Last Airbender: "Zuko Alone"] pig-headed deer with pig legs, bushy tail and antlers

deer-bunny: see jackalope, doe

deerfly: [Xanth series by Piers Anthony] giant 4-legged, insectoid with antlers and brown eyes from Land of Flies, Xanth or [Xanthian mondegreen] Xa, Thia system

deerwig: [deer-earwig portmanteau] hooved and antlered ruminant with pair mandibles and antennae

deerwigator: [deerwig alligator portmanteau] alligator-like predator whose bite morphs victim into deerwig

degu: [*National Geographic Encyclopedia of Animals*] large rodent from Chile, Terra (alpha Zodiaci III), [*Dell Crossword Puzzle Dictionary*] see cavy, paca, coypu, agouti

deichsor: [*The City of a Thousand Traps* by William Voltz] dangerous predator from Gevonia (Targo II)

deinococcus: extremophilic bacterium resistant to radiation, vacuum, dryness, vacuum, see rubrobacter, pyrococcus

deinonychus: [*A Field Guide to Dinosaurs* by Henry Gee and Luis V. Rey] aka incorrectly as velociraptor [*Jurassic Park* by Michael Chrichton], ["terrible claw", *Feathered Dinosaurs: The Origin of Birds* by John Long and Peter Schuten] 3-meter dromaeosaur with large slashing claws, able to stiffen tail for balance

deinothere: [*After the Dinosaurs* by Donald R. Prothero] mastodont with characteristic downward-turned tusks from Miocene

Deiran turkey: ["Never Enough Dark"] 1.3-meter magenta-furred turkey-like ornithoids from Deira

dekawatt: [Outernauts] yellow, red-eyed arrowhead-shaped electrical creature, see watt, killawatt, gigawatt

deleater: [delete eater mondegreen] surreal creature that eats letters causing creature name elisions and mondegreens

delp: [*Wyst: Alastor 1716* by Jack Vance] especially vicious black creature used as watchdog from Wyst

delphini: [piscium extrapolation] egg-laying dolphin-like cetacean

delpinusaur: sea serpent-like dinosaur from Delphinus constellation

deltagar: [*Jandar of Callisto* by Lin Carter] sabretoothed tiger-like predator from jungle moon of Thanator with whip-like serrated tail, remarkably fast for its size, shaggy scarlet fur, 2 fantastic curling horns, neck ruff

demi-pachyderm: [Warhammer 40,000] large meat animal from Flint, Angelus subsector, Scarus sector

demiguise: [*Fantastic Beasts and Where to Find Them* by Newton Artemis Fido Scamander] herbivorous pongid with long, fine, silky, silver fur and large black eyes, sometimes invisible

demon squid: [*Capt. Proton: Defender of the Earth* by D. W. "Prof." Smith] monstrous cephalopodan, in common and giant varieties, from Grayhawk II

demon wasp: ["The March through the Underworld" by Ernst] 1-meter wasp-like burrowing insectoid with faceted eyes, poisonous stinger from Cronot

demondog: see hellhound

demondogator: [demondog alligator portmanteau] alligator-like predator whose bite morphs victim into demondog

demorr: [Albanian dem-morr portmanteau] bull-louse, large, aggressive, louse-like insectoid with horns

Denarian parasite: [*Grave Matter* by Justin Richards] parasite able to keep host "alive" even after death, identified by pale-eye

Denevan neural parasite: ["Operation: Annihilate" by Steven W. Carabotsos] amorphous, gelatinous parasitic gestalt that devastated beta Portola, Levinius V, theta Cygni XII, Ingraham B and finally Deneva

dennimla: [James Cooke Brown's Loglan denro nimla (dangerous animal) compound] dangerous animal from Logla, Brown's system

Denobian lemur: ["Enterprise" series] furry quadruped, mostly one-headed, valued for its tasty liver from Denob

dentic: ["Farscape" series] teeth-cleaning insectoid from Farscape galaxy

deodath: [Thongor series by Lin Carter] dragon-cat with 2 brains, 3 hearts from Lemuria

depotoped: [mynynym] creature with legs that can be deposited and then regrown

der: [baldnander mondegreen] shapeshifting creature from Baldna system: [-der mondegreens, red der palindrome] red flame-resistant sauroid from Salama, Ga systems or [zarander mondegreen] elephant-like porcoid from Zara system or [scamander or gerrymander mondegreens] fantastic creature from Scama system or Gerryma system

Derbyshire ram: ["The Derbyshire Ram"] gigantic ram, like Norstilian sheep that symbolizes the greatness of God

derer: [wanderer mondegreen] ornithoid that deres (eats seeds, leaves and invertebrates), see wan

derfi: [James Cooke Brown's Loglan dertu ficli] ground fish

derling: [sanderling mondegreen] invertebrate-eating ornithoid from arctic Sa, the Leech Planet

derlingator: [derling alligator portmanteau] alligator-like predator whose bite morphs victim into derling

deroo: [wanderoo mondegreen] large megapodan from Wa system

derpo: [James Cooke Brown's Loglan dertu porju] groundhog

derr: [copper red derr eppoc palindrome] red variety of eppoc

derra: [Albanian derr-rra portmanteau] pig-worm, leg-less, pig-like scavenger from Alban system

derv: [dervish backformation] dustdevil-like desert creature

desbreko: [The Legend of Zelda] large variety of skullfish with escort skullfish from Hyrule

deseret: [*Dell Crossword Puzzle Dictionary*] honeybee

desert croc: see zintal

desert hopper: [*The Future Is Wild* by Dougal Dixon] turret-eyed land shelled mollusc with one three-toed foot, scaly skin and drill-like proboscis that must hop to breath

desert lizard: [desert lizard malapropism] sweet, food reptilian

desert shark: [Dougal Dixon] virtually hairless, insectivorous worm-like burrowing quadruped

desert-devil: ["The Quality of Mercy" by J. Michael Straczinski] creature from Miaplacida

deserter: [*Dell Crossword Puzzle Dictionary*] rat

desh: ["The Door to Saturn" by Clark Ashton Smith] greater variety, semi-transparent extra-dimensional with slim, fish-like body, 4 knotted limbs, wide mouth with many curved 6-inch teeth, several lidless, plate-like eyes in crescent; lesser variety, large, silvery extradimensional with tadpole-like body, limp toothless mouth, several beady eyes across a narrow head, long, tough and springy limbs, destroys brain when used as portal

destroyer bird: [frigate bird extrapolation] large frigate bird-like ornithoid

deti: [Albanian gjeldeti mondegreen] rooster-turkey, parthenogenic ornithoid ancestral to turkey and rooster

deuteroceratops: [protoceratops extrapolation] missing link between protceratops and triceratops

devanaan: ["Target: Morpheus System" by Marc A. Herren] swarming, helicopteryx-like insectoid that drop lava chunks from Orontes, Morpheus system

devi bun: [Monster Galaxy] bat-winged, white rabbitoid with gray furry collar from Libra constellation

devil croc: horned crocodilian, see ceratosuch

devil monkey: [*Monster Spotter's Guide to North America* by Scott Francis] 1.5-meter gray simian with baboon-like face, kangaroo-like legs, small forearms, bushy tail

devil-swine: ["Drums on Fire Mt." by Graeme Morris and Tom Kirby] monstrous porcoid

devil's dreck: [*Worlds Apart: Nat. Hist. of Furaha and Earth* by Souren Nyoroge]

arboreal predator fond of bushhog from Meralgia, Furaha (alpha Phoenicis IV)

devil's corkscrew: large helical worm (or just giant beaver holes, not fossils)

devilfish: [Xanth series by Piers Anthony] reddish horned fish able to walk on water balancing on its curved, barbed tail predatory against angelfish from Xanth or [Xanthian mondegreen] Xa, Thia system

devourosaur: ["Flash Gordon" series] sea serpent from Mongo

devourotaur: [devourosaur minotaur portmanteau] see man-eating cow

dew: [*Dell Crossword Puzzle Dictionary*] jackdaw

dewback: ["Star Wars IV: A New Hope" by George Lucas] large reptilian herbivore used as beast of burden and guard creature in arid ecosystems like Tatooine, Jedi galaxy

dewbear: [dewberry backformation] dew-bear-like pegasoid

dexut: [tuxedo dexut palindrome] black furry with white legs, belly and chest

dhedeen: ["Guardians of the Intrawelt" by Herbert Haensel] 4-cm, long-winged, chick-like, yellow ornithoid with needle-sharp transparent beak used as translator from Intrawelt

dheja: ["Death in the Turquoise Ocean" by Andreas Findig] marine animal from Auroch-Maxo-55, Segafrendo galaxy

dhenrro: [Albanian rrodhen mondegreen] sheep-leech, blood-sucking parasite of sheep

dhiccer: ["The Anti-Molkex Bomb" by Hans Kneifel] blue-black flying squirrel with mouse-like head, empathic (fur turns white if near nervous breakdown)

dhiriq: [Albanian dhi-iriq portmanteau] goat-hedgehog, horned, hedgehog-like creature with goatee

dhog: [dog-hog portmanteau] caninoid with short snout, curly tail from Stiria, Airit system, Galaxiki

dhogator: [dhog alligator portmanteau] alligator-like predator whose bite morphs victim into dhog

dhole: ["The Dream-Quest of Unknown Kadath" by Howard Phillips Lovecraft] enormous slimy, rustling, crawling, burrowing nocturnal creatures from the Pnoth valley, Isle of Oriab, Southern Sea, Dreamworld; [*Dell Crossword Puzzle Dictionary*] wild dog

dhuguluk: ["The Hour of the Centaurs" by H. G. Ewers] semi-organic, garment-like symbiot of Asdis that heals and camoflauges

dhushbar: [Perry Rhodan] aka ruuk, noted for 30-day generations from Lennyth, Thootis system, Dakkardim balloon galaxy

di: [mi extrapolation] millipede-like creature with 501 legs, see dioid; [idnatao ananymondegreen] vulture-like ornithoid from Oata system

dilli: [Cherokee] skunk-like mammaloid from Tsalagi system

diacodexis: [*After the Dinosaurs* by Donald R. Prothero] early deer-like artiodactyl with long hind legs for running and hopping from Eocene Tethys Sea, Terra (alpha Zodiaci III)

diamond lizard: [Perry Rhodan] food reptilian from Troy, Helena system

dianoga: ["Star Wars IV: A New Hope" by George Lucas] 10-meter long 7-tentacled omnivore from shallow pool and murky swamps with one eyestalk, Jedi galaxy

dianogator: [dianoga alligator portmanteau] alligator-like predator whose bite morphs victim into dianoga

diaper viper: ["Glad Rags to Riches" by Jack Hayes and Charles Lamont] deadly snake that hides in diapers

diatryma: [*After the Dinosaurs* by Donald R. Prothero] 2-meter, flightless "terror crane", related to gastornis from Paleocene Europe [*The Mistaken Extinction* by Lowell Dingus and Timothy Rowe] or Eocene S. America, Terra (alpha Zodiaci III)

dib: [Far Side: "Dibs!" by Gary Larson] easy prey, plump, short-legged antelope

dibeh-yazzie: [Navaho] small sheep-like creature from Diné system

dibeh: [Navaho] sheep-like ruminant from Diné system

dicerathere: [*After the Dinosaurs* by Donald R. Prothero] two-horned rhino from early Miocene

dicoot: [bandicoot mondegreen] rodentoid from Ba system

dicyanodon: mammal-like amphibious reptile of Permian

didgeridodo: [trumpeter swan backformation] swan-dodo ornithoid with didgeridoo-like call

dieb: [*Dell Crossword Puzzle Dictionary*] jackal from N. Africa, Terra (Soll III)

diefret: [Afrikaans dief-fret portmanteau] buzzard-ferret, burrowing griffinoid predator

digalinv'hidv: [Cherokee] donkey-like equinoid from Tsalagi system

digdogger: [The Legend of Zelda] giant one-eyed sea urchin from kingdom of Hyrule

diger: [*Monster Manual* by Skip Williams, etal.] underground-dwelling ooze

digester: [*Monster Manual* by Skip Williams, Jonathan Tweet and Monte Cook] velocirapter-like beast with bony head, feeding tendrils and acid-squirting head tube

digger: ["Seed of Reason" by Daniel Hatch] burrower from Chamal, [Perry Rhodan] fast, dangerous burrowing worm from Tabatau

diggle: [Xanth series by Piers Anthony] worm-like sub-vole ten times the size of a wiggle able to phase through bedrock without affecting it under Xanth

digworm: [*Han Solo's Revenge* by Brian Daley] small burrowing worm whose digestive juices can dissolve rock from planet Kamar, Jedi galaxy

diine: ["diine at times emit taeniid" palindrome] host of telepathic parasite

dikironium cloud creature: ["Obsession" by Art Wallace] space-faring gaseous bloodthirsty predator able to phase shift to become invisible

dil: [Albanian qen kandil deti mondegreen] sea ornithoid ancestral to deti and jellyfish

dilion: [dandilion mondegreen] aerial scavenger from Da system

dilldapp: [museumofhoaxes.com by Alex Boese] hamster-like wolperting from Sweden, Terra (alpha Zodiaci III)

dillion: [dandillion mondegreen] floating puffball from Da system

dilly: [dilly-bug backformation] creature that dilly-bug bug from Wyst

dilly-bug: [*Wyst: Alastor 1716* by Jack Vance] tittering insectoid from Wyst

dilly-bugator: [dilly-bug alligator portmanteau] alligator-like predator whose bite morphs victim into dilly-bug

dilong: ["emperor dragon", Feathered Dinosaurs: The Origin of Birds by John Long and Peter Schuten] 1.6-meter tyrannosaurid from Jurassic China, Terra (alpha Zodiaci III)

dilongator: [dilong alligator portmanteau] alligator-like predator whose bite morphs victim into dilong

dilophosaur: [*The Mistaken Extinction* by Lowell Dingus and Timothy Rowe] ceratosaur descendant along with coelophysis, carnotaur

dilophotaur: [dilophsaur minotaur portmanteau] ceratotaur variant

dilyra: [ardylide dilyra palindrome] yellow ornithoid

dim: [midnight hgin dim] hgin predator

dimat: [gandimat mondegreen] magpie-like ornithoid from Ga system

dimepede: [Xanth series by Piers Anthony] related to nicklepede with smaller more painful bite from Xanth

dimeroo: [buckaroo backformation] smaller quarteroo

dimetrodon: [*The Mistaken Extinction* by Lowell Dingus and Timothy Rowe] short-legged dinosaur with sail from Permian

dina: [Azerbaijani sardina mondegreen] sardine-buzzard goose-like flying ornithoid, ancestral to buzzard and small ichthyoid

dindun: [Fr. Johann Martin Schleyer's Volapük] turkey-like ornithoid from Schleyer's system

dine: [sardine, an ondine mondegreens] off-white long-necked fish-mammal amphibian

dingar: [*Dell Crossword Puzzle Dictionary*] wild honeybee from E. Indies, Terra (alpha Zodiaci III)

dingo: [*National Geographic Encyclopedia of Animals*] wild dog from Australia, Terra (alpha Zodiaci III)

dingonak: [John Alfred Jordan] 5.5-meter scaly river monster with reptilian claws, scorpion tail, walrus tusks from Maggori river, Kenya, Terra (alpha Zodiaci III), [Here Be Monsters almanac] and mane with feelers, fangs

dinho: [Monster Galaxy] gray donkey-like equinoid with buckteeth, black mane and yellow chest

dinko: [*Han Solo at Star's End* by Brian Daley] palm-sized venomous creature with powerful hind legs covered with serrated spurs, 4 "arms", needle-like fangs that secretes a foul-smelling liquid to mark territory and discourage predators, Jedi galaxy

dino: [dinosaur mondegreen] dinosaur-like animal toy animaled by Love, see partysaurus

dinoc: [dinocroc mondegreen] predatory roc

dinocroc: ["Dinocroc vs. Supergator" by Jim Wynordski, Mike MacLean] crocodilian dinosaur

dinofelis: [*After the Dinosaurs* by Donald R. Prothero] sabre-toothed cat from Miocene

dinoflagellate: [*The Big Bad Book of Beasts* by Michael Largo] sphere with long string-like flagella (tails)

dinohyus: [*After the Dinosaurs* by Donald R. Prothero] renamed daeodon

dinoid: [Grk. "whirling"] see strom

dinoshark: ["Dinoshark" by Frances Doel, Guy Prevost] shark ancestor

dinscher: short-haired caninoid with small ears and tail from Poberma

dioid: [mynynym] di-like creature

Diomedean horse: [Diomedes] flesh-eating horse

dioskylos: ["Clash of the Titans"] 2-headed hellhound, see eberus

dip: [Catalana] vampiric canine with one lame leg

diphong: [Perry Rhodan] food ichthyoid from Centaurus A galaxy

diphongator: [dphong alligator portmanteau] alligator-like predator whose bite morphs victim into diphong

diplocynodon: [*After the Dinosaurs* by Donald R. Prothero] 1.5-meter caiman-like alligator from Paleocene

diplodocus: ["double-beam"] large, herbivorous dinosaur with long neck and tail from early Cretaceous

diplovertubron: ["The Monster of Piedras Blancas by C. Haile Chace] 1.8-meter tall scaly anthropoid with large claws, 2 blunt horns, large flared nostrils, fleshy shoulder pads, lumpy, varicose chest veins

dipper: [*After Man* by Dougal Dixon] long-necked, aquatic bird that become flightless as it matures; [*National Geographic Encyclopedia of Animals*] invertebrate and fruit-eating songbird from N. and Meso-America, Terra (alpha Zodiaci III)

diprotodon: [*After the Dinosaurs* by Donald R. Prothero] rhino-sized wombat from Pliestocene

dipsas: [Xanth series by Piers Anthony] serpent whose bite causes unquenchable thirst from Mt. Parnaaus foothills, Xanth

diricawl: [*Fantastic Beasts and Where to Find Them* by Newton Artemis Fido Scamander] non-extinct variety of teleporting dodo

dirosaur: ["The Prince and the Pirate" by Keith Laumer] forest sauroid with long neck and chin spike hunted on Elora

dirotaur: [dirosaur minotaur portmanteau] forest bovinoid with long neck and chin spike

dirt-dragon: ["Tremors" by S. S. Wilson and Brent Maddock] aka tu-long, graboid

dirtcreeper: see mudder

dirus: [canis dirus] giant wolf from Pleistocene, see dog-bear, waheela, amarok

Disench ant: [disenchant mondegreen] ant-like insectoid said to be good for removing curses and possessions from Disench system

dishley: [*Dell Crossword Puzzle Dictionary*] sheep from Leicester, Terra (alpha Zodiaci III)

disky: [frisky dog spoonerism] energetic, playful gliding batrachoid

dismembee: [dismember backformation] regenerative, segmented bee-like insectoid

dispare squid: ["Red Dwarf: Back to Reality" by Rob Grant and Doug Naylor] dysempathic cephalopod that caused mass suicide of *Esperanto* crew

displacer beast: ["The Ecology of the Displacer Beast" by David Cook, etal.] blue-black puma-like beast with 2 long black shoulder-tentacles with horny edges, 2 or 4 extra limbs, able to "displace" (appear meter from actual position), related to couerl

dissac: [*After the Dinosaurs* by Donald R. Prothero] large, hoofed mesonychid (whale ancestor) from Paleocene

distarterops: [*After Man* by Dougal Dixon] marine walrus-like rodent with tusks and one clawed limb

dito: [bandito mondegreen] green biped from Ba system

ditry: [banditry mondegreen] symbiotic nyzel, farrn and drohs from Ba system

divto: ["Ewok" series] 3-meter, 3-headed nocturnal venomous snake from Endor's moon, Jedi galaxy

dīwe: antimal-faced shapeshifting ogre with large tusks and horns from Persia, Terra (alpha Zodiaci III)

dizard: [desert lizard portmanteau] desert-dwelling reptilian from Lesert system

dlab: [bald dlab palindrome] hairless mammaloid; [baldnander ananymondegreen] red shapeshifter from Na system

dlas: ["Destination Base" by Micahel Marcus Thurner] deadly owl from Ertrus (Kreit III)

dlef: [feldgrau arg dlef, feldspar aps dlef palindrome] arg or aps variants

dlog: [gold dlog palindrome] reddish yellow furry

dlogator: [dlog alligator portmanteau] alligator-like predator whose bite morphs victim into dlog

dly: [deadly spawn mondegreen] worm-like creature ancestral to dea and deadly spawn

dnazd: [*Killing Machine* by Jack Vance] centipede-like creature with large poison-tipped mandibles from Misk Mts. of Thamber

do: [Basque mando mondegreen] mule-like beast of burden from Ma system; [sando mondegreen] mammaloid sea monster from Sa, the Leech Planet; dodo nasna (merged into left-footed dodo); [Jap. anpasando mondegreen, &] 2-D das-like creature from Anpasa system

dobbie: ["The Roots of the Dinosaurs: by Arndt Ellmer] stinking caninoid from Tullama

dobermantis: [Doberman-manta portmanteau] pale green centauroid with powerful grasping forelimbs, antennae

dococrile: [crocodile spoonerism] large amphibious carnivore

dodicka: see sisimite

doddlebug: bombeetle-like insectoid

doddlebugator: [doddlebug alligator portmanteau] alligator-like predator whose bite morphs victim into doddlebug

dodg: [dodgy backformation] elusive prey

dodgator: [dodg alligator portmanteau] alligator predator whose bite morphs victim into dodg

dodriped: mutant with 75% as many legs

doe: [*Dell Crossword Puzzle Dictionary*] female rabbit or deer or jackalope

dog-bird: [*The Travels and Adventures of William Bingfield, Esq.*] great flightless ornithoid from Bingfield's Island with shaggy hair, greyhound-like head, pig-like tail, long legs with panther-like claws, lays eggs and gives milk

dog-fish: [dogfish mondegreen] amphibian with forelimbs with non-retractable claws, no whiskers or backfin, see cat-shark

dogator: [dog-alligator portmanteau] canine-like amphibious sauroid

dogg: [doggish, doggy backformation] bloodhound-like caninoid

doggator: [dogg alligator portmanteau] alligator-like predator whose bite morphs victim into dogg

dogie: [*Dell Crossword Puzzle Dictionary*] motherless calf

dogopus: [Sheldon Cooper in "Big Bang Theory"] cross between dog and octopus

dogopuss: [dogopus puss portmanteau] dog-octopus-cat chimera

dogosaur: [*Dogosaurus Rex* by Anna Staniszawski] domesticatable dinosaur, less so with larger rex variety, see dino

dogotaur: [dogosaur minotaur portmanteau] domesticatable bovine, less so with larger rex variety

dograt: [*King of Argent* by John Phillifent, dog-rat portmanteau] scavenger from Argent, Alcone II

dogwoodchuck: [dogwood-woodchuck portmanteau] burrowing caninoid

dogy: see dogie

dök: [Fr. Johann Martin Schleyer's Volapük] duck-like ornithoid from Schleyer's system

dolabratops: ["pickaxe-faced", *The New Dinosaurs* by Dougal Dixon] sprintosaur with pickaxe-shaped crest

dolit: [Haitian zandolit mondegreen] reptilian from Za system

dolly: [*The Big Bad Book of Beasts* by Michael Largo] aka dolichorhynchops, 4.5-meter air-breathing sea reptile with long neck, paddle-like fore-fins and powerful rear fins

dolman: ["Attack of the Dinosaur" by Dirk Hess] 3-meter, 6-legged, armored, purple predatory serpentine with ears from Cronot, Heith system

dolph: [dolphish backformation] fish-mimicking cetacean

dolphish: [dolphinfish portmanteau] dolphin-mimicking ichthyoid

dom: [phandom mondegreen] one-horned, one-eyed cephalopodan from Pha system

domestical: ["People from the Retort" by H. G. Ewers] breeding marine animal from Refuge (Ubiger VIII)

domo-kun: brown, rectangular, bipedal furry with large mouth that attacks small animals like kittens from Japan, Terra (alpha Zodiaci III)

doney: [*Dell Crossword Puzzle Dictionary*] hedge sparrow

dong: [budong mondegreen] large lavender space-dwelling ichthyoid

dongator: dong alligator portmanteau] alligator-like predator whose bite morphs victim into dong

donin: [dah-nes-tsa, tsa-e-donin-ee mondegreen] ram-fly relative

donkey-lizard: see allosaur

donkiwi: [donkey-kiwi bird portmanteau] griffinoid with long ears, long slender bill and vestigial wings

doodlebug: divining rod-like Y-shaped walkingstick-like insectoid

doodlebugator: dooglebug alligator portmanteau] alligator-like predator whose bite morphs victim into dooglebug

doodlesacker: [trumpeter swan backformation] bagpiper swan variant with goatskin-like plumage

doodpecker: [doodlebug woodpecker portmanteau, descent of woodpeckers] doodlebug predator

dool: [dool blood palindrome] leech prey

doolaga: [*The Yowie: In Seach of Australian Bigfoot* by Tony Healy and Paul Cropper] see yowie

doolb: [bloody doolb palindrome] possum-like mammaleoid noted for blood-sweating faux death

doomfang: [*A Hero's Guide to Deadly Dragons* by Hiccup Haddock III] gigantic, yet very fast, black dragon with blue, frozen-fire breath from Barbarian archipelago

doomfangator: [doomfang alligator palindrome] alligator-like creature whose bite morphs victim into doomfang

door-sturgeon: [Theodore Sturgeon mondegreen] sturgeon-like ichthyoid able to travel through portals from Theo system

doorab: [door dorab portmanteau] ichthyoid able to travel through portals, see doorado, door-sturgeon, see doorado, doorab

doorado: [door dorado portmanteau] goldfish able to travel through portals, see doorab, door-sturgeon

doorgone: [door dorgone portmanteau] sandworm able to travel through portals

dooril: [door doril portmanteau] beast able to travel through portals

doorilope: [dooril antelope portmanteau] dooril with antlers, see PNB

doormouse: [dormouse mondegreen] mouse-like rodentoid able to travel through portals

doorudon: [door dorudon portmanteau] whale-like cetacean able to travel through portals

doorthygale: [Dorothy Gale mondegreen] gale variety able to open an extradimensional portal

dor-mouse: ancestor of insecto-mammaloid griffins, and flying squirrels, see dor

dor: [*Dell Crossword Puzzle Dictionary*] June bug; [tandor mondegreen] mammoth from Ta system

dorab: [*Dell Crossword Puzzle Dictionary*] marine fish from E. India, Terra (alpha Zodiaci III)

dorado: [piscium extrapolation] egg-laying goldfish-like ichthoid

dore: [*Dell Crossword Puzzle Dictionary*] walleyed pike; [hash-dore-tso mondegreen] lion relative from Diné system

dore-sturgeon: [Theodore Sturgeon mondegreen] pike-like door-sturgeon mimic from Theo system

doreign: [pandoreign mondegreen] narwhal-like sea creature with see-through skin from Pa system, see dorus

dorgone: ["Servant of Perfection" by Marianne Sydow] 7-meter sand worm with many legs, large eyes, mandibles from Pthor

doril: [mandoril mondegreen] wild beast from Ma system

dorilope: [doril antelope portmanteau] doril with antlers

dork: ["Thetryonic Alliance" by Susan Schwartz] domesticatible predator with sloping back, long spiny tail and hair except on legs, chunky skull, snubnosed muzzle, 6 tusks (2 above, 4 below), long purple tongue, huge triangular ears from Ganroj, Thagg system, Stardust galaxy

dormmouse: [dormouse mondegreen] rodentoid adapted to dorm-living

dormouse: [*Dell Crossword Puzzle Dictionary*] squirrel-like mammal

dornhai: ["Gene Death" by Michael Nagula] dogfish-like ichthyoid from Pegasus Major
dorshevell: [Perry Rhodan] dolphin-like sea creature from Occreshija
dorten: ["The Star Pilot" by H. G. Francis] swarming, nesting reptilian from Urirgi
dorudon: [*After the Dinosaurs* by Donald R. Prothero] whale ancestor related to basilosaur and mysticetes
doruemic pinnipex: ["Face To Face With Planet Scanodon" by Rocky Strone] variety of crawling worm from Scanodon, Croft system
dorus: [pandorus mondegreen] narwhal-like sea creature with see-through skin from Pa system, see doreign
dosa: [Cherokee] mosquito-like insectoid from Tsalagi system
dosvdali: [Cherokee] ant-like insectoid from Tsalagi system
doto: [*Dell Crossword Puzzle Dictionary*] sea slug, see elysia
dottle: ["The Book of Ptath" by A. E. Van Vogt] sleek, scarlet, one-horned quadrupedal steed from Gonwonlane
double-beam: see diplodocus, behemoth
double-ellipsoid: smooth, gray, telepathic creature like rotating circles from Sombrero galaxy
double-mouth: [four-mouth extrapolation] leg-less variety of four-mouth with 2 leg-like lips with feeding mouth between and balancing tail, related to hophead, chin-chilla and chinpanzee, from Thuban (alpha Draconis)
doublivore: [*Another World* by Jean-Ignace-Isidore Gérard] sterile chimera with heads on both ends, such as apelicans, elephantoads, bullizards, etc., often omnivores with both a herbivorous and a carnivorous head to compensate for no anus, from Gérard's world
douc langur: [*National Geographic Encyclopedia of Animals*] monkey from S. E. Asia, Terra (alpha Zodiaci III)
douc: [*Dell Crossword Puzzle Dictionary*] monkey from China, Terra (alpha Zodiaci III)
Douglass' deer: [*After the Dinosaurs* by Donald R. Prothero] dromomeryx with large-bottomed inward-curving horns

dourada/o: [female Galician peixa-dourada backformation, male Portuguese piexe-dorado] ichthyoid ancestral to goldfish
dove: [*Dell Crossword Puzzle Dictionary*] pigeon, see barb, nun, pouter, roller
downed hog: [hound dog spoonerism] burrowing pigasus with vestigial wings
downed hogator: [downed hog alligator portmanteau] alligator-like predator whose bite morphs victim into downed hog
dóya: [Cherokee] beaver-like amphibian from Tsalagi system
doyouthinkhesaurus: [Do you think he saw us? modegreen] dangerous, nearsighted male pterosaur from Godville
doyouthinkshesaurus: [Do you think she saw us? modegreen] dangerous, nearsighted female pterosaur from Godville
dozare: [tandozare mondegreen] long-necked sirenian from Ta system
dozer: [Terra Monster] rotund burrower from Terrarium
draagax: [*Creatures of the Galaxy* by Phil Brucato, Bill Smith, Rick D. Stuart, Chuck Truett] grassland pack hunter of ronrentoids, most dangerous in dry season fed on sentinel plant, from Relkass, Jedi galaxy
draak: ["Beasts of the Underworld" by Kurt Mahr] geneered 5-meter arachnoid with dozens of rope-like legs, ir vision, black fur from Afzot
dracoid: dragon-like creature, in winged lizard (pterosaur) and monster lizard (dinosaur) varieties
draconis: [OviPets] egg-laying dracoid
dracosaur: see dragonosaur
dracuc: [Catalan drac-cuc portmanteau] dragon-worm, larval form of metamorphosizing dracoid
dragoff: [dragon backformation] dragon predator that drags off prey
dragon bird: [Perry Rhodan] flying serpentoid from Campopas (Sheneka II)
dragon horse: [Xanth series by Piers Anthony] horse-dragon, rare creature with horse-like front and dragon-like rear from Xanth

dragon of the Up-and-Out: ["The Game of Rat and Dragon" by Cordwainer Smith, aka Rat] "hungry vortex of aliveness, hate and tenuous interstellar matter", able to teleport a million miles in just under two milliseconds (virtual 2700c) and able to "tear the soul out of a body with its roots dripping", see Rat

dragon snake: [*Creatures of the Galaxy* by Phil Brucato, Bill Smith, Rick D. Stuart, Chuck Truett] long, ferocious serpentine from Dagobah, Jedi galaxy

dragon turtle: [*Odin's Quest* by Cleon Jones] dragon-like turtle

dragon-slug: ["Star Wars" series by Archie Goodwin and Al Williamson, *Prophets of the Dark Side* by Paul and Hollace Davids] slug-like lumni-spice eating cavern dweller from Hoth VI, Jedi galaxy

dragon-slugator: [dragon-slug alligator portmanteau] alligator-like predator whose bite morphs victim into dragon-slug

dragon: hellfire-breathing serpent in flying [Isa 14:29] and non-flying [Num 21:6] varieties

dragonet: [*National Geographic Encyclopedia of Animals*] reef fish from Indo-Pacific; [Pern series by Ann McCaffrey] six-legged lizard from which dragonkin were geneered from Pern (Rukbat (alpha Sagittarii) III)

dragoneye: ["False Flag" by Clark Darlton] large cetacean with 2-meter, slightly hypnotic eyes from Okul, Sagittarius contellation

dragonflare: [Terra Monster] segmented, six-winged insectoid with hot tailbulb from Terrarium, see dragonfry

dragonfly: ["dragonfly from another world", *Adventures of the Fly*] dragon-like hellfire-breathing, 5.5-meter tall, 11-meter long insectoid with purple skin, 4 legs, 2 heads, 2 wings; [Xanth series by Poul Anderson] small hellfire-breathing insectoid dragon from Xanth

dragonfry: [Terra Monster] small, 4-winged insectoid with hot tailbulb from Terrarium, see dragonflare

dragonkin: [Pern series by Ann McCaffrey] includes watch-whers, fire lizards and dragonriders' thread-fighting dragons (blue, brown, bronze, gold, green, white) geneered from dragonets from Pern (Rukbat (alpha Sagittarii) III

dragonne: [*Monstrous Compendium, Vol. 2* by David Cook, etal.] lion-like desert dracoid

dragonnewt: [*White Bear and Red Moon* by Greg Stafford] newt-like dracoid from Glorantha

dragonosaur: [Abbott and Costello Cartoon Show: "Save a Cave"] aka dracosaur, dragon-like dinosaur

dragonsnail: [*White Bear and Red Moon* by Greg Stafford] snail-like dracoid from Glorantha

draid: ["The Shadowless" by Horst Hoffmann] forest animal from Novatho, Jamondi cluster

drake: [Xanth series by Piers Anthony] small, ornate, but fierce and crafty hellfire-breathing dragon with large, streamlined wings from Xanth

drakken: [*The Face of the Waters* by Robert Silverberg] top predator, with rammerhorn, from the waterworld Hydros

drakrab: [Czech drak-krab portmanteau] dragon-crab, triphibious crustacean

dram: [Armenian voskedram mondegreen] finch-like ornithoid

Drambon carpet: [*Major Operation* by James White] irridescent/translucent leech from Drambo (aka Meatball)

drang: ["The Monster From Krypton"] large, purple, flying serpentine with one white horn on dinosauroid head from Krypton, Rao system

drangator: [dran alligator portmanteau] alligator-like predator whose bite morphs victim into dran

drannit: ["Farscape"] vile, noisome, uncouth creature from the Farscape galaxy

dras: [Lithuanian gandras mondegreen] stork-like ornithoid from Ga system

Drascue bacterium: [*Encyclopedia Galactica*] mutant strain that destroyed all organics on Drascue facility of Procyon (alpha Canis Majoris) IV

drass: [drove of asses spoonerism, drassonax mondegreen] bear-ass centauroid with baboon-like rump

drassonax: [*After the Dinosaurs by* Donald R. Prothero] bear-like pinniped ancestor
dratricu: [James Cooke Brown's Loglan draka tricu (dark tree) compound] bloodsucking tree-mimic from Logla, Brown's system
Dravidian firebird: ornithoid with shiny, metallic plumage from Dravidia
dre: [dre herd palindrome, scalandre mondegreen] large herding beetle sometimes used as steed from Scala system
dread: [Xanth series by Piers Anthony] invisible monster with haunting voice, less terrorizing if named, from Xanth
dreamer: ["The Winged Dreamers" by Jennifer Guttridge] furry, transparent-winged flier that "exists for living their dreams", telepathic gestalt on Durban's world; [*Dell Crossword Puzzle Dictionary*] puffbird from Brazil, Terra (alpha Zodiaci III)
dreamstealer: [*The Stealers of Dreams* by Stevbe Lyons] aerial hallucinogenic bacteria from Arkannis Major
drebbin: [*The Courtship of Princess Leia* by Dave Wolverton] horned predator of rancors from Jedi galaxy
dree: [drift of bees spoonerism, dreemer bee portmanteau] bee-grizzly-like griffinoid with 6 legs, large fangs
dreemer bear: ["In the Land of Dreemer" by H. G. Francis] 9-meter, grizzly-like predator with 6 legs, large fangs, 2 spines on skull from Clearwater
dreemer: ["In the Land of Dreemer" by H. G. Francis] 1.5-meter, green scaly, beaver-like amphibian with mole-like head with moose-antler-like sideblades, 6 limbs from Clearwater
dreep: [dragon sheep portmanteau, drove of sheep spoonerism] dragon-headed sheep-like ruminant
drefiala: [fandrefiala mondegreen] spear-headed snake from Fa (iota Orionis) system
dreizebra: [Germ. trizebra, aka hexacamel, fairy chess] 6-legged black-and-white-striped camelopardian
drekavac: [Slavic "yeller"] dog- or fox-like caninoid with kangaroo-like legs from Kriavicka river valley, including krilati (winged) and long-necked vira (whirlpool) varieties
dreldrake: [dropping of sheldrake spoonerism, dragon sheldrake portmanteau] black and white dragon-duck
drella: ["Wolf in the Fold" by Robert Bloch] love-eater from Canopus (alpha Carinae) V; [wandrella mondegreen] omnivorous worm from Wa system
dremetze: ["Operation CV Embinium" by Horst Hoffmann] felinoid predator from Akron
drexl: ["The Sith Lords"] large, usually green, flying steeds of Beast-riders of Onderon, Jedi galaxy
drexlope: [drexl antelope portmanteau] drexl with antlers
drezup: ["The Setchenen" by Susan Schwartz] heat-seeking, palm-sized, poisonous stinging, brown fly-like nocturnal predator from Quarantimo, Salmenghast galaxy
drig: ["Squirrel Cage" by Robert Sheckley] predator that eats slegs from Seer; [dragon pig portmanteau, drift or drove of pigs] dragon-like porcoid
drigator: [drig alligator portmanteau] alligator-like predator whose bite morphs victim into drig
driggist: ["Face To Face With Planet Scanodon" by Rocky Strone] aka trundle bed, mobile as larva, from Scanodon, Croft system
drillbit: [*The Integral Trees* by Larry Niven] dangerous parasite from Smoke Ring, LeVoy's system
driller-dragon: [*A Hero's Guide to Deadly Dragons* by Hiccup Haddock III] black, winged dragon with swiveling drill-like nosehorn from Barbarian archipelago
drillrat: ["Robot Hugs" by R. Hugs'] burrowing rodentoid with drillsnout
drine: [drift of swine spoonerism] raft-like seapig
drirrel: [dray of squirrels spoonerism, drill squirrel portmanteau] ground squirrel-like rodentoid with drillsnout
driver dragon: [*A Hero's Guide to Deadly Dragons* by Hiccup Haddock III] enormous

white dragon with sabre-like fangs and headspikes from Barbarian archipelago

dro: [alejandro and dro- mondegreens] ancestor of iomimus, maeosaurs, mice, momeryx, mornis, ngo and ubavit from Aleja system

drogg: ["The Soul Hoarders" by Leo Lukas] multifunctional cyban from Intrawelt

droggator: [drogg alligator portmanteau] alligator-like predator whose bite morphs victim into drogg

drohs: ["The Great Silence" by Marianne Sydow] manipulative and senging symbiot in banditry, see nyzel, farrn

drok: ["Flash Gordon" series] stegosauroid from Mongo

dromaeosaur: ["running lizard", *A Field Guide to Dinosaurs* by Henry Gee and Luis V. Rey, *Feathered Dinosaurs: The Origin of Birds* by John Long and Peter Schuten] bird-like dinosaur with relatively large teeth, including bambiraptor, rahonavis, sinornithosaur, deinonychus (or velociraptor), utahraptor

dromaeotaur: [dromaeosaur minotaur portmanteau] bird-bull-like griffinoid

dromiceiomimus: ["emu-mimic", *Feathered Dinosaurs: The Origin of Birds* by John Long and Peter Schuten] 4-meter ornithomimosaur

dromomeryx: [*After the Dinosaurs* by Donald R. Prothero] deer relative with bony horn cones that diversified in Miocene, see cranioceras, Douglass' deer, Gregory's deerlet, Lull's deerlet, procranioceras, Rak's deer, sinclairomeryx, Sinclair's deer

dromornis: ["running bird", After the Dinosaurs by Donald R. Prothero] 3-meter flightless bird from Miocene

dromozoon: ["A Planet Named Shayol" by Cordwainer Smith] mutagenic parasite from Shayol

drongo: [*National Geographic Encyclopedia of Animals*] insectivorous bird-mimicking bird with forked tail from Sub-Sahara, Terra (alpha Zodiaci III)

droon: [*Border Princes* by Dan Abnett] small, long-legged, dark blue sinus-cavity-dwelling insects hatching from pale blue eyes

dropbear: large, vicious carnivorous koala from Australia, Terra (alpha Zodiaci III)

drork: [drok-rork portmanteau] monstrous stegasauroid

droth: [Superman mythos] large, sea ornithoid that feeds on silten sea weed from Krypton, Rao system

droub: ["The First" by Peg Robinson] jumping creature from Shadrasi's world

droub-avit: ["The First" by Peg Robinson"] steed of the Shadrasi

droxen: [drove of oxen spoonerism, dragon-oxen portmanteau] 8-legged, 2-headed ox-like dracoid, see toxen, yoxen

druail: [dragon quail portmanteau, drift of quails spoonerism] dragon-quail-like ornithoid

drullock: [drove of bullocks spoonerism] bovinoid-like antler-less dryx

drumse: [drumstick mondegreen] host of parasitic drumse tick

drurtle: [dragon turtle portmanteau] see dragon-turtle

dryopithecus: [*After the Dinosaurs* by Donald R. Prothero] European primate vanished in Miocene

dryworm: ["Who Mourns for Adonais?" by Gilbert Ralston] giant worm-like creature from Antos IV

drywystrys: [Welsh dryw-wystrys portmanteau] barnacle goose-like wren-oyster from Pharr, Farpt system, Galaxiki galaxy

dryx: [an ondryx mondegreen] off-white antlered herd creature

dschiggetai: ["In the Light of Vega" by Christopher Montillon] ass from Asia

dsipraen: [Perry Rhodan] house-sized creature with 50 long tentacles tipped with suckers and drillbits from Jaimbor, Mbor system, Hercules cluster

dū paikar: 2-faced sea monster from China Sea, Terra (alpha Zodiaci III)

du: [mandu mondegreen] mountain felinoid from Ma system

duan: [Bill Gibbons] larger than ropen with phosphorescent underbelly and bony crest like pteranodon

dubb: [*Dell Crossword Puzzle Dictionary*] bear from Syria, Terra (alpha Zodiaci III)

duckbill: see hadrosaur, platypus

duckbill deer: [duck builder mondegreen] deer-like ruminant with duck bill, see duckbillope, duckbilly

duckbillope: [duckbill antelope portmanteau] with antlers, see duckbill deer, duckbilly

duckbilly: [duckbill billygoat portmanteau] duckbilled goat-like creature, see duckbillope, duckbill deer

ducrot: ["Formula of Death" by Hans Kneifer] lizard-like predator whose scales are used as currency from Capucinu

duesp: [pseudoduesp palindrome] predator mimicked by pseudoduesp

dugbog: [*Fantastic Beasts and Where to Find Them* by Newton Artemis Fido Scamander] log-like amphibian with webbed paws, sharp teeth that eats mandrakes

dugbogator: [dugbog alligator portmanteau] alligator-like predator whose bite morphs victim into dugbog

dugerún: [Perry Rhodan] beetle-like insectoid from Bench, Heperés system

duglithen: ["Robot City" by H. G. Ewers] omnivore like gray-brown whip-like cords

dugong: [*Dell Crossword Puzzle Dictionary*] sea cow, see manatee

dugongator: [dugong alligator portmanteau] alligator-like predator whose bite morphs victim into dugong

duiker: [*National Geographic Encyclopedia of Animals*] antelope relative from Africa, Terra (alpha Zodiaci III)

duirg: ["Bastion of Parrakh" by Michael Nagula] rust-colored, oval, grooming louse-like insectoid from Roewis, Nubecula

duirgator: [duirg alligator portmanteau] alligator-like predator whose bite morphs victim into duirg

duitra: ["The Ambergris Element" by Margaret Armen] aka sur-snake, red tentacled, whale-sized venomous sea monster from Argo

dula: [sardula mondegreen] horned lion ancestor

dullahan: headless undead monster from Ireland, Terra (alpha Zodiaci III)

dumbo: [*The Integral Trees* by Larry Niven] dangerous predator in Smoke Ring, LeVoy's system

dump creature: [*Fortean Times*] 5-cm fuzzy worm with blue eyes

dun: [*Dell Crossword Puzzle Dictionary*] May fly

dun pudding: [*Monster Manual* by Skip Williams, etal.] desert-adapted pudding-thick ooze, not related to dun

dunaliella: extremophilic bacterium resistant to extreme saltiness, see halobacterium

dunebug: [dunebuggy backformation] large beetle-like desert steed

dunebugator: [dunebug alligator portmanteau] alligator-like predator whose bite morphs victim into dunebug

dung beetle: [Xanth series by Piers Anthony] insect make dung smell like sweet violets and roses from Xanth or [Xanthian mondegreen] Xa, Thia system

dung furry: ["Rhodan Times a Thousand" by Hans Kneifel] fist-sized scavenger of giant snail dung from Trafalgar (fka Magadona), Victory system, Demetria cluster

dunka: [James Cooke Brown's Loglan dunmu katma/kangu (ape cat/dog) compound] ape-headed nimravoid from Logla, Brown's system

dunkasni: [James Cooke Brown's Loglan dunmu kasni (ape cow) compound] centauroid with ape upper body and cow lower body from Logla, Brown's system

dunli: [James Cooke Brown's Loglan dunmu clika (ape-like) compound] pongoid from Logla, Brown's system

dünon: ["The Instinct Warrior" by H. G. Francis] arachnoid predator, prey of instinct warrior from Zentapher

dunpo: [James Cooke Brown's Loglan dunmu porja (ape pig) compound] centauroid with ape upper body and pig lower body from Logla, Brown's system

dunsi: [James Cooke Brown's Loglan dunmu simba (ape lion) compound] centauroid with ape upper body and lion lower body from Logla, Brown's system

duntigra: [James Cooke Brown's Loglan dunmu tigra (ape tiger) compound] centauroid with ape upper body and tiger lower from Logla, Brown's system

duocorn: [*The Stars Are Ours* by Andre Norton] blue-gray bicorn with silver horns from Astra, Deutero-Sol II

duplgoose: [*Amazing Logic Puzzles* by Norman D. Willis] goose-like ornithoid that lays eggs in pairs from Dranac

duppypog: [puppydog spoonerism] small caninoid related to even smaller poggle

duppypogator: [duppypog alligator portmanteau] alligator-like predator whose bite morphs victim into duppypog

duracrete slug: 10-meter slug able to feed on duracrete, using indigestible bits as armor

durdon: ["The Dreamers of Oth" by Marianne Sydow] giant lion-like felinoid from Pthor

Duriel caterpillar: ["Covenant of Dealer" by Rüdiger Schäfer] voracious 9-segmented caterpillar-like insectoid from Duriel V

durkii: ["Droids" series] hideous, 3-meter reptilian megapodan with baboon face

duroc: [*Dell Crossword Puzzle Dictionary*] red pig

durok: ["Battle for Alana" by Bernie Krigstein] steed adapted to icy cold

durtle: [turtle dove portmanteau, dole or dule of turtles spoonerism] cliff-dwelling winged tove

durzog: [The Elder Scrolls III: Tribunal] powerful reptilian with slashing claws and sharp teeth

durzogator: [alligator portmanteau] alligator-like predator whose bite morphs victim into durzog

duschio: [Hildegard of Bingen's Lingua Ignota] sea ornithoid from Ignota, Hildegard's system

dusk amoeba: 50-meter space amoeba from planetless Cathex Som system, aka Dusk, Galaxiki galaxy

dusk beast: [*Manual of the Planes* by Jeff Grubb, etal.] 2-headed, human-sized shadow-lizard

dust bunny: see ashi-magari, [Godville] rabbit-like desert lizard, see thed, skovisaur

dustdevil: see thirsty vortex

dust waiburn: [Tokyo Mew Mew] geneered moth-like insect that spreads poison dust from its wings

duster: ["The Parasite Planet" by Stanley G. Weinbaum] giant moth-like insectoid

dustosaur: see skovisaur

dustotaur: see skovitaur

dwalker: [sandwalker mondegreen] camel-eating crustacean from Sa, the Leech Planet

dwarf megalosaur: [*The New Dinosaurs* by Dougal Dixon] island subspecies about a third the size of normal megalosaur

dwarfsnouter: [The Snouters by Harald Stümpke] small sand-dwelling snouter from Wisi-Wise, Hi-Yi-Yi Islands, Terra (alpha Zodiacl III)

dwark: [Thongor series by Lin Carter] large tyrannosaur-like jungle sauroid

dwarmari: [Perry Rhodan] wingless (except for queen) ant-like, omnivorous insectoid with venomous string, including pygmy variety, from Taloris, Hayok system

dwayl: [land-whale mondegreen] large, land predator from La system

dwaylope: [dwayl antelope portmanteau] dwayl with antlers

dweebit: small, reddish-brown, beetle-like insectoid from Yuuzhan Vong galaxy, made Beladan uninhabitable with noxious gases

dwhale: [land whale mondegreen] large carnivore from La system

dxkcan: [Thai *] 2-D pentapus or hexapus

dy: [crowdy mondegreen] crow-camel pegasoid; [candy ananymondegreen] orange-red ornithoid from Ca system

Dylan Thomas sheep: ["The Return of the Kangaroo Rex" by Janet Kagat] blue-wooled sheep adapted to Mirabile

dylion: [dandylion mondegreen] felinoid from Da system

dyna: [dynamite mondegreen] small, but powerfully toxic insectoid

dynafly: [Outernauts] immature voltifly

dyryth: [Pellucidar series by Edgar Rice Burroughs] arboreal, sloth-like, elephant-sized shaggy-haired herbivore with bark-slashing claws, defensive tail

dysphonia: [euphonia antonym] large, carnivorous bird with white noise call that blocks other birdcalls

dzebe: [James Cooke Brown's Loglan dzeli beldu] jelly-belly from Logla, Brown's system

dzefi: [James Cooke Brown's Loglan dzeli ficli compound] jellyfish-like sea creature from Logla, Brown's system

dzeh: [Navaho] elk-like rumninant from Diné system

dzesuate: [James Cooke Brown's Loglan dzeli sua te (gelatinous-to-the-third) compound] gelatinous cube from Logla, Brown's system

dzharel: see jarel

dzi: [sardzi mondegreen] spider-horse ancestor

dzizh: [Armenian dzi-izh portmanteau] horse-cobra, dracoid with horse hooves, mane and tail

dzoka: [James Cooke Brown's Loglan dzoru kanru (walking stick) compound] walkingstick insect from Logla, Brown's system

dzu-teh: [Tib. "cattle bear"] brown bear of Himalyalas, see yeti

dzuko: ["Where the Gods Live" by E. G. Ewers and "Dying Worlds" by Hans Kneifel] gnu-like mount with cow-like head, antelope legs from Koetanor Delp, Myrguuk system

e'rrh: [i-less ei'rrh] poisonous hummingbird-like cave ornithoid from Friatica, Friaticalida system, Galaxiki galaxy

e: [dah-nes-tsa, tsa-e-donin-ee mondegreen] ram-fly relative

e-i-chahār-sar: [beheaded be-i-chahār-sar] winged berus

ea: [argea mondegreen] gray, arboreal hexapod, [Aranea aenara ananym] arachnoid from Aenara system

eagle-condor: ["Frog in the Mountains" by R. A. Lafferty] eagle-headed condor-like prey of shasos from the mountains of Paravata

eagowl: [eagle owl portmanteau] predatory ornithoid

eagull: [eagle-gull portmanteau] orinthoid with long wings, webbed feet, hooked beak and sharp eyesight

ealubu: [ealubu nubulae mynynum] space-dwelling cloud creature

ean: [*Dell Crossword Puzzle Dictionary*] lamb, ewe, yean

ear golem: golem made from ears

earfin: [earwing extrapolation] flightless, aquatic earwalker with ears adapted for swimming

earleaper: [earwing extrapolation] flightless earwing with ears adapted for leaping

earthbat: [Robot Hugs] dracoid with earthworm-like body and bat-like wings

earthborer: ["The Puppets of Areffa" by Peter Griese] like brown, egg-laying cross between rabbit and Plophos mole that communicated by beeping with yellow larva with 24 legs, protruding eyes and paddle-like teeth from Areffa, Manam Turu galaxy

earthpig: see woodchuck

earthpigator: [earthpig alligator portmanteau] alligator-like predator whose bite morphs victim into earthpig

earthsnake: ["Red Sun over Ruby" by Detlev G. Winter] 2-meter burrowing serpentoid from Ruby (Omega II)

earthzwack: ["Spaceship in Need" by William Voltz and Peter Griese] mouse-like rodentoid on Sol

earwalker: [earwing extrapolation] flightless earwing with ears adapter for walking

earwax golem: golem made from earwax, see wax golem

earwing: [*The Snouters* by Harald Stümpke] hummingbird-like, iridescent snout leaper with large ears adapted for gliding, vestigial tail from Hi-Yi-Yi Islands, Terra (alpha Zodiaci III)

earwingator: [earwing alligator portmanteau] alligator-like predator whose bite morphs victim into earwing

Easter bunny: see lepus
eavra: [eavra larva palindrome] insectoid
ebek: [nebek elision] hairy tyger-like felinoid
ebirah: ["Godzilla vs. the Sea Monster"] 110-meter lobster from Letchi Island, Terra (alpha Zodiaci III)
ebma: [amber ebma palindrome] orangish yellow ornithoid
ebmit: [timber ebmit palindrome] forest-dwelling caninoid
ebmul: [Crayola lumber ebmul palindrome] pale tan ornithoid from Crayol A
ebur: [ruber ebur palindrome] purplish-red ornithoid
ebye: [Afrikaans perdebye mondegreen] hornet-horse pegasoid
ec: [Czechoslovakian kanec mondegreen] boar-like porcoid from Ka system; [klokanec mondegreen] kangaroo-boar from Kloka system; [vážkanec mondegreen] dragonfly-boar pegasoid from Vazhka system, [Slovenian piščanec mondegreen] chicken like ornithoid from Pišca system
ecalypse: [*Manual of the Planes* by Jeff Grubb, etal.] shadow-equinoid
ecap: [raced ecap palindrome] furry with narrow stripe down middle of face, see epirt
echid gnat: [echidna-gnat portmanteau mondegreen] echidna-like gnat with spines, slender snout
echidna: [*Dell Crossword Puzzle Dictionary*] porcupine anteater
echis: [*Dell Crossword Puzzle Dictionary*] viper
eci: [eci lice/mice palindromes] mouse-louse, see reb, mrehpo
eclipse fish: see pla rahu
ecroo: [ecru kangaroo portmanteau] yellowish-gray macropodan
ecup: [puce ("flea") ecup palindrome] dark red to grayish purple insectoid
edlog: [golden edlog palindrome] white furry with brown hairtips, see orn
edlogator: [edlog alligator portmanteau] alligator-like predator whose bite morphs victim into edlog
edac: [cadet edac palindrome] gray ornithoid

edednod: [dandelion oil edednod palindrome] yellowish orthinoid noted for oily secretion
edentate: includes sloths, armadillos and anteaters
edest: [*The Big Bad Book of Beasts* by Michael Largo] "scissor-mouth shark" with long, many-toothed snout
edge sparrow: [hedgesparrow elision] cliff edge-dwelling sparrow-like ornithoid
Edge wraith: [*Edge Chronicles* by Paul Stewart and Chris Riddell] ferocious, white chiropteran from Edgeworld, Cerulea system
edgehog: [fairy chess, array of hedgehogs spoonerism] cliff edge-dwelling porcoid
edgehogator: [edgehogalligator portmanteau] alligator-like predator whose bite morphs victim into edghog
edkcelf: [flecked edkcelf palindrome] furry with small patches or spots, see elkcep, ekcit, otleb
ednad: [dandelion oil ednad palindrome] yellow ornithold
edne: [lavender edne val palindrome] purplish val
edraob: [bearded edraeb portmanteau] bearded male goat-like ruminant, see eldraeb
edrornj: [red-orange spoonerism] red-orange ornithoid
edspu: [Upsdell edspu palindrome] brownish red ornithoid
edusa: [medusa spoonerisms] medusa-like sea creature from Makhaar and Malma systems
edwoh: [edwoh chowder palindrome] food molluscoid
edyenoh: [honeydew edyenoh palindrome] pale green creature
ee: [dah-nes-tsa, tsa-e-donin-ee mondegreen, erst of bees spoonerism] ram-fly relative; [beheaded mee] mee gan ceean
eed: [deer eed palindrome] brown antlered ruminant
eedle: [needlefish elision] small, swordfish-like ichthyoid
eeh: [Crayola sheen eehs palindrome] light green ornithoid from Crayol A

eek: [keel eek palindrome] screaching, red ocher ornithoid, see eik, evit

eela: [waheela (bear-dog) mondegreen] warg-like canine

eelbird: ["Amok Time" by Theodore Sturgeon] 9-meter, dracoid with snake-like body, feathery wings and tail, 2 large clawed legs, light prismatic blue underbelly, noted for its 11-yr migration to western caves from Arodi (Regulus A V)

eelddar: [raddle eelddar palindrome] red ocher eel-like watersnake, see eelddur

eelddur: [ruddle eelddur palindrome] red ocher eel-like watersnake, see eelddar

eelephant: [eel-elephant portmanteau] elephant-like quadruped with serpentine "trunk"

eelk: [eel-elk portmanteau] large grayish-brown ruminant with antlers and serpent-headed tongue, see eelope

eelope: [eel antelope portmanteau] legless, eel-like ruminant with antlers, see eelk

eelpard: [Afrikaans/Dutch kameelpard mondegreen] eel-like seahorse ancestral to giraffe from Kam

een: [taneen mondegreen] dracoid from Ta system

eendief: [Afrikaans eend-dief portmanteau] duck-ferret, burrowing and aquatic griffinoid

eeno: [The Legend of Zelda] small, snow creature able to meld and split from Termina

eerg: [neon green eerg noen palindrome] green noen; [greenasaur ananymondegreen] green, bipedal dinosaur from Ruasa system

eergator: [eerg alligator portmanteau] alligator-like predator whose bite morphs victim into eerg

eessacir: [eessacir fricassee palindrome] food animal

eew: [bittersweet eew srett ib, tumbleweed eew elbmut palindromes] orange furry, see srettib, elbmut

ef: [fenar ananymondegreen] reptilian from Ra system

éfac: [café au lait ialua éfac, café noir ion éfac palindromes] brown creature, in ialed and ion varieties

effoc: [coffee effoc palindrome] brown-to-black ornithoid

effut: [stuffed effuts palindrome] food animal

efreet: ["Tales of the Outer Planets" ed. by Gary L. Thomas] Outer Planet creature

eft: [*Dell Crossword Puzzle Dictionary*] newt or small lizard from Europe, see evet, triton, gecko

eg: [genasaur ananymondegreen] cerapod from Ruasa system

egahippus: [beheaded megahippus] leaf-eating gan ceann

egassa sarphagum: [Cyclopedia of Worlds] 15-meter jellyfish-like creature with 150-km mat, related to sarmus, from Dakka, Neptune system

egasua: [egasua sausage palindrome] food porcoid related to azzi

egdirbmac: [Cambridge egdirbmac palindrome] pale blue ornithoid

egdod: [Dodger egdod palindrome] blue ornithoid

egger: [*Dell Crossword Puzzle Dictionary*] moth

eglo: [bereglo mondegreen] gnawing mammal

egnikcot: [stockinged egnikcot palindrome] furry with leg marking above sock or boot

egne: [scavenger egne vacs palindrome] immature vacs

egnig: [ginger egnig palindrome] yellow-orange ornithoid without black

egnigator: [egnig alligator portmanteau] alligator-like predator whose bite morphs victim into egnig

egret: [*Dell Crossword Puzzle Dictionary*] wading bird, see ibis, rail, crane, heron, stilt, avocet, avoset, jacana, flamingo

ehcaop: [poached ehcaop palindrome] food animal

ehco: [ocher ehco palindrome] yellow ornithoid

ehctap: [patched ehctap palindrome] furry with patches of red over another color

ehctolb: [blotched ehctolb palindrome] furry with blotchy markings

ehsae: [seashell ehsaes palindrome] pale pinkish off-white ornithoid

ehsgge: [eggshell ehsgge palindrome] off-white ornithoid

ei'rrh: [nei'rrh elision] poisonous hummingbird-like ornithoid

eider: [*Dell Crossword Puzzle Dictionary*] sea duck, see cooyt, scaup, scoter

eight-biter: ["In the Realm of the Torture King" by Clark Darlton"] small, but voracious, 8-legged insectoid with strong mandibles from Gaberaan

eight-clawed bear: ["Demon of the Red Dwarf" by Ernst Vlcek] delicacy food animal from frozen wastes of Ottoljim

eihcoo: [eihcoo poochie palindrome] poochie-like amphisbæna

eik: [kiel eik palindrome] screaching, red ocher arachnoid, see eek, evit, a-beyn, zech

eika-beyn: ["The Death of a Magniden" by Hans Kneifel] palm-sized arachnoid

eikzech: ["The Goddess of the Symbionts" by H. G. Ewers] 25-meter, armored predator with 8 column-like legs, arched back, inflatable cheeks, horns and poison gas-emitting tubes that sucks out dissolved interiors of prey from Tonturst (Lignan II)

eilllej: [jellied eillej portmanteau] food animal

eipto: [eipto pot pie palindrome] food animal

eirf: [fried eirf palindrome] food animal related to rettab from Pharr, Farpt system, Galaxiki galaxy

eir: [carrier eirrac palindrome] rac used as messenger

eirf: [fried eirf palindrome] food animal

eirruc: [curried eirruc palindrome] food animal

eitio: ["eitio at times emit taoitio" palindrome] pot-like gestalt

ej: [jet ej palindrome] black ornithoid

ejdra: [Dutch ejdra ape-ez zeepaardje palindrome] ape-like sea-centauroid descended from seahorse

ejiron: [nejiron elision] rock-like, underground-dwelling lumbering, rolling, explosive creature

ejron: [i-less ejiron] rock-like creature from Friatica, Friaticalida system, Galaxiki galaxy

ek: [ek elision] caninoid with 3-clawed feet, sold on black market for nek

ekab: [baked ekab palindrome] food animal

ekao: [soaked ekaos palindrome] amphibian rarely on land

ekcit: [ticked ekcit palindrome] furry with small patches or spots, see edkcelf, elkcep, otleb

ekco: [socked ekcos palindrome] furry with leg marking below stocking, see etoob

eki: [eki-like mynynym backformation] ekioid-like creature

ekioid: eki-like creature

eknod: [donkey eknod palindrome] brown ornithoid

ekomata: [nekomata elision] 2-tailed monster cat

eksam: [masked eksam palindrome] furry with dark raccoon-like marking around eyes

el-bat: [stable el-bats palindrome] riding chiropteran

el: [Romanian catel mondegreen] felinoid producing puppy-like young; [scarlet elracs mondegreen] orangish-red rac from Oita system

ela-egel: [Perry Rhodan] marine ectoparacite

elacroc: ["The Cryer of Crystal" by Joseph Green] creature as big as an elephant with teeth like a crocodile from Crystal

elagnit: [elagnit hgin nightingale palindrome] variety of hgin

elaphine: [*Dell Crossword Puzzle Dictionary*] red deer

elaps: [*Dell Crossword Puzzle Dictionary*] garter snake from S. Africa, Terra (alpha Zodiaci III)

elasmosaur: [*The Big Bad Book of Beasts* by Michael Largo] long-necked plesiosaur, "sea giraffe"

elasmotaur: [elasmosaur minotaur portmanteau] long-necked plesiotaur

elb: [bubbles elb bub palindrome] pale blue spheroid related to bub, ugelb, see aborpmi, ahcuotnu, aveilebnu, idercni, ignatni, isivni, issopmi, isualp

elba: [sable elbas palindrome] black ornithoid

elbmut: [tumbleweed eew elbmut palindrome] pale orange eew

elbow leech: [Avatar: The Last Airbender: "The Swamp"] large segmented leech with white dot per segment

elbowalker: [snouter extrapolation] snouter with atrophied legs and nasarium adapted to walking on elbows to free its hands for grabbing prey

elbram: [marbled elbram portmanteau] furry with whorls or spiral markings, see elrem, elppad

eldda: [saddled elddas palindrome] furry with back marking, see eteknalb

elderbear: [elderberry backformation] long-lived ursinoid, see youngbear

eldnirb: [brindle eldnirb palindrome] furry with black/blue/live/lilac stripes over red/yellow/cream

eldraeb: [beardless eldraeb portmanteau] beardless female goat-like ruminant, see edraeb

elea-ina: swarming ant-like insectoid from Zonder-Myry

elec: [celestial Ait's elec palindrome] celestial blue creature from Ait system

electrex: [Monster Legends] electrical land eel with spikes

electria: [Outernauts] immature electrifoal

electrifly: [Outernauts] mature voltifly

electrifoal: [Outernauts] electrical equifoal with yellow, lightningbolt-horn, see electrina, electria

electrina: [Outernauts] mature electrifoal

electripine: [Terra Monster] small quadruped with electromagnetic barbs, see sporkupine, from Terrarium

electrophor: aka electic eel, long, bioelectricity-generating fish

electrosaur: [electrophor-alectrosaur portmanteau] electric marine dinosaur

electrotaur: [electrosaur minotaur portmanteau] electric marine bovinoid

electrotter: [Monster Galaxy] electric ceature with z-shaped tail, ancestor of spwinder from Gemini constellation

elenu: [*The Howling Stones* by Alan Dean Foster] ichthyoid from Parramat archipelago, Senisran

elepah: [shapeless elepahs palindrome] large amorph

elephant: ["The Blind Men and the Elephant"] chimera with wall-like body, pillar-like legs, fan-like ears, thick snake-like trunk, spear-like tusks and rope-like tail

elephant bird: aka aepyornis, large flightless bird from Madagascar; [*Horton Hatches an Egg* by Theodore Seuss Geissel] elephamimornis, elephant-mimicking bird

elephant koi: [Avatar: The Last Airbender: "The Warriors of Kyoshi"] 12-meter orange and yellow koi fish

elephant rat: [Avatar: The Last Airbender: "Avatar Day"] small, black rodent with elephant-like trunk, raccoon-like white-ringed eyes

elephant-bee: [*Through the Looking-glass and What Alice Found There* by Charles Ludwidge "Lewis Carroll" Dodgeson] insect with nectar-gathering proboscis from Looking-glass world

elephant-bird: [Atkanda-lihiniya] huge bird able to hold elephants in talons, from Sri Lanka and Nepal, Terra (alpha Zodiaci III), see rukh

elephant-cat: [*If I Ran the Zoo* by Theodore Seuss Geissel] 4.8-meter elephant-headed creature with flat feet, horse-like tail, long neck

elephant-cow: elephant-headed cow-like bovinoid, see calf

elephant-fish: [Hindi] fish with elephant-like head and forelegs

elephant-tiger: [*1001 Arabian Nights*] tiger-like felinoid with elephantine head and wings

elephant-whale: elephant-headed whale-like cetacean, see calf

elephanteater: [elephant anteater portmanteau] creature that eats elephants, see rukh

élephantortue: [élephant-tortue portmanteau, Another World by Jean-Ignace-Isidore Gérard] aka elephanturtle, carapaced pachyderm from Gérard's world

elephent: [elephant-ent portmanteau] see nicor

eleroo: [Wuz series by Douglas Hutchison] elephantine megapodan from Wuz

eles: [ateles mondegreen] light brown spider monkey

elgnap: [spangled elgnaps palindrome] spotted (spangled, maculate) creature

elgnuj: [jungle elgnuj palindrome] jungle-adapted creature

eliob: [boiled eliob palindrome] food crustacean

eliobster: [eliob lobster portmanteau] lobster-like crustacean

eliorb: [broiled eliorb palindrome] food creature

elbirroh: [horrible elirroh palindrome] monstrous creature

elived: [deviled elived portmanteau] food animal

Elizabth Lake monster: [*Monster Spotter's Guide to North America* by Scott Francis] bat-winged griffinoid from Elizabeth Lake, CA, Terra (alpha Zodiaci III)

elk-coon: [Gene L. Coon mondegreen] creature with elk-like head and coon-like body from Ji system

elk-lizard: ["Queen of the Panther World" by Berkeley Livingston] elk-headed reptilian from Pola

elkcep: [speckled elkceps palindrome] furry with small patches or spots, see edkcelf, ekcit, otleb

ellf: [i-less ellif] cave insectoid from Friatica, Friaticalida system, Galaxiki galaxy

ellif: [Welsh ellifant mondegreen] large insectoid

ellik: [killer ellik palindrome] carnivorous elk-like predator

ellim: [smitten ellims palindrome] dark pinkish purple rekab prey

Elmendorf monster: [*Monster Spotter's Guide to North America* by Scott Francis] short, mottled bluish-gray caninoid with overbite from S. Texas, Terra (alpha Zodiaci III)

eloiv: [violet eloiv palindrome] violet ornithoid

elolan: massive, purple herbivore from Pakuri, Takrone system, Ambriador galaxy

eloressa: [eloressa casserole palindrome] food animal

elppa: [apple elppa, candyapple elppa ydnac palindromes] chartreuse green variety of ydnac

elppad: [dappled elppad palindrome] furry with medium patches or spots, see elbram, elrem

elprup: [purple elprup palindrome] purple ornithoid

elrah: [harlequin iuq elrah palindromes] yellowish green iuq

elrem: [merle elrem palindrome] furry with patches or spots, see elbram, elppad

elsiap: [paisley elsiap palindrome] ornithoid with colorful swirling markings

elsie: [*Monster Spotter's Guide to North America* by Scott Francis] humped lake snake from Lake Elsinnore, CA, Terra (alpha Zodiaci III)

elt: [*Dell Crossword Puzzle Dictionary*] small pig, see grice

eltop: [spotless eltops palindrome] furry without spots

eltrym: [myrtle eltrym palindrome] greenish ornithoid

eltsiht: [thistle eltslht palindrome] pale purplish ornithoid

eltt: ["eltt at times emit tattle" palindrome] parrot-like ornithoid gestalt

elttob: [bottle elttob palindrome] translucent green ornithoid

eltobster: [elttob lobster portmaneau] greenish ornithoid, see cobster

elttom: [mottled elttom palindrome] mottled creature

elysia: [*Dell Crossword Puzzle Dictionary*] sea slug, see doto

elytratker: ["The End of the Crib" by H. G. Francis] arachnoid from Alkordoom galaxy

elzzadelzzar: [Crayola razzle dazzle elzzadelzzar palindrome] magenta-rose ornithoid from Crayol A

em sponge: 30-cm lenticular creature with fine hair-like suckered tentacles, symbiotic with omnivorous em amoebae from Emshen cluster, Canis Venatici

em(e)u: [*Dell Crossword Puzzle Dictionary*] ostrich-like bird, see ratite

emac: [cameo emac] furry with red-tipped white hair or [camel emac palindrome] light brown ornithoid

emaerc: [creamed emaerc palindrome] food animal, see emarac

emarac: [caramel emarac] gray-pinkish (blue-fawn) furry, see emaerc

embrac: [*Monster Manual* by Skip Williams, Jonathan Tweet and Monte Cook] illithidae variant

embrithopod: [*After the Dinosaurs* by Donald R. Prothero] see arsinothere

emh: ["The Altar of Redemption" by Anne Laurie Logan] large creature of the jauneans

emis: [nemis elision] mosquitoid from Ta system

emmet: [*Dell Crossword Puzzle Dictionary*] pismire ant

emmop: [pomme emmop] mop-like creature with green spots

emmu: [summer emmus portmanteau] hibernating emu-like ornithoid

emoester: [Afrikaans emoe-oester portmanteau] emu-oyster, barnacle goose-like ornithoid

emoose: [emu-moose portmanteau] shaggy quadruped with moose-like body and antlers and emu-like neck and head

emparasend: [Hind. &] 2-D das-like creature

emuda: [beheaded remuda] saddled gan ceann

emyd: [*Dell Crossword Puzzle Dictionary*] terrapin or fresh water tortoise

emydosaur: turtle-lizard

emydotaur: [emydosaur minotaur portmanteau] turtle-bull

emys: [*Dell Crossword Puzzle Dictionary*] marsh tortoise

en: [nen elision] dove-like ornithoid

enantiornis: ["opposite bird", *The Mistaken Extinction* by Lowell Dingus and Timothy Rowe] misidentified as non-avian dinosaur, small swallow-sized with characteristic backward feet

encantado: [*The Big Bad Book of Beasts* by Michael Largo] snake-like parasites that infest pink dolphins or humans from Amazonia, Terra (alpha Zodiaci III)

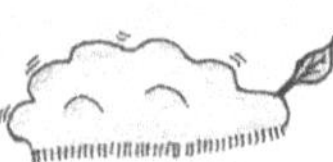

encephalophant: ["The Prospectors of Cigro" by Peter Terrid] 6-meter, gray-white shimmering clump with photosynthetic tail, hundreds of small legs, used for prospecting, transportation and shelter from Cigro, Manam Turu galaxy

endac: [Croatian crvendac mondegreen] aka enka

endrop: [Physiologus] seahorse-like horse-fish from Rumania, Terra (alpha Zodiaci III)

energ: [enegy backformation] rarely materialized energy creature

energator: [energ alligator portmanteau] alligator predator whose bite morphs victim into energ

energy creature: ["The Ordeals of Dimension Z" by Leo Dorfman] energy creature from Z dimension

energy monster: [WordGirl: "Becky and the Bard", "The Birthday Girl's Monstrous Gift"] living electricity

energy-leech: ["Call of the Cosmos" by Cary Burkett] energy-draining parasite threatening Shatou

enet(te): [beheaded genet(te)] small gan ceann

enfield: ["Xoology" by Kittenbaker] griffinoid with fox-like head, greyhound-like chest, eagle-like wings, wolf-like legs and tail from Szurane

eng: [ateng mondegreen] light brown bison-like ruminant

engator: [eng alligator portmanteau] alligator-like predator whose bite morphs victim into eng

enil: [linen enil palindrome] white ornithoid

eniojnoc: [conjoined eniojnoc palindrome] Siamese twin creature

enka: [cervenka mondegreen] robin-worm, aka endac, ornithoid with worm-like hatchling

Enki ape: [Enki ape-hak kahepaikhe portmanteau] pongoid ancestral to amphibious hak from Enki system

enleipapuun: [Johanneksenleipäpuun mondegreen] locust-like insectoid from Joha, Nek system, related to nesbröd

ennedi: [*Here Be Monsters almanac*] striped sabertoothed cat from Chad, Terra (alpha Zodiaci III)

ennet: [beheaded jennet] small gan ceann, see enet(te)

énnet: [tenné énnet palindrome] tawny ornithoid

enoh: [honey enoh palindrome] ruddy brown ornithoid

enormoose: [enormous moose palindrome] giant moose

enormouse: [enormous mouse portmanteau] moose-sized rodentoid

enottub: [buttoned enottub palindrome] furry with belly patches

enrag: [garnet enrag palindrome] aka unbluebird, ornithoid in dark red or brown, black, green yellow varieties, but not blue

enragator: [enrag alligator portmanteau] alligator-like predator whose bite morphs victim into enrag

enretsap: [pasterned enretsap palindrome] furry with leg marking above coronet

enroc: [Cornell enroc palindrome] brownish red roc

enroh: [horned enroh palindrome] horned owl-like ornithoid

entelodont: [*After the Dinosaurs* by Donald R. Prothero] pig-like artiodactyl with bony warts on lower jaws from Priabonian

enterorhinus: [*The Snouters* by Harald Stümpke] allsnouter with ciliated epithelium

eohippo: [eohippus hippo portmanteau] eohippoid from Noy, Cihpma system, Galaxiki galaxy

eohippus: ["dawn horse", *After the Dinosaurs* by Donald R. Prothero] hyrax-like 3-toed perissodactyl mistaken for Eocene horse

eon-coral: [neon-coral elision] long-lived brilliantly glowing sea creatures living in colonies from Snobaal, Laabon system, Galaxiki galaxy

eon: [pigeon mondegreen] pig-like griffinoid from Adiusa, Goodiusa system, Galaxiki galaxy

eopie: ["The Gugan Frontier" by Chris McCubbin] 1.7-meter tall, pale-skinned, short-trunked cameloid herd beast of burden from Jedi galaxy

eosaur: ["dawn lizard", lambeosaur mondegreen] early dinosaur

eot: [toenayo ananymondegreen] licorn from Oya rogue planet

eotaur: [eosaur minotaur portmanteau] early bovinoid

eotyrannus: [*Feathered Dinosaurs: The Origin of Birds* by John Long and Peter Schuten] 8-meter tyrannosaurid with long arms and fingers from Eurasian jungles, Terra (alpha Zodiaci III)

eozoon: [John William Dawson] giant foraminiferan

ep: [torep backformation] predatory bull-bird griffinoid

ópagneul-tortue. [*Another World* by Jean-Ignace-Isidore Gérard] carapaced spaniel-like caninoid from Gérard's world

epidendrosaur: ["on-tree lizard", *Feathered Dinosaurs: The Origin of Birds* by John Long and Peter Schuten] scansoriopterygid with long grub-grabbing finger

epihippo: [epihippus hippos portmanteau] eohippoid from Noy, Cihpma system, Galaxiki galaxy

epihippus: [*After the Dinosaurs* by Donald R. Prothero] beagle-sized three-toed horse from middle Eocene

epirt: [striped epirt, pinstriped epirt snip palindromes] furry with thin stripes and snippers

epmi: [imperial air epmi palindrome] purple ornithoid in flying and flightless varieties

epo: [epolope backformation] epolope without antlers

epolope: [mynynym] epo with antlers

eporhtnanthrope: [mynynym] aka 'thrope, anthrope from Eporhta system

eppek: [keppel palindrome] cyan-colored ornythoid

eppin: [snipped eppins palindrome] furry with marking between nostrils

eppoc: [copper eppoc palindrome] reddish brown creature, see ynnep, derr

epollac: [scalloped epollacs palindrome] food animal

equiflora: [Outernauts] mature equifoal

equifoal: [Outernauts] green, herbivorous bicorn-like creature, see equiflora, equina

equina: [Outernauts] immature equifoal

equinair: [Terra Monster] small equiness from Terrarium

equiness: [Terra Monster] flying pink equinine with green eyes, white mane and tail, rear anklewings from Terrarium

equinox: [equine-ox portmanteau] horse-like bovine

equulei: [piscium extrapolation] small, egg-laying horse-like quadruped

equuleusaur: small, horse-like dinosaur from Equuleus constellation

equus: [OviPets] egg-laying equinoid

er: [courser mondegreen, red er palindrome] insect and seed-eating, red bird from Cour system; [renahippus ananymondegreen] gan ceann from Suppiha system; [renar ananymondegreen] fox-like caninoid from Ra system

eralc: [claret eralc palindrome] claret wine-colored purple ornithoid

erank: ["The Planet-lock" by Marianne Sydow] large, scaly sea horse from Guhmo (Nurshug IV), Black galaxy

erazo: [erazo dozare palindrome] dozare-like amphisbæna

erberus: [beheaded cerberus] 2-headed hellhound, see dioskylos

erca: [sacred ercas palindrome] inedible bovine

erd: [nerd elision] flat-footed biped with striped neck, muttonchops and crest; [*Dell Crossword Puzzle Dictionary*] shrew, see tartar

erdkat: [Afrikaans seekat antonym] land octopus, non-aquatic cat-like cephalopodan, see octopuss

erdmeeu: [Afrikaans seemeeu backformation] burrowing cuckoo-like ornithoid

erehtothere: [mynynym] aka beast from Ereht system

erekcam: [mackerel erekcam palindrome] ichtyoid with thin vertical stripes

ereltra: [antlered ereltra palindrome] antlered creature

eremothere: [*After the Dinosaurs* by Donald R. Prothero] 6.3-meter ground sloth from Pleistocene

ereppik: [kippered ereppik palindrome] food ichthyoid

erf: [nerf elision] domesticated herbivore bred for meat and pelts

erffaz: [zaffre erffaz palindrom] blue erf predator

erg: [greater eta erg palindrome] large worm from eta Majoris, see essel

ergal: [at mondegreen] light brown nightingale-like ornithoid

erator: [erg alligator portmanteau] alligator-like predator whose bite morphs victim into erg

erhco: [ochre erhco palindrome] pale brownish-yellow ornithoid

eri(a): [*Dell Crossword Puzzle Dictionary*] silkworm from Assam, Terra (alpha Zodiaci III)

erif: [fire engine nigne erif, firebrick cirb erif palindrome] red creature, see nigne, cirb

erkle: [nerkle elision] biped with powderpuff tail, long thin beak and neck

erlikosaur: [*Feathered Dinosaurs: The Origin of Birds* by John Long and Peter Schuten] 6-meter therizinosaur with peg-like teeth, long snout

erllen: [Cornell red erllen roc palindrome] red roc

ern(e): [*Dell Crossword Puzzle Dictionary*] sea eagle, see gull, skua, scaup, tern, fulmar, gannet, petrel, scoter

ernanodon: [*After the Dinosaurs* by Donald R. Prothero] sloth-like from Cenozoic

erovore: [mynynym] erotic- energy-eater

erowl: [generowl backformation] eagle-goose ornithoid

erpillar: [caterpillar mondegreen] larval felinoid

erpine: [beheaded serpine] winged dracoid
erplex: [beheaded serplex] 2-headed, winged dracoid
errat: [starred errats palindrome] furry with marking between or above eyes
erro: [sorrel erros palindrome] brownish-orange to light brown ornithoid, see omannic
ERRV: [endogenous retroretrovirus, *The Land That Time Forgot* by Edgar Rice Burroughs] virus that reverses ERV's "reboot"
ert: [tree ert palindrome, galaxiki.org] arboreal creature from Troctopia, Qujhtba system, Galaxiki galaxy, see ert sib
Ertrus bear: ["Radio Free Ertrus" by Robert Feldhoff] 1.2-meter, 4-tonne ursinoid from Ertrus (Kreit III)
Ertrus centipede: ["The Rat of the Jersey City" by Frank Böhmert] 20-cm, red, blue and green, centipede-like nocturnal pest with poisonous bite adapted to high pressure from Ertrus (Kreit III)
Ertrus gnu: [*Alpha Alarm* by H. G. Francis] gnu geneered for Ertus (Kreit III)
erua: [aureolin ilo erua palindrome] yellow ornithoid associated with ilo, see erual
erual: [laurel erual palindrome] greenish erua-like ornithoid
erum: ["erum at times emit tamure" palindrome] snapper fish-like ichthyoid gestalt
erumpent: [*Fantastic Beasts and Where to Find Them* by Newton Artemis Fido Scamander] gray rhinoid with explosive horn and rope-like tail
ERV: [endogenous retrovirus, "Martian Autumn" by Stephen Baxter] virus causing "reboot" to ancestral form when triggered by ecocatastrophe
eryx: [*Dell Crossword Puzzle Dictionary*] sand snake or ["Base Thunder God" by H. G. Francis] predator spider-snake with 6 multi-faceted eyes and pinchers, 8 gray, hairy legs, greenish scales
és-jel: [Hung. &] 2-D das-like creature
esara: [Catalan esarabat mondegreen] roach-like chiropteran
esarb: [i-less esiarb] food animal from Friatica, Friaticalida system, Galaxiki galaxy

esbröd: [nesbröd elision] aka esbrød [esbrød], locust-like insectoid
escargot-phaléne: [*Another World* by Jean-Ignace-Isidore Gérard] snail-headed moth from Gérard's world
esd: [moonesd mondegreen] cow-like bovinoid from Luna (alpha Zodiaci IIIb)
esee: [esee geese palindrome] goose-like ornithoid
eseeh: [esseh cheese palindrome] milk animal
eseel: [esee eel portmanteau] eel-headed triphibian
esgi: [kananésgi mondegreen] arachnoid from Kana system
esher: [*The Dumb Robot* by Hans Kneifel] serpentoid from Chephren Nova, Pharaoh system
esiarb: [braised esiarb palindrome] food animal
esillag: [Hung. *] 2-D pentapus or hexapus
esillagator: [esillag alligator portmanteau] alligator-like predator whose bite morphs victim into esillag
Eskarian oviparum: [*Investigations* by Jerri Taylor] oviparous creature of Eskar, Delta Quadrant
eskirte: ["Mountain Mage" by Clark Darlton] 3-meter, grizzly-like ursinoid from Pthor
esmarg: ["The Sun's Death" by Uwe Anton] parasitic, swamp-dwelling scavenger from Holter
esmargator: [esmarg alligator portmanteau] alligator-like predator whose bite morphs victim into esmarg
ESO: [Enormous Space Octopus acronym] space octopus used for space travel
esohippus: [beheaded mesohippus] 3-toed gan ceann
esoo: [esoo moose/goose palindrome] antlered griffinoid
espeed: [deep sea espeed palindrome] fast, psychic creature of the ocean depths from Snobaal, Laabon system, Galaxiki galaxy
esperluette: [Fren. &] 2-D das-like creature
ess: [*Dell Crossword Puzzle Dictionary*] S-shaped worm, see tinea

essel: [lesser essel palindrome] ess-like worm in larger and smaller varieties from eta Minoris, see aerg

esserp: [pressed esserp palindrome] food serpentoid from Snowi, Nejstea system, Galaxiki galaxy

esset: [nesset elision] venomous 3-fanged serpentinoid

essur: [russet essur palindrome] reddish-orange brown ornithoid

esupam: ["Rescue Operation Tekayl" by H. G. Francis] very poisonous serpentoid

et: [Norwegian manet mondegreen] jellyfish-like sea creature from Ma system; [net elision] ornithoid [pianet, toucanet mondegreens] from Pia or [toucanet mondegreen] Touca system, see avoc, bloodhorn, horn, ka, lipp, zanig varieties

et-merrki: [Fin. &] 2-D das-like creature

et-techen: [Scot. &] 2-D das-like creature

et-zei: [et-zeichen backformation] large et-zeichen

et-zeichen: [Germ. &] 2-D das-like creature

etan: ["etan at times emit tanate" palindrome] wild dog gestalt

etch: [netch elision] herd air jellyfish-like creature that hovers

etee: [eter backformation] non-jellyfish-like sea creature from Ma system

etekcol: [locketed etekcol palindrome] furry with white chest

etekcolope: [etekcol antelope portmanteau] etekcol with antlers

eteknalb: [blanketed eteknalb palindrome] furry with back marking, see eldda

eteno: [coroneted eteno roc palindrome] roc with leg marking below pastern

eter: [Swedish maneter mondegreen] jellyfish-like predator from Ma system

etfut: [tufted etfut portmanteau] creature in tufted and other varieties

etha: [gaasyendietha mondegreen] inedible yendi from Gaa system

etibneg: [etibneg agebbite palindrome] agenbite-like amphisbæna

etibnegator: [etibneg alligator portmanteau] alligator-like predator whose bite morphs victim into etibneg

etir: [etir krite palindrome] krite-like amphisbæna

etjie: [Afrikaans verkleurmannetjie mondegreen] chameleon-like reptilian from Verkleurma system

ētli: [Cherokee] mink-like mammaloid from Tsalagi system

etoob: [booted etoob palindrome] furry with leg marking below stocking, see ekco

etoobster: [etoob lobster portmanteau] etoob with lobster-like claws

etserc: [crested etserc palindrome] ornithoid noted for its crest

ettabtnuom: [Mountbatten ettabtnuom palindrome] grayish mauve creature, see tomylp

ette: [genette backformation] goose-horse pegasoid

etter: [Irish setter spoonerism] silky-haired reddish-brown caninoid from Sirish system

ettim: [mitted ettim palindrome] furry with white front paws

ettodaklop: [polka-dotted ettodaklap palindrome] creature marked by dots

ettop: [spotted ettops palindrome, "Rudolph the Red-nosed Reindeer and the Island of Misfit Toys" by Michael Aschner] white, elephant-like animated toy animal with red spots

etvor: [Czech/Slovak netvor elision] monstrous creature

etwep: [pewter etwep palindrome] blue-gray-silver creature

eucebra: [eucebra barbecue palindrome] food animal

eucerathere: [*After the Dinosaurs* by Donald R. Prothero] shrub oxen from Pleistocene

eugno: [eugno tongue palindrome] food animal noted for tongue

eule-chat: [*Another World* by Jean-Ignace-Isidore Gérard] owl-headed, cat-bodied griffinoid from Gérard's world

eulec: [eule-chat mondegreen] owl-cat-in-a-hat

euparkeria: [*The Mistaken Extinction* by Lowell Dingus and Timothy Rowe] typical archosaur with possible antorbital air sac

euphonia: [*National Geographic Encyclopedia of Animals*] small, herbivorous bird with call like tinkling bell from Caribbean, Terra (alpha Zodiaci III)

euphoniumbird: [trumpeter swan backformation] large tuba swan-like ornithoid with euphonium-like call

evaeb: [beaver evaeb palindrome] brown aquatic creature

ever bird: [never bird elision] aka New Jerusalem bird

evet: [*Dell Crossword Puzzle Dictionary*] newt, see eft, triton

evillya: [Mushroom Planet series by Eleanor Cameron] insectoid from Basidium (alpha Zodiaci IIIc)

evir: [river evir palindrome] hippopotamus-horse ancestral to horse and hippopotamus, related to aeco and ekal

evit: [tiver evit palindrome] screaching, red ocher ornithoid, see eik, eek

evli: [silver evlis palindrome] pale furry with dark-tipped hairs

evoni: [sinovenator ananymondegreen] long-legged troodont from Rota system, see osuni

ewolf'n: [cornflower ewolf'n roc palindrome] blue roc

ewopdnap: [pomp and power ewopdnap mop palindrome] purplish mop-like land cephalopodan

ewt: [newt elision] salamander-like amphibian

ewyn: [babewyn mondegreen] blue pongoid

execution bird: ["Drang the Destroyer" by Leo Dorfman] predatory ornithoid from Cyclon

Exmoor beast: [exmoorotherium, *Unexplained!* by Jerome Clark] 2.4-meter, black or tan cat-like creature from Exmoor, Devonshire, Eng., Terra (alpha Zodiaci III)

exogorth: ["The Empire Strikes Back" by George Lucas] aka space slug, 1000- to 10-meter silicon-based gastropod with root-like tail, found in caysh (planetoid burrow) from Jedi galaxy

exogyra: spirally-shaped oyster from Cretaceous

exterminator: [*A Hero's Guide to Deadly Dragons* by Hiccup Haddock III] semi-transparent, packhunting dragon with sword-talons and 2 hearts from Barbarian archipelago

eyas: [*Dell Crossword Puzzle Dictionary*] unfledged bird

eye-lizard: see opthalmosaur

eye-ra: [*The Ultimate Monster Guide* by Jaymond] blob with large red eye

eyecleaner: ["Castle of Secrets" by H. G. Ewers] 50-cm, nocturnal animal from Dorkh

eyesah: [Outernauts] cephalopoid with 5 eyestalks, pink crest

eyesaur: [Outernauts] land cephalopodan with many eyestalks, walking tentacles, red crest

eyesee: [Outernauts] immature eyesah with just 3 eyestalks, walking tentacles

eyeseel: [eyesee eel portmanteau] eyesee-like conjoined triplet eels

eyh: [hyena-swine ananymic mondegreen] pig-headed hyena-like caninoid from Eniwsa system; [hyenat ananymondegreen] isectoid from Ta system

eyra: [*Dell Crossword Puzzle Dictionary*] wildcat from S. America, Terra (alpha Zodiaci III)

ez: [Dutch ejdra ape-ez zeepaardje portmanteau] ape-seahorse ancestral to ejdra and seahorse

ezalb: [blazed ezalb palindrome] furry with stripe down middle of face

ezkahla: ["The March through the Underworld" by Ernst Vlcek] large predator from Tratta

eznorb: [bronze eznorb palindrome] coppery brown to tawny buff ornithoid

F-4 virus: ["No Exit" by Kate Orman] deadly virus that leaves survivors sterile

f'tan: ["Seed of Reason" by Daniel Hatch] porcine from Chamal

fabool: [*Star Wars - the Essential Guide to Planets and Moons* by Daniel Wallace] baboon-like simian from Dantarian savannah, Dantooine, Jedi galaxy

faboolope: [faboo antelope portmanteau] faboo with antlers

fachen: shapeshifting creature, often black-feather-maned mare from Scotland, Terra (alpha Zodiaci III)

fae: [seafoam aofaes palindrome] silver-gray ornithoid, related to ao

fafazon: ["Battle of Ferrol" by Michael Marcus Thurner] wild beast from Ferrol (Vega (alpha Lyrae) VIII)

fagah: ["The Children of the Robot" by H. G. Ewers] sauroid from Vurla, Vurla system

fagflaki: [James Cooke Brown's Loglan fagro flaki compound] firefly from Logla, Brown's system

fagnirda: [James Cooke Brown's Loglan fagro nirda compound] firebird from Logla, Brown's system

fahigh: [buffahigh mondegreen] shaggy, lavender, long-horned, long-necked bovinoid

fairy: ["Rhodan Times a Thousand" by Hans Kneifel] nocturnal, swarming insectoid from Trafalgar (fka Magadona), Victory system, Demetria cluster

falanx: [*After Man* by Dougal Dixon] wolf-like predatory rodent

falcarius: ["sickle-maker", *Feathered Dinosaurs: The Origin of Birds* by John Long and Peter Schuten] 4-meter early herbivorous therizonosaur

falcoff: [falcon backformation] falcon predator

falconfly: [*The Future Is Wild* by Dougal Dixon] large flutterbird-eating wasp with both grasping and slashing legs

falipa: ["The Psi-fighter" by Achim Mehnert] small, furry rodentoid from Trilith Okt's homeworld

falled-in: [dolphin spoonerism] amphibious cetacean

falok: [Fr. Johann Martin Schleyer's Volapük] falcon-like ornithoid from Schleyer's system

falta: ["The Law of the Idols" by H. G. Francis] tiger-like, reddish-blue felinoid with 8 legs

faltani: [James Cooke Brown's Loglan falta nirda] liar bird from Logla, Brown's system

faltcec: ["The Wrong Grossart" by Hans Kneifel] 16-cm, long-legged insectoid with 4 wings

faltechse: ["Planet of Storms" by Michelle Stern] basilisk-like 2-headed bird predator from Thersunt

falumpaset: ["The Gungan Frontier" by Chris McCubbin"] herd quadruped with distinctive bellow, used as mount, from Naboo swamps and plains, Jedi galaxy

fambaa: ["The Gungan Frontier" by Christ McCubbin] large, scaly, amphibious, herbivorous beast of burden from Gungan, Jedi galaxy

fanamin-pitoloha: 7-headed hydra from Madagascar, Terra (alpha Zodiaci III), see pitoloha

fanback: ["The Gungan Frontier" by Chris McCubbin] egg-laying sauroid with dorsal spine, lower-jaw tusks from Jedi galaxy

fandrefiala: spear-headed snake of Malagasy

fang: [*The Ultimate Monster Guide* by Jaymond] venomous, red insectoid with scorpion-like stinger, metallic legs, fangs

fangator: [fang alligator portmanteau] alligator-like predator whose bite morphs victim into fang

fangryf: [fanged gryphon portmanteau, "Day of Burning" by Poul Anderson] winged creature from Merseia, between Betelgeuse and Rigel, Orion constellation

fant: [Maltese iljunfant mondegreen] elephant-lion ancestral to lion and elephant; [buffant mondegreen] lavender elephantoid

faol: [faol tae meatloaf palindrome] food animal related to sllab and tae

faolope: [faol antelope portmanteau] faol with antlers

Far-Go chicken: ["Famine in Far-Go" by Michael Pricedeadly] radioactive, mutant chicken

Farmer City monster: [*Monster Spotter's Guide to North America* by Scott Francis] 2.4-meter nape with yellow eyes from Farmer City, IL, Terra (alpha Zodiaci III)

farmian: [Terra Monster] from Terrarium

farnoth: ["In the Walls from Eryx" by Howard Phillips Lovecraft and Kenneth Sterling] fly-like insectoid

farrn: ["The Great Silence" by Marianne Sydow] locomotive symbiot of banditry, see nyzel, drohs

fasticalon: ["Murder Under Glass" by Bob Liddel] beast immune to poisonous rose and hunted on Kilgari

fastiga: ["The Three-cornered Wheel" by Poul Anderson] long-eared, long-snouted equinoid from Ivanhoe system

fastigator: [fastiga alligator portmanteau] alligator-like predator whose bite morphs victim into fastiga

fat bat: [Cloudstone] nearly flightless, square-shaped chiropteran

fathla: [Thongor series by Lin Carter] awful, cat-sized arboreal leech from Lemuria, Terra (alpha Zodiaci III)

fatoceros: ["L'il Abner" by Al Capp] bloated pachyderm vulnerable to addictive mockaroni

fatsnake: [*After Man* by Dougal Dixon] venomous viper-like cobra with enlarged baseball bat-like tail

fatty: [*Syzygy and Brontomek* by Michael G. Coney] tuna-like ichthyoid, primary food source of colonists from Arcadia

fatu-liva: [*The Cruise of the Kawa* by Walter E. Traprock (George Sheperd Crappel), museumofhoaxes.com by Alex Boese] cubical-egg-laying bird from Filbert Islands, see oo-er

faust: [Monster Galaxy] white pegasoid with purple markings

faux bois golem: [Fren. "false wood"] golem of faux bois

favvinta: ["The Dark Zero" by Rainer Castor] wrinkly, maneless, teleporting packrat-like baboonoid from Clurmertakh

fawcrish: [crawfish spoonerism] predatory crustacean from Snobaal, Laabon system, Galaxiki galaxy

faynaa: ["The Gungan Frontier" by Chris McCubbin] fast-moving, carnivorous lute-shaped ichthyoid from Jedi galaxy

faz: [Afrikaans/Dutch fazant mondegreen] feathered insectoid

feather boa: large, constricting snake with feathers

feather-wing beetle: [Xanth series by Piers Anthony] insect with feather-like wings from Xanth

featherfoot: [*After Man* by Dougal Dixon] hopping desert rodent immune to plant toxins which it spits out for defense

feaver: [family of beavers spoonerism, featherfoot beaver portmanteau] beaver-like creature immune to plant toxins which it spits out for defense

feeder: ["Fungi from Yuggoth" by Howard Phillips Lovecraft] fractal-dimensional like spiked sphere cluster, minion of Yog-Sothoth

Feejee mermaid: [Phineas T. Barnum] monkey-fish, primitive ichthropoid

feem: ["Milk Run" by Robert Sheckley] noted for freezing-point parthenogenesis, like queel

fehed: [*Dead Diver* by Wim Vandermaan] blue sauroid with long legs that spews sticky black prey-luring goo from Lepso, Firing system

feist: [*Dell Crossword Puzzle Dictionary*] small dog, see pom, pug, peke, pup

fejl'n: ["Pilot of the Chaotarchs" by Leo Lukas] 6-legged racing caninoid from Hangay galaxy

feld: [German Feldlerche mondegreen] lark-like ornithoid from Adulala, moon of Fyver, Neccobit's system, Galaxiki galaxy

felinodore: [*Eyes of the Overworld* by Jack Vance] felinoid

felisaur: cat-like lizard from Hiye (Koloris IV), Galaxiki galaxy

felitaur: [felisaur minotaur portmanteau] cat-headed bovinoid

fell beast: [*Lord of the Rings* by J. R. R. Tolkien] carrion-eating pterosaur-like steed of the Nazgûl from Middle Earth

feltervi: ["Persecuted and Outlaws" by Falk-Ingo Klee] brown (summer), white (winter) mountain marten-like ornithoid from Arklard, Suuma system, Manam Turu (Krelquan) galaxy

femtogurp: [centigurp extrapolation] pink furball able to bounce, roll, fond of spheres, and be in fifteenplex places at once, see gurp

fenar: ["In the Hand of the Executioner" by Clark Darlton] reptilian from Zercasholpek

fêng-huang: [Chinese] beautifully feathered bird with enchanting cry, ssu ling of the South, see benu, phoenix

fêng-huangator: [fêng-huang alligator portmanteau] alligator-like predator whose bite morphs victim into fêng-huang

fennec fox: [Perry Rhodan] wolf-like caninoid from Chephren Nova, Pharaoh system

fenris: ["Rise of the Cynos" by H. G. Ewers] 40-cm, blue, shaggy caninoid with stubby tail, cropped ears from Kamash (Paternal VII)

ferbe: [James Cooke Brown's Loglan fer beldu] ironbelly from Logla, Brown's system

fere: [*The Dirdir, The Pnume* by Jack Vance] dangerous gulch creature from Sibol

ferm: lake lizard that reproduces via symbiotic flies from Habitat (Iestonian Spiral IV), Galaxiki galaxy

fern bicker: [*Creatures of the Galaxy* by Phil Brucato, Bill Smith, Rick D. Stuart, Chuck Truett] solitary pongoid from Kashÿyÿk, Jedi galaxy

Ferrol cat: [Odyssey series] turquoise and white cat with beard and golden eyes from Ferrol (Vega (alpha Lyrae) VIII)

ferti: [James Cooke Brown's Loglan fer titci] iron-eater from Logla, Brown's system

feyr: ["Nothing to Fear" by Kevin N. Haw] large brain-like cephalopodan with many large, golden eyes and needle-toothed mouths, dies on exposure to sunlight unless the great feyr variety

fez ant: [pheasant mondegreen] burrowing insectoids whose hills are fez-shaped

ffes: [Welsh ffesant mondegreen] feathered insectoid

ffoc: [coffee ffoc palindrome] brown-to-black ornithoid

ffonagort: [ffonagort Stroganoff palindrome] beefy food animal

fibbee: [fibber backformation] bee-like insectoid agitated when lied to

ficli: [James Cooke Brown's Loglan] ichthyoid from Logla, Brown's system

fiddler fly: [Xanth series by Piers Anthony] from Land of Flies, Xanth

field nickel: ["Quartier Lemurica" by Michael Marcus Thurner] edible, garden pest size of rodent's head from Arcane Raphan, Nagigal trinary system

fierson: [Jets*Rockets*Spacemen Trading Cards #89-90] ravenous, fanged ursinoid with apish face from Kroto, Sirius (alpha Canis Majoris) system

fiery horse: [Sirach 48:9] plasmoidal steed

fifer: [trumpeter swan backformation] small flute swan-like ornithoid with fife-like call

figgy pudding: [pudding extrapolation] brownish pudding-thick ooze

fiil: ["Imperator of Akron" by Rainer Castor] space worm from Ay

fil: [one-i fiil] one-eyed space worm

filagin: [Azaerbaijani fil-lagin portmanteau] elephant-falcon, pegasoid with both wings and earwings from Peggassa, Hippocrenea system, Galaxiki galaxy

filcher: [*Monster Manual* by Skip Williams, Jonathan Tweet and Monte Cook] white, interdimensional creature with dark green back and hands, 4 eyes and large stomach-mouth on torso, 2 eyes and round mouthhole on bauble-like head, 1 leg with 4 toes and 4 arms, usually found underground

fillt: ["In the Land of Beasts" by H. G. Francis] prey of orhil from Umshuyr (Netse-Tana II)

fin lizard: [*After Man* by Dougal Dixon] bipedal lizard with fin-like skinflaps

finchworm: [finch-inchworm portmanteau] finch-like ornithoid's leg-less, wingless hatchling

findow: [*There's a Wocket in My Pocket* by Theodore Seuss Geissel] 3-meter orange biped with long ears, antlers

finfoot: [*National Geographic Encyclopedia of Animals*] sea bird from Indonesia, Terra (alpha Zodiaci III)

fingal: ["Believer's" by David Gerrold] noted for eggs

finger leech: [leech finger backformation] leech fond of fingers, particularly ring finger

fingerprint fish: [*Bardín the Superrealist* by Max] fish with fingerprint-like markings

fingershell: [*A Door into Ocean* by Joan Slonczewsky] used to control fingershell parasites by colonists on Shora, the Ocean Moon of Valedon

fingerwalker: [snouter extrapolation] snouter adapted for walking on fingers with atrophied arms, legs and nasarium

fingger: [finger mondegreen] pink segmented inchworm-like predator that finggs

finicky: [icky fin spoonerism] slimy, inedible ichthyoid

finikor: [*The Spawn of Fashan* by Kirby Lee Davis] creature from Boosboodle

fink: [*The Ultimate Monster Guide* by Jaymond] arachnoid with praying mantis-like forelimbs, retractable head, and carapace from Amazonia, Terra (alpha Zodiaci III)

fippler: [trumpeter swan backformation] flute swan-like ornithoid, see fluter

fird: [flock of birds spoonerism] ornithoid gestalt that flies as rectilinear solid

fire beetle: [Jets*Rockets*Spacemen Trading Card #24] enormous insectoid with snake-like hypnotic powers and adapted to high temperatures

fire bug: "The Instinct Warrior" by H. G. Francis] fiery insectoid from Zentapher

fire bugator: [fire bug alligator portmanteau] alligator-like predator whose bite morphs victim into fire bug

fire dragon: ["The Headquarters of the Irregulars" by Conrad Shepherd] winged dracoid with fire-generating organ from Boulktat (Boul III), Nubecula Minor

fire fly: [Odd Squad: Sector 21] fiery fly-like insectoid prey of fire toad

fire lizard: ["The Power of the Sun" by H. G. Francis] deadly 2-meter lizard with flame skin

pattern from Ailand (aka Zwottertracht, Zwotta II); [Pern series by Ann McCaffrey] small dragonkin in blue, brown, bronze, gold and green varieties

fire muräne: ["The Psi-fighter" by Arndt Drechler] dangerous sea creature from Trilith Okts homeworld

fire slug: [*Fantastic Beasts and Where to Find Them* by Newton Artemis Fido Scamander] poisonous slug from Brazil, Terra (alpha Zodiaci III)

fire slugator: [fire slug alligator portmanteau] alligator-like predator whose bite morphs victim into fire slug

fire toad: [Odd Squad: Sector 21] fiery toad-like batrachoid that eats fire flies, see flaming frog

fire-crab: [*Fantastic Beasts and Where to Find Them* by Newton Artemis Fido Scamander] tortoise-like creature with gem-studded carapace that expels flaming methane from rear like gamera from Fiji, Terra (alpha Zodiaci III)

fire-man: [fireman mondegreen] anthopomorphic fiery plasmoid

fireball: [*Fantastic Beasts and Where to Find Them* by Newton Artemis Fido Scamander] pig-eating, scarlet fire-breathing dragon from China, Terra (alpha Zodiaci III)

fireball loon: [fireball balloon portmanteau] fiery red loon-like ornithoid that can puff up like pufferfish

fireballope: [fireball antelope portmanteau] fireball dracoid with antlers

firebat: hellfiery chiropteran from Clodios (Iestonian Spiral VII), Galaxiki galaxy

firebird: ["At the Zoo" by Rick Shelley] supergaudy pheasant-like ornithoid from Fennich; another from Orion VII; [*The Reefs of Space* by Frederik Pohl and Jack Williamson] multitudinous prey of the pyropods

firebug: ["Bug" by William Castle, Thomas Page, "The Nest"] mutant, fire-starting cockroach

firebugator: [firebug alligator portmanteau] alligator-like predator whose bite morphs victim into firebug

firedog: [Xanth series by Piers Anthony] fire-breathing, volcanically hot devil dog from Xanth; see hellhound

firedogator: [firedog alligator portmanteau] alligator-like predator whose bite morphs victim into firedog

firedragon: ["Flash Gordon" by Frederick Stephani, George Plympton, Basil Dickey, Ella O'Neill, based on Alex Raymond's strip] hellfiery dracoid from Mongo

firefly: [Xanth series by Piers Anthony] domesticatable flying insect with flaming tail from Xanth or [Xanthian mondegreen] Xa, Thia system

firekong: [Monster Legends] hellfiery gorilla-like ape

firekongator: [firekong alligator portmanteau] alligator-like predator whose bite morphs victim into firekong

firemouth: [*Edge Chronicles* by Paul Stewart and Chris Riddell] venomous moth from Edgeworld, Cerulea system

firenaught: [Terra Monster] armored, winged insectoid predator, see firmitaur, from Terrarium

firepuppy: [Monster Legends] small hellhound

firequacker: [Rainbeau's Riddles and Rhymes] cross between duck and firefly

firesaur: [Monster Legends] aka pyrosaur, hellfiery bipedal dinosaur

firestilt: ["The Black Time" by Wim Vandermaan] creature from Jonathon, Jonah system, Charon nebula

firgel: ["Milk Run" by Robert Sheckley] big, croaking, cold-fixing lizard, that becomes dormant with sudden temperature or pressure changes

firgelope: [firgel antelope portmanteau] firgel with antlers

firmitaur: [Terra Monster] armored, armed, cave-dwelling hexapod with thick antennae, see firmian and firenaught, from Terrarium

first mast: [fourth mast backformation] relative of fourth mast from Emeris, Sheel-Sen system

firsthand: [handbird backformation] variety of handbird

fischaf: [German Fisch-Schaf portmanteau] fish-sheep, wooly amphibian from polar seas of Germa system

fish lizard: [Space: 1889] ichthyosauroid from Venus (alpha Zodiaci II)

fish-goose: [church of Zillis] fish-headed goose-like ichthyornithoid

fish-snake: ["The Man Who Saved Kal-El's Life" by Robert Bernstein] venomous eel-like creature from Fire Falls, Krypton, Rao system

fishbird: [*The Reefs of Space* by Frederik Pohl and Jack Williamson] aka ichthyornis, multitudinous prey of pyropods from Orion VII

fishcrow: [fish crow mondegreen] crow-likw ichthyornis

fishie: [Lobo #3] aka space-dwelling dolphin-like creature

fiskur: [Icelandic gullfiskur backformation] fish-gull triphibian, ancestral to fish and goldfish

fkyd: ["The Altar of Redemption" by Anne Laurie Logan] quadruped of the jauneans

fla: [manfla mondegreen] fly-like insectoid from Ma system

flabbee: [flabby mondegreen] bee-like insectoid with flesh-colored dewlap

flag-lizard: see vexillosaur

flagg: [flaggy backformation] limb, almost boneless creature

flaggator: [flagg alligator portmanteau] alligator predator whose bite morphs victim into flagg

flaif: [portmanteau] see flitter waif

flallow: [flying swallow portmanteau, flight of swallows spoonerism] leg-less murre-swallow-like ornithoid

flame devil: ["Graveyard of Ships" by Cathrin Hartmann] blue plasmoid that feeds on death fear through forehead to reproduce by division from Pakuri, Takrone system, Ambriador galaxy

flame-monster: ["The Ordeals of Dimension Z" by Leo Dorfman] monstrous fire-adapted creature from Z dimension
flamebeast: [Superman mythos] flaming, pyrothere-like creature from Krypton, Rao system
flamebird: [Superman mythos] red, yellow, orange, green ornithoid with red crest from Krypton, Rao system
flaming frog: [Odd Squad: Sector 21] fiery frog-like batrachoid, see fire toad, combustible tadpole
flaming frogator: [flaming frog alligator portmanteau] alligator-like predator whose bite morphs victim into flaming frog
 **flamoose**: [Terra Monster] moose with flaming antlers and tail, see ignitler, from Terrarium
flan: [Final Fantasy] ooze between pudding and jelly thickness in amarillo (yellow), azabache (jet black), azul (blue), blanco (white), palido (pale, pearl) and rojo (red) varieties; [flight of swans spoonerism, flying swan portmanteau] leg-less murre-swan-like ornithoid
flan tick: [flan, flantic mondegreen] tick that infests flan inducing tics
flantic: [*Rhialto* by Jack Vance] long-necked forest-dweller
flapaloo: ["L'il Abner" by Al Capp] scrawny bird, now extinct, able to lay 1000 eggs per minute, which dissolve into gasoline
flape: [portmanteau] see flying ape
flapper: [Sky Ocean] rokh-like ornithoid from Sios
flare-wing: [*Completely Unofficial Star Wars Encyclopedia*] flying creature from Alderaan, Jedi galaxy
flare-wingator: [flare-wing alligator portmanteau] alligator-like predator whose bite morphs victim into flare-wing
flarmian: [Terra Monster] small, red-brown insectoid with thick antennae, see firmitaur, from Terrarium
flarmiblue: [Terra Monster] creature from Terrarium

flarn: ["Babylon 5: The Parliament of Dreams" by J. Michael Straczynski] delicacy from Antares (alpha Scorpii) system
flarp: [*The New Dinosaurs* by Dougal Dixon] 1-meter pterosaur with vestigial wingflap for display
flash spider: ["The Space Circus" by Hans Kneidel] regeneered arachnoid that spins almost unbreakable thread
flashback parasite: [Rick and Marty: "Total Rickall" by Mike McMahan] parasite that reproduce via flashbacks
flat eel: ["Exile of the Oracle" by Michael Marcus Thurner] flat eel-like ichthyoid from Baikal (Cain I)
flat food monster: ["Dawn over Hellworld" by Hans Kneifel] flat, camouflaged ground predator edged with grasping claws from Ereshkigal (Hellworld), Adad system
flatcat: [*The Rolling Stones* by Robert A. Heinlein] small, furry, omnivorous, empathic symbiot, dormant when not eating
Flathead monster: [*Monster Spotter's Guide to North America* by Scott Francis] 18-meter, black, smooth-skinned, eel-like lake snake from Flathead Lake, MT, Terra (alpha Zodiaci III)
flatt: [flattish backformation] tapetoid, see carpet-thing
flatwing: [*The Jesus Incident* by Frank Herbert and Bill Ransom] dangerous ground dweller from Pandora
flatwingator: [flatwing alligator portmanteau] alligator-like predator whose bite morphs victim into flatwing
Flatwoods monster: [*Unexplained!* by Jerome Clark] gliding creature with head like ace of spades, foul odor from Flatwoods, WV, Terra (alpha Zodiaci III)
flauriz: [Hildegard of Bingen's Lingua Ignota] pelican-like ornithoid from Ignota, Hildegard's system
flaxet: ["The Golderin" by Susan Schwartz] creature from Whirlpool galaxy
flaygrub: [*Ghost-Walker* by Barbara Hambly] flaying grub-like creature from Midgwis (Elcidar Beta III)

flear: [portmanteau] see flying bear

fled: [fleddox mondegreen] wild ox-like griffinoid

fleddox: ["The Feme Singer" by Arndt Ellmer] flying mount with purple veins, raptor head, with pointed white beak, huge yellow eyes, using ultrasound echolocation from Ash-Irthumo, Ash system, Jamondi cluster

fleder: [Germ. Fledermaus mondegreen] common ancestor to rodentoids and chiropteroids from Germa system

fledg: [fledgy backformation] feathered creature

fledgator: [fledg alligator portmanteau] alligator predator whose bite morphs victim into fledg

fleel: [portmanteau] see flat eel

fleep: [portmanteau, flock of sheep spoonerism] see flying sheep

fleeter: ["The Fantastic Voyage of *Francis Drake-4*" by Clark Darlton] small, pearly white, fruitivorous rodentoid from Typhoon (Kuros Kuros II), Nubecula Minor

flellyfish: [flyingfish jellyfish portmanteau, fluther of jellyfish spoonerism] flying jellyfish

flendag: [*Ghost-Walker* by Barbara Hambly] creature that nests in streams from Midgwis (Elcidar Beta III)

flendagator: [flendag alligator portmanteau] alligator-like predator whose bite morphs victim into flendag

fleopard: [flying leopard portmanteau, Dan. 7:6] 3-headed, 4-winged leopard-like griffinoid

fleratii: [*The Howling Stones* by Alan Dean Foster] large, silvery flying-fish-like ichthyoid from Parramat archipelago, Senisran

flesh eater: ["The Flesh Eaters" by Arnold Drake] microbes that grow upon electrification into glowing lumpy oval 6-by-12-meters with 9 feeding tendrils, 1 white eye spot, poisoned by blood

flesh jelly: [*Monster Manual* by Skip Williams, etal.] flesh-eating jelly-thick ooze

flib: [Fr. Johann Martin Schleyer's Volapük] flea-like insectoid from Schleyer's system

flice: [flock of lice spoonerism] small woolyworm-like creature, see heep

flicker: [flickertail mondegreen] squirrel-like creature noted for its near-invisibity

flig: [flying pig portmanteau] see pigasus

fligator: [flig alligator portmanteau] alligator-like predator whose bite morphs victim into flig

fling: magenta creature from Bubblefire, Phoenix system, Galaxiki galaxy

flion: [fly-lion portmanteau] griffinoid with insect-like wings, antennae and cat-like body

flippisk: ["Farscape" series] decapod, tasty if prepared correctly, but dangerous when not from Farscape galaxy

flird: [flock of birds spoonerism] classical song ornithoid

flish: [flying fish portmanteau, *The Future Is Wild* by Dougal Dixon] air-breathing ichthyopteryx with insulating hollow scales with protusile (horizontally moving) jaws, horizontal tail

flit: [*The Barber of Aldebaran* by William Moy Russell] insignificant seeming creature but producing an astonishingly potent pheromone to which other creatures, humans, and even robots are not resistant from Aldebaran (alpha Tauri) system

flitamug: [Fr. Johann Martin Schleyer's Volapük] bat-like flying mammaloid from Schleyer's system

flitamugator: [flitamug alligator portmanteau] alligator-like predator whose bite morphs victim into flitamug

flitter waif: [*Edge Chronicles* by Paul Stewart and Chris Riddell] waif with 3 curved fangs from Edgeworld, Cerulea system

flitterbick: [*Monster Spotter's Guide to North America* by Scott Francis] nearly invisible flying squirrel, see flicker

flitty: [flying kitty portmanteau] see felinopteryx

floater: ["Fungi from Yuggoth" by Howard Phillips Lovecraft] fractal-dimensional like short, sturdy clubs with many fin-like blades, minion of Yog-Sothoth

floatgoat: lighter-than-air goat

flobber: [flobberworm backformation] ornithoid that flobs (follows slime trail)

flobberworm: [*Fantastic Beasts and Where to Find Them* by Newton Artemis Fido Scamander] thick, brown, slimy 2.5-cm worm that secrets slime from both ends

flockopi: [flying octopi portmaneau] aerial cephalopodan gestalt

flofox: [Terra Monster] small pale blue and white fox, see wintail, from Terrarium

flog: [flying frog portmanteau, spoonerism] insectivorous, batrachopteryx-like triphibian, best when fried

flogator: [flog alligator portmanteau] alligator-like predator whose bite morphs victim into flog

flolf: [mynynym, flying wolf portmanteau] see wolf-like caninopteryx

flomar: ["Foray into Intrawelt" by Christian Montillon] gray, edible forest-dwelling quadruped from Intrawelt

flongboo: [*Rootabaga Stories* by Carl Sandburg] yellow, nocturnal predator with luminous tail that lives in hollow trees of Saskatchewan, Terra (alpha Zodiaci III)

floob-boober-bab-boober-bub: [*On Beyond Zebra* by Theodore Seuss Geissel] cross between 10-meter, 4-tentacled, dog-faced, red-nosed cephalopodan, see bab, boober, bub and floob

floob: [*The Howling Stones* by Alan Dean Foster] short-legged, brown-furred creature of Parramat archipelago, Senisran, related to bab, boober and bub

floobster: [floob lobster portmanteau] floob with lobster-like claws

flood blea: [blood flea spoonerism] parasitic insectoid that appears during flooding

floodplain sailer: ["Escape to Talanis" by Hubert Haensul] creature with larger, colorful females from Stardust, Far Away cluster, Shapley supercluster

flooer: [*After Man* by Dougal Dixon] flightless chiropteran with flower-like nose and ears

floridaceras: [*After the Dinosaurs* by Donald R. Prothero] acerathere from Miocene

floundder: [flounder backformation] flounder-like amphibian

flounddeer: [flounder backformation] deer-like floundder

flove: [flight of doves spoonerism] ornithoid that coos

flower-faced snouter: [*The Snouters* by Harald Stümpke] snouter with petaled nasarium in long stem-like tails, short-tailed and tail-less varieties from mountains of Mitadina, Hi-Yi-Yi Islands, Terra (alpha Zodiaci III)

flowercat: ["The Last General" by H. G. Francis] felinoid from Lyberjan IV

flox: [portmanteau] see flying-fox

flub-a-dub: ["The Howdy Doody Show"] octochimera from eight animals with spaniel's ears, cat's whiskers, duck's bill, giraffe's neck, dachshund's torso, seal's flippers and elephant's memory

flügelhorner: [trumpeter swan backformation] swan-like ornithoid with flügelhorn-like call

flugskerne: [*Star of Astarte* by Hans Kneifel] predator of anchorwhip snake from Venus (alpha Zodiaci II)

flumsh: [*Sugar and Spike* #90] 9-meter long, 6-meter tall dracoid, pink with blue spots, red crest and back plates, fangs, yellow forehead horn, vestigial yellow wings, 4 short legs, with forked red tongue, able to fix anything (by touch chronoplasty)

flunkey: [*After Man* by Dougal Dixon] gliding simian

flunlin: [fling of dunlins] brown and white sandpiper-like ornithoid

flunnel: [*On Beyond Zebra* by Theodore Seuss Geissel] 1.1-meter bushy-tailed megapod with long ears and neck with double collar and two-fingered forepaws

flunnelope: [flunnel antelope portmanteau] flunnel with antlers, see jackalope

flusshai: ["Battle of Ferrol" by Michael Marcus Thurner] dangerous predator from Ferrol (Vega (alpha Lyrae) VIII)

flustard: [*If I Ran the Zoo* by Theodore Seuss Geissel] horn-less, yellow giraffe-cat from the Zombo-ma-Tant Mts.

fluster: [Terra Monster] long-tailed yellow hexapod with brown extremities from Terrarium, see mothball, motharch

fluter: [trumpeter swan backformation] tuba swan-like ornithoid with flute-like call, see fipper

flutter crab: ["Fighter for Garbesh" by H. G. Ewers] small, dark brown crustacean from Arpa Chai (Wahiat II)

flutter monkey: ["The World of the Disembodied "and "Flagship in Need" by H. G. Ewers] small simian with leathery wings, hands, glowing golden eyes, black lips, songbird-like voice with from Pigell (Vega (alpha Lyrae) VI)

flutter valve: ["Return of the *Sol*" by H. G. Francis] creature from Ovaron's world, Finder Maelstrom between Ploohn-Nabyl and Mahagoul galaxies

flutterbird: [*The Future Is Wild* by Dougal Dixon] tropical petrel-like ornithoid that includes roachcutter, spitfire, false spitfire, etc.

flutterfly: [flutter of butterflies spoonerism] yellow-winged insectoid

flutternatter: ["The Cathedral of Rhoarx" by Michael Marcus Tharn] flying creature from Dwingloo galaxy

flying fish: [Xanth series by Piers Anthony] jet-propelled, rigid finned ichthyopteryx from Xanth or [Xanthia mondegreen] Xa, Thia system

flyingfish: [Odd Squad: Sector 21] aka ichthyopteryx, see hovering haddock

fly-man: ["The Fly" by George Langenlaan] fly-headed anthropoid, sometimes also with fly's leg

fly-fisher: [fly fishing backformation] carnivorous pegasoid with insectoid wings and dark brown fur

flyg: [*Worlds Apart: Nat. Hist. of Furaha and Earth* by Souren Nyoroge] short snake-like dracoid with 4 wings with 45-cm wingspan, males gold and blue, females brown and gray from Furaha (alpha Phoenicis IV)

flygator: [flyg alligator portmanteau] alligator-like predator whose bite morphs victim into flyg

flying ape: ["The Confrontation" by H. G. Francis] bluish ichthyopteryx with small arms from Gaea (Prov III), Provcon Fist nebula

flying bear: see ursapteryx

flying frog: see batrachopteryx

flying frogator: [flying frog alligator portmanteau] alligator-like predator whose bite morphs victim into flying frog

flying grizzly: [*The World of Synnabarr* by Raymond C. S. McCracken] geneered grizzly bear cyban with feathered wings and lazer-eyes from Synnabarr (fka Mars (alpha Zodiaci IV)

flying sheep: [Xanth series by Piers Anthony] ovinopteryx from Xanth

flying snake: [Xanth series by Piers Anthony] sometimes poisonous herpetopteryx related to dragons from Xanth

flying snow otter: lutrapteryx adapted to cold from Sappire (Eno III), Galaxiki galaxy

flying threat: ["Flying Threat" by David H. Keller] plane-sized insectoid

flying-fox: [flying fox mondegreen] see vulpopteryx

fnetar: ["Shadows over Ferrol" by Hermann Ritter] furry farm animal

fo: [bufo mondegreen] lavender toad-like batrachian

fog-eater: see grava

foklom: [*The Spawn of Fashan* by Kirby Lee Davis] creature from Boosboodle

folding eel: ["Exile of the Oracle" by Michael Marcus Thurner] toxic, snake-like ichthyoid from Baikhal (Cain V)

fond-crested eagle: [*Hitchhiker's Guide to the Galaxy* by Douglas Adams] eagle-like desert ornithoid noted for paper mâché nests from Damogran

Foochow dog: [*Boris Karloff's Tales of Mystery* #48: "The Laughing Dog of Foochow"] giant dog, deadly even blindfolded

food-beast: [*Titan* by Jack Vance] beast used for food

foodcock: [fall of woodcocks spoonerism, foodhen antonym] edible rooster-salmon-like ichthyopteryx

foodhen: [foodcock antonym, extrapolation] edible variety of hen (chicken-salmon) ichthyopteryx

fogg: [foggy backformation] fog-like cloud crature

foggator: [fogg alligator portmanteau] alligator predator whose bite morphs victim into fogg

footpad: ["Mortal Nature" by Stephen Dedman] greenish ambush predator with huge soft paw and algae symbiot in fur from Northbergen

footworm: larger variety of inchworm with twelve segments

forfi: [James Cooke Brown's Loglan fo fitpi (four feet) compound] quadruped from Logla, Brown's system

fork fish: [knife fish extrapolation] swordfish-like ichthyoid with forked "sword"

forkafi: [James Cooke Brown's Loglan forka ficli] fork fish from Logla, Brown's system

formaldé: [formaldehyde mondegreen] orcature noted for preservative hide

formisaur: [*The New Dinosaurs* by Dougal Dixon] ant-like dinosaur

forntarch: [*Planets of the Galaxy* by Greg Farshtey, Bill Smith, Ed Stark] carnivorous, arboreal rodentoid with razor-sharp forecraws from Gorsh, Jedi galaxy

floshawk: [flight of goshawks spoonerism, flying goshawk portmanteau] leg-less, murre-goshawk-like ornithoid

forsorlu: [James Cooke Brown's Loglan fo sorlu (four ear) compound] four-eared earwalkerfrom Logla, Brown's system

fossa: [*National Geographic Encyclopedia of Animals*] feline predator of lemurs from Madagascar, Terra (alpha Zodiaci III)

fortcela: [James Cooke Brown's Loglan fo tcela (four wing) compound] four-winged dracoid from Logla, Brown's system

fotserpi: [James Cooke Brown's Loglan fotpa serpi] fatsnake from Logla, Brown's system

Fouke monster: [*Monster Spotter's Guide to North America* by Scott Francis, "The Legend of Boggy Creek"] 3-meter, 3-toed amphibious gigantanthropoid from Sulphur River, Arkansas, Terra (alpha Zodiaci III)

fouligator: [Terra Monsters] malodorous, black, bipedal, swamp-dwelling reptilian with yellow underbelly and white-striped bushy tail, see allistinker, from Terrarium

four-ear: [tailwalker extrapolation] earwalker with 4 long ears adapted for walking from Hi-yi-yi Islands

4-F virus: [F-4 virus extrapolation] virus that leaves survivors unable to fight

four-headed snake: [John Gorraeus] snake with 4 heads from Ceylon, Terra (alpha Zodiaci III)

four-mouth: ["The Wondrous Works of His Hands" by Jayge Carr] noted for great appetite from Thuban (alpha Draconis) system

four-tail: [tailwalker extrapolation] tailwalker adapted to walking on 4 prehensile tails from Hi-yi-yi Islands

four-winged bat: [Scanodonian bat mondegreen] 4-winged cheiropteran from Sca, Odo system

tourth mast: see big mast

fouse: [fieldmouse spoonerism] burrowing rodentoid pest

fox-bear: [*Island of Dr. Moreau* by Herbert George Wells] fox-headed ursinoid mutant

fox-fish: [Church of Zillis] fox-headed vulpichthyoid

fox-hound: [foxhound mondegreen] fox-headed hound dog

fox-snake: [fox snake mondegreen] fox-headed snake

fox-squirrel: [fox squirrel mondegreen] fox-headed squirrel

fox-swallow: [fox swallow mondegreen] vulpopteryx with fox-like head and swallow-like body

foxfirefly: [foxfire-firefly portmanteau] bioluminescent flyingfox-like creature

foxpaw: [Terra Monster] purple fox, see pranktail, from Terrarium

fragon: [fire dragon spoonerism] dire-like dracoid

frallop: [*Earth in Twilight* by Doris Piserchia] jungle-dwelling mutant
francolin: [*National Geographic Encyclopedia of Animals*] chicken relative from Middle East and Asia, Terra (alpha Zodiaci III)
frankenfish: ["Frankenfish" by Simon Barrett, Scott Clevenger] monstrous fish
frankenstoat: ["Frankenstoat" by Leigh Loveday] monstrous stoat
frankenswine: [*Mirabile* by Janet Kagan] monstrous porcoid from Dragon's Tooth
frankilla: [Terra Monsters] greenish, electric pongoid, see gorillastein, from Terrarium
frayoomnairo: [Mushroom Planet series by Eleanor Cameron] egg-sized mushroom-like creature from Basidium (Soll IIIc)
freezard: [The Legend of Zelda] cold-breathing dracoid which when shot shatters into 2 to 5 mini-freezards from Hyrule
frelimard: [Continuum] 3-meter giant dragonfly from Idengal, Belverius Helenis system
frell: ["The Wreck of the Godspeed" by James Patrick Kelly] food animal from which sausage is made on Harvest
frella: ["Prince of Peril" by Otis Adelbert Kline] hairless sheep-like food animal from Zarovia (Venus (alpha Zodiaci II))
frellope: [frell antelope portmanteau] frell with antlers
freshwater shark: [Resident Evil] genineered ichthyoid from Racoon University
fretro: [Star Frontiers] large, 4-eyed, green-haired carnivore from Artule
fried-egg jellyfish: ["The Worm Turns" by Gregory Benford] space creature like both fried egg and jellyfish from HD209458 system
frier: [Xanth series by Piers Anthony] hen that lays fried eggs from Xanth
fris bee: [Xanth series by Piers Anthony] disc-shaped, striped honey-producing insectoid that spins as it flies from Xanth
fristigo: ["Investments" by Walter John Williams] food animal
frizzap: [Outernauts] mature frizzee
frizzee: [frizzy mondegreen, Outernauts] long-legged llama-like creature. see frizzap, fuzzoo

frizzer: [frizze backformation] predator that electrocutes and frizzes hair of prey
frog-dog: caninoid with batrachian head, see worrt
frog-dogator: [frog-dog alligator portmanteau] alligator-like predator whose bite morphs victim into frog-dog
frogator: [frog alligator portmanteau] alligator-like predator whose bite morphs victim into frog-dog
frogg: [froggy backformation] batrachoid
froggator: [frogg alligator portmanteau] alligator predator whose bite morphs victim into frogg
frogger: ["Seed of Reason" by Daniel Hatch] animal from Chamal
frog-man: [frog man mondegreen] frog-headed anthropoid
frogmouth: [*National Geographic Encyclopedia of Animals*] predatory bird of S. W. Pacific, Terra (alpha Zodiaci III)
frôlion: [Code Lyoko] geneered leg-less, 10-winged mosquitoid with laser-stinger and poison-spitting proboscis
fromp: [*Edge Chronicles* by Paul Stewart and Chris Riddell] creature with striped, prehensile tail, curving claws, proboscis, rabbit-like ears, comical warning shutter-cough (except giant fromp) from Edgeworld, Cerulea system
froodle: [French poodle spoonerism] caninoid with thick curly hair from Pench system
froopflap: [Outernauts] mature froopie
froopie: [Outernauts] green sea creature with lure stalk, see froopy, froopflap
froopy: [Outernauts] immature froopie
frosaur: [frozen dinosaur portmanteau, Outernauts] mature, plump frozodon
frost beast: ["The Ordeals of Dimension Z" by Leo Dorfman] beastly cold-adapted creature from Z dimension
frost worm: [*Monster Manual* by Gary Gygax] worm-like dracoid with armored head, black spider-like eyes, able to freeze nearby with mandibles or paralyze more distant with howl

frothing trumpet snouter: [*The Snouters* by Harald Stümpke] variety of trumpet snouter that uses froth to hide and capture prey from Hi-Yi-Yi Islands, Terra (alpha Zodiaci III)
frozard: [frozen lizard portmanteau, Outernauts] immature, lean frozodon
frozodon: [Outernauts] reptilian with bushy, bluish tail, toothed beak, see frozard, frosaur
frozzilla: [Outernauts] mature frozzling with three eyes, 1 antenna
frozzling: [Outernauts] greenish blob with 2 eyes, 1 antenna, see frozzo, frozzilla
frozzlingator: [frozzling alligator portmanteau] alligator-like predator whose bite morphs victim into frozzling
frozzo: [Outernauts] immature frozzling with 1 eye, 1 antenna
frroh: [i-less ifirroh] mutant cave pongoid
frunch: [free lunch portmanteau] ornithoid that nests only on windward cliffs
frutwux: [*The Unofficial Questarian Guide*] aka bloodtick, food insectoid from Tev'meck, Warvan system
fu t'ou: [*Dragon's Honor* by Kij Johnson and Greg Cox] wagon-pulling herbivore from Pai, Dragon nebula
fu-hsi: ox-headed snake
fud: [Maltese qanfud mondegreen] hedgehog-like burrower from Qa system
fudnik: [*Tears of the Oracle* by Justin Richards] parasitic creature that feeds on host's fud [fear, uncertainty and doubt] and on non-host's lifeforce from Paracletes
fugl: [Danish sommerfugl mondegreen] bird-mimicking butterfly
fugu: [*Dell Crossword Puzzle Dictionary*] fish from Japan, Terra (alpha Zodiaci III), see tai
fujarabird: [trumpeter swan backformation] flute swan-like ornithoid with fujara-like call from Wintria, Pfetea system, Galaxiki galaxy
fulmar: [*National Geographic Encyclopedia of Animals*] long-lived sea bird, [*Dell Crossword Puzzle Dictionary*] sea bird, see ern(e), gull, skua, scaup, tern, gannet, petrel, scoter

fumado: [*Dell Crossword Puzzle Dictionary*] see pilchard, sardine
funazz: [Aliens in the Family: "You Don't Have to Be a Pet to Be Popular"] pet from Harnaz
fungaxx: [Outernauts] 'shroom-headed slug from Guinica, see fungoo
fungoo: [Outernauts] immature fungaxx
Fuolornis fire dragon: [Hitchhiker's Guide to the Galaxy series by Douglas Adams] salamander-like dracoid hunted to extinction as alleged aphrodisiac from Brequinda
fuoma: ornithoid with flowery tail, conical beak and antler-like crest from Terropas
furbee: [furby backformation] fuzzy bee-like insectoid
furby: [Tiger Electronics] small, furry creature with yellow beak, long ears
furiosa kato: [Thousand Stars] aggressive feline from Noxind
furmid: [Fr. Johann Martin Schleyer's Volapük] ant-like insectoid from Schleyer's system
furmo: [Outernauts] see smoof, slowrax
furnoc: [*Creatures of the Galaxy* by Phil Drucato, Bill Smith, Rick D. Stuart, Chuck Truett] pack hunting sauroid from Geston, Jedi galaxy
furry crab: [*Shards of Honor* by Lois McMaster Bujold] many-legged creature with yellow, razor-sharp beak and 4 beady eyes
furry scorpion: scorpion-like crustacean with fur from Aren, Galaxiki galaxy
fursnake: [Robot Hugs] furry boa-like snake
fusa: [Maltese hanfusa backformation] beetle-like insectoid from Ha system
fusorian: [*The Reefs of Space* by Frederik Pohl and Jack Williamson] single-cell interstellar space dweller that fuses free hydrogen into heavier elements forming the Reefs of Space
fuster: [Catalan ocell fuster mondegreen] woodpecker-like ornithoid
fususaur: [*The New Dinosaurs* by Dougal Dixon] burrowing dinosaur like sandle
fuzzoo: [Outernauts] short-legged, electric spheroidal, immature frizzee

fuzzy crab: [*Shards of Honor* by Lois McMaster Bujold] vampiric balloon-like spheroid with maroon tentacles

fvai: [pl. fvaiin, *The Romulan Way* by Terisa Halekala-LoBrotto, *The Disinherited* by Diane Duane and Peter Morwood] pet from ch'Rihan, Eisn (128 Trianguli) system

fwoilto: [Fwoumies' zoilto spoonerism] food animal from Zoumi system

fwooper: [*Fantastic Beasts and Where to Find Them* by Newton Artemis Fido Scamander] brightly-colored bird with maddening song (fwoop) from Africa, Terra (alpha Zodiaci III)

fworm: [puffworm mondegreen] puf larva

fynock: [*Creatures of the Galaxy* by Phil Brucato, Bill Smith, Rick D. Stuart, Chuck Truett] leg-less murre-like ornithoid with snake-like tail, face suckers from Talus, Jedi galaxy

G-larva: [Resident Evil] parasite that morphs host into G-type mutant (acid-spitting, clawing, burrower with many tentacles and teeth)

ga: [changa mondegreen] mole-cricket from Cha system; [Filipino tanga mondegreen, sage gas palindrome] gray-green moth-like insectoid from Ta; [Indonesian/Malay serangga mondegreen] insectoid from Sera, [Stardrift Empires Nova] or system 416, Third galaxy

gaarnokh: [Flandry series by Poul Anderson] horned creature from Starkad

gaasyendietha: [Seneca, "Sea Serpents of Canada" by Charles Alexander Moffat] hellfire-breathing, fresh-water dragon that leaves a firetrail from Canada, Terra (alpha Zodiaci III)

gabbledictum: ["Space Patrol" series] voice-mimicking parrot-like ornithoid from Mars (alpha Zodiaci IV), see lazoon

gabey: [mangabey mondegreen] simian from Ma system

gaccoon: [gaze of raccoons, gah raccoon portmanteau] rabbit-raccoon-like burrower

gagh: ["A Matter of Honor" by Wanda M. Haight, Gregory Amos and Burton Armus] "serpent worms" by Klingons eaten either live or stewed from Qonos

gagria: [Hildegard of Bingen's Lingua Ignota] goose-like ornithgoid from Ignota, Hildegard's system

gah: [Navaho] rabbit-like burrower from Diné system

gaid: [*Book of Dreams* by Jack Vance] 6-meter ichthyoid with luminifer-tipped dorsal spines from Aloysius

gaija beast: [Malibu Deep Space 9 #21: "Fadeout"] large, furry, purple beast

gajasimha: [Sinhalese] monstrous elephant-lion from Sri Lanka, Terra (alpha Zodiaci III), see gajavirāla

gajavirāla: monster with lion and elephant characteristics, see gajasimha

galaga: [*The Yowie: In Seach of Australian Bigfoot* by Tony Healy and Paul Cropper] see yowie

galago: [*National Geographic Encyclopedia of Animals*] "bush babies", small lemur with large, pointy ears from Africa, Terra (alpha Zodiaci III)

galané: ["The First Thort" by Michelle Stern] orange fruit-eating chiropteran with triangular body from Zarbik, moon of Groll, Vega (alpha Lyrae) system

gale: [gam of whales spoonerism] see blackengale, bitingale, dorthygale, ightengale, whitengale

galegi: [Cherokee] blacksnake from Tsalagi system

galiva: [Continuum] 8-meter sea crocodilian from Amarillon, Nogullon system

gallimimus: ["fowl-mimic", Feathered Dinosaurs: The Origin of Birds by John Long and Peter Schuten] 6-meter, 440-kg ornithomimosaur with short arms, toothless beak

galliwumpus: [Samuel "O. Henry" Porter] mammal with backfin and 18 toes

galliwumpuss: [galliwumpus puss portmanteau] felinoid with backfin and 18 toes

galloro: [Catalan gall-lloro portmanteau] gull-parrot, bright-colored sea ornithoid

gallynipper: large mosquito that nips gallies

galo: [bugalo mondegreen] lavender milkbeetle

galoomp: ["The Gungan Frontier" by Chris McCubbin] rattle-tailed, hoofed, herbivorous bipedal reptilian mammaloid from Tatooine, Jedi galaxy

galschia: [Hildegard of Bingen's Lingua Ignota] dove-like ornithoid from Ignota, Hildegard's system

galuisdi: [Cherokee] bedbug-like insect from Tsalagi system

galumpf: [*The Invasion of the Planet Wampetter* by Samuel H. Pillsbury] steed with colored spirals and wing-like spray from Lake Wacawawawoo, Wampetter

galushaceras: [*After the Dinosaurs* by Donald R. Prothero] acerathere from Miocene

gam: [magnolia ailon gam, telemagenta atne gam elet, magenta atne gam, magic mint nimci gam palindromes] whitish ailon, purplish-red atne or greenish nimci, see elet

gamelon: ["Camping with Xavier" by Steve Poling] beast from Bunyan

gamera: ["Gamera the Invisible" by Nizo Takahashi] 60-meter energy-eating, green-blooded, space tortoise with nearly invulnerable carapace, upward-pointing tusks, flyes by retracting legs and shooting jets of 2 or 4 legholes

gamoo: [kangamoo mondegreen] milk-producing macropodan from Ka system

gan: [game swan portmanteau, game of swans spoonerism] long-necked game ornithoid, see gargan

gan ceann: [Ire. "without head"] headless horse, see ceann

gananoid: [*The First Kingdom* by Jack Katz] very long necked quadruped

ganbalea: [Basque ganba-balea portmanteau] prawn-whale, crustacean-eating cetacean

gandder: [gander mondegreen] goose-like predator that gandds

gandimat: [*After Man* by Dougal Dixon] skua-like magpie

ganjuko: [*Creatures of the Galaxy* by Phil Brucato, Bill Smith, Rick D. Stuart, Chuck Truett] 3-5-meter tall, furry predator with thick skullplate and beak from Filve sector and Bothan worlds, Jedi galaxy

Gankarian auroch: [*Our Man in Space* by Kurt Mahr] wild auroch-like creature from Gankar

ganna: [Irish meánranganna mondegreen] locust-like insectoid from Ra, Mea system

gannet: [*National Geographic Encyclopedia of Animals*] sea bird from N. Atlantic, Terra (alpha Zodiaci III), [*Dell Crossword Puzzle Dictionary*] sea bird, see ern(e), gull, skua, scaup, tern, fulmar, petrel, scoter

gannetwhale: [*The Future Is Wild* by Dougal Dixon] walrus-like flightless seabird

gantala: [i-less giantala] giant sloth-like cave megapod from Friatica, Friaticalida system, Galaxiki galaxy

ganute: [*Earth in Twilight* by Doris Piserchia] 3-eyed, black, wooly, blue-mouthed jungle-dwelling mutant

ganzer: ["Mindswap" by Robert Sheckley] egg-layer from Melde II

gyaos: ["Gamera vs. Gyaos" aka "Return of the Giant Monsters" by Fumi Takahashi] 61-meter tall nocturnal biped with small, powerful claws, flat bird-like head, stiff neck, leathery wings, big yellow eyes with red irises, bright pink blood, able to shoot destructive yellow sonic beam from double throat, regenerate injured body parts, put out fires with yellow vapor, but vulnerable to ultraviolet light

gappa: ["Gappa, the Triphibian Monster", aka "Monster from a Prehistoric Planet" by Iwao Yamazak and Ryuzo Nakanishi] 90-meter bipedal hellfire-breathing dracoid with bat-like wings, fat horn, beak

gar: ["gar at times emit tarag" palindrome] sabre-toothed tiger gestalt; [Icelandic mangar mondegreen] mongoose-like burrower, related to goest, gosta, gouste, gust, gusta, gustë, gustiniai, gusto, hust, from Ma system [*Dell Crossword Puzzle Dictionary*] needlefish

gara: [tjangara mondegreen] pongoid from Tja system

Garanian bolite: ["A Man Alone" by Michael Pillar] bolide from Garan

garbill: [*Dell Crossword Puzzle Dictionary*] merganser duck, see smew

garboyl: [Super Smash Bros.] harmless pokémon

gardaix: [Catalan llangardaix mondegreen] reptilian from Lla system

gardenworm: [*The Future Is Wild* by Dougal Dixon] 45-cm crevice-dwelling polychaete (bristleworm) with fern-like algae-filled "branches" able to dissolve terabyte glue

gardon: ["Teenagers from Outer Space" by Tom Graeff] lobster-like crustacean that feeds on air and people

garel-orum: [*On Beyond Zebra* by Theodore Seuss Geissel] 10-meter biped with whiskers, collar

garf: [garfish backformation] garfish mimic

garg-worm: [*Reteif to the Rescue* by Keith Laumer] worm-like source of garg, food of the Ynnezadoogians

gargan: [*The Dirdir, The Pnume* by Jack Vance] game ornithoid from Sibol, see gan

gargoyle: [*Fabulous Beasts and Demons* by Heinz Mode] dragon-monster golem that turns back to stone when exposed to sunlight

Garko gas creature: ["Supergirl's Fortress of Solitude" by Jerry Siegel] gaseous creature from Garko

garkurma: [James Cooke Brown's Loglan gardi kurma compound] gardenworm from Logla, Brown's system

garliktho: scaly, flying dracoid

garn: [Dutch garnaal mondegreen] prawn-eel, shelled, serpentine ichthyoid

garoo: [kangaroo mondegreen] megapod from Ka system

garooster: [kangarooster mondegreen] large, flightless ornithoid with large hopping legs from Ka system

garral: [*Creatures of the Galaxy* by Phil Brucato, Bill Smith, Rick D. Stuart, Chuck Truett] wolf-like caninoid from Wayland and Chalganna, Jedi galaxy

garralope: [garrol antelope portmanteau] garrol with antlers

garro: [Basque birigarro, oilagarro mondegreen] thrush/woodcock-like ornithoid ancestral to oila and woodcock

gart(r)o: [*Creatures of the Galaxy* by Phil Brucato, Bill Smith, Rick D. Stuart, Chuck Truett] small, harmless, omnivorous ornithoid with bat-like wings, spiked tails and teeth from Coruscant, Jedi galaxy

garthim: [*The Dark Crystal* by Jim Henson] vicious, black-shelled crustacean with no internal organs animated by the Skeksis

garthok: [*Coneheads* by Tom Davies and Dan Aykroyd] elephantine hexapod with spiked tail from Remulak, Cone nebula

gartuo: [Crayola outrageous uoe gartuo palindrome] orange male uoe from Crayol A

garuda: [Hindu] large, eagle-like bird with white face, red wings and golden body

garudimimus: [*Feathered Dinosaurs: The Origin of Birds* by John Long and Peter Schuten] 3-meter toothless ornithomimosaur without toeclaw

garue: [kangarue mondegreen] blue variety of garooster from Ka system

gase: [*There's a Wocket in My Pocket* by Theodore Seuss Geissel] 60-cm yellow biped with pink collar and cuff fringe

gashadokuro: [Mighty Morphin Power Rangers] 23-meter bone golem detected by ringing-in-ear sound from Japan, Terra (alpha Zodiaci III)

gashant: [Space: 1889 RPG] 2.5-meter bipedal iguana-like steed with eagle-like beak from Mars (alpha Zodiaci IV)

gastornis: [*After the Dinosaurs* by Donald R. Prothero] large flightless "terror crane" from Paleocene, related to diatryma

gastropod: [*Dell Crossword Puzzle Dictionary*] snail, abalone

gata: [Filipino ngumagata mondegreen] felinoid ruminant from Nguma; [*Dell Crossword Puzzle Dictionary*] nurse shark

gathra: [*Fiend Folio* 3rd Ed.] dangerous black bovinoid beast of burden with boar-like head, inward-curving horns, straight upward-pointing tusks from Avernus, Bantor

gator: [-gator compounds] alligator-like predator whose bite morphs victim from Bloomsla, Boomsla, Da, Dada, Doomfa, Dra, Fa, Fenghua, Ha, Meringueua, Pta, Sa,

Salada, Selada, Siama, Sla, Slada, Sra, Tentafa, Tha, Tikbala and Ua systems, see gator gar

gator gar: [*A History of Fishes* by J. R. Norman, [*River Monsters* by Jeremy Wade] 12-meter "very despised, hated fish"; gar-like ichthyoid whose bite morphs victim into gator

gatoroid: ["Megapython vs. Gatoroid" by Naomi I. Selfman] giant alligator

gatortoise: [alligator-tortoise portmanteau] amphibious sauroid with high, rounded carapace, powerful jaws

gau: [Indonesian/Malay bangau mondegreen] heron-like ornithoid from Ba

gaudybird: [*Palace without Chairs* by Brigid Brody] aka bobby-dazzler, brightly-colored finch from Evarchia, Balkan penisula, Terra (alpha Zodiaci III)

gaunch: [Wyst: Alastor 1716 by Jack Vance] forest monster from Wyst

gauntling: [*Frostworld* and *Dreamfire* by John Morressy] river creature from Hraggcllon (Duruos II)

guantlingator: [guauntling alligator portmanteau] alligator-like predator whose bite morphs victim into guantling

gaur: [*Dell Crossword Puzzle Dictionary*] wild ox from India, see gour, zebu, gayal, s(a/e)ladang

gava: [savage gavas palindrome] dangerous predator

gavinger pudding: [Langavinger pudding mondegreen] pudding-thick ooze that gavings from La system

gaviocetus: [*After the Dinosaurs* by Donald R. Prothero] whale ancestor related to takracetus and basilosaur

gaya: ["Shadow Lord" by Laurence Yep] long-haired, 3-meter long goat-like herd creature from Angira; [tsasgaya mondegreen] yellowjacket-like insectoid from Tsa system

gayal: [*Dell Crossword Puzzle Dictionary*] wild ox from India, Terra (alpha Zodiaci III), see gaur, gour, zebu

gayalope: [gayal antelope portmanteau] gayal with antlers

gaylor: [Armenian gayl-lor portmanteau] wolf-quail, pack-hunting, predatory quail-like ornithoid

gazanggh: [Armenian gazan-anggh portmanteau] beast-vulture, vulture-like griffinoid that eats both dead and living

Gazanian salamander: ["The Last Tribble" by Kevin L. Davis] salamander-like creature that both crawls and slides from Gazania

gazolt: [Terra Monster] small buzzgrass grazer, see volteer and shadowvolt, from Terrarium

gazun: [Hildegard of Bingen's Lingua Ignota] hen-like ornithoid from Ignota, Hildegard's system

gë: [Albanian merinangë mondegreen] arachnoid from Merina system

ge: [ge leg palindrome] food ornithoid; [Norwegian slange mondegreen] serpentoid from Sla system

gebird: [-orangebird mondegreens] chameleon-like ornithoid that can become any color of the rainbow from Ora system

Geerb ox: [gearbox mondegreen] noisy ox-like bovine from Geerb system

gecobra: [gecko-cobra portmanteau] small venomous sauroid with padded suction-cup feet and flattened hood

ged(d): [*Dell Crossword Puzzle Dictionary*] pike from Scotland, Terra (alpha Zodiaci III)

geegy: ["Vengence on Varos" by Phillip Martin] fly-like insectoid from Varos, Cetus constellation

geejaw: ["The Gungan Frontier" by Chris McCubbin] bat-winged, large-beaked small insectovorous ornithoid that mimics other ornithoids from Naboo and Endor's moon, Jedi galaxy

geeling: [*If I Ran the Zoo* by Theodore Seuss Geissel] green biped with yellow collar, long ears

geelingator: [geeling alligator portmanteau] alligator-like predator whose bite morphs victim into geeling

gëemadhe: [Albanian merinagë e madhe mondegreen] tarantula-like arachnoid from Merina system

gekko: [OviPets] egg-laying geckoid
gekkoe: [Dutch gekko-koe portmanteau] gecko-cow, milk reptilian
gel: [The Legend of Zelda] 2-eyed blob, in ambushing green and slow, red dividing varieties, related to chuchus and zol, from Hyrule; [xac-gel mondegreen] xac-gel ancestor
gelagrub: [*Creatures of the Galaxy* by Phil Brucato, Bill Smith, Rick D. Stuart, Chuck Truett] large, beetle-like insectoid from Felucia, Jedi galaxy
gelatinous cube: ["The Ecology of the Gelatinous Cube" by Ed Greenwood] jelly-thick cubical ooze, related to qyoob
geldarm: [Jap. gerudoaamu, *The Legend of Zelda*] large, vertical-attacking sand worm from Hyrule
gelk: [gang of elks] antlered ruminant
gen: [Fr. Johann Martin Schleyer's Volapük] goose-like ornithoid from Schleyer's system
genasaur: [*The Mistaken Extinction* by Lowell Dingus and Timothy Rowe] cerapod ancestor
generowl: [Terra Monster] large, eagle-like ornithoid with armored head, see hootenant, from Terrarium
genet(te): [*Dell Crossword Puzzle Dictionary*] small horse, aka jennet
genser: ["A Final Unity" by Spectrum HoloByte] creature geneered Dr. Vi Hynh-Foertsh from Morassia (epsilon Chysule II)
gentoo: [*National Geographic Encyclopedia of Animals*] fast-swimming variety of penguin
genyornis: flightless bird
gep: [German shepherd spoonerism mondegreen] herding caninoid from Sherma system
ger: [granger mondegreen] caninoid from Gra system; [snozzwanger mondegreen] creature with unique snout from Snozzwa system; [Vanger mondegreen] cormorant-like triphibian from Va system
gerblin: gerbil-like rodentoid from Naic III, Galaxiki galaxy
gerbull: [gerbil-bull portmanteau] small, long-tailed rodentoid with horns

gerde: [wine dregs gerde niw palindrome] brownish red niw prey
gerenuk: [*National Geographic Encyclopedia of Animals*, Somali "giraffe-necked"] long-legged, long-necked gazelle from Somalia, Terra (alpha Zodiaci III)
gernaute: [*Alter Ego* ed. by Patrick and Michael Phillips, Eric Lautier. Bernard Jullian, Jean-René Jelteon] geneered gerbil-like companion
gerrymander: [Elbridge Gerry] large, monstrous salamander-like dracoid
gestalt: many creatures acting as one; [*The New Dinosaurs* by Dougal Dixon] black arbrosaur with white spots and sensory hairs, whose 1-meter queen lays 10 eggs per 10 days in thatched nest for each poisonous head-spined male, see formisaur (ant-lizard)
get: [i-less iget, igeti] cave-dwelling ape-stingray
geta: [Armenian getadzi mondegreen] hippopotamus-horse amphibian
gettle: ["Chain of Command" by Frank Abatemarco] wild herd creature from Cardassia
Gevaudan beast: [gevaudathere, *Unexplained!* by Jerome Clark] cow-sized hyena-like wolf/warg
gewey: [Atbash] see re'em, unicorn
ghair: [*There's a Wocket in My Pocket* by Theodore Seuss Geissel] 2-meter, canine with curly green fur, long ears and very long tail and yellow tuff
ghastly: [Xanth series by Piers Anthony] slimy, nearly indestructible creature that looks like a squashed caterpillar with many legs and tentacles that bites, belches and spits purple venom from Xanth
ghastozar: [Callisto series by Lin Carter] seagull-sized flying predator from Thanator
ghat: ["Lost Sorceress of the Silent Citadel" by Michael Moorcock] scaly creature from Mars (alpha Zodiaci IV)
ghee: [Outernauts] immature ghiroo

gherkin: [*If I Ran the Zoo* by Theodore Seuss Giessel] 1.5-meter cloven-hooved, yellow quadruped with orange spots, mustache and T-shaped antlers

ghest: [*Creatures of the Galaxy* by Phil Brucato, Bill Smith, Rick D. Stuart, Chuck Truett] large, reptilian predator of swamps of Rodia, Jedi galaxy

ghidorah: ["Ghidrah" by Shinichi Sekizawa] 14-meter tall, 3-headed, long-necked dracoid with leathery wings, back spines, 2 tails, golden scales, able to spit lightning

ghiroo: [Outernauts] phantom with orange eye, bat wings, short arms, see ghee, ghyst

ghoat: [ghost goat portmanteau] ultradimensional goat-like ruminant

ghole: ["Vaster Than Empires and More Slow" by Ursula K. LeGuin] experimental creature from Hain; [*After Man* by Dougal Dixon] bone-eating mammal

ghost waif: [*Edge Chronicles* by Paul Stewart and Chris Riddell] thin, pale waif with very long barbels

ghost-jelly: [*Starcross* by Philip Reeve] ghostly, jellyfish like space-dwelling creature

ghyst: [Outernauts] winged, tailed mature ghiroo

gi: [Cherokee Tsalagi mondegreen] monkey-like simian from Giyía system; [golbangi mondegreen] snail-like 2-D creature from Golba system; [Haitian zangi mondegreen] eel-like ichthyoid from Za system; [ignatni ananymondegreen] electric sphere from Inta system

gi'i: [Cyclopedia of Worlds] sulfide-based animal with long, multi-branched jaws, lined with hard, sharp scraping teeth from Omuch, T'Canidew system

giant bee: [*Mysterious Island* by Jules Verne, gigantapis; [*The Scarlet Empress* by Paul Magrs] honey-producing insectoid from Hyspero

giant bird: [*Last Man Running* by Chris Boucher] giant ornithoid from Lentic empire

giant bird louse: [*Last Man Running* by Chris Boucher] giant louse-like insectoid on giant ornithoids from Lentic empire

giant claw: ["The Giant Claw" by Samuel Newman and Paul Gargelin] vulture-like ornithoid with 60-meter wingspan, pear-shaped body, long neck, large head protected by antimatter shield but neutralizable by muon beam

giant duck: [Madnight Movies: "It Quacked the World"] giant duck-like ornithoid, related to hadrosaur

giant electric penguin: [Monty Python's Flying Circus: "Scott of the Sahara" 6-meter tall desert-dwelling penguin-like biped with glowing eyes and 2 long green tentacles from Sahara, Terra (alpha Zodiaci III)

giant fly: [Avatar: The Last Airbender: "The Swamp"] brown-green, flight-less, edible fruitfly with red eyes, small translucent wings, 8 legs

giant hornet: [You Might Be A Zombie and Other Bad News] large hornet that sprays flesh-eating acid-phermone from Japan, Terra (alpha Zodiaci III)

giant jellyfish: [Voyage to the Bottom of the Sea: "Graveyard of Fear" by Robert Vincent Wright, "No Escape from Death" by William Welch] very large jellyfish

giant leech: ["Attack of the Giant Leeches" by Leo Gordon] very large, blood-sucking leech

giant llam: [small llams palindrome, llama contraction] large variety of lamb-headed llama-like ruminant

giant mousaka: ["Attack of the Giant Mousaka" by Panos Evagellidis and Yorgos Korontsis] very large Greek food turns on diners

giant mutant fire clam: [*World of Synnabarr* by Raymond C. S. McCracken] large mutant clam adapted to fire from Mars (alpha Zodiaci IV)

giant nit: [tiny nit palindrome] large, louse-like insectoid

giant octopus: [*Unexplained!* by Jerome Clark] 6-meter tentacle span that washed up at St. Augustine, FL, Terra (alpha Zodiaci III)

giant rock snake: boulder-like food animal from Mercury (alpha Zodiaci I)

giant sea spider: ["Monsters of the Antarctic" by D. Trull, Voyage to the Bottom of the Sea: "The Monster's Web" by Al Gail] thousand-times normal from Antarctica, Terra (alpha Zodiaci III)

giant shrew: ["Radio Free Ertrus" by Robert Feldhoff] 2-meter shrew from Ertrus (Kreit III), see killer shrew

giant snail: ["Rhodan Times a Thousand" by Hans Kneifel] 15-meter shelled snail with man-sized molars from Trafalgar (fka Magadona), Victory system, Demetria cluster

giant vulture: ["Attack of the Giant Vulture" by Leslie Chueng and Jessica May Liu] very large vulture-like ornithoid

giant virus: ["Attack of the Giant Virus" by PhilipMerrick] virus accidentally macroscopically enlarged

giant ymgyp: [pygmy ymgyp portmanteau backformation] large creature also in small variety

giantala: [*After Man* by Dougal Dixon] giant sloth-like macropod

gib: [*Dell Crossword Puzzle Dictionary*] tomcat

gibbee: [gibber backformation] bee-like insectoid prey of gibber and ingbird

gibber: [gibberish backformation] insectivorous mock ingbird from Ing system

gibberling: [*Fiend Folio* ed. by Don Turnbull] gestalt in shape of pale, hunchbacked, pointy-eared anthropoid with black mane, black eyes, that reproduces by injecting gibberslugs during bite, eat even own dead

gibberlingator: [gibberling alligator portmanteau] alligator-like predator whose bite morphs victim into gibberling

gibberslug: [*Fiend Folio* ed. by Don Turnbull] larval gibberling

gibberslugator: [gibberslug alligator portmanteau] alligator-like predator whose bite morphs victim into gibberslug

gibik: [*Highway* by Neal Barrett, Jr.] extraordinarily vicious lemming-like predator

gibling: [Superhero City] rodentoid pest from Gibbi

giblingator: [gibling alligator portmanteau] alligator-like predator whose bite morphs victim into gibling

gidni: [indigo gidni palindrome] blue-violet ornithoid

gieb: [beige gieb palindrome] light grayish brown or grayish yellow ornithoid

gigan: ["Godzilla vs. Gigan" by Jun Fukuda and Shinichi Sekizawa, "Godzilla vs. Megalon"] 120-meter biped with large claws, tail, 3 flimsy but utile wings, armor plating particularly on forehead (from which destructive beam comes), shoulders, thighs, kneepads, beak and mandibles, one large red eye, neckspikes, buzzsaw in chest from Hunter nebula

gigant: ["The Giants of Pigell" by Wim Vandemaan] 1.5-meter jungle-dwelling anthropoid from Pigell (Vega (alpha Lyrae) VI)

gigantelope: [After Man by Dougal Dixon] 10-tonne elephant-like antelope in hairless tropical, wooly polar varieties with plow-like horns and long-necked, short-horned variety, horrane prey

gigantillocutus: [T. C. Harbaugh of Casstown, OH, Middletown, MD *Valley Register*] monstrous creature

gigantobacterium: ["The World of Giant Germs" by Robert Bernstein] giant germ-like creatures

gigantoblattoid: ["The Cockroach that Ate Cincinnati" by Rose and the Arrangement] worst monster of all

gigantocricetus: ["Three, Two, One -- Penguins!"] aka giant space hamster (GSH), brown-bear-sized rodentoid used as food and spaceship power source by Tinker Gnomes from Krynn, in sabre-toothed, carnivorous flying, hellfire-breathing and miniature ("normal" hamster) varieties

gigantomimus: [gigantomus backformation] sizeshifting mouse-like rodentoid

gigantomus: ["The Monster Mouse" by Robert Bernstein, "Odd Squad: the Movie"] mutant giant mouse, see ginor

gigantorca verdis: ["Multi-Man Strikes Again"] killer whale made large and green

gigawasp: [gigawatt malapropism, Continuum] 7-cm dungwasp from Lemur (aka Korina)

 **gigawatt**: [dekawatt extrapolation] giant, arrow-shaped electrical creature with 2 eyes

gigelorum: very small, mite-ear-dwelling creature from Scotland, Terra (alpha Zodiaci III)

gigram: [Monster Legends] fox-like monster with white collar

gila: [*Dell Crossword Puzzle Dictionary*] beaded lizard, see gecko, guana, skink, varan, iguana

gilacorn: [Avatar: The Last Airbender: "Appa's Last Days"] once giant gila monster with unicorn-like horn

gilam: [malignant amoeba ananymondegreen] giant amoeba from Abeomatna system

gilgonnoal: food pachyderm from Gizmonian Steepes (Edonian cluster II), Galaxiki galaxy

Gilly boat: [billygoat spoonerism] small, nautiloid with horned, goateed masthead from Gilly system

gilt: [*Dell Crossword Puzzle Dictionary*] small female hog, see shoat, shote

gilvo: ["New Ground" by Grant Rosenberg] rare stick-like tree-dweller from rain forests of Corvan II

ginea: [Basque ginea txerri mondegreen] Guinea pig-pig, see gini, mar, meri, tsova, uk

gingersnapdragon: [ginger snap-snapdragon portmanteau] red-headed, snapping dracoid

gini: [Filipino gini-baboy mondegreen] Guinea pig-pig ancestor from Adiusa, Goodiusa system, Galaxiki galaxy, see ginea, mar, meri, tsova, uk

ginis: [Lithuanian banginis mondegreen] cetacean from Ba system

ginor: [ginormous mondegreen] moose-sized mouse-like rodentian

girafe-coléoptére: [*Another World* by Jean-Ignace-Isidore Gérard] giraffe-beetle, carapaced camelopardoid with insectoid legs from Gérard's world

girallon: [Monster Manual by Skip Williams, etal.] 4-armed white gorilla-like pongoid with dinosaur's tail that walks semi-erect

girbil: [giraffe-gerbil portmanteau] small yet long-legged, long-necked, long-tailed rodentoid

girbilope: [girbil antelope portmanteau] girbil with antlers

giriffin: [giraffe-griffin portmanteau] quadruped with long neck and legs, tan with orange-brown blotches, short horns, eagle-like head, lion-like body

git'woa: [Star Trek] amphibian from T'Khasi, Nevasa (40 Eridani) system

githyanki: ["Tales of the Outer Planets" ed. by Gary L. Thomas] creature from Outer Planet

gitli: [Cherokee] caninoid from Taslagi system

gitshou: cranny-dwelling ovaloid from Tincityie (Edonian cluster VII), Galaxiki galaxy

giu tie: [Fringe] segmented anaerobic metallophage with suckers and pinchers

givol: [Continuum] pink, horned, ostrich-like ornithoid mount from Sotkaard, Galunis system, Firehorse constellation

gixauh: [huaxignathus ananymondegreen] long-handed compognathoid from Suhta system

giyísgi: [an'dalesgiyísgi mondegreen] aka Dale's simian from rogue planet A

gizka: [Knights of the Old Republic] very adaptable, prolific, small, frog-like creature from Jedi galaxy

glacierin: [Terra Monsters] ice-adapted quadruped with one horn from Terrarium

gladehawk: [Edge Chronicles by Paul Stewart and Chris Riddell] hawk-like ornithoid

gladehawk: [*Edge Chronicles* by Paul Stewart and Chris Riddell] hawk-like ornithoid

gladrat: ["The Return of the Kangaroo Rex" by Janet Kagan] pesty rodentoid from Mirabile

glærke: [Danish sanglærke mondegreen] skylark-like ornithoid from Sa, the Leech Planet

glagon: ["Deadly Planet" by James Opie] Lurgi steed from Kalthar

glar: [rouglar mondegreen] creature ancestral to rou and rouglar

glass bird: [Xanth series by Piers Anthony] ornithoid golem made from glass from Looking Glass Land, Xanth

glass cow: [Xanth series by Piers Anthony] bovine-like golme made from glass from Looking Glass Land, Xanth

glass deer: [Douglass' deer mondegreen] deer-like golem made of glass from Dou system

glass unicorn: [Xanth series by Piers Anthony] unicorn-like golem made from glass from Looking Glass Land, Xanth

glat: [*City of the Chaschby* Jack Vance] dangerous, heavy jungle creature able to merge with shadows from Shattorak

glatisant beast: [*Le Morte d'Arthur* by Thomas Malory] beast with serpent's head, leopard's body, haunches of lion, feet of hart

gle: [elgnap ananymondegreen] spotted creature from Pa system

gled(e): [*Dell Crossword Puzzle Dictionary*] kitebird, see elanet

glee: [strangler backformation mondegreen] prey of strangling predators from Stra system

gleek: ["Mork and Mindy" series] poodle-like creature from Ork; ["The All-New Super Friends Hour" series] blue simian

glef: [janglefish mondegreen] ichthyoid from Ja system

gli: [one-eyed glii] cyclops ornithoid

glider squid: [*A Door into Ocean* by Joan Slonczewsky] red-blooded cephalopodan from Shora, the Ocean Moon of Valedon

gliffer: ["Rhodan Times a Thousand" by Hans Kneifel] black ornithoid that gliffs, prey of hymeri from Trafalgar (fka Magadona), Victory system, Demetria cluster

glificli: [James Crooke Brown's Loglan glida ficli] pilot fish from Logla, Brown's system

glii: [boranglii mondegreen] purple ornithoid from Bora system

glikasni: [James Cooke Brown's Loglan gliso kasni compound] glass cow from Logla, Brown's system

glikker: [*If I Ran the Zoo* by Seuss] 6-cm blue and white striped biped that glikks

glim worm: [*Creatures of the Galaxy* by Phil Brucato, Bill Smith, Rick D. Stuart, Chuck Truett] 1-meter burrowing, predatory worm with sharp, scaly skin and glue-like slime (glim)

glimmer: [Resident Evil: "Dead Aim"] 20-eyed, flat-headed garbage-eating bioluminescent scavenger

glinirda: [James Cooke Brown's Loglan gliso nirda compound] glass bird from Logla, Brown's system

glister: [*The Curse of the Gloamglozer* by Paul Stewart and Chris Riddell] large, ever-changing shape-shifter feeding on strong emotions, in larger and deadlier blood-red variety

glitch: aka saboteur bug

glitterfire: [*Monster Manual* by Skip Williams, etal.] glittering, fiery ooze

glob: ["The Outrageous Okona" by Les Menchen, Lance Dickson and David Landsberg] fly-like insectoid half the size of a Terran mosquito but with loud buzzing sound from Qonos

globoid: ["The Globoid Terror" by R. F. Starzl] 12-meter, large-mouthed, gelatinous spheroid with feeding tentacles

globster: [beached St. Augustine, FL 1896] whale-squid-like globular sea creature from Atlantic, Terra (alpha Zodiaci III)

glockensp: [Glockenspiel mondegreen] eel-like ichthyoid noted for mating song

gloe-ih: [Navaho] weasel-like creature from Diné system

glook: [Space Patrol: "The Rangers"] strange insectoid from Dictum Forest

gloomworm: [*The Future Is Wild* by Dougal Dixon] cave-dwelling bacteria-eating polychaete (bristleworm), prey of slickribbon

gloppit: [Babylon 5: "Believers" by David Gerrold] legendary egg-layer from Placibo

glossina: [*Dell Crossword Puzzle Dictionary*] tsetse fly, see mau, kivu

Gloucester monster: [*Monster Spotter's Guide to North America* by Scott Francis] 30-meter, dark basilosauroid from Gloucester, Mass., Terra (alpha Zodiaci III)

glowat: glowworm-like chiropteran from Youmisian Homeland (Edonian cluster III), Galaxiki galaxy

glowfly: [Avatar: The Last Airbender: "The Swamp"] housefly-like insectoid with blindingly bright firefly-like glow

glowino: [Terra Monster] mutant shino with electrical power, see gloyew, from Terrarium

glowpossum: [*Starman Jones* by Robert Heinlein] bioluminescent rodent-like marsupial from Charity

gloyew: [Terra Monster RPG] radiation-eating rhinoid with backspikes, see glowino, from Terrarium

glum: [bugglum mondegreen] lavender spheroidal biped with antennae

glumbumble: [*Fantastic Beasts and Where to Find Them* by Newton Artemis Fido Scamander] furry, nettle-eating insect whose bite induces melancholy from N. Europe, Terra (alpha Zodiaci III)

glydeer: [glider deer portmateau] ancestor of deer-like pegasi

glyptodont: [*After the Dinosaurs* by Donald R. Prothero] huge armadillo-like creature from Miocene

gnadnaf: [fandango gnadnaf palindrome] purplish ornithoid

gnalsmoo: [gnalsmoo boomslang palindrome] boomslang-like amphisbæna

gnalligator: [gnaw of alligators spoonerism] awesomely colorfully (ganalligating) feathered dracoid

gnant: [gnat-ant portmanteau] small, biting, 2-winged social insectoid

gnar: ["Seed of Reason" by Daniel Hatch] rodentoid from Chamal

gnaro: [neon orange gnaro noen palindrome] orange noen

gnarsh: ["A Vision of Venus" by Otis Adelbert Kline] man-eating flying creature from Zarovia (Venus (alpha Zodiaci II))

gnart: [strange gnarts palindrome] indescribable creature

gnarth: ["Detour" by Mike Sekowsky] vicious predator from Chalandor

gnarwhale: [Monster Galaxy] large flying ichthyoid with feathery wings from Pisces constellation

gnew: [wenge gnew palindrome] brownish gray ornithoid

gnewt: [gnu-newt portmanteau] small, slender, brightly colored amphibious quadruped with drooping mane and beard, long tuffed tail, curved horns

gni: [flamingo gni malf, gni wing palindromes] pink malf-like food pegasoid, see gnilhcta

gniling: [mynynym] immature gni

gnik: [gnik a la king palindrome] food ornithoid

gnilhcta: [gnilhtca hatchling] egg-laying gni

gnim: [gnim aerc's screaming palindrome] aerc noted for its scream

gnint: [lightning gnint ghil palindrome] electric variety of ghil

gnirp: [springy gnirps palindrome] frog-bunny, creature with batrachoid head on lapoid body

gnnayh: [*Travels into Several Remote Nations of the World* by Lemuel Gulliver] bird of prey from Houyhnhnm Island

gnoc: [Congo gnoc palindrome] pink ornithoid

gnorl: ["Land of No Return" by Bill Finger] energy-eating monster

go: [Filipino hunyango mondegreen] chameleon-like reptilian from Hunya system; [Portuguese frango mondegreen] chicken-like ornithoid from Fra system; [ognam ananymondegreen] orange gnat from Ma system

go pudding: [mango pudding mondegreen] always moving pudding-thick ooze from Ma system, see hasty pudding

gó: [Hungarian pillangó mondegreen] butterfly-like insectoid from Pilla system

goanna: [*After the Dinosaurs* by Donald R. Prothero] monitor lizard

GOAT: [greatest of all time acronym] gigantocapra

goat gorilla: [Avatar: The Last Airbender: "The King of Omashu"] 3-meter dark pongoid with gorilla-like face, 2 upward-pointing fangs, rabbit-like ears, 2 horns, backhump, hooved hindlegs

goatalope: [goat antelope portmanteau] goat-headed antelope-like rumninant, see kid
gobbleglop: ["L'il Abner" by Al Capp] teddybear-like porcoid omnivore that prefers garbage and rubbish
gobi: [Jap.] five-tailed whale-horse
gobiathere: ["Gobi beast", *After the Dinosaurs* by Donald R. Prothero] beast with huge inflated snout supported by bone
gobmag: [gamboge gobmag palindrome] saffron or mustard yellow ornithoid
gobmagator: [gobmag alligator portmanteau] alligator-like predator whose bite morphs victim into gobmag
gocko: ["Flash Gordon" by Frederick Stephani, George Plympton, Basil Dickey, Ella O'Neill, based on Alex Raymond's strip] 9-meter long, green, underground-dwelling dracoid with serpentine torso, 6 taloned feet, lobster-like claws, beak with nostrils and forked tail from Mongo
godwit: [*National Geographic Encyclopedia of Animals*] insectovorous bird from N. America, Terra (alpha Zodiaci III)
goest: [Dutch mangoest mondegreen] mongoose-like burrower, related to gar, goest, gosta, gouste, gust, gusta, gustë, gustiniai, gusto and hust from Ma system
goff: [*Creatures of the Galaxy* by Phil Brucato, Bill Smith, Rick D. Stuart, Chuck Truett] purple, pteradactyloid with 100-meter wingspan, feathered chest, secretes reddish attractant from Naboo, Jedi galaxy
gogh: [Monster Galaxy] Mayan glyph-like creature with crest and back markings from Gemini constellation
gohma: [The Legend of Zelda] cyclops monster crab from Hyrule
gojirasaur: ["Godzilla" by Inoshira Honda and Takeo Murata] 120-meter tall radioactive bipedal sauroid with jagged back plates, able to breathe hellfire
gok: ["A Race through Dark Places" by J. Michael Straczynski] felinoid from Minbar
gokül: [Fr. Johann Martin Schleyer's Volapük] chicken-like ornithoid from Schleyer's system

gōl: [i-less iigōli] cave-dwelling perch-like ichthyoid
golbangi: [Kor. @] 2-D snail-like at, see chioccda
golbrorn: [*Dragon Annual* #1] smaller, pack-hunting version of bulette
gold bear: bear-like golem made from gold, see golden bear
gold bug: [Xanth series by Piers Anthony] insect similar to but slightly less dangerous than the midas fly that gold-plates whatever touches it from Xanth; fly-like golem made from gold
gold bugator: [gold bug alligator portmanteau] alligator-like predator whose bite morphs victim into gold bug
goldem: [gold golem portmanteau] golem made of gold
golden bear: [Shawnee and Wyandot] 700-kg, golden-colored bear from Kansas, Terra (alpha Zodiaci III)
golden beetle: [Gor series by John Norman] rhino-sized insectoid with meter-wide mandibles, golden mane, feeds primarily on priest-kings
golden snow virus: [Power Ranger] virus used by Algolian gas-drinkers on Leslie
golden goose: ["The Goose and the Golden Eggs" by Aesop, "The Story of Jack Spriggins and the Enchanted Bean", "The Golden Goose" by Grimm brothers] golden goose that lays golden egg and resists be plucked
golem: [Heb.] artificially animated creature made from inanimate (clay, water) or dead gestalt, see bone gashadokuro, blood kekkai, tentacle nyraala, fat waste, etc.
goliath: [*The Big Bad Book of Beasts* by Michael Largo] bird-eater spider, also eats bats and rodents
golin: [pangolin mondegreen] armadilloid from Pa (eta Serpentis) system
golla: [allognathosuch ananymondegreen] small, crocodillian from Hcusohta system
golob: [bonognawer ananymondegreen] small, cylindrical insectoid from Rewa system
golobster: [golob lobster portmanteau] small, cylindrical crustracean

golp panther: [heraldry] monstrous felinoid with purple spots, flaming mouth and ears

golpher: [caddy backformation] lake monster that golphs (induces purple spots and flaming mouth and ears), see caddy

gomorra: [The Tick: "Paul the Samuri"] 15-meter gigantogecko from Monster Island

gomphothere: [*After the Dinosaurs* by Donald R. Prothero] mastodont that migrated from Miocene Eurasia to America

Gonalian moth: ["Disaster" by Ron Jarvis and Philip A. Scorza] swarming insectoid from Gonal IV

gonarch: [Half-Life] last-stage 3-meter headcrab with 4 razor-sharp legs, exoskeleton but vulnerable in sac

gonchong: [*Island of the Lizard King* by Ian Livingstone] parasite that controls host via proboscis in skull

gongchongator: [gongchong alligator portmanteau] alligator-like predator whose bite morphs victim into gongchong

gondar: [*The Courtship of Princess Leia* by Dave Wolverton] creature from Hoth, Jedi galaxy

gonera: [Catalan sangoera mondegreen] leech-like parasite, related to guessuga, guijuela, guissuga and si, from Sa, the Leech Planet

gonmoose: [mongoose spoonerism] musteloid with antler-like growths

goo: electric eel-like ichthyoid with blue venom that solidifies into yellow glue

Goober peacock: [goober pea-peacock portmanteau] brightly-colored ornithoid with peanut-shaped body from Goober system

goodger: [badger backformation] herbivorous badger-like burrower

goose-bear: [gooseberry backformation] goose-headed ursinoid

goomba: [The Legend of Zelda: "Link's Awakening"] aka kuriboe; brown, bipedal chestnut-like creature from Koholint Island, Hyrule

goonch: [*River Monsters* by Jeremy Wade] 200-kg leathery, slug-like fish with broad, tooth-filled head

goony bird: aka albatross, mollyhawk

gooroo: [guru mondegreen] goo-eating owl-headed macropodan

gootch: [*If I Ran the Zoo* by Theodore Seuss Geissel] giraffe-cat with foot tufts and tall crest

gopher bear: [Avatar: The Last Airbender: "City of Walls and Secrets"] burrowing ursinoid

gopher-tortoise: [gopher tortoise mondegreen] burrowing tortoise with gopher-like head

gopher: [gopher backformation] predator that gophs (burrows)

gopogo: [i-less igopogo] cave-dwelling, dog-headed ichthyosaur

goraffe: [gorilla-giraffe portmanteau] tan centauroid with orange-brown blotches, ape-like upper body and 4 long legs

gorg: [*Creatures of the Galaxy* by Phil Brucato, Bill Smith, Rick D. Stuart, Chuck Truett] domesticated batrachian from Tatooine, Jedi galaxy

gorgator: [gorg alligator portmanteau] alligator-like predator whose bite morphs victim into gorg

gorgon: [*Historie of Foure-Footed Beastes* by Edward Topsell] catoblepas-like creature with hairy head, cow-like snout, scales, hooves, curly tail

gorgonster: [gorgon monster portmanteau] creature more monstrous than gorgon

gorgops: [*After the Dinosaurs* by Donald R. Prothero] huge species of hippo with eyestalks from Pleistocene

gorgosaur: ["Gorgo" by Carson Bingham] 75-meter tall bipedal sauroid with large ears, red eyes, armored back and tail from Nara Island; [*Feathered Dinosaurs: The Origin of Birds* by John Long and Peter Schuten] 9-meter, 1-tonne albertosaur-like tyrannosaurid

gorhen: [*Dell Crossword Puzzle Dictionary*] moorhen

gorillamp: [Terra Monsters] large, black-and-blue electric pongoid, see ampint and frankilla, from Terrarium

gorillasaur: [Mighty Samson series] large fanged pongoid with lizard-like legs and tail

gormander: [*Le cinquiesme et dernier livre des faicts et dicts du bon Pantagruel* by François Rabelais] brightly colored bird able to change colors chameleon-like from Ringing Island

gornis: [yandangornis mondegreen] lizard-bird from Ya, Da system

gorog: pongoid with bony knobs and horns on head and two hearts from Cato Neimodia, Jedi galaxy

gorogator: [gorog alligator portmanteau] alligator-like predator whose bite morphs victim into gorog

gorolla: [*The Barber of Aldebaran* by William May Russell] fierce animal from Toxicurare

gorrick: ["Turning Point" by Josepha Sherman] source of leather from Thallon, Thollonian empire

gorth: [*Ultra Klutz* by Jeff Nicholson] 4-armed, large, hairy, mumblimg anthropoid

gorwol: [*Frostworld* and *Dreamfire* by John Morressy] silver-furred creature huntable only by Onhla from Starside Hraggellon (Dunuos II)

gorwolope: [gorwol antelope portmanteau] gorwol with antlers

gos: [goshawk backformation] hawk-like ornithoid

goshawk: [*National Geographic Encyclopedia of Animals*] carnivorous bird

goshi: [ba-goshi mondegreen] sea-cow ancestor

gospmoc: [compsognathus ananymondegreen] bird-like dinosaur from Suhta system

gossamer tiger: ["On the High Frontier" by Michael F. Flynn] predator of jellybelly that hides in hypoholes and attacks with particle beams

gosta: [Catalan/Italian/Spanish mangosta mondegreen] mongoose-like burrower, related to gar, goest, gouste, gust, gusta, gustë, gustiniai, gusto, hust, from Ma system

gotca: [James Cooke Brown's Loglan] goat from Logla, Brown's system

gotli: [James Cooke Brown's Loglan gotca clika (goat-like) compound] goat-like ruminant from Logla, Brown's system

gotu: ['gotu'at times emit tautog" palindrome] oysterfish gestalt

goud: [Afrikaans/Dutch goudvis mondegreen] ichthyoid related to guld from Snobaal, Laabon system, Galaxiki galaxy

gour: [*Dell Crossword Puzzle Dictionary*] wild ox from India, see gaur, gayal and zebu

gourmai: [*National Geographic Encyclopedia of Animals*] reef fish from Asia, Terra (alpha Zodiaci III)

gouste: [French mangouste mondegreen] mongoose-like burrower from Ma system, related to gar, goest, gosta, gust, gusta, gustë, gustiniai, gusto and hust

gowk: elusive bird like snipe or hoodwink from Scotland, Terra (alpha Zodiaci III)

grabanster: ["The Big Game" by Sandy Schofield] thick furred, chattering, rat-like tribble predator with wet-dog B. O.

grabbit: [green rabbit portmanteau, "The Trap" by Finn O'Donovon] green rabbit with grabbing lobster claws from Asidia's world

grabfoot: [*Uhura's Song* by Janet Kagon] underground-dwelling chicken-sized dinosauroid from Sivao

graboid: ["Tremors" series] aka tu-long, dirt-devil, giant blind worm with mouthed tongues, see tilpasaran

grahl: [The Elder Scroll III: Morrowind] large, powerful, white-furred cave-dwelling creature with large tusks and claws, red eyes from Solstheim

graiveh: [*Creatures of the Galaxy* by Phil Brucato, Bill Smith, Rick D. Stuart, Chuck Truett] 2.5-meter, dangerous, bipedal predator from Ealor, Jedi galaxy

grakel: ["Learning Curve" by Ronald Wilkerson] creature noted for its "milk", Delta Quadrant

grakelope: [grakel antelope portmanteau] grakel with antlers

grakk: [Thongor series by Lin Carter] large, scaly, green-blooded "lizard-hawk" dracoid with 12-meter wingspan, long neck, barbed tail, hideous head, hooked beak, scarlet eyes, blue spiny crest from Lemuria

grakka: [Brick Bradford series] bipedal saurian with powerful arms, jaw and tail, horn on back of head, back spikes, bullet-proof hide

grakurma: [James Cooke Brown's Loglan grani kurma compound] dryworm from Logla, Brown's system

gral: [large gral palindrome] grasshopper-like insectoid in large and small varieties

grallow: [grasshopper swallow portmanteau] swallow-like ornithoid with grasshopper-like insectoid head and legs

grampus: [*Dell Crossword Puzzle Dictionary*] whale, see orc, ork, cet(e), beluga

grampuss: [grampus puss portmanteau] large, catfish-like ichthyoid

granger: ["A Final Unity" by Spectrum HoloByte] caninoid geneered by Dr. Vi Hynh-Foertsh from Morassia (epsilon Chysule II)

grank: ["The Gungan Frontier" by Chris McCubbin] large-mouthed bulldog-like creature from Jedi galaxy

grantchester: [*Mothstorm* by Philip Reeve] variety of ichthyomorph

graouilli: [*Fabulous Beasts and Demons* by Heinz Mode] monstrous dragon from Metz, Terra (alpha Zodiaci III)

grape jelly: [jelly extrapolation] purple jelly-thick ooze

grapefruit jelly: [jelly extrapolation] jelly-thick ooze

graphorn: [*Fantastic Beasts and Where to Find Them* by Newton Artemis Fido Scamander] large, grayish-purple bicorn with humped back from Alps, Terra (alpha Zodiaci III)

grarbler: [grasshopper warbler portmanteau] warbler-like ornithoid with grasshopper-like insectoid head and legs

gras: [*Dell Crossword Puzzle Dictionary*] gypsy horse, gri, gry

grass hopper: grasshopper mondegreen] hopper golem made from grass

graul: [*Creatures of the Galaxy* by Phil Brucato, Bill Smith, Rick D. Stuart, Chuck Truett] large, green to reddish-orange pongoid from Dantooine, Jedi galaxy

graulope: [graul antelope portmanteau] graul with antlers

grava: ["The Curse of the Microcosm" by Conrad Shepherd] aka fog-eater, huge, sickle-shaped dracoid with 100-meter wings, large tentacles, silver-blue leathery skin from Dnofftrie, Microcosm

gravedigger: [Resident Evil 4] victim of T-virus, huge graboid-like worm with 4 long mandibles, bloodsucking young

gravel-maggot: ["Star Wars IV: A New Hope" by George Lucas] worm-like creature that feeds on rotting flesh from hills and rocky badlands of Tatooine, Jedi galaxy

gravornis: ["heavy bird", *The New Dinosaurs* by Dougal Dixon] large, flightless bird like cold-adapted tromble

grawlinx: [Outernauts] pink, immature grawlox

grawllon: [Outernauts] rotund, purple horny toad-like mature grawlox with horns, more spikes

grawlox: [Outernauts] batrachoid with 4 short feet, see grawlinx, grawlion

gray ooze: [*Monster Manual* by Skip Williams, etal.] viscous, gray 4-meter puddle unable to climb walls, but immune to fire and cold

great eagle: see thoron

great feyr: see feyr

Great Lake snake: large, freshwater serpentine monster from Great Lakes, Terra (alpha Zodiaci III)

greath: [green death portmanteau, spoonerism] green maggot from Dea system

grec: [*Worlds Apart: Nat. Hist. of Furaha and Earth* by Souren Nyoroge] flightless, tail-less yellow ornithoid with 4 vestigial wings, clam-like head from Nullarbor Plain, Auralgia, Furaha (alpha Phoenicis IV)

gredbird: [grue-bleen extrapolation] green bird that turns red, not to be confused with bledbird, gebird, greenbird, grellowbird, grindigobird, grioletbird, gruebird, redbird, reenbird, rellowbird, rindigobird, rioletbird, ruebird, vedbird or yedbird from Ora system

gree: [agree mondegreen, grist of bees, green bee portmanteau] green, bee-like insectoid
greel: [squeaky wheel gets the grease spoonerism] predator that lures wheases by squeaking
greelope: [greel antelope portmanteau] greel with antlers
green ape: [Boris Karloff's Tales of Mystery #76] green pongoid planimal with big, black eyes and fangs that grows from seeds like plant
green death: [*The Green Death* by Malcolm Hulke] green maggot that leaves deadly slime trail from Metebelis III
green goo: [*Encyclopedia Galactica*] aka bionano, geneered creature as opposed to non-biological grey goo
green slime: ["The Green Slime" by Charles Sinclair, William Finger and Tom Rowe, *Monster Manual* by Skip Williams, etal.] ooze that looks like green blood that metamorphs into bipedal, 3-clawed footed, 2-armed mound with red orb on top, double boney back ridge, electrogenic pincers for self-cauderizing wounds
greenasaur: [Monster Legends] green bipedal dinosaur
greenbird: [grue-bleen extrapolation] bird that remains green, not to be mistaken for bleenbird, gebird, gredbird, grellowbird, grindigobird, grioletbird, gruebird, reenbird, veenbird or yeenbird from Ora system
greeny: [*Monster Spotter's Guide to North America* by Scott Francis] 9-meter, green eel-like lake snake from Finger Lakes, NY, Terra (alpha Zodiaci III)
greep: [Motie series by Larry Niven] crab-like quadruped from Maxroy's Purchase
greeshka: ["A Song for Lya" by George R. R. Martin] cave-dwelling parasite able to give pseudo-immortality to empathic Shkeen in 10-year Joining
Gregory's deerlet: [*After the Dinosaurs* by Donald R. Prothero] dromomeryx without horns but with fangs

greibble: ["The Greibble" by Steven Speilberg] floppy giant with pink and purple fur that eats inanimate objects
grejo: [Spanish cangrejo, Portuguese carangrejo mondegreen] crab-like crustacean from Ca and Cara systems
grelbon: [*Coneheads* by Tom Davies and Dan Aykroyd] carrion-eating heron-like ornithoid with half-meter wingspan from Remulak, Cone nebula
grelbonster: [grelbon monster portmanteau] carnivorous grelbon
grellowbird: [grue-bleen extrapolation] green bird that turns yellow, not to be confused with bleen, blellowbird, gebird, gredbird, greenbird, grellowbird, grindigobird, grioletbird, gruebird, reenbird, rellowbird, veenbird, vellowbird, yedbird, yeenbird, yellowbird, yindigobird, yioletbird or yuebird from Ora system
gremlinoid: [Thousand Stars] 2-kg gremlin-like creature from Khao Thap
gremur: [group of lemurs spoonerism] long-tailed, very communal, arboreal pongoid
greti: [*Encyclopedia Galactica*] untamable carnivore from Helicon, Arcturus (gamma Boötis) system
greylag: [*National Geographic Encyclopedia of Animals*] goose from Europe and Africa, Terra (alpha Zodiaci III)
greylagator: [greylag alligator portmanteau] alligator-like predator whose bite morphs victim into greylag
greysor: [*Creatures of the Galaxy* by Phil Brucato, Bill Smith, Rick D. Stuart, Chuck Truett] simian pet from Naboo, Mimban, Chalganna, Jedi galaxy
greywaif: [*Edge Chronicles* by Paul Stewart and Chris Riddell] smooth-skinned gray waif with 2 barbels
gri: [*Dell Crossword Puzzle Dictionary*] gypsy horse, see gry, gras
gribaka: [Filipino grib-baka portmanteau] grebe-horse, griffinoid with hooves, mane, webbed feet
grice: [*Dell Crossword Puzzle Dictionary*] small pig from Scotland, Terra (alpha Zodiaci III), see elt

grick: [*Monster Manual* by Skip Williams, etal.] 2.4-meter green and white slug with vulture-like beak, rubbery hide and 4 barbed feeding tentacles

griffi-saur: [*Sea Devils* #32] 5-meter orange-skinned biped with lion-like head and mane, feathery wings, scaly skin

griffin: [*The Big Bad Book of Beasts* by Michael Largo] "eagle-lion", [Adrienne Mayor] related to wingless proceratops

griffletae: ["The Dashing About Flying Box People" by Uncle River] sleepy, sluggish creature from Craton V

grii: [ny'ghan grii mondegreen] spheroid from Nygha system

grilleguan: [German Grille-Leguan portmanteau] long-legged, hopping cricket-headed iguana-like reptilian

grilse: [*Dell Crossword Puzzle Dictionary*] small salmon, see parr

grimb: ["The Book of Ptath" by A. E. van Vogt] 3.6-meter tall creature with small 3-horned head on long yellow neck on green body with bluish-violet tail from Gonwonlane

grimworm: [*The Future Is Wild* by Dougal Dixon] larval bumblebeetle which hatches from flish carcass, reproduces both sexually and parthenogenetically, dominant female eats all others and then pupates

grindigobird: [grue-bleen extrapolation] green bird that turns indigo, not to be confused with bleenbird, blindigobird, gebird, gredbird, greenbird, grellowbird, grindigobird, grioletbird, gruebird, reenbird, rindigobird, veenbird, vindigobird, yeenbird, yindigobird from Ora system

grindylow: [*Fantastic Beasts and Where to Find Them* by Newton Artemis Fido Scamander] green, horned lake cephalopodan

gring: [*Metamorphosis* by Jean Lorrah] purplish fanged pongoid with 4-fingered hands from Elysia

gringator: [gring alligator portmanteau] alligator-like predator whose bite morphs victim into gring

grinirda: [James Cooke Brown's Loglan grisi nirda (gray bird) compound] gray ornithoid from Logla, Brown's system

grioletbird: [grue-bleen extrapolation] green bird that turns violet, not to be confused with bleenbird, blioletbird, gebird, gredbird, greenbird, grellowbird, grindigobird, grioletbird, gruebird, reenbird, riolet, vedbird, veenbird, vindigobird, violetbird, yeenbird, yioletbird or vuebird from Ora system

grither: ["Seasons of Belief" by Michael McDowell] proud, hateful, large-eared beast that griths (hates its name spoken aloud)

grivet: [*Dell Crossword Puzzle Dictionary*] monkey from Africa, see mona, waag

grizzleel: [grizzly (bear)-eel portmanteau] ursinoid with snake-like tongue from Skjoob, Bjosko system, Galaxiki galaxy

groack: [Callisto series by Lin Carter] towering, scaly, flippered "river dragon" from Callisto (Jupiter (alpha Zodiaci Vd))

goat: herding herbivore noted for groatle (shaggy hair) from Fulacin, Rhylanor subsector

groath: [*After Man* by Dougal Dixon] goat-like hornhead, plate-like horns on males, pyramid-like horns on females

grob: ["grob at times emit taborg" palindrome] crayfish-spider gestalt

grobbit: [*After Man* by Dougal Dixon] rodent with hooves, long tail and raccoon-like hands

grobrabekti: [James Cooke Brown's Loglan groku brani bekti (big brown thing) compound] large, slimy man-eater from Logla, Brown's system

grobster: [grob lobster portmanteau] crayfish-spider-lobster chimera

grofitpi: [James Cooke Brown's Loglan groda fitpi (big foot) compound] pongoid from Logla, Brown's system

grog: [groundhog spoonerism] tiny, parasitic canine insectoid

grogator: [grog alligator portmanteau] alligator-like predator whose bite morphs victim into grog

grogg: [groggy backformation] sloth-like arboreal

groggator: [grogg alligator portmanteau] alligator predator whose bite morphs victim into grogg

groke: [*Muumipappa merellä, Muumipappan urotyöt* by Tove Jansson] aka mårran and mörkö, blue, pear-shaped creature with large, round eyes fascinated by lamps, whose loneliness causes ground to freeze

grol: [grol slorg palindrome] slorg-like amphisbæna

gromble: ["Aaahh!!! Real Monsters" series] monster with green beard and fur, black hands, yellow teeth, bulging eyes and bright red lips

gromgor: [Outernauts] mature grumba

grompus: [Superman mythos] one-eyed creature from Krypton, Rao system

grompuss: [grompus puss portmanteau] cyclops felinoid

gron: ["Vaster Than Empires and More Slow" by Ursula K. LeGuin] "scapegoat" from Hain

gronckle: [*A Hero's Guide to Deadly Dragons* by Hiccup Haddock III] slow and stupid, snot green, bogie beige and pooey brown dragon with mace-tipped tail, wings, spikes from Barbarian archipelago

gronirda: [James Cooke Brown's Loglan groda nirda compound] big bird from Logla, Brown's system

grono: [*Vampirella* #1 by Forrest J. Ackerman and James Warren] vampiric, boar-like porcoid from Draculon

gronster: [gronckle/grono monster portmanteau] vampiric dracoid with mace-tipped tail

grooze: [grey ooze portmanteau] see grey ooze

gropper: ["Bird-watchers' Slang" by Paul Beale] grasshopper warbler

grored trorti: [James Cooke Brown's Loglan groda redro troku titci (big red rock eater) compound] big, red trorti from Logla, Brown's system

grotseth: [*Planets of the Galaxy* by Greg Farshtey, Bill Smith, Ed Stark] 4-meter, predatory, pack hunting ichthyoid covered in razor-sharp shells from Baralou

grou: [i-less igriou] cave-dwelling white millipede

grouillard: [*Worlds Apart: Nat. Hist. of Furaha and Earth* by Souren Nyoroge] cackler with greenish-yellow rump, foul spittle from S. Paleogea, Furaha (alpha Phoenicis IV)

ground fish: [*Rainbeau's Riddles and Rhymes*: "Wouldn't It Be Better?"] fish adapted to burrowing in the ground

ground hog: [groundhog mondegreen] burrowing porcoid

ground hogator: [ground hog alligator portmanteau] alligator-like predator whose bite morphs victim into ground hog

grounder: [*Highway* by Neal Barrett, Jr.] insidious threat to Lemmits

groupie: [Xanth series by Piers Anthony] fattish fish with large, soft extremities and kiss of death from Xanth

grub-bee: [grubby backformation] bee-like insectoid that metamorphs from grub-like larva

grudgeon: [Outernauts] mature gruglox

grue: [*Zork* by Dave Lebling, Godville] photophobic predator ironically with luminescent fur

gruebird: [grue-bleen extrapolation] green bird that turns blue, not to be confused with bledbird, bleenbird, blellowbird, blindigobird, blioletbird, bluebird, gebird, gredbird, greenbird, grellowbird, grindigobird, grioletbird, greenbird, ruebird, veenbird, vuebird, yeenbird or yuebird from Ora system

grugling: [Outernauts] immature gruglox

gruglingator: [grugling alligator portmanteau] alligator-like predator whose bite morphs victim into grugling

gruglox: [Outernauts] mock-rocky, red-eyed batrachoid, see grugling, grudgeon

gruis: [grus, piscium extrapolation] crake-like ornithoid

grumba: [Outernauts] purple-winged, green dracoid with yellow spikes, see grunny, gromgor

grumphurr: [Continuum] catcus-eating, malodorous, but edible, rodentian from

Sotkaard, Galunis system, Firehorse constellation

grumpy converter: [*Empire of a Thousand Planets*] living replicator used as counterfeiter from Bluxte (Valeria)

grundler: ["Exile of the Oracle" by Michael Marcus Thurner] rainbow-colored freshwater predatory ichthyoid with big green eyes from Tan-Jamondi II

grunny: [Outernauts] purple-winged, green immature grumba

grusaur: crane-like dracoid from Grus constellation

gruutf: [bergruutf mondegreen] frilled herbivore

gry: [*Dell Crossword Puzzle Dictionary*] gypsy horse, see gri, gras

gryf: [fangryf mondegreen] toothless, beaked griffinoid from Fa (iota Orionis) system; [*Tarzan the Terrible* by Edgar Rice Burroughs] 6-meter triceratops-like dinosauroid with blue body, yellow face and belly, blue bands around eyes, red hood, 3 bony back ridges (yellow, red and yellow), used as steed in Pal-ul-don, Zaire

gryken: [*The Future Is Wild* by Dougal Dixon] scroflet-eating mustelid with long, thin body and sharp teeth that lives in grykes (limestone fissures)

gryllus: [Bosch Cretensis, Kato Zakro] monster with incongruous body parts, chimera, doublivore, mosaic animal

grynn: [Terra Monster] carnivorous donkey-like equine, see heckyll, from Terrarium

gryon: goat-like ruminant from Daxon (Yonith I), Galaxiki galaxy

gryonster: gryon monster portmanteau] carnivorous goat-like creature

gryph: [Monster Galaxy] griffinoid from Leo constellation

gryphorg: [*Fly Man* #34] 12-meter long omnivorous dracoid conjured by Evilo with 12-meter bat-like wings, gray skin, nearly useless forearms, long neck and back plate

gryphorgator: [gryphorg alligator portmanteau] alligator-like predator whose bite morphs victim into gryphorg

gryphus: [OviPets] egg-laying griffinoid

gu: [nukkangu mondegreen] desert caninoid from Nukka system; [kangu mondegreen] caninoid from Ka system, [katkangu mondegreen] nimravoid from Katka system; [nirangu mondegreen] bird-headed caninoid from Nira system; [pangkarlangu mondegreen] pongoid from Pangkarla system

Guaca mole: [guacamole mondegreen] small, geenish, venomous, burrowing marsupial from Guaca system

gualama: [*Creatures of the Galaxy* by Phil Brucato, Bill Smith, Rick D. Stuart, Chuck Truett] docile, swift herd quadruped with long tail, horns, smaller relative of gualara, from Naboo, Jedi galaxy

gualara: herd quadruped with long tail, horns, larger relative of gualama, from Naboo, Jedi galaxy

guan: [*National Geographic Encyclopedia of Animals*] chicken relative from S. America, Terra (alpha Zodiaci III), [Dell Crossword Puzzle Dictionary] see jacu, sylph, turco, seriema

guana: [*Dell Crossword Puzzle Dictionary*] lizard, see gila, gecko, skink, varan, iguana; [Perry Rhodan] living spaceships bred by Guanaar from giant worms from Louipaz galaxy

guanaco: [*National Geographic Encyclopedia of Animals*] desert ruminant related to llama

guanat: [i-less iguanat] small cave-dwelling lizard from Friatica, Friaticalida system, Galaxiki galaxy

guanlong: ["crown dragon", *Feathered Dinosaurs: The Origin of Birds* by John Long and Peter Schuten] 3-meter tyrannosaur ancestor with backward-facing hollow crest, U-shaped teeth

guanlongator: [guanlong alligator portmanteau] alligator-like predator whose bite morphs victim into guanlong

guapena: [*Dell Crossword Puzzle Dictionary*] ribbonfish

guar: [*The Eldar Scrolls III*: "Morrowind"] domesticated beast of burden called "tigers" because Deshaan Plain variety are striped from Morrowind, related to alit and kagouti

guava jelly: [jelly extrapolation] jelly-thick ooze, see rum jelly

guay: [The Legend of Zelda] creature similar to keese, crow and pterodactyl, including flightless variety, from Hyrule

gubba: [*The Yowie: In Seach of Australian Bigfoot* by Tony Healy and Paul Cropper] see yowie

guchod: [*Cyclopedia of Worlds*] docile sea creature, similar to predatory bamoda, from Dakka, Neptune system

guck: [badling of ducks antonym] flightless, landuck

guejo: [Portuguese/Galician caranguejo backformation] crab-like crustacean from Cara system

guera: [anhangüera mondegreen] hellfire-breather from Anha system

guessuga: [Galician/Portuguese sanguessuga backformation] leech-like parasite, related to gonera, guijuela, guissuga and si, from Sa, the Leech Planet

guessugator: [guessuga alligator portmanteau] alligator-like predator whose bite morphs victim into guessuga

gugai: [Cherokee] tick-like insectoid from Tsalagi system

gugurunz: [Hildegard of Bingen's Lingua Ignota] ostrich-like ornithoid from Ignota, Hildegard's system

guh: [huge guh palindrome] giant, quail-like ornithoid

guhgwe: [Cherokee] quail-like ornithoid from Talagi system

guicol: ["Battle of Ferrol" by Michael Marcus Thurner] dangerous mimicking predatory insectoid from Ferrol (Vega (alpha Lyrae) VIII)

guijuela: [Spanish sanguijela backformation] leech-like parasite, related to gonera, guessuga, guissuga and si, from Sa, the Leech Planet

guilala: ["The Big Space Monster Guilala" aka "The X of Outer Space" by Kazui Nihonmatsu, Eibi Motomochi, Moriyoshi Ishida] 60-meter tall sauroid biped with lumpy skin, large leg frills, claws, beak, 2 flat body projections from sides from face, 2 antennae, 1 horn, shrinks when exposed to guilalium

guiled woose: [wild goose spoonerism] variety of woose

guilla: meganguilla mondegreen] sea serpent from Mega system

guillemot: [*National Geographic Encyclopedia of Animals*] fish-eating bird from N. Atlantic, Terra (alpha Zodiaci III)

guiron: ["Gamera vs. Guiron" aka "Attack of the Monsters" by Fumi Takahashi] 60-meter long biped shaped like a butcher's knife with eyes on sides, brawny arms, stumpy legs

guironster: [guiron monster portmanteau] gamera-guiron-like monster

guissuga: [Italian sanguissuga backformation] leech-like parasite, related to gonera, guessuga, guijuela and si, from Sa, the Leech Planet

guissugator: [guissuga alligator portmanteau] alligator-like predator whose bite morphs victim into guissuga

guitarf: [guitarfish backformation] guitarfish mimicking ichthyoid

guitarfish: [*National Geographic Encyclopedia of Animals*] mollusc and crustacean-eating ray

guld: [Danish guldfisk backformation] ichthyoid ancestral to fish and goldfish, related to goud

gulder: [*Cyclopedia of Worlds*] large-eyed, hermaphroditic marsupial with small-mouthed snout from zeta Reticuli system

gull: [*Dell Crossword Puzzle Dictionary*] sea bird, see ern(e), skua, scaup, tern, fulmar, gannet, petrel, scoter

gull-deer: [gulder mondegreen] deer-like griffinoid with gull-like head and wings

gullipud: ["The Gungan Frontier" by Chris McCubbin] squishy, fast-breeding self-inflatable swamp-dweller used as gulliball from Jedi galaxy

gulo: [*Dell Crossword Puzzle Dictionary*] wolverine

gulon: aka jerff, ravenous dog-sized beast with head, ears, claws of cat, fox-like tail and thick shaggy brown fur from Scandinavia, Terra (alpha Zodiaci III); ["Xoology" by Kittenbaker] aka lion-hyena from Szurane

gulonster: [gulon monster portmanteau] jerff-gulon-like chimera

gulp worm: [Resident Evil: "Code Veronica"] T-virus victim like mandible-less gravedigger

gulper: [*National Geographic Encyclopedia of Animals*] fish-eating eel from E. Atlantic, Terra (alpha Zodiaci III)

gulphog: ["Alien Animal Planet" by Sean Cooper] biped with vibration-sensitive tusks and uv-sensitive parietal eye from Aurelia

gulphogator: [gulphog alligator portmanteau] alligator-like predator whose bite morphs victim into gulphog

gumbe: [gumberoo backformation] bear-like kangaroo ancestor

gumberoo: [*Monster Spotter's Guide to North America* by Scott Francis] 1.8-meter thick-skinned, hairless ursinoid

gumi: [Swahili nyangumi backformation] cetacean from Nya [yangumi mondegreen] or Ya systems

gummie: shark

gummy worm: [Here Be Monsters almanac] worm used to catch phantom catfish

gummy wyrm: [Godville] monstrous, gelatinous worm said to have caused extinction of dinosaurs and dodos

gundark: ["The Empire Strikes Back" by Donald E. Glut] strong, wild, 4-armed 1.5-meter long pongoid whose ear-pulling was a rite of initiation from Poiu-Trewq, Jedi galaxy

Gunji jackdaw: ["If Wishes Were Horses" by Neil McCue Crawford and William L. Crawford] ostrich-like ornithoid

guppeacock: [guppy-peacock portmanteau] small, iridescent blue-green triphibian

gupsin: ["FthinraKathi" by Dale Murphy] venomous serpentine dracoid from T'Khasi, Nevasa (40 Eridani) system

gur: [douc langur mondegreen] simian from Doucla system; [kangur mondegreen] macrapodan from Ka system

gura: ["Star Pirate" by Len Dodson] giant egg-laying creature

gurkey: [gang of turkeys spoonerism, giant turkey portmanteau] turkey-like gigantovis

gurp: [Odd Squad: "The Trouble with Centigurps" by Guy Toubes] pink furball able to bounce, roll, fond of spheres, able to multilocate

gurrath: [*After Man* by Dougal Dixon] jaguar-like mongoose

gusset: [*If I Ran the Zoo* by Theodore Seuss Geissel] 1.2-meter, yellow bird with long neck, long pointed beak and large crest

gust: [Estonian/Armenian mangust backformation] mongoose-like burrower from Ma system, related to gar, goest, gosta, gouste, gusta, gustë, gustiniai, gusto and hust

gusta: [Polish/Romanian mangusta backformation] mongoose-like burrower from Ma system, related to gar, goest, gosta, gouste, gust, gustë, gustiniai, gusto and hust

gustë: [Albanian mangustë] mongoose-like burrower from Ma system, related to gar, goest, gosta, gouste, gust, gustiniai, gusta, gusto and hust

gustiniai: [Lithuanian mangustiniai mondegreen] mongoose-like burrower from Ma system, related to gar, goest, gosta, gouste, gust, gustë, gustiniai, gusto and hust

gusto: [Galician mangusto backformation] mongoose-like burrower from Ma system, related to gar, goest, gosta, gouste, gust, gustë, gustiniai and hust

gutnimla: [James Cooke Brown's Loglan gutra nimla (weird animal) compound] weirdo from Logla, Brown's system

guyascutus: [*Monster Spotter's Guide to North America* by Scott Francis] 3-meter armored, mountain-climbing gator-like or rabbit-deer-like creature with dorsal spikes

guze panther: [heraldry] monstrous felinoid with blood-red spots and flaming mouth and ears

gvhe: [Cherokee] bobcat-like felinoid from Tsalagi system

gvna: [Cherokee] turkey-like ornithoid from Tsalagi system

gvnigetsuli: [Cherokee] black fox-like creature from Tsalagi system

gwak: ["Flash Gordon"] large, monstrous equine from Mongo

gwiazdka: [Pol. *] 2-D pentapus or hexapus

gwyfyn-cwcwyddrywystrys: [Welsh] barnacle goose-like griffinoid ancestral to moth and cwcwyddrywystrys

gwythaint: [Prydain series by Lloyd Alexander] huge black bird used as spy and executioner by Arawn, defeated by crows

gy: [Hungarian varangy backformation] toad-like amphibian from Vara system

gya: [Hungarian hangya backformation] ant-like insectoid from Ha system

gyaos: ["Gamera vs. Gyaos" by Fumi Takihashi] 61-meter tall nocturnal biped with small, powerful claws, flat bird-like head, stiff neck, leathery wings, big yellow eyes with red irises, bright pink blood, able to shoot destructive yellow sonic beam from double throat, regenerate injured body parts, put out fires with yellow vapor, killable with ultraviolet light

gybbon: [Georges-Louis Leclerc, Comte de Buffon] aka gibbon, arboreal pongoid with long arms

gybbonster: [gybbon monster portmanteau] carnivorous gibbon-like pongoid

gynip: [spinygnateater ananymondegreen] insectovore with spines from Retaeta system

gyorg: [The Legend of Zelda] pink, spiky shark-like ichthyoid from Hyrule

gyorgator: [gyorg alligator portmanteau] alligator-like predator whose bite morphs victim into gyorg

gyphus: [OviPets] egg-laying griffinoid

gyter: [tyger spoonerism] black felinoid with orange stripes

gyüki: multi-legged, bull-headed dracoid with sword-like tail from Japan, Terra (alpha Zodiaci III)

ha: [boisha mondegreen] food ruminant from Boi system; [Galician/Portuguese aranha mondegreen] arachnoid, related to ya, from Ara constellation; [piranha mondegreen] predatory pack ichthyoid from Pira system;

haha nasna; [hanadak ananymondegreen] grizzly-baboon creature from Kada system

ha-as-tso-si: [Navaho] mouse-like rodentoid from Diné system

ha-gnat: [piranha-gnat mondegreen] tiny, swarming carnivorous insectoid from Pira system

ha-inu: ["winged dog"] blue caninopteryx, see ao-inu, huckleberry hound

haasluk: [Afrikaans haas-sluk modegreen] hare-swallow, burrowing griffinoid related to haasmous, haaspecht, haaswaan and haasvoël

haasmous: [Afrikaans haas-smous mondegreen] hare-hawk, burrowing griffinoid related to haasluk, haaspecht, haaswaan and haasvoël

haaspecht: [Afrikaans haas-specht portmanteau] hare-woodpecker, burrowing griffinoid related to haasluk, haasmous, haaswaan and haasvoël

Haast eagle: see poukoi

haasvoël: [Afrikaans haas-aasvoël mondegreen] hare-vulture griffinoid related to haasluk, haasmous, haaspecht and haaswaan

haaswaan: [Afrikaans haas-swaan mondegreen] hare-swan, burrowing griffinoid related to haasluk, haasmous, haaspecht and haasvoël

hach: [hachat mondegreen] light brown pongoid

hachibi: [Jap.] eight-tailed, horned cephalopod

hackblunter: [black hunter spoonerism] parasite that preys on writers

hackrabbit: [husk of jackrabbits spoonerism] lapoid with hatchet-like nose horn

haddo: [*Dell Crossword Puzzle Dictionary*] humpback salmon, see holia

hadger: [hog/honey badger portmanteau] burrowing, honey-loving porcoid

hadhayosh: [Persian, *The Bundahishn* transl. by E. W. West] aka sarsaok, related to behemoth, source of immortality beverage hush

hadrak: [Czech had-drak portmanteau] snake-dragon, leg-less, wing-less dracoid

hadrocodium: proto-mammal brainier than morganucodon from Jurassic

hadrosaur: dinosaur with duck-like bill and webbed feet, related to crested lambeosaur, see giant duck

hadruk: [Belarussian had-druk portmanteau] skunk-seal, malodorous sirenian from Skjoob, Bjosko system, Galaxiki galaxy

haetae: lion-like, fire-eating canine, sometimes with one horn, bull-dog-like jaw from Korea, Terra (alpha Zodiaci III)

hagfish: fish with 4 hearts, toothed tongue, one nostril

haggot: [*Wyst: Alastor 1716* by Jack Vance] food ichthyoid from Wyst

haha: [*The Last Yggdrasill* by Robert F. Young] ornithoid from New America (Genji V), fed by Quantextils, made extinct with the cutting of the last Yggdrasill tree, see ha-ha

haho: ["Prince of Peril" by Otis Adelbert Kline] large, mottled green and orange hyena-like nocturnal creature with 3 horns, spines from Zarovia (Venus (alpha Zodiaci II))

haidh: [nhaidh elision] cockroach-like insectoid

haietlik: [Nootka] sharp-headed sea serpent able to shoot electricity from tongue

hairball loon: hairball loon portmanteau] loon-like ornithoid with hairy, kiwi-like feathers that can puff up like a pufferfish

hairy ghost: [*Oregon's Ghosts and Monsters* by Mike Helm] elusive, 2.1-meter, white, bear-like nape with webbed feet from Conser Lake nr. Albany, Ont., Terra (alpha Zodiaci III)

hairyoddity: [Nehemiah Grue and Peter MacInnis] arboreal, bipedal lapois that feeds on palm seeds and cocoanuts from Ugly Islands

haischa: [Hildegard of Bingen's Lingua Ignota] turtle dove-like ornithoid from Ignota, Hildegard's system

haishravas: [beheaded chaishravas] 5-headed wingless pegasoid

hak: [Enki ape-hak kahepaikhe palindrome] amphibious pongoid from Enki system

hake: [*National Geographic Encyclopedia of Animals*] deep-sea fish from Europe, Terra (alpha Zodiaci III)

haku: [*Dell Crossword Puzzle Dictionary*] kingfish, see opan

hal-bird: [halberd mondegreen, Xanth series by Piers Anthony] very thin bird with very large, narrow axe-beaked head from Xanth

hale: [beheaded whale] whale mimicking schish gestalt

hali toad: [*Edge Chronicles* by Paul Stewart and Chris Riddell] frog-like reptilian with poisonous breathe

haliaeetus: [OviPets] eagle-like ornithoid

hall minotaur: [Godville] minotaur adapted from labyrinths to hallways

hallowienie: [Halloween wienie palindrome] dachshund-like devil dog

hallucinogenia: [*Wonderful Life* by Stephen Jay Gould, *The Big Bad Book of Beasts* by Michael Largo] invertebrate with 14 pincher-tipped tentacles and 16 defensive spikes without eyes, ears or mouth from Cambrian

halobacterium: extremophile bacterium resistant to extreme saltiness, see dunaliella

halrus: [herd of walruses spoonerism] mocking walrus-like amphibian

hameh: ["Xoology" by Kittenbaker] ornithoid that springs from murder victim's blood from Szurane

hamerkop: [*National Geographic Encyclopedia of Animals*] frog- and fish-eating chicken relative from Afro-Arabia, Terra (alpha Zodiaci III)

hamites: ammonite that uncoils from shell into hairpin shape from Cretaceous

hammel: [hammelhorn backformation] hornless hammelhorn

hammelope: [hammel antelope portmanteau] hammel with antlers

hammelhorn: [*Edge Chronicles* by Paul Stewart and Chris Riddell] shaggy, domesticated, black herd animal with large "sadface", 3 hooves per foot

hammerfly: [Xanth series by Piers Anthony] night construction insect from Land of Flies, Xanth

hammie: [*The Tree of Life* by Mark Michalowski] vicious pongoid predator symbiotic with trees of Life whose brains were absorbed when threatened by Tollipian virus
hammond: [ham and eggs mondegreen] egg-laying creature
Hampstead horror: ["The Adventure of the Lost World" by Dominic Green] trombone-crested hadrosaur, formerly from Maple White Land
hamsteer: [hamster-steer portmanteau] small rodentoid with large cheek pouches, horns and short tail
hamster: [hamster backformation] hamster-like predator that hamsts (stores food in cheek pouch)
hamstercat: [Cloudstone] hamster-like felininoid
han: [herd of swans spoonerism, handbird swan portmanteau] akateko-swan-like ornithoid
hanadak: ["Ewoks" series] ferocious creature like grizzly-baboon from Endor's moon, Jedi galaxy
handbird: [*The Right Hand of Dextra* by David J. Lake] hand-like ornithoid, in righthand, lefthand, firsthand, secondhand, hourhand, minutehand, onehand, otherhand varieties from Dextra, see akateko
handwalker: [snouter extrapolation] snouter adapted to walk on hands with atrophied feet and nasarium
hane: [herd of cranes spoonerism] ornithoid with long legs, long neck and long bill
hang: ["Squirrel Cage" by Robert Sheckley] flying predator that eats slegs from Seer
hangator: [hang alligator portmanteau] alligator-like predator whose bite morphs victim into hang
hantel: [hanelope backformation] antler-less handelope
hantelope: [herd of antelopes spoonerism] hantel with antlers
hanzo: [Monster Galaxy] rat-headed, blue biped with large, clawed hands, red wings with blue tips from Sagittarius

hapalops: [*After the Dinosaurs* by Donald R. Prothero] ground sloth from Miocene
Hapiazan clam: ["happy as a clam" mondegreen] smileyface clam from Hapiaza system
hapyxelor: [*Monster Spotter's Guide to North America* by Scott Francis] 7.5-meter sirenian with 3 eyes, aka mussie from Muskrat Lake, Ont., Terra (alpha Zodiaci III)
haran: [Star Trek] legendary "fire beast" from T'Khasi, Nevasa (40 Eridani) system
hāranka: [beheaded bhāranka] ornithoid
hardhat: [The Legend of Zelda] non-rock-spitting, rubbery beetle related to octorok, red much harder to kill than blue from Hyrule
hardim: [*Dell Crossword Puzzle Dictionary*] starred lizard, see agama
hareng: [Fr. Johann Martin Schleyer's Volapük] herring-like ornithoid from Schleyer's system
haregator: [hareg alligator portmanteau] alligator-like predator whose bite morphs victim into hareg
harger: [beheaded charger] war gan ceann
harikap: [*Palace of Love, Star King* by Jack Vance] large bristly biped from Sarkoy
haribou: [herd of caribou spoonerism, harikapt-caribou portmanteau] harikapt-headed caribou-like centauroid
harikapt: [harikap-apt portmanteau] bristly pongoid with white fur, 2 arms, 4 legs, hippo-like mouth with 2 large slightly curving tusks, large multi-lidded compound eyes
haringtonhippus: aka stilt-legged horse, but actually a horse mimic unrelated to horses, asses or zebras
harmonium: [*The Sirens of Titan* by Kurt Vonnegut, Jr.] kite-like, asexual, somewhat telekinetic, blind and deaf chiropteran from Mercury (alpha Zodiaci I)
harpymimus: [*Feathered Dinosaurs: The Origin of Birds* by John Long and Peter Schuten] 3-meter ornithomimosaur with beak with few teeth
harrekki: [*Wizard of Earthsea* by Ursula K. LeGuin] small dracoid the size of a girl's hand with wings and talons, feeding on worms,

wasps and sparrow's eggs from Iffish, Earthsea

harrot: [hawk parrot portmanteau] hawk-headed parrot-like ornithoid

harrow: [host of sparrows spoonerism, hawk-sparrow portmanteau] harrowing hawk-headed sparrow-like ornithoid

hash: [hash-dore-tso mondegreen] lion relative from Diné system

hash-dore-tso: [Navaho] lion-like felinoid from Diné system

hass: [herd of asses spoonerism] long-eared equinoid, see drass

hasty pudding: [pudding extrapolation] fast-moving pudding-thick ooze, see go puddling

hatazi: [Azerbaijani hata-tazi portmanteau] bug-greyhound, large, long-legged, carapaced beetle-like insectoid

hatrack coon: [hat raccoon mondegreen] domesticated raccoon adapted to nesting in hatracks

hattifattener: [*Finn Family Moonintroll* by Tove Janssen] aka hattifnattar and hattvatit, tall, thin, tubular, white, vibration-sensitive creature with side tentacles, grown from seeds

hattle: [herd of cattle spoonerism] bovinoid

haurok: [Star Trek] ornithoid from T'Khasi, Nevasa (40 Eridani) system

hawk: [National Geographic Encyclopedia of Animals] carnivorous bird

hawk-bat: [*Creatures of the Galaxy* by Phil Brucato, Bill Smith, Rick D. Stuart, Chuck Truett] purple or red with nooked beak and leathery wings from Coruscant or Taris, Jedi galaxy

hawk-owl: [hawk owl mondegreen] hawk-headed owl-like ornithoid

hawkbower: [*After Man* by Dougal Dixon] predatory bowerbird, male with flesh-tearing beak for attracting flies for females

hawkoon: [hawk-'coon portmanteau, "Robot Hugs" by R. Hugs'] griffinoid like hawk and raccoon

haxopod: [*Frostworld and Dreamfire* by John Morressy] beast of burden from Hraggellon (Dunuos II)

hayalit: [Star Trek] small, burrowing creature from T'Khasi, Nevasa (40 Eridani) system

haÿyoth: [*Angels* by Malcolm Godwin] fire-breathing yet heavenly beast

hcam: [Doria hcam machairod palindrome] sabre-toothed felinoid from Doria system

hcegila: [unhcegila backformation] non-man-eating dragon, see chivalrous shark

hdoretso: [hash-dore-tso mondegreen] lion-like felinoid from Ha rogue planet

he: [Indonesian/Malay hebat backformation] mammoth-bat griffinoid

headcrab: [Half-Life] aka head-humper, small, round parasite with 2 mottled tan and reddish hind limbs and 2 clawed forelimbs and beak between, in several varieties: watermelon-sized, both toxin- and radiation-resistant land and non-resistant aquatic, fast wall-walking and black or dark green poisonous with white knees and rattle-sound, controls host by covering face or whole head ("mawling") and substituting "chestmaw"

headwiggle: aka polliwog

heasant: [beheaded pheasant, head of pheasants spoonerism] pheasant gan ceann

heath-hound: headless hell-hound, 'ell-'ound

heaven hound: ["The Hound of Heaven" by Gerard Manley Hopkins] opposite of hell hound, see heptacorn

hebra: [herd of zebras spoonerism, horse zebra portmanteau] horse-headed zebra-like equinoid, see zorse

heckkius: voracious insectoid from Nytrino, Locomoto system, Galaxiki galaxy

heckyll: [Terra Monster] black, one-horned caninoid, see grynn and cackyll, from Terrarium

heckyllope: [heckyll antelope portmanteau] heckyll with antlers

hedamnu: [Hurrite] amphibious snake-dragon

heder: [*Dell Crossword Puzzle Dictionary*] unshorn sheep, see hogg

hedorah: ["Godzilla vs. Hedorah" aka "Godzilla vs. the Smog Monster"] 60-meter "flying pancake" garbage-eater with bulging eyes that leaves a sulphuric acid trail that grew into 120-meter amorph with red eyes, stumpy legs, pseudopods, long flat tail

heela: [*Warriors of Mars* by Edward Powys Bradbury and Michael Moorcock] 8-legged hyena-sized creature with 6 curved talons, long neck with 2 heads each with 4 eyes, razor-like teeth, 2 tails, barrel-like torso, that feeds on own dead when prey unavailable from Kane's world (Mars (alpha Zodiaci IV))

heep: [Cape Hope, herd or hurtle of sheep spoonerisms, beheaded sheep] sheep-like gan ceann from Cape Shope

heer: [herd of deer, spoonerism] antlered ruminant

hegetothere: [*After the Dinosaurs* by Donald R. Prothero] rabbit-like toxodont from Miocene

heid: [Afrikaans luiheid backformation] sloth-lui ancestral to lui (leopard-horse) and sloth

helicat: [GreenSpace] scavenger felinoid helicopteryx

helicoid: ["Mathematical Zoo" by Martin Gardner] creature shaped like helix or spiral, such as mumps virus

helicoprion: [*The Big Bad Book of Beasts* by Michael Largo] "buzz-saw shark", shark with saw-like rows of teeth

helicopteryx: [snouter extrapolation] hummingbird-like earwing with nearly-invisible rotating rather than flapping wing-ears, see helicat, rotorohippus

heliopath: [*Fantastic Beasts and Where to Find Them* by Newton Artemis Fido Scamander] tall, fiery creature

hellhound: aka demondog, calf-sized dark, shaggy canine with glowing red eyes, sometimes headless, from hell via Suffolk or Norfolk; see heath-hound, blackdog

hellbender: [*National Geographic Encyclopedia of Animals*] salamander from America, Terra (alpha Zodiaci III)

hellephant: [hellhound extrapolation, herd of elephants spoonerism] fire-breathing elephant

Hellguard virus: [*Pandora Principle* by Carolyn Clowes] silicon-based virus that bonds very fast with oxygen, but countered by fool's gold dust

hellspider: [sourceforge.net] hellish transdimensional arachnoid

hellworm: ["From Within" by Jonathan Glassner] parasitic worm that induces lust and violence

hemauchenia: [*After the Dinosaurs* by Donald R. Prothero] aka Blancan llama from Pliocene

hemicyon: [*After the Dinosaurs* by Donald R. Prothero] long-legged running bear from early Miocene

hemiped: mutant with half the usual number of legs, 2-legged quadruped, 3-legged insectoid, 6-legged arachoid, balaseli or crustacean, 8-legged ornad, 18-legged hocust

hen: [*Dell Crossword Puzzle Dictionary*] female chicken or salmon or chicken-salmon (chalmon) or salmon-chicken (sicken) ichthyopteryxes; [herd of wrens spoonerism]

hephalumph: [*Reignbeau's Riddles and Rhymes*: "The Hephalumph"] 4-meter, 3-eared, though deaf, pachyderm with red eyes, blue tail, turquoise nose and fondness for honey from Wildesmere

heptaskylos: [hexaskylos extrapolation] 7-headed hellhound

Heptops: [Grk. seven-eyed, Rev. 5:6] aka Septicorn, Jesus, the Lamb of God

her: [thrasher mondegreen] insect and berry-eating ornithoid from Thra system, see him

Heraclitus virus: [Warhammer 40,000] deadly virus used against Tyranids on Tarsis Ultra

herbil: [horde of gerbils spoonerism] small but ferocious horned rodentoid

heretic-ant: [Warhammer 40,000] omnivorous ant-like insectoid that eats from feet upward from Catachan

hericane: [hurricane mondegreen] female aerial dinoid sea monster, see himicane, strom

herill: [*Nomenclator Aquatitium Animantium* by Conrad Gesner] aka scweynwal quadrupedal ichthyoid with pig-like snout and ears

hermit: [*Diaspora* by Greg Egan] molluscoid with interferometer vision from the janus tree forests of Poincaré

heron: [*Dell Crossword Puzzle Dictionary*] wading bird, see ibis, rail, crane, egret, stilt, avocet, avoset, jacana, flamingo

heronster: [heron monster portmanteau] giant carnivorous heron-like ornithoid

herpetopteryx: ["snake-wing"] aka flying snakes, winged snake, related to dracoids

herrerasaur: [*The Mistaken Extinction* by Lowell Dingus and Timothy Rowe] 2.5-meter bipedal dinosaur or dinosauromorph

herrerataur: [herrerasaur minotaur portmanteau] bipedal bovinoid

herring-gull: [herring gull mondegreen] ichthyornis with herring-like head and gull-like body

Hesiodian chimera: chimera with heads of three different species

hesperocyon: [*After the Dinosaurs* by Donald R. Prothero] early weasel-like canine from Eocene

hesperopithicus: ape with pig-like prosthennops teeth from Pliocene

hesperornis: [*The Mistaken Extinction* by Lowell Dingus and Timothy Rowe] long-legged, long-necked, flightless diving bird from Cretaceous, related to ichthyornis

hessi: [Cyclopedia of Worlds] aka barn beetle, food 8-legged arthropod with iridescent plates from Cathole, Barnard system

heteroceratops: [homoceratops antonym] herbivorous ceratopsian dinosaur on Palul (Lar Don), the Dinosaur Planet

heterodontosaur: [*The Mistaken Extinction* by Lowell Dingus and Timothy Rowe] ornithopod descendant

heterothere: [heterothere antonym] toothless felinoid

hexa-puma: ["Ms. Midshipwoman Harrington" by David Weber] hexapodal puma-like felinoid from Sphinx

hexacamel: [N. M. Gibbons] bimorph aka trizebra, 6-legged zebral-like camel or 3-legged camel-like zebra

hexacamelope: [hexacamel antelope portmanteau] hexaccamel with antlers

hexagiraffe: [fairy chess] bimorph aka double zebra, 6-legged zebra-like camelopardoid or 8-legged giraffe-like zebra

hexaprotodon: [*After the Dinosaurs* by Donald R. Prothero] hippo from Miocene

hexapteryx: [*The Snouters* by Harald Stümpke] creature with 6 wings, such as Hi-Yi-Yi damselfly

hexaskylos: [pentaskylos extrapolation] 6-headed hellhound

hexip: [*The Right Hand of Dextra* by David J. Lake] equinoid from Dextra

heyuannia: [*Feathered Dinosaurs: The Origin of Birds* by John Long and Peter Schuten] crestless oviraptorosaur

hfeeder: ["The Worm Turns" by Gregory Benford] aka hydrophage, hydrogen-eating space creature with spokes, beams, rhomboids, fat curves, rough skin, prickly shells, rubbery rods and slick mirrors

hgi: [timber hgi high rebmit palindrome] mountaintop variety of rebmit

hgiliwt: [twilight hgiliwt palindrome] twilight variety of ad

hgin: [night hgin palindrome] nocturnal variety of diurnal ad, insectoid

hgkatha: [*Pawns and Symbols* by Majliss Larson] 6-legged, mahogany-colored burrower with slender muzzle from Tsorn

hi: [ba-goshi mondegreen] bovine from Bagonia, Bago system, see buffahi; [beheaded chi] large dracoid with red eyes green back and 3 heads

hia: [*Dell Crossword Puzzle Dictionary*] hawk parrot

hibex: [herd of ibexes spoonerism] high-flying ibex-like ornithoid

hicken: [headless chicken] chicken-like ornithoid except headless

Hickerson turtle: [Dean Hickerson in Game of Life] space-faring turtle capable of c/3

hickwall: [*Dell Crossword Puzzle Dictionary*] green woodpecker

hidebehind: [*Monster Spotter's Guide to North America* by Scott Francis] man-eater never seen until it's too late because of its ability to hide behind trees or rocks

hider: ["Fungi from Yuggoth" by Howard Phillips Lovecraft] fractal-dimensional like tiny tentacled blob, usually within other fractal, minion of Yog-Sothoth
hierocosphinx: falcon-headed lion
hierof: [hierophant mondegreen] ant-like insectoid that kills even when not hungry
highdeer: [hider mondegreen] rarely seen deer of mountain peaks
hiirnahr: [Estonian nahrhiir backformation] mouse-bat, ancestral to nahr (bat-mouse) and mouse
hiku: [*Dell Crossword Puzzle Dictionary*] scabbard fish from New Zeeland
him: [*Monster Spotter's Guide to North America* by Scott Francis] 2.1-meter, long-armed skunk ape from Hawley, TX, Terra (alpha Zodiaci III), see her
himamanāv: [Nepal. "snow man"] see yeti
himbur: dark brown furry with black extremities
himera: [beheaded Hesiodian chimera] chimera with heads of 2 different species
himicane: [hurricane backformation] aerial dinoid sea monster, see male strom, hericane
hiploop: [The Legend of Zelda] man-sized insectoid from Hyrule
hipokampus: [hipocampus mondegreen] creature from Romula, Galaxiki galaxy, see kampus, hyperkampus
hipparion: [*After the Dinosaurs* by Donald R. Prothero] last 3-toed horse from Pleistocene
hippodontia: [Cyclopedia of Worlds] 4-meter tall, long-legged quadruped on Palul (Lar Don), the Dinosaur Planet
hippogryph: horse-like griffinoid with eagle head and wings
hippopotamonstrosequiped: [hippopotamonstrosesquipedian backformation] monstrous hippoid with 2 extra legs
hippopotamoose: [hippopotamus-moose portmanteau] hippoid with moose-like antlers
hippopotamouse: [hippopotamus-mouse portmanteau] river-dwelling hippo-sized rodentoid

hipporcupine: [hippopotamus-porcupine portmanteau] hippoid with long, sharp, erectile quills
hiri: hiri-hiri nasna
hiri-hiri: [*After Man* by Dougal Dixon] predatory marsupial with snake-like prehensile tail
hirnahr: [one-eyed hiirnahr] one-eyed flittermouse
hirschwan: [German Hirsch-Schwan portmanteau] deer-swan griffinoid
hirsuk: [Dudekors "Hairy monster"] amphibious suk with thick matted hair and tough hide
hive-rat: [*King David's Spaceship* by Jerry Pourelle] fierce oviparous rodentoid from Makassar
hlai: [pl. hlaiin, *The Romulan Way* by Terisa Halekala-LoBrotto] large flightless food ornithoid from Eisn (128 Trianguli) system
hlinga: [*Double, Double* by Michael Jan Friedman] emotion-sensitive glowworm from Rythria
hlingator: [hlinga alligator portmanteau] alligator-like predator whose bite morphs victim into hlinga
hlorg: ["Contamination Crew" by Alan Nourse] pink omnivorous blob absorbs energy on atomic level via nuclear enzyme, particularly fond of carbon doubling in 8 hrs. but edible
hlorgator: [hlorg alligator portmanteau] alligator-like predator whose bite morphs victim into hlorg
hlvdaji: [Cherokee] lion-like felinoid from Tsalagi system
hlvdatsi: [Cherokee] tiger-like felinoid from Tsalagi system
hnoiyika: [pl. hnoiyikar] vicious weazel-like predator from ch'Rihan, Romulan Empire
hoatzin: [*National Geographic Encyclopedia of Animals*] "stinkbird", nearly flightless bird of Amazon, Terra (alpha Zodiaci III)
hobab: [Fr. Johann Martin Schleyer's Volapük] ox-like bovine from Schleyer's system
hobby horse: aka stick or cock horse, stick with horse's head, sometimes with wheel at rear

hocetus: [rodhocetus mondegreen] aerial dolphin-like relative of rod

hockroach: [hissing cockroach spoonerism] roach-like insectoid noted for kissing its victims to death

hodag: [*Monster Spotter's Guide to North America* by Scott Francis] 2.4-meter, black, horned creature with backspikes, spear-like tail in cave and shovel-nose varieties from Wisc., Terra (alpha Zodiaci III)

hodagator: [hodag alligator portmanteau] alligator-like predator whose bite morphs victim into hodag

hodgee: [*Monster Spotter's Guide to North America* by Scott Francis] 6-meter, long-necked lake snake with flippers, prey of hodging predators, from Lake Hodges, CA, Terra (alpha Zodiaci III)

hodgeel: [hodgee eel portmanteau] small hodgee-like lake eel

hog monkey: [Avatar: The Last Airbender: "Jet"] baboon-like simian with red eyes, dark face with pig-like snout, thicker upperhair, upward-pointing tusks

hogator: [hog alligator palidrome] alligator-like predator whose bite morphs victim into hog

hoggator: [hogg alligator palindrome] alligator-like predator whose bite morphs victim into hogg

hogg: [*Dell Crossword Puzzle Dictionary*] unshorn sheep, see heder; [hoggish backformation] omnivorous porcoid, see pigg, swin

hoggator: [hogg alligator portmanteau] alligator-like predator whose bite morphs victim into hogg

hogoose: [hog-goose portmanteau] long-necked griffinoid with cartiginious snout, four legs with hooves, see bargans

hohokum: ["The Gungan Frontier" by Chris McCubbin] fast-swimming, insectoid with wide flippers, short eyestalks and mandibles from Jedi galaxy

hokoratata: poisonous ichthyoid, mimicked by non-poisonous mock hokoratata, both from Deepsea (Phoenix IV), Galaxiki galaxy

hokuwa: [*Monster Spotter's Guide to North America* by Scott Francis] long-necked, small-headed lake snake from Devil's Lake, Wisc., Terra (alpha Zodiaci III)

hol: [athol mondegreen] light brown fish-eating chiropteran

holey cow: [Piers Anthony, holy cow mondegreen] brainless bovine full of holes, yet used as steed, from Xanth

holia: [*Dell Crossword Puzzle Dictionary*] humpback salmon, see haddo

holmesina: [*After the Dinosaurs* by Donald R. Prothero] giant armadillo from Pleistocene

Homeside magpie: ["From Galaxy to Galaxy" and "Ghost Ship Chrest IV" by Kurt Mahr] shaggy, gray, 1.5-meter ornithoid with spherical head, button eyes, long beak, one leg, 6-fingered arm, communicates via radiowaves from Virgo A galaxy

homoceratops: [Cyclopedia of Worlds] carnivorous ceratopsian dinosaur on Palul (Lar Don), the Dinosaur Planet

homodontosaur: [heterodontosaur antonym] ornithopod ancestor

homomys: [heteromys antonym] mouse-like rodentoid

homothere: [*After the Dinosaurs* by Donald R. Prothero] dirk-toothed cat from Pleistocene

homy: [Monster Galaxy] sardonic, multicolored molluskoid

hónatata: [*The Snouters* by Harald Stümpke] berry-eating snoutwalker with 4 nasaria from Hi-Yi-Yi Islands

Honey Island Swamp monster: [*Monster Spotter's Guide to North America* by Scott Francis] aka "wookie", 2.1-meter, gray, amphibious nape with yellow eyes, 4-toed feet from Honey Island swamp, LA, Terra (alpha Zodiaci III)

honeyrabbit: [honey bee-bunny rabbit portmanteau] aka honeybunny, rabbit-like burrowing creature that yields a honey-like excretion

honeysucker: [*Worlds Apart: Nat. Hist. of Furaha and Earth* by Souren Nyoroge] armored creature with long tail, neck and snout that eats both honey and larval aurae from Furaha (alpha Phoenicis IV)

honeytail: [*The Snouters* by Harald Stümpke] bee-eating snouter that secretes solidifying sella from nasarium and honey-like secretion from tail from Mitadina, Hi-Yi-Yi Islands

honkey: [hog monkey portmanteau] pig-headed simian that honks

honon: [aethonon mondegreen] bluish-green pegasus

hononster: [honon monster portmanteau] monstrous honon

hooded dasher: [*The Jesus Incident* by Frank Herbert and Bill Random] dangerous ground-dweller from Pandora

hoodwink: [M. F. Meikeljohn] bird too elusive to be seen or heard clearly or captured, see gowk, snipe [Terra Monster RPG] from Terrarium

hooey hound: [Popeye] aka painted wolf from Africa

hook spider: ["Realm of Fear"] Talarian arachnoid with half-meter legs from Talar

hoon: [*Eyes of he Overworld* by Jack Vance] grue-like predator

hoop snake: [*Monster Spotter's Guide to North America* by Scott Francis] venomous black serpent up to 4.5-meters, able to move quickly by biting its tail and rolling, from American Southwest, Terra (alpha Zodiaci III) or [*The Children Star* by Joan Slonczewski] L'li, see ouroboros, tzuchinoko

hoopworm: [Xanth series by Piers Anthony] worm able to move quickly by biting its tail and roll from Xanth

hoorah bird: [Xanth series by Piers Anthony] colorful, though ugly, bird that collects debris and bric-a-brac from Xanth

hoose: [herd of moose spoonerism, horse-moose portmanteau] horse-headed moose-like ruminant

hoot: [*Planiverse* by Alexander Dewdney] 2-D sea animal from Arde, Shems system, see ara and robor hoot

hootenant: [Terra Monster] owl-like ornithoid with armored head, see generowl, from Terrarium

Hoover hog: [slang] armadillo

Hoover hogator: [Hoover hog alligator portmanteau] alligator-like predator whose bite morphs victim into armadillo

hoover: [*Star Wars: Return of the Jedi* by James Kahn] quadruped with long, disproportionate snout and large eyes

hop'n'bop: [Odd Squad: Sector 21] triangulovorous, blue centauroid with red crest and tuff with hunger chest markings

hophead: double-mouth adapted to hopping, see chin-chilla, jawbreaker, from Thuban (alpha Draconis) system

hopiak: [*The Howling Stones* by Alan Dean Foster] flying creature like bird and bat with pink eye below and above short beak from Parramat archepelago, Senisran

hoplophoneus: [*After the Dinosaurs* by Donald R. Prothero] sabre-tooth-like nimravid from Oligocene

hopper: [*The Stars Are Ours* by Andre Norton] kangaroo rat-like creature that hopps (both hops and burrows) from Astra (Deutero-Sol II)

hoppie: [slang] flea

hopping fish: ["Return of the Kangaroo Rex" by Janet Kagan] rice-loving fish able to leap 3.6 meters from Mirabile

hopping hawk: [Peter MacInnis] flightless bird with winghooks from Ugly Islands

hoppolophorus: [propaleohoppolophorus mondegreen, hoppopotamus lophorus portmanteau] hoppopotamus relative

hoppopotamimus: [hoppopotamus backformation] hippo-like rabbit

hoppopotamus: [Wuz series by Douglas Hutchison] rabbit-like hippoid from Wuz

horeb: [Callisto series by Lin Carter] vile rodentoid from Thanator

horja: ["Planet of Lizard" by Bernd Perpline] mosquito-like insectoid from Topid

horker: [The Elder Scrolls III: "Morrowind"] white furred, tusked, water-breathing sirenians from near Solstheim

horklump: [*Fantastic Beasts and Where to Find Them* by Newton Artemis Fido Scamander] pinkish mushroom-like creature with black bristles that eats earthworms

horn adon: [hornadon mondegreen] adon with horns

hornadon: [*The First Kingdom* by Jack Kate] 2.1-meter, horned, fanged anthropoid

horned bear: [*Boris Karloff's Tales of Mystery* #50] bear with horns

horn et: [hornet mondegreen] et with horn-like call, see bloodhorn et

hornhead: [*After Man* by Dougal Dixon] see groath, moose-like antelope in helmeted variety with axe-shaped horns and water variety with branched horns and spade-shaped mouth

hornswoggle: [*Charlie and the Chocolate Factory* by Ronald Dahl] dangerous creature from Loompaland, Africa, Terra (alpha Zodiaci III)

horntail: [*Fantastic Beasts and Where to Find Them* by Newton Artemis Fido Scamander] 5-meter black, omnivorous dragon with bronze horns, spiked tail from Hungary, Terra (alpha Zodiaci III)

hornterror: [Perry Rhodan series] egglayer of which one egg can defoliate a planet, but secret molkex used as armor in Blue Empire ships

hornworm: [Xanth series by Piers Anthony] predatory worm with 4 horns that usually protrude above the surface attacks with corrosive poison strong enough to shatter stone from Xanth

horrane: [*After Man* by Dougal Dixon] cheetah-like gigantelope-eating primate with sharp teeth, curved claws

horria auss: ["Face To Face With Planet Scanodon" by Rocky Strone] auss from Scandon, Croft system

horse-fly: horse-headed fly-like insectoid

horse-hawk: horse-headed hawk-like ornithoid, see hurrok

horse-man: [horseman mondegreen] horse-headed anthropoid

horse-rhino: [*The Island of Dr. Moreau* by Herbert George Wells] horse-headed rhinoceros mutant

horswine: [horse-swine portmanteau] long-legged horse-like porcoid

hort: ["The Face of Evil" by Chris Boucher] piranha-like crustracean from Xoanon's world

hortabud: [Outernauts] immature hortasprout

hortakong: [Outernauts] mature hortasprout with fangs

hortakongator: [hortakong alligator portmanteau] alligator-like predator whose bite morphs victim into hortakong

hortasprout: [Outernauts] green planimal with six legs, see hortabud, hortakong

horust: ["Face To Face With Planet Scanodon" by Rocky Strone] large, terrestrial scavengers with 12 to 36 legs and multi-fingered antennae at both ends, pink chitinous plates up to 5 meters from Scandon, Croft system

hoska: [*Planets of the Galaxy* by Greg Farshtey, Bill Smith, Ed Stark] herding food ruminant from Essowin, Jedi galaxy

hotdog: [hot dog mondegreen] caninoid adapted to extreme heat

hoto: [Portuguese gafanhoto backformation] grasshopper-like insectoid from Gafa system

hotpepperfish: [pepperfish extrapolation] hot variety of pepperfish

hou tie: [Fringe] armored, anaerobic metallophage with tentacles, prey of kun tie

houndeye: [Half-Life] yellow-green triped with electric blue stripes, large black compound eyes, high-pitched bark, destructive pack harmonics, mouth on underbelly, related to panthereye

hourhand: [minutehand extrapolation] larger and slower variety of minutehand

horse-rad: [horseradish backformation mondegreen] horse-mimicking planimal

hout: [hover of trout spoonerism, hover trout portmanteau] trout-hummingbird like ichthyopteryx

houtou: [*Dell Crossword Puzzle Dictionary*] motmot from S. America, Terra (alpha Zodiaci III)

hovering haddock: [Odd Squad: Sector 21] haddock-like ichthyopteryx

hoverworm: [*Edge Chronicles* by Paul Stewart and Chris Riddell] 1-meter poisonous worm that explosively expels toxic gas

how: [horde of crows spoonerism] black predatory ornithoid

howboy: [cowboy hat spoonerism] rather large felinoid with wide brim for protecting its light-sensitive eyes from the sun

howl: [how owl portmanteau] owl-like ornithoid that says "how?" rather than "who?"

howler cat: ["Shabazzas Death Track" by H. G. Francis] forest felinoid from Lepso (Firing V)

howler caterpillar: ["The Element of Cold" by Arndt Ellmer] roaring, 30-cm, white and pink spotted caterpillar-like insectoid with need for uv from Azyrk

howler dog: ["Beasts of the Underworld" by Kurt Mahr] jungle caninoid from Geron

howler dogator: [howler dog alligator portmanteau] alligator-like predator whose bite morphs victim into howler dog

howler: [*Monster Manual* by Skip Williams, etal.] fur-less, violetish-gray, sickly-dog-like simian with misshapened shoulders, legquills and maddening howl, trained as mounts with difficulty, or carnivorous, reptilian quadruped from Yavin 5, Jedi galaxy

howlk: [hawk owl portmanteau] predatory ornithoid

howlrunner: [*Han Solo's Revenge* by Brian Daley] wild, canine-like omnivore from Kamar with humanoid-skull-like head

hownow: ["How now, brown cow"] brown bovinoid

hoxney: [Heliconia trilogy by Brian W. Aldiss] creature from Helliconia, Batalix-Freyr system

Hoylean dog: ["Dog Star" by Will Richardson (Bill DuBay)] giant, tentacled monster like that owned by Cable Renshaw named Nebraska from Hoyle

hplovec: [H. P. Lovecraft] raft-like water surface predator

hravas: [beheaded shravas] wingless pegasoid

hreshnik: [Armenian hresh-shnik portmanteau] monster-pig, giant, ferocious porcoid fro Adiusa, Goodiusa system. Galaxiki galaxy

hridon: [bothridon mondegreen] triphibious porcoid with fly-like wings

hridonster: [hridon monster portmanteau] monstrous flying porcoid

hrochrt: [Czech hroch-chrt portmanteau] hippopotamus-greyhound, large, gray, aquatic caninoid

hrotr: ["The Altar of Redemption" by Anne Laurie Logan] flying creature of the jauneans

hrtvor: [Croatian hrt-tvor portmanteau] greyhound-skunk, fast, malodorous mammaloid

hrumph: ["The Gungan Frountier" by Chris McCubbin] large herbivore beast of burden with antlers from Jedi galaxy

hsalf: [flashy hsalf] brightly colored oloc

hsel: [hsel klesh palindrome] klesh-like amphisbæna

hsi-fu: [fu-hsi backformation] snake-headed ox-like bovine

hsigo: ["Xoology" by Kittenbaker] winged simian from Szurane

hssiss: aka dark side dragon, large, dark gray reptilian, nearly invisible, from Stenness, Jedi galaxy

hsub: [bush hub palindrome] creature of jungle undergrowth

htar: [bishtar mondegreen] elephantine beast of burden from Bi system

htee: [htee teeth palindrome] right of passage quest beast

htif: [filthy htif palindrome] mudhen-like creature noted for filthiness

htyhr: [rhythm htyhr palindrome] blue-gray ornithoid

huaxignathus: ["old Chinese jaw", Feathered Dinosaurs: The Origin of Birds by John Long and Peter Schuten] 1.8-meter compsognathid with very long hands

hucklebear: [huckleberry backformation] see bluebear

hüen: [Fr. Johann Martin Schleyer's Volapük] hyena-like caninoid from Schleyer's system

huey: [Monster Galaxy] blue vulpinoid from Gemini constellation

huffalo: [herd of buffalo spoonerism, curtailed huffalon] tail-less huffalon

huffalon: [*Amazing Logic Puzzles* by Norman D. Willis] beast of burden from Dranac
huffalonster: [huffalon monster portmanteau] monstrous huffalon
hugger: [*The Barber of Aldebaran* by William Moy Russell] exotic life-form
huggernaut: [Godville] monster that kills by hugging, not crushing like juggernaut
hugl: ["The Chosen People" by Robert Randall] invested Nidor, see wiggle-worm until edris powder discovered
huhnerz: [German Huhn-Nerz portmanteau] chicken-mink, egg-laying, furry burrower with beak from Germa system
huhu: [Cherokee] yellow mockingbird-like ornithoid from Tsalagi system
huilliches: aka Chilean basilisk, long mouse-like rodent with rooster-like head
huit: [Fr. Johann Martin Schleyer's Volapük] oyster-like sea creature from Schleyer's system
huli jing: [Here Be Monsters almanac] 9-tailed fox aka kitsune in Japan and kurniho in Korea, Terra (alpha Zodiaci III)
hull rat: [Cyclopedia of Worlds] thin hexapod up to half-meter from gas giant Chassana
hum sow: [somehow spoonerism] hummingbird-like porcoid with wings that hum as it flies
huma: [*Music of Life* by Hazrat Inayat Khan] androgynous, carrion-eating phoenix from Persia, Terra (alpha Zodiaci III)
humar: [Fr. Johann Martin Schleyer's Volapük] lobster-like crustacean from Schleyer's system
humbaba: [*Here Be Monsters almanac*] hellfire-breathing gianthropoid with lion's mane, horns, feline face from Mesopotamia, Terra (alpha Zodiaci III)
humbug: [*The Phantom Tollbooth* by Norton Juster] large beetle-like insectoid in lavish coat, striped trousers, checkered waistcoat, spats and derby; insectoid mosaic; [hummingbird bug mondegreen] hummingbird-like insectoid

humbugator: [humbug alligator portmanteau] alligator-like predator whose bite morphs victim into humbug
humdinger: [*Fantastic Beasts and Where to Find Them* by Newton Artemis Fido Scamander] blibbering creature
hummelch: [German Hummel-Elch portmanteau] bumblebee-elk/moose, griffinoid with antlers and humming from Ahla, Ojikh system, Galaxiki galaxy
hummer: [Xanth series by Piers Anthony] mysterious humming flying creature from stagnant water whose hum is especially annoying to demons in Xanth
humming dog: ["The Glowing Eggs of Titan"] oviparous hummingbird-like caninoid from Titan (alpha Zodiaci VIa)
humming dogator: [humming dog alligator portmanteau] alligator-like predator whose bite morphs victim into humming dog
humming peeper: ["Ewoks" series] small, flying swamp-dweller with sleep-inducing hum from Endor I's forest moon, Jedi galaxy
hummingcow: aka hummingbird-cow griffinoid, see libri
humped man: [*The Night Land* by William Hope Hodgson] anthropoid from the Night Land
humpedback lizard: ["Liberation in Camouflage" by Michael Marcus Thurner] large sauroid with backhump from Sadik
humpf-humpf-a-dumpfer: [*If I Ran the Zoo* by Theodore Seuss Geissel] creature with very large, wide-set eyes
humrož: [Czech humr-mrož portmanteau] lobster-walrus, six-legged, eyestalked serenian with tusks and whiskers
humung: [humungous mondegeen] giant goose-like ornithoid
humungator: [humung alligator portmanteau] alligator-like predator whose bite morphs victim into humung
hunanothere: [*After the Dinosaurs* by Donald R. Prothero] giraffe near relative
hungry hairball: [hungry hippo extrapolation, "TerrorVision" by Ted Nicolaou] alien trash-eater

hungry hippo: ["Hungry, Hungry Hippo"] omnivorous hippoid
huou: [Vietnamese con huou backformation] creature ancestral to con and giraffe from Disa system
hurlew: [herd of curlews spoonerism] brownish, long-legged shore ornithoid
hurrok: [Tortall series by Tamora Pierce] aka "horse-hawk" predatory pegasus with claws rather than hooves
hurt panther: [heraldry] monstrous felinoid with blue spots with flaming mouth and ears
hurtle: [Cloudstone portmanteau] hare-turtle, lapoid-headed burrowing turtle
husavec: [Czech husa-savec portmanteau] goose-mammal, goose-like triphibious mammaloid
huse: [*Dell Crossword Puzzle Dictionary*] white whale from Caspian, Terra (alpha Zodiaci III), see beluga, huso
hush: [*High Stakes* by David Peters] somewhat like animated bearrug with coarse, matted brown fur
huso: see huse
hust: [Belarussian manhust backformation] mongoose-like burrower from Ma system, related to gar, goest, gosta, gouste, gust, gustë, gustiniai
hutia: [*National Geographic Encyclopedia of Animals*] lizard-eating rodent from Cuba, Terra (alpha Zodiaci III)
hviezdička: [Slovak *] 2-D pentapus or hexapus
hyaenodon: [*After the Dinosaurs* by Donald R. Prothero] primitive creodont from Oligocene
hyaenodonster: [hyaenodon monster portmanteau] hyena-like monster
hycust: [locust antonym] swarming mountain insectoid
hydra: [*The Big Bad Book* of Beasts by Michael Largo] snake-like dracoid with 7 regenerating heads from Greece, Terra (alpha Zodiaci III)
hydrae: [piscium extrapolation] egg-laying hydra

hydraclops: [Odd Squad: "Rise of the Hydraclops"] large, one-eyed, tentacled seamonster
hydralic ram: [Xanth series by Piers Anthony] large, curly horned, wooly sheep-like ruminant, related to battering ram, from Xanth
hydrapoid: [*The Microbots* #1] 4.5-meter tall gray-furred creature with mammoth-like body, tusks, 2 tentacle-like "trunks", 3 slimy, suckered feeding tentacles on either side of face
hydrarchos: [Alber Koch] 34-meter sea serpent
hydrusaur: sea serpent from Hydrus constellation
hyena-swine: [*Island of Dr. Moreau* by Herbert George Wells] hyena-headed porcine mutant
hyenat: [hyena-gnat portmanteau] small scavenger insectoid with powerful mandibles, short hind legs
hyla: [*Dell Crossword Puzzle Dictionary*] toad
hylighter: [*The Jesus Incident* by Frank Herbert and Bill Random] orange jellyfish-like lighter-than-air carnivore from Pandora
hymeri: ["Rhodan Times a Thousand" by Hans Kneifel] gliffer-eating forest lizard that gives off foul, nocturnal gas bubbles from Trafalgar (fka Magadona), Victory system, Demetria cluster
hyper lynx: [Godville] lynx-like plasmoid able to travel at lightspeed
hypercoryphodon: [*After the Dinosaurs* by Donald R. Prothero] rhino-sized coryphodon
hyperfish: [The Tick: "Pan-Celestial Challenge of Champions"] air-breathing hyperdimensional ichthyoids that travel in space-time in schools of up to 27 members
hypergriffin: [Final Crisis Aftermath: Run #4] hyperdimensional griffin-like monster
hyperkampus: [hipokampus backformation] hyperdimensional kampus
i: [beheaded hi] large dracoid with red eyes green back and 2 heads
ialp: [plaid ialp palindrome] plaid ornithoid
ialua: [café au lait ialua éfac, café noir ion éfac palindromes] light brown éfac

iao: [*Dell Crossword Puzzle Dictionary*] honey eater bird, see moho, manuao; [beheaded niao] 2-headed bird of ill omen
iaryt: [Tyrian iaryt palindrome] purplish brown ornithoid
iatnuom: [niatnuom elision] mountain goat-like ruminant
ib: ["The Amazing Carnival of Complaining" by Nathan Carlson and Phil Lollar] creatures with red nape (back of neck), see muloc, oloc, rab, rallod, reg
ibid: [*Dell Crossword Puzzle Dictionary*] lizard from Phillipines, see ibit
ibis: [*Dell Crossword Puzzle Dictionary*] wading bird, see rail, crane, egret, heron, stilt, avocet, avoset, jacana, flamingo
ibit: see ibid
ibla: [nibla elision] white ornithoid
ibling: [nibling (neice/nephew) elision] red-naped, immature unk
iblingator: [ibling alligator portmanteau] alligator-like predator whose bite morphs victim into ibling
ibong adarna: [*The Big Bad Book of Beasts* by Michael Largo] eagle-sized songbird with peacock tail and coma-inducing droppings from Philippines, Terra (alpha Zodiaci III)
ibrot: [torbie ibrot palindrome] furry with patchy markings of "red" (yellow-orange)/brown on "blue" (gray)/cream (very pale yellow-orange)
ic: [abannic mondegreen] red-orange creature from Aba, Taurus
ice crab: [Winx Club] cold-adapted crustacean
ice dragon: dracoid adapted to extreme cold from Sappire (Eno III), Galaxiki galaxy or [Odd Squad: Sector 21] Sector 21
ice screamer: [ice cream screamer portmanteau] screamer adapted to cold
ice shark: ["Ice Sharks" by Emile Edwin Smith] hibernating shark from Arctic, Terra (alpha Zodiaci III), see upland shark
ice snake: [Winx Club] ice-breathing serpentoid from Omega dimension, see snowsnake

ice-ant: ["Flight on Titan" by Stanley G. Weinbaum] cold-adapted insectoid from Nivia colony, Titan (Saturn (alpha Zodiaci VI)d)
ice-burro: [Edgar Rice Burroughs mondegreen] burro-like eguinoid adapted to arctic from Edgar system
ice-dragon: ["Once a Legionnaire" by Gerry Conway] dracoid from frigid Wondil IX
ice-wolf: ["Courier" by Keith Laumer] cold-adapted caninoid from Sköne or Vasa, Jorgensen's system
icebeast: ["Cauldron of the Transmitter" by Dirk Hess] 3-meter, slim, gray predator with 4 legs, long furry tail, broad head with 2 fangs from Kledzak-Mikhon
icegedunk: [*Monster Spotter's Guide to North America* by Scott Francis] flipper-less sirenian with wheel-like rear appendages
icegiant: large cold-adapted creature from Stiemond (Papiloma IV), star maelstrom between Ploohn-Nabyl and Mahagoul galaxies
icegoat: ["Demon of Red Dwarves" by Ernst Vlcek] goat-like ruminant adapted to cold from Ottooljim, Ottrahr system, Perseus arm
icespider: ["Ice Spiders" by Eric Miller] arachnid adapted to cold
icevia: [Monster Galaxy] serpentine with crystalline horn and mane
iceworm: [E. J. "Stroller" White] worms living in glacial ice, ["The Peace Mission" by Hubert Haensel, "The Ysterone" by Kurt Mahr] 30-meter, slimy variety from Worsian IV, All-Mohandot galaxy
ichibi: [Jap.] one-tailed tanuki (raccoon-dog)
ichneumon: [*Historia Animalium* by Conrad Gesner] aka Egyptian mongoose, long-tailed crafty enemy of dragons
ichthropoid: [ichthyo- anthropoid portmanteau, "The Creature from the Black Lagoon" by Maurice Zimm] fish-man creature
ichthyoid: fish-like creature
ichthyopteryx: ["fish-wing"] fish with wings, ancestor of ichthyornis
ichthyornis: ["fish-bird", *The Mistaken Extinction* by Lowell Dingus and Timothy

Rowe] seabird from Cretaceous, related to hesperornis, ichthyopteryx

ichthyosaur: ["fish-lizard"] fish-like aquatic dinosaur of Cretaceous, including opthalmosaur

icor: [nicor elision] creature like both elephant and ent

icosohedroid: ["Mathematical Zoo" by Martin Gardner] creature shaped like icosohedron including herpes, measles, and triola viruses

ichthyomorph: [*Starcross* by Philip Reeve] space-dwelling fish-like creature

id monster: ["Forbidden Planet" by Irving Block and Allen Adler] nearly invisible, large, hairy, ground sloth-like pre-Krell with hook-like claws materialized via brain energy from Altair (alpha Aquilae) IV, see brain beast

id na tao: [Filipino qanid na tao backformation] vulture-like ornithoid from Qa system

id nob: [Bondi idnob palindrome] blue ornithoid, see nob

idek: [Star Trek] creature from T'Khasi, Nevasa (40 Eridani) system

idercni: [incredible elb idercni palindrome] fantastic variety of elb-like spheroid, see aveilebnu

idhoggr: [nidhoggr elision, "id-tearer"] telepathic dracoid

idico: [nidicolous elision mondegreen] louse-like insectoid remaining in nest until able to fly

idifu: [nidifugous elision mondegreen] goose-like ornithoid whose hatchlings soon leave the nest

idigat: [Continuum] black, pack hunting leonid, both sexes maned from Amarillon, Nogullon system

idigator: [idigat alligator portmanteau] alligator-like predator whose bite morphs victim into idigat

idoffad: [Crayola daffodil idoffad palindrome] daffodil yellow creature from Crayol A

idrev: [verdigris irg idrev palindrome] blue-green irg

iduani: [inaudible elb iduani palindrome] seen but never heard variety of elb-[ke spheroid

ie: [tiffanie mondegreen] felinoid from Tiffa system

iec: [ceil iec palindrome] blue ornithoid

iellä: [Finnish niellä elision] swallow-like ornithoid

iffler: [niffler elision] iffling predator

ifirroh: [Horrific ifirroh palindrome] horrible monster

igar: [budgerigar mondegreen] mutant jungle-dwelling parrot-like ornithoid

igbekti: [nigbekti elision] man-eater

igelch: [German Igel-Elch portmanteau] hedgehog-elk/moose, burrower with digging antlers from Egeland [Afrikaansor Dutch egel-eland portmanteau]

iger: [beheaded tiger, ambush of tigers spoonerism] headless tiger-like gan ceann

iget: [zanigret mondegreen] mountain predator from Za system

Igeti ape: [Basque, Igeti ape-epaitegi portmanteau] ape-stingray ancestral amphibian to ape and stingray from Igeti system

igficli: [nigficli elision] man-eater

iggle: see bald iggle

ightingale: [nightingale elision] nightingale-like gan ceann

Igi snake: [Igi lab baligi palindrome] geneered baligi-like amphisbæna from Igi laboratories

igitz: ["The Gungan Frontier" by Chris McCubbin] small blue batrachian with webbed hind feet and clawed forefeet and hind fins

igjanto: [nigjanto elision] triphibian predator

ignatni: [intangible elb ignatni palindrome] electric variety of elb-like spheroid, see ahcuotnu

ignitler: [Terra Monster] small flamoose from Terrarium

igōli: [anigōli mondegreen] perch-like ichthyoid from A system

igopogo: [*Monster Spotter's Guide to North America* by Scott Francis] 21-meter gray, dog-headed, air-breathing creature with flippers from Lake Simcoe, Ont., Terra (alpha Zodiaci III), related to Beaverton bessie and Kempenfet Bay kelly varieties

igret: [zanigret mondegreen] mountain predator from Za system

igrifani: [milligrifani mondegreen] green millipede

igriou: [Grondo "lazy"; *La Découverte de L'Empire de Cantahur* by De Varennes de Mondasse] white donkey-like person-shy equinoid from Cantahar Island that needs dog for motivation

igobird: [blindigobird mondegreen] blind-as-a-bat cave ornithoid with sonar

iguana: [*Dell Crossword Puzzle Dictionary*] lizard, see gila, gecko, guana, skink, varan

iguanadon: [Gideon Mantell] large herbivorous dinosaur, quadruped (or not), with nose-horn (or thumb-claw)

iguanadonster: ["The Giant Gila Monster" by Ray kellogg] iguanadon monster portmanteau] iguana-like monster

iguanat: [iguana-gnat portmanteau] small, 6-legged sauroid

igum: [igum imugi palindrome] imugi-like amphisbæna

ihc: [china animal ananymondegreen] animated china creature from Laminaa system

ihcnat: [tanchinaro ananymondegreen] black-and-silver ornithoid from Ora system

ihcro: [orchid ihcro palindrome] purplish pink ornithoid, see ihscuf

ihi: [*Dell Crossword Puzzle Dictionary*] stitchbird

ihscuf: [fucshia ihscuf palindrome] pinkish purple creature, see ihcro

ihselttab: [battleship ihselttab palindrome] metallic gray ornithoid

ijamo: [omajinakoos ananymondegreen] brown lake snake with rat's tail from Sooka system

ik: [botik mondegreen] small pongoid with fly-like wings; [bulanik mondegreen] from Bulga system

ikka: [ikkas isakki palindrome] wild caninoid

iknit: [stinking niknits palindrome, elision] malodorous arachnoid

ikopi: ["The Gungan Frontier" by Chris McCubbin] long-legged quadruped with question-mark-shaped horns (said to cure shaupat bite) and long hollow tongue from Naboo plains, Jedi galaxy

ikpmup: [pumpkin inpmup palindrome] orange ornithoid

ikthos: ["Prince of Peril" by Otis Adelbert Kline] hideous, scaly pet with tusks, long tail from Zarovia (Venus (alpha Zodiaci II))

ikun: ["ikun at times emit tanuki" palindrome] raccoon-dog gestalt

il: [nil elision] hippopotamus-horse

ila: [agan ila kalinaga palindrome] kalinaga-like amphisbæna from Aga system

ilager: [regalia ilager palindrome] purplish ornithoid that ilages

ilc: [cliff ilc mondegreen] cliff-dwelling ornithoid

ilgai: [nilgai elision] antelope-like ruminant

ilgfee: [red ilgfee reef glider palindrome] red reef glider-like creature

ilgfeel: [ilgfee eel portmanteau] non-red ilgfee-like eel

iliboru: [urobilin iliboru palindrome] brownish orange creature

ilijah: [*The Gods of the Underworld* by Stephen Cole] voracious lizard with parasitic young geneered by Boor and later by Venedel

ilingoceras: [*After the Dinosaurs* by Donald R. Prothero] pronghorn with straight spiral horns from Miocene

iliphint: three-eyed pachyderm

ilj: [Dutch niljpaard backformation elision] hippopotamus-horse ancestral to horse and hippopotamus

ill: [llinav ananymondegreen] yellowish, off-white ornithoid from Va system

illa: [vanilla moose mondegreen] moose-like ruminant from Va system

illard: [grouillard mondegreen] crackler with millipede-like larvae

iller quail: small ornithoid with mottled plumage and short tail from Iller

illica: [illica bacilli palindrome] microscopic disease organism

illithida: [pl. illithidae, *Monster Manual* by Skip Williams, etal.] Illithid-like creature including cessirid, embrac, kigrid and saltor

illuyanka: [Hittite] hydra-like 7-headed dracoid

ilma kabosh: [*Planiverse* by Alexander Dewdney] 2-D sea animal from Arde, Shems system

ilo: [olid ilo, solitary rat ilos palindromes] malodorous lone-wolf rodentoid, see nar, see erua

ilop: [Catalan antilop backformation] elk/moose-antelope, ruminant ancestral to elk or moose and antelope

ilope: [il antelope portmanteau] il with antlers

ilski: [Croatian nilski konj elision backformation] hippopotamus-horse ancestral to horse and hippopotamus

ilut: [tulip ilut] pink ornithoid

im: ["The Stranger" by H. G. Ewers] insectoid symbiot in chelao gestalt, see thread devils and membrillas

imac: [caminalcole ananymondegreen] spotted triped without claws or unspotted, quadruped with claws from Elocla system

imdugud: griffin from Mesopotamia

imoba: [abominable Elban imoba palindrome] monstrous creature from Elba system

imretxe: [exterminator ananymondegreen] semi-transparent dracoid from Rota system

imugi: large python-like water or cave snake from Korea, Terra (alpha Zodiaci III)

in'hhui: [*The Romulan Way* by Terisa Halekala-LoBrotto] ichthyoid from ch'Rihan, Eisn (128 Trianguli) system

ína: [Icelandic canína backformation] lapoid from Ca system

ínadv: [Cherokee] snake-like creature from Tsalagi system

inadzuk: [Armenian sardinadzuk backformation] sardine-spider, sea arachnoid ancestral to land spider and small ichthyoid

inafrog: predatory batrachian with poison gas bubbles from Bubblefire, Locomoto system, Galaxiki galaxy

inafrogator: [inafrog alligator portmanteau] alligator-like predator whose bite morphs victim into inafrog

inága: [beheaded linága] 997-headed snake

inágator: [inága alligator portmanteau] alligator-like predator whose bite morphs victim into inága

inata: [satanic inatas palindrome] Tasmanian devil-like omnivore

incisivosaur: [*Feathered Dinosaurs: The Origin of Birds* by John Long and Peter Schuten] 1-meter primitive oviraptorosaur with buckteeth

indigobird: [grue-bleen extrapolation] bird that remains indigo, not to be confused with blindigobird, gebird, grindigobird, rindigobird, vindigobird or yindigobird from Ora system

indri: [*National Geographic Encyclopedia of Animals, Dell Crossword Puzzle Dictionary*] short-tailed lemur from Madagascar, Terra (alpha Zodiaci III), see maki

indricotherium: [*The Big Bad Book of Beasts* by Michael Largo] hornless rhino with horse-like legs, see Persian ass

ined: [denim ined palindrome] blue ornithoid

inesra: [arsenic inesra palindrome] gray ornithoid

infinity worm: [*Keys of Infinity* by Clifford A. Pickover] worms with highly variable life expectancies from short-lived greens (11.86 yrs.), through goldens, grays (13.17 yrs.), blues (237 yrs.), violets (391 yrs.), crimsons (147,000 yrs.) and virtually immortal blacks and transparents from Callisto (Jupiter (alpha Zodiaci Vd))

ingbird: [mockingbird mondegreen] parrot-like ornithoid predator of gibbee from Ing system, see gibber

ingen: [ningen elision] cuckoo-rabbit, long-eared burrowing griffinoid

ingenia: [*Feathered Dinosaurs: The Origin of Birds* by John Long and Peter Schuten] 2-meter oviraptorosaur with low crest, short arms

inipollac: [inipollac scallopini palindrome] food animal

inippus: [beheaded minippus] small gan ceann

inisid-isda: [Filipino maninisid-isda backformation] cormorant-like ornithoid from Ma system

inkanyamba: ["Animal X"] horse-headed serpentoid from Howick Falls, S. Africa, Terra (alpha Zodiaci III) [Here Be Monsters almanac] or 2 antelope heads

inki: [ninki-nanka elision] creature ancestral to nanka and inki-nanka

inkt: [Dutch inktvis backformation] squid-fish, feeding-tentacled ichthyoid ancestral to fish and squid

inlarga: [Outernauts] mature inlargamorph

inlargamorph: [Outernauts] 6-legged, brain-eating parasite with nosehorn, spikes, see inlargapup, inlarga

inlargapup: [Outernauts] immature inlargamorph

inlargator: [inlarga alligator portmanteau] alligator-like predator whose bite morphs victim into inlarga

inlati: [*Doomsday World* by Carmen Carter, Peter David, Michael Jan Friedman and Robert Greenberger] spicy-tasting ichthyoid

inoceramimus: [inoceramus backformation] clam-mouthed bottom fish

inoceramus: 2-meter flat clam from Cretaceous

inoli: [Cherokee] badger-like burrower from Tsalagi system

insinuosaur: [*The New Dinosaurs* by Dougal Dixon] coneater-mimicking jinx

inspector: ["Fungi from Yuggoth" by Howard Phillips Lovecraft] magic-eating fractal-dimensional like thin spiky tube with blob at one end, minion of Yog-Sothoth

instinct warrior: ["The Instinct Warrior" by H. G. Francis] predator from Zentapher

intellect devourer: [*Monster Manual* by Skip Williams, etal.] bred by Illithid, [*The World of Synnabarr* by Raymond C. S. McCracken] very dangerous relative of shoo monster from Synnabarr, fka Mars (alpha Zodiaci IV)

interro: [interro gator backformation] bloodhound-parrot-like ornithoid

interro gator: [interrogator mondegreen] alligator-like predator whose bite morphs victim into interro

into: [beheaded pinto] piebald or mottled gan ceann

investi: [investigator backformation] bloodhound-like caninoid

investi gator: [investigator mondegreen] alligator-like predator whose bite morphs victim into investi

invisible: ["Superman under the Red Sun"] large land octopus from Krypton, Rao system

io: [*Dell Crossword Puzzle Dictionary*] peacock butterfly or moth, see kiho

io-hippus: [beheaded miohipppus mondegreen] horse-like pegaoid with butterfly or moth-like wings

iocaudate: [cardiocaudate mondegreen] red butterfly with heart shaped wings

ioceras: [procranioceras mondegreen] horned dinosaur from Procra system

iomahc: [chamois iomahc palindrome] yellow or grayish yellow ornithoid

iomimus: [dromiceiomimus mondegreen] butterfly/moth mimicking hummingbird-like ornithoid

ion: [café au lait ialua éfac, café noir ion éfac palindromes] dark brown éfac

ionster: [ion monster portmanteau] monstrous dark brown éfac

ip: [spinach ananymondegreen] non-man-eating spinach mimic

ipal: [lapis lazuli Luzal's ipal palindrome] blue ornithoid from Luzal system

ipe: [sepia ipes palindrome] old ivory furry with dark brown ticking

ipogo: [manipogo mondegreen] lake snake from Ma system

iponi: [sinopia iponi palindrome] dark reddish brown ornithoid

ipparion: [beheaded hippion] 3-toed gan ceann

Ipsllean spider: ["Red Ipslle Bell Spider"] red Bell spider-like space creature from Ipslle system

iput: [stupid iputs palindrome] lemming-like rodentoid

ir: [telp ir triplet palindrome] telp-like mammaloid with three breasts

iraco: [ocarinabird ananymondegreen] ocarina bird-like ornithoid from Driba system

iram: [iram aramari palindrome] aramari-like amphisbæna

irap: [Paris irap palindrome] toxic emerald green ornithoid

irati: [Slovenian šikanirati backformation] caninoid from Šika system

Iratus bug: ["Star Gate: Atlantis" series] large insectoid that morphs more and more into its prey from Pegasus galaxy

Iratus bugator: [Iratus bug alligator portmanteau] alligator-like predator whose bite morphs victim into Iratus bug

irba: [nirba elision] aquatic reptilian with large head and foreclaws and long tail

iree: [eerie iree palindrome] eerie black ornithoid

ireel: [iree eel portmanteau] eel-headed iree-like ornithoid

iretsiw: [wisteria iretsiw palindrome] lavender ornithoid

irg: [sangria irg nas mondegreen] reddish purple na, see idrev

irgator: [irg alligator portmanteau] alligator-like predator whose bite morphs victim into irg

iri: [iris iri palindrome] blue ornithoid

iriaze: [*Creatures of the Galaxy* by Phil Brucato, Bill Smith, Rick D. Stuart, Chuck Truett] brown, furry, bipedal ungulate with one horn, long 'roo-like tail from Muunilist and Dantooine. Jedi galaxy

Irish elk: [megaloceras giganteius, *After the Dinosaurs* by Donald R. Prothero] moose-like deer with 3.6-meter antlers

irkangu: [nirkangu elision] bird-headed caninoid

irli: [nirli elision] orthinoid aka early bird

iron horse: large, powerful knightmare

iron-eater: ["The Bio-breeder" by Peter Terrid] insectoid from Ohhgras that excretes iron

ironbelly: [*Fantastic Beasts and Where to Find Them* by Newton Artemis Fido Scamander] metallic gray, 6-tonne dragon with deep red eyes from Ukraine, Terra (alpha Zodiaci III)

irpac: [capri itrpac palindrome] light sky blue ornithoid

irukk: ["irukk at times emit takkuri" palindrome] buzzard gestalt

irzibaj: [jabizri ananym] flying beetle with pale blue back and glossy black underbelly with bright red spots from Ahla, Ojikh system, Galaxiki galaxy

isaacasi: [Isaac Asimov mondegreen] moth-like insectoid gestalt

isak: [pl. isakki, *Fortune's Light* by Michael Jan Friedman] wild, toothy, black caninoid from Imprima, muzza ("bitch")

ischyrosmilus: [*After the Dinosaurs* by Donald R. Prothero] sabre-toothed cat from Zanclean age (early Pliocene)

iserri: [irresistable Elbit's iserri palindrome] cerise creature from Elbit system

iset: [janiset mondegreen] weasel-like predatory rodent from Ja system

ishcuf: [neon fuchsia ishcuf palindrome] purplish red noen

íshinú: [níshinú elision] herring-headed amphibious caninoid

ishravas: [beheaded aishravas] 3-headed wingless pegasoid

ishu: [ishu fu-hsi palindrome] fu-hsi-like amphisbæna

isivni: [invisible elb isivni palindrome] never-seen but heard variety of elb-like spheroid, see iduani

isopod: [*The Big Bad Book of Beasts* by Michael Largo] aka pillbug, crustacean able to curl into pill-shape

isser: [isser cressi palindrome] cressi-like amphisbæna

istes: [dalanistes mondegreen] amphibean with long snout from Dala system

isualpmi: [implausible elb isualpmi palindrome] rare variety of elb-like spheroid, see aborpmi

it: [tinamou ananymondegreen] flightless, game ornithoid from Uoma system

it-kutch: [*If I Ran the Zoo* by Theodore Seuss Geissel] flat-footed quadruped with crest, puffy tail and large eyes

it: [valit mondegreen] red burrower, related to it and kutch, [kanitt mondegreen] furball from Ka system

ita: [Filipino pugita backformation] octopus-dog ancestral to dog and octopus

itch beetle: [Alien Pet: "I Was A Teenage Bearded Boy" by Japhet Asher] small beetle-like insectoid from Confirma

itch-a-pod: [*On Beyond Zebra* by Theodore Seuss Geissel] furry biped with striped neck, itchy feet

itchfly: [Xanth series by Piers Anthony] from Land of Flies, Xanth

itchyworm: [*A Hero's Guide to Deadly Dragons* by Hiccup Haddock III] small, chili red, blood-sucking pack-hunting dracoid with painful sting from Barbarian archipelago

itcra: [antarctic, arctic itcra palindrome] arctic ant-like insectoid

ite: [mesite mondegreen] insect, seed and invertebrate-eating ornithoid from Me system

itnam: [mantis itnam palindrome] greenish insectoid

Itnatan shrimp: [Atantia itnata palindrome] shrimp-like sea creature from Itnata system

itoare: [Romanian ciocanitoare mondegreen] woodpecker-like ornithoid from Cioca system

itreraptor: [buitreraptor mondegreen] lavender dinosaur

itrot: [tortie itrot palindrome] furry with tortoiseshell (black, "red" (yellow-orange), cream) markings

ittehgap: [spaghetti ittehgaps palindrome] long, thin red and white worm

ity: [wality mondegreen] green gopher-like burrower

iuq: [Quinacridone Nodircan iuq palindrome] from Nodirca system, see elrah, noj

iutouniao: [beheaded jiu tou niao mondegreen] 8-headed bird of ill omen

iv: [vinagroon ananymondegreen] scorpion-like creature from Nooraga system

ival: [nival elision] ptarmigan-partridge ornithoid

ivaz: [zavinac ananymondegreen] herring-like ichthyoid from Ca system

ivedder: [red devil ivedder palindrome] dark crimson ornithoid that iveds

ivil: [livid ivil palindrome] blue-gray ornithoid

ivory sail: ["The Worm Turns" by Fregory Benford] ivory-colored solar sail with spars from HD209458 system

ivory sailfish: [ivory sail sailfish portmanteau] sailfish-like golem made from ivory

ivto: [beheaded divto] 2-headed, nocturnal, venomous snake

iwedi: [niwedi elision] red sidewinder-like amphisbæna

iwha: [taniwha mondegreen] sea monster from Ta system

iwhsa: [niwhsa elision] ashwinder-like amphisbæna

ixxen: ["The Dogtown Tourist Agency" by Jack Vance] blind fox-like animal that sometimes raise wild Gomaz children on Long Bones steppes, Maz

iylf: [niylf elision] flying dracoid

iynx: wryneck woodpecker

izard: [lizard spoonerism] reptilian from Labydo, Lant, Lelk systems, in eye

izlard: [lizard spoonerism] fatty reptilian

j: [Xanth series by Piers Anthony] cheery, crested bird in blue, green and red varieties from Xanth

j'suna: ["The Menace of Mystery Island", "Cosmo turns Traitor"] alien pet of D'jann

ja: [pl. j'ja, *Tarzan the Terrible* by Edgar Rice Burroughs] sabre-toothed, yellow-and-black striped lion-like felinoid from Pal-ul-don, Zaire, Terra (alpha Zodiaci III); ["Confluence" by Brian Aldiss] depraved underground from Myrin; [Slovenian kanja backformation] buzzard-like ornithoid from Ka system; [curtailed jay] blue, tail-less ornithoid

ja kacka: [Belarussian dzika ja kacka backformation] boar-duck, tusked triphibian

jabberwock: [*Through the Looking-Glass* by Charles Ludwidge "Lewis Carroll" Dodgeson, illustrated by John Jenniel] 6-meter tall creature with thin legs, 3-toed dinosaur-like foot, thin arms with 3 long furry claws, long rat-like tail, bat-like wings, pear-shaped body, serpentine neck, fish-like head with fins jutting from lower jaw and tendrils from sides of mouth, bug-eyes, antennae, scales, but no nose

jabizri: [*The Voyages of Dr. Dolittle* by Hugh Lofting] 7.5-cm flying beetle with glossy black back with bright red spots and pale blue underbelly

jaboon: ["The Gungan Frontier" by Chris McCubbin] slow long-eared, fork-tailed quadrupedal herbivore with leathery hide from Jedi galaxy

jacana: [*National Geographic Encyclopedia of Animals*] large-footed, leaf-hopping bird from India and S. E. Asia, Terra (alpha Zodiaci III), [*Dell Crossword Puzzle Dictionary*] wading bird, see ibis, rail, crane, egret, heron, stilt, avocet, avoset, flamingo

jackalope: [*Monster Spotter's Guide to North America* by Scott Francis] aka deer-bunny, "warrior rabbit", 1.2-meter lapoid with antlers from Wyoming, Terra (alpha Zodiaci III) or [*Monster Galaxy*] batwinged variety from Leo constellation; [jackal antelope portmanteau] jackal with antlers

jackass-rabbit: [contracted to jackrabbit] jackass-headed lapoid, see mule rabbit

jacu: [*Dell Crossword Puzzle Dictionary*] bird from S. America, see guan, sylph, turco, seriema

jaculus: [The Big Bad Book of Beasts by Michael Largo] "lance snake", flying serpent that kills by impaling

jaeger: [*Dell Crossword Puzzle Dictionary*] gull, see skua, allan

jaekelopterus: [*The Big Bad Book of Beasts* by Michael Largo] 2.4-meter sea arthropod with 16 crawling legs, front pincher-claws from Permian

jag: [Monster Galaxy] leopard-spotted, 4-legged landshark

jagar: [jaguar cougar portmanteau] jaguar-headed cougar-like felinoid

jagator: [jag alligator portmanteau] alligator-like predator whose bite morphs victim into jag

jagg: [jaggy backformation] jagged rock mimic

jaggator: [jagg alligator portmanteau] alligator-like predator whose bite morphs victim into jagg

jaglui: [Afrikaans jagluiperd backformation] cheetah-horse ancestral to horse and cheetah

jaguon: [Jets*Rockets*Spacemen Trading Card #45] lion-like felinoid adapted to high temperatures

jaguonster: [jaguon monster portmanteau] monstrous jaguaon

jaiga: ["Gamera vs. Jiger", aka "Gammera vs. Monster X" by Fumi Takahashi] 60-meter long stregosauroid that can spit quill-like spears, shoot heat ray, fly using jets under neck shield

jaigator: [jaiga alligator portmanteau] alligator-like predator whose bite morphs victim into jaiga

Jaiwanese frog: [*Genius Loci* by Ben Aaronovitch] ritually burned giant batrachian beast-of-burden from Jaiwan

jak: [Fr. Johann Martin Schleyer's Volapük] shark-like ichthyoid from Schleyer's system

jakabird: ["The Beast with a Billion Backs" by Eric Kaplan] angeloid that feeds off parasites from electro-matter bubble universe

jakal: [Fr. Johann Martin Schleyer's Volapük] jackal-like caninoid from Schleyer's system

jakalope: [jakal antelope portmanteau] jakal with antlers

jakrab: [*Creatures of the Galaxy* by Phil Brucato, Bill Smith, Rick D. Stuart, Chuck Truett] hare-like rodentoid from Tatooine, Jedi galaxy

jamod: [Fr. Johann Martin Schleyer's Volapük] camel-like desert quadruped from Schleyer's system

jan: [jelly flan portmanteau] flelly ooze between jelly and flan thickness

janais: [*Timeless* by Stephen Cole] pet from Gallifrey which exhales time, but apparently dies in Big Bang after eating Time Vortex wraiths

janglefish: musical ichthyoid from Atnam, moon of Tamanta, Stamanta system, Galaxiki galaxy

janiset: [*After Man* by Dougal Dixon] weasel-like predatory rodent

janoid: Janus-like two-faced creature

janther: [jaguar panther portmanteau] jaguar-headed panther-like felinoid

japote: [Babylon 5: "Knives" by Lawrence G. DiTillio] food animal from Centauri Prime

jaq: [Outernauts] pumpkin-beast with purple eyes, see jaqopee, jaqgrowl

jaqgrowl: [Outernauts] mature jaq with more spikes

jaqopee: [Outernauts] immature jaq

jarel: [Ili-Golik dzharel] small horned equinoid from T'Khasi, Nevasa (40 Eridani) system

jarelope: [jarel antelope portmanteau] jarel with antlers

Jarvis' sea-monster: [*Four-Day Planet* by H. Beam Piper] source of tallow wax, main export from Fenris

jasimha: [gajasimha mondegreen] gray-green elephant-lion, elephant-headed lion-like felinoid

jastrike: [Terra Monster RPG] large, predatory ornithoid, not as stealthy as striken, from Terrarium

javelina: [museumofhoaxes.com by Alex Boese] prehistoric horned porcoid, ancestor of rackabore

jawalker: [snouter extrapolation] snouter with atrophied legs and nasarium and "double-jaw" adapted for both walking up to and then swallowing prey

jawbreaker: [hophead extrapolation] large hophead with jaws adapted for pouncing on and stunning or crushing prey from Thuban (alpha Draconis)

jawflipper: [snouter extrapolation] predatory snouter with atrophied legs and nasarium adapted to backflipping upon unsuspecting prey by opening jaw

jay-hawk: [jay hawk mondegree] jay-headed hawk-lik ornithoid from Kansas, Terra (alpha Zodiaci III)

je-june bug: [jejune june bug portmanteau, Xanth series by Piers Anthony] dull, uninteresting insect from Xanth

je-june bugator: [je-june bug alligator portmanteau] alligator-like predator whose bite morphs victim into je-june bug

jebei noion: ["The Mysterious Barbarian" by Peter Terrid] war ornithoid

jeep: [Popeye] hyperdimensional, bipedal painted wolf hydrid with bear-like head, large nose, long tail able to teleport from Africa

(yellow with black spots), Indiana (blue and gray) or (red and black) Ohio, Terra (alpha Zodiaci III)

jeholornis: [*Feathered Dinosaurs: The Origin of Birds* by John Long and Peter Schuten] l-meter long-tailed bird from early Cretaceous, see shenzhouraptor

jello: [Outernauts] immature jellocto

jellocerator: [Outernauts] mature jellocto

jellocto: [jellyfish-octopus compound, Outernauts] venomous, jellyfish-like sea creature with double crests, see jello, jellocerator

jelly: [*Monster Manual* by Skip Williams, etal.] jelly-thick ooze

jelly-belly: ["On the High Frontier" by Michael F. Flynn] like jellyfish, whale, tent caterpillar and radio, and unlike all of them, source of stardust, prey of gossamer tigers

jellyf: [jellyfish backformation] jellyfish mimic

jellyfish-spider: [*Imperial Moon* by Christopher Bulis] lo-gee creature like jellyfish and spider from Phiadora

jen: [Romanian paianjen backformation] arachnoid from Paia system

jennet: [Dell Crossword Puzzle Dictionary] small horse, see gennet, genette

jenny: female donkey, wren or donkey-wren-like pegasoid

jequard: [*Pawns and Symbols* by Majliss Larson] creature from Aldebaran (alpha Tauri) system

jerff: [Swedish] see gulon

Jerrya hern: [Jerry Ahern mondegreen] hern-like ornithoid from Jerrya system

Jersey Devil: [Alex Crow, James Harding, *Monster Spotter's Guide to North America* by Scott Francis] egg-laying creature with long pointed bill, 4 clawed (or cloven) legs, bat-like wings, mule-like head, one eye and armored body resembling tiger, vampire and bovalupus from Pine Barrens, NJ. Terra (alpha Zodiaci III)

jestar: [Terra Monster] purple bipedal fox-like, teleporting creature with jester-like crest, see pranktail, from Terrarium

jeval: [Fr. Johann Martin Schleyer's Volapük] horse-like quadruped from Schleyer's system
jevalope: [jeval antelope portmanteau] jeval with antlers
ježirafa: [Croatian jež-žirafa portmanteau] hedgehog-giraffe, small, giraffe-like burrower with clawed forelegs and shovel-like horns
jha: bipedal, silver wolf-like caninoid from Jharv, Golden Axe system, Galaxiki galaxy
jhimn: [*The Romulan Way* by Terisa Halekala-LoBrotto, *The Disinherited* by Diane Duane and Peter Morwood] serpentinoid from ch'Rihan, Eisn (128 Trianguli) system
jibeinia: [*Feathered Dinosaurs: The Origin of Birds* by John Long and Peter Schuten] 12-cm enantiorn with wishbone, small wing-claws
jigok: [Fr. Johann Martin Schleyer's Volapük] hen-like ornithoid from Schleyer's system
jikan-to-jikan-o-mōichido-gyo: [Jap. "time-and-time-again-fish", The Tick: "Karma Tornado"] air-breathing, chronoporting grouper
jimbra: [*The Yowie: In Seach of Australian Bigfoot* by Tony Healy and Paul Cropper] see yowie
jime: [jelly slime portmanteau] slelly ooze between jelly- and slime-thickness
Jiminy cricket: [The Adventure of *Pinocchio* by Carlo Collodi] cricket-like insectoid symbolic of Jesus Christ from Gemini constellation
jinfengopteryx: ["golden-phoenix-wing", *Feathered Dinosaurs: The Origin of Birds* by John Long and Peter Schuten] 55-cm very bird-like troodontid with rounded snout, slashing toe, relatively long arms, but without leg feathers
jingo: [*Worlds Apart: Nat. Hist. of Furaha and Earth* by Souren Nyoroge] angular hexapod with backsails, black fringe from Furaha (alpha Phoenicis IV)
jinx: [*The New Dinosaurs* by Dougal Dixon] aka insinuosaur, predatory coneater mimic with teeth, killing claw and only 3 fingers
jip: [Fr. Johann Martin Schleyer's Volapük] sheep-like rumninant from Schleyer's system

jipülavultur: [Fr. Johann Martin Schleyer's Volapük] bearded vulture-like ornithoid from Schleyer's system
jiroo: [Outernauts] immature, bluish jirumph
jirooph: [Outernauts] mature white jirumph with black tail, mane
jirumph: [Outernauts] whiter llama-like creature, see jiroo, jirooph
jitter: [danjitter mondegreen] hawk-like ornithoid that jitts (dances) from Da system
jitterbug: [jitter backformation] insectoid pest of jitter bird
jitterbugator: [jitterbug alligator portmanteau] alligator-like predator whose bite morphs victim into jitter
jiu tou niao: 9-headed bird of ill omen from China, Terra (alpha Zodiaci III)
joat: [*If I Ran the Zoo* by Theodore Seuss Geissel] 3.6-meter giraffe-cat with S-shaped horns, cow-like head from Motta-fa-Potta-fa-Pell
jobberknoll: [*Fantastic Beasts and Where to Find Them* by Newton Artemis Fido Scamander] tiny, blue, speckled bird whose death knell includes every sound its every heard
joe: ["The Cage" by Bertram Chandler] small, multicolored furball scavenger with retractable tentacles from Hawkins' world
joey: [*Dell Crossword Puzzle Dictionary*] small kangaroo
jog: [jumping frog spoonerism] brightly-colored, fast roadrunner-like ornithoid
jogator: [jog alligator portmanteau] alligator-like predator whose bite morphs victim into jog
jogg: [jogg-oon mondegreen] oon relative, jogg-oon ancestor
jogg-oon: [*On Beyond Zebra* by Theodore Seuss Geissel] 2.4-meter biped with large head, mane and feet
joggator: [jogg alligator portmanteau] alligator-like predator whose bite morphs victim into jogg
jolter mite: [joltermite mondegreen] small electric insectoid related to volter mite

joltermite: [Terra Monster] electrical black beetle-like insectoid with yellow markings, see voltermite, from Terrarium

joogabinna: [*The Yowie: In Seach of Australian Bigfoot* by Tony Healy and Paul Cropper] yowie from New South Wales, Australia, Terra (alpha Zodiaci III)

jor: [Monster Galaxy] horned, black bovinoid with white head and frill that eats children from Libra or [rojo jor palindrome] red creature

Joranian ostrich: ["Past Prologue" by Kathryn Powers] bird noted for hiding head under water, sometimes too long

jraf: [giraffe contraction] short-necked, short-legged camelopardian, see qilin

jr̊rtol: [J. R. R. Tolkien kine pun] bovinoid gestalt

jub: jubjub nasna

jubjub: [*Through the Looking-Glass* by Charles Ludwidge "Lewis Carroll" Dodgeson] bird with terrifying, shrill, screaming song but exquisite when cooked from Snark Island, Looking-glass world

juck(le): dog

jugger: [juggergnat backformation] pitcherplant-mimicking predator that juggs

juggergnat: [juggernaut gnat portmanteau] gnat-like insectoid related to squashbug that infests juggers

juhiyama: 8-legged creature with wheel-like feet from Nagui archipelago, Nemodia, Hlatteld system, Galaxiki galaxy

jukfitpi: [James Cooke Brown's Loglan jukto fitpi compound] grabfoot from Logla, Brown's system

juko: [ganjuko mondegreen] large, furry, beaked predator from Ga system

jump-at-a-body: [Xanth series by Piers Anthony] small hairy, multi-legged monstrous creature formerly from Mundania later from Xanth

jumpee: [jumpy, jumper backformation] prey of jumping predators

junco: [*National Geographic Encyclopedia of Animals*] seed and invertebrate-eating songbird from N. America, Terra (alpha Zodiaci III)

jungle-bunny: camouflaged lapoid

juoon: generic atmospheric monster from Alest (Kalamon VIII), Galaxiki galaxy

juras: [Latvian juras cuba, juras cucina, juras zirdzinš backformation] chimera ancestral to cuka, porpoise, Guinea pig and seahorse

juraventor: ["Jura mt. hunter", *Feathered Dinosaurs: The Origin of Birds* by John Long and Peter Schuten] 80-cm compsosaur

jurrawarra: [*The Yowie: In Seach of Australian Bigfoot* by Tony Healy and Paul Cropper] see yowie

juru: [Lithuanian juru kiaules, juru kiaulyte, juru arkliukas, juru veplys backformation] chimera ancestral to kiaules, porpoise, Guinea pig, seahorse and walrus

jynx: aka wryneck woodpecker, ill-omen bird

jyÿkle: solitary, but tempermental, vulture-like ornithoid from Mimban and Kashÿyÿk, Jedi galaxy

k'boodl: [kit 'n' kaboodle mondegreen] small, furball-like felinoid

k'lor: ["The Old Republic"] large, omnivorous slug-like worm from Korriban, Jedi galaxy

k'nurt. [Star Trek] rabbit-like rodentoid from T'Khasi, Nevasa (40 Eridani) system

k'zana: ["Captives of Alien Beasts"] beastly creature

ka: [illuyanka mondegreen] hydra from Illuya system; [ninki-nanka mondegreen] snake-croc from Ninkina system; [Polish kijanka backformation] tadpole-like creature from Kija system; [Lithuanian slanka backformation] woodcock-like ornithoid from Sla system; [kaet] food ornithoid from or Pia or Touca systems

ka'ineth: [Atbash] see leviathan

kaadu: ["The Gungan Frontier" by Chris McCubbin] flightless ornithoid steed from Naboo swamps, Jedi galaxy

kabe: [urikabe backformation] force-field-projecting parrot-like ornithoid ancestral to uri and urikabe

kabosh: see ilma kabosh

kade: [*Dell Crossword Puzzle Dictionary*] sheep tick, see ked

kadeko: [*Eros Descending* by Michael Resnick] beast of burden from Grotamana, Quinellus cluster

kae: [*Dell Crossword Puzzle Dictionary*] jackdaw from Scotland, Terra (alpha Zodiaci III)

kaet: [kaet steak palindrome] food variety of et from Pia or Touca systems

kaeuq: [squeaky kaeuqs palindrome] small burrowing creature

kaf: [fake kaf palindrome] calf-like predator mimicked by pseudokaf

kagar: [lanka'gar mondegreen] chiropteran from La system

kagouti: [The Elder Scrolls III: "Morrowind"] short-tailed biped with triangular snout, forward-pointing tusks, related to alit and guar

kaha: [*Dell Crossword Puzzle Dictionary*] proboscis monkey

kahk: [khaki kahk palindrome] camoflage brown ornithoid

kahla: [ezkahla mondegreen] amphibious predator

kai-wip: [Cyclopedia of Worlds] aka zatcher or ther, 4-meter two-winged torpedoid with horizontal tail fins, 2.7-meter wingspan from Emeris, Sheel-Sen system

kail: [*Dell Crossword Puzzle Dictionary*] ibex, see kyl, tur

kailiauk: [Gor series by John Norman (John F. Lange, Jr.)] large, lumbering, gregarious and dangerous, shaggy, trident-horned 2-tonne ruminant with 4 stomachs, 8-valved heart 2.5-meter at shoulder

Kainji nightingale: [*Across the Universe* by Pamela Sargent and George Zebrowski] nightingale-like ornithoid from Kainji mts., Merope (23 Tauri) IV

kaioso: [Basque kaio-oso portmanteau] seagull-bear, clawed, billed triphibian from Skjoob, Bjosko system, Galaxiki galaxy

kaison: [Cyclopedia of Worlds] bright-colored flying grass-dwellers (yellow-green bar k., blue and yellow sheet k., black and blue fad k. vatrieties) from Shuttleworth, Amon Alpha system

kaisonster: [kaison monster portmanteau] mostrous kaison

kakapo: [*National Geographic Encyclopedia of Animals*] parrot from New Zealand, Terra (alpha Zodiaci III)

kakar: [*Dell Crossword Puzzle Dictionary*] deer, see muntjac, ratwa

kākissa: [Finnish kāki-kissa portmanteau] cuckoo-cat, griffinoid with retractable claws, fosters eggs in other griffins nests

kakuru: [*The New Dinosaur* by Dougal Dixon] aka rainbow lizard, coelurosaur ancestral to cribrusaur

kalaboo: [Cloudstone] pesty grass-eaters

kalak: [Star Trek] 2.35-meter, very stupid reptilian with thick hide from Mobus, Jedi galaxy

kalanoro: 1-meter tall, 3-toed, 3-fingered, hairy, telepathic creature with large eyes, backward feet

kalidah: [*The Wonderful Wizard of Oz* by L. Frank Baum] bear-lion forest creature from Munchkin Country, Oz

kalināga: [Hindi] 1000-headed snake

kalināgator: [kalināga alligator portmanteau] alligator-like predator whose bite morphs victim into kalināga

kalkatma: [James Cooke Brown's Loglan kolpi katma compound] copycat from Logla, Brown's system

kallikantzari: long-tailed mammals that steal food and put out fires during winter from Greece, Terra (alpha Zodiaci III)

kamaitachi: aka "sickle weasel", burrowing predator with very thin sharp claws, born in triplets from Japan, Terra (alpha Zodiaci III)

kamakolia: ["Message from a Star"] lizard with metal-strong horn from Delta, alpha Centauri system

kamama: [Cherokee] butterfly-elephant griffinoid from Tsalagi system

kamelch: [German Kamel-Elch portmanteau] camel-elk/moose, desert moose from Germa system

Kamese eel: [Afrikaans kameel backformation] desert eel from Kam system

kampus: [hipokampus backformation] ancestor to hipokampus and hyperkampus

kan: [taaraankan mondegreen] 2-D pentapus or hexapus from Taaraa system

kan'nuna: [Cherokee bullfrog-like amphibian from Tsalagi system

kanair: [Fr. Johann Martin Schleyer's Volapük] canary-like ornithoid from Schlayer's system

kananésgi: [Cherokee] arachnoid from Tsalagi system

kanatsisdatsi: [Cherokee] wasp-like insectoid from Tsalagi system

Kandorian hound: [Superman mythos] yellow, telepathic caninoid with wolf-like tail, boar-like snout from Kandor, Krypton, Rao system

kanficli: [James Cooke Brown's Loglan kangu ficli compound] dog-headed ichthyoid from Logla, Brown's system

kangamoo: [kangaroo-moo (cow) portmanteau] macropod-like milk producer

kangaroo rex: [*Mirabile* and "The Return of the Kangaroo Rex" by Janet Kagan] tyrannosaur-like macropodan mutant from Dragon's Tooth, Mirabile

kangarooster: [kangaroo-rooster portmanteau] large macropod-like flightless ornithoid

kangarue: [blue kangaroo synthetic rhyme] blue macropodan

kangu: [James Cooke Brown's Loglan] dog from Logla, Brown's system

kangur: [Fr. Johann Martin Schleyer's Volapük] macropodan from Schleyer's system

kaniok: [Belarussian marskoj kaniok backformation] seahorse-like creature ancestral to marshoj and seahorse

kanitt: [Continuum] furball-like catcus from Sotkaard, Galunis system, Firehorse constellation

kanka: [James Cooke Brown's Loglan kangu katma (dog cat) compound] dog-headed cat-like nimravoid from Logla, Brown's system

kanko: ["The Fox and the Badger in Japanese Folklore" by M. W. de Visser] aka koda-gitsune, rat-sized fox with vertical eyes, thin hair

kankrelat: [Code Lyoko] aka roachster, cling with 4 pointy legs, carapace, laser-eye geneered by Xana

kanli: [James Cooke Brown's Loglan kangu clika (dog-like) compound] caninoid from Logla, Brown's system

kannirda: [James Cooke Brown's Loglan kangu nirda compound] dog-headed bird from Logla, Brown's system

kanscho: [Hildegard of Bingen's Lingua Ignota] hawk-like ornithoid from Ignota, Hildegard's system

kao tzu: ["Dragon's Honor" by Kij Johnson and Greg Cox] slug from Pai, Dragon nebula

kapeklacervus: [candiacervus extrapolation] deer with chair-like antlers

kaplumbaga: [Turkish kaplumbaga güvercin backformation] dove-like ornithoid ancestral to pigeon and turtle dove

kaplumbagator: [kaplumbaga alligator portmanteau] alligator-like predator whose bite morphs victim into kaplumbaga

kapnorvalni: [James Crooke Brown's Loglan kapli norma valni compound] Perfectly Normal Beast from Logla, Brown's system

kappa: [*Oriental Adventures* by Gary Gygax, etal., "Xoology" by Kittenbaker] furless, green-skinned, beaked simian with exposed cerebrospinal fluid, carapace, stretchable limbs from Japan, Terra (alpha Zodiaci III)

napper: [catnapper mondegreen] felinoid that napps, see ypeel

Kara bat: [Turkish karabatak backformation] chiropteran ancestral to ak and cormorant from Kara system

karapeet: [parakeet spoonerism] small, colorful ornithoid

karavi: [Albanian karavidhe backformation] lobster-goat ancestral to a goat and lobster

karikot: quadrupedal beast of burden with blue-black fur from Ikranaka, Spica (alpha Virginis) system

karip: [Fr. Johann Martin Schleyer's Volapük] carp-like ichthyoid from Schleyer's system
karipede: [karikot centipede portmanteau] karikot with many legs
karix: [*The Goddess of Ganymede* by Michael D. Resnick, Donald M. Grant] lion-like day-blind creature the size of a grizzly with retractable suction cups on foot, with loud roar from Thane's moon
karkaddan: [The Arabian Nights] 1-horned, antelope-like pegasoid intermediate in size between elephant and rukh from Camphor island
Karlek virus: deadly virus from Karlek, Aronshok, Galaxiki galaxy
Karn beast: ["The Beasts of Karn" by Ken Koonce and Michael Merton] chiropteroid from Karn
karpoun: [Trullion: Alastor 2262 by Jack Vance] wild tiger-like beast of Shamshin volcanoes
karura: hellfire-breathing eagle-headed anthropoid, enemy of dragons, from Japan, Terra (alpha Zodiaci III)
kaskangu: [James Cooke Brown's Loglan kasma kangu compound] bull-headed caninoid from Logla, Brown's system
kasli: [James Cooke Brown's Loglan kasli clika (cow-like) compound] bovine from Logla, Brown's system
kasni: [James Cooke Brown's Loglan] cow from Logla, Brown's system
kastodon: [sarkastodon mondegreen] creodont ancestor
kastodonster: [kastodon monster portmanteau] creodont-like monster
kat: [Fr. Johann Martin Schleyer's Volapük] cat from Schleyer's system
katficli: [James Cooke Brown's Loglan katma ficli compound] cat-headed ichthyoid from Logla, Brown's system
katkangu: [James Cooke Brown's Loglan katma kangu (cat dog) compound] cat-headed dog-like nimravoid from Logla, Brown's system

katli: [James Cooke Brown's Loglan katma clika (cat-like) compound] felinoid from Logla, Brown's system
katnirda: [James Cooke Brown's Loglan katma nirda (cat bird) compound] cat-headed ornithoid from Logla, Brown's system
katogle: [*Dell Crossword Puzzle Dictionary*] eagle owl, see bubo
katyr: [Danish kat-tyr portmanteau] cat-bull, small, furry, horned bovinoid from Draapaa, Albina system, Galaxiki galaxy
kautūhala: [Hindi] two-creature chimera, e.g., elephant-lion, deer-lion, etc.
kavak: [bukavak mondegreen] lavender, nocturnal water monster
kavead: [Fr. Johann Martin Schleyer's Volapük] Guinea pig-like creature from Schleyer's system
kawama: [The Elder Scrolls III: "Morrowind"] tunneling hive-creature
kawk: [kawōni hawk portmanteau, kettle of hawks spoonerism] duck-headed hawk-like ornithoid
kawōni: [Cherokee] duck-like ornithoid from Tsalagi system
kaycro: 20-meter, 4.5-tonne fast, food mammaloid from Agills
kazmortel: [Perry Rhodan] fist-sized sparrow-like ornithoid with button eyes, that communicates via near ultrasonic from Kazmortul
kea: [*Dell Crossword Puzzle Dictionary*] large, sheep-killing parrot from New Zeeland, see lory, vasa, vaza
keblak: [Sumatran] aka ghost cockerel
ked: [*Dell Crossword Puzzle Dictionary*] sheep tick from Scotland, see kade
keese: [The Legend of Zelda] chiropteroid controlled by Vire from Hyrule
kekkai: [Jap. "blood lump"] blood golem
kektci: [James Cooke Brown's Loglan kekti tsini] kickchin from Logla, Brown's system
kelenken: [*The Big Bad Book of Beasts* by Michael Largo] 3-meter flightless bird with large hawk-like head from Argentina, Terra (alpha Zodiaci III)

kelep: [*Dell Crossword Puzzle Dictionary*] stinging ant

kell: [Dark Forces] slightly stockier dracoid related to krayt from Jedi galaxy

kellope: [kell antelope portmanteau] kell with antlers

kelly: [*Monster Spotter's Guide to North America* by Scott Francis] igopogoid from Kempenfet Bay, Ont., Terra (alpha Zodiaci III)

kelpie: aka water-horse, black horse with red eyes from the sea around Scotland, Terra (alpha Zodiaci III)

kelpling: [Outernauts] immature kelpoid

kelplingator: [kelpling alligator portmanteau] alligator-like predator whose bite morphs victim into kelpling

kelpoid: [Outernauts] green kelp mimic with blue tentacles, see kelpling, kelrog

kelrog: [kelp-balrog portmanteau, Outernauts] mature kelpoid with, teeth and lure, see kelpoid, kelpling

kelrogator: [kelrog alligator portmanteau] alligator-like predator whose bite morphs victim into kelrog

kemili: [Cherokee] camel-like desert quadruped from Tsalagi system

kên: [Vietnamese con kên kên backformation] trisexual creature ancestral to con and vulture from Disa system

kenel: [FthinraKathi by Dale Murphy] equinoid from T'Khasi, Nevasa (40 Eridani) system

kenelope: [kenel antelope portmanteau] kenel with antlers

kenfish: [frankenfish mondegreen] monstrous icthyoid from Fra system

keo: [James Cooke Brown's Loglan] kappa from Logla, Brown's system

kep-mok: [Tev'Meckian "devouring-mother"] mother bloodtick from Tev'meck, Warvan system

kepard: ["Empire Star" by Samuel R. Delany] dangerous animal from Rhys, Tyre's moon, tau Ceti system

keratoro: [*Space Ark* by A. M Lightner] golden-horned unicorn from Shikai

kermitoid: [*Worlds Apart: Nat. Hist. of Furaha and Earth* by Souren Nyoroge] bipedal batrachoid from Furaha (alpha Phoenicis IV)

kermospi: [James Cooke Brown's Loglan kerku mospi] hairy ghost from Logla, Brown's system

kernimla: [James Cooke Brown's Loglan kerko nimla (hairy animal) compound] mammaloid from Logla, Brown's system

kerril: [*Dell Crossword Puzzle Dictionary*] sea snake from Asia, Terra (alpha Zodiaci III)

kestrel: [*National Geographic Encyclopedia of Animals*] predatory bird from Africasia, Terra (alpha Zodiaci III)

kete: ["Ewoks" series] large dragon-fly-like insectoid that builds spiral mounds made with sticky marshmallow-like substance from Endor I's moon, Jedi galaxy; [eteknalb ananymondegreen] furry with black markings from Bla system

keukegen: [Jap. "fluffy hair appearance", Mujara 2 by Shigeru Mizuki] originally long-haired canine, then any rare creature

khaan: [*Feathered Dinosaurs: The Origin of Birds* by John Long and Peter Schuten] 1.5-m conchoraptor-like oviraptorosaur with sharper head-neck angle

khat: [Tev'Meckian] ant-like insectoid from Tev'Meck, MakTar system

khiffah: [*After Man* by Dougal Dixon] herd pongoid

khmer: long-haired furry without white feet (socks)

khrukai: [Flandry series by Poul Anderson, "swordwing"] swarming insectoid from Starkad

ki: [githyanki mondegreen] creature from Githya system; [beheaded uki] headless, red-and-gray ornithoid

ki'i: [Haw. *] 2-D pentapus or hexapus

kiau: [Lithuanian juru kiaules, juru kiaulyte backformation] porpoise-Guinea pig, ancestral to les, porpoise and Guinea pig

kiaules: [Lithuanian juru kaiules backformation] cetacean ancestral to juru and porpoise

kiaulyte: [Lithuanian juru kiaulyte backformation] rodentoid ancestral to juru and Guinea pig
kickchin: [chicken spoonerism] large aggressive flightless ornithoid
kid: young goat, antelope or goatelope
kida: [Continuum] 30-cm sandspider able to jump 3 meters from Sotkaard, Galunis system, Firehorse constellation
kigeon: [kit of pigeons spoonerism, killer pigeon] pit-dwelling, killer pigeon-wigeon-like ornithoid
kigeonster: [kigeon monster portmanteau] monstrous kigeon
kigrid: [*Monster Manual* by Skip Williams, etal.] illthida variant
kiho: [*Dell Crossword Puzzle Dictionary*] io butterfly

kiiloks: [Estonian kiil-loks portmanteau] dragonfly-rattler, 4-winged, leg-less murre-like dracoid with rattle-tipped tail
kik: kik-kik nasna
kik-kik: ["Shadow Lord" by Laurence Yep] giant beetle with luminous "eyes" in rat niche from Angira
kilin: ["Xoology" by Kittenbaker] one-horned dracoid with lion's mane, stag's body, ox's tail from Szurane
kilison: slug hunted for sport from Lestonian Lushland (Edonian cluster V), Galaxiki galaxy
kilisonster: [kilison monster portmanteau] monstrous slug
Kilkenny cat: feline able to fight until just claws and tail tip from Kilkenny, Ireland, Terra (alpha Zodiaci III)
kill-adder: [*Witch of the Dark Gate* by John Jakes] snake thick as man's arm with large fangs, threeked tongue
killa: [frankilla mondegreen] greenish pongoid from Fra system
killawatt: [Outernauts] mature dekawatt
killdeer: [*National Geographic Encyclopedia of Animals*] insectovorous bird from Americas, Terra (alpha Zodiaci III)
killer: [srel-like killers palindrome] deadly srel mimic

killer bee: [Warwick E. Kerr] swarming, aggressive African-American bees
killer donut: ["Attack of the Killer Donuts" by Nathan Dalton, Chris De Christopher and Rafael Diaz-Wagner] food that turns on its eaters, see giant mousaka
killer hare: [Godville] carnivorous hare, distinguishable from killer rabbit by tattoolessness
killer hog: ["Attack of the Killer Hogs" by Agustin Cavalieri and Marcos Meroni] hog turned killer
killer lamprey: ["Blood Lake: Attack of the Killer Lampreys" by Anna Rasmussen and Delondra Williams] voracious lamprey that turns from fish prey to Human prey from Blood Lake
killer mantee: ["Attacjk of the Killer Manatee" by Wes Horn] manatee turned carnivorous
killer penguin: [*Orcbusters* by Ken Rolston] penguin than kills
killer rabbit: [Godville, "Monte Python and the Holy Grail"] carnivorous rabbit, distinguishable from killer hare by skin tattoos, [*The Night of the Lepus* by Russell Braddon] in giant variety
killer shrew: ["The Attack of the Killer Shrews" by Jay Simms] giant, yet still voracious, mutant shrew from Baines Island, Terra (alpha Zodiaci III)
killer turd: ["Attack of the Killer Turds" by Matt Molloy] bad meat turns worse, killing restaurant patrons
kilok: [one-eyed kiiloks] one-eyed dragonfly-rattler dracoid
kimogila: large, vicious, dark green lizard with double row of spikes from nose to tail from Lok, Jedi galaxy
Kimonian lizard-bird: ["Immigrant" by Clifford Simak] tinshemet-like saurornithoid from Kimon
kinrath: [Knights of the Old Republic 2: "The Sith Lords"] large, venomous archnoid from Dantooine and Kashÿyÿk, Jedi galaxy
kip: [valkip mondegreen] red falcon-chicken-like ornithoid

kiskadee: [*National Geographic Encyclopedia of Animals*] large flycatcher from America, Terra (alpha Zodiaci III)
kistadeel: [kistadee eel portmanteau] eel-headed kistadee-like ornithoid
kiskader: [kiskadee backformation] predator that kiskades
kite: [Laurence Doyle and Manoj Joshi] multi-mouthed insectivore with jellyfish-like tendrils and tether from Blue Moon, see box kite
kitsune: [Here be Monsters almanac] 9-tailed fox from Japan, aka huli jing in China and kurniho in Korea, Terra (alpha Zodiaci III)
kitton: ["Mother Hitton's Littul Kittons" by Paul "Cordwainer Smith" Linebarger] fiercest, smallest, craziest telepathic mink from Norstrilia (aka Old North Australia)
kitty-hawk: [Xanth series by Piers Anthony] cat-headed and legged ornithoid with feathered tail from Xanth
kiu-lung: hornless dragon from China, Terra (alpha Zodiaci III)
kiu-lungator: [kiu-lung alligator portmanteau] alligator-like predator whose bite morphs victim into kiu-lung
kivu: [*Dell Crossword Puzzle Dictionary*] tsetse fly, see mau, glossina
kiwi: [*National Geographic Encyclopedia of Animals*, Maori kiwi-kiwi] rarite ornithoid from New Zealand, Terra (alpha Zodiaci III)
kiyūga: [Cherokee] chipmunk-like rodentoid from Tsalagi system
kiyūgator: [kiyūga alligator portmanteau] alligator-like predator whose bite morphs victim into kiyūga
kjingyow: [Sambahsa] goldfish
kkryÿtch: [*Creatures of the Galaxy* by Phil Brucato, Bill Smith, Rick D. Stuart, Chuck Truett] seed-eating ornithoid from Kashÿyÿk, Jedi galaxy
kkught: [Armenian kku-ught portmanteau] cuckoo-camel, desert pegasus with hump, fosters eggs in other pegasi nests

Klabnian eel: ["QPid" by Randee Russell and Ira Steven Behr] snake-like ichthyoid from Klabnia
klakatma: [James Cooke Brown's Loglan klada katma compound] cloud cat from Logla, Brown's system
klake: [*Nick and the Glimmung* by Philip K. Dick] horned creature from Plowman's planet
klammer: [klammerraffer backformation] simian relative from Germa system
klammerraffer: [Ger. @ "Klammerrraffer"] 2-D clinging-monkey-like at
klatitci: [James Cooke Brown's Loglan klada titci compound] cloudeater from Logla, Brown's system
kldets'ots'ia: [Georgian tst'elp'rtian kldets'ots'ias backformation] partridge-like ornithoid from Tst'elp'rt system
klesh: [Navaho] snake-like creature from Diné system
kli: [kli milk palindrome] domesticated bovine
klizzie: [Navaho] goat-like ruminant from Diné system
kllhe: [*The Romulan Way* by Terisa Halekala-I oBrotto] dungworm from ch'Rlhan, Eisn (128 Trianguli) system
klokanec: [Czech klokan-kanec portmanteau] kangaroo-boar, large hopping porcoid
klok: [i-less kiiloks] cave-dwelling dragonfly-rattler dracoid
knah: [knah shank palindrome] food animal
knake: [knot of snakes spoonerism, khah snake portmanteau] food snake, see nake
knal: [knal flank palindrome] food animal
knalope: [knal antelope portmanteau] knal with antlers
knarl: [*Fantastic Beasts and Where to Find Them* by Newton Artemis Fido Scamander] lactose intolerant hedgehog
knarlope: [knarl antelope portmanteau] knarl withe antlers
kneazle: [*Fantastic Beasts and Where to Find Them* by Newton Artemis Fido Scamander] cat with large ears, spots and lion-like tail
knid: [*Charlie and the Great Glass Elevator* by Ronald Dahl] huge, dark, spaceship-attacking pack ovoid

knife fish: [*The Big Bad Book of Beasts* by Michael Largo] electric eel-like fish with static bubble-shield

knightaur: [Monster Galaxy] armored bovine from Taurus constellation

knightbeast: [night beast mondegreen] armored, bipedal sauroid

knightcrawler: [nightcrawler mondegreen] large, armored worm-like dracoid, see knightswimmer

knighthowler: [nighthowler mondegreen] armored simian

knightlemuel: [nightlemuel mondegreen] armored lemuel

knightmar: [nightmar mondegreen] armored mar

knightmare: [nightmare mondegreen] armored dracoid steed

knightowl: [nightowl mondegreen] owl-likw nightwing

knightstalker: [nightstalker mondegreen] armored, flightless, pack-hunting cheiropteroid

knightswimmer: [nightswimmer mondegreen] aquatic knightcrawler

knightwaif: [nightwaif mondegreen] armored waif

knightwalker: [nightwalker mondegreen] armored anthropoid

knightwing: [nightwing mondegreen] armored, flightless ornithoid, see knightowl

knightwingator: [knightwing alligator portmanteau] alligator-like predator whose bite morphs victim into knightwing

knim: [mink knim palindrome] furry with dark extremities

knine: [Monster Galaxy] cyberdog from Leo constellation

knip: [pink knip palindrome] light red ornithoid

knish: [knife fish portmanteau] see knife fish

knivor: [*Coldheart* by Trevor Baxendale] carnivorous chiropteran from Eskon

knoad: [knot of toads spoonerism] small toad-like batrachoid gestalt, see noad

knobbee: [knobby mondegreen] knobby bee-like insectoid

knobby: [*Monster Spotter's Guide to North America* by Scott Francis] 1.8-meter nape from Cleveland Co., N. C., Terra (alpha Zodiaci III)

knobby white: [*Creatures of the Galaxy* by Phil Brucato, Bill Smith, Rick D. Stuart, Chuck Truett] large arachoid that at maturity roots itself into ground as gnarl tree from Dagobah system, Jedi galaxy

knoe shoshu: [Space: 1889] sly predator from Mars (alpha Zodiaci IV)

knot: [Dell Crossword Puzzle Dictionary] small, red sandpiper, see pume, stint

knurd: [drunk tank nat knurd palindrome] pink nat predator

ko: [kanko mandegreen] rat-sized fox-like mammalian from Ka system; koko nasna

koala-shrew: [*The Pollinators of Eden* by John Boyd] symbiot to siren tulips from Flora

koalaotter: [Avatar: The Last Airbender: "The Waterbending Master"] creature like both koala and otter

koanaf: [Fr. Johann Martin Schleyer's Volapük] shellfish-like sea creature from Logla, Brown's system

kobe: [Swahili kobe njiwa backformation] turtle dove-pigeon ornithoid

kobor hoot: [*Planiverse* by Alexander Dewdney] 2-D sea animal from Arde, Shems system

kockanec: [Czech kocka-kanec portmanteau] cat-boar, nocturnal, predatory porcoid with retractable claws

koda-gitsune: [Jap. "pipe-fox"] see kanko

kodius: 1-tonne kodiak subspecies bred for Human compatibility by Kodius Co. ("Exploration Team" by Murray Leinster)

kodkod: [*National Geographic Encyclopedia of Animals*] small cat from Chile, Terra (alpha Zodiaci III)

koek: [Dutch koekoek backformation] cuckoo-cow, milk griffinoid that fosters eggs in other griffinoid nests

kōga/i: [Cherokee] crow-like ornithoid from Tsalagi system

kohcitra: [artichoke kohcitra palindrome] green ornithoid

kohun: [*Creatures of the Galaxy* by Phil Brucato, Bill Smith, Rick D. Stuart, Chuck

Truett] centipede-like insectoid with stinger and teeth from Mimban and Indoumodo, giant Naboo variety shoots poisonous puffs, Jedi galaxy

koira: [Finnish lammaskoira backformation] sheep-dog ancestral to both sheep and sheepdog

koko: [*Dell Crossword Puzzle Dictionary*] parson bird from New Zeeland, Terra (alpha Zodiaci III)

kol bata: [bol kata spoonerism] dangerous piranha-like ichthyoid

kola: [*Dell Crossword Puzzle Dictionary*] jackal from India, Terra (alpha Zodiaci III)

kolezia: [Hildegard of Bingen's Lingua Ignota] thrush-like ornithoid from Ignota, Hildegard's system

kolkatma: [James Cooke Brown's Loglan kolro katma compound] colour cat from Logla, Brown's system

kolponomos: [*After the Dinosaurs* by Donald R. Prothero] aka beach bear, semi-aquatic mollusk-eating bear from Miocene

kolvalni: [James Cooke Brown's Loglan kolro valni compound] colour beast from Logla, Brown's system

kom: [smoke koms palindrome] furry with pale coat with gradually darkening tips

komarac: [Croatian obican komarac backformation] gnat-like insectoid from Obica system

komnair: berkomnair mondegreen] pachedermoid

Komodo rhino: [Avatar: The Last Airbender: "The Warriors of Kyoshi"] Komodo dragon-like reptilian with large frontal horn and 2 more at temples, claws, not actually from Komodo

kongamato: ["boat-breaker", *Witchbound Africa* by Frank Melland] pterodactyl-like creature from Jiungu swamp, Africa, Terra (alpha Zodiaci III)

kongres: [Code Lyoko] piranha-headed eel with laser eyes, vulnerable in pod on blue tail geneered by Xana

konjež: [Croatian konj-jež portmanteau] horse-hedgehog, large hedgehog-like steed

kook: [cuckoo contraction] cuckoo-like ornithoid

kookaburra: [National Geographic Encyclopedia of Animals] bird from Australia, Terra (alpha Zodiaci III)

kookaburro: [kookaburra'cuckoo-burro portmanteau] burro-like griffinoid

koolokamba: see sisimite

koon: ["Killer Koons from Outer Space"] monstrous raccoon-like predator

koop: [spooky koops palindrome, fly the koop] ultradimensional kite-like ornithoids

köpegi: [Turkish çobanköpegi backformation] sheepdog-like caninoid from Çoba system

kor: [roknatree fungus ananymondegreen] fungoid from Sugnufeerta system

kora: [*Dell Crossword Puzzle Dictionary*] water cock

korat: ["purple-gray"] trim, short-haired seafoam (silver-"blue" (gray)) furry with tall ears, heart-shaped head, large green eyes

korclser: [James Crooke Brown's Loglan korci serpi compound] ropesnake from Logla, Brown's system

korfla: [James Cooke Brown's Loglan korma flaki (horse fly) compound] horse-fly pegasoid from Logla, Brown's system

koriena: [*Creatures of the Galaxy* by Phil Brucato, Bill Smith, Rick D. Stuart, Chuck Truett] "zebra dog", striped, pack hunting canine from Jedi galaxy

korli: [James Cooke Brown's Loglan korma clika] horse-like quadruped from Logla, Brown's system

korm: [Danish ko-orm portmanteau] cow-worm, boneless bovinoid

korpo: [James Cooke Brown's Loglan korma porju] horse-swine from Logla, Brown's system

kosmoceratops: [Odd Squad: Sector 21] fringed dinosaur with 15 horns

kotka: [Finnish korppikotka backformation] vulture-raven, omnivorous ornithoid

kotur: [Fr. Johann Martin Schleyer's Volapük] quail-like ornithoid from Schleyer's system

koutalacervus: [candiacervus extrapolation] deer with ladle-like antlers

koutalicervus: [candiacervus extrapolation] deer with spoon-like antlers

krab: [Fr. Johann Martin Schleyer's Volapük] crab-like crustacean from Schleyer's system

krabes: [Code Lyoko] large crab-like crustacean with 4 scythe-like legs, 2 tri-lasers and a pulse laser geneered by Xana

krabik: [Bulgarian krab-bik portmanteau] crab-bull, horned crustacean

krabken: [Terra Monster] crab-like crustacean from Terrarium

krait: [*National Geographic Encyclopedia of Animals*] eel and fish-eating sea snake

krakana: [*Creatures of the Galaxy* by Phil Brucato, Bill Smith, Rick D. Stuart, Chuck Truett] sea creature with many, pincher-tipped tentacles from Mon Calamari, Jedi galaxy

kraken: [Germ. colossal squid, *The Museum of Hoaxes* by Alex Boese] 9-meter (or larger) cephalopod with razor-sharp hooks: [Odd Squad] wiggle-worm-like egg-laying variety

krank: [*The Resurrection Casket* by Justine Richards] shark-like space-dwelling ichthyoid

krayt: ["Star Wars IV: A New Hope" by George Lucas] 10-legged, carnivorous dracoid, great variety 100-meter long, with blue scales, from Jundland mts., Tatoonine, Jedi galaxy

kreefout: [Afrikaans kreef-fout portmanteau] crab-bug, flightless insectoid with large pinchers

kreetle: ["The Gungan Frontier" by Chris McCubbin] omnivorous, long-tailed, decapodal, beetle-like insectoid trained as nutcracker from Jedi galaxy

kref: [Fr. Johann Martin Schleyer's Volapük] crayfish-like sea creature from Schleyer's system

krelat: [kankrelat backformation] 4-legged insectoid from Ka system

krelk: [*Pawns and Symbols* by Majliss Larson] aka llamaroo, dun with black back stripe, black eyes and nose, long prehensile-tipped tail, kangaroo-like legs, llama-like head and neck

krelor: [Armenian krel-lor portmanteau] bear-quail-like ursinopteryx from Skjoob, Bjosko system, Galaxiki galaxy

Krempeltierchen: [Germ.] curl-up from Germa system

krenshar: [Monster Manual 3.5] 1.5-meter felinoid with shaggy, spotted (maculate) fur, bristly hair, bushy tail, terrifying screech

kresch: ["The Gungan Frontier" by Chris McCubbin] parrot-like mollusk that repeats what it hears from Jedi galaxy

Kriegspian eel: [Kriegspiel mondegreen] electric eel-like ichthyoid used as a weapon from Kriegsp system

krik: [Fr. Johann Martin Schleyer's Volapük] cricket-like insectoid from Schleyer's system

krikül: [Fr. Johann Martin Schleyer's Volapük] grasshopper-like insectoid from Schleyer's system

krill: [Norw. kril ("young fry of fish"), *The Big Bad Book of Beasts* by Michael Largo] "large" zooplankton, especially ichthyoid hatchlings

krite: [*Dell Crossword Puzzle Dictionary*] snake from India, see cobra, daboia, daboya

krith: [*The Ring of Ritornel* by Charles L. Harness] winged spider, most fearsome predator from the Deep in the Twelve Galaxies

krobaa: see venom

kroger: ["Prince of Peril" by Otis Adelbert Kline] 1.8-meter mottled green and yellow, reptile, 2/3 mouth, pouch behind head, 2 legs below ears with 3-taloned feet, back-curving teeth from Zarovia (alpha Zodiaci II)

krolig: [Fr. Johann Martin Schleyer's Volapük] rabbit-like burrower from Schleyer's system

kroligator: [krolig alligator portmanteau] alligator-like predator whose bite morphs victim into krolig

kroll: ["The Power of Kroll" by Robert Holmes] giant mutant squid with 250-meter head and more than 50 tentacles mistakenly worshipped by Swampies exiled to delta Magna III's moon

krotasnek: [Fr. Johann Martin Schleyer's Volapük] rattlesnake from Schleyer's system, see noidülasnek

kroter: [Thongor series by Lin Carter] fleet horse-sized reptilian steed from Lemuria

krov: [Fr. Johann Martin Schleyer's Volapük] crow-like ornithoid from Schleyer's system
kroyie: [*Heir to the Empire* by Timothy Zahn] huge, canopy-dwelling ornithoid from Kashÿyÿk, Jedi galaxy, attracted to bright lights, hunted for food by Wookiees
krrunkku: [Armenian krrunk-kku portmanteau] crane-cuckoo ornithoid from Armen system
krupik: ["Help Needed" by Kirill Bulychev] small, gray creature under fir tree, not rabbit, hare, kangaroo or squirrel from Remotus (distant) constellation
Kryonian tiger: ["Imaginary Friend" by Jean Louise Matthias and Ronald Wilkerson and Richard Fliegel] tiger-like felinoid in xoo on Brentalia
Kryptonian mole: [Superman mythos] large metallovorous mole-like creature from Krypton, Rao system
ku: kuku nasna
kubanochoerus: [*After the Dinosaurs* by Donald R. Prothero] aka unicorn pig from Mlocene
kud: [Duke kud palindrome] blue ornithoid
kudu: [*National Geographic Encyclopedia of Animals*] antelope relative from Africa, Terra (alpha Zodiaci III)
kuguguk: [Turkish kugu-guguk portmanteau] swan-cuckoo, long-necked aquatic ornithoid that fosters eggs in other's nests
kuhai: [German Kuh-Hai portmanteau] cow-shark, not easily tamed ichthyoid that secretes milk-like liquid
kulture: [kettle of vultures spoonerism, culture mondegreen] barnacle-goose-like ornithoid that grows from swamp bottom scum and eats dead
kukpeti: [James Cooke Brown's Loglan kukpe titci] intellect devourer from Logla, Brown's system
kuku: [*Dell Crossword Puzzle Dictionary*] fruit pigeon from N. Z., Terra (alpha Zodiaci III)
kukuk: [Fr. Johann Martin Schleyer's Volapük] cuckoo-like ornithoid from Schleyer's system
kulan: [*National Geographic Encyclopedia of Animals*] horse from Mongolia, Terra (alpha Zodiaci III)

kulshedra: hellfire-breathing serpentine dracoid with 9 tongues, horns, spines and large wings from Albania, Terra (alpha Zodiaci III)
kulta: [Finnish kultakala backformation] ichthyoid ancestral to fish and goldfish
Kulyhean turtle: [*Shadow World Atlas* by Terry K. Amthor] chelonian large enough to build houses on from Kulyhea
kumo: [*The Big Bad Book of Beasts* by Michael Largo] reclusive, giant vampiric spider from Japan, Terra (alpha Zodiaci III)
kumquat jelly: [jely extrapolation] jelly-thick ooze
kun: [Fr. Johann Martin Schleyer's Volapük] cow-like quadruped from Schleyer's system
kun tie: [Fringe] 1.5-tonne, predatory, anaerobic mellophage with spear-like proboscis
kuni: [Outernauts] more purplish electrical creature with U-shaped head in shocker variety, see punl, uni
kuribou: see goomba
kurniho: [*Here Be Monsters almanac*] 9-tailed fox from Korea, aka kitsune in Japan, huli jing in China, Terra (alpha Zodiaci III)
kurtavuk: [Turkish kurt-tuvuk portmanteau] wolf-chicken, flightless omnivorous griffinoid
kusfla: [James Cooke Brown's Loglan kusfa flaki (house/pet fly) compound] housepetfly from Logla, Brown's system
kushel: [*Creatures of the Galaxy* by Phil Brucato, Bill Smith, Rick D. Stuart, Chuck Truett] fowl from T'Khasi, Nevasa (40 Eridani) system
kuskatma: [James Cooke Brown's Loglan kusfa katma compound] housecat from Logla, Brown's system
kuspic: [Shona, Zimbabwe cipsuka (red/orange/purple) kuspic palindrome] red, orange or purple ornithoid
kusrat: [Dutch muskusrat backformation] muskrat-mouse rodentian from Mu system
kusu: [Azerbaijani balabankusu backformation] bittern-like ornithoid from Balaba system

kutch: [it-kutch backformation] relative of it and it-kutch

kutoro: [Filipino kuto-toro portmanteau] louse-bull, 6-legged bugalo-like food creature with carapace

kutrub: [*The Arabian Nights*] creature with long forefeet

kutterfly: [kaleidoscope of butterflies spoonerism] fly-like insectoid that kutts (psychokinetically cuts) up food

kuyutha: [Final Fantasy VII] gigantic bull-bear monster

kvgwóha: [Cherokee] sapsucker-like ornithoid from Tsalgi system

kvgwóha: [Cherokee] sapsucker-like ornithoid from Tsalagi system

kvtli: [Cherokee] raccoon-like scavenger from Tsalagi system

kwandaioha: [Cherokee] cobra-like serpent from Tsalagi system

Kwean bee: [queen bee mondegreen] bee-like insectoid from Kwea, Kwe system

kwekaweau: ["The Hunt for the Kwekaweau"] giant gecko from N. Z., Terra (alpha Zodiaci III)

kwyjibo: [Bart Simpson] big, dumb, nape

kybuck: fast, ruminant, males horned, from Kashÿyÿk, Jedi galaxy

kyl: [*Dell Crossword Puzzle Dictionary*] ibex, see kail, tur

Kylerian goat: ["Death Wish" by Michael Pillar] goat-like ruminant noted for "milk" from Kyler, Delta Quadrant

kyptoceras: [*After the Dinosaurs* by Donald R. Prothero] protoceras with nose horns and foreward-curving forehead horns

kyren: [*Creatures of the Galaxy* by Phil Brucato, Bill Smith, Rick D. Stuart, Chuck Truett] small, leg-less, swarming, herbivorous insectoid from Ansion, Jedi galaxy

kyuubi: [Jap.] nine-tailed fox, see cat o' nine tails, yoake

kyyhky: [Finnish turturikyyhky backformation] turtle dove-pigeon ornithoid ancestral to turturi and turtle dove

la: [manla mondegreen] louse-like insectoid from Ma system; [Vietnamese con la backformation] creature ancestral to con and mule from Disa; [wol-la-chee mondegree] ant-like insectoid

laa: [*Creatures of the Galaxy* by Phil Brucato, Bill Smith, Rick D. Stuart, Chuck Truett] anglerfish-like ichthyoid from Naboo, Jedi galaxy; [laa n'aal palindrome] n'aal-like amphisbæna

lab chicken: [Syfy Monster Island] mutant fire-breathing, electric chicken with tentacles for legs

labbeetle: ["Protective Mimicry" by Alguis Bulgess] selectively vampiric beetle-like insectoid in A, B, AB and O varieties from Deneb XI

labbit: [litter of rabbits sponnerism, labbeetle rabbit portmanteau] selectively vampiric beetle-rabbit in A, B, AB and O varieties

laboc: [cobalt laboc palindrome] metallic blue ornithoid

labyrithodon: [aka sithig, Pellucidar series by Edgar Rice Burroughs] amphibian with crocodile-like jaws, toad-like body

lacc: [sarlacc mondegreen] beast with feeding tentacles

lacertae: [piscium extrapolation] egg-laying lizard

lackdog: [beheaded blackdog] blackdog lacking a head

ladder: [ladder mondegreen] tall giraffe-like predator that ladds

ladma: [James Cooke Brown's Loglan ladzo manti (louse-ant) compound] louse-headed ant-like insectoid from Logla, Brown's system

lady-bug: [ladybug mondegreen] beetle-like insectoid with skirt-like carapace

lady-bugator: [lady-bug alligator portmanteau] alligator-like predator whose bite morphs victim into lady-bug

laf: [falu laf palindrome] deep red ornithoid

lag monster: [Godville] extradimensional with time-slowing aura

Lagafljót worm: [*The Big Bad Book of Beasts* by Michael Largo] thin, 90-meter lake snake from Iceland, Terra (alpha Zodiaci III)

lagar: ["The Cloud" by Tom Szollosi] egg-layer from Takar, Delta Quadrant

lagardo: ["Dear Mom" by Stephen C. Fisher] 1-meter tall blue-black sauroid biped with beak and no arms, that spreads its wattles when excited from La Paz
Lagartan gecko: ["Carnival Night" by Warren Hammond] scavenger lizard from Lagarta
lago: [galago mondegreen] gray-green lemur
lagosuchus: [*The Mistaken Extinction* by Lowell Dingus and Timothy Rowe] dinosauromorph, not actually a dinosaur
laifah: ["Battle of Ferrol" by Michael Marcus Thurner] carnivore from Ferrol (Vega (alpha Lyrae) VIII)
laigrek: [*Creatures of the Galaxy* by Phil Brucato, Bill Smith, Rick D. Stuart, Chuck Truett] large arachnoid with painful, but not poisonous bite, fond of dark and dank, from Dantooine, Jedi galaxy
laith quine: [Irish éanlaith quine backformation] Guinea fowl-like ornithoid from Ea system
lajazell: [Callisto series by Lin Carter] small winged dracoid from seashore, Thanator, related to zell
lajazellope: [lajazell antelope portmanteau] lajazell with antlers
lake cow: underwater-dwelling bovine from Lake Albert, E. Africa, Terra (alpha Zodiaci III)
Lake Iliamna monster: [*Monster Spotter's Guide to North America* by Scott Francis] 9-meter silver fish with black stripes, blunt barracuda-like head from Lake Iliamna, Alaska, Terra (alpha Zodiaci III)
Lake Leelanau monster: [Monster Spotter's Guide to North America by Scott Francis] 6-meter lake snake with long neck like cedar branch from Lake Leelanau, Mich., Terra (alpha Zodiaci III)
Lake Manitou monster: [*Monster Spotter's Guide to North America* by Scott Francis] 18-meter lake snake with round eye, forked tongue from Lake Manitou, IN, Terra (alpha Zodiaci III)
lake snake: [*Monster Spotter's Guide to North America* by Scott Francis] aka naitaka, freshwater basilosauroid or giant eel
Lake Utopia monster: [*Monster Spotter's Guide to North America* by Scott Francis] 15-meter, eel-like lake snake from New Brunswick, Terra (alpha Zodiaci III)
Lake Worth monster: [*Monster Spotter's Guide to North America* by Scott Francis] "fishy man-goat", amphibious biped with goat-like legs, white fur, scaly face from Lake Worth, TX, Terra (alpha Zodiaci III)
lalu: [*Minions of the Wankh* by Jack Vance] wild creature from Long Bones steppe, Maz
lamarin: [lion tamarin portmanteau] simian as large as a lion, males with mane
Lamb of God: [Jn. 1:19, Rev. 5:12, 6:16, 7:14, 12:11, 13:8] ultimate Sacrifice, Jesus
lambeosaur: crested hadrosaur
lambo: [Monster Galaxy] lamb-like wooly ruminant with red heart-shaped markings
lambprey: [lamb-lamprey portmanteau] small, wooly quadruped with jawless sucking mouth with rasping teeth from Woolarra III, Galaxiki galaxy
lamec: [*Encyclopedia Galactica*] beast of burden from Helicon, Arcturus (gamma Boötis) system
Lamington beetle: [Peter MacInnis] large carnivorous, dark brown click beetle with white spots, huge mandibles and hinged head from Ugly Islands
lamoster: ["In the Light of Vega" by Christopher Montillon] Fantan toothbrush-like creature
lampray: [lamprey-ray portmanteau] ichthyoid with horizontally flattened body, narrow tail, and jawless sucking mouth with rasping teeth
lampshell: see brachiopod
lancey: ["Bird-watchers' Slang" by Paul Beale] lanceolated warbler
land kraken: [Xanth series by Piers Anthony] guards the Love-Lies-Bleeding monument in Isle of View, Xanth
land-eel: [*This Moment of the Storm* by Roger Zelazny] eel-like land creature from Tierra del Cygnus, 72 Cygni system
land-whale: ["Superman under the Red Sun"] carnivorous whale re-adapted to land
landbeaver: see woodchuck

landine: [*Relative Dementias* by Mark Michalowski] geneered shapeshifting "guarddog" from Annarene

landstrider: [*The Dark Crystal* by Jim Hensen] cream-colored, long-legged, floppy-eared quadrupedal steed with coilable proboscis

lank: [*The New Dinosaurs* by Dougal Dixon] 4-meter, giraffe-like hadrosaur with ankleclaws

lanka'gar: ["night flyer"] chiropteran from T'Khasi, Nevasa (40 Eridani) system

lanmola: [The Legend of Zenda] monstrous centipede from Hyrule

lantern bird: ["Ewoks" series] large, beautiful ornithoid with shimmering nest, iridescent tail feathers used in medicinal potions from Endor's moon, Jedi galaxy

lantern fish: [Xanth series by Piers Anthony] luminescent fish with goggling eyes from Xanth

lantern shark: [*The Big Bad Book of Beasts* by Michael Largo] small shark with bioluminescence

lao shu: [*Dragon's Honor* by Kij Johnson and Greg Cox] rodentoid

lapago: [galapago mondegreen] gray-green tortoise

lapin-escargot: [*Another World* by Jean-Ignace-Isidore Gérard] rabbit-headed, rabbit-sized snail from Gérard's system

lapling: ["The Most Toys" by Shari Goodhartz] small creature with long snout thought extinct but discovered not quite

laplingator: [lapling alligator portmanteau] alligator-like predator whose bite morphs victim into lapling

lapók: [Hungarian tellapók backformation] large arachnoid ancestral to tel and tellapók, related to tel, tola, tul, tule, twla, from Tara system

lapon: [*Dell Crossword Puzzle Dictionary*] scorpion fish

laponster: [lapon monster portmanteau] monstrous scorpion fish

lapwing: [*National Geographic Encyclopedia of Animals*] insectovorous bird from S. America, Terra (alpha Zodiaci III)

lapwingator: [lapwing alligator portmanteau] alligator-like predator whose bite morphs victim into lapwing

lar: [*Dell Crossword Puzzle Dictionary*] monkey from Malaysia, Terra (alpha Zodiaci III), see marmoset, sai

lara: [*Vulcan's Forge* by Josepha Sherman and Susan Shwartz] dazzlingly blue desert ornithoid from T'Khasi, Nevasa (40 Eridani) system

lareme: [emerald lareme palindrome] green ornithoid

larg: [largish backformation] sizeshifter, see blowf, bigg

largator: [larg alligator portmanteau] alligator-like predator whose bite morphs victim into larg

larl: [Gor series by John "Norman" F. Large Jr.] white-furred, panther-like felinoid with meter-wide head and paralyzing roar

larlope: [larl antelope portmanteau] larl with antlers

larpa: [*The Cry of the Onlies* by Judy Klass] hooting camel-like beast of burden with long muzzle from Boaco IV

larrow: [lark sparrow partmanteau] ornithoid with lark-like head and sparrow-like body

larth: [Thongor series by Lin Carter] sea serpent "twice ship-size" with lashing tail, claws, fangs from Lemuria

larva: [Lat. "mask"] immature form of polymorphic creature, like caterpillar form of insectoid

laschiz: [Hildegard of Bingen's Lingua Ignota] eagle-like ornithoid from Ignota, Hildegard's system

laser chicken: [Odd Squad: Sector 21] giant chicken with laser-eyes

lasher: see venom

lashlarm: ["How Aliens Work" by Craig Freudenrich] toilet-shaped beach predator with large mouth, sensory tendrils and 3 short stool-like legs

lasphine: ["Keepsakes" by Mike Resnick] Ragobad symbiot

lasset: [*Dell Crossword Puzzle Dictionary*] white ermine, see miniver

lat: [lab rat spoonerism] rodentoid from Rab system

lataceratops: [Cyclopedia of Worlds] ceratopsian dinosaur up to 12 meters, with 6-meter hornspan on Palul (Lar Don), the Dinosaur Planet

latch: [arglatch mondegreen] metallic gray predator

laud: [Fr. Johann Martin Schleyer's Volapük] lark-like ornithoid from Schleyer's system

lauia: [*Dell Crossword Puzzle Dictionary*] parrot-fish, see loro, scarid

lava flea: [*Creatures of the Galaxy* by Phil Brucato, Bill Smith, Rick D. Stuart, Chuck Truett] domesticated, hard-shelled arthropod from Mustafar, Jedi galaxy

lava fly: ["Macrocosm" by Brannon Braga] fly-like insectoid from Rinax

lavyrm: [Terra Monster] black-headed pink, lava-eating wyrm, see magmawyrm, from Terrarium

lawk: [lease of hawks spoonerism, lark-hawk portmanteau] lark-headed hawk-like ornithoid

lazoon: ["Fireball XL5" by Garry and Sylvia Anderson] mimicking pongoid from Mars (alpha Zodiaci IV), see gabbledictum

lazybird: aka cowbird

le-matya: [*Worlds of the Federation* by Shane Johnson, FthinraKathi tematla] yellow and green nimravid-like desert predator with diamond-like side markings, striped tail, poisonous fangs, leathery skin, faced single-handedly in kahs-wan ritual, from T'Khasi, Nevasa (40 Eridani) system

le: [tangelo le nat palindrome] dark orange gnat, see nire

leaf hopper: [leafhopper mondegreen] hopper-like golem made from leaves

leaf leaper: [*The Snouters* by Harald Stümpe] snouter with tail with bristly sole-plate on leg-like tail along with nasarium for leaping both forward and backward from Hy-yi-yi Islands

leafy sea dragon: [*The Big Bad Book of Beasts* by Michael Largo] seaweed-like seahorse able to change colors

leap dog: [*The Monstrous Regiment* by Storm Constantine] hazard of Mireway Artemis, Shamberel-Guimo system

leap dogator: [leap dog alligator portmanteau] alligator-like predator whose bite morphs victim into leap dog

leaper: [*After Man* by Dougal Dixon] large, desert-dwelling, fat-storing rodent

leapfrogg: [leapfrogging backformation] chronoporting batachian

leapfroggator: [leapfrogg alligator portmanteau] alligator-like predator whose bite morphs victim into leapfrog

leaping devil: [*After Man* by Dougal Dixon] round, short-faced insectovorous mammal with long tail, long legs

leaping sphagnum: [*Mothstorm* by Philip Reeve] variety of sphagnum or nibbling sporran which leaps from Uranus (alpha Zodiaci VI)

Lear deer: ["King Lear" by William Shakespeare] rodent-sized deer

lednirda: [James Cooke Brown's Loglan ledri nirda compound] thunderbird from Logla, Brown's system

ledvalni: [James Cooke Brown's Loglan ledri valni] lightning beast from Logla, Schleyer's system

leech phage: [Resident Evil 4] regenerate leech-like phage

leech zombie: [Resident Evil 0] leech gestalt that mimics James Marcus who merged the queen leech with the progenitor virus, soaks victims with acid, explodes when threatened

leet: groundhog-like creature from Rubi-Ka

leever: [The Legend of Zelda] red or blue 4-horned gumdrop-like energy-eater from Hyrule

lefthand: [handbird backformation] variety of handbird

legg: [leggy backformation] long-legged stork-like ornithoid

leggator: [legg alligator portmanteau] alligator predator whose bite morphs victim into legg

legghorn: [leghorn mondegreen] long-legged legg with horn-like leg spurs

leghorn: chicken without horns from Leghorn, Italy, Terra (alpha Zodiaci III)

leidyosuch: [*After the Dinosaurs* by Donald R. Prothero] alligator ancestor from Paleocene

lelk: [sealelk mondegreen] amphibious mammaloid with antlers, flippers and fluke from Skjoob, Bjosko system, Galaxiki galaxy

leltutce: [James Cooke Brown's Loglan leltu tcela] lapwing-like ornithoid from Logla, Brown's system

lelyo: [yellow spoonerism] yellow canary-like ornithoid

lemkin: [*Edge Chronicles* by Paul Stewart and Chris Riddell] small, blue pet with "Wai-kha!" call

lemon jelly: [jelly extrapolation] yellow jelly-thick ooze

lemur: [*Dell Crossword Puzzle Dictionary*] small monkey with large eyes

leodragerus: see lóng, lion-headed dragon

leohoppolophorus: [propaleohoppophorus mondegreen] lion-like hoppolophorus, see propa

leon: [Fr. Johann Martin Schleyer's Volapük] lion-like felinoid from Schleyer's system

leonatoar: [Fr. Johann Martin Schleyer's Volapük] sealion-like sirenian from Schleyer's system

leonis: [piscium extrapolation] egg-laying lion-like felinoid

leonster: [leon monster portmanteau] monstrous lion-like felinoid

leontocephalus: [*Odin's Quest* by Cleon Jones] walrus-like sealion with mane

leopard-shark: [*Dreadnaught!* by Diane Carey] iridescent spotted (matulate) fish with 12 gills from Proxima Centauri

leopard-tortoise: [leopard tortoise mondegreen] carnivorous, spotted, cat-headed tortoise

leopard: [*Dell Crossword Puzzle Dictionary*] tree tiger

leopardvark: [leopard-aardvark portmanteau] large, spotted (matulate) anteater

lep: [Fr. Johann Martin Schleyer's Volapük] pongoid or simian from Schleyer's system

lepon: [Jets*Rockets*Spacemen trading card #17] 2.1-meter long carnivore like both lion and flying squirrel with webbed paws adapted to low gee

leponster: [lepon monster portmanteau] monstrous lepon

leppee: [lepper backformation] racing rabbit

lepper: racing dog

leptauchenia: [*After the Dinosaurs* by Donald R. Prothero] little semi-aquatic oreodont from Oligocene

lepticid: [*After the Dinosaurs* by Donald R. Prothero] small, insectivorous mammal with elephant-like trunk and kangaroo-like legs from Eocene

leptomeryx: [*After the Dinosaurs* by Donald R. Prothero] tiny deer-like grazer from Oligocene

leptophoca: [*After the Dinosaurs* by Donald R. Prothero] with praepusa, crytophoca, pontophoca, the first true seals from Miocene

lepus: [OviPets] aka Easter bunny, egg-laying rabbit-like burrower

lepusaur: [lepus-saur portmanteau] burrowing dinosaur from Lepus constellation

lepuss: [lepus puss portmanteau] egg-laying, rabbit-cat

leputaur: [lepusaur minotaur portmanteau] rabbit-headed cow-like bovinoid

lerwa: [*Dell Crossword Puzzle Dictionary*] snow partridge

les: [Lithuanian juru kiaules backformation] amphibian ancestral to kiau and kiaules

leshe: [*The Suns of Caresh* by Paul Saint] giant carnivorous insect that travels on icebergs

lesothosaur: [*The Mistaken Extinction* by Lowell Dingus and Timothy Rowe] bipedal dinosaur

lesothotaur: [lesothosaur minotaur portmanteau] bipedal bovinoid

lethifold: [*Fantastic Beasts and Where to Find Them* by Newton Artemis Fido Scamander] black, cloak-like carnivore from Papua, New Guinea, Terra (alpha Zodiaci III)

lette: [bulette mondegreen] lavender armadillo/shark/snapping turtle-like monster

leucotrix: ["Mathematical Zoo" by Martin Gardner"] long thin bacterium that reproduce by tying itself in knots to divide
leucrotta: [*Monster Manual* by Gary Gygax] 2-meter tall, dark, badger-headed creature with beige lion-like torso, stag's legs and bony ridges not teeth, able to sound like woman, child or animal in distress
leviacuda: [leviathan-baracuda portmanteau, Terra Monster] armored predatory ichthyoid, see scuda and predacuda, from Terrarium
leviathan: [Heb. Job 40:25-41:26] large wild, armored, hellfire-and-steam breathing sea monster with back spikes; [Monster Galaxy] sea serpent with purple fringe, many teeth and 2 antennae from Pisces constellation
leviosaur: ["The Door of His Face, the Lamps of His Mouth" by Roger Zelazny] leviathan-like lizard
leviotaur: [leviosaur minotaur portmanteau] leviathan-like bovinoid
levitating lobster: [Odd Squad: Sector 21] psychokinetic lobster-like crustacean
lha-cha-eh: [Navaho] caninoid from Diné system
li: [Turkish delikanli backformation] small caninoid from Delika system
liäm: [Fr. Johann Martin Schleyer's Volapük] lamb-like ruminant from Schleyer's system
liar bird: [Peter MacInnis] aka rubbish bird, small, greenish, mimicking bird from Ugly Islands
liati: [Babylon 5: "Knives" by Lawrence G. Tillio] wild Centauri creature
libelul: [Fr. Johann Martin Schleyer's Volapük] dragonfly-like insectoid from Schleyer's system
libri: [Danish kolibri backformation] aka hummingcow (hummingbird-cow), small milk griffinoid ancestral to cow and hummingbird
licat: [*Ghost-Walker* by Barbara Hambly] small predator from Midgwis (Elcidar Beta III)
licorne: [French] horse-bodied unicorn
lida-eniquine: [Continuum] striped, flexible camelopardian from Nogullon system

lidi: [Pellucidar series by Edgar Rice Burroughs] diplodocus-like beast of burden of the Thurians, Pellucidar
lief: [Monster Galaxy] blue quadruped with leafy green ears, collar and tail; [field lief palindrome] leaf mimic in both field and other varieties
lieto: see ocama
liev: [Fr. Johann Martin Schleyer's Volapük] hare-like burrower from Schleyer's system
lifeleech: [Gary Gygax in *Monster Manual III*] variety of otyugh, ferocious with supernatural healing powers and super-tetanus bite
lifette: debatably living creatures adapted to extreme cold from Froze, Locomoto system, Galaxiki galaxy
liger: [lion tiger portmanteau] lion-headed tiger-like felinoid
lightning beast: [Mighty Samson series] giant reptilian that can unleash a high-voltage charge
lightning bug: [Xanth series by Piers Anthony] insectoid with electricity generating ability of electric eel from Xanth or [Xanthian mondegreen] Xa, Thla system
lightning bugator: [lightning bug alligator portmanteau] alligator-like predator whose bite morphs victim into lightning bug
lightsabre-toothed tiger: [Godville] cybernetic tiger with lightsabre fangs
liguhldisgi: [Cherokee] mud dauber-like insectoid from Tsalagi system
lija: [*Dell Crossword Puzzle Dictionary*] leatherfish or unicorn fish
like like: [The Legend of Zelda] yellowish, cylindrical shield-eaters
lilysnouter: [*The Snouters* by Harald Stümpke] plant-mimicking snouter with rigid tail, including miracle or glowing lilysnouter varieties from Hi-Yi-Yi Islands
lim: [milk lim palindrome] small wooly mammaloid
limicoline bird: [*Dell Crossword Puzzle Dictionary*] snipe, plover
limimus: [gallimimus mondegreen] gray-green beaked dinosaur with short arms

limpkin: [*National Geographic Encyclopedia of Animals*] ail and mussel-eating bird from Caribbean and S. America, Terra (alpha Zodiaci III)

limrev: [vermillion oil limrev portmanteau] insectoid with long thin proboscis that secretes vermillion oil

lin: [Navaho] horse from Diné system

linãga: [beheaded alinãga] 998-headed snake

linãgator: [linãga alligator portmanteau] alligator-like predator whose bite morphs victim into kalinãga

lindorm: [*Unexplained!* by Jerome Clark] 6-meter, black snake with yellow belly from Norway, Terra (alpha Zodiaci III)

lindwurm: ["Xoology" by Kittenbaker] green-gold serpentine dracoid from Szurane

ling: [Danish musling backformation] clam-mouse, shell-dwelling rodentoid ancestral to mouse and clam

lingator: [ling alligator portmanteau] alligator-like predator whose bite morphs victim into ling

lingon: [lingonberry (cowberry, mountain cranberry) backformation] red cow-like mountain ursinoid

lingonster: [lingon monster portmanteau] monstrous lingon

liobear: [Mighty Samson #1, lion bear portmanteau] golden furred, 3-meter tall lion-headed ursine, see cub

lioloph: [beheaded plioloph] gan ceann from Ypresia, Ypres system

Lion of Judah: [Gen. 49:9, Jdg. 14:-6, 1 Sam. 17:34-36, 2 Sam 23:20] symbol of strength and so the Strong One of Israel, Jesus, from Holy Land, Terra (alpha Zodiaci III)

lion turtle: [Avatar: The Last Airbender: "The Library"] lion-like turtle

lion-dog: [China] bushy-tailed lion-like creature occasionally with wings or one horn from Fo

lion-dogator: [lion-dog alligator portmanteau] alligator-like predator whose bite morphs victim into lion-dog

lion-fish: [Church of Zillis] lion-headed ichthyoid

lion-hyena: see Szuranian gulon

lion-wolf: lion-headed wolf-like caninoid, see cub

liondragon: [*Fantastic Beasts and Where to Find Them* by Newton Artemis Fido Scamander] see lóng

liopleurodon: [*The Big Bad Book of Beasts* by Michael Largo] 11-meter sea reptile with long snout, paddle-fins

liovet: [violet spoonerism] violet lion-maned creature

lipp: [lippet mondegreen] small variety of et from Pia or Touca systems

lippet: [*The Dirdir* by Jack Vance] small, defenseless animal from Carabas, Sibol

lira: [Monster Galaxy] ornithoid with antlers and purple-and-white stripes from Libra

liret: [sterile lirets palindrome] mule-like equinoid

lis: [cornsilk lis roc palindrome] cornsilk white roc

liškanec: [Czech liška-kanec portmanteau] fox-boar, bushy-tailed porcoid

lithling: [Outernauts] immature lithog

lithlingator: [lithling alligator portmanteau] alligator-like predator whose bite morphs victim into lithling

lithog: [Outernauts] snogg-like burrower, see lithling, lithosaur

lithogator: [lithog alligator portmanteau] alligator-like predator whose bite morphs victim into lithog

lithosaur: [Outernauts] mature lithog; dinosaur-like golem made from rock

lithotaur: [lithosaur minotaur portmanteau] bull-like golem made from rock

litkurma: [James Cooke Brown's Loglan litpo kurma compound] glowworm from Logla, Brown's system

litoptern: [*After the Dinosaurs* by Donald R. Prothero] camel/horse-like hoofed mammal from Paleocene

litten: [litter of kittens spoonerism, lit kitten portmanteau] small, luminescent felinoid

litter bug: [Godville] small, carapaced packrat-like insectoid with 6 legs, able to carry much in its hyperdimensional sacs

litter bugator: [litter bug alligator] alligator-like predator whose bite morphs victim into litter bug

lituusbird: [trumpeter swan backformation] trumpeter swan-like ornithoid with curved neck and lituus-like call

Liuvian builder: [red Liu's Builder palindrome] red builder-like creature from Liu system

liva: [galiva mondegreen] gray-green crocodilian

living blasphemy: [*Monster Manual* by Skip Williams, etal.] especially ugly ooze

living rock: [Richard Demonde in *World Wide News*] rock with very slow metabolism, weeks for breathing cycle

liw: [wild liw palindrome] beastly creature

lizard-bird: saurornithoid or pterosaur, see tinshemet

lizard-snake: [Perry Rhodan] 3.5-meter reptilian with prehensile tail, croc-like legs, scorpion-like mandrel on tail tip from Lumbagoo, moon of Ajaton, Lumbagoo system

lizzard: [lizard-buzzard portmanteau] lizard-headed buzzard-like griffinoid

ljah: [l-less iljah] cave-dwelling lizard from Friatica, Friaticalida system, Galaxiki galaxy

llam: [small llams palindrome] llamba-like ruminant in large and small varieties

llama: [Span. "name"] shaggy mountain ruminant

llamaroo: [llama-kangaroo portmanteau] cross between llama and kangaroo, see krelk

llamba: [llama-lamb portmanteau] small long-necked wooly ruminant from Woolarra III, Galaxiki galaxy

llem: [smelly llems palindrome] skunk-like creature

llerb: [acronym] see brell, rellb

llihcnihc: [chinchilla llihcnihc palindrome] white furry with black-tipped hairs

llinav: [vanilla llinav palindrome] yellowish off-white ornithoid

llion: [llama-lion portmanteau] tawny long-necked, wooly-haired felinoid with mane and tufted tail

llionster: [llion monster portmanteau] monstrous, 2-headed llion

llir: [llir krill palindrome] ichthyoid

lllama: [3-l lama, llama extrapolation] 2-headed pyrogenic llama

llof: [folly llof palindrome] rosy crimson ornithoid

lloh: [Hollywood oowy lloh, squares erauqs palindromes] barnacle-like parasite infesting oows and oow-gods

llopoll: [Catalan llop-poll palindromic portmanteau] wolf-louse, insectoid of insectoid-canine symbiot hunting in co-operative packs, see pollop

llorocell: [Catalan lloro-ocell portmanteau] parrot-bird, parrot-like bird, often confused with ocelloro

llurg: [grullo llurg palindrome] dun or mouse-colored furry

llurgator: [llurg alligator portmanteau] alligator-like predator whose bite morphs victim into

lluyanka: [beheaded, i-less illuyanka] cave-dwelling, hydra-like, 6-headed dracoid

llwyf-cwcwyddrywystrys: [Welsh] barnacle goose-like ornithoid ancestral to magpie and cwcwyddrywystrys

llyff: [Welsh llyffant backformation] amphibious insectoid

loa: [*Dell Crossword Puzzle Dictionary*] eye-infesting worm from Africa, Terra (alpha Zodiaci III)

loan shark: [Xanth series by Piers Anthony] shark fond of arms and legs of Girard Giant river of blood, hypnogourd world, Xanth

lob: [bole lob palindrome] brownish ornithoid

lobalug: [*Fantastic Beasts and Where to Find Them* by Newton Artemis Fido Scamander] poisonous cephalopodan from North Sea, Terra (alpha Zodiaci III)

lobalugator: [lobalug alligator portmanteau] alligator-like predator whose bite morphs victim into lobalug

lobo: [*Dell Crossword Puzzle Dictionary*] gray timber wolf

lobo-sa: [lobosa mondegreen, *Kursaal* by Peter Anghelides] virus causing lycanthropism from Kursaal, Cronus system
lobosa: [*Dell Crossword Puzzle Dictionary*] protozoan
lobsteer: [lobster-steer portmanteau] horned crustacean with stalked eyes, long antennae, 8 legs and 2 pinchers
Loch Moose monster: [*Mirabile* by Janet Kagan] moose-like lake monster mutant from Dragon's Tooth, Mirabile
locnil: [Lincoln locnil palindrome] deep warm olive green ornithoid
loga: ["The Little Wanderer" by Joe Gill] space ornithoid
Logan bear: [loganberry backformation] ursinoid from Loga system
logator: [loga alligator portmanteau] alligator-like predator whose bite morphs victim into loga
logworm: [*Edge Chronicles* by Paul Stewart and Chris Riddell] large, brown, log-mimicking, non-venomous hoverworm
lole: [labo(u)r of moles spoonerism, low mole portmanteau] deep-burrowing mole
loligo: [*Dell Crossword Puzzle Dictionary*] squid
lolo: [Cherokee] locust-like insectoid from Tsalagi system
lomo: parroting simian from Clodios (Iestonian Spiral VII), Galaxiki galaxy
long-mā: [Vietnamese] horse-dragon with horn
long-necked muzzle: ["Capt'n Virgil, Sportsman in Space" by David Brooks] muzzle-like sea creature with long neck
lóng: hellfire-breathing dragon with golden lion-like neck spikes, snub-snout from China, Terra (alpha Zodiaci III)
lóngator: [lóng alligator portmanteau] alligator-like predator whose bite morphs victim into lóng
longhorn: [*Fantastic Beasts and Where to Find Them* by Newton Artemis Fido Scamander] dark green dragon with long tail, glittering gold horn from Romania, Terra (alpha Zodiaci III)

longicorn: beetle with long antennae
longisquama: [*The Big Bad Book of Beasts* by Michael Largo] lizard with feather-like back spines
longspur: [*National Geographic Encyclopedia of Animals*] aquatic insect and seed-eating songbird from N. America, Terra (alpha Zodiaci III)
lonk: [*Dell Crossword Puzzle Dictionary*] black-faced sheep from England, Terra (alpha Zodiaci III)
looc: [cool black calb looc palindrome] calb variant
loomi: [Space Patrol: "The Swamps of Jupiter"] creatures valued for their heat-retaining skins from Jupiter (alpha Zodiaci V)
loomp: [galoomp mondegreen] gray-green rattle-tailed, bipedal herbivore
lootsman: [*Dell Crossword Puzzle Dictionary*] pega, remora suckerfish
lopelier: [French antilopelier backformation] bone-eater adapted to eating antlers
lopenbär: [German antilopenbär backformation] anti-antelope-bear, creature that eats antelope-bears from Germa system
loper: [*Galaxy Guide 2: Yavin and Bespin*] small, red, furry, possum-like rodentoid with hairless bony, barb-tipped tail from Yavin 4 alligator portmanteau] alligator-like predator whose bite morphs victim into
lophorus: [propaleohoppolophorus mondegreen] hoppopotamus relative
loplac: [Cal Poly loplac palindrome] dark green ornithoid
lora: [*Dell Crossword Puzzle Dictionary*] tree snake
lori(s): [*National Geographic Encyclopedia of Animals*] that secrets toxic oil from Sri Lanka, Terra (alpha Zodiaci III), [*Dell Crossword Puzzle Dictionary*] see aye-aye, Ceylonese lemur
lork: ["The Astronautical Revolution" by Leo Lukas] from Yezzikan Rimba (Rimba III), Dommrath galaxy, see thunderlork
loro: [*Dell Crossword Puzzle Dictionary*] mock parrot or parrot-fish, see lauia, scarid

lorshara: aquatic mammal larger than whale from Mya (Airajah IV)

lory: [*National Geographic Encyclopedia of Animals*] parrot from Maluku, Indonesia, Terra (alpha Zodiaci III), [*Dell Crossword Puzzle Dictionary*] see kea, vasa, vaza

lossine: [*Voyage au center de la terre*] 1.8-meter leathery sauroid used as watchdog from Albur, Pluto

lotheo: [Terra Monster] aquatic rodentian with large rudder-like ears, long tail, clawed "fins", see hytheo, from Terrarium

lotis: [Terra Monster RPG] insectovorous plant mimic, see mantislash, from Terrarium

lotor: [OviPets] egg-laying raccoon-like creatures

Lotron dragon: ["Patron of Time" by H. G. Ewers] T. rex-like dinosaur

lou carcolh: [*Giants, Monsters and Dragons* by Carol Rose] cave-dwelling serpent-like mollusk with very long, slimy tentacles from France, Terra (alpha Zodiaci III), related to darkmantle, piercer and roper

lounge lizard: [Godville] lizard adapted to lounging, usually in front of television, see parlor snake

loupie: [Fren. loup-pie portmanteau, *Another World* by Jean-Ignace-Isidore Gérard] wolf-magpie, pack-hunting chattering griffinoid with long tail from Gérard's world

loupoisson: [Fren. loup-poisson portmanteau] wolf-headed ichthyoid from Gérard's world

louporc: [Fren. loup-porc portmanteau] wolf-head porcoid from Gérard's world

loupoule: [Fren. loup-poule portmanteau] wolf-headed chicken-like ornithoid

love bug: [Xanth series by Piers Anthony] glowing, brightly colored insect from Xanth; ["What's So Bad About Feeling Good" by Tedd Pierce, Robert Pirosh and George Seaton based on "I am thinking of my darling" by Vincent McHugh] euphoria-inducing virus carried by toucans

love bugator: [love bug alligator portmanteau] alligator-like predator whose bite morphs victim into love bug

Loveland frog: [*The Big Bad Book of Beasts* by Michael Largo] 1-meter bipedal frog with humanoid eyes and nose

lowder: [louder homonym, The Legend of Zelda] small, blue beetle from Hyrule

lowland beluga: [upland beluga antonym] variety of amphibious beluga, see upland beluga

lox: [leash of foxes spoonerism, loupie fox portmanteau] wolf-fox-magpie-like chimera

lu: lulu nasna; [ulnatit ananymondegreen] yellow ornithoid from Tita system

luachsh: [Cabyle legend] wild monster

luce(t): [Dell Crossword Puzzle Dictionary] full-grown pike

luchusa: ["La Mujer Luchusa" (The Owl Witch)] gigantic, footless blackbird seen only by evil people from Robstown, nr. Corpus Christi, TX, Terra (alpha Zodiaci III)

luckdragon: [*The Neverending Story* by Michael Ende] hellfire-breathing, dog-headed wing-less dragon which flies via accelerated levitation

Lucky Pierre: [**The Snouters** by Harald Stumpke] earthworm-eating burrowing snouter from Hi-Yi-Yi Islands

luffabo: [buffalo spoonerism] bison-like bovinoid

lug: [*Knight Moves* by Walter Jon Williams] large-headed, bug-eyed non-hopping megapodan that grazes on grass-like moss, able to teleport, on Amaterasu

lug bizard: [bug lizard spoonerism] insectovorous reptilian beast-of-burden

lugator: [lug alligator portmanteau] alligator-like predator whose bite morphs victim into lug

luggage: ["Uncharted Territory" by Connie Willis] extraordinarily sedentary sloth-like creature from Boohte

luhimuh: [*Travels into Several Remote Nations of the World* by Lemuel Gulliver] wild rat from Houyhnhnm Island

lui: [Afrikaans luiperd, luiheid backformation] leopard-horse, ancestral to horse and leopard, related to heid sloth

lül: [Fr. Johann Martin Schleyer's Volapük] owl-like ornithoid from Schleyer's system

Lull's deer: [*After the Dinosaurs* by Donald R. Prothero] dromomeryx with branch-like horns

lulu: [*Dell Crossword Puzzle Dictionary*] barn owl from Samoa, Terra (alpha Zodiaci III)

lum: [mulberry yrreb lum palindrome] pinkish purple yrreb

lumba-lumba: [Indonesia/Malay ikan lumba-lumba backformation] dolphin-fish, ichthyoid ancestral to fish and dolphin from Ik system

Lumenian cat: ["Planet of Light"] crystalline felinoid pet killed by oxygen from Lumenia

lumette: [*L'Automne à Pékin*] small, yellow, sand-dwelling snail from Exopotamia

lumir: [Action Comics #314] six-legged pet from Krypton, Rao system

lummox: large ox-like bovine that distracts especially during finals

lumpf: [galumpf mondegreen] gray-green steed

lumpskull: [*Edge Chronicles* by Paul Stewart and Chris Riddell] mysterious creature

luna: [*Dell Crossword Puzzle Dictionary*] green moth

lunatick: [Power Rangers: "Survival of the Silver"] insectoid from Kadix

lundu: [James Cooke Brown's Loglan lunli dunmu (wooly ape) compound] wooly pongoid from Logla, Brown's system

lung: [Chinese] hellfire-breathing, scaly, horned dragon, see lóng

lungator: [lung alligator portmanteau] alligator-like predator whose bite morphs victim into lung

lunk: [If I Ran the Zoo by Theodore Seuss Geissel] simian with dark collar, long tuffed tail and hairy crest and paws

lunka: [James Cooke Brown's Loglan lunli kangu/katma (wooly dog/cat) compound] wooly nimravoid from Logla, Brown's system

lunku: [James Crooke Brown's Loglan Lun kurma] moon worm from Lunli, moon of Logla, Brown's system

lunva: [James Crooke Brown's Loglan Lun valni] moon beast from Lunli, moon of Logla, Brown's system

luon: [Vietnamese con luon backformation] sea creature ancestral to con and eel from Disa

luonster: [luon monster portmanteau] monstrous luon

lupow: [Outernauts] mature luoror

luproo: [Outernauts] immature lupror

lupror: [Outernauts] gray wolverine-like creature with tusks, red backstripe, see lupoo, lupow

lupus: [OviPets] egg-laying wolf-like caninoid

lupusaur: wolf-like, pack-hunting dinosaur from Lupus constellation

lupuss: [lupus puss portmanteau] egg-laying wolf-cat

luputaur: [lupusaur minotaur portmanteau] egg-laying wolf-headed bovinoid

lurg: [*Dell Crossword Puzzle Dictionary*] marine annelid used as bait, see sao, nereis

lurgator: [lurg alligator portmanteau] alligator-like predator whose bite morphs victim into lurg

lurker: [Resident Evil 0] progenitor virus-infected giant frog with small eyes, nearly invulnerable skin and sharp tongue

lurkfish: [*The Future Is Wild* by Dougal Dixon] 4-meter, lumpy, camouflaged swamp-dweller with motion-sensing barbels, protective plates, able to generate kilovolt charge

lurkworm: ["Face the Raven" by Sarah Dollard] glowworm that also gives off misdirection field that makes surrounding seem normal

lurtle: [leatherback/lion turtle spoonerism] chelonian with mane and tethered lurtlings on its carapace

luschia: [Hildegard of Bingen's Lingua Ignota] duck-like ornithoid from Ignota, Hildegard's system

lushaceras: [galushaceras mondegreen] gray-green acerathere

lutie: [*After Man* by Dougal Dixon] nocturnal, mouse-like rabbit

lutrapteryx: ["otter-wing"] otter-like furry with wings

lutscher: ["Mother's Day" by Astrid Julian] with large sowbug-like larvae from Sheelar

luxzia: [Hildegard of Bingen's Lingua Ignota] locust-like insectoid from Ignota, Hildegard's system

luyanka: [beheaded lluyanka] 5-headed hydra-like dracod

lyabani: [Azerbaijani qulyabani backformation] monstrous swan

lyam: [*Dell Crossword Puzzle Dictionary*] bloodhound from Scotland, Terra (alpha Zodiaci III)

lycanthropic virus: see lobo-sa

lychbug: [*Marune: Alastor 933* by Jack Vance] stinging insectoid of Marune

lychbugator: [lychbug alligator portmanteau] alligator-like predator whose bite morphs victim into lychbug

Lycosa tarantula: ["Realm of Fear"] wolf spider from Taranto, Italy, Terra (alpha Zodiaci III)

lyena: [laughing hyena spoonerism] caninoid able to reproduce by splitting after gorging

lyhannh: [*Travels into Several Remote Nations of the World* by Lemuel Gulliver] large swallow-like bird from Houynhhnm Island

lying cat: [Saga] feline able to detect lying, like cetaceans do with sonar

lylek: [*Creatures of the Galaxy* by Phil Brucato, Bill Smith, Rick D. Stuart, Chuck Truett] tall predator with protective exoskeleton, tentacles, spear-footed limbs, paralyzing poison-tipped tail-tentacle from Ruloth, Jedi galaxy

lynar: ["Chain of Command" by Frank Abatemarco] chiropteroid from Celtris III

lyncis: [piscium extrapolation] lynx-like, egg-laying felinoid

lynel: [The Legend of Zenda] lion-headed centaur

lynelope: [lynel antelope portmanteau] lynel with antlers

lynipper: [gallynipper mondegreen] gray-green mosquitoid

Lyoko mite: [Code Lyoko] sphere with tentacles that spits yellow energy balls

Lyoko scorpion: [Code Lyoko] biped with transparent skin, thick forelegs, thick muscular neck, large beak and large tail with stinger, related to creeper

Lyoko tarantula: [Code Lyoko] spider-like quadruped with 6 small red eyes and foreleg lasers geneered by Xana, vulnerable at top of head

Lyraxian cat: ["Squirrel Cage" by Robert Sheckley] felinoid with enhanced senses of smell and hearing though virtually blind from Lyrax

lyrebird: bird with lyre-like tail

lyrehorn: see croizetoceras

Lysenkan mole: [*Enemies of the System* by Brian Aldiss] bipedal mole mutant from Lysenka II

lytcadactyl: [mynynym] creature with unique toes from Lytca system

lyte: [Lithuanian juru kialyte backformation] rodentian ancestral to kiau and kiaulyte

ma: [Ygamese ma palindrome, surma mondegreen] reddish brown caninoid with prehensile, snake-like tail

ma-e: [Navaho] fox-like caninoid from Diné system

ma'pek: ["The Web" by Michelle Stern] man-eating simian

macaque: [*Dell Crossword Puzzle Dictionary*] see bruh, rhesus

macboon: [*Fantastic Beasts and Where to Find Them* by Newton Artemis Fido Scamander] large, hairy carnivorous quintaped or hairless herbivorous quintaped from Isle of Drear

machairod: [*After the Dinosaurs* by Donald R. Prothero] sabre-toothed cat from Miocene

machin: [*Dell Crossword Puzzle Dictionary*] monkey from Phillipines, Terra (alpha Zodiaci III)

machshund: [moxie of dachshunds spoonerism] supersonic caninoid

macrauchenia: [*After the Dinosaurs* by Donald R. Prothero] camel-like litoptern with long, tapir-like proboscis from Pliocene

macropodan: large-footed kangaroo-like marsupial
macropodus: [OviPets] egg-laying kangaroo-like marsupial
macrovirus: ["Macrocosm" by Brannon Braga] giant virus-like organism from Delta quadrant
madder: [*Dell Crossword Puzzle Dictionary*] red turkey
mado: [*Dell Crossword Puzzle Dictionary*] trumpeter perch
maeosaur: [dromaeosaur mondegreen] bird-like dinosaur
maeosaur: [maerosaur minotaur portmanteau] bovinoid pegasoid with bird's wings
maer: [cream maer] pale yellowish or tan furry
mafedet: snake-lion from Egypt, Terra (alpha Zodiaci III)
mag: [*Dell Crossword Puzzle Dictionary*] titmouse, see pagus, magg
magator: [mag alligator portmanteau] alligator-like predator whose bite morphs victim into mag
mag(g): [*Dell Crossword Puzzle Dictionary*] magpie, see pie(t), piot, pyot, pyet, ninut, pi(an)et
mag(g)ator: [mag(g) alligator portmanteau] alligator-like predator whose bite morphs victim into mag(g)
måged: [Danish måge-ged portmanteau] seagull-goat, goateed, horned triphibian
magic carpet: see xirdoor
magic-sniffer: [Xanth series by Piers Anthony] short quadruped with long flexible tapir-like snout that snootles in presence of anything magical, especially magic berries, from Xanth
magicaneo: [Terra Monsters] magic creature from Terranium
magma creature: ["The Caves of Androzani" by Robert Holmes] subterranean creature from Androzani Minor, Sirius (alpha Tauri) system
magma: ["Gorath" by Takeshi Kimura] 75-meter tall walrus with glowing eyes able to use flippers for defense

magmawyrm: [Terra Monsters] 4-legged, white winged, heat-resistant red dracoid, see lavyrm, from Terrarium
magnoped: ["Flash Gordon" series] large pachyderm with pair of crushing tusks from rogue planet Mongo
magon: [dragon spoonerisms] dracoid from Drica or Drood systems; [tormagon backformation] bull-like creature
magonster: [magon monster portmanteau] monstrous magon
magoo: [Space: 1889] mysterious predator from Mars (alpha Zodiaci IV)
magraclop: large headed cyclops from Valley of Monsters, Amazonia, Terra (alpha Zodiaci III) ("Mystery of the Magraclop", "The Lost Skeleton Returns Again" by Larry Blamire)
magtail: [The Legend of Zelda: "The Wind Waker"] small, one-eyed, hi-temp centipede with large jaws, curls up when threatened
maha: [*Dell Crossword Puzzle Dictionary*] sambar deer, see rusa
mahseer: [*River Monsters* by Jeremy Wade] 90-kg fish from Himalayas, Terra (alpha Zodiaci III)
maillekal: [Lake Lliamna monster ananymon-degreen] large ichthyoid with black stripes from Retsnoma system
maiti: [uzamaiti mondegreen] non-blue grizzly-like ursinoid
maja: [*Dell Crossword Puzzle Dictionary*] spider crab
makant: ["Ewoks" series] large, playful insectoid like both mantis and cricket from Endor's forest moon, Jedi galaxy
makara: [Hindi] croc-like, elephant-like, snake-like chimera
maki: [*Dell Crossword Puzzle Dictionary*] lemur, see indri
makl: [*The Spawn of Fashün* by Kirby Lee Davis] creature from Boosboodle
mako: [*Dell Crossword Puzzle Dictionary*] long-nosed shark
Makrian eel: [Afrikaans/Dutch makreel backformation] eel-like ichthyoid from Makr system

Malachi's Boots: [*Double, Double* by Michael Jan Friedman] dangerous, poisonous, soft, tentacled beast of Tranquility 7
malaclaw: [*Fantastic Beasts and Where to Find Them* by Newton Artemis Fido Scamander] poisonous, but not-deadly, lobster-like crustacean
malf: [flame malf palindrome] furry with "red" (yellow-orange)-tipped hair, see gni
malficli: [James Crooke Brook's Loglan malna ficli compound] milk ichthyoid from Logla, Brown system
malia: [*Creatures of the Galaxy* by Phil Brucato, Bill Smith, Rick D. Stuart, Chuck Truett] swift, nocturnal, blue-gray furry with long tapered snouts with triple row of yellow teeth from Ragoon 6, Jedi galaxy
malignant amoeba: ["The Ship That Dared Not Land" by Otto Binder] giant, omnivorous amoeboid
Mamese moth: [mammoth backformation] giant moth-like insectoid from Mam system, [Rus. mamuth] large, shaggy pachyderm
mammontops: [*The Snouters* by Harald Stümpke] aka shaggyfaced snouter, 1.3-meter snout walker with 4 short, thick walking nasaria and 2 feeding nasaria from Mitadina, Hi-Yi-Yi Islands
mammoth chicken: ["Far Side" by Gary Larson] giant chicken-like ornithoid with upward-turned tusks, nosehorn and bonecrest
mammothball: [mammoth mothball portmanteau] mammoth-like creature able to curl up like curl-up
mamuta fiso: [Thousand Stars] 200-kg mammoth from Khorkalon
man-eating cow: [The Tick: "Man-eating Cow"] carnivorous bovine, hornless variety of bicorn, see carnotaur
man-eating spinach: [Mad Magazine: *My First Scary Reader, twisted little thoughts for warped little minds*] giant, mobile spinach that eats men, women and especially children
man: [pl. mans, Azerbaijani manat backformation] manta-horse, seahorse-like amphibian ancestral to horse and manta ray, not to be confused with male Human
manakin: [*National Geographic Encyclopedia of Animals*] fruit-eating bird from S. and Meso-America, Terra (alpha Zodiaci III)
manateel: [manatee-eel portmanteau] long, thin aquatic mammaloid with broad, flattened tail and paddle-like flippers
manda: ["Atoragon" (Atragon) by Shinichi Sekizawa] 6-meter long aquatic snake with 4 small vestigial limbs, 4 straight horns, 180-centimeter fangs, snout tendrils, short brown mane on back, yellow eyes from Mu
mandoril: [*Araminta Station* by Jack Vance] wild creature from Cadwel
mandu: [Katmandu backformation] mountain feline
manfla: [James Cooke Brown's Loglan manti flaki (ant fly) compound] ant-headed fly-like insectoid from Logla, Brown's system
mangá: [Vietnamese mang-gá backformation] flightless bear-chicken griffinoid, related to mangông
mangabey: [*National Geographic Encyclopodia of Animals*] monkey from W. Africa, Terra (alpha Zodiaci III)
mangaroo: [mob of kangaroos spoonerism, mongabey-kangaroo portmanteau] monkey-like megapod
mangông: [Vietnamese mang-gá backformation] flightless bear-goose griffinoid, related to mangá
mangôngator: [mangông alligator portmanteau] alligator-like predator whose bite morphs victim into mangông
manipogo: [*Monster Spotter's Guide to North America* by Scott Francis] 15-meter muddy brown, humped lake snake from Manitoba lakes, see winipogo
maniraptor: [*The Mistaken Extinction* by Lowell Dingus and Timothy Rowe] featherless ancestor of both dromaeosaurs and birds
mankasni: [James Cooke Brown's Loglan manti kasni compound] antcow from Logla, Brown's system
manla: [James Cooke Brown's Loglan manti ladzo (ant-louse) compound] ant-headed

louse-like insectoid from Logla, Brown's system

manli: [James Cooke Brown's Loglan manti clika (ant-like) compound] from Logla, Brown's system

manshark: [Xanth series by Piers Anthony] shark-headed anthropoid with gills and large fin on neck from Xanth

mansimba: [James Cooke Brown's Loglan manti simba] antlion from Logla, Brown's system

mantella: [*National Geographic Encyclopedia of Animals*] insectivorous frog from Madagascar, Terra (alpha Zodiaci III)

manteri: [Terra Monster, young manticub] quadruped with ringed, pincher-tipped tail and both electrical and poisonous, see manticub and amperor, from Terrarium

mantigrue: ["Ewoks" series] hideous, dracoid with leathery wings, sharp claws, long pointed beak from Endor's moon, Jedi galaxy

mantislash: [Terra Monster] plant-mimicking insectoid with petalclaws, see lotis, from Terrarium

mantitci: [James Cooke Brown's Loglan manti titci (ant eater) compound] anteater from Logla, Brown's system

manuao: [*Dell Crossword Puzzle Dictionary*] honeybee, see deseret, moho

manul: [*Dell Crossword Puzzle Dictionary*] wild cat from Siberia or Tibet, Terra (alpha Zodiaci III)

manulope: [manul antelope portmanteau] manul with antlers

manx: cat, not crabbit, without tail

mao: [*Dell Crossword Puzzle Dictionary*, Kipling] peacock, see pavo

mapingari: [Dr. David Oren, "Sightings"] 1.8-meter, 270 kg ground sloth from Amazonia, Terra (alpha Zodiaci III)

mapo: [*Dell Crossword Puzzle Dictionary*] small goby from Atlantic

mapon: [mew of capons spoonerism] mapo-like ichthyoid with forked tail

maponster: [mapon monster portmanteau] monstrous mapon

mar: [Danish marsvin backformation] Guinea pig-pig, see ginea, gini, meri, tsova, uk; [çakalamar mondegreen] coyote-squid from Çakala system; [clezmar mondegreen] spherical sponge from Clez system; [comar mondegreen] giant bovinoid from Co system

mara: [*National Geographic Encyclopedia of Animals*] herbivorous rodent from Patagonia, Terra (alpha Zodiaci III); [Croatian bubamara mondegreen] beetle ancestor to Ahla, Ojikh system, Galaxiki galaxy

marabou: [*Dell Crossword Puzzle Dictionary*] stork

marabounta: [Code Lyoko] gray sphere that multiplies by digital mitosis geneered by Jeremie, see tornade, shabom, rover

maracan: [*Dell Crossword Puzzle Dictionary*] macaw from Brazil, Terra (alpha Zodiaci III)

maramu: [*Creatures of the Galaxy* by Phil Brucato, Bill Smith, Rick D. Stuart, Chuck Truett] ram-headed rooid from Genesia and Cholganna, and Endor's moon, Jedi galaxy

marauder: ["Fungi from Yuggoth" by Howard Phillips Lovecraft] parasitic fractal-dimensional like stringy mass of fine tendrils, minion of Yog-Sothoth

marax: [*The Maracot Deep* by Arthur Conan Doyle] 75-cm crayfish

marí: [Basque corb marí backformation] cormorant-raven ornithoid ancestral to raven and cormorant

Markoffian sea lizard: [" Deja Q" by Richard Danus] aquatic sauroid from Markoff

marling: [murmuration of starlings spoonerism, mar backformation] Guinea pig-piglet, small relative of mar

marlingator: [marling alligator portmanteau] alligator-like predator whose bite morphs victim into marling

marmelot: ["Prince of Peril" by Otis Adelbert Kline] horse-sized hairless, scaly, mottled orange and black saber-toothed felinoid from Zarovia (Venus (alpha Zodiaci II))

marmont: [*The Dirdir, The Pnume* by Jack Vance] large, braying bovinoid from Sibol

marmoset: [*Dell Crossword Puzzle Dictionary*] monkey, see lar, sai

marmot: [*Dell Crossword Puzzle Dictionary*] woodchuck, see moonack

mårran: [Swedish] see groke

mars: [Monster Galaxy] turquoise spheroid with crest and 2 eyes

marshkoj: [Belarussian marshoj kaniok, marshoj svinki mondegreen] seahorse-Guinea pig amphibian ancestral to kaniok and seahorse and Guinea pig

marsupilani: [André Franquin] yellow, block-spotted primate with very long prehensile tail, large, round black nose, floppy rabbit-like ears from Palombia

marthresant: ["The Colonel Returns to the Stars" by Robert Silverberg] walrus-like sea creature from Phosphor

Martian mandrill: ["The Menace of the Martian Mandrills" by Jack Miller] mandrill-like creature with superpowers from Mars (alpha Zodiaci IV)

martilki: [Turkish marti-tilki portmanteau] seagull-fox, coastal griffinoid with furry tail from Draapaa, Albina system, Galaxiki galaxy

martyaxvar: [Pers. "maneater"] manticore

marvint: [varmint spoonerism] small insectoid pest

maržyrat: [Belarussian maržy-žyrat portmanteau backformation] walrus-giraffe amphibian

mas: [Indonesian/Malay ikan mas mondegreen] ichthyoid ancestral to goldfish, see arany, kulta

massiff: [*Creatures of the Galaxy* by Phil Brucato, Bill Smith, Rick D. Stuart, Chuck Truett] pet and guard animal in Jedi galaxy

mastig: [*Deep Domain* by Howard Weinstein] dragoid from Rannica III

mastigator: [mastig alligator portmanteau] alligator-like predator whose bite morphs victim into mastig

masu: [*Dell Crossword Puzzle Dictionary*] salmon from Japan, Terra (alpha Zodiaci III)

mat: [mischief of rats, mouse-rat portmanteau] cross between mouse and rat, see rouse

matagot: demonic black cat said to cough up a gold coin per day from France, Terra (alpha Zodiaci III)

matanoo roc: [beheaded and curtailed amata-no-oroch] 6-headed, 6-tailed, roc-like dracoid with red eyes and mossy, forested back

matouchi: [*Mémoires De Sir George Wallop* by Pierre Chevalier Duplessis] deer from Aprilis, New Britain Islands

mattle: [mob of cattle spoonerism] bovinoid

mau: [Egyptian] aka ocicat, spotted (spangled, matulate) cat; [*Dell Crossword Puzzle Dictionary*] tsetse fly, see kivu, glossina

maulotaur: [Heretic-HeXen] minotaur variant that uses maul (large hammer) and serpent-like pyrokinesis

maulverine: [Terra Monsters] large wolvus relative from Terrarium

maustier: [German Maus-Stier portmanteau] mouse-bull/beast, beastly creature with horns and large round ears

mavie/s: see missel

maya: [*Dell Crossword Puzzle Dictionary*] weaverbird, see baya, taha

Maylb ox: [mailbox mondegreen] papyrus-eating ox-like bovine from Maylb system

mblelu: [*Unexplained!* by Jerome Clark] stegosauroid from Africa, Terra (alpha Zodiaci III)

mbyllizogojer: [Alb.] wolf-like caninoid that mbyllizogojs (eats quickly)

meaching: [*After Man* by Dougal Dixon] small, burrowing lemming-like rodent, prey for ravenes, booties and gandimots

meachingator: [meaching alligator portmanteau] alligator-like predator whose bite morphs victim into meaching

measle: [*Dell Crossword Puzzle Dictionary*] tapeworm larva

meaterworm: [inchworm extrapolation mondegreen] 1-meter, flesh-eating worm

meatgoat: ["Planet of the Zombies" by Dirk Hess] lean goat-like ruminant with long curved horns from Aramar's world, Microcosm

mecrim: [*The Menagerie* by Martin Day] deadly, heat-seeking predator geneered in Menagerie of Ukkazaal

mecrim gut bacterium: [*The Menagerie* by Martin Day] bacterium in mecrim gut that killed its geneers on Ukkazzal

medusa-bird: ["Wonder Girl's Decision of Doom" by Robert Kanigher] bird with medusa-like crest from Paradise Island

medusa: [*The Sign of the Mute Medusa* by Ian Wallace] endangered azure aerial life-form from Turquoise (Gannet IV)

mee: [muster of peacocks spoonerism] ornithoid in meecock and meehen varieties, see ee and pree

meercan: [*Vulcan's Glory* by D. C. Fontana] steed from Areta (beta Circini III)

meese: [goose extrapolation] moose gestalt

mega bite: [Resident Evil: "Outbreak File #2"] giant, blood-sucking mutant flea with queen as large as subway

mega-grasshopper: Hitchhiker's Guide to the Galaxy series by Douglas Adams] large grasshopper-like insectoid from Arcturus (gamma Boötis) system

megachasma: [The Big Bad Book of Beasts by Michael Largo] 5.4-meter shark

megadonkey: [Hitchhiker's Guide to the Galaxy by Doug Adams] large donkey-like equinoid from Arcturus (gamma Boötis) system

megagecko: ["Monster Manatee vs. Giant Gecko" by Satanus666] giant gecko

megager acrix: ["Face To Face With Planet Scanodon" by Rocky Strone] large predatory cressi from Scanodon, Croft system

megahippo: [megahippus hippo portmanteau] giant hippoid from Mega system

megahippus: [*After the Dinosaurs* by Donald R. Prothero] leaf-eating horse from Miocene

megalania: [*After the Dinosaurs* by Donald R. Prothero] giant monitor lizard from Pleistocene

megaloceras: [*After the Dinosaurs* by Donald R. Prothero] Irish elk ancestor

megaloceratops: [Cyclopedia of Worlds] carnivorous ceratopsian dinosaur on Palul (Lar Don), the Dinosaur Planet

megalodon: ["giant tooth", *After the Dinosaurs* by Donald R. Prothero, "Megashark vs. Giant Octopus" by Ace Hannah] see

whale-eating, 17-meter species of carcharocles (great white shark)

megalon: ["Godzilla vs. Megalon" by Jun Fukuda and Shinichi Sekizawa] 120-meter tall biped with head and blotchy-yellow beetle wings, 2 thick mandibles, short spiked tail, leaf-like plates, conical burrowing "arms", large red side-viewing eyes, floppy antennae, horn with startip that shoots lightning bolt, able to spit fireballs

megalonyx: [Thomas Jefferson "giant claw", *After the Dinosaurs* by Donald R. Prothero] large ground sloth

megalosaur: [William Buckland] large ancestor to tyrannosaur

megalotaur: [megalosaur minotaur portmanteau] large bovine

megamanatee: ["Monster Manatee vs. Giant Gecko" by Satanus666] giant killer manatee

meganguilla: [Greco-Spanish] giant eel, sea serpent

megantereon: [*After the Dinosaurs* by Donald R. Prothero] sabre-toothed cat from Zanclean age (early Pliocene)

megaphone bird: [*The Snouters* by Harald Stümpke] thrush-sized slime snouter predator of Eeza-zofa, Hi-Yi-Yi Islands

megapillar: giant, but quick, caterpillar-like worm from Habitat (Iestonian Spiral IV), Galaxiki galaxy

megapiranha: ["Megapirahna" by Naomi L. Selfman] giant piranha

megapython: ["Megapython vs. Gatoroid" by Naomi L. Selfman] giant python

megashark: ["Megashark vs. Giant Octopus" by Jack Perez, "Megashark vs. Crocosaurus" by Naomi L. Selfman] giant shark, see supershark

megaspider: ["Eight Legged Freaks" by Jesse Alexander, Ellory Elkayem, "Tarantula" by Robert M. Fresco, Martin Berkeley] giant man-eating spider

megasquid: [*The Future Is Wild* by Dougal Dixon] 8-tonne land cephalopodan with 8 short cylindrical legs, 2 feeding tentacles, one lung and frog-like croak

megathere: giant Pleistocene sloth (see mylodon, mapingari)
megatick: ["Bird-watchers' Slang" by Paul Beale] very rare bird; giant tick-like crustacean
megatrociraptor: ["giant cruel raptor"] giant variety of atrociraptor
meh: [Monster Galaxy] fluffy, green goat-like ruminant from Capricorn constellation
mei long: ["soundly sleeping dragon", *Feathered Dinosaurs: The Origin of Birds* by John Long and Peter Schuten] 53-cm troodontid that slept curled bird-like, with large nostrils, closely packed teeth, related to sinoventor
meilmir: [*Odin's Quest* by Cleon Jones] melanic (dark) porcupine
mela ntouka: ["elephant-killer", *Unexplained!* by Jerome Clark] rhino-like creature from Lake Tele, Congo, Terra (alpha Zodiaci III)
meliaceratops: [Cyclopedia of Worlds] ceratopsian dinosaur on Palul (Lar Don), the Dinosaur Planet
mellitus: ["Wolf in the Field" by Robert Bloch] gaseous when in motion, solid when still from alpha Majoris system
mellivora: [*After the Dinosaurs* by Donald R. Prothero] aka honey badger from Pleistocene
melodee: [Monster Galaxy] horrible, pink biped with fluffy white wings
melure: [lemur spoonerism] easily caught, large-eyed, arboreal simian
membrilla: ["The Stranger" by H. G. Ewers] skin-like symbiot in chelao gestalt, see ims and thread devils
memphre: [*Monster Spotter's Guide to North America* by Scott Francis] 21-meter, dark, humped lake snake from Lake Memphremagog, VT, Terra (alpha Zodiaci III)
menigirri: [*Fortune's Light* by Michael Jan Friedman] plump, cobalt-colored sauroid with pleasant scent from Imprima
menoceras: [*After the Dinosaurs* by Donald R. Prothero] sheep-sized rhino with two nose-horns on males which migrated to America in early Miocene
menura: [*Dell Crossword Puzzle Dictionary*] lyrebird

mera: [gamera mondegreen] gray-green space tortoise; [triply beheaded Hesiodian chimera] see gan ceann
meraffe: [mer-giraffe contraction] giraffe-like sea monster with long neck, short horns and tan with orange-brown blotches
meraps: [*Stranger from the Stars* by Nancy Etchemendy] cloud-like creature from Seldor, theta Scorpii system
Mercurio's ichthyosaur: ["Tourish Attraction" by Dean Riesner] large-headed lungfish with clawed arm-like fins and ability to focus sound from Crater Lake, San Paulos
mercury ooze: [*Monster Manual* by Skip Williams, etal.] thick, silvery ooze
merganser: black and white duck, aka sheldrake
merhorse: [merman extrapolation] seahorse larege enough to be used as steed
meri: [Estonian merisiga backformation] Guinea pig-pig, see ginea, gini, mar, tsova, uk
meringue-utang: [*Reignbeau's Riddles and Rhymes*, meringue orangutang portmanteau] white, fluffy relative of the orangutang
merino: [*Dell Crossword Puzzle Dictionary*] sheep
merlank: [*Trullion: Alastor 2262* by Jack Vance] sauroid from Trullion
merlette: [heraldry] aka leg-less duck, air-dwelling ornithoid, see murre
merlin: [*Dell Crossword Puzzle Dictionary*] pigeon hawk, [*National Geographic Encyclopedia of Animals*] variety of falcon eating smaller birds from N. Hemisphere, Terra (alpha Zodiaci III)
merling: [*Trullion: Alastor 2262* by Jack Vance] night-hunting amphibian riverback burrower from Tullion
merlingator: [merling alligator portmanteau] alligator-like predator whose bite morphs victim into merling
mermoalornis: [*After the Dinosaurs* by Donald R. Prothero] large flightless bird from Miocene
merycoidodon: [*After the Dinosaurs* by Donald R. Prothero] sheep-sized oreodon
mes: [seme mes palindrome] starry furry

mesa: [Hausa, Nigeria] hose-python
mesite: [*National Geographic Encyclopedia of Animals*] insect, seed and invertebrate-eating bird from Africa, Terra (alpha Zodiaci III)
mesohippo: [mesohippus hippo portmanteau] three-toed hippoid from Meso system
mesohippus: [*After the Dinosaurs* by Donald R. Prothero] three-toed horse
mesonyx: wolf-like ungulate pakicetus ancestor
messelobunodon: [*After the Dinosaurs* by Donald R. Prothero] primitive artiodactyl
messi: [Monster Galaxy] tan felinoid with shaggy dark hair, fond of kicking balls, from Leo constellation
messie: [*Monster Spotter's Guide to North America* by Scott Francis] large lake snake from Lake Murry, S. C., Terra (alpha Zodiaci III)
metal-eater: [Superman mythos] large tapir-like metallovore from Krypton, Rao system
metallovore: [Space Family Robinson: Lost in Space comic] 12-meter long beetle-like creature with metallic scales, long smooth neck, 6 stocky legs (hind legs thinner), rat-like tail, red eyes, vulnerable to rust from Altair (alpha Aguilae) system
metridiochoerus: [*After the Dinosaurs* by Donald R. Prothero] warthog-like artiodactyl with 1-meter shoulder height, long curved upper and lower tusks from Pleistocene
metti: [James Crooke Brown's Loglan metli titci compound] metal-eater from Logla, Brown's system
meushiká: [Jap. meushi-shiká portmanteau] cow-deer ruminant
mew: [*Dell Crossword Puzzle Dictionary*] sea gull from Europe, Terra (alpha Zodiaci III)
mewmel: [*Edge Chronicles* by Paul Stewart and Chris Riddell] felinoid with spiky tail, poisonous spittle, see cactus cat
mewmelope: [mewmel antelope portmanteau] mewmel with antlers
mhal: [shermhal backformation] shermhal descendant related to sher

mhor: [*Dell Crossword Puzzle Dictionary*] whale-shark
mhorse: [morse-horse portmanteu] land walrus-like steed
mi: [ci extrapolation, Roman MI] unmillipede
miacid: [*After the Dinosaurs* by Donald R. Prothero] small, weasel-like ancestral carnivore from Paleocene
miam: [*Book of Dreams* by Jack Vance] fly-like insectoid noted for musk from McVann's star system
mica dragon: [Warhammer 40,000] dracoid with chainsaw-like teeth from Luther McIntyre IX
mico: [*Dell Crossword Puzzle Dictionary*] marmoset
micorb: [Catalan mico-corb portmanteau] ape-crow, hairy, arboreal, black winged pongoid
microgurp: [centigurp extrapolation] pink furball able to bounce, roll, fond of spheres, and be in a million places at once, see gurp
microraptor: [*Feathered Dinosaurs: The Origin of Birds* by John Long and Peter Schuten] 77-cm bird-like dinosaur with gliding arm-wings and leg-wings and long feathered tail
microrcim: [mynynym] very small orcim
midas fly: [Xanth series by Piers Anthony] insect that turns whatever touches it into solid gold, related to gold bug, from Xanth
midj: large tourist-eating insectoid from Isle of Storms (Hailstorm I), Galaxiki galaxy
midwife toad: ["Death Wish" by Michael Pillar] batrachian from Gorok, Delta Quadrant
miin: insectoid from Meri (Kalamon III), Galaxiki galaxy
mikaio: [Basque mika-kaio portmanteau] magpie-seagull, aquatic ornithoid
mikardi: [Basque mika-ardi portmanteau] magpie-sheep, small, wooly pegasoid
mikie: ["The Probe" by Seeley Lester] giant tentacled blob-like mutant microbe
mil: [lime mil, slimy mils palindromes,] light green slug

milchgrub: [Edge Chronicles by Paul Stewart and Chris Riddell] large insectoid that excretes honey-like milch

millennial bug: [Buzz Lightyear of Star Command: "Millennial Bugs" by Nicholas DuBois] large, dangerous ex-extinct insectoid stopped with belly-tickling

millennial bugator: [millennial bug alligator portmanteau] alligator-like predator whose bite morphs victim into millennial bug

milligrifani: [Continuum] 50-cm poison-clawed millipede from Lemur (aka Korina)

milligurp: [centigurp extrapolation] pink furball able to bounce, roll, fond of spheres, and be in a thousand places at once, see gurp

mimic-dog: [Xanth series by Piers Anthony] canine that mimics whatever it sees or hears from Xanth

mimic-dogator: [mimic-dog alligator portmanteau] alligator-like predator whose bite morphs victim into mimic-dog

mimiknik: ["L'il Abner" by Al Capp] mockingbird-like songbird from Lower Slobbovia

mimoboar: [minotaur, mimosaur malapropism] shape-shifting porcoid

mimosaur: [ornithomimosaur backformation, *Boris Karloff's Tales of Mystery #42*] shape-shifting chameleon-like lizard

mimotaur: [mimosaur minotaur portmanteau] shapeshfting bull

mimple: [Monster Galaxy] pink sheep-like ruminant with yellow wings from Aries constellation

min: [one-eyed miin] cyclopean insectoid

mincer: [mincer backformation] predator that minces

minchenella: [*After the Dinosaurs* by Donald R. Prothero] tethythere relative from late Paleocene, ancestral to elephants, manatees and dugongs

mind monster: [Boris Karloff's Tales of Mystery #27] infradimensional monster spawned from hatred

mind worm: [*Monster Manual* by Skip Williams, etal.] purple worm-like creature created by Illthid attack with probe worms

minhocão: [Brazillian "big earthworm"] 50-meter giant worm lizard with scaly black skin, see graboid, titanoboa

mini-freezard: see freezard

minimimus: [minimus backformation] sizeshifting insectoid

minimus: [*Dell Crossword Puzzle Dictionary*] small creature, see mite

minina: [minina taninim palindrome] small sauroid, see neenina

mininim: [mynymym] aka rutai, small variety of nim

minippus: [*After the Dinosaurs* by Donald R. Prothero] small horse from Yprerian age (early Eocene)

minitaur: [Godville] minotaur 4.8-meter tall with fangs

miniver: [*Dell Crossword Puzzle Dictionary*] squirrel or white ermine, from Siberia, Terra (alpha Zodiaci III), see lasset

mink snake: [Avatar: The Airbender: "The Deserter"] furry boa-like serpentine

minka: [Peramangks] harbinger-of-death bird from Mt. Barker, Australia, Terra (alpha Zodiaci III)

minoboar: [minotaur malapropism] boar/pig-headed anthropoid

minosaur: [minotaur dinosaur portmanteau] lizard-headed anthropoid

minotaur: bull-headed anthropoid from Crete, Terra (alpha Zodiaci III)

minstyngar: [*Creatures of the Galaxy* by Phil Brucato, Bill Smith, Rick D. Stuart, Chuck Truett] insectoid from Kashÿyÿk and Mimban, Jedi galaxy

minutehand: [secondhand extrapolation] larger and slower variety of secondhand

miohippo: [miohippus hippo portmanteau] hippoid from Mio system

miohippus: [*After the Dinosaurs* by Donald R. Prothero] small, archaic horse

miracinonyx: [*After the Dinosaurs* by Donald R. Prothero] cheetah from Zanclean age (early Pliocene)

mird: [medusa-bird portmanteau, spoonerism] azure ornithoid with medusa-like crest from Bedusa system

miri nugri: ["dark dwarves", "Horror from the Hills" by Frank Belnap Long] dark, mute dwarf of toad origin, minion of Chaugnar
miro: [*Dell Crossword Puzzle Dictionary*] wood robin from New Zeeland, Terra (alpha Zodiaci III)
mirti: [James Cooke Brown's Loglan mitro titci (meat eater) compound] carnivore from Logla, Brown's system
mishibizhiw: [*Kitchi-Gami: Life Among the Lake Superior Ojibway* by Johann Kohl] water panther or copper cat with deer's or bison's horns, snake's scales, bird's feathers
miškamp: [Croatian miš-škamp portmanteau] mouse-prawn, small, burrowing, land crustracean
missel: [*Dell Crossword Puzzle Dictionary*] thrush, see veery, mavie, mavis
miššiš: [Croatian šišmiš backformation] mouse-šiš, ancestral to šiš (bat-mouse) and mouse
mite: [*Dell Crossword Puzzle Dictionary*] small, parasitic insect, see acarid, minimus
mitgo: [James Crooke Brown's Loglan mitro gotca compound] meatgoat from Logla, Brown's system
miukumauka: [Finn. @] 2-D sleeping-cat-like at
mnemonicus: [*Monster Manual* by Skip Williams, etal.] memory-enhancing symbiot from Illithid or their slaves (Urophion, Tzakandi, Mozgriken, Mindwitness)
mnemosite: [*Society of Dreamers* ed. by Malthijs Holter] dream-eating parasite
moasi: [Navaho] felinoid from Diné system
mobe: [mobile mondegreen, Sebomese mobes palindrome] eel-like jellyfish gestalt from Sebom system
moby: [The Legend of Zelda II] orange, dive-bombing predatory bird from Hyrule
mockrock: see pseudo-rock
mock turtle: [*Through the Looking Glass, and What Alice Found There* by Charles "Lewis Carroll" Dodgson] cow-turtle from Looking Glass world

mock walrus: [museumofhoaxes.com by Alex Boese] roach-eating molerat-like insectovore from Tasmania, Terra (alpha Zodiaci III)
modron: ["Tales of the Outer Planets" by Gary L. Thomas] Outer Planet creature
modronster: [modron monster portmanteau] monstrous modron
moerthere: [*After the Dinosaurs* by Donald R. Prothero] primitive pig-like mastodont with short tusks and no trunk from Eocene
mog: ["Early Model" by Robert Sheckley] green-furred caninoid from Tels IV
mogator: [mog alligator portmanteau] alligator-like predator whose bite morphs victim into mog
mogai: [*The Disinherited* by Diane Duane and Peter Morwood] large, carnivorous ornithoid from ch'Rihan, Eisn (128 Trianguli) system
mogo: ["Droids" series] large, black-furred creature with undulating worm-like body, ten legs and camel-like head from Roon, Jedi galaxy
moguz: [Hildegard of Bingen's Lingua Ignota] gull-like ornithoid from Ignota, Hildegard's system
mogwik: ["Bless the Beasts" by Karen Haber] purple quadruped with many eyes from Sardal, Delta quadrant
moho: [*Dell Crossword Puzzle Dictionary*] honey eater bird, see iao, manuao
moke: [*Fantastic Beasts and Where to Find Them* by Newton Artemis Fido Scamander] usually small, but size-shifting, lizard, see mokele-mbembe
mokele-mbembe: [*Unexplained!* by Jerome Clark] sauropod from Central Africa, Terra (alpha Zodiaci III)
mokey: [*Halflife* by Mark Michalowski] green simian related to night beast from Espero
mokreb: [borkomnair ananymondegreen] elephantine creature from Ria system
mola: [aloma mola palindrome] red-yellow, [lanmola mondegreen] large centipede-like insectoid from La system; [Dell Crossword Puzzle Dictionary] sunfish, see bream

molamok: [Filipino mola-lamok portmanteau] mule-mosquito, griffinoid with long, pointy ears, blood-sucking proboscis

moldorm: [The Legend of Zelda] giant worm from Hyrule

mole snouter: [*The Snouters* by Harald Stümpke] snouter with nasarium adapted for burrowing from Mairúvili, Hi-Yi-Yi Islands, includes glans-nosed and gravel-dwelling narrow-nosed varieties

moleosaur: [Godville] underground-dwelling dinosaur

moleotaur: [moleosaur minotaur portmanteau] underground-dwelling bovinoid

moleskito: [moleday.org] tiny, blood-sucking, winged mole

mollyhawk: [Dut. Mollemok "stupid gull"] see albatross

molonne: [Continuum] 4-meter house-carrying beast of burden from Igendal, Belverius Helenis system

molto: [Outernaut] immature, yellow moltovo, in venomous and non-venomous varieties

moltovo: [Outernaut] orange, fiery creature, in venomous and non-venomous varieties

mølus: [Danish møl-lus portmanteau] muskox-louse, ruminant parasite

momeryx: [dromomeryx mondegreen] antler-less deer relative, see daderyx

momo: [Missouri monster] 3-toed, black skunk ape with no neck, red eyes from Missouri, Terra (alpha Zodiaci III)

mona: [*Dell Crossword Puzzle Dictionary*] monkey from Africa, Terra (alpha Zodiaci III), see waag, grivet

monal: [*Dell Crossword Puzzle Dictionary*] pheasant from India, Terra (alpha Zodiaci III)

monasa: [*Dell Crossword Puzzle Dictionary*] puffbird

monase: [*Dell Crossword Puzzle Dictionary*] nunbird

monene: [nguma monene mondegreen] quadruped with serrated backridge from Nguma

money ha-ha: ["L'il Abner" by Al Capp] creature with taxi-horn-shaped ears that lays American currency from Pincus II, see altama, golden goose, haha

mong: [contraction] mongrel dog

mongator: [mong alligator portmanteau] alligator-like predator whose bite morphs victim into mong

mong-goose: [mongoose mondegreen] dog-headed goose-like griffinoid

mongoose dragon: [Avatar: The Last Airbender: " Chase"] large lizard steed with yellow eyes, mongoose-like ears and elongated neck

mongosaur: [neimongosaur mondegreen, mongoose diosaur portmanteau] mongoose-lizard griffinoid

mongotaur: [mongosaur minotaur portmanteau] mongoose-bull griffinoid

monitor: [*Dell Crossword Puzzle Dictionary*] large lizard, uran

monkey-cat: ["Day of Burning" by Poul Anderson] gray, arboreal creature with high-pitched trilling hiss

monkey-lizard: [*Creatures of the Galaxy* by Phil Brucato, Bill Smith, Rick D. Stuart, Chuck Truett] 60-cm, furry with large ears, beak, tail from Kowak, Jedi galaxy

monkeyshine: [Piers Anthony] agile, little, gleaming brown simian from Xanth

mono: [*Dell Crossword Puzzle Dictionary*] howling monkey, see araba

monoceratis: [piscium extrapolation] egg-laying unicorn-like quadruped

monocerous: [Xanth series by Piers Anthony] huge, monstrous broad-sided unicorn from Xanth

monocyanic quantum bacterium: [Quasi-Scientific Ponderings: "Greatest Failure" by David Sagus] unusual bacterium from Archemelar III, Horsehead nebula

monolith monster: ["The Monolith Monsters" by Robert M. Fesco and Jack Arnold] 4.5-meter black obelisk-like bengilbertite lifeform that reproduces by falling and shattering, feeds on water and sand, turns carbon-based lifeforms into sandstone, growth stunted by salt

mononykus: ["one-claw", *The Mistaken Extinction* by Lowell Dingus and Timothy Rowe, *Feathered Dinosaurs: The Origin of Birds* by John Long and Peter Schuten] 1-meter flightless therapod related to alvarezsaur, with olecranon ("funny bone") from Cretaceous

monstee: [monster backformation] any prey of monsting (frightening) predators

monster bird: see teratorn

monster lizard: aka dinosaur, see dragon

monster locust: [*Pictures of Flying Creatures of Many Kinds* by Nicolaas de Bruyn] locust with usual long proboscis, feathery antennae, but with 4 bird-like wings, 6 webbed mammalian legs

monster men: ["The Monster Men" by Edgar Rice Burroughs] monsters created by Prof. Maxon, including #1, a mountain of deformed ashen flesh with white hair, pink mismatched eyes, a gaping hole for a nose, twisted mouth, long mismatched arms and legs, large flat feet; and #3, somewhat more anthropoid with long black hair

monster of Disaster: [The Adventures of the Fly] multi-armed giant batrachoid

monster: [backformation] creature that monsts (frightens), of 6 kinds [Philip van Doren Stern]: M1K, invisible; M2K, shapeless; M3K, small, nasty, swarmy; M4K: large, powerful, dangerous, old; M5K: ordinary turned dangerous; M6K: man turned against man

monsturd: [monster turd portmanteau, Outernaut] mature ploppah

monstrous leech: [*The Dalek Factor* by Simon Clark] monstrous leech from Pelt's world, Quadrille system

monty python: [Monty Python, Godville] large snake that emits a gas that causes its prey to die laughing

moo sow: [Avatar: The Last Airbender: "Zuko Alone"] pig-headed bovine with pig legs

mood-dragon: [*A Hero's Guide to Deadly Dragons* by Hiccup Haddock III] long dragon (skyserpent) with backspikes, and wings that changes color with mood: blue-black (angry), orange-red (excited), pale green (nervous) from Barbarian archipelago; [mood ring chart] black (fearful, depressed), yellow (anxious, cautious, mellow), orange (stressed, confused, challenged), peridot (restless, worried), light green (jealous, envious), blue-green (upbeat, pleased, optimistic, calm, peaceful), violet (amorous, mischievious, sensual), pink (infatuated, curious, very happy)

mooka: [*The Lost City of the Jedi, Prophets of the Dark Side* by Paul and Hollace Davids] 4-eared, furry and feathered pet from 4th moon of Yavin III, Jedi galaxy

moolwurm: [*The Web* by Michelle Stern] worm-like creature, secretion used in beverages**moon bear**: [sun bear backformation] small ursinoid with crescent-shaped collar from Luna (alpha Zodiaci IIIb)

moondog: [sundog backformation] caninoid from Luna (alpha Zodiaci IIIb)

moondogator: [moondog alligator portmanteau] alligator-like predator whose bite morphs victim into moondog

moonfish: [sunfish backformation] ichthyoid from Luna (alpha Zodiaci IIIb)

moongwas: [sungwas backformation] wolf-weasel from Luna (alpha Zodiaci IIIb)

moontiger: [suntiger backformation] striped felinoid from Luna (alpha Zodiaci IIIb)

moon worm: ["Futurama"] large, omnivorous, sometime ridden, worm from Luna (alpha Zodiaci IIIb)

moon-beast: ["War Against the Moon-Beast" ed. by Murray Boltinoff] alien creature from moon

moon-calf: [Blount] shapeless lump like a cow's aborted fetus deformed by lunar or demonic forces

moonack: [*Dell Crossword Puzzle Dictionary*] marmot, woodchuck

moonesd: cow-like bovinoid from Youmisian Homeland (Edonian cluster III), Galaxiki galaxy

moongoose: [mongoose malapropism] goose-like ornithoid from Luna (alpha Zodiaci IIIb)

moonhopper: ["Hey Diddle-diddle"] space-faring moon-calf-like bovinoid

moonling: ["The Moon Creatures" by Bob Haney, starling extrapolation] extinct creature revived from moon dust

moonlingator: [moonling alligator portmanteau] alligator-like predator whose bite morphs victim into moonling

moonroon: creature from Bubblefire, Phoenix system, Galaxiki galaxy

moor cock: [Michael Moorcock mondegreen] cock-like ornithoid adapted to moors from Mykl system

Moorf owl: [moorfowl mondegreen] swamp-dwelling owl-like ornithoid from Moorf system

moorvleerno: [Mushroom Planet series by Eleanor Cameron] small flying dragon from Basidium

moose-lion: [Avatar: The Last Airbender: "Bitter-Work"] large, brown felinoid with 2 sabre-like upper fangs, antlers on both genders

mooyarf: [frayoomnairo ananymondegreen] shroom-like snail from Oria, Or system

morag: [*Unexplained!* by Jerome Clark] lake snake from Lake Mora, Scotland, Terra (alpha Zodiaci III)

moragator: [morag alligator portmanteau] alligator-like predator whose bite morphs victim into morag

morak: [*Strange Tales* by Steve Ditko and Stan Lee] aka "the thing behind the wall", 6-meter, watermelon-shaped creature with arms, legs, face and sideburns from Black dimension

mordbear: (*Intergalactic Adventure Mazes* by Dick Smith) ursinoid from Mord, Gyron galaxy

morganucodon: [*The Mistaken Extinction* by Lowell Dingus and Timothy Rowe] brainy proto-mammal from Jurassic

morgril: [Star Trek] wolverinoid with anpsi (animal psychic powers) from T'Khasi, Nevasa (40 Eridani) system

morgrilope: [morgril antelope portmanteau] morgril with antlers

morgu: ["Welcome Home, Daughter -- Now Die" by Cary Bates] monstrous creature from Orando

morhc: [chrome morhc palindrome] metallic yellow ornithoid

morii orfiidane: extinct, horned bear-like creature with venomous armpits and tailclub from Relegooturnia (Phoenix IV), Galaxiki galaxy

mork: [mustering of storks spoonerism] wading ornithoid

mörkö: [Finnish] see groke

morlak: ["The Twilight World of No Return" by Jerry Seigel] caninoid from Krypton, Rao system

mormuk: [Armenian morm-muk portmanteau] tarantula-mouse, 6-legged rodentoid

mornis: [dromornis, mo(u)rning dove/warbler mondegreens] grayish brown or yellow-and-olive morning-singing ornithoid

moropus: [*After the Dinosaurs* by Donald R. Prothero] horse-like chalicothere with long clawed forelimbs and short hind legs; ["Gone to Glory" by R. Garcia y Robertson] large, horse-headed, long-necked, rhino-sized, tuber-digger with trunk-like limbs from Glory, delta Eridani

mororfdane: [i-less morii orfiidane mondegreen] horned cave-dwelling ursinoid

Morrison virus: [Sheila Morrison, "From Within" by Jonathon Glassner] deadly zombifying virus

morrt: [*Star Wars Sourcebook* by Bill Slavicsek and Curtis Smith] loyal, friendly, cuddly, mouse-sized blood-sucking parasite from planet Gamorr, Jedi galaxy, considered status symbol by Gamorreans (20 for warlords)

morse: [*Dell Crossword Puzzle Dictionary*] walrus; [moose-horse, *Heiro's Journey* by Sterling Lanier] antlered equine

mort: [*Dell Crossword Puzzle Dictionary*] 3-year-old salmon

morticoccus: ["Killer Germ" by Jack Kirby] geneered bioweapon

morvalni: [James Cooke Brown's Loglan mortu valni compound] death beast from Logla, Brown's system
moržirafa: [Croatian morž-žirafa portmanteau] walrus-giraffe, long-necked seamonster with tusks, flippers, short horns and whiskers
mosasaur: aquatic dinosaur from Cretaceous
mosataur: [mosasaur minotaur portmanteau] aquatic bovinoid
moschops: [*The Big Bad Book of Beasts* by Michael Largo] 1-tonne cow-toad
moseurg: [gruesome moseurg palindrome] monstrous creature
moseurgator: [moseurg alligator portmanteau] alligator-like predator whose bite morphs victim into moseurg
moshtaol: [loathsome moshtaol palindrome] loathsome creature
moshtaolope: [moshtaol antelope portmanteau] moshtaol with antlers
mospidze: [James Cooke Brown's Logla mospi dzeli] ghost jelly from Logla, Brown's system
moss piglet: see water bear
mossbird: [*Edge Chronicles* by Paul Stewart and Chris Riddell] aka skullpecker, tiny, florescent emerald green, bird that attacks eyes
mossbunker: [*Dell Crossword Puzzle Dictionary*] pogy or menhaden fish
mosser: mosquito, insect that mosses
mosura: ["Mothra", "Godzilla vs. Mothra" by Shinichi Sekizawa] 60-meter long caterpillar that can shoot incredibly strong and sticky webbing that grows into moth-like insectoid with 120-meter wingspan from Infant Island
mot: motmot nasna
moth hawk: [Xanth series by Piers Anthony] stealthy predatory insect with taloned feet from Xanth
moth head hawk: [hawk head moth cancrine] hawk-like ornithoid with moth-like head
motharch: [Terra Monster] predatory insectoid with yellow wings and antennae, orange head, green eyes and brown extremities from Terrarium

mothball: [Terra Monster] yellow flower-mimic with brown face, see motharch and fluster, from Terrarium
mothball loon: [mothball balloon portmanteau] loon-like ornithoid that smells like mothballs and can puff up like a pufferfish
motherhen: [mother hen mondegreen] parthenogenic moth-eating chicken-like ornithoid
mothorse: [moth horse mondegreen] moth-horse-like grinninoid
mothman: 2-meter, black cheiropteroid with long legs, glowing red eyes, 3-toed feetfrom W. V., Terra (alpha Zodiaci III)
mothra: see mosura
motmot: [*National Geographic Encyclopedia of Animals*] insect and fruit-eating bird from Meso-America, Terra (alpha Zodiaci III); [*The Courtship of Princess Leia* by Dave Wolverton] shaggy herd animal of Toola, Kaelta system, Hapes cluster, Jedi galaxy
mott: ["The Gungan Frontier" by Chris McCubbin] fast, keen-nosed, easily domesticated, orange-tan, white-stripped rhinoid with snouthorn, from Naboo and Mimban, Jedi galaxy
mouf: [*Creatures of the Galaxy* by Phil Brucato, Bill Smith, Rick D. Stuart, Chuck Truett] sociable ursinoid from Jedi galaxy
mouflon: [*Dell Crossword Puzzle Dictionary*] horned wild sheep
mouflonster: [mouflon monster portmanteau] monstrous horned, wild sheep
moundflea: [*Starship Warrior* by Stephen Mooser] small insectoid from Lov
mountain ant: [*Travels* by Sir John Mandeville] dog-sized, gold-digging with 6 [Hortus Sanitatis] or 4 legs
mountain tiger: ["The World of the Blessed" by H. G. Ewers] tiger-like felinoid from Homy, Quendolin system
mountainhopper: [grasshopper extrapolation] grasshopper-like pegasoid from Peggassa, Hippocrenea system, Galaxiki galaxy
mouse-bird: [mousebird mondegreen] bat-mimicking ornithoid

mouse-crab: [pl. mice-crabs, ice-crab backformation] mouse-headed crab-like crustacean

mouse-bunny: ["A Dark and Stormy Night" by Larry Blamire] burrowing mammal like both mouse and bunny from Tagunga

mouse-burro: [pl. mice-burroes, ice-burro backformation] mouse-headed burro-like equinoid

mouse-dragon: [pl. mice-dragons, Odd Squad: Section 21] small, mouse-headed dracoid

mouse-goat: [pl. mice-goats] mouse-headed goat-like ruminant

mouse-gopher: see wocket

mouse-snake: [pl. mice-snakes] mouse-headed serpentoid

mouse-wolf: [pl. mice-wolves] small, mouse-headed wolf-like caninoid

mousebird: [*Dell Crossword Puzzle Dictionary*] see coly, shrike

mouth: [*The Face of the Waters* by Robert Silverberg] predator from waterworld Hydros

möv: [Fr. Johann Martin Schleyer's Volapük] seagull-like ornithoid from Schleyer's system

mow: [murder of crows spoonerism] black predatory ornithoid

moxtail: [Terra Monster] mischievious red fox-like creature, see vextail, from Terrarium

moxtailaope: [moxtail antelope portmanteau] moxtail with antlers

moz: [zomp moz palindrome] bluish green ornithoid

mozg: [Treks Not Taken: "A Clockwork Data" by Steve R. Boydett] leech-like creature from Betazed (Cyndriel, beta Veldonna V)

mozgator: [mozg alligator portmanteau] alligator-like predator whose bite morphs victim into mozg

mozoon: [dromozoon mondegreen] moz-infecting parasite

mozzur: mosquito

mraw: [mraw swarm palindrome] swarming insectoid

mrehpo: [eci mrehpo gopher-mice palindrome] gopher-like rodentoid, see wocket

mrodni: [mrodni lindorm palindrome] lindorm-like amphisbæna

mrofla: [James Cooke Brown's Loglan mroza flaki compound] hammerfly from Logla, Brown's system

mroflaki: [James Cooke Brown's Loglan mroza flaki compound] hammerfly from Logla, Brown's system

mrotosku: [James Cooke Brown's Loglan mroza tosku compound] hammerhead shark from Logla, Brown's system

mrouse: [mouse-grouse portmanteau] small, plump rodentoid with mottled brown or grayish coloring, beak

muaddeeb: mouse-like rodentoid from Pandia, Nyx system, Galaxiki galaxy

mucharty: [Belarussian much-charty portmanteau] housefly-greyhound griffinoid

mucilator: [Ben 10: Omniverse: "It Was Them" by David McDermitt] large yet fast, gray, silicon-based frog-like predator with pink-purple sticky spheres on its body from Orthopterra

mud ball: [Cloudstone] pesty living mud

mud blaggot: [blood maggot spoonerism] mud-dwelling bottom-feeder

mud monster: [Strange Stories, Amazing Facts] 1.5-meter, slimy nape with light brown fur, smelling of dead fish from Big Muddy River, Murphyboro, Ill., Terra (alpha Zodiaci III)

mud-gulper: [*After Man* by Dougal Dixon] hippoid swamp rat

mudball loon: [mudball balloon portmanteau] brown loon-like ornithoid that can puff up like a pufferfish

mudbutt: [*Worlds Apart: Nat. Hist. of Furaha and Earth* by Souren Nyoroge] prey of sawjaw from Furaha (alpha Phoenicis IV)

mudcrab: [The Elder Scrolls III: "Morrowind"] large, edible crustacean in marine, coastal, cave and varieties

mudder: ["Echo of the Lost" by Hans Kneifel] aka dirtcreeper, 2-meter, oval, pale yellow, slimy worm, with spidery legs, mandibles at each end from Zartiryt, moon of Lumbagoo (Ajatan), Lumbagoo system

mudfish: [*Titan* by Jack Varley] ichthyoid from Titan (Saturn (alpha Zodiaci VIa))

mudhen: [Xanth series by Piers Anthony] small, plump mud-splashing bird from Xanth

mudmen: ["Droids" series] semi-solid anthropoid from Roon that tickle victims and then take their shiny objects packrat-like

mudpod: ["Alien Animal Planet" by Sean Cooper] shovel-nosed hexapod with serrated claws that feeds on and builds dams with stinger fans from Aurelia

mudpuppy: [*National Geographic Encyclopedia of Animals*] seafood-eating salamander from Mid-America, Terra (alpha Zodiaci III)

mudrat: ["Seed of Reason" by Daniel Hatch] mud-dwelling rodentoid from Chamal; [Peter MacInnis] rodent of Big Ugly River, Big Ugly Island

muf: [uo muf mondegreens] grey and reddish brown uo

mug: [Fr. Johann Martin Schleyer's Volapük] mouse-like prey of mugger from Schleyer's system

mugato: ["A Private Little War" by Gene Roddenberry] 2-meter, 440-kilogram white-furred bipedal pongoid with dorsal spines and cranial horn, poisonous bite (treatable with mako root assisted blood transfusion) from Neural (zeta Bootis) III

mugator: [mugato alligator portmanteau] alligator-like predator whose bite morphs victim into mugato

mugger: [mugger backformation] predator that muggs (faceshifts)

muglump: [*Edge Chronicles* by Paul Stewart and Chris Riddell] 6-legged, carnivorous frog with snorkle-like nose

muisvle(e)r: [Afrikaans vlermuis, Dutch vleermuis backformation] mouse-vle(e)r ancestral to vle(e)r (bat-mouse)

mukku: [Armenian muk-kku portmanteau] mouse-cuckoo, bat-like ornithoid with tendency to foster eggs in other birds nests that moos and coos

mukov: [Armenian muk-kov portmanteau] mouse-cow, large milk rodentoid

mule rabbit: aka jackass-rabbit

mull: ["Frankenstein Meets the Space Monster" by George Garrett] 1.8-meter guard-slave anthropoid with long dark hair, 3-clawed hands, pointy ears, stone-like flesh, large eyes, double-slit nose, fangs

mulligatawny: [*If I Ran the Zoo* by Theodore Seuss Geissel] quadruped with long ears and snout, flat feet from Zind desert

mul: [mulish backformation] beastly beast-of-burden

mulbear: [mulberry backformation, mul-bear mondegreen] ursinoid beast-of-burden

muloc: [Columbia ib muloc palindrome] blue owl-like ornithoid with red nape (back or neck)

mulope: [mul antelope portmanteau] mul with antlers

mumblebee: [bumblebee backformation] bee-like insectoid that makes mumbling sound

mummic: [mummichog mondegreen] catfish-like ichthyoid with cartiginous snout

mummichog: [*National Geographic Encyclopedia of Animals*] catfish relative from W. Atlantic, Terra (alpha Zodiaci III)

mummichogator: [mummichog alligator portmanteau] alligator-like predator whose bite morphs victim into mummichog

mumpa: [*The Perfect Planet* by Edward Packard] tusked, clawed buffaloid from Utopa (Achnar V), Gallatin quadrant

mumre: [James Crooke Brown's Loglan] sailor from Logla, Brown's system

munacure: [museumofhoaxes.com by Alex Boese] miniature water buffalo nearly hunted to extinction for horns from Manchuria, Terra (alpha Zodiaci III)

munch: [munchkin backformation] voracious, long-legged munchkin relative

munchkin: short-haired furry with short legs

munling: [Mun diminuative] sole surviving lifeform from Demerjian, Inq Centralis system, Galaxiki galaxy

munligator: [munling alligator portmanteau] alligator-like predator whose bite morphs victim into munling
munnin: [Monster Galaxy] raven-like ornithoid from Aquarius constellation
muntjac: [*National Geographic Encyclopedia of Animals*] deer from S. Asia, Terra (alpha Zodiaci III)
muntjac: [*Dell Crossword Puzzle Dictionary*] deer, see kakar, ratwa
munya: [Monster Galaxy] green sheep-like ruminant from Aries constellation
murbri: James Crooke Brown's Loglan murki brili] monkeyshine from Logla, Brown's system
murdersquito: [Godville] small, fast, deadly mosquito-like blood-sucking insect that causes humps, lumps and mumps
murgo: [James Cooke Brown's Loglan murki gotma (monkey-goat) compound] centauroid with monkey upper body and goat lower body from Logla, Brown's system
murkatma: [James Crooke Brown's Loglan murki katma compound] monkey-cat from Logla, Brown's system
murli: [James Cooke Brown's Loglan murki cliki compound] simian from Logla, Brown's system
murpo: [James Cooke Brown's Loglan murki porju (monkey-pig) compound] centauroid with monkey upper body and pig lower body from Logla, Brown's system
murr(e): [*Dell Crossword Puzzle Dictionary*] razor-billed auk, see alca
murra: [James Cooke Brown's Loglan murki ratcu (monkey-rat) compound] monkey-headed rodentoid from Logla, Brown's system
murre: leg-less bird, see merlette
murrolet: [*National Geographic Encyclopedia of Animals*] fish-eating bird from N. Pacific, Terra (alpha Zodiaci III)
mursa: [James Cooke Brown's Loglan murki sarpi (monkey-serpent) compound] monkey-headed snake from Logla, Brown's system
murtigra: [James Cooke Brown's Loglan murki tigra (monkey-tiger) compound] centauroid with monkey upper body and tiger lower body from Logla, Brown's system

murtlap: [*Fantastic Beasts and Where to Find Them* by Newton Artemis Fido Scamander] rat-like creature with anemone-like growth on back
mus: [sarmus mondegreen] beastly jellyfish, see musdze
muscae: [piscium extrapolation] egg-laying fly-like insectoid
musdze: [James Cooke Brown's Logla musmi dzeli] flesh jelly from Logla, Brown's system, see mus
musetter: [trumpeter swan backformation] bagpipe swan-like ornithoid with musette-like call
mush: [mutation of thrushes spoonerism] polar husky-like griffinoid
mushiká: [Japanese mushi-shiká portmanteau] insect-deer griffinoid
mušhuššu: [Revelation 12:3] fire-red horned dragon with lion forefeet, eagle hindfeet, scorpion stinger tail from Babylonia
muskcat: [Joyce Muscat mondegreen] felinoid with musk gland from Joiss system
muskfox: [muskox-fox portmanteau] caninoid with broad, flat curved horns, upright ears, pointed snout, long shaggy, musky hair and long bushy tail
muskit: [Fr. Johann Martin Schleyer's Volapük] mosquitoid from Schleyer's system
muskrattler: [muskrat-rattler portmanteau] large, brown, aquatic rodentoid with musk glands and rattle on tail
mussie: see hapyxebor
mustard jelly: [*Monster Manual* by Skip Williams, etal.] mustard-colored, jelly-thick ooze
mustela: [OviPets] egg-laying ferret-like furry
mutacamel: ["Space Rats of the CCC" by Harry Harrison] 3-meter mutant camel with impervitium claws and teeth
mutriok: [*Creatures of the Galaxy* by Phil Brucato, Bill Smith, Rick D. Stuart, Chuck Truett] quadruped prey of tra'cor from Socorro, Jedi galaxy
mutterfly: [Monarch butterfly spoonerism] mockingbird-like fly that mutters from Bonarch system

muzza: ["bitch", *Fortune's Light* by Michael Jan Friedman] female isak from Imprima
muzzle: ["Capt'n Virgil, Sportsman in Space" by David Brooks] long-necked ichthyoid from Arizant
mwa: [mwa yawm palindrome] yawm-like amphisbæna
mya: ["The Chase" by Terry Nation] man-eating land cephalopodan with short eyestalks from Aridius
mycosporg: parasitic fungus from Fhelh, Orihbe system, Galaxiki galaxy
mycosporgator: [mycosporg alligator portmanteau] alligator-like predator whose bite morphs victim into mycosporg
mylagaulid: [*After the Dinosaurs* by Donald R. Prothero] rodent with two pointed horns on snout that dug corkscrew-shaped burrows
mylohyus: [*After the Dinosaurs* by Donald R. Prothero] warthog-like peccary from Zanclean age (early Pliocene)
mynewt: [minute homonym] small newt-like amphibian
myngaun: [*The Yowie: In Seach of Australian Bigfoot* by Tony Healy and Paul Cropper] see yowie
mynock: [*Star Wars Sourcebook* by Bill Slavicsek and Curtis Smith, *The Empire Strikes Back* by Donald F. Glut] black, 1.6-meter chiropteran, silicon-based, energy parasite with 1.25-meter wingspan, armored skull, fangs, able to attach to spaceship with suckers, reproduce by splitting, from Jedi galaxy
myriapede: worm-like insectoid with more legs than millipede
myrigurp: [centigurp extrapolation] pink furball able to bounce, roll, fond of spheres, and be in ten thousand places at once, see gurp
myrlochars: [Monster of Faerün] giant brownish-green arachnoid with 8 red eyes, demonic servants of Lolth
mysery: [Outernauts] mature mystroo
mystroo: [Outernauts] stormcloudcreature, see mysty, mysery

mysticetes: [*After the Dinosaurs* by Donald R. Prothero] whale related to dorudon and odontocetes
mysty: [Outernauts] immature mystroo
n'aal: [Kane's world series by Michael "Edward Powys Bradbury" Moorcock] giant snake-like creature from Kane's world
n'hhu: [i-less in'hhui] cave-dwelling ichtyoid
na: [Haitian kanna mondegreen] duck-like ornithoid from Ka system; [Irish réinfhianna mondegreen] reindeer-like ruminant from Réinfhia; [ganna, sand nas mondegreens] gray-green or tan locust-like insectoid; [phranna mondegreen] food fish from Phra system, see irg
na'a!: ["na'a! at times emit ta!a'an" palindrome] bone eater gestalt
Na'ka'leen feeder: ["Grail" by Christy Marx] triped that feeds on brainwaves (preferably older ones), moving very fast during attack, discovered by Centauri on Na'ka'leen
naardvark: [an aardvark elision] insectovore
naastsosi: [Navaho] mouse-like rodentoid from Diné system
nab: [Crayola banana nab palindrome] yellow creature from Crayol A
nabbit: [nest of rabbits, nab rabbit portmanteau] yellow rabbit-like lapod
nablofi: [James Cooke Brown's Loglan nablo ficli] knife fish from Logla, Brown's system
naca: [nacarat mondegreen] red rodentoid from Aca system
nachteg: [Dutch nachtegaal mondegreen] eel-nightingale, leg-less murre-like, nocturnal dracoid from Stiria, Airit system, Galaxiki galaxy
nachtegator: [nachteg alligator portmanteau] alligator-like predator whose bite morphs victim into nachteg
nade: [tornade backformation] horned sphere-like fractal creature
nadzuk: [i-less inadzuk] cave sardine-arachnoid with small ichthyoidal hatchlings from Friatica, Friaticalida system, Galaxiki galaxy

naemun: [Fr. Johann Martin Schleyer's Volapük] anemone-like creature from Schleyer's system

naffit: [Tiffany naffit palindrome] greenish-blue ornithoid

nāgali: [vannāgali] 2-D das-like creature from Va system

naggartura: ["mountain-carver"] moorhen likely infested with schamir worms

naghta: [naghta cathgan palindrome] cathgan-like amphisbæna

nago: [mahogany nago ham palindrome] reddish brown porcoid

nagor: [*Dell Crossword Puzzle Dictionary*] reedbuck

nahoor: [*Dell Crossword Puzzle Dictionary*] wild mountain sheep from Tibet, Terra (alpha Zodiaci III), see sha, sna, rasse, urial, bharal, oorial

nahr: [Estonian nahrhiir mondegreen] bat-mouse, ancestral to mouse and bat

naig: [giant naig palindrome] insignificant creature, except for giant variety, see tnagig, tommam

naigator: [naig alligator portmanteau] alligator-like predator whose bite morphs victim into naig

nairo: [Nairobi mondegreen] bee-like insectoid

naitaka: [*Monster Spotter's Guide to North America* by Scott Francis] lake snake of Lake Okanagan, BC, which with flippers and back serrations is rather unsnake-like, more a freshwater basilosauroid

nake: [nest of snakes spoonerism]

naked bear: ["Fuzzy-wuzzy" by Henry Wadsworth Longfellow] hairless ursinopongoid

nakhur: [Persian] camel needing tickling to give milk

naktivilik: [Eskimo] mature walrus

nalpgge: [eggplant nalpgge palindrome] purple creature

Namalan salamander: [red Namala's salamander palindrome] red salamander-like amphibian from Namala system

namazu: giant catfish from Japan, Terra (alpha Zodiaci III) or Uzama, Galaxiki galaxy

namoeba: [an amoeba mondegreen] amoeba-like creature

Nandi bear: 1.5-meter bear-like brain-eater from Nandiland, Kenya, Terra (alpha Zodiaci III)

nane: [*The Closed Worlds* by Edmond Hamilton] anthropoid with large, softly glowing eyes, no nose, small mouth, white skin, flexible (because boneless)

nanka: [ninki-nanka backformation] creature ancestral to ninki and ninki-nanka

nannippus: [*After the Dinosaurs* by Donald R. Prothero] primitive horse from Zanclean age (early Pliocene)

nannosquila: small crustacean that moves like tank-track

nannybear: [nannyberry backformation] see sheep-bear

nanobacterium: creature only 50 nm across, said to cause extra-skeletal calcification

nanogurp: [centigurp extrapolation] pink furball able to bounce, roll, fond of spheres, and be in a billion places at once, see gurp

nant: [an ant mondegreen, nest of ants spoonerism] large, non-social insectoid

nanteater: [an anteater mondegreen] nant predator

nap: [panfried eirfnap palindrome] eirf prey, also food animal

nape: [Loren Coleman, "North American ape portmanteau, *Monster Spotter's Guide to North America* by Scott Francis] includes sasquatch, skunk ape, etc. from N. America, Terra (alpha Zodiaci III)

naphid: [an aphid mondegreen] sap-sucking insectoid

napu: [*Dell Crossword Puzzle Dictionary*] animal from Indo-Malaysia, Terra (alpha Zodiaci III)

nar: [Monster Galaxy] pink, plant-like crab with 4 arms, 4 legs and snake-like neck and head from Scorpio constellation; [rank nar palindrome] malodorous creature, see ilo

nargah: [*Legacy* by Michael Jan Friedman] egg-layer of Merkaans

narglatch: ["The Gungan Frontier" by Chris McCubbin] fierce hunter from Jedi galaxy

nargle: [*Fantastic Beasts and Where to Find Them* by Newton Artemis Fido Scamander] packrat-like pest, from Elgra

nark: [*Dell Crossword Puzzle Dictionary*] stool pigeon

narlzak: ["Return to Karn" by Bill Motz] large mealworm-like burrower from Karn or Kazlra

narwalrus: [narwhal-walrus portmanteau] 4-flippered amphibian with long spirally twisted tusk, tough, wrinkled skin and bushy, drooping mustache

narwhalimbus: [Cloudstone] see air-whale, skywhale

narwhalite: [Terra Monsters] narwhal-like cetacean from Terrarium

nashtah: [*Han Solo's Revenge* by Brian Daley] 6-legged, bloodthirsty, green, sleek-skinned sauroid with triple row of teeth, diamond-hard claws, long barbed tail from Dra III, Jedi galaxy

nasicorn: [*Dell Crossword Puzzle Dictionary*] black rhinoceras, see borele

nasna: [*Temptation of St. Anthony* by Flaubert] half-creatures, see ansan

nasp: [an asp mondegreen] asp-like serpentoid

nass: [an ass mondegreen] ass-like equinoid

nast: [dessert sand nast resed palindrome] pinkish brown resed

nasutoceratops: "big-nosed longhorn" dinosaur from Late Cretaceous

nat: [Jets*Rockets*Spacemen trading card #51] space-faring pterodon-like creature from planet Ex, see knurd; gas-dwelling creatures from Clodios (Iestonian Spiral VII), Galaxiki galaxy

nata: [i-less inata] cave-dwelling Tasmanian devil-like omnivore

natch: [*If I Ran the Zoo* by Theodore Seuss Geissel] bushy-footed squirrel-like creature with large eyes, snout and crest

natdzofo: [James Crooke Brown's Loglan natli dzofo] nightwalker from Logla, Brown's system

natmafle: [James Cooke Brown's Loglan natli mafle] night flier from Logla, Brown's system

natronobacterium: extremophilic bacterium resistant to extreme acid, see clostridium, bacillus

natterjack: [*National Geographic Encyclopedia of Animals*] insectivorous toad from Europe, Terra (alpha Zodiaci III)

natvalni: [James Crooke Brown's Loglan natli valni] night beast from Logla, Brown's system

nauga: [naugahyde backformation] animal noted for its durable hide

naugator: [nauga alligator portmanteau] alligator-like predator whose bite morphs victim into nauga

naurok: ornithoid from T'Khasi, Nevasa (40 Eridani) system

nav: [Vanese nav, van nav palindromes] white ornithoid from Va system

nava: [savannahwalker ananymondegreen] large ruminant from Reklawha system

navi: [navigator backformation] homing pigeon-like ornithoid

navi gator: [navigator mondegreen] alligator-like predator whose bite morphs victim into navi

nazdzoru: [James Cooke Brown's Loglan nazbi dzoru compound] snouter from Logla, Brown's system

nazeb: [bezant nazeb, Bezan nazeb palindromes] monster with gold spots with flaming mouth and ears from Beza system

ne: [atne mondegreen] light brown gam

nea: [a noyance of fleas spoonerism] small pesty insectoid

nea's ant: [nest, nide or nye of pheasants spoonerism] ant-like nea predator

neahsjsh: [Navaho] owl-like ornithoid from Diné system

nebek: hairy tyger-like felinoid

nebelung: blue-black furry with silver tipped hairs

nebelungator: [nebelung alligator portmanteau] alligator-like predator whose bite morphs victim into nebelung

necic: [Shona, Zimbabwe cicena (yellow/yellow-green) necic palindrome] yellow or yellow-green ornithoid

neck-less giraffe [Far Side: "The Evolution of the Giraffe" by Gary Larson] early giraffe with virtually no neck but very long legs, see short-necked giraffe
necsevalf: [flavescent necsevalf palindrome] pale brownish yellow ornithoid
nedom: [modena nedom palindrome] purple ornithoid, see vuam, airyt
neebray: [Clone Wars series] giant manta-like space creature that breeds in nebulae, Jedi galaxy
needle snake: ["Projections" by Brannon Braga] serpentine from Delta Quadrant
neek: [*Creatures of the Galaxy* by Phil Brucato, Bill Smith, Rick D. Stuart, Chuck Truett] small, fast, flocking, bipedal, reptilian herbivore with short sleep cycle from Ambria, Jedi galaxy
neel: [an eel mondegreen] eel-like segmented sea creature
neen: ["neen at times emit taneen" palindrome] reptile gestalt
neenina: [neenina tanineen palindrome] larger sauroid, see minina, neen
neerwolf: ["A Final Unity" by Spectrum HoloByte] caninoid geneered Dr. Vi Hynh-Foertsh from Morassia (epsilon Chysule II)
negdze: [James Cooke Brown's Loglan negda dzeli] egg-jellyfish, in fried-egg, poached-egg and scrambled-egg varieties
Nehcorleh cat: [Nehcorleh cat Stachelrochen] stingray-felinoid amphibian from Nehcorleh system
nei'rrh: [*The Romulan Way* by Terisa Halekala-LoBrotto] poisonous hummingbird-like ornithoid from ch'Rihan, Eisn (128 Trianguli) system
neimongosaur: ["inner mongolian lizard", *Feathered Dinosaurs: The Origin of Birds* by John Long and Peter Schuten] 2.5-meter herbivorous ornithischian dinosaur
neitapab: [Fr. Johann Martin Schleyer's Volapük] moth-like insectoid from Schleyer's system
nejiron: [The Legend of Zelda: "Majora's Mask"] rock-like, underground-dwelling lumbering, rolling, explosive creature from Hyrule
nejironster: [nejiron monster portmanteau] monstrous nejiron
nek: [Star Wars: Dark Empire series by Tom Veritch and Cam Kennedy] muscular, hairless caninoid with 3-clawed feet, sold on black market for illegal fights from Cyborrean system, Jedi galaxy
neko-mata: [Jap. "forked-cat"] cat with two tails aka nibi
neleph: [an elephant mondegreen] large ant-like insectoid
nelk: [an elk mondegreen] elk-like ruminant
nelphan: [Fr. Johann Martin Schleyer's Volapük] elephant-like creature from Schleyer's system
Nematode: [Man-eating Cow #8] giant insectoid
nemegtomaia: ["nemegt mother", *Feathered Dinosaurs: The Origin of Birds* by John Long and Peter Schuten] 2-meter oviraptorid with short beak, large crest
nemi: [Maltese tan-nemis backformation] mosquitoid from Ta system
neml: see tahti neml
nemu: [an emu mondegreen] large, flightless emu-like ornithoid
nen: [Finnish kyyhkynen backformation] dove-like ornithoid ancestral to kyyhky and pigeon
neon-coral: [Xanth series by Piers Anthony] brilliantly glowing sea creatures living in colonies from Xanth
neothelid: [*Monster Manual* by Skip Williams, etal.] worm-like Illithid tadpole yet to eat a brain (ceremorph) with 4 feeding tentacles and immense (but non-sentient) mental powers
nepa: [*Dell Crossword Puzzle Dictionary*] needle bug or water scorpion
nerd: [*If I Ran the Zoo* by Theodore Seuss Geissel] flat-footed biped with striped neck, muttonchops and crest
nereis: [*Dell Crossword Puzzle Dictionary*] sea worm, see sao, lurg
nerf: [*The Empire Strikes Back* by Donald F. Glut] 1-meter domesticated though grumpy,

antlered herbivore with long, but dull horns, bred for meat and pelts from Jedi galaxy

nerkle: [*If I Ran the Zoo* by Theodore Seuss Giessel] biped with powderpuff tail, long thin beak and neck

nerve runner: [*The Jesus Incident* by Frank Herbert and Bill Ransom] dangerous ground dweller from Pandora

nerve swimmer: [*Monster Manual* by Skip Williams, etal.] immature neothelid used for torture and interrogation

nesbröd: [Swedish johannesbröd backformation] aka nesbrød [Danish], locust-like insectoid from Joha, Nek system, related to enleipäuun

nesra: [i-less inesra] gray, cave-dwelling creature

nesset: ["Sacred Ground" by Lisa Klink] venomous 3-fanged serpentinoid

nessiteras: ["Ness monster"] plesiosaur-like lake snake of Loch Ness, Scotland, Terra (alpha Zodiaci III)

nesst: [nest egg mondegreen] non-venomous, egg-laying relative of nesset

net: [gannet mondegreen] sea ornithoid from Ga system

netwhale: [gannetwhale mondegreen] whale with net-like lips for filtering prey from Ga system

netch: [The Elder Scrolls III: "Morrowind"] herd air jellyfish-like creature that hovers via gassacs, smaller, territorial, polyandrous female, larger poisonous male

netwing: [Xanth series by Piers Anthony] insect with net-like air-capturing wings from Xanth

netwingator: [netwing alligator portmanteau] alligator-like predator whose bite morphs victim into netwing

neurobat: vampire bat-like cheropteroid that feeds on brain impulses

neurovore: [*The Wine of Violence* by James Morrow] savage, desert-dwelling brain-eater from Carlotta, Malnovian belt, UW Canis Majoris system

never bird: [*Peter Pan, or the Boy Who Wouldn't Grow Up* by James Matthew Barrie] lagoon-dwelling bird that nests in hat from Never-never Land

New Texan cattle: ["A Planet for Texans" by H. Beam Piper and J. McGuire] 15-tonne, 1.2-meter tall bovinoid from New Texas

nex: [nex oxen palindrome] ox-like bovinoid

nexi: [nexi vixen palindrome] pathenogenic fox-like caninoid

nexu: [*Attack of the Clones* by George Lucas and Jonathan Hales] domesticatable arboreal creature with tan-brown (prairie) or striped (jungle) fur, 2 extra ir eyes on spade-shaped, toothy head, slit-tipped tail, climbing suckers from Cholganna, Jedi galaxy

ng loob: [Filipino masiraan ng loob backformation] quail-like ornithoid from Masiraa

ngo: [drognu mondegreen] mockingbird-like ornithoid

nguma monene: ["large python", *Unexplained!* by Jerome Clark] quadruped with serrated backridge from Dongu-Mataba river, Congo, Terra (alpha Zodiaci III)

nhaidh: [*The Romulan Way* by Terisa Halekala-LoBrotto, *The Disinherited* by Diane Duane and Peter Morwood] cockroach-like insectoid from ch'Rihan, Eisn (128 Trianguli) system

ni: [panni mondegreen] planimal from Pa (eta Serpentis) system

niao: [beheaded uniao] 3-headed bird of ill omen, see p'eng-niao

nibbling sporran: see sphagnum

nibi: [Jap.] two-tailed cat aka neko-mata

nibla: [albino nibla palindrome] white ornithoid

nible: [James Cooke Brown's Loglan] inspector from Logla, Brown's system

nibur: [rubine nibur palindrome] reddish ruby ornithoid

nic: [omannic mondegreen] reddish-brown ornithoid from Oma, see erro; [cinnabunny ananymondegreen] light brown lapoid from Ynnuba system

nickleodeon: [Xanth series by Piers Anthony] dumpy box-like nickepede predator that makes music as it feeds from Xanth

nicklepede: [Xanth series by Piers Anthony] insectoid with 500 legs and deadly sharp pincers that gouge out nickel-sized pieces of flesh from Xanth

nickleroo: [dimeroo backformation] smaller dimeroo

nicor: ["Queen of Air and Darkness" by Poul Anderson] creature like both elephant and ent, [*Roland*] "elephent"

nidhoggr: ["corpse-tearer"] dragon near Lower Niflheim

nifflee: [niffler backformation] prey of niffling (packrat-like burrowing) predators

niffler: [*Fantastic Beasts and Where to Find Them* by Newton Artemis Fido Scamander] packrat-like with spade-like forepaws

nifid: see ra nifid

nigbekti: [James Cooke Brown's Loglan nigro bekti (black thing) compound] man-eater from Logla, Brown's system

nigeel: [*The World of Synnabarr* by Raymond C. S. McCracken] eel-like creature from Synnibarr, fka Mars (alpha Zodiaci IV)

nigficli: [James Cooke Brown's Loglan nigro ficli] black ichthyoid from Logla, Brown's system

night beast: ["Star Wars" series by Archie Goodwin and Al Williamson] murky green, bipedal, clawed sauroid with flat skull, fish-like lips, many teeth from Yavin IV, Jedi galaxy used as guard by Massassi; [*Halflife* by Mark Michalowski] more intelligent re-geneered mokey with snuffling sound from Espero

night howler: [*The Stars Are Ours* by Andre Norton] moth-eating monkey with huge eyes from Astra (Deutero-Sol II)

night monster: [*The Navy vs. the Night Monsters* by Murray Leinster] tree mimic omnivore that hunts at night from Antarctica, Terra (alpha Zodiaci III)

night stalker: [*After Man* by Dougal Dixon] 1.5-meter flightless pack bat that walks on forelimbs, slashes with hindlegs, hunts by echolocation

night-lemuel: [*Edge Chronicles* by Paul Stewart and Chris Riddle] arboreal creature with lemkin-like call

night-owl: ["Simulated Trainer"] nocturnal ornithoid

night-walker: ["Exploration Team" by Murray Leinster] troublesome creature that dislikes light or cold from Loren II

nightcrawler: ["Star Wars IV: A New Hope" by George Lucas] small, nocturnal insectoid from Tatooine, Jedi galaxy; [*Lost Empires of Faerün* by Travis Stout] huge, black worm from Plane of Shadows

nightglider: [*After Man* by Dougal Dixon] gliding, predatory weasel with chest quills

nighthaunt: [*Lost Empires of Faerün* by Travis Stout] gargoyle-like creature from Plane of Shadows

nightjar: [*National Geographic Encyclopedia of Animals*] insectivorous bird that plays possum from S. E. Asia, Terra (alpha Zodiaci III)

nightling bug: [lightning bug spoonerism] small, telepathic insectoid able to cause localized blindness

nightling bugator: [nightling bug alligator portmanteau] alligator-like predator whose bite morphs victim into nightling bug

nightlizard: [*Ghost-Walker* by Barabara Hambly] nocturnal sauroid from Midgwis (Elcidar Beta III)

nightmar: [nightmarish backformation] mar shapeshifter that can mimic coyote-squid, Guinea pig-pig, giant bovine or spherical sponge

nightmare: [*A Hero's Guide to Deadly Dragons* by Hiccup Haddock III] emerald green, brilliant scarlet and deepest purple dragon with retractable claws, slightly poisonous from Barbarian archipelago

nightswimmer: [*Lost Empires of Faerün* by Travis Stout] aquatic nightcrawler from Plane of Shadows

nightwaif: [*Edge Chronicles* by Paul Stewart and Chris Riddell] short nocturnal waif

nightwalker: [*Lost Empires of Faerün* by Travis Stout] anthropoidal horror of darkness from Plane of Shadows

nightwing: [Superman mythos] Prussian blue magpie-like bird from Krypton, Rao system;

[*Lost Empires* of Faerün by Travis Stout] cheiropteran from Plane of Shadows

nightwingator: [nightwing alligator portmanteau] alligator-like predator whose bite morphs victim into nightwing

nigjanto: [James Cooke Brown's Loglan nigro janto (black hunter) compound] triphibian predator from Logla, Brown's system

nigne: [fire engine nigne erif palindrome] orangish red erif

nigrebua: [aubergine nigrebua palindrome] dark purple ornithoid

niguana: [an iguana mondegreen] iguana-like sauroid

nihc: [Chinese nihc palindrome] vermillion ornithoid

nihgual: [laughing nihgual portmanteau] hyena-like caninoid

nihgualope: [nihgual antelope portmanteau] nihgual with antlers

nikcoh: [shocking nikcoh palindrome] bright pink electric ornithoid

nikin: [mynynym] ni relative

niknit: [stinking nitknits palindrome] malodorous creature

nil: [German Nilpferd backformation] hippopotamus-horse, river-dwelling equinoid from Wintria, Pfetea system

nilatac: [Catalina nilatac palindrome] blue ornithoid

nilbraw: [warbling nilbraw portmanteau] warbling ornithoid

nilem: [meline nilem palindrome] yellow creature

nilgai: [*National Geographic Encyclopedia of Animals*] "blue bull", antelope relative from India, Terra (alpha Zodiaci III)

nilkrap: [sparkling nilkraps palindrome] lightningbug-like insectoid

nillapa: [apalling nillapa palindrome] monstrous creature from Wintria, Pfetea system, Galaxiki galaxy

nillebasi: [isabelline nillebasi palindrome] pale grayish-yellow ornithoid

nilope: [nil antelope portmanteau] nil with antlers

nim: [mininim backformation, carmine nim rac palindrome] vivid red rac from Oita system, see rutai

nimby: [Outernauts] immature cirrius

nimci: [magic mint mimci gam palindrome] greenish gam

nimolap: [palimino nimolap palindrome] brown equine with cream-colored tail and mane

nimrav: [nimravid backformation] nimravid-like creature from Noy, Cihpma system, Galaxiki galaxy

nimravid: [*After the Dinosaurs* by Donald R. Prothero] sabertooth cat-like predator from Eocene

nimsaj: [jasmine ninsaj palindrome] pale yellow ornithoid

ningen: [*The Big Bad Book of Beasts* by Michael Largo] whale-like sea creature with humaoind face and arms or [Welsh cwningen backformation] cuckoo-rabbit, long-eared burrowing griffinoid ancestral to cw and rabbit, almost indistinguishable from cw from Pharr, Farpt system, Galaxiki galaxy

ninih: [shining ninihs palindrome] glowworm-like creature, see niremmih

nink: [*The Wocket in My Pocket* by Theodore Seuss Geissel] 1-meter yellow, hairy, large-snouted biped

ninki-nanka: swamp-dwelling, horse-faced, snake/croc with mirror-like scales, skin-crest from Gambia, Terra (alpha Zodiaci III), [*Here Be Monsters almanac*] with webbing on head and arms able to stiffen into sharp blades

ninn: ["ninn at times emit tannin" palindrome] dracoid gestalt

ninut: [*Dell Crossword Puzzle Dictionary*] magpie, see mag(g), pie(t), piot, pyot, pyet, pi(an)et

nio: [nio loin portmanteau] food amimal

nip: [pink nip palindrome] pale reddish ornithoid

nipe: [cerise pink nipe sirec palindrome] pinkish sirec

niper: [nest of vipers spoonerism, nipe backformation] nipe predator

nippan: [snapping nippans palindrome] guard turtle

niptune: [Terra Monster] fish-eating blue fox, see aquanine and carnivice from Terrarium

niram: ["niram at times emit tamarin" palindrome] marmoset gestalt

nirama: [aquamarine nirama uqa palindrome] variety of paler blue uqa

nirao: [soaring niraos palindrome] rarely landing, insectivorous ornithoid

nirba: ["How Aliens Work" by Craig Freudenrich] aquatic reptilian with large head and foreclaws and long tail

nirda: [James Cooke Brown's Loglan] bird from Logla, Brown's system

nire: [tangerine nire gnat palindrome] orange gnat-like insectoid, see le

niremmih: [shimmering niremmihs palindrome] glowworm-like creature, see ninih

niretci: [icterine niretci palindrome] yellowish ornithoid

nirevih: [shivering nirevihs palindrome] penguin-like ornithoid

nirkangu: [James Cooke Brown's Loglan nirda kangu compound] bird-headed caninoid from Logla, Brown's system

nirli: [James Cooke Brown's Loglan nirda clika (bird-like) compound] ornithoid from Logla, Brown's system

nirmartlu: [ultramarine nirmartlu palindrome] dark blue ornithoid

nirtic: [citrine nirtic palindrome] yellow ornithoid

níshinú: [Japanese níshin-inú portmanteau] herring-dog amphibian

nit: [drannit mondegreen] pest from Dra system

nitargim: [migrating nitargim palindrome] migratory prey of rotargim

nitnuh: [hunting nitnuh palindrome] hounddog-like caninoid

nitnazyb: [Byzantine nitnazyb palindrome] purplish ornithoid

niuqelrah: [harlequin niuqelrah palindrome] 50-to-75% white furry

nival: [Spanish perdiz nival backformation] ptarmigan-partridge ornithoid ancestral to partridge and ptarmigan

nivilo: [olivine nivilo palindrome] grayish olive ornithoid

niw: [niw twin palindrome] mammaloid with two breasts that usually has offspring in pairs, see telp; [wine niw palindrome] brownish red gerde predator

niwedi: [red niwedi sidewinder palindrome] red sidewinder-like amphisbæna

niwhsa: [niwhsa ashwinder palindrome] ashwinder-like amphisbæna

niwi: [periwinkle elk niwi rep, persimmon Ommi's rep palindromes] pale lavender blue elk-like creature from Ommi system

niylf: [flying niylf palindrome] flying ornithoid

nizo: ["nizo at times emit taozin" palindrome] insectoid gestalt

no: [beheaded and curtailed anoo] 2-headed, 2-tailed, very large dracoid with red eyes and mossy, forested back

no-see-'em: aka punkie, midge, tiny gnat-like insect

noad: [nest of toads spoonerism, beheaded knoad] toad-like gan ceann

noao: [Rotcurt's noao boa constructor palindrome] boa constructor-like amphisbæna from Rotcurt system

nob: [bone nob palindrome] bone-colored off-white ornithoid;[bonnacon anamondegreen] large, armored dracoid from Noca system

nobe: [ebony nobe palindrome] black ornithoid

nobster: [nob lobster portmanteau] bone-colored, armored dracoid with lobster claws

noc: [sad noc anacondas palindeome] large, melancholic, constricting serpentoid

noca: [noca bacon palindrome] food porcoid

nododon: [mynynym] creature noted for its knot-like teeth

nodosaur: ["knot-lizard"] dinosaur with spikes

nodotaur: [nodosaur minotaur portmanteau] bull with spikes

noen: [neon orange gnaro noen, neon fuchsia ishcuf noen, neon green eerg noen palindromes] see gnaro, ishcuf and eerg

nog: [knot of frogs spoonerism] amphibious ovoid

nogator: [nog alligator portmanteau] alligator-like predator whose bite morphs victim into nog

nogoodnik: ["L'il Abner" by Al Capp] aka bad schmoo, sickly green, eye-eyed, yellow-toothed schmoo predator

noidülasnek: [Fr. Johann Martin Schleyer's Volapük] rattlesnake-like serpentoid from Schleyer's system, see krotasnek

noil: [lion noil palindrome] tan ornithoid

noio: [*Dell Crossword Puzzle Dictionary*] tern from Hawaii, Terra (alpha Zodiaci III)

noitolgninn: ["at times emit ta" palindrome] creature that produces tanning lotion

noj: [jonquil iuq noj, Nacridone Nodirca iuq palindromes] yellowish iuq from Nodirca system

nok: ["The Flash -- Fact or Fiction" by Cary Bates] aura-eater that knocks prey into alternate reality; [tornok backformation] bull-like creature

nōkísí: [Cherokee] meadowlark from Tsalagi system

nolb: [blond nolb palindrome] pale yellow ornithoid

nolimku: [James Cooke Brown's Loglan no nu limji kurma] infinity worm from Logla, Brown's system

nomaid: [diamond nomaid palindrome] pale blue ornithoid

nomitna: [antimony nomitna palindrome] reddish yellow ornithoid

nomla: [almond nomla palindrome] almond-colored ornithoid

nonasus: [tyrannonasus mondegreen] predatory snouter from Tyra

nonny: songbird that flies perpendicularly -- "All day she chirps her joysome odes and if she goes too far explodes."

nonu: [Perry Rhodan] noted for neurotoxin from Honur, Thatrel system

noocoonah: [*The Yowie: In Seach of Australian Bigfoot* by Tony Healy and Paul Cropper] see yowie

noot owl: [newt-hoot owl portmanteau] nocturnal, large-headed, large-eyed, slender, brightly-colored amphibian with hooked claws and beak

nooth grush: [*There's a Wocket in My Pocket* by Seuss] 1.5-meter multicolored bird with a long neck, stripes and bulleye markings

Norco energy beast: ["It Crawled Out of the Woodwork" by Joseph Stephano] small electrical cloud that kills indiscriminately in quest for more energy from Norco energy research center

norebo worm: [*Nightdreamers* by Tom Arden] psychevore space creature that generates gravity fields to draw prey and feeds on their dreams

normae: [piscium extrapolation] 2-D, oval-laying square

normenki: [James Cooper Brown's Loglan norji menki] orange-eye from Logla, Brown's system

normie: [*Monster Spotter's Guide to North America* by Scott Francis] 9-meter lake snake from Lake Norman, N. C., Terra (alpha Zodiaci III)

normrenu: [James Cooke Brown's Loglan norka mrenu (blind man) compound] long-legged, clawed predator from Logla, Brown's system

nornet: [nest of hornets spoonerism, noru hornet portmanteau] hornet-like pest of nornus

nornirda: [James Cooke Brown's Loglan norji nirda (orange bird) compound] orange ornithoid from Logla, Brown's system

Norstrilian sparrow: [*The Planet Buyer* by Cordwainer Smith] 20-kg flightless sparrow from Norstrilia

norto: [James Crooke Brown's Loglan no tosku] orse from Logla, Bown's system

noru: ["noru at times emit tauron" palindrome] bovine gestalt

nós: [Irish ligean nós mondegreen] plover-like ornithoid from Ligea system

noshingra: ["The Peacefulness of Vivyan" by James Tiptree, Jr.] bimorphic shellfish aka come-and-go animal

nostrich: [an ostrich mondegreen] ostrich-like ornithoid

nothocyon: [*After the Dinosaurs* by Donald R. Prothero] bear-like pinniped ancestor

nothronychus: ["sloth-claw", *Feathered Dinosaurs: The Origin of Birds* by John Long and Peter Schuten] 3.6-meter tall therizinosaur with short tail, small head, 10-cm claws from N. America, Terra (alpha Zodiaci III)

nothrothereiops: [*After the Dinosaurs* by Donald R. Prothero] ground sloth smaller than eremothere from Pleistocene

notili: [notili ziliton palindrome] ziliton-like amphisbæna

notoungulate: [*After the Dinosaurs* by Donald R. Prothero] hippo/rhino-like hoofed mammal from Paleocene

notsnoom: [moonstone notsnoon palindrome] bluish ornithoid

notter: [an otter mondegreen] otter-like amphibious mammaloid

nottoc: [cottoncandy ydnacnottoc palindrome mondegreen] pale red ydnac

nowl: [an owl mondegreen] owl-like nocturnal ornithold

nox: [an ox mondegreen] ox-like bovinoid

noyster: [an oyster mondegreen] sea predator that noysts (camouflages) cephalopod-like to catch prey

nozia: [Hildegard of Bingen's Lingua Ignota] tawny owl-like ornithoid from Ignota, Hildegard's system

nqwebasaur: [*Feathered Dinosaurs: The Origin of Birds* by John Long and Peter Schuten] 1-meter coelurosaur with long thumb

nrab: [barn nrab portmanteau] owl-like ornithoid

nu: [yutyrannus mondegreen] titanosauroid from Yutyra system

nu-kwa: ox-headed snake from Japan, Terra (alpha Zodiaci III)

nuatnu: ["nuatnu at times emit tauntaun" palindrome] horned, furry quadruped gestalt

nuclear watchdog: [Godville] see radiation dog

nuclear watchdogator: [nuclear watchdog alligator portmanteau] alligator-like predator whose bite morphs victim into nuclear watchdog

nudj: [*Creatures of the Galaxy* by Phil Brucato, Bill Smith, Rick D. Stuart, Chuck Truett] chameleon-like swamp lizard from Dagobah, Jedi galaxy

nue: monkey-headed tanuki (raccoon dog) with tiger's legs, snake's tail able to become black, flying cloud from Japan, Terra (alpha Zodiaci III)

nukkangu: [James Cooke Brown's Loglan nukli kangu (dirty dog) compound] desert caninoid from Logla, Brown's system

numbat: [*National Geographic Encyclopedia of Animals*] insectivorous mammal from S. Australia

numidothere: [*After the Dinosaurs* by Donald R. Prothero] mastodont with short tusks and no trunk from Eocene

nuna: ["The Gungan Frontier" by Chris McCubbin] aka swamp turkey, flightless, neck-less scaly-backed ornithoid with fleshy "whiskers", dwarf variety extinct, from Naboo (more aggressive) or Tatooine, Jedi galaxy; [kan'nuna mondegreen] bullfrog-like amphibian from Ka system

nunbird: [*Dell Crossword Puzzle Dictionary*] monase, see barb, dove, pouter, roller

nunk: [*Nick and the Glimmung* by Philip K. Dick] creature from Plowman's planet

nup: [*The Unofficial Questarian Guide*] gnu-like ruminant from Tev'meck, Warvan system

nupboard: [*There's a Wocket in My Pocket* by Theodore Seuss Geissel] 30-cm, yellow, round-headed biped

nureau: [*There's a Wocket in My Pocket* by Theodore Seuss Geissel] 1-meter, blue bipedal lapoid without external ears, see bureau thread

nurikabe: aka whomp, creature able to project blocking or misdirecting "wall" from Japan, Terra (alpha Zodiaci III)

nurp: [prune nurp palindrome] mature, brownish ulp

nutara: [Eskimo] baby walrus

nutch: [*If I Ran the Zoo* by Theodore Seuss Geissel] furry, green neckless biped
nutria: [*Dell Crossword Puzzle Dictionary*] web-footed rodent from S. America, Terra (alpha Zodiaci III)
nwad: [dawn nwad] insectoid from Agcaqa, Neccobit's system, Galaxiki galaxy
nwarc: [scrawny nwarcs palindrome] inedible egg-layering creature
nwat: [tawny nwat palindrome] brownish-orange ornithoid
ny'ghan grii: ["The Invaders" by Henry Kuttner] extradimensional, translucent, leprosy-white oblate spheroid covered with slender, squirming tentacles, 1 great faceted eye, puckered mouth accompanied by extreme cold, slide when magic is practiced, able to devolve victim
nyak: [*Encyclopedia Galactica*] huge flying game bird from Samia, Anacreon sector
nyl: [lynx nyl palindrome] feline with reddish-brown stripes on "blue" (gray) or cream (pale yellow-orange)
nylope: [nyl antelope portmanteau] nyl with antlers
nyork: ["The Gungan Frontier" by Chris McCubbin] jumping mollusk from Jedi galaxy
nyraala: [*Monster Manual* by Skip Williams, etal.] flailing, slimy tentacle golem made by Illithid as guard dogs and attack dogs
nyzel: ["The Great Silence" by Marianne Sydow] communicating symbiot in banditry, see farrn and drohs
o: [Esp. asterisko mondegreen, *] 2-D pentapus or hexapus; [beheaded ao] headless bird of ill omen; [onactornis ananymondegreen] flightless ornithoid from Sinrotca system; [onager ananymondegreen] hunchbacked, wild ass-like equinoid from Rega system; [onax ananymondegreen] ass-like equinoid from Xa system
o-grab-me: [embrago ananym] tentacled shore predator
oa: [Basq. asteriskoa mondegreen, *] 2-D pentapus or hexapus

oakbat: [*Edge Chronicles* by Paul Stweart and Chris Riddell] arboreal chiropteran
oakhen: [*Midnight Over Sanctaphrax* by Paul Stewart and Chris Riddell] arboreal creature
oakleaf toad: [*After Man* by Dougal Dixon] brown or green if infected with parasitic fluke) toad with oakleaf-like skinflaps, worm-like tongue
oaklore: [Terra Monsters] planimal from Terranium
oan: [beheaded roan] red gan ceann
oao: [noao elision] boa constructor-like amphisbæna
oarion: [Terra Monster] creature from Terrarium
oarionster: [oarion monster portmanteau] monstrous oarion
oast: [*The Dying Earth* by Jack Vance] 2.7-meter anthropoid with yellow hair, watery blue eyes, used as beast of burden by villagers and eaten "properly braised and kettled"
obdurodon: [*After the Dinosaurs* by Donald R. Prothero] ancient platypus
obelttil: [little boy obelttil palindrome, Little Boy] dangerous, deep baby blue ornithoid
obispo: [*Dell Crossword Puzzle Dictionary*] spotted stingray
obloot: [Crayola toolbox obloot] purplish blue ornithoid from Crayol A
obmu: [obmu gumbo palindrome] food animal
oboa: [titanoboa mondegreen] large serpentoid from Tita system
oboer: [trumpeter swan extrapolation, *Across the Universe* by Pamela Sargent and George Zebrowski] swan-like ornithoid with sound of oboe from Merope (23 Tauri) IV
obsk: [*If I Ran the Zoo* by Theodore Seuss Geissel] long-necked, flightless, yellow bird with large feet, pointed beak, wide bottom and red crest
obtusewhale: [obtuse anglewhale mondegreen] anglewhale that turns in greater than right angles
obtuseworm: [obtuse angleworm mondegreen] angleworm that turns in greater than right angles

oc: [cobalt lab oc palindrome, noc elision] geneered metallic blue anaconda-like amphisbæna; ococ nasna

ocabussó: [Catalan oca-cabussó portmanteau] goose-grebe, aquatic ornithoid with pointed bill

ocama: [Cyclopedia of Worlds] aka toca, lieto, 3-meter aquatic, anguilliform predator that uses Guyman's electrosensors more than eyes from Dakka, Neptunes system

ocarinabird: [trumpeter swan backformation] swan-like ornithoid with ocarina-like call

occamy: [*Fantastic Beasts and Where to Find Them* by Newton Artemis Fido Scamander] 4.5-meter winged, leg-less murre-like dracoid that lays silver eggs

ocean phantom: [*The Future Is Wild* by Dougal Dixon] 10-meter long siphonophore (jellyfish) with sail-fins, airsacs and waterjets, symbiot to algae and spindletroopers, hunting with suction bell, feathery sensors, eyestalk-ringcd tentacles

ocelloro: [Catalan ocell-lloro portmanteau] bird-parrot, parrot-like bird, often confused with llorocell

ochi: [beheaded rochi] large dracoid with red eyes green back and 6 heads

ochoer: [kubanocherus mondegreen] one-horned porcoid from Kuba system

ochokochi: see alma

ochre jelly: [*Monster Manual* by Skip Williams, etal.] golden-colored jelly-thick ooze

ocicat: see mau

ocileuqoc: [coquelicot ocileuqoc palindrome] red-orange ornithoid

ocirpa: [apricot ocirpa palindrome] pale brown ornithoid

ococ: [cocoa ococ, cocoanut unococ palindromes] light brown omnivorous creature

ocsab: ["ocsab at times emit ta" palindrome] creature that produces tabasco-like secretion

octibullus: sprintosaur with eight-knobbed crest

octo balloon: [The Legend of Zelda: "A Link to the Past"] air cephalopodan that explodes into dozens of small ones when attacked

octo-ooze: [*The Ultimate Monster Guide* by Jaymond] slimy, large-mouthed, blue cephalopodan with eyestalks

octobear: [Godville, octopus-bear portmanteau] grizzly-like ursine with 8 legs, suckers and exuding bacony slime

octobeaver: ["Robot Hugs" by R. Hugs'] beaver-like amphibian with octopus-like tentacles

octogiraffe: [fairy chess] octopedal camelopardian

octoped: 8-legged creature, see arachnoids, crustaceans, heela, hessi, juhiyama, sardzi, sagsār, sharabha, thoat, etc.

octopin: [*Monster Manual* by Skip Williams, etal.] 6-tentacled, purple-skinned monster with one eye made by Illithid

octopuss: [octopus-puss portmanteau] 8-legged amphibious felinoid, see erdkat

octorok: [The Legend of Zelda] red or blue land octopodan able to spit rocks from Hyrule

octosak: ["Flash Gordon" by Frederick Stephani, George Plympton, Basil Dickey, Ella O'Neill, based on Alex Raymond's strip] reptilian octopus from Mongo

octtolopus: [*Valley Register*] noted for snallygaster-like screech

octule: [noctule elision] large, reddish-brown insectivorous chiropteran

ocyne: [cyanocyne mondegreen] caninoid from Cya system

od: ["od at times emit tado" palindrome] snake gestalt

odah: [Crayola shadow odahs palindrome] brownish gray ornithoid from Crayol A

odalec: [celalon odalec palindrome] sea green or blue ornithoid

odder: ["The Return of the Kangaroo Rex" by Janet Kagan] neo-otter that eats canal clogweed (aka oddee) from Mirabile

odi: [peridot odi rep, persimmon Ommi's rep palindromes] yellow rep from Ommi system

odon: [atanodon mondegreen] toothed dragonfly-like insectoid from Ata system; [dicanodon mondegreen] amphibious reptile from Dica system; [ern, ernanodon] sloth-like sea eagle from Erna system

odonster: [odon monster portmanteau] monstrous odon

odontotyrannus: [Alexander romance] 3-horned monster

odorip: [Crayola spiral disco ball Aboc's idorips palindrome] greenish blue ornithoid from Aboc system

Oduri leech: [Odurihirudo palindrome] leech-like creature from Oduri system

oel: [*Big Planet* by Jack Vance] swamp-dwelling, 2.1-meter biped with narrow head, 4 horns, black dorsal carapace, 12 folding clawed arms, able to be trained to dance the mazurka; [leonatoar ananymondegreen] sealion-like sea creature from Raota system

oeluràta: [Continuum: "Callicrates"] flying, one-horned tortoise from Atlantis, see gamera

oesophagus: ["uniform eater", "A Double-Barrelled Detective Story" by Mark Twain] bird

ofile: [pilofile backformation] insectovorous eel

off: [ffonagort ananymondegreen] food animal from Troga system

og: [Aubrey's dog spoonerism] flying caninoid from Daubrey system; [army of frogs spoonerism, og-tegn mondegreen] 2-D tegn relative; [gonarch ananymondegreen] crab-like creature from Hcra system

og-tegn: [Dan. &] 2-D das-like creature

ogator: [og alligator portmanteau] alligator-like predator whose bite morphs victim into og

oga: [dianoga mondegreen] eyestalked heptapodan from Dia system

ogator: [oga alligator portmanteau] alligator-like predator whose bite morphs victim into oga

ogg: dog-like porcoid, see cherry-ogg, hogg, dhog

oggator: [ogg alligator portmanteau] alligator-like predator whose bite morphs victim into ogg

oggie: [*Monster Spotter's Guide to North America* by Scott Francis] 6-meter salamander-like amphibian from Onondaga Lake, NY, Terra (alpha Zodiaci III)

ogle: [katogle backformation] griffinoid ancestral to cat and owl

ognam: [Crayola tango mango gnat ognam palindrome] orange gnat parasite from Crayol A

ognid: [dingonar ananymondegreen] river monster from Ra system

ogno: [Congo ogno palindrome] Congo pink flamingo-like ornithoid

ogopogo: [W. H. Brimblecombe, *Monster Spotter's Guide to North America* by Scott Francis] aka naitaka, dark blue-black, humped, creature with horse-like head, flippers, back serrations, white underbelly from Lake Okanagan, BC, Terra (alpha Zodiaci III)

ogreon: [*The First Kingdom* by Jack Katz] 6-meter tall, horned, devil-faced bipedal man-eater

ogrillion: ["The Gauntlet" by Graeme Morris] creature

ogrillionster: [ogrillion monster portmanteau] monstrous ogrillion

ogrim: [The Elder Scrolls III: "Morrowind"] fat, green, scaly daedra with large twisted horns above small eyes

oh: ["oh at times emit taho" palindrome] cave lion gestalt

óh: [hónatata ananymondegreen] 4-nasaria snoutwalker from Atata system

ohctopus: [OH octopus] small freshwater octopus from Ohio river, Terra (alpha Zodiaci III), see oktopus

ohctopuss: [ohctopus puss portmanteau] catfish-like octopus from Ohio river

oikpavocervus: [candiacervus extrapolation] deer with pitchfork-like antlers

oil snake: [snake oil backformation] snake from which healing snake oil comes

oila: [Basque oilagarro mondegreen] woodcock-like ornithoid

oir: [rionnag ananymondegreen] 2-D pentapod or hexapod from Ga system

oj: [canoj mondegreen, Foppan canoj spoonerism] "guard dog" with square skull, 2 tusks from Foppa system

oji: [Outernauts] immature squibat

ok: [Filipino manok, Fr. Johann Martin Schleyer's Volapük torok mondegreens, nok elision] chicken-like dracoid that eats auras and knocks prey into alternate reality

okeecho: [Okeechobee mondegreen] swamp-dwelling bee-like insectoid from Ahla, Ojikh system, Galaxiki galaxy

okonihcuz: [okonihcuz tzuchinoko palindrome] tzuchinoko-like amphisbæna

oktopus: [OK octopus portmanteau, *Monster Spotter's Guide to North America* by Scott Francis] 6-meter, reddish brown, leathery, freshwater octopus from Oklahoma lakes (Thunderbird, Oologah, Tenkiller), possibly related to smaller WV, KY (okytopus) and Ohio River (ohctopus) varieties

oktaskylos: [heptasklos extrapolation] 8-headed hellhound

okytopus: [KY octopus] small freshwater octopus from Kentucky, see oktopus

ol: [berol mondegreen] beetle-like insectoid; [slow ols palindrome] flightless owl-like ornithoid

ola: [i less oila] woodchuck-like creature from Friatica, Friaticalida system, Galaxiki galaxy

oldfather: [Perry Rhodan] mature bron-klyth from Arpa Chai, Wahiat Zont system

oldt: [newt antonym] mature newt-like amphibian

olebok: [Skobeloff oleboks palindrome] dark blue-green antelope-like creature

olem: [melon olem palindrome] pinkish ornithoid

olgnu: [sunglow olgus palindrome] orangish yellow ornithoid

olhp: [plox olhp palindrome] florescent purple ornithoid

oligobunis: [*After the Dinosaurs* by Donald R. Prothero] weasel-like carnivore that migrated to America in Miocene

olingo: [*National Geographic Encyclopedia of Animals*] raccoon relative from S. America, Terra (alpha Zodiaci III)

oliphaunt: [*The Lord of the Rings* by J. R. R. Tolkien] giant war elephant

oliphent: [Superman mythos] large, warm-blooded, egg-laying beast of burden from Krypton, Rao system

olla: [allosaur ananym] dinosauroid from Rua system

ollaf: [fallow ollaf palindrome] pale brown ornithoid

ollemnu: [Crayola unmellow ollemnu palindrome] florecent orangish yellow ornithoid from Crayol A

olley: [yellow olley palindrome] yellow ornithoid

ollirpi: [ollirpi viprillo palindrome] aka "ollie", viprillo-like amphisbæna

ollopom: ["The Gungan Frontier" by Chris McCubbin] aka pseudo-pom, floats lily-pad-like from Jedi galaxy

oloc: [bicolor oloc ib palindrome] furry with two colors, see hsalf, ehctap, dexut

olor: [*Dell Crossword Puzzle Dictionary*] whistling swan

om: [akinom, moss om mondegreen] fruit-eating, blue-green or green ornithoid; [monal ananymondegreen] pheasant-like ornithoid; [monasa anaymondegreen] puffbird-like iornithoid from Asa system; [monase ananymondegreen] nunbird-like from Esa system

omajinaakoos: ["ugly one"] 30-cm brown, lake monster with rattail from Big Trout Lake, Ont., Terra (alpha Zodiaci III)

omannic: [cinnamon omannic palindrome] reddish-brown creature, see erro

omao: [*Dell Crossword Puzzle Dictionary*] thrush from Hawaii, Terra (alpha Zodiaci III)

omel: [lemon omel palindrome] yellowish ornithoid, see resal

omenester: ["Squirrel Cage" by Robert Sheckley] sleg predator from Seer

omla: [salmon omlas pormanteau] pale pinkish orange ornithoid

ommoc: [common ommoc portmanteau] creature in common and uncommon varieties

omnethoth: [*The Fall of Yquatine* by Nick Walters] gestalt gaseous creature geneered as acid rain producer, re-geneered into beautiful golden gasclouds from Yquatine

omnivoracius: [Ben 10: Omniverse: "Showdown" by Marty Isenberg] tall, purple predatory ornithoid, extinct by climate change, from Galva

omnivore: [*Omnivore* by Piers Anthony] most ferocious of the 1-eyed, 1-legged creatures from Nacre, see nasna

omnivorous bat: ["Bats" by John Logan] mutant bat that will eat anything, fruit, insects, mammals

omoichidogyo: [jikan-to-jikan-o-mōichido-gyu mondegreen] air-breathing, chronoporting grouper-like flying ichthyoid from Jika, Tojika system

omomys: lemur-like primate which replace plesiadapid from late Paleocene

on: [snow ons, turanon palindromes] flightless, off-white ornithoid from Tura system; [nonasus ananymondegreen] predatory snouter from Susa system

onactornis: [*After the Dinosaurs* by Donald R. Prothero] large flightless bird with hunched back and J-shaped neck from Miocene

onager: [*Dell Crossword Puzzle Dictionary*] wild ass from Asia, see quagga

onatit: [titanonatit ananymondegreen] large natit from Tita system

onax: [drassonax mondegreen] ass-like pinniped ancestor

ondine: [*The Perfect Planet* by Edward Packard] green, long necked amphibian from Utopa (Achnar V), Gallatin quadrant

ondo: [Swahili nondo elision] moth-like insectoid

ondryx: [*Exiles* by Howard Weinstein] herd creature with spindly legs, shoulder humps, complex forward-extending antlers, trunk from Kejor VI

one-eye: [*Monster Spotter's Guide to North America* by Scott Francis] giant lake snake from Lake Granbury, TX, Terra (alpha Zodiaci III)

onehand: [handbird extrapolation] variety of handbird, see otherhand

ong: [Filipino pagong mondegreen] tortoise-pug, caninoid with carapace ancestral to pug and tortoise; [Vietnamese con ong mondegreen] creature ancestral to con and bee from Disa

ongator: [ong alligator portmanteau] alligator-like predator whose bite morphs victim into ong

Onihc cat: [Ohihc cat tacchio portmanteau] cat-turkey griffinoid ancestral to cat and turkey from Onihc system

onny: [nonny elision] exploding creature

onster: [beheaded monster] see gan ceann

onza: [*Unexplained!* by Jerome Clark] aka cuitlamiztli, wolf-like cat or nimravid from Sierra Madre Mts., Mex., Terra (alpha Zodiaci III)

oo: [noocoonah ananymondegreen] large, bipedal raccoon-like from Ha system; [maroon oo ram palindrome] dark brownish red sheep

oo-er: [museumofhoaxes.com by Alex Boese] cubical-egg-laying bird from Australia, Terra (alpha Zodiaci III), see fau-liva

oob: [*The Mathematics of Oz* by Clifford A. Pickover] 1.4-meter serpentoid with spindly arms and gross oversized head from Zyph, Betelguese (alpha Orionis) system

oobster: [oob lobster portmanteau] serpentoid with large head and lobster claws

oogaher: [trumpeter swan extrapolation] swan-like ornithoid with oogah sound

oogl: ["Eripmav" by Damon Knight] aka "meat tree" whose flesh petrifies rapidly with exposure to air, used for construction on Veegle, Fomalhaut (alpha Piscis Austrini) system

ooh: [hooded ooh portmanteau] creature in hooded and unhooded varieties, with "Ooh!" cry

ook: [*Alien Secrets* by Annette Curtis Klause] pet from Shoon (aka Aurora, tau Ceti II)

ookaris: [babookaris mondegreen] blue simian

oomfer: [*Warrior of Llarn, Theif of Llarn* by Gardner F. Fox] giant ornithoid steed from Llarn that oomfs (flies while ridden)

oon: [jogg-oon mondegreen] jogg relative, ancestor of jogg-oon

oopik: [*Creatures of the Galaxy* by Phil Brucato, Bill Smith, Rick D. Stuart, Chuck Truett] sauroid with vestigial wings, echolocation, great variety with gas toxin sac and ultrasonic stun, from Paramatan, Jedi galaxy

oor: [roonat ananymondegreen] rodentoid from Ta system

oorial: [*Dell Crossword Puzzle Dictionary*] wild mountain sheep from Tibet, see sha, sna, rasse, urial, bharal, nahoor

oorialope: [oorial antelope portmanteau] oorial with antlers

oorochi: [yamata-no-orochi mondegreen] 8-headed, 8-tailed, very large dracoid with red eyes and mossy, forested back from Yamata system

oort: [*Monster Manual* by Skip Williams, etal.] large, small-brained aggressive creature from which Illithid bred oortlings

oortling: [*Monster Manual* by Skip Williams, etal.] docile, large-brained food anthropoid bred by Illithid from oort

oortlingater: [oortling alligator portmanteau] alligator-like predator whose bite morphs victim into oortling

ootter: 2-headed aquatic mammaloid

oow: [wood oow palindrome] owl-like forest ornithoid

oow-god: [dogwood oowgod palindrome] large, rose owl-like ornithoid

oow-ylrub: [burlywood oowylrub palindrome] pale orange oow relative

ooze: [*Monster Manual* by Skip Williams, etal.] includes ever more viscous slime, jelly, flan, pudding and blobs, usually blind and acid-secreting

oozefish: [*Edge Chronicles* by Paul Stewart and Chris Riddell] foul, sluggish, vile-tasting mudskipper-like ichthyoid

opaleye: [*Fantastic Beasts and Where to Find Them* by Newton Artemis Fido Scamander] sheep-eating, iridescent dragon with pupil-less, multi-colored eyes from Australia or New Zealand, Terra (alpha Zodiaci III)

opan: [*Dell Crossword Puzzle Dictionary*] kingfish, see haku

opee: [*Creatures of the Galaxy* by Phil Brucato, Bill Smith, Rick D. Stuart, Chuck Truett] large, anglerfish-like ichthyoid from Jedi galaxy

opeel: [opee eel portmanteau] anglerfish-like ichthoid with eel-like lure

opelet: [*Dell Crossword Puzzle Dictionary*] sea anemone

opelter: [argopelter mondegreen] grey arboreal pelter

oph: large horned serpent whose blade-ridged spine slashes

ophiacodon: low, 3.7-meter sauroid with long hindlegs, large toothed jaw

opinicus: creature with serpent's body, lion's legs, long bill, pointy ears, eagle's wings, camel's tail

opose: small warbear used by Quan from Hoan (Acram II), Galaxiki galaxy

oppihippo: [mynynym] hippoid from Oppi system

opthalmosaur: ["eye-lizard] variety of ichthyosaur

opus: [walopus mondegreen] green cephalopoid

opyli: ["opyli at times emit tailypo" palindrome] caninoid gestalt

or: [Armenian tsovaoror mondegreen] sea ornithoid ancestral to tsova and seagull; [carrot or rac palindrome] orange variety of rac from Oita system

Oramese beast: ["The Creature that Slept a Million Years" by E. Nelson Bridwell] dangerous beats from Oram

orang-pendek: [*Unexplained!* by Jerome Clark] see sedapa

orange eyes: [*Monster Spotter's Guide to North America* by Scott Francis] 3.3-meter nape from Mansfield, OH, Terra (alpha Zodiaci III)

orange jelly: [jelly extrapolation] orange jelly-thick ooze

orangopoid: [orangutan-anthropoid portmanteau, "Flash Gordon" by Frederick Stephani, George Plympton, Basil Dickey, Ella O'Neill, based on Alex Raymond's strip] horned long-armed anthropoid

orbalisk: [*Darth Bane: The Rule of Two* by Drew Karpyshyn] barnacle-like parasite with rage-inducing toxin from Beast Moon of Dxun, Jedi galaxy

orbz: [Monster Galaxy] web-spinning arachnoid with 4 long legs, 2 hands from Cancer constellation

orc: [*Dragons, Unicorns and Other Magical Beasts* by Robin Palmer] man-eating sea creature with impenetrable scales, tusks; [*Lord of the Rings* by J. R. R. Tolkien] goblin-like land orc; [*Dell Crossword Puzzle Dictionary*] whale, see ork, cet(e), beluga, grampus

orcat: [orca-cat portmanteau] large black and white amphibious predatory felinoid

orchidsnouter: [*The Snouters* by Harald Stümpke] plant-mimicking snouter with rigid tail from Hi-Yi-Yi Islands

orcim: [microrcim backformation] small whale-like cetacean

ördegi: [Azerbaijani yaban ördegi mondegreen] widgeon-like ornithoid from Yaba system

ordzook: ["Prince of Peril" by Otis Adelbert Kline] bluish-green amphibian with yellow head and neck with red neckring, spiny ridges from Zarovia (Venus (alpha Zodiaci II))

orea: pongopteryx from Relegooturnia (Phoenix IV), Galaxiki galaxy

orek: [Czech norek elision] mink-like mammaloid

oreodon: herding ruminant from Oligocene

oreodonster: [oreodon monster portmanteau] monstrous hering ruminant

orepavicervus: [candiacervus extrapolation] deer with sickle-like antlers

orf(e): [*Dell Crossword Puzzle Dictionary*] yellow fish

orffa: [saffron orffas palindrome] orangish-yellow ornithoid

org: [*This Moment of the Storm* by Roger Zelazny] contraction from "organism-with-a-long-name-I-can't-remember"] 3-meter long, segmented body, wide head, traffic-signed eyes, pale little legs, razor-sharp teeth from Tierra del Cygnus, 72 Cygni system

orgator: [org alligator portmanteau] alligator-like predator whose bite morphs victim into org

órga: [Irish iasc órga mondegreen] ichthyoid ancestral to fish and goldfish

órgator: [órga alligator portmanteau] alligator-like predator whose bite morphs victim into órga

orhin: [stephanorhinus mondegreen] rhinoid from Stepha system

orhinus: [tichorhinus, stephanorhinus mondegreens] rhinoid tich relative from Stefa system

Orion parasite: ["Operation: Annihilate" by Steven W. Carabatsos] gelatinous, colorless, football-sized amorph gestalt that drives host mad with pain, destroyed Aldebaran Magnus V, Ingraham B and Deneva

ork: [*The Sword of Lankor* by Howard L. Cory] 3-headed ornithoid from Lankor; [*The Scarecrow of Oz* by L. Frank Baum] ornithoid with 4 legs and 4 wings and propeller-like tail; [*Dell Crossword Puzzle Dictionary*] whale, see orc

orka: [*Dell Crossword Puzzle Dictionary*] killer whale

orluck: [Barsoom series by Edgar Rice Burroughs] yellow-and-black striped elephantine beast from Mars (alpha Zodiaci IV)

ormrenu: [normrenu elision] long-legged, clawed predator

orn: [goldenrod orn ed-log palindrome] variant of ed-log

ornad: [*Earth in Twilight* by Doris Piserchia] 9-meter long jungle-dwelling 16-legged, green and yellow, caterpillar with long head with long floppy ears, teeth worse than tail stinger, able to shoot webbing, lives in oval nest

orned: [Crayola goldenrod orned log palindrome] yellowish log-like creature from Crayol A

ornirda: [nordirda elision] orange ornithoid

ornithoid: bird-like creature

ornitholestes: ["bird-robber", *Feathered Dinosaurs: The Origin of Birds* by John Long and Peter Schuten] 2-meter, 15-kg ornitomimosaur from Wyoming, Terra (alpha Zodiaci III)

ornithomimosaur: ["bird-mimic", *The Mistaken Extinction* by Lowell Dingus and Timothy Rowe, *Feathered Dinosaurs: The*

Origin of Birds by John Long and Peter Schuten] coelurosaur descendant
ornithomimotaur: [ornithomimosaur minotaur portmanteau] bird-mimicking bull-like pegasoid
ornithopod: ["bird-footed", *The Mistaken Extinction* by Lowell Dingus and Timothy Rowe] ancestor of heterodontosaur, camptosaur, edmontosaur, parasauroloph
ornithorhynchus: aka platypus ["flatfoot"], egg-laying, furry quadruped with duckbill, webbed feet, poisonous footspike, beaver's tail, see puggle, obdurodon
oro: [kalanoro mondegreen] small hairy anthropoid from Kala system
orochi: [*Sacred Texts: The Kojiki — The Eight-forked Serpent* tr. by B. H. Chamberlain, *Here Be Monsters almanac*] aka yamata-no-orochi "big snake of 8 branches"] 8-headed, 8-tailed, very large dracoid with red eyes and mossy, forested back
orohippo: [orohippus backformation] beagle-sized eohippoid from Noy, Cihpma system, Galaxiki galaxy
orohippus: [*After the Dinosaurs* by Donald R. Prothero] beagle-sized, three-toed horse from middle Eocene
orok: [Slovak norok elision] mink-like mammaloid
orole: amphibian from Relegooturnia (Phoenix IV), Galaxiki galaxy
orphan bird: [*The Big Bad Book of Beasts* by Michael Largo] 1-meter bird with heron-like body, hawk's beak, red, white and black striped feathers that lays its eggs on water
orray: [*Creatures of the Galaxy* by Phil Brucato, Bill Smith, Rick D. Stuart, Chuck Truett] horse-alligator-like creature from Jedi galaxy
orse: ["The Legend of Sleepy Hollow" by Washington Irving] headless horse from Sleepy Hollow, NY, Terra (alpha Zodiaci III), see gan ceann
orsu: [Finnish norsu elision] pachyderm
orsuk: [Durdekors "supermonster"] giant anthropoid with sharp teeth and broken ugly face

orthopoi: [Pellucidar series by Edgar Rice Burroughs] small, 3-toed equine from Pellucidar
ortic: [citron ortic palindrome] yellowish green ornithoid
otili: [notilli elision] ziliton-like amphisbæna
oryx: [*National Geographic Encyclopedia of Animals*] antelope relative from Arabia, Terra (alpha Zodiaci III)
os: [sonak ananymondegreen] 1-eyed quadruped from Ka system; [sonarkne ananymondegreen] 1-eyed quadruped with 2 antennae from Enkra system
osaur: [titanosaur mondegreen] amphibious bipedal lizard from Tita system
otaur: [osaur minotaur portmanteau] amphibious bipedal bovinoid
osc: [pronounced "usk"] little, gentle creature that swims on river's surface during day, feeding on "fluff and water-weed which other creatures do not need", hangs bat-like at night
oscar: [*Monster Spotter's Guide to North America* by Scott Francis] aka beast of Busco, 1.8-meter turtle from Lake Fulk, Ind., Terra (alpha Zodiaci III)
oscine: [*Dell Crossword Puzzle Dictionary*] songbird
óserp: [Catalan ós-serp portmanteau] bear-snake, furry, boa-like dracoid with claws
osh: [beheaded posh] giant, long-legged gan ceann
osi(c): [Slovenian/Polish nosi(c) elision] ursinoid
oslet: [*Planets of the Galaxy* by Greg Farshtey, Bill Smith, Ed Stark] 3-meter tall, timid, arboreal creature, used as mount, from Sio jungle on Joralia, Jedi galaxy
osmilus: [prosansanosmilus mondegreen] cat-like nimravid from Sa, Prosa system
osmirc: [crimson osmirc palindrome] crimson red ornithoid, see rolgn
ossard: [drassonax ananymondegreen] sea bear from Xa system
ossolb: [cherry blossom ossolb yrrehc palindrome] light pink yrrehc
oston: [not so hairy riah oston palindrome] short-haired riah

ostonster: [oston monster portmanteau] monstrous short-haired riah
ostrich horse: [Avatar: The Last Airbender: "The Spirit World"] steed with short feathers, ostrich-like legs, wings and feet, hairy tail, horse-like neck and head, beak
osuni: [sinusonasus ananymondegreen] long-legged troodont from Susa system, see evoni
ot: [toy ot palindrome] small, otter-like pet
otaria: [pithanotaria mondegreen] sea lion from Pitha system
otary: [*Dell Crossword Puzzle Dictionary*] seal with ears
ote: [Eton ote palindrome] greenish blue ornithoid
oteltsac: [Castleton oteltsac palindrome] green ornithoid
othere: [hunanothere, titanothere mondegreens] rhinoid beast from Tita, giraffe-like beast from Huna system
otherhand: [handbird extrapolation] variety of handbird, see onehand
otleb: [belton otleb palindrome] furry with small patches or spots, see edkcelf, elkcep, ekcit
otornis: [notornis elision] ear-winged ornithoid
otselrahc: [Charleston otselrahc palindrome] dark green ornithoid
otsi: [tsuganotsi mondegreen] centipede from Tsuga system
otter-fowl: [Arkarian waterfowl spoonerism] predatory weasel-bird from Warkar system
otter-penguin: [Avatar: The Last Airbender: "The Boy in the Iceberg"] amphibian with seal-like face, otter's tail and 4 flippers
ottern: [otter-tern portmanteau] otter-like amphibious ornithoid
otvi: [otvi divto palindrome] divtoid amphisbæna
otylop: [titanotylopus mondegreen] cameloid from Tita system
otyugh: [Gary Gygax in *Monster Manual III*] 2.4-meter, sewer-dwelling creature with rock-hard brownish-gray skin, 3 thick legs, 3 eyes on leaf-like stalk, 2 long tentacles with bony torn-like ridges, related to lifeleech

ouar: [anouar mondegreen] white, furry, nocturnal predator with red eyes from A
oucher-poucher: [*National Geographic Picture Atlas of Our Universe* by Michael Whelan] metallophagous life-form that moves by inflating pouch-like hydrogen sac and making bouncing landings from Venus (alpha Zodiaci II)
ouija creature: [Linda Moore's daughter] black creature with red eyes, triangular head, pointy fingerless arms that move spider-like
ounce: [*Dell Crossword Puzzle Dictionary*] snow leopard or panther
ouniao: [beheaded touniao] 5-headed bird of ill omen
ouroboros: [Piers Anthony] black-and-white water dragon from Xanth, see hoop snake
ous: [quadrumanous mondegreen] 4-armed pongoid from Quadruma system
overboard: [upboard extrapolation] queen board, see board, upboard, underboard
overland snail: [Xanth series by Piers Anthony] fast-moving variety of snail used for message transport from Xanth
overworm: [*Greyhawk Monstrous Compendium Appendix* by Mike Breault, etal.] giant worm in service to Kyuss the Worm King from Greyhawk
ovis: [OviPets] egg-laying cow-like bovinoid
ovus: [OviPets] bispheroid with headspikes and beak
ow: [curtailed owl] flightless owl-like ornithoid
owf: [snowflake ooze spoonerism mondegreen] sleep-inducing freshwater ichthyoid from Rovarga, Gravor system, Galaxiki galaxy
owl-fly: [Xanth series by Piers Anthony] large-eyed, tufted, stealthy insect from Xanth
owl-monkey: [owl monkey mondegreen] owl-mimicking winged simian
owlbear: ["The Ecology of the Owlbear" by Jonathan M. Richards] aka wildkin, 2.5-meter, carnivorous griffinoid
owlreed: [Monster Galaxy] book-eating, purple and white owl-like ornithoid from Aquarius constellation

owltiger: ["The Hunting" by Doris Beetem] owl-like ornithoid with ears and beak-like fangs

owon: ["Time Squared" by Maurice Hurley] brown chicken-like egg-layer

owonster: [owon monster portmanteau] monstrous, brown chicken-like ornithoid

owriss: ["Ewoks" series] large, harmless amorph from Endor's moon, Jedi galaxy

oxyaena: [*After the Dinosaurs* by Donald R. Prothero] jaguar-sized, small-brained creodont from late Paleocene and early Eocene

oysteer: [oyster-steer portmanteau] amphibian with oyster-like shell and retractable hooved legs and horned head

oystercracker: [oyster cracker mondegreen] aquatic predator of oysters that cracks rather than mere prys open oyster shell

oyster-man: [oysterman mondegreen] oyster-headed anthropoid

ozama: [Amazon ozama palindrome] green ornithoid

ozuma: [*Ozuma* by Leiji Matsumoto] giant sand-whale

ozoa: telepathic, asexual jellyfish-like sea creature with 24 eyes from Polypo (Viola-Stauro III), Galaxiki galaxy

ozorbo: [ozorbo cobrozo palindrome] corbrozo-like amphisbæna

P-rex: [Outernauts] aka pataraur rex, mature pataraur

p'eng-niao: thunderbird from China, Terra (alpha Zodiaci III)

pa: [gappa mondegreen] gray-green dracoid

pab: [Fr. Johann Martin Schleyer's Volapük] butterfly-like insectoid from Schleyer's system

paca: [*Dell Crossword Puzzle Dictionary*] rodent from S. America, Terra (alpha Zodiaci III), see cavy, degu, coypu, agouti

pacd: [*Les Adventures de Jacques Sadeur* by Gabriel Foigny] gregarious songbird from Terre Australe

pacer: [*The Anoma* by Jack Vance] draft creature from Durdane descended from bullocks

pachycephalosaur: ["boneheaded lizard"] 4.6-meter bipedal sauroid with thick knobby skull from Cretaceous

pachycephalotaur: pachycephalosaur minotaur portmanteau] bovinoid with thick knobby skull

packrabbit: [pack rat-jackrabbit portmanteau] rabbit-like burrowing, borrowing creature

packrattler: [pack rat-rattler portmanteau] snake-like borrowing burrower with rattle on tail, related to siiloks

packtail: [Pern series by Ann McCaffrey] food ichthyoid from Pern (alpha Sagittarii) III)

paco: [OviPets] egg-laying llama-like ruminant

pacolet: [*Dell Crossword Puzzle Dictionary*] swift horse

paddelfin: [Danish padde-delfin portmanteau] aka paddlefin, amphibian-dolphin, amphibious sirenian-like cetacean

paddler: [*Monster Spotter's Guide to North America* by Scott Francis] lake snake with flippers from Lake Pend Oreille, Idaho, Terra (alpha Zodiaci III)

pädrit: [Fr. Johann Martin Schleyer's Volapük] partridge-like ornithoid from Schleyer's system

paf: [Fr. Johann Martin Schleyer's Volapük] peacock-like ornithoid from Schleyer's system

pafkurma: [James Cooke Brown's Loglan pafto kurma compound] digworm from Logla, Brown's system

pagen: [*Creatures of the Galaxy* by Phil Brucato, Bill Smith, Rick D. Stuart, Chuck Truett] blue and red swamp ornithoid from Windsor, Jedi galaxy; [dragon spoonerisms] dangerous dracoid from Dranzer system or harmless one from Driffer system

paguar: [panther jaguar portmanteau] panther-headed jaguar-like felinoid

paiku suru: [*Cyclopedia of Worlds*] 136-meter, smoky pink or orange superpredator with 4 paddle-like fins, claw-like mandibles, hunted for "dakkasword" and paiki soup from Dakka, Neptune system

pairodd: [The Legend of Zelda] teleporting parrot-like ornithoid from Koholint Island, Hyrule

pake: [pit of snakes spoonerism, pakicetus snake portmanteau] snake-like pakicetus relative

pakicetus: [*After the Dinosaurs* by Donald R. Prothero] whale ancestor related to mesonynch and ambulocetus

pal: [pal-rai-yûk mondegreen] seaserpent-like tizheruk ancestor

pale whale: [pod of whales, Moby Dick spoonerisms] aka doby mick, missing link between white and gray whales

paleoryct: [*After the Dinosaurs* by Donald R. Prothero] shrew-like insectivorous mammal from Paleocene

paleorys: [*After the Dinosaurs* by Donald R. Prothero] giraffe ancestor from Chattian age (late Oligocene)

paleosaur: ["The Giant Behemoth" by Robert Abel and Allen Adler] 1.2-meter tall, 1.8-meter long, long-necked quadrupedal reptilian amphibian

paleotaur: [paleosaur minotaur portmantreau] long-necked, long, amphibious bovinoid

palido: [Final Fantasy] pale, pearl flan-thick ooze

palla: [Finnish ruijanpallas mondegreen] halibut-like ichthyoid from Ruija system

paloma: [*Dell Crossword Puzzle Dictionary*] dove from Spain, Terra (alpha Zodiaci III)

palooski: [*If I Ran the Zoo* by Theodore Seuss Geissel] white-headed blue bird with red crest, blue collar, from Russia, Terra (alpha Zodiaci III)

palorchestes: [*After the Dinosaurs* by Donald R. Prothero] sloth-like marsupial from Pleistocene

palrus: [pod of walruses spoonerism, pal walrus portmanteau] flipper-less walrus-like seaserpent

pamingo: [pink flamingo spoonerism] long-legged, long-necked ornithoid from Flink system

pamola: [Abenaki] aka bmola, moose-headed anthropoid with eagle's wings and feet

pamthret: [*After Man* by Dougal Dixon] puma-like forest pack weasel

pan: [Tev'Meckian] gnu-like ruminant from Tev'Meck, MakTar system; [puddling flan portmanteau] fludding ooze between puddling and flan thickness

pandaken: [Monster Legends] monstrous panda

panda mite: [pandamite mondegreen] small insectoid that infests pandas

pandamite: [Terra Monster] small, red, white and yellow panda-like volcano-dwelling creature, see pandora and pandorum, from Terrarium

pandora: [Terra Monster] red, white and yellow panda-like molten rockeater, see pandamite and pandorum, from Terrarium; [Outernauts] immature pandorus

pandoreign: [Outernaut] mature pandorus

pandorus: [Outernaut] narwhal-like sea creature with see-through skin, see pandora, pandoreign

pandorum: [Terra Monster] large, red, white and yellow lava-eating panda-like creature, see pandamite and pandora, from Terrarium

panee: [Outernauts] immature panso

pangbourne: [*Mothstorm* by Philip Reeve] variety of icthyomorph

pangkarlangu: [*The Yowie: In Seach of Australian Bigfoot* by Tony Healy and Paul Cropper] see yowie

pangolin: scaly anteater that curls and rolls

pann: [Outernauts] mature panso

panni: [James Cooke Brown's Loglan panta nimla (plant-animal) compounds] planimal from Logla, Brown's system

panso: [Outernauts] quadruped with black horn, orange body, yellow mane, see panee, pann

pansy dragon: [Godville] young panzer dragon

panther: [panther backformation] felinoid predator that panths

panti: [James Cooke Brown's Loglan panta titci (plant eater) compound] from Logla, Brown's system

pantolambda: [*After the Dinosaurs* by Donald R. Prothero] dog-sized mammal from Danian age (early Paleocene)

pantolestid: [*After the Dinosaurs* by Donald R. Prothero] swimming and burrowing otter-like mammal from Paleocene
panzer dragon: [Godville] 1-meter dragon that tastes better than chicken, young called pansy dragon
paon: [*Dell Crossword Puzzle Dictionary*] blue peacock
paonster: [paon monster portmanteau] monstrous, blue peacock
papag: [Fr. Johann Martin Schleyer's Volapük] parrot-like ornithoid from Schleyer's system
papagator: [papag alligator portmanteau] alligator-like predator whose bite morphs victim into papag
papaki: [Grk. @ duckling] 2-D, duck-like at
paracerathere: [fka baluchithere] 5.5-meter at shoulder hornless, long-legged rhinoid with longish neck
paracosoryx: [*After the Dinosaurs* by Donald R. Prothero] pronghorn with long-stemmed Y-shaped horns from Miocene
Paradise virus: ["Lost Sorceress of the Silent Citadel" by Michael moorcook] flesh-eating virus in water and "grass" from Mars (alpha Zodiacl IV)
parailurus: [*After the Dinosaurs* by Donald R. Prothero] panda from Zanclean age (early Piocene)
paraka: ["Warlord" by Lisa Klink] winged creature from Delta Quadrant
parapara parsite: [Tokyo Mew Mew] causes gigantism
paraque: [*National Geographic Encyclopedia of Animals*] potoo relative from S. and Meso-America, Terra (alpha Zodiaci III)
parasauroloph: [*The Mistaken Extinction* by Lowell Dingus and Timothy Rowe] ornithopod descendant
parashrew: [*After Man* by Dougal Dixon] shrew-like mammal with umbrella-like tail used for parachuting
paratoceras: [*After the Dinosaurs* by Donald R. Prothero] protoceras with small nose-horns, short, wide-bottomed horns over eyes and V-shaped horns behind ears

paravane: [*Dell Crossword Puzzle Dictionary*] otter
parc: [scarpy parcs palindrome] fighting-cock-like ornithoid
parg: [Crayola grape parg palindrome] purplish creature from Crayol A, see rebye
pargator: [parg alligator portmanteau] alligator-like predator whose bite morphs victim into parg
pargo: [*Dell Crossword Puzzle Dictionary*] porgy from Europe, Terra (alpha Zodiaci III)
parictis: [*After the Dinosaurs* by Donald R. Prothero] bear-like pinniped ancestor
parlor snake: snake adapted to parlor, see lounge lizard
parmops: [Estonian parm-mops portmanteau] horsefly-pug, ugly, small griffinoid fond of horses
parody: [Xanth series by Piers Anthony, parrot-chickadee portmanteau] green-winged mimicking bird with downward curved beak from Xanth
parr: [*Dell Crossword Puzzle Dictionary*] young salmon, see grilse, skegger
parrot fish: [parrotfish mondegreen] colorful, beaked ichthyoid
parrot-lizard: see psittacosaur
parrotter: [parrot-otter, par-rotter portmanteau] triphibian with hooked bill, webbed feet, dense, dark brown fur-like feathers and secreting a decay accellerant (par)
parrowl: [parrow-owl portmanteau] lark-sparrow-owl-like ornithoid
Party Beach monster: ["The Horror of Party Beach" by Richard L. Hilliard] mutant sea creature combined with human corpse in form of blood-thirsty humanoid with large scales, claws, dorsal fin, spiny-ray ears, bursts into flame with contact with sodium
partysaurus: [Toy Story Toons: "Partysaurus Rex" by Mark A, Walsh] dinosaur-like toy animal animated by love of partying
parus: [*Dell Crossword Puzzle Dictionary*] titmouse, see mag
paschathere: [*After the Dinosaurs* by Donald R. Prothero] earliest tethythere (elephant and

manatee ancestor) from late Paleocene, related to minchenella

pat: [pounce of cats, a counts of pats spoonerism]

patao: [*Dell Crossword Puzzle Dictionary*] mojerra fish

pataraur: [Outernauts] green lizard with red backspikes, see patchoo, P-rex

patas: [*Dell Crossword Puzzle Dictionary*] red monkey from S. Africa, Terra (alpha Zodiaci III)

patchoo: [Outernauts] immature pataraur

patriofelis: [*After the Dinosaurs* by Donald R. Prothero] leopard-sized creodont from Ypresian age (early Eocene)

pavo: [Dell Crossword Puzzle Dictionary] peacock, see mao

pavonis: [piscium extrapolation] peacock-like ornithoid

pawk: [pigeon-hawk portmanteau] see pigeon-hawk

pay: [party of jays spoonerism, pavo bluejay portmanteau] blue peacock-like ornithoid

PBO: [Planetary Bacteria Organism acronym, *Introduction a la Nouvelle Bacteriologie* by Dr. Sorin Sonea and Dr. Maurice Panisset] intelligent, but non-sentient, super-organism able to terraform planets and resist antibiotics,

pe: [Serbocroatian pecat mondegreen] seal-cat or sea-cat ancestral to cat and seal from Skjoob, Bjosko system, Galaxiki galaxy

peach jelly: [jelly extrapolation] jelly-thick ooze

peacockatoo: [peacock-cockatoo portmanteau] blue-green iridescent ornithoid with long erectile crest and fan-like tail

peacock-fish: [peacock fish] peacock-like ichthyopteryx

peacockroach: [peacock-cockroach portmanteau] blue-green iridescent insectoid with long erectile crest and fan-like tail

Peaf owl: [peafowl mondegreen] peacock-like owl from Peaf system

peafyx: [Monster Galaxy] vulpine with peacock feather collar and tail from Taurus constellation

peak bear: ["Ms. Midshipwoman Harrington" by David Weber] bear-like creature from Sphinx

peakcock: [proud as a peacock mondegreen] mountain-dwelling cock-like ornithoid from Prowdaza system

peal: [pod of seals, pea-green seal portmanteau] light green seal that makes a bell-like cry

peanut butter jellyfish: [Godville] jellyfish that tastes vaguely like peanuts

pear jelly: [jelly extrapolation] jelly-thick ooze

peascorp: [Monster Galaxy] blue, herbivorous scorpion-like creature with 5 stingers with eye-like spots from Scorpio

peasel: [pack of weasels spoonerism, peascorp weasel portmanteau] weasel-like predator with eye-like spots

pechav: [pechavy backformation] small, yellow-furred slug-like creature

pechavy: [*Big Planet* by Jack Vance] sluggish, yellow-furred sheep-sized creature from the Big Planet

peekin' pom: [*Rainbeau's Riddles and Rhymes*] cross between Pekinese and Pomeranian canines

peele: [*Dell Crossword Puzzle Dictionary*] reebok

pega: [*Dell Crossword Puzzle Dictionary*] suckerfish, see remora, lootsman

pegasaur: pterosaur with bird-like wings

pegasi: [piscium extrapolation] egg-laying pegasoid

pegasus: [Greek] equinopteryx with bird-like wings

pegataur: ["Top Ballista" by Carl Sargent] bovinopteryx with bird-like wings

peixinxa: [Catalan peix-xinxa portmanteau] fish-bedbug, riverbed-dwelling, bloodsucking parasite

pejin: [Fr. Johann Martin Schleyer's Volapük] pigeon-like ornithoid from Schleyer's system

peke: [*Dell Crossword Puzzle Dictionary*, Pekinese contraction] small dog, see pug, pup, feist, pom

peko: [backformation] peko peko-like nasna

peko peko: ["The Gungan Frontier" by Chris McCubbin] large, purple, long-tailed reptilian with venomous blood and mimicry
pelecanimimus: ["pelican-mimic", Feathered Dinosaurs: The Origin of Birds by John Long and Peter Schuten] bird-like dinosaur with 220 teeth
pelek: [Fr. Johann Martin Schleyer's Volapük] pelican-like ornithoid from Schleyer's system
pelficli: [James Cooke Brown's Loglan pelpi ficli] leatherfish from Logla, Brown system
pelgrane: [*Rhialto* by Jack Vance] subdyvolt with white fangs, clawed hands, black horn, hard leathery gargoyle-like body, great hatchet-like beak, leering eyes
pelorovis: [*After the Dinosaurs* by Donald R. Prothero] giant ram with 2-meter horn span from Pleistocene
pelüd: [Fr. Johann Martin Schleyer's Volapük] octopus-like cephalopodan from Schleyer's system
peluda: [Giants, Monsters and Dragons by Carol Rose] green dragon with poisonous quills, snake's head, neck and tail, large tortoise-like feet, in hellfire or water or acid breathing varieties from La Ferté-Bernard, France, [*Here Be Monsters almanac*] "shaggy beast' with poisonous saliva
pen: [*Dell Crossword Puzzle Dictionary*] female swan, see penguin and pendrill
pendrill: [Terra Monster] large flightless ornithoid with wings adapted as drills, see turanon and chillbeak, from Terrarium
pengator: [penguin-alligator portmanteau, The Legend of Zelda: "A Link to the Past"] polar predator that attacks by sliding on belly
pengoo: [Monster Galaxy] pig-like iglooid adapted to cold
penguinsect: [penguin-insect portmanteau] black and white amphibious insectoid
pentabrach: [*Trillion: Alaster 2262* by Jack Vance] small, edible, 5-limbed sea creature
pentagiraffe: [fairy chess] camelopardian with leg-like tail
pentapus: [Avatar: The Last Airbenders: "Return of Omashu"] tiny, purple, sewer-dwelling hand-like cephalopodan with suckered tentacles
pentapuss: [pentapus puss portmanteau] felinoid with leg-like tail
pentaskylos: [tetraskylos extrapolation] 5-headed hellhound
pepperfish: [*Blue World* by Jack Vance] ichthyoid from the Blue World, in hotpepper variety
peraceras: [*After the Dinosaurs* by Donald R. Prothero] acerathere from Miocene
perceb: [*Wyst: Alastor 1716* by Jack Vance] small mollusc of sub-surface rocks on shore of Moaning Ocean, delicacy when fried in nut oil with aiole from Wyst
perdaas: [Afrikaans perd-daas portmanteau] horse-horsefly, small insectoid pegasus
Perfectly Normal Beast: [Hitchhiker's Guide to the Galaxy series by Douglas Adams] migratory bovinoid able to travel trough portals from Anhondo plain, Lamuella, etc., see kapnorvalni, doorilope
pern: [*Dell Crossword Puzzle Dictionary*] honey buzzard
perpent: [polar-serpent spoonerism] snake-like plasmoid creature from alpha Zodiaci, not to be confused with flare
Persian ass: [*The Big Bad Book of Beasts* by Michael Largo] horse-like triped with nose-bump, 4 eye (2 on back), related to indricotherium
peryton: ["The Ecology of the Peryton" by Nigel Findley] blue-black and dark green stag-headed eagle with 7.5-meter wingspan, obsidian antlers, that smells like Human, eats humanoid hearts ["Xoology" by Kittenbaker] from Szurane, [*Here Be Monsters almanac*] Europe, Terra (alpha Zodiaci III)
pesanat: [Catalan] nocturnal, black, hairy large dog, cat or nimravid with steely claws and holey paws
peshkorb: [Albanian peshk-korb portmanteau] fish-raven, triphibous black ornithoid
petelen: [Bulgarian petel-elen portmanteau] rooster-deer, pegasoid with antlers, crest and

wattle pegasoid from Peggassa, Hippocrenea system, Galaxiki galaxy

peto: [*Dell Crossword Puzzle Dictionary*] wahoo fish

petrel: [*Dell Crossword Puzzle Dictionary*] sea bird, see ern(e), gull, skua, scaup, tern, fulmar, gannet, scoter, [*National Geographic Encyclopedia of Animals*] from S. Pacific, Terra (alpha Zodiaci III)

pett: [pettish backformation] small, insecotivore

peuchen: [*Chilota, Chiloe Misterioso* by Oscar Martinez Vilches] gigantic, vampiric, serpentine flying dragon that whistles, with petrifying gaze

pezosiren: [*After the Dinosaurs* by Donald R. Prothero] sirenian ancestor with hands and feet from Eocene Tethys Sea

pfit: [*After Man* by Dougal Dixon] anteater-like insectivorous mammal small enough to waterwalk

pfph: [*Star Rangers* by Andre Norton] beast of burden from Falthar

pfrdffl: ["Space Rats of the CCC" by Harry Harrison] nitrogen-breathing creature noted for drunkenness from Planizz

pfugux: [*Ghost-Walker* by Barbara Hambly] herding creature from Midgwis (Elcidar Beta III)

Phaaxan goose: [fox and goose mondegreen] goose-like ornithoid from Phaaxa system

phage: ["eating"] see venom; ["Phage" by Timothy DeHaas, "The Offering" by Dan Simmons] aka cancer vampire, extradimensional insectoidal grub that eats organs

phaléne-porcépic: [*Another World* by Jean-Ignace-Isidore Gérard] moth-headed porcupine from Gérard's world

phandom: [Outernauts] orange, one-horned, one-eyed ultradimensional cephalopoid

phantar: [Outernauts] mature phandom

phantom bird: invisible predatory bird from Beloro (Rod Brown of the Rocket Rangers: "The Phantom Birds of Beloro")

phantom catfish: [Here Be Monsters almanac] catfish caught with gummy worms

phantoo: [Outernauts] immature phandom

pharm animal: animal useful for pharmecology

pharple: [*Creatures of the Galaxy* by Phil Brucato, Bill Smith, Rick D. Stuart, Chuck Truett] small to medium-sized game ornithoid from Lok, Jedi galaxy

phase spider: [*Monster Manual* by Skip Williams, etal.] giant, 2-eyed green-and-white spider

phenacodont: [*After the Dinosaurs* by Donald R. Prothero] horse-like from Paleocene/early Eocene

Phillip cay duck: [Phillip K. Dick pun] duck from Phillip cay

phoebe: [*National Geographic Encyclopedia of Animals*] insect, fish and berry-eating flycatcher bird from Americas, Terra (alpha Zodiaci III)

Phoenix flu viroid: ["Invasion" by Robin Cook] meteorite-protected mutagenic virus-like creature that transforms into scaly-skinned, 4-armed, bug-eyed monster

phoenicis: [piscium extrapolation] phoenix-like ornithoid

phoenix: [Greek] bird with yellow neck, red-purple body, blue-with-rose tail, large plume that hatches egg by self-cremation between 350 and 12,994 years, see benu, fêng-huang

phog: ["Phog" by Poul Anderson] scummy, stinking, deadly gaseous creature from Phoebus system

phogator: [phog alligator portmanteau] alligator-like predator whose bite morphs victim into phog

phorusrhacos: 2-meter tall eagle-beaked creature from Patagonia, Terra (alpha Zodiaci III)

photh: [Thongor series by Lin Carter] scarlet vampire bat

phranna: ["Courtesan of the Empire" by Alexander Huiskes] 3-meter food fish from mangrove forest of Jusimal

phroomis: [Babylon 5: "Duet for Human and Narn in C Sharp" by David Gerrold] Narn delicacy

phryix: ravenous, aquatic rodentoid from Zlay, Golden Axe system, Galaxiki galaxy

pi uao: one-horned lion-like pterosaur with no anus

pi(an)et: [*Dell Crossword Puzzle Dictionary*] magpie, see mag(g), pie(t), piot, pyot, pyet, ninut

piasa: [Illini "giant bird that devours man", *Monster Spotter's Guide to North America* by Scott Francis] scaly, antlered, man-eating pterosaur with long, poisoned-barbed tail

piatek: [Armeniana] large mammal with hair sticking out and large beak from Armenia, Terra (alpha Zodiaci III)

piccoloer: [trumpeter swan backformation] small flute swan-like ornithoid with piccolo-like call

picdar: [*La Découverte de L'Empire de Cantahar* by De Varennes dc Mondasse] green, bear-sized, creature with white spots, leopard-like head, hunted though dangerous from Cantahar Island

piche: [*Dell Crossword Puzzle Dictionary*] monkey from S. America, Terra (alpha Zodiaci III)

pici: [*Dell Crossword Puzzle Dictionary*] woodpecker

picken: [Avatar: The Last Airbender: "Zuko Alone"] pig-headed hen with pig legs, see pigster

picklepuss: [Xanth series by Piers Anthony] feline with green, prickly snout that pickles with its salty tears from Xanth

picktooth: [*After Man* by Dougal Dixon] rabbuck with 2 tusks and foreleg spurs

picogurp: [centigurp extrapolation] pink furball able to bounce, roll, fond of spheres, and be in nineplex places at once, see gurp

picture-winged fly: [Xanth series from Piers Anthony] small butterfly-like insect with wings mimicking various art forms including charcoal, crayon-drawing, cubist, naturalistic, oil, pastel chalk, pastoral, pen-and-ink, still-life, surrealistic, watercolor from Xanth

picule: [*Dell Crossword Puzzle Dictionary*] small woodpecker

pie(t): [*Dell Crossword Puzzle Dictionary*] magpie, see mag(g), piot, pyot, pyet, ninut, pi(an)et

piebald rat: [*Edge Chronicles* by Paul Stewart and Chris Riddell] black and white spotted, inedible sewer rat

piercer: [*Monster Manual* by Gary Gygax] stalactite-mimicking gastropod with second slow-digesting stomach, in black, gray, green or blue varieties, tastes like snail, related to darkmantle, roper and lou carcolh

piffilosaur: [*Dr. Doolittle and the Secret Lake* by Hugh Lofting] diploducus-like dinosaur from No-Man's-Land

pigadillo: [picadillo malapropism, "Robot Hugs" by R. Hugs'] armadillo-like armored porcoid

pigasus: [Godville] aka flying pig, pegasus-like porcoid from Cincinnati, OH, Terra (alpha Zodiaci III)

pigator: [pig-alligator portmanteau] aquatic carnivorous sauroid with cloven hooves and cartilaginous snout from Adiusa, Goodiusa system, Galaxiki galaxy

pigeon-hawk: [pigeon hawk mondegreen] ornithoid with pigeon-like head with hawk-like body

pigeon-toad: [pigeon-toed mondegreen] pigeon-headed triphibious batrachoid

pigg: [piggish, piggy backformation] omnivorous porcoid, see hogg, swin

piggator: [pigg alligator portmanteau] alligator-like predator whose bite morphs victim into pigg

piggy-back: [Xanth series by Piers Anthony] plump, pink-skinned porcoid steed from Xanth

pigmole: [Tengen Toppe Gurren Lagunn] pig-like mole burrower

pigmy hippo: [*History of the Great Island of Madagascar* by Étienne de Flacourt] small hippopotamus from Madagascar, Terra (alpha Zodiaci III)

pigmy pompom: small furball with mouth and eyes from Callisto, Jupiter (alpha Zodiaci Vd)

pigmy puff: [*Fantastic Beasts and Where to Find* Them by Newton Artemis Fido Scamander] small pink or purple variety of puffskein

pigoose: [pig-goose portmanteau] griffinoid with longish neck, short, pointed beak and cloven hooves from Adiusa, Goodiusa system, Galaxiki galaxy

pigster: [Avatar: The Last Airbender: "Zuko Alone"] pig-headed rooster with pig legs, that pigsts, see picken

pihippus: [beheaded epihippus] small, 3-toed gam ceann

pihwaya: [papaya whip pihwaya pap palindrome] pale orange ornithoid that regurgitates food for its young

pihwrohena: [pihwrohena anchorwhip palindrome] anchorwhip-like amphisbæna

pika: [*National Geographic Encyclopedia of Animals*] small rabbit relative from Asia, Terra (alpha Zodiaci III), [*Dell Crossword Puzzle Dictionary*] rabbit-like rodent, "rat hare"

pike-man: [pikeman mondegreen] ichthropoid with pike-like head

pikka: [Hitchhiker's Guide to the Galaxy series by Douglas Adams] magpie-like ornithoid unsurprized by the Perfectly Normal Beasts' interplanetary migrations from Lamuella

pikobi: ["The Gungan Frontier" by Chris McCubbin] web-footed therapod with long beak and tail from Naboo, Jedi galaxy

pil: [Fr. Johann Martin Schleyer's Volapük] eel-like ichthyoid from Schleyer's system

pilchard: [*Dell Crossword Puzzle Dictionary*] see fumado, sardine

pililli: [*Mémoires De Sir George Wallop* by Pierre Chevalier Duplessis] blue and red dove from Aprilis, New Britain Islands

pilkatma: [James Cooke Brown's Loglan pilni katma] flatcat from Logla, Brown's system

pillar snouter: [*The Snouters* by Harald Stümpke] crab-eating stationary snouter in symbiosis with secretion-loving suctorial snout leaper from Hi-Yi-Yi Islands

pillbug: aka roly-poly, slater, sowbug, wood louse that moves by curling and rolling

pillbugator: [pillbug alligator portmanteau] alligator-like predator whose bite morphs victim into pillbug

pilofile: [*After Man* by Dougal Dixon] insectivore with sharp summer beak and hairy funnel for catching insects, with long winter beak for probing for insects

pilot fish: [Xanth series by Piers Anthony] arboreal ichthyoid fond of plane trees from Xanth

piltcela: [James Cooke Brown's Loglan pilni tcela] flatwing from Logla, Brown's system

pinch: [Xanth series by Piers Anthony] little ornithoid with large beak from Xanth

pinclaw: [Terra Monster] creature from Terrarium

pind: [Danish pindsvin mondegreen] hedgehog-pig, burrowing porcoid ancestral to pig and hedgehog

pineapple jelly: [jelly extrapolation] jelly-thick ooze

pink elephant: ["Pink Elephants on Parade" by Ned Washington] pink elephant-like hyperdimensional

pink panther: [Pink Panther series] pink panther-like bipedal felinoid adapted to pink desert sand

pinnipex: [Cyclopedia of Worlds] 3.5-meter, crawling worm-like swamp-dweller from Scanodon, Croft system

pinocchio frog: [National Geographic] long-nosed frog from New Guinea, Terra (alpha Zodiaci III)

pinocchio frogator: [pinocchio frog alligator portmanteau] alligator-like predator whose bite morphs victim into pinocchio frog

pintano: [*Dell Crossword Puzzle Dictionary*] sier-like damselfish

pinto: [*Dell Crossword Puzzle Dictionary*] piebald or mottled horse

piot: [*Dell Crossword Puzzle Dictionary*] magpie, see mag(g), pyot, pie(t), pyet, ninut, pi(an)et

pipee: [sandpiper backformation] sand-dwelling insect prey of sandpiper

pipi: [*Dell Crossword Puzzle Dictionary*] mollusk from New Zeeland, Terra (alpha Zodiaci III)

pipit: [*Dell Crossword Puzzle Dictionary*] titlark

pipius: ["Matter of Honor" by Burton Armus] Klingom food animal

pippohotamimus: [pippohotamus backformation] non-fire-resistant from Pippo-no-Pungu jungle

pippohotamus: [hippopotamus spoonerism] fire-resistant hippoid from Pippo-no-Pungu jungle

piraiba: ["evil mother of all fishes", *River Monsters* by Jeremy Wade] 3.3-meter, 200-kg fish with 40-cm mouth from Amazonia, Terra (alpha Zodiaci III)

piranha bird: [Showcase #91: "The Planet of Death"] voracious pack-hunting ornithoid

piranhamouse: [Mad Magazine: "Woodlore"] voracious pack-attacking field mouse with red armpit marks

pirarucu: ["redfish", *River Monsters* by Jeremy Wade] arapaima from Amazonia, Terra (alpha Zodiaci III)

pird: [pod of birds spoonerism, pirarucu bird portmanteau] red ichthyormithoid

pirounicervus: [candiacervus extrapolation] deer with fork-like antlers

piscium: [OviPets] egg-laying ichthyoid

pismire: [Geoffrey Chaucer] ant attracted to urine, see emmet

pistolwig: [whistlepig spoonerism] anteater-like creature with tubular snout and wig-like crest

pistolwigator: [pistolwig alligator portmanteau] alligator-like predator whose bite morphs victim into pistowig

pithanotaria: [*After the Dinosaurs* by Donald R. Prothero] sea lion ancestor from Miocene

pitoloha: [fanamin-pitoloha mondegreen] amin-like hydra from Pa (iota Orionis) system

pitta: [*National Geographic Encyclopedia of Animals*] forest-dwelling bird from Australasia, Terra (alpha Zodiaci III)

pitwing: [Outernauts] mature rotwing, in ice variety

pitwingator: [pitwing alligator portmanteau] alligator-like predator whose bite morphs victim into pitwing

pla rahu: [Thai "eclipse fish", *River Monsters* by Jeremy Wade] 90-kg sea or river stingray

plaga: [pl. plagas, *Resident Evil 4*] includes blade plage, centipede plage, leech plage, spider plage, whip plage

plagator: [plaga alligator portmanteau] alligator-like predator whose bite morphs victim into plaga

plague crawler: [Resident Evil 0] 2-meter insectoid victim of T-virus

plaise: [*National Geographic Encyclopedia of Animals*] mollusc-eating perch relative from Europe, Terra (alpha Zodiaci III)

plantimal: [plant animal portmanteau, Blackhawk #218] 21-meter long plant-like creature with mossy body, 4 thin legs, 3-toed feet, frog-like head, 6 tentacles with twin end-tendrils from Ezz; any plant mimic

plateosaur: [*The Mistaken Extinction* by Lowell Dingus and Timothy Rowe] sauropodomorph, not actually a sauropod

platybelodon: ["shovel-tusk"] elephant ancestor with broad blade-like lower teeth

platygonus: [*After the Dinosaurs* by Donald R. Prothero] warthog-like peccary from Zanclean age (early Pliocene)

platyplus: [platypus-plus portmanteau] platypus-like creature with two duckbilled heads and beavertail

platypus bear: [Avatar: The Last Airbender: "The Fortuneteller"] creature with bear's, teeth-lined bill, flat webbed hind feet, beaver-like tail, bear-like body

playsaurus: [Cloudstone] playful plesiosaurus-like sea monster

plesiadapid: [*After the Dinosaurs* by Donald R. Prothero] primitive primate with rodent-like head and ground squirrel-like body from Danian age (early Paleocene), replaced by omomyid and adapid

plesiocyon: [*After the Dinosaurs* by Douglas R. Prothero] bear-like pinniped ancestor

plesiosaur: ["near-lizard"] aquatic dinosaur with long neck, unfluked tail, and flippers

plesiotaur: [plesiosaur minotaur portmanteau] aquatic bovinoid with long neck, unfluked tail, and flippers

plimpie: [*Fantastic Beasts and Where to Find Them* by Newton Artemis Fido Scamander] spherical biped sea bottom-dweller

Pliocene clam: [Jeff Jones] ravenous man-eater said to have roamed wetland

plioceras: [*After the Dinosaurs* by Donald R. Prothero] pre-pronghorn with short wide horns from Miocene

plioloph: [*After the Dinosaurs* by Donald R. Prothero] horse from Ypresian age (early Eocene)

pliosaur: whale-like plesiosaur

pliotaur: [pliosaur minotaur portmanteau] whale-like bovinoid

plodder: [plodder backformation] slow-moving, but well-armored, chelonian that plodds (moves slowly)

plofle: [i-less pilofile] cave-dwelling ornithoid with summer and winter bills from Friatica, Friaticalida system, Galaxiki galaxy

plog: [golp plog palindrome] monster with purple spots, flaming mouth and ears

plogator: [plog alligator portmanteau] alligator-like predator whose bite morphs victim into plog

ploppah: [Outernaut] light brown blob with top curl, see pudoo, monsturd

plovee: [plover backformation] insect prey of plover

pluck: [plump of ducks spoonerism, plucked duck portmanteau] featherless, aquatic ornithoid

plum jelly: [jelly extrapolation] purplish jelly-thick ooze

pmah: [shampoo pmahs palindrome] pink poo-mimic

pmu: [pmu rump palindrome] food animal

PNB: [acromyn] see Perfectly Normal Beast

po: [police mondegreen] peace-keeping lice-like insectoid

poa: [Thongor series by Lin Carter] 30-meter long river-dragon with translucent flesh from Lemuria

poad: [pigeon-toad portmanteau] see pigeon-toad

pob: [pudding blob portmanteau] bludding ooze between pudding and blob thickness

pocket gopher: [*After the Dinosaurs* by Donald R. Prothero] small gopher from Eocene

pocket mouse: [*After the Dinosaurs* by Donald R. Prothero] see heteromys

poe: [*Dell Crossword Puzzle Dictionary*] parson bird, see tue, tui, koko

poëbrothere: humpless camel ancestor from Oligocene

poemakreel: [Dutch poema-makreel portmanteau] cougar-mackerel, amphibious predator

pog: [passel or parcel of hogs spoonerism] pig-hog, difficultly tamed porocid; [pack of dogs spoonerism] caninoid

pogator: [pog alligator portmanteau] alligator-like predator whose bite morphs victim into pog

poggle: [*The Future Is Wild* by Dougal Dixon] small, furry cave-dwelling mammalian which feed on seeds gathered by silverspiders who eat their flesh and drink their blood

pogonodon: [*After the Dinosaurs* by Donald R. Prothero] saber-toothed nimravid from Oligocene

pogosaur: [pogostick dinosaur portmanteau] dinosaur with 4 spring-like legs, see brontëosaur

pogotaur: [pogosaur minotaur portmanteau] bovinoid with 4 spring-like legs, see brontëotaur

pogy: [*Dell Crossword Puzzle Dictionary*] menhaden or mossbunker fish, see sardine

poinsetter: [*Rainbeau's Riddles and Rhymes*] cross between pointer and setter canines

poisson d'Avril: [Fren.] easily caught ichthyoid from Avril system

pok: [*Once Burned* by Peter David] large, hairy steed used by Danteri

polar mite: ["Nest" by Scott Peters] tiny, maddening insects from Arctic

polar monkey: ["Crazy as Can Be"] simian adapted to extreme cold

polar mouse: [Avatar: The Last Airbender: "The Boy in the Iceberg"] hamster-like creature with flattened cat's tail, cat-like ears, triangular head
polar-serpent: [*A Hero's Guide to Deadly Dragons* by Hiccup Haddock III] white dragon with faint gray markings able to windsurf very fast across ice from Barbarian archipelago
polarcat: [Jets*Rockets*Spacemen trading card #58] of polar caps from planet Ex
poletake: ["Face To Face With Planet Scanodon" by Rocky Strone] nocturnal hive animal from Scandon
polip: [Fr. Johann Martin Schleyer's Volapük] polyp-like creature from Schleyer's system
poljska: [Croatian poljska ševa mondegreen] lark-like ornithoid
polkadot flu virus: [Odd Squad] virus that induces polkadot markings
pollard: [*Dell Crossword Puzzle Dictionary*] hornless stag
pollarilla: [polar gorilla portmanteau, "The Future Begins" by Roberto Orci and Alex Kurtzman] arctic gorilla-like pongoid from Delta Vega (alpha-4 Lyrae)
pollop: [Catalan poll-llop palindromic portmanteau] louse-wolf, wolf-like caninoid insectoid symbiot hunting in co-operative packs, see llopoll
pollymorph: [polly polymorph portmanteau] shapeshifting parrot-like ornithoid
polopony: ["The Honeymooners" polo pony malapropism] small equinoid
polphin: [pod of dolphins spoonerism] cetacean with paw-like fins
polutan: [*The Howling Stones* by Alan Dean Foster] short, cute biped with dark mournful eyes, ornate feathery crown of Parramat archipelago, Senisran
polve: [pack of wolves spoonerism] wacky caninoid that wacks wabbits
polyceratops: ["many-horned", Monstrorum Historiae by Ulisse Aldrovandi] deer with foliage-like antlers
polytick: [politic mondegreen] tick-like insectoid parasitic gestalt

pom: [*Dell Crossword Puzzle Dictionary*, Pomeranian contraction] small dog, see pug, pup, peke, feist
pomegranate jelly: [jelly extrapolation] tough-skinned, reddish jelly-thick ooze
pomhopper: ["The Gungan Frontier" by Chris McCubbin] large-footed quadrupedal waterwalker that hops to escape poms
pomme panther: [heraldry] monstrous felinoid with green spots, flaming mouth and ears
pongo: huge tiger seashark; man-eating gorilla-like anthropoid
ponik: [*Monster Spotter's Guide to North America* by Scott Francis] 12-meter, dark lake snake with humps, barbels from Lake Pohenegamook, Ontario, Terra (alpha Zodiaci III)
pontophoca: [*After the Dinosaurs* by Donald R. Prothero] with praepusa, crytophoca, leptophoca, the first true seals from Miocene
ponyhopper: ["Protector II: The Aftermath" by Lil Prancer] macropodam equinoid from Theramin
poo: [shampoo pmah mondegreen] fluffy, non-pink ornithoid, see pmah
poochie: ["Lair of the Grimalkin" by G. H. Irwin] feathered serpent
poodle monkey: [Avatar: The Last Airbender: "The Tales of Bas Sing Se"] poodle-like simian
pooh: [Winnie-the-Pooh series by A. A. Milne] bear-like toy animal animated by Love
pook: [parliment of rooks, poo rook portmanteau] fluffy, non-pink rook-like ornithoid
poolic: swamp-dwelling amphibian from KraShur (Krur III), Galaxiki galaxy
popper: [X-COM: Apocalypse] small, blue biped that explodes to attack
poppycock: rooster addicted to poppy seeds, noted for strange cacklings
poraquê: [*River Monsters* by Jeremy Wade] electric "eel" knifefish from Amazonia, Terra (alpha Zodiaci III)
porca: [*The Mammoth Book of Astounding Word Games* by David Richards and Daniel Cohen] killer porcoid

porcabra: [Catalan porc-cabra portmanteau] pig-goat, horned, goateed porcoid
porcanard: [Fren. porc-canard portmanteau] pig-headed duck
porchat: [Fren. porc-chat portmanteau] pig-headed felinoid from Gérard's world from Gérard's world
porcc: [porc-chat mondegreen] pig-cat-in-a-hat
porcideer: ["Robot Hugs" by R. Hugs'] antlered porcupine
porcoq: [French porc-coq portmanteau] pig-rooster, griffinoid with wattle, beak, hooves and short, curly tail from Gérard's world
pore: [yolianpore mondegreen] dust-like omnivore from Yolia, Yol system
porgotca: [James Cooke Brown's Loglan porju gotca [pig/hog/swine goat compound] pig-headed goat from Logla, Brown's system
porgy: [*Dell Crossword Puzzle Dictionary*] fish, see scup
porka: [James Cooke Brown's Loglan porju kangu/katma (pig cat/dog) compound] pig-headed nimravid from Logla, Brown's system
pormurki: [James Cooke Brown's Loglan porju murki] pig monkey from Logla, Brown's system
pornirda: [James Cooke Brown's Loglan porju nirda (pig bird) compound] pig-headed ornithoid from Logla, Brown's system
poro: ["The Pathways of Desire" by Ursula K. LeGuin] food animal from Yirdo
Poroccan oviparum: ["Flashback" by Brannon Braga] oviparous creature from Poroccus IV, Delta Quadrant
porpin: [*After Man* by Dougal Dixon] dolphin-like penguin
porpuss: [porpoise-puss portmanteau] small cetacean with catfish whisker-like barbels
porsimba: [James Cooke Brown's Loglan porju simba (pig lion) compound] pig-headed lion from Logla, Brown's system
portoileh: [heliotrope portoileh palindrome] pink ornithoid
portschen: ["Investments" by Walter John Williams] food animal

posh horse: ["Feast Your Minds"] giant, long-legged horse
posset: [*After Man* by Dougal Dixon] marsupial rainforest pig
possum chicken: [Avatar: The Last Airbender: "The Swamp"] griffinoid with possum's face and prehensile tail, chicken's stubby wings, taloned feet
postdater: [predater backformation] predater descendant
postmort: [post mortum, mort extrapolation] salmon older than 3 years
pota: [potatoes mondegreen] food porcoid with big feet
potak: ["Parturation" by Tom Szollosi] dunghill ornithoid noted for potable glandular secretions from Potak II, Delta Quadrant
potfish spider: [Genius Loci by Ben Aaronovitch] arachnoid from Jaiwan
potoo: [*National Geographic Encyclopedia of Animals*] insectivorous bird from S. America, Terra (alpha Zodiaci III)
potoroo: [*National Geographic Encyclopedia of Animals*] forest mammal from Australia, Terra (alpha Zodiaci III)
Potter moth: [*Mothstorm* by Philip Reeve] moth with loathsome, man-eating grubs from Luna (alpha Zodiaci IIIb), see moon worm
potter: [*Dell Crossword Puzzle Dictionary*] red-bellied terrapin, see slider
potto: [*National Geographic Encyclopedia of Animals*] small primate with Human-like fingers from Africa, Terra (alpha Zodiaci III)
pouch: [*The New Dinosaurs* by Dougal Dixon] aka saccosaur, fish-eating coelurosaur with pelican-like pouch, black-and-white striped tail, webbed feet, armflaps, in river, sea and swamp varieties
pougoowa: squid-like cephalopodan from Deepsea (Phoenix X), Galaxiki galaxy
poukui: [Maori] 140-kg flightless raptor, possibly same as Haast eagle, only predator of dinornis, from New Zealand, Terra (alpha Zodiaci III)

poulec: [poule-chat mondegreen] chicken-cat-in-a-hat

poulechat: [Fren. polecat] chicken-cat, chicken-headed cat-like griffinoid from Gérard's world

poulp: [*Vingt Mille Lieues Sous les Mers* by Jules Verne] 7-meter long cuttlefish with 8 suckered tentacles, large green eyes, parrot-like beak

poulpe: [*Dell Crossword Puzzle Dictionary*] octopus

poultra: ["Jimmy Neutron, Boy Genius" by John A. Davis and Steve Oedekerk] large chicken-like ornithoid with 3 eyestalks from Yelkus

pouter: [*Dell Crossword Puzzle Dictionary*] pigeon, see nun, barb, dove, roller

power-cat: ["Friday's Child" by D. C. Fontana] brick-red, brown bear-sized felinoid with golden eyes, short tail, brown back spines, fast as cheetah, able to throw a 200-volt charge 6 meters, from Kohath (Capella (alpha Auriga) IV) system

powl: [parliament of owls spoonerism] powerful owl-like ornithoid

poyote: [pack of coyotes spoonerism] caninoid

praepusa: [*After the Dinosaurs* by Donald R. Prothero] with pontophoca, crytophoca, leptophoca, the first true seals from Miocene

prairie elephant: ["Futurama"] rare long-legged, burrowing pachyderm

pranktail: [Terra Monster] 2-tailed fox with pink and white tailtip, see foxpaw, from Terrarium

pranktailope: [pranktail antelope portmanteau] pranktail with antlers

prantis: [praying mantis spoonerism] insectoid from Mei-Ying system

pratincole: [*National Geographic Encyclopedia of Animals*] insect and spider-eating bird from S. Pacific, Terra (alpha Zodiaci III)

praxa: [*The Maracot Deep* by Sir Arthur Conan Doyle] partially organic, partially gaseous greenish cloud creature with luminous core that eats eyes

prayery dog: [prairie dog mondegreen] praying mantis-like burrowing canine

prayery dogator: [prayery dog alligator portmanteau] alligator-like predator whose bite morphs victim into prayery dog

predator: ["Fungi from Yuggoth" by Howard Phillips Lovecraft] magic-eating fractal-dimensional like bundles of spiky stafts able to shoot tiny bolts of energy, minion of Yog-Sothoth

preducor: ["Ewoks" series] 4-meter clawed quadruped with razor-sharp mane hair, long, spiked tail, glowing eyes, vestigial wings from moon of Endor I, Endor system, Jedi galaxy

preed: stratosphere-dwelling star-shaped creature from Geosia prime, Epheran system, Galaxiki galaxi

pree: [curtailed preep, pride of peacocks spoonerism] preep without a tail

preep: [*If I Ran the Zoo* by Theodore Seuss Geissel] short-legged, flat-footed, dog-faced ornithoid with crest and stripes

prepostoroa: [preposterous mondegreen] rhinoid with spiked head-like tail

pressie: [*Monster Spotter's Guide to North America* by Scott Francis] 23-meter, dark lake snake with barbels and fluke from Lake Superior, nr. Presque Island River, Terra (alpha Zodiaci III)

prickle snake: [Avatar: The Last Airbender: "The Southern Air Temple"] serpentine with quills

prinscho: [Hildegard of Bingen's Lingua Ignota] kite-like ornithoid from Ignota, Hildegard's system

printer: [*Nick and the Glimmung* by Philip K. Dick] creature from Plowman's planet sought by the invisible Glimmung

prion: [pride of lions spoonerism, mondegreen] lion mimic from Lyd system

prionster: [prion monster portmanteau] monstrous prion

priscileo: [*After the Dinosaurs* by Donald R. Prothero] lion-like marsupial with huge stabbing lower canines and long blade-like cheek teeth from Miocene

pristichamps: crocodilian with serrated blade-like teeth from Paleocene

prober: [*Worlds Apart: Nat. Hist. of Furaha and Earth* by Souren Nyoroge] 1-meter, yellow hexapod with club-like "arms", long jaws from Furaha (alpha Phoenicis IV)

proboscipede: aka sclerorrhinus ("hard-nose"), includes jumping and hopping snouters

proceratosaur: ["1st horned lizard", *Feathered Dinosaurs: The Origin of Birds* by John Long and Peter Schuten] 3-meter, 250-kg horned coelurosaur with many curved teeth, snout crest from Middle Jurassic

proceratotaur: [procertosaur minotaur portmanteau] bovinoid with snout crest

procranioceras: [*After the Dinosaurs* by Donald R. Prothero] dromomeryx with straight horns over eyes and curved horns behind ears

profogg: [*Creatures of the Galaxy* by Phil Brucato, Bill Smith, Rick D. Stuart, Chuck Truett] prairiedog-like burrower from Tatooine, Jedi galaxy

profoggator: [profogg alligator portmanteau] alligator-like predator whose bite morphs victim into profogg

promerycochoerus: [*After the Dinosaurs* by Donald R. Prothero] semi-aquatic, pig-like oreodont with short legs and proboscis

prong-headed snake: ["Whooo-ooo Flupper!" by Nicholas Fisk] burrowing serpentine with prong-shaped head from Positos

prong: [pronghorn backformation] ruminant noted for thin pointed pitchfork-like horns

prongator: [prong alligator portmanteau] alligator-like predator whose bite morphs victim into prong

pronghorn moose: ["Unification" by Rick Berman and Michael Pillar] moose-like ruminant with pronged horns, noted for loud, horrible call from Bardakia

pronglet: [*After the Dinosaurs* by Donald R. Prothero] small pronghorn, Merriam's variety has fan-like horns from Miocene

proo: [*If I Ran the Zoo* by Theodore Seuss Giessel] long-necked caninoid with short legs, large feet and very long, furry ears

propaleohopplophorus: [*After the Dinosaurs* by Donald R. Prothero] armadillo-like glyptodont from Miocene

propa: [propaleopplophorus mondegreen] leohopplophorus relative

propa gator: [propagator mondegreen] alligator-like predator whose bite morphs victim into propa

prosansanosmilus: [*After the Dinosaurs* by Douglas R. Prothero] cat-like nimravid from Miocene

protarchaeopteryx: ["1st ancient wing", *Feathered Dinosaurs: The Origin of Birds* by John Long and Peter Schuten] 60-cm incisivosaur relative

prothylacynus: [*After the Dinosaurs* by Donald R. Prothero] wolf-like marsupial from Miocene

protoceras: [*After the Dinosaurs* by Donald R. Prothero] artiodactyl with two short nose-horns and two short forehead-horns on males, distantly related to camel from Oligocene

protoceratops: [*The Mistaken Extinction* by Lowell Dingus and Timothy Rowe] ceratops with characteristic frill, relative of triceratops

protorohippo: [protorohippus hippopotamus portmanteau] small hippoid with four front and three hind toes from Protoro system

protorohippus: [*After the Dinosaurs* by Donald R. Prothero] beagle-sized horse with four front and three hind toes from Ypresian age (early Eocene)

proty: [protoplasm contraction, Legion of Super-Heroes] pet telep polymorph from Durla

prowlgrin: [*Edge Chronicles* by Paul Stewart and Chris Riddell] sperm whale-like mount

pryligu: [Superman mythos] sea monster from Krypton, Rao system

psar: [raspberry yrreb psar palindrome] purplish pink yrreb

pseudailurus: [*After the Dinosaurs* by Douglas R. Prothero] first true cat from Miocene

pseudo-rock: ["The Long Night" by John Christopher] aka mockrock, ferrophagous creature, rock-like in nocturnal state, otherwise spherical with retractable pseudopods, reproduces by fission

psittaco: [OviPets] parrot-like ornithoid

pseudoci: [ci mimic palindrome] ci mimic

pseudoduesp: [mynynym] duesp mimic

pseudokaf: [fake kaf palindrome] predatory calf-like mimic of kaf

pseudoslaf: [false slaf palindrome] slaf mimic

psittacosaur: [*The Mistaken Extinction* by Lowell Dingus and Timothy Rowe, "parrot-lizard"] bipedal ceratops with characteristic beak; parrot-lizard-like griffinoid

psittacotaur: [psittacosaur minotaur portmanteau] parrot-bull-like griffinoid

psobb: [psomo antanym] puffy spheroid of benevolent blue

psomo: ["The Worm Turns" by Gregory Benford, Puffy Sphere of Malevolent Orange acronym] puffy orange malevolent spheroid from HD209458 system

psychrobacter: extremophilic bacterium resistant to extreme alkaline and cold, see vibio, arthrobacter

ptang: ["Prince of Peril" by Otis Adelbert Kline] giant sloth-like creature with sharp, upcurved claws

ptangator: [ptang alligator portmanteau] alligator-like predator whose bite morphs victim into ptang

pteracuda: ["Sharktopus vs. Pteracuda" by Matt Yamashita] pterodactyl-barracuda, monstrous ichthyopteryx

pterodactyl: short-tailed pterosaur that replaced long-tailed rhamporhynchus

pterosaur: ["winged lizard", *Han Solo's Revenge* by Brian Daley] carnivorous, flying dracoid of Ammudd, Jedi galaxy; see pterodactyl, rhamporhynchus

pterotaur: [Far Side: "When Cows Ruled" by Gary Larson, pterosaur minotaur portmanteau] winged bull, see bovinopteryx, winged buffalo

ptitza: [zhar-ptitza mondegreen] ornithoid related to zhar and ancestral to zhar-ptitza

ptolemaia: [*After the Dinosaurs* by Donald R. Prothero] wolf-sized predatory insectovore from Oligocene

ptuksit: [Delaware origin of "tuxedo"] round-footed wolf

puat: [taupe puat palindrome] dark grayish brown ornithoid

puck: [paddling of ducks spoonerism] small, cylindrical shellfish adapted to icy water

pudamef: [*The Queen of Zambia* by L. Sprague de Camp] 6-legged cold-adapted reptilian (see shan) of Krishna, tau Ceti system

pudamefling: small pudamef-like creature from Rovarga, Gravor system, Galaxiki galaxy

pudameflingator: [pudamefling alligator portmanteau] alligator-like predator whose bite morphs victim into pudmefling

pudding: pudding-thick ooze

puddingator: [pudding alligator portmanteau] alligator-like predator whose bite morphs victim into pudding

pudding worm: [*Mothstorm* by Philip Reeve] raisin-like larval form of pudding bug which infests Christmas puddings and other desserts

pudelhund: [Germ. poodle] waterfowl-hunting dog

pudoo: [Outernauts] immature ploppah

puf: [Fr. Johann Martin Schleyer's Volapük] louse-like insectoid from Schleyer's system

puffadoo: [Outernauts] mature puffala with puffier crest and tail

puffala: [Outernauts] pink, pufferfish-like ichthyoid with yellow fins, see puffaloo, puffadoo, puffalo, puffeero, puffoloo

puffalo: [Outernauts] immature puffoloo

puffaloo: [Outernauts] immature puffala

puffeero: [Outernauts] mature puffoloo

puffin: [*Dell Crossword Puzzle Dictionary*] sea bird from Northern hemisphere, Terra (alpha Zodiaci III)

puffoloo: [Outernauts] light blue pufferfish-like ichthyoid, see puffalo, puffeero, puffaloo, puffadoo, pufala

puffskein: [*Fantastic Beasts and Where to Find Them* by Newton Artemis Fido Scamander] custard-colored, furry, omnivorous spheroid with long thin tongue

puffworm: [*Wyst: Alastor 1716* by Jack Vance] creature sold by vendors from Wyst

pug jumpers: insectoid from Kashÿyÿk, Jedi galaxy

puggle: young platypus from Australia, Terra (alpha Zodiaci III)

pugot: headless head-hunting pongoid from Philippines, Terra (alpha Zodiaci III)

pugwing: [Outernauts] immature rotwing, in ice variety

pugwingator: [pugwing alligator portmanteau] alligator-like predator whose bite morphs victim into pugwing

pugwis: [*Monster Spotter's Guide to North America* by Scott Francis] ichthropoid possibly related to Thetis Lake monster, from Puget Sound, Terra (alpha Zodiaci III)

puli: [*Dell Crossword Puzzle Dictionary*] dog from Hungary, Terra (alpha Zodiaci III)

pullmi-pushu: llama-like doublicaud with two tails and no heads

puma: [*Dell Crossword Puzzle Dictionary*] mountain lion

pumaferno: [Outernauts] mature pumasear

pumaflar: [Outernauts] immature pumasear

pumasear: [Outernauts] hot-blooded puma-like felinoid, see pumasear

pumaus: [German Puma-Maus portmanteau] cougar-mouse, large predatory rodentoid from Germa system

pume: [*Dell Crossword Puzzle Dictionary*] small sandpiper, see stint, knot

pumferno: [Outernauts] purple felinoid with fiery tail and crest, and spiked, beaver-like tail

puni: [Outernauts] pink, round, immature kuni with antennae in shocker variety

punkie: aka midge, no-see-'em, tiny gnat-like insect

punkin: ["Drop Dead" by Clifford Simak] small omnivore that makes unholy racket when hungry and always hungry from Polaris (alpha Ursa Minoris) system

punkle: [*Hagerstown Mail*] shellfish whose shells are polish by Umbopelanders with snallygaster hide

pup: [*Dell Crossword Puzzle Dictionary*] small dog or seal

puppen: ["Outlands" by Adam de la Peña] cutest, but deadly, teddy-bear-like creature

pur: [longspur mondegreen] aquatic insect and seed-eating songbird from Long system

purgatorius: [Purgatory Hill, MT] first primate

purple cow: [Gelett Burgess] mineral-deficient bovine from Florida State Nutrition Lab, Terra (alpha Zodiaci III)

purple frog: aka hasikabatrachus, burrowing frog with pointed snout

purple frogator: [purple frog alligator portmanteau] alligator-like predator whose bite morphs victim into hasikabatrachus

purrip: [*After Man* by Dougal Dixon] eye-less bat with facial ears

purrpetal: [Terra Monster] felinoid with thorny tailtip, see dandylion and vioness, from Terrarium

purrpetalope: [purrpetal antelope portmanteau] purrpetal with antlers

purtle: [pitying of turtles, purple turtle portmanteau] purple chelonoid

pus hog: ["Projections" by Brannon Braga] disgusting creature partially domesticated by the Kazon, Delta Quadrant

pus hogator: [pus hog alligator portmanteau] alligator-like predator whose bite morphs victim into pus hog

pusghetti: [spaghetti spoonerism] long, thin worm fond of pus

pushmi-pullyu: [*The Story of Dr. Doolittle* by Hugh Lofting] shy horned doublivore like both gazelle and chamois, possibly related to llamall, see pullmi-pushu

puttikan: [*The Yowie: In Seach of Australian Bigfoot* by Tony Healy and Paul Cropper] see yowie

pussum: [puss-possum portmanteau] felinoid marsupial

pwee: [Monster Galaxy] green dracoid with pink star tuff from Pisces constellation
pwytyn-cwcwyddrywystrys: [Welsh] barnacle goose-like griffinoid ancestral to pug and cwcwyddrywystrys
pyet: [*Dell Crossword Puzzle Dictionary*] magpie, see mag(g), pie(t), piot, pyot
pyg: [pygarg mondegreen] gray porcoid dlef
pygator: [pyg alligator portmanteau] alligator-like predator whose bite morphs victim into pyg
pygarg: [Dt. 14:5] deer-like ruminant
pygargator: [pyrarg alligator portmanteau] alligator-like predator whose bite morphs victim into pygarg
pylat: [*Creatures of the Galaxy* by Phil Brucato, Bill Smith, Rick D. Stuart, Chuck Truett] white and black cockatiel-like ornithoid from Neimoidia, Jedi galaxy
pyot: [*Dell Crossword Puzzle Dictionary*] magpie, see mag(g), pie(t), piot, pyet
pyradon: [Outernauts] pyrosaur variant, see pyrzard, pyrasaur
pyralli: [aka pyrotocone, *Inventorum Natura* by Pliny the Elder] dracoid with insectoidal wings that lives in and feeds on fire from Pyrallis Island
pyrasaur: [Outernauts] mature pyradon
pyrataur: [pyrasaur minotaur] pyrotaur variant
Pyrithian bat: ["Doctor's Orders" by Chris Black] chiropteran from Pyrith
pyrococcus: extremophilic bacterium resistant to extreme radiation, see rubrobacter, deinococcus
pyrolobus: extremophilic bacteria resistant to extreme termerature and pressure from Mid-Atlantic ridge, Terra (alpha Zodiaci III)
pyropod: [*The Reefs of Space* by Frederik Pohl and Jack Williamson] aggressive squid-like omnivore from the Reefs of Space
pyrosaur: lizard adapted to extreme heat, see firesaur, fire-lizard, pyrasaur, salamander
pyrotaur: [pyrosaur minotaur portmanteau] bovinoid adapted to extreme heat
pyrothere: ["fire-beast", *After the Dinosaurs* by Donald R. Prothero] small mastodon-like non-proboscidean marsupial from Chattian (late Oligocene), see flamebeast
pyrotocone: see pyralli
pyrzard: [Outernauts] immature pyradon
pysantilla: [*The Dirdir, The Pnume* by Jack Vance] dangerous creature of chasms on Sibol
pytheron: [*After Man* by Dougal Dixon] predatory seal-like rodent
pytheronster: [pytheron monster portmanteau] monstrous, predatory, seal-like rodentoid
Qara bat: [Azerbaijani qarabatdaq mondegreen] cheiropteran ancestral to daq and cormorant from Qara system
Qatzan dog: [cats and dogs mondegreen] flying caninoid nimravid from Qatza system
qefla: [*Bloodthirst* by J. M. Dillard] aka Rigelian rat, cat-like rodentoid from Rigel (beta Orionis)
qilin: short-necked giraffe from China, Terra (alpha Zodiaci III), see jraf
qilqmao: [milk cow spoonerism] bovinoid
qiqirn: [Inuit] large, mangy dog with hairy feet, ears, mouth and taillip that induces fits from Arctic, Terra (alpha Zodiaci III)
qooqur: [cook your goose mondegreen] goose-like food ornithoid
quadribullus: [*The New Dinosaurs* by Dougal Dixon] sprintosaur with four-knobbed crest
quadrumanous: [Space Family Robinson: Lost in Space #54] 2.4-meter tall pongoid with one eye, large mouth, shaggy brown hair, 3-toed feet and 4 arms from Alpha 34
quagga: [*Dell Crossword Puzzle Dictionary*] wild ass from Africa, see onager
quaggator: [quagga alligator portmanteau] alligator-like predator whose bite morphs victim into quagga
quandary: [*If I Ran the Zoo* by Seuss] symmetrical, orange, sea amygdaloid (almond-shaped) with crest-like tail
Quarll's deer: reddish-brown fawn-like ruminant mammalian twice hare-size with goat-like face and

feet from Quarll's Island, Pacific, Terra (alpha Zodiaci III)

quarm: [Edge Chronicles: "The Winter Knights"] tree-dweller with distinctive squeal or variety from Troctopia, Qujhtba system, Galaxiki galaxy

quartado: [pintado backformation] large seir-like fish

quarterpede: [Xanth series by Piers Anthony] five times as deadly as a nicklepede from Xanth

quarteroo: [buckeroo backformation] smaller buckeroo

quarti-freezard: one of four mini-freezards

quartiped: mutant with 25% as many legs

quata: [*Dell Crossword Puzzle Dictionary*] spider monkey, see coaita, ateles

quatch: [sasquatch mondegreen] large, hairy anthropoid from Sa, the Leech Planet

queel: ["Milk Run" by Robert Sheckley] small sheep adapted to hi-gee with oily, metallic wool reproduce feemishly (like feems) from Tensis V

queelope: [queel antelope portmanteau] queel with antlers

queetar: [*The Perfect Planet* by Edward Packard] web-footed creature from Utopa (Achnar V), Gallatin quadrant

quella: ["The First" by Peg Robinson] egg-layer from Shadrasi's world

quetzalcoatl: [*The Big Bad Book of Beasts* by Michael Largo] pterosaur with 3-meter wingspan

quica: [*Dell Crossword Puzzle Dictionary*] oppossum from S. America, Terra (alpa Zodiaci III)

quiffin: [*Liselott and the Quiffin* by Hans Peterson] flying llama from Scandinavia, Terra (alpha Zodiaci III)

quinkin: [*The Yowie: In Seach of Australian Bigfoot* by Tony Healy and Paul Cropper] yowie from Queensland, Australia, Terra (alpha Zodiaci III)

quinotaur: [*The Big Bad Book of Beasts* by Michael Largo] bull-headed fish-tailed amphibian with 5 horns, dark brown fur, dark nose

quintaped: ["five-legged", Abraham Lincoln] donkey with tail adapted into fifth leg, see hairy macboon

quinti-freezard: one of five mini-freezards

quintibullus: [quadribullus extrapolation] sprintosaur with five-knobbed crest

quirkat: [quicky cat, Terra Monster] felinoid from Terrarium

quirl: see couerl

quoll: [*National Geographic Encyclopedia of Animals*] carnivorous mammal from Australia, Terra (alpha Zodiaci III)

quorl: [*Trullion: Alastor 2262* by Jack Vance] beach mollusk

qupine: [torqupine backformation] winged bull-like pegasoid, related to winged buffalo

quskuns: [Azerbaijani qus-skuns portmanteau] bird-skunk, ornithoid noted for malodorous aerial spray

quurtoise: [turquoise spoonerism] turquoise ornithoid

qwhale: [quail-whale portmanteau] huge penguin-like triphibian with mottled brown markings and short tail

qyoob: ["The Ecology of the Gelatinous Cube" by Ed Greenwood] aka gelatinous cube, 9-cubic meter, transparent omnivore that paralyzes with electric shock, reproducing by budding small snub cubes, adapted to dungeons from gelatinous non-cube, so-called from its cry

ra: [burra mondegreen] lavender lungfish

ra nifid: [*Planiverse* by Alexander Dewdney] 2-D sea animal from Arde, Shems system

raad: [*Dell Crossword Puzzle Dictionary*] thunderfish

raafuut: [Dutch raaf-fuut portmanteau] raven-grebe, ornithoid

raänid: [Fr. Johann Martin Schleyer's Volapük] arachnoid from Schleyer's system

rab: [Barbie ib rab, barn rab palindrome]s barn-dwelling, pink furry with red nape (back of neck)

rabbiroo: [Avatar: The Last Airbender: "Tales of Ba Sing Se"] rabbit-headed kangaroo with multiple births in pouch

rabbit-fish: [rabbitfish mondegreen] prolific, burrowing amphibian

rabboon: [*After Man* by Dougal Dixon] tyrannosauroid baboon

rabbuck: [*After Man* by Dougal Dixon] giant, hoofed deer-like rabbit in running and hopping varieties, including strank, watoo and picktooth

rac: [carnation Oitan rac, scary racs palindrome] frightening pink, rokh-like predatory ornithoid from Oita system, in ailen, anid, anilo, eir, el, nim, or and rutai varieties; [carnage anamnymondegreen] psychic killer from Ega system

rac-coon: [raccoon mondegreen] raccoon-like pegasoid

raccoon-shark: [Racoon shark malapropism] amphibious landshark with raccoon mask and arms

racer: [*Dell Crossword Puzzle Dictionary*] black snake

rackabore: [museumofhoaxes.com by Alex Boese] mountain goat-like porcoid in rightward and leftward varieties like sidehill gouger and hoofer, see javelina

racket: [Terra Monster] see ratchet and racruel, from Terrarium

rackleg: [*City of the Chasch* by Jack Vance] dangerous jungle creature able to merge with shadows from Shattorak

racklegator: [rackleg alligator portmanteau] alligator-like predator whose bite morphs victim into rackleg

racnifla: [James Cooke Brown's Logla racni flaki] itchfly from Logla, Brown's system

racniku: [James Cooke Brown's Logla racni kurma] itchyworm from Logla, Brown's system

racruel: [Terra Monster] large, green and black forest-dwelling fruit-eater, see racket and ractchet. from Terrarium

rad: [radish backformation] radish mimicking planimal

raddler: [raddle rattler portmanteauu] red ocher rattlesnake, see ruddler

radiation dog: [Appointment with F. E. A. R. by Steve Jackson] radioactive canine, see nuclear watchdog

radiation dogator: [radiation dog alligator portmanteau] alligator-like predator whose bite morphs victim into radiation dog

radinskya: [*After the Dinosaurs* by Donald R. Prothero] most primitive perissodactyl (horse, rhino, tapir ancestor) from Paleocene

radiojack: [Monster Galaxy] creature with large, batwing ears, smaller back wings, arrowhead-tipped tail from Leo constellation

radiolarium: [*The Challenger Radiolaria* by Ernest Haeckel] polyhedral creatures with pseudopods at vertices

radiovore: ["Just Deserts" by Michael Jan Friedman] radiation-eating creature that visited Utalabria

radnim: [mindaro radnim palindrome] pale chartreuse ornithoid

radon: [pteranodon contraction, aka rodan] 100-tonne dracoid with 150-meter wingspan, chest spikes, able to fly at supersonic speeds, feeds on 6-meter long insects

raep: [pearl raep palindrome] pale pinkish off-white creature

raft: ["Grandpa" by James Schmitz] broad, green, leathery hat-shaped with pineapple-like center and stinging ribbon-like tentacles, armor-plated "head", long kinky leafless vines, red buds, short thick paddle-like leaves, slimy nettle-streamers from Sutang

rag pudding: [pudding extrapolation] rag-dwelling pudding-thick ooze

ragdoll: limp, pain-insensitive furry

ragewyrm: [Terra Monsters] blue, quadrupedal dracoid with white wings and underbelly, see snowyrm, from Terrarium

ragno: [ragno bongar palindrome] bongar-like amphisbæna

ragoji: [*Dragon's Honor* by Kij Johnson and Greg Cox] food animal

rahc: [charm rahc, charcoal aoc rahc palindromes] pink or gray rokh

rahgid: [*Dragon's Honor* by Kij Johnson and Greg Cox] food animal

rahonorvis: [*A Field Guide to Dinosaurs* by Henry Gee and Luis V. Rey] bird-like dromaeosaur

rai: [pal-rai-yûk mondegreen] seaserpent-like tizheruk ancestor
raidybug: [rash of ladybugs spoonerism] eyelash-dwelling dustmite-like insectoid
raidybugator: [raidybug alligator portmanteau] alligator-like predator whose bite morphs victim into raidybug
rail: [*Dell Crossword Puzzle Dictionary*] marshbird, wading bird, see ibis, crane, egret, heron, stilt, avocet, avoset, jacana, flamingo
rain sucker: [beheaded brain sucker] insectoid that sucks moisture from air threatening cloud creatures (chog, cirrius, meraps, mysteron, mysery, mysty, praxa), see cloudeater
rainbird: [*Stations of the Tide* by Michael Swanwick] lowtide whose high-tide form is the sparrowfish dimorph from Miranda, Prospero system
rainbow beast: ["The Rainbow Beast" by Bill Finger] large, multicolored anthropoid able to burn, freeze, bidimensionalize and mistify
rainbowbird: see gebird
rainbow lizard: [*The New Dinosaurs* by Dougal Dixon] see kakuru
rainbow squid: [*The Future Is Wild* by Dougal Dixon] long-lived 40-meter flish-eating cephalopodan
rainburn: [Monster Galaxy] black dracoid with long rainbow tail, feathery wings from Ares constellation
raindeer: [reindeer homonym, Xanth series by Piers Anthony] horned quadruped with personal storm cloud from Xanth
Rak's deer: [*After the Dinosaurs* by Donald R. Prothero] dromomeryx with nearly semi-circular horns
rakazzak: ["Ewoks" series] 3-meter tall arachnoid steed from Endor I's moon, Jedi galaxy
rakrab: [Czech rak-krab portmanteau] crayfish-crab, amphibious crustacean
rallod: [dollar bill ib rallod palindrome] green furry with red nape (back of neck)
ramingo: [regiment of flamingos spoonerism, ram flamingo portmanteau] ram-flamingo-like griffinoid

rammerhorn: [*The Face of the Waters* by Robert Silverberg] top predator, along with drakken, from the waterworld Hydros
Rammin dog: [*Contacting Aliens* illustrated by Kevin Lenagh] bushy-tailed, two-toed biped with trunk-like "head" from Ramm
ramp ant: [rampant mondegreen] flying ant-like insectoid that builds ramps on its anthills
rampant: [Code Lyoko] aka creeper, anthropoid with mechanical snake-like tail, 2 pulling legs, large mouthflap and laser eye geneered by Xana
ramph: ["Prince of Peril" by Otis Adelbert Kline] great, hairless, green scaly bear-like creature with greenish-yellow underbelly from Zarovia (Venus (alpha Zodiaci II))
ramt: [nightmare ramt hgin palindrome] predatory hgin
ranac: [canary ranac palindrome] yellow ornithoid
rancor: [*Return of the Jedi* by James Kahn] fierce, solitary 5-meter carnivorous biped sauroid with sharp and long claws, arms, fangs from Dathomir, Lehon, and Felucia, Jedi galaxy
rangakoo: [kangaroo spoonerism] macropodan with chime-like call and backpouch
rangifer: [OviPets] egg-laying reindeer-like ruminant
ranine: [umbranine mondegreen] creature ancestral to umbranine
Rannian sea serpent: ["The Beast With the Sizzling Blue Eyes" by Gardner Fox] 2-headed sea serpent with sizzling blue eyes from Rann, alpha Centauri system
rapide: [*After Man* by Dougal Dixon] cheetah-like predatory rodent
rapierfish: [swordfish extrapolation] ichthyoid with rapier-like snout
rapsecap: [Crayola, Deep Space Sparkle elk rapsecap speed palindrome] fast elk-like metallic-colored ruminant from Crayol A
raptor-wolf: ["Oil and Water" by Robert T. Jerschonek] winged warg from Rigel system
raptortongue: [*A Hero's Guide to Deadly Dragons* by Hiccup Haddock III] dragon able

to camouflage and flatten itself into near invisibility in crevices from Barbarian archipelago

rarnozbi: [James Cooke Brown's Loglan ra nozbi (all nose) compound] allsnouter from Logla, Brown's system

rarnsuk: aka stone-monster, [Dudekors] suk golem that turns back to stone upon exposure to sunlight, see gargoyle

rarref: [Ferrari rarref palindrome] red non-marten-like ornithoid, see rarten

rarten: [richness(e) of martens spoonerism], non-red martin-like rarref

rarti: [James Cooke Brown's Loglan ra titci (all eater) compound] omnivore from Logla, Brown's system

ras: ["ras at times emit tasar" palindrome] silkworm gestalt; [beheaded gras] gypsy gan ceann, see ri, ry

rasher: [*Dell Crossword Puzzle Dictionary*] rockfish, see tambor

raskadik: [Arthur Porges] wildcat-like carnivore with quills, large tender nose from Faraday, 4 Ceti system

raspbear: [raspberry backformation] raspy ursinold

rasse: [*Dell Crossword Puzzle Dictionary*] wild mountain sheep from Asia, Terra *alpha Zodiaci III), see sha, sna, urial, bharal, nahoor, oorial, argali

rast: [*Monster Manual* by Skip Williams, etal.] dog-sized, blood-sucking creature with 14 or more brown spidery legs with rust-red claws, large rust-colored head like snake, vulture and goblin, paralyzing gaze, able to use only 4 claws at a time

rastipod: ["Progress" by Peter Allan Fields] rast-footed carnivore variety or more graceful herbivorous variety from Bajor

rat-dog: [*Briefing for A Descent into Hell* by Doris Lessing] brown caninoid with monkey-like head, long, scaly rat-like tail, poor sight, communicating in barks and whistles, females with scarlet-edged genital markings from Watkinsland, Latin America, Terra (alpha Zodiaci III)

ratdogator: [ratdog alligator portmanteau] alligator-like predator whose bite morphs victim into ratdog

rat-mule: [*Treks Not Taken*: "One Beamed on the Cuckold's Nest" by Steve R. Boydett] creature like both rat and mule from Cardassia

rat-snake: [rat snake mondegreen] rodent-headed serpent

Rat: see Dragon

ratbird: [*Edge Chronicles* by Paul Stewart and Chris Riddell] small, flying scavenger rodent from sky pirate ships, related to snicket

ratchet: [Terra Monster] black, gray and green appleseed-eating biped with bushy tail, see racket and racruel, from Terrarium

ratli: [James Cooke Brown's Loglan] rodentoid from Logla, Brown's system

ratel: [*Dell Crossword Puzzle Dictionary*] honey badger

ratelope: [ratel antelope portmanteau] ratel with antlers

rath: [*Through the Looking-Glass* by Charles Ludwidge "Lewis Carroll" Dodgeson] green porcoid that makes a noice between a bellow and whistle with sneeze in middle

ratite: [*Dell Crossword Puzzle Dictionary*] ostrich-like bird, see em(e)u

ratsum: [mustard ratsum palindrome] yellowish rodentoid

ratt: [rattish backformation] rodentoid

rattenkaiser: ["rat-king", "Last Rites" by Marc Platt] rodentian gestalt from Epajaenda

ratti: [James Cooke Brown's Loglan ratcu titci (rat eater) compound] rat-eater from Logla, Brown's system

rattleback: [*The Future Is Wild* by Dougal Dixon] rodent with flameproof armored matted-hair plates and sidequills that feeds on fire-cooked carakiller eggs

rattler: [*Dell Crossword Puzzle Dictionary*] rattlesnake, see crotalus

rattus: [OviPets] egg-laying rodentoid

ratwa: [*Dell Crossword Puzzle Dictionary*] deer, see muntjac, kakar

rau: [rawhide mondegreen] skin-eating parasite

raulicaucis: [Cyclopedia of Worlds] 3.6-meter pack predatory quadruped on Palul (Lar Don) the Dinosaur Planet

rauq: [square rauqs palindrome] checkerboard-like barnacles, see oowylloh

rauracki: [museumofhoaxes.com by Alex Boese] wolpertinger from Thuringia, Terra (alpha Zodiaci III)

ravene: [*After Man* by Dougal Dixon] fox-like predatory rodent

ravid: [*Monster Manual* by Skip Williams, etal.] 2.1-meter, whitish-violet, levitating serpentoid with small arm behind head with claw whose touch can animate inanimate and energize (or over-energize) animate from Positive Energy Plane

ravin: [*Dell Crossword Puzzle Dictionary*] prey

ray-rat: ["Lost Sorceress of the Silent Citadel" by Michael Moorcock] rat-like and ray-like amphibian from Mars (alpha Zodiaci IV)

rayl: [*Captain's Peril* by William Shatner] eel-like ichthyoid with 6 arms, sharp teeth and spikes from Bajor

razor-bat: ["Guest of Honor" by Robert Reed] razor-winged chiropteran from Erindi III

razorback pig: [Xanth series by Piers Anthony] porcoid with razor-sharp back spines from Xanth

razorbeast: ["Rascals" by Ward and Diana Dru Botsford and Michael Pillar, "Imaginary Friend" by Jean Louise Matthias, Ronald Wilkerson and Richard Filegel] huge, brown-furred creature with large spiny wings noted for jumping from Tarkass

raztsi: [James Crooke Brown's Loglan raznu tsito] reason stealer from Logla, Brown's system

razzilb: [Crayola, blizzard razzilb palindrome] pale greenish-blue ornithoid from Crayol A

re: [ernanodon ananymondegreen] sloth-like arboreal from Nodona system

re'em: [Heb. Num. 23:22, 24:8, Dt. 33:71, Job 39:9, Ps. 22:2, 24:6, Isa. 34:7] one-horned auroch, see unicorn

re(i)na: [*Dell Crossword Puzzle Dictionary*] rockfish from California, Terra (alpha Zodiaci III)

rea: [aero rea palindrome] sky blue ornithoid

real: [Catalan ànec real mondegreen] mallard duck-like ornithoid

reaper: [X-COM: UFO Defense] large, ferocious, brown-furred biped

reason stealer: [*Monster Manual* by Skip Williams, etal.] maddening ooze

reb: [iceberg reb eci palindrome] pale blue louse-like mouse parasite

rebmit: [timberwolf low rebmit palindrome] pale gray creature from below timberline, related to white hgi

rebye: [Crayon cyber grape pargrebye palindrome] parg variant from Crayol A

reca: [reca racer palindrome] racer-like amphisbæna

recoy: [Atbash] golem

Rectilian vulture: ["Phage" by Skye Dent and Brannon Braga] vulture-like ornithoid from Rectil, Delta Quadrant

Rectyne monopod: ["The Icarus Factor" by David Assael] 2-tonne one-footed creature

red eel: [*The Maracot Deep* by Sir Arthur Conan Doyle] poisonous red eel

red pudding: [pudding extrapolation] red pudding-thick ooze

redbat: ["Invasive Procedures" by John Whelpley and Robert Hewett Wolfe] red cheiropteroid from Andoria

redbird: [grue-bleen extrapolation] red bird that remains red, not to be confused with bledbird, gebird, gredbird, reedbird, rellowbird, rindigobird, rioletbird, ruebird, vedbird, yedbird from Ora system

redd: [reddish backformation] red shapeshifter

redfish: [Pern series by Ann McCaffrey] food ichthyoid from Pern (Rukbat (alpha Sagittarii) III)

rednirli: [James Cooke Brown's Loglan redro nirda (red bird) compound] red ornithoid from Logla, Brown's system

ree(ve): [*Dell Crossword Puzzle Dictionary*] sandpiper, see ruff, stib, stint

reed-eel: [Edge Chronicles: "Midnight Over Sanctaphrax" by Paul Stewart and Chris Riddell] thin, green reed-like eel with yellow eyes and flower-like sucker-tip

reedstilt: [*After Man* by Dougal Dixon] large horse-like, fish-eating mammal with elongated neck, sharp teeth, slender hairy heron-like legs

reef glider: [*The Future Is Wild* by Dougal Dixon] bulbous, teardrop-shaped algae-eater with long tongue, 6 flippers, colorful gill-tail, compound eyestalks and scent-detecting rhinophores

reek: ["Attack of the Clones" by George Lucas and Jonathan Hale] large, quadrupedal mammaloid with cheek tusks and nose horn from plains of Yelsia or its moon, Hutt space, Jedi galaxy

reenbird: [grue-bleen extrapolation] redbird that turns green, not to be confused with bledbird, gebird, gredbird, greenbird, grellowbird, grindigobird, grioletbird, gruebird, redbird, reenbird, rellowbird, rindigobird, riloetbird, ruebird, vedbird or yedbird from Ora system

reesn: very good food newt from Lestonian Lushland (Edonian cluster V), Galaxiki galaxy

ref: [fern ref palindrome] greenish plantimal

reg: [gerbil ib reg] gerbil-like furry with red nape (back of the neck)

regguh: [huggernaut anamondegreen] ursinoid that hugs Tua system

regoniosu: pack-hunting predatory ornithoid from Betonia (Edonian cluster V), Galaxiki galaxy

regova: ["Destiny" by David S. Cohen and Martin A. Winer] egg-layer from Cardassia

rehctacta: [rehctacta ratcatcher palindrome] felinoid

rehtou: [Southern rehtou portmanteau] rehtron-like creature from northern hemisphere

rehtron: [Northern rehtron portmanteau] rehtou-like creature from southern hemisphere

rehtronster: [rehtron monster portmanteau] monstrous rehtron

réiltin: [Irish *] 2-D pentapus or hexapus

reindog: [reindeer dog portmanteau, *How the Grinch Stole Christmas* by Theodore Seuss Geissel] caninoid with antlers

rekab: [Baker-Miller ellim rekeb palindrome] pink ellim predator, see uahc

reklawli: ["reklawli at times emit tailwalker" palindrome] tailwalker gestalt

relddu: [relddu ruddler palindrome] ruddler-like anæbsihpma

rellb: [acronym] see brell

rellowbird: [grue-bleen extrapolation] redbird that turns yellow, not to be confused with bledbird, blellowbird, gebird, gredbird, grellowbird, redbird, reenbird, rellowbird, rindigobird, rioletbird, ruebird, yedbird yeenbird, yellowbird, yindigobird, vellowbird, yioletbird or yuebird from Ora system

reltta: [reltta rattler palindrome] rattler-like anæbsihpma

relwarct: [relwarct hgin nightcrawler palindrome] nocturnal predator

remora: ["Dreadnaught" by Gary Holland] suckerfish-like sea creature from Proxima (beta Centauri) system; [*Dell Crossword Puzzle Dictionary*] shark parasite, see pega, lootsman

remorhaz: [*Age of Worms Overlord* by Erik Mona] 6-meter, bluish-white segmented snowworm with many long legs, webbed spines like cobra's fan, 2 glowing-red heat-radiating lumps-per-segment, 4 antennae

remuda: [*Dell Crossword Puzzle Dictionary*] fresh saddle horse

ren: [Fr. Johann Martin Schleyer's Volapük] reindeer-like ruminant from Schleyer's system

renahippus: [beheaded arenahippus] gan ceann from Dania, Dan system

renar: [Fr. Johann Martin Schleyer's Volapük] fox-like caninoid from Schleyer's system

render: [*Monster Manual* by Skip Williams, etal.] 2.7-meter swamp-dweller with short tail, 6 eyes, gray clay-like hide, that reproduce by budding, but carries young in pouch, adopts other creatures whose enemies it renders and eats

renic: [cinereous uoe renic palindrome] brownish gray female uoe from Crayol A system

rep: [Peru rep palindrome, per- mondegreens] see ffoc, talocohc, odi, niwi from Ommi system
repaelli: ["repaelli at times emit tailleaper" palindrome] tailleaper gestalt
reppil: [slippery reppils palindrome] slimy snake-like reptilian
repsargli: ["repsargli at times emit tailgrasper" palindrome] parasitic tailgrasper gestalt
reptarapter: [palindrome, First Kingdom comics] rapter from Repta system
reptile bird: [Avatar: The Last Airbender: "The Waterbending Scroll"] green, basilisk-like lizard with parrot-like beak and tail, backspines, clawed wing-hands
reptilicus: [*Reptilicus* by Dean Owen] 30-meter long, snake-like dracoid with armored plates, 2 vestigial hands, wings, able to spit green poison
reptisaur: ["Reptisaurus" by Jeremiah Campbell, aka "Sky Fighter"] giant pterosaur
reptitaur: [reptisaur minotaur portmanteau] giant, flying bovinoid
resal: [Crayola laser lemon omelresal palindrome] florescent yellow omel from Crayol A
resed: [desert reset palindrome] brown desert creature, see nast
reta: [reta egg-eater palindrome] egg-layer
retantos: food rodentoid from Gizmonian Steepes (Edonian cluster II), Galaxiki galaxy
retaw: [waterspout Uop's retaw palindrome] bluish green sea creature from Uop system
reth: [red yeth portmanteau] corpse-animating symbiot with 2 red "eyes", see yeth
retnu: [retnu hunter palindrome] game creature
retrovirus: vieus that causes host to devolve into an ancestral form
retsa: [pl. retsae, Eastern retsae portmanteau] retsew-like creature from west
retsew: [Western retsew portmanteau] retsa-like creature from east
Retsno monster: [palindrome] monstrous creature from Retsno system
rettab: ["batter-fried eirf-rettab"] food animal related to eirf from Pharr, Farpt system, Galaxiki galaxy

rettalf: [flattery rettalf palindrome] brown ornithoid
rettir: [rettir fritter palindrome] food animal
rettulf: [flutternatter ananymondegreen] flier from Retta system
revavuaa: [*The Howling Stones* by Alan Dean Foster] purple ichthyoid with feathery gill from Parramat archipelago, Senisran
revil: [liver revil, silver revils palindromes] brown or metallic gray furry
revilope: [revil antelope portmanteau] revil with antlers
rex: furry with sparse, short, wavy fur
rhadari: [Kane's world series by Michael "Edward Powys Bradbury" Moorcock] 1.8-meter tall, 3.6-meter long carnivore with wide toothy mouth, claws, viscous crystalline "flesh" from Kane's world
rhamphorynchus: pterosaur succeeded by pterodactyl
rhea: [*Dell Crossword Puzzle Dictionary*] ostrich from America, Terra (alpha Zodiaci III)
rhedosaur: ["The Beast from 20,000 Fathoms"] 15-meter tall quadrupedal amphibian with toxic blood
rhedotaur: [rhedosaur minotaur portmanteau] amphibious bovinoid with toxic blood
r(h)eebok: [*Dell Crossword Puzzle Dictionary*] see peele
rhen: [wren-hen portmanteau] small brownish singing ornithoid with rounded wings, slender bill short tail
rhesus: [*Dell Crossword Puzzle Dictionary*] bruh, macaque
rheti: [Kane's world series by Edward Powys Bradbury (Michael Moorcock)] rodentoid the size of a half-grown elephant from Kane's world
rhiniciris: [four-i rhinoceros] four-eyed rhinoid
rhino-beast: ["Murder Under Glass" by Bob Liddil] armored land-whale from Grantin
rhinocéras-coléoptére: [*Another World* by Jean-Ignace-Isidore Gérard] rhinoceros-beetle, rhinoid with insectoid legs and carapace from Gérard's world

rhinoceros beetle: [Xanth series by Piers Anthony] giant bulldozer-like insectoid from Xanth

rhinograde: [*The Snouters* by Hal Stümpke] shrew-like mammals with specially adapted noses from Hi-Iay Islands

rhinokey: [rhinoceros-monkey palindrome, Wuz series by Douglas Hutchison] creature both rhinoceros-like and monkey-like

rhinoplatyx: [Outernauts] creature with horned duckbill and spiked tail, see rhinopus, saberpus

rhinopus: [Outernauts] immature rhinoplatatyx

rhinopuss: [rhinoceras puss portmanteau] felinoid with nosehorn

rhinosaur: ["nose-lizard"] tiny, cave lizard adapted to noses

rhinotaur: [rhinoceras minotaur portmanteau] rhinoceras-headed bull-like bovinoid

rhinowl: [rhinoceras owl portmanteau] rhinoceras-headed owl-like ornithoid, see shinnow

rhiyew: [Terra Monster] larger variety of rhinoid with backspikes from Terrarium

rhodsaur: large dinosauroid from Nytrino, Locomoto system, Galaxiki galaxy

rhubarb jelly: [jelly extrapolation] jelly-thick ooze

Rhulian flu virus: [*Infection* by John Gregory Betancourt] geneered virus that causes Rhulian influenza, deadly to Archarians, Terok Nor, Bejorans, Romulans and Helenans

ri: [beheaded gri] gypsy gan ceann, see ras, ry

riah: [hairy riah palindrome] furry in long-haired yrev and short haired oston varieties

riava: [riava caviar palindrome] ichthyoid noted for edible eggs

ribbonfish: [Xanth series by Piers Anthony] very wide, flat eel-like fish that captures by scooping and sliding along its length from Xanth

ribe: [*Dell Crossword Puzzle Dictionary*] lean animal from Scotland, Terra (alpha Zodiaci III), see scrag

rice pudding: [pudding extrapolation] pudding-thick ooze with rice-like solid parts

rid: [Crayola dirt rid palindrome] dirty brown ornithoid from Crayol A

ridgeback: [*Fantastic Beasts and Where to Find Them* by Newton Artemis Fido Scamander] large mammal-eating, black dragon with bronze horns, but unlike horntail venomous, from Norway, Terra (alpha Zodiaci III)

riding croc: [riding crop malapropism, "The Blue Giraffe" by L. Sprague de Camp] mutant long-legged crocodilian

Rigelian anteater: ["Collection Team" by Robert Silverberg] smelly anteater-like creature with unmusical honking/bleating from Rigel (beta Orionis) system

rigfrid: lemur-like creature with red stripe and large ears from Relegooturnia (Phoenix IV), Galaxiki galaxy

righthand: [handbird backformation] variety of handbird

rightwail: [rightwhale mondegreen] righthand variety with wailing call

rightwhale: [right whale mondegreen] anglewhale that turns in right angles

rightworm: [angleworm extrapolation] angleworm that moves in right angles like pacman

rihppa: [sapphire rihppas palindrome] bright blue ornithoid

riih: [hiirnahr ananymondegreen] mouse-bat from Rha system

rilf: [flirt rilf palindrome] purplish ornithoid

rillan: [*Dictionaria Vulcaniana*] source of fat used in ancient rumarie ritual from T'Khasi, Nevasa (40 Eridani) system

rimi: [*Unexplained!* by Jerome Clark] Babylonian auroch or unicorn, see re'em

rinchenia: [*Feathered Dinosaurs: The Origin of Birds* by John Long and Peter Schuten] 2.5-meter clam-cracking oviraptorosaur with large crest

rindigobird: [grue-bleen extrapolation] red bird that turns indigo, not to be confused with bledbird, blindigobird, gebird, gredbird, grindigobird, indigobird, redbird, reenbird, rellowbird, rindigobird, rioletbird, ruebird, vedbird, vindigobird, yedbird, yindigobird from Ora system

ringdocus: aka skunka warakin, hyena-like wild dog, possibly related to boraphage or thylacine, from Great Plains, Terra (alpha Zodiaci III)

rioletbird: [grue-bleen extrapolation] redbird that turns violet, not to be confused with bledbird, blioletbird, gebird, gredbird, grioletbird, redbird, reenbird, rellowbird, rindigobird, ruebird, vedbird, veenbird, vellowbird, vindigobird, violetbird, vuebird, yedbird or yioletbird from Ora system

rionnag: [Scot. *] 2-D pentapus or hexapus

rionnagator: [rionnag alligator portmanteau] alligator-like predator whose bite morphs victim into rioonag

riot: see venom

ripsnorter: [Davy Crockett] bear-like creature that rips and snorts

ripsnouter: [ripsnorter snouter portmanteau] snouter predator able to rip with four claws at once

rised: [desire resed palindrome] red ornithoid

ritoodolorum: [*First Lensman* by E. E. Smith] ferocious 6-legged tiger-like felinoid from Aldebaran (alpha Tauri) II

riuschiz: [Hildegard of Bingen's Lingua Ignota] vulture-like ornithoid from Ignota, Hildegard system

river devil: [The Legend of Zelda II] large arachnoid from Hyrule

rizia: [Italian pigrizia mondegreen] pig-sloth ancestral to pig and sloth

rnalixis: [Continuum] flying, 3-meter, 4-eyed eel-like dracoid from Ral'xi Sea, Antrxzs, Andromede, red giant star system

ro-roo: [*Creatures of the Galaxy* by Phil Brucato, Bill Smith, Rick D. Stuart, Chuck Truett] lemur-like simian from Kashÿÿÿk and Mimban, Jedi galaxy

ro: [oro ro palindrome] golden creature from Spain, Terra (alpha Zodiaci III); [garro mondegreen] gray-green thrush-woodcock-like ornithoid; 16-legged, green and yellow caterpillar from Da system

roa: [*Dell Crossword Puzzle Dictionary*] kiwi

roachcutter: [*The Future Is Wild* by Dougal Dixon] turret-eyed, short-winged, forest-dwelling insectivorous flutterbird

roachster: see kankrelat

roadkill: ["Uncharted Territory" by Connie Willis] extraordinarily sedentary creature from Boohte

roan: [*Dell Crossword Puzzle Dictionary*] white-flecked horse, see bay

roara prawn: [Peter MacInnis] land amphipod that lays eggs in river, feeds on sinking duck feathers of Finnegan's Lake, Big Ugly Island, so-called from its mating call

roargilla: [gorilla spoonerism] large ichthyoid with lion-like roar

robber-fly: [Xanth series by Piers Anthony] packrat-like insect able to lift many times their own weight from Xanth

robbin: [robin mondegreen] packrat-like red ornithoid

robinsect: [robin-insect portmanteau] large beaked, red-breasted insectoid

robinsect: [robin-insect portmanteau] large beaked, red-breasted insectoid

robo-beast: [Superhero City] cyberneticized beast used by Zigonians, see cyban

roc: [corn roc palindrome] yellow giant ornithoid, see avod, enroc, ewol'n, lis'n, rokh

rochi: [beheaded orochi] large dracoid with red eyes green back and 7 heads

rociraptor: [atrociraptor mondegreen] light brown roc-like dromaeosaur

rock breaker: ["The Headhunter" by Klaus Fischer] rockeater with snaggle-toothed funnel-snout

rock crab: [GreenSpace] conical rock-mimicking crab-like scavenger that hides behind other rock crabs like a hidebehind; crab-like golem made from rock

rock eel: ["The Lonely Time" by Andreas Findig] waterfall-dwelling eel from Orllyndie; eel-like golem make from rock

rock fish: [rockfish mondegreen] fish-like golem made from rock

rock hopper: [rockhopper mondegreen] hopper-like golem made from rock
rock hound: [Xanth series by Piers Anthony] dog made of living stone from Xanth; (hell)hound-like golem made from rock
rock lion: ["Our Man in Space" by Kurt Mahr] predatory felinoid from Gankar; lion-like golem made from rock
rock mussel: ["The Planet-lock" by Marianne Sydow] mollusc whose shell is used for knife blades from Guhmo (Nurshug IV), Black galaxy; mussel-like golem made from rock
rock rat: ["The Arkonide and the Ruler" by H. G. Francis] 15-cm, dangerous pack animal with dense, dark brown fur, large spherical head from Säggallo; rat-like golem made from rock
rock-eater: see saxiphage
rock-rack: [*Throy* by Jack Vance] food ichthyoid from Throy
rockadillo: [*Mad Magazine*: "Woodlore"] "mock rock", armadillo with rock-like backshell
rockchuck: see woodchuck
rockchucker: [rockchuck extrapolation] mountain-dwelling creature that chucks rocks on passersby
rocket fish: [*Extraterrestrial Zoology* by Robert A. Freitas, Jr.] fish able to propel itself out of water squid-like
rockfish: ["Rockfish" by Tim Miller and Jeremy Cook, Paul Talor, Chuck Wojthiewicz] magma-dwelling game ichthyoid
rockhopper: [*National Geographic Encyclopedia of Animals*] variety of penguin from Antarctic, Terra (alpha Zodiaci III)
rocking horse: ["The Rocking Horse Winner" by D. H. Lawrence"] toy animal that becomes winning race horse, see hobby horse
rocking-horse fly: [*Through the Looking-glass and What Alice Found There* by Lewis Carroll] wooden insect that swings between branches feeding on sawdust and sap from Looking-glass world
rockness monster: [sockness monster variation] lake snake-like stone golem
rod: see skyfish

rodden: [Roddenberry backformation] fruit bat especially fond of roddenberries
rodhocetus: [*After the Dinosaurs* by Donald R. Prothero] dolphin-like whale ancestor related to dalanistes and takracetus
rodporju: [James Cooke Brown's Loglan rodlu porju (road hog/pig/swine) compound] roadhog, roadrunner-like porcoid from Logla, Brown's system
roh: [shore rohs palindrome] amphibious creature; horned, fanged anthropoid from Noda system
rohippus: [beheaded orohippus] small, amphibious gan ceann
rojam: [Majorelle rojam palindrome] blue ornithoid
rojjer: [Buck Rogers mondegeen] predator that rojjes male deer
rojo: [Final Fantasy] red flan-thick ooze
rokh: [Sindbad] giant bird, said to feed elephants and rhinos to young, see rac, roc, rohc, rokling
rokling: [Outernauts] immature rokrol
roklingator: [rokling alligator portmanteau] alligator-like predator whose bite morphs victim into rokling
rokna tree fungus: ["Ewoks" series] blue fungus on rokna trees that causes amnesia and rapid aging from Endor I's moon, Jedi galaxy
rokrol: [Outernauts] blue and gray ornithoid, see rokling, rokh
rokubi: [Jap.] six-tailed seahorse-like slug with branching nettles
rolg'n: [crimson glory rolg'n osmirc palindrome] osmirc variant
roller: [*Major Operation* by James White] hermaphroditic, xenophilic waterworm without heart that must roll to circulate blood; [*Dell Crossword Puzzle Dictionary*] pigeon, see nun, barb, dove, pouter; [*National Geographic Encyclopedia of Animals*] insect and amphibian-eating bird from Indiasia, Terra (alpha Zodiaci III); [Pern series by Ann McCaffrey] woodlouse-like insectoid from Pern (Rukbat (alpha Sagittarii) III)

rolmtrokl: [*The Spawn of Fashün* by Kirby Lee Davis] creature from Boosboodle
rolt: [rag or rake of colts] small equinoid
rolve: [rout(e) of wolves spoonerism] wolf-like caninoid with antlers
roly-poly: aka pillbug, slater, sowbug, wood louse that moves by curling and rolling
romanticore: [Godville, romantic manticore portmanteau] manticore with lion-like body, scorpion tail and romance-craving heart
rompo: [*Here Be Monsters almanac*] creature with rabbit-like head, strange ears, thin body, powerful badger- or bear-like arms
Roncadorian hummingbird: [*The Green Child* by Herbert Read] hummingbird found in Roncador, S. America, Terra (alpha Zodiaci III)
rondor: ["The Super-Revenge of the Phantom Zone Prisoner" by Edmond Hamilton] unicorn-like creature from Krypton, Rao system
rondoor: [rondor door portmanteau] unicorn-like creature able to travel through portals
rong: [*Creatures of the Galaxy* by Phil Brucato, Bill Smith, Rick D. Stuart, Chuck Truett] boar-like porcoid from Minban, Jedi galaxy
rongator: [rong alligator portmanteau] alligator-like predator whose bite morphs victim into rong
ronto: ["The Gungan Frontier" by Chris McCubbin] quadruped beast of burden noted for humped neck and sidebeards, poor eyesight, from Tatooine, Jedi galaxy
roo: [OviPets] egg-laying macropodan
roobee: ["Galaxy Quest: A New Adventure" by Tony Lee Healey] ruby-like insectoid
roof lizard: see stegosaur
roofhound: [Russian wolfhound spoonerism] stegosaur-like caninoid from Wussia, Wuss system
roogie: [Space: 1889] ravenous predator from Mars (alpha Zodiaci IV)
roonat: [*The Courtship of Princess Leia* by Dave Wolverton] rodentoid from Jedi galaxy
roosteer: [rooster-steer portmanteau] griffinoid with four hoofed feet, beak, comb, horns and feathered head and neck

rootsucker: [*After Man* by Dougal Dixon] burrowing rodent with compressed-hair shell and faceplate
ropen: pterosauroid with green hair on head, black or brown hide that eats clams, fish, corpses from Vaboi I., New Guinea, Terra (alpha Zodiaci III), see duan
roper: ["The Ecology of the Roper" by Jonathan M. Richards] gray rope-like stalactite-mimic, related to darkmantle, piercer and lou carcolh
ropesnake: [*Starman Jones* by Robert Heinlein] rope-like serpentinoid from Charity
rora: [savory roras palindrome] food animal
rork: [*Rork!* by Avram Davidson] monstrous, elusive feeder on valuable redwing plant
rorku: [James Cooke Brown's Loglan rorno kurma] hornworm from Logla, Brown's system
rorse: [riding horse spoonerism] solitary equinoid noted for its roar
rortilba: [James Cooke Brown's Loglan rorno tilba] horntail from Logla, Brown's system
rortoise: [rockery of tortoises spoonerism] tail-wagging, roaring, carapaced amphibians
rortu: [James Cooke Brown's Loglan rorno tosku] hornhead from Logla, Brown's system
ros: [Danish hvalros, German Walroß-Wal backformation] aka roß, walrus-whale, amphibious cetacean with tusks and whiskers, ancestral to whale and walrus
rosip: [Fr. Johann Martin Schleyer's Volapük] toad, see bufod
rosselbock: [museumofhoaxes.com by Alex Boese] jackalope-like wolpertinger from N. Hessia, Terra (alpha Zodiaci III)
rosso: [Italian pesce rosso mondegreen] ichthyoid ancestral to goldfish
rot: [aetrot mondegreen] hellfire-breathing bluish-green equinoid; [tornade ananymondegreen] large, orange sphere from Eda system
rotader: [rotader predator palindrome] prey animal that rotades its prey
rotagator: [mynynym] alligator-like predator whose bite morphs victim of other gators back to their original form

rotargim: [migratory rotargim] ornithopteryx predator of gnitargim
rotini worm: [Flonk News: "A 'Rotini Worm' Fossil on Mars?"] vermoid from Mars (alpha Zodiaci IV)
rotorohippus: [beheaded protohiipus] equinoid helicopteryx
rotparaptor: [mynynym] packrat-like creature from Rotpa system
rotsa: [rotsa ruck] ruck relative
rotstsud: [dust storm rotstsud palindrome] pinkish gray ornithoid
rottee: [rotter backformation] sea bottom-dwelling prey of rotters from Snobaal, Laabon system, Galaxiki system
rotteel: [rottee eel pormanteau] rotte-like eel
rotter: [romp of otters spoonerism] maloderous bottom-feeding aquatic mammaloid
rotwing: [Outernauts] cheiropteroid in ice variety, see pugwing, pitwing
rotwingator: [rotwing alligator portmanteau] alligator-like predator whose bite morphs victim into rotwing
rou: [tamarou mondegreen] creature ancestral to tama and rouglar
rouge: [French poisson rouge mondegreen] red ichthyoid ancestral to goldfish
rouglar: [*The Galactic Gourmet* by James White] big, slow, stupid, nearly extinct ruminant from Wemar
roulenboule: [Fren.] see curl-up
rouse: [rat-mouse portmanteau] cross between a rat and a mouse
rove: ["The Star Bastard" by Robert Feldhoff] pollen-eating, beetle-like insectoid from Creiff
rover: [The Legend of Zelda] see shabom, tornade
rovi: [ivory rovi palindrome] off-white creature
rowhcni: [Crayola inchworm palindrome] greenish vermoid from Crayol A
rown: [red-brown spoonerism] bread-eating reddish-brown urban creature
rrod: [Albanian rrodhen mondegreen] blood-sucking chicken-like ornithoid

rrodhen: [Albanian rrodhe-dhen portmanteau] leech-sheep, blood-sucking, wooly mammal from Woolarra III, Galaxiki
ru: [buru mondegreen] lavender crocodilian
ruasosaur: [mynynym] dinosaur-like creature from Ruasus system
ruatotaur: [mynynym] bovinoid from Ruat system
rubb: [rubbish backformation] junky golem
rubber chicken: [Rich "(Son of) Svengoolie" Koz] thin, chicken-like toy animal animated by Love, see toothed chicken
rubber duckie: ["Rubber Duckie" by Jeff Moss] duck-like toy animal made of rubber animated by Love
rubbish bird: see liar bird
rubrobacter: extremophilic bacterium resistant to radiation, see deinococcus, pyrococcus
rubua: [auburn rubua palindrome] reddish brown ornithoid
rubusaur: ["bramblebush-lizard", The New Dinosaurs by Dougal Dixon] aka bricket
rubutaur: [rubusaur minotaur portmanteau] aka "bramblebush bull"
ruck: [raft of ducks spoonerism] aquatic ornithoid with duckbill, see rotsa
ruda: [garuda mondegreen] large gray-green eagle-like ornithoid
ruddler: [ruddle rattler portmanteau] red ocher water snake with rudder-tipped tail
rudimimus: [garudimimus mondegreen] gray-green toothless dinosaur
rudistid: toilet-shaped reef-forming bivalve with inverted conical bottom and hinged lid from Cretaceous
ruebird: [grue-bleen extrapolation] red bird that turns blue, not to be confused with bledbird, bleenbird, blellowbird, blindigobird, blioletbird, bluebird, gebird, gredbird, redbird, reenbird, rellowbird, rindigobird, rioletbird, ruebird, vedbird or yedbird from Ora system
ruff: [*Dell Crossword Puzzle Dictionary*] sandpiper, see ree(ve), stib, stint
rugfish: [*Big World* by Jack Vance] ichthyoid whose skin is used for sandal leather

rugger: [*Creatures of the Galaxy* by Phil Brucato, Bill Smith, Rick D. Stuart, Chuck Truett] small, furry rodentoid from forest moon of Endor, Jedi galaxy
rugkatt: [Swedish] Siberian forest cat from Siberia, Terra (alpha Zodiaci III)
ruinfly: [Outernauts] long-tailed, flying insectoid with pick ball-tipped tail, see banefly
rukh: [*Alf layah wa laylah* aka *The Thousand and One Nights*] huge bird with 2 horns, 4 back humps, that feeds elephants to its young
rum jelly: [jelly extrapolation] jelly-thick ooze, see guava
rumblesnout: [*Trullion: Alastor 2262* by Jack Vance] bugsucker from Trullion
rumpifusel: thin, furry arboreal creature like fur scarf, but dangerous when disturbed, from North Woods
rumpifuselope: [rumpifusel antelope portmanteau] rumpifusel with antlers
rundihorn: [*After Man* by Dougal Dixon] gi antelope-like rhinoid with 4 conical horns
runner: see runnerbeast
runnerbeast: [Pernese] horse from Pern (Rukbat (alpha Sagittaurii) III)
rurkey: [rafter of turkeys spoonerism, red turkey portmanteau] red, turkey-like ornithoid
rusa: [National Geographic Encyclopedia of Animals] deer from Java, Terra (alpha Zodiaci III), [*Dell Crossword Puzzle Dictionary*] deer or elk from India, see sambar, maha
rust monster: ["The ecology of the Rust Monster" by Ed Greenwood] 1.5-meter rust-colored cave-dwelling crustacean with yellowish-tan underbelly, prehensile antennae that instantly oxidize iron, gold or silver, propeller-tail, sometimes in symbiotic relation with carrion crawler
rutai: [miniature rutai nim palindrome] aka mininim, small nim variety of rac
ruuk: see drushbar
ruumet breehr: [Space: 1889] large, but gentle, beast of burden from Mars (alpha Zodiaci IV)
ruvf: ["The Altar of Redemption" by Anne Laurie Logan] roaring felinoid of the jauneans

ruza: [azure ruza palindrome] light purplish blue ornithoid
ry: [beheaded gry] gypsy gam ceann, see ras, ri
rybyka: [Belarussian byry-ryka portmanteau] fish-bull, horned amphibian from Akyby, Rybyka system, Galaxiki galaxy
rycrit: [*Star Wars Sourcebook* by Bill Slavicsek and Curtis Smith] bovine from Ryloth, Jedi galaxy
rykor: [Barsoom series by Edgar Rice Burroughs] headless anthropoid used as steed by arachnoid Kaldane from Mars (alpha Zodiaci IV)
rype: [*Dell Crossword Puzzle Dictionary*] ptarmigan
ryth: [*Tanar of Pellucidar* by Edgar Rice Burroughs] Amiocap Island cave bear
ryu: triphibious dragon from Japan, Terra (alpha Zodiaci III)
s'ris: [*Double, Double* by Michael Jan Friedman] tentacled, soft, poisonous den-dwelling creature from Tranquility 7, Gatheta (gamma Theta) system
sa: [ash sa palindrome] gray-white to black ornithoid; [dansa mondegreen] giant headless heptapus from Da system
sa(i)miri: [*Dell Crossword Puzzle Dictionary*] monkey from S. America, Terra (alpha Zodiaci III)
sabalo: [*Dell Crossword Puzzle Dictionary*] milkfish, see awa
saberpus: [Outernauts] mature, hunchbacked rhinoplatatyx with fangs
saberpuss: [saberpus puss portmanteau] sabertootooth housecat
sabre-tooth sand crab: [Starcross by Philip Reeve] from Mars (alpha Zodiaci IV)
sabre-tooth squirrel: ["Ice Age" by Michael J. Wilson, etal.] squirrel with sabre-like fangs
sabrefish: [swordfish extrapolation] ichthyoid with sabre-like snout from Akyby, Rybyka system, Galaxiki galaxy
saccosaur: [*The New Dinosaurs* by Dougal Dixon] see pouch
saccotaur: [saccosaur minotaur portmanteau] marsupial bovinoid

sackbuter: [trumpeter swan backformation] trombone swan-like ornithoid with sackbut-like call

Sadalsuudian moth: ["Intelligent Life Elsewhere" by Stephen Bowkett] furry, sparrow-sized moth with blackberry-like eyes from Sadalsaad (beta Aquarii) system

sadu: [tsisadu backformation] wren-rabbit griffinoid

safat: [*Dragons, Unicorns and Other Magical Beasts* by Robin Palmer] ever-flying bird, whose eggshell induces madness

sagayl: [Armenian sag-gayl portmanteau] goose-wolf, pack-hunting, predatory caninopteryx

sagaylope: [sagayl antelope portmanteau] sagayl with antlers

sagibi: [aosagibi montegreen] heron-like ornithoid, related to ao

sagsār: [*Mahābhārata*] 8-legged deer-like mountain-dweller

saguin: [*Dell Crossword Puzzle Dictionary*] monkey from S. America, Terra (alpha Zodiaci III)

sai: [*Dell Crossword Puzzle Dictionary*] capuchin monkey, see marmoset, lar

saia-wip: [*Cyclopedia of Worlds*] kai-wip relative from Emeris, Sheel-Sen system

saiga: [*National Geographic Encyclopedia of Animals*] antelope relative from Asia, Terra (alpha Zodiaci III)

saigator: [saiga alligator portmanteau] alligator-like predator whose bite morphs victim into saiga

sailor: ["The Winged Dreamers" by Jennifer Guttridge] furry brown sausage with bright amber eyes, flat furry face, 3-clawed toe per foot from Durban's world

sajou: [*Dell Crossword Puzzle Dictionary*] monkey from S. America, Terra (alpha Zodiaci III)

sak: [beheaded tsak] bovinoid

saki: [*Dell Crossword Puzzle Dictionary*] monkey from S. America, Terra (alpha Zodiaci III)

saku: ["The Web" by Michaelle Stern] flying creature with oval ring body, builds mulch nests in caves

saladang: see sladang

saladangator: [saladang alligator portmanteau] alligator-like predator whose bite morphs victim into saladang

salakamar: [*Loglan* by James Cook Brown] çalakamar from Brown's world, Logla system

salamander: [*Here Be Monsters almanac*, Paracelsus] unstable lizard-like creature of living flame whose shed skin becomes coal, related to semi-stable efreet

saligugi: [Cherokee] snapping turtle from Tsalagi system

salika: [*The Perfect Planet* by Edward Packard] unicorn from Utopa (Anchar V), Gallatin quadrant

sallard: [sord or su(i)te of mallards spoonerism, salamander-mallard portmanteau] flame-resistant mallard-like ornithoid]

sallur: [*Planiverse* by Alexander Dewdney] see ra sallur

salm: [Fr. Johann Martin Schleyer's Volapük] salmon-like ichthyoid from Schleyer's system

salmon-bear: [salmonberry backformation] salmon-headed, amphibious ursinoid

saloli: [Cherokee] squirrel-like creature from Tsalagi system

salor: [*Monster Manual* by Skip Williams, etal.] illithidae variant

salp: [*Dell Crossword Puzzle Dictionary*] small sea creature

salpinxer: [trumpeter swan backformation] ivory-colored swan-like ornithoid with salpinx-like call

Salt Lake snake: large, serpentine monster from Salt Lake, UT, Terra (alpha Zodiaci III)

saltfish: [pepperfish antonym] salty sea food ichthyoid

saltik: [czasaltik mondegreen] insectivore

saltimbocca: schmoo-like creature

Salvanese gecko: [*Encyclopedia Galactica*] geckoid from Salvan

samad: [damask samad palindrome] flamingoid

samari panther: see sinha
sambar: [*National Geographic Encyclopedia of Animals*] deer from S. Asia, [*Dell Crossword Puzzle Dictionary*] elk from India, Terra (alpha Zodiaci III), see maha, rusa
samjogo: ["Three-Legged Bird to replace Phoenix on State Seal"] 3-legged bird from Korea, Terra (alpha Zodiaci III)
samorael: ["samorael at times emit tastable aromas" palindrome, Jeff Grant in *Word Ways*] unusual chiropteran that emits stable aromas rather than ultrasound
samothere: [*After the Dinosaurs* by Donald R. Prothero] giraffe relative with shorter neck, longer horns
sanbi: [Jap.] aka umibouzu, green turtle with three tails
sand flapjack: [*After Man* by Dougal Dixon] flat-tailed rodent with dew-condensing stone-and-twig burrow plug
sand shark: ["Sand Shark" by Cameron Larson] shark adapted to burrowing through sandy beaches ["Far Side" by Gary Larson] and deserts; ["The Invisible Enemy" by Jerry Sohl] sand-dwelling predator that tracks prey by sound from Mars (alpha Zodiaci IV)
sand sloth: ["Droids" series] rhino-muskox-like beast of burden from Annoo, Jedi galaxy
sand toad: from New Caledonia ("Ligdon and the Young Pretender" by Walter Jon Williams)
sandbat: ["The Empath" by Joyce Muskat] predator that appears as inanimate rock crystals until it attacks from Manark IV
sandeater: ["The Curse of the Microcosm" by Conrad Shepherd] desert creature from Duofftrie microcosm
sanderling: [*National Geographic Encyclopedia of Animals*] invertebrate-eating bird from Arctic, Terra (alpha Zodiaci III)
sanderlingator: [sanderling alligator portmanteau] alligator-like predator whose bite morphs victim into sanderling
Sanderson's crab: ["A Walk in the Dark" by Arthur C. Clarke] crustacean known by the clicking of its claws, feeds on rock not actually greenhorns from beyond Carver's Pass, Sanderson's world, near Canopus (alpha Carinae)
sandking: ["Sandkings" by George R. R. Martin] scorpion-like creature from Mars (alpha Zodiaci IV)
sandkingator: [sandking alligator portmanteau] alligator-like predator whose bite morphs victim into sandking
sandle: [*The New Dinosaurs* by Dougal Dixon] red, burrowing, desert fususaur with black stripes, white underbelly and paralyzing saliva
sandman: [Xanth series by Piers Anthony] shape-shifting living sand able to assume humanoid and other shapes and induce sleepiness from Xanth
sando: [Satr Wars] 200-meter omnivorous sea mammaloid from Naboo, Jedi galaxy
sandwalker: giant, camel-eating, nocturnal crustacean with sharp beak and scorpion-like tail
sane: [se(d)ge of cranes spoonerism] ornithoid with long legs, long neck and long bill
sang: [Danish sanglærke mondegreen] lark-like ornithoid
sangator: [sang alligator portmanteau] alligator-like predator whose bite morphs victim into sang
sao: [*Dell Crossword Puzzle Dictionary*] sea worm, see lurg, nereis
saor: [roast saor palindrome] food ornithoid related to tsaorto
sapajou: [*Dell Crossword Puzzle Dictionary*] monkey from S. America, Terra (alpha Zodiaci III)
sapeornis: [Society for Avian Paleontology and Evolution, *Feathered Dinosaurs: The Origin of Birds* by John Long and Peter Schuten] bird with 1-meter wingspan but no sternum from Cretaceous
sapo de loma: ["toad of the hills"] deadly poisonous bird-eating batrachian of Andes Mts., S. America, Terra (alpha Zodiaci III)
sapo: [*Dell Crossword Puzzle Dictionary*] toadfish

Sapontian basilisk: ["The Emperor and the Maula" by Robert Silverberg] basilisk-like creature from Sapont I., Sea of Miaule, Grand Binella, Ansaar empire

sapress: [Terra Monster] creature from Terrarium

sar: [dabbē-i-chahār-sar mondegreen] creature ancestral to dabbē-i-chahār-sar

sardine: [*Dell Crossword Puzzle Dictionary*] young pogy or menhaden fish, see fumado, pilchard

sardula: [Kesava temple, Somnathpur] horned leonine

sardzi: [Armenian sard-dzi portmanteau] spider-horse, 8-legged equinoid

sarecoceras: [mynynym] deer-like ruminant with sarex-shaped horns

sareteras: [mynynym] monster from Sare system

sarg: [grassland Nal's sarg, Grasslan Nal's sarg palindromes] ruminant from Grassla, Nal system

sargan: [*Warrior of Llarn, Theif of Llarn* by Gardner F. Fox] sharp-clawed, half-tonne, white furball from Llarn

Sargasso sea monster: [*Boris Karloff's Tales of Mystery* #29: "Creature of the Sargasso Sea"] 20-meter, one-eyed, cephalopoid seaweed gestalt animated by a meteorite from mid-Atlantic, Terra (alpha Zodiaci III)

sargator: [sarg alligator portmanteau] alligator-like predator whose bite morphs victim into sarg

sark: ["Pen Pals" by Melinda M. Snodgrass] Klingon steed from Qonos

sarkastodon: see creodont

sarlacc: ["Return of the Jedi" by Lawrence Kasdan and George Lucas] sand-dwelling 30-meter carnivore with many feeding tentacles around its 2.4-meter toothed beak and barbed tongue, giant variety from Felucia several kilometers, Jedi galaxy

sarmimus: [sarmus backformation] jellyfish-like cephalopod

sarmus: [Cyclopedia of Worlds] jellyfish-like relative of egassa sarphagum from Dakka, Neptune system

sarpi: [James Cooke Brown's Loglan] serpent from Logla, Brown's system

sarsaok: [Koa's Ra's sarsaok palindrome] from Ra, Koa system, see hadhayosh

saspi: [saspi dipsas palindrome] dipsas-like amphisbæna

sasquatch: [*Monster Spotter's Guide to North America* by Scott Francis] aka bigfoot, 3-meter nape from N. E. Pacific coast, Terra (alpha Zodiaci III)

satauqa: [aquatasnap ananymondegreen] shark-like ichthyoid from Pa system

sâu: [Vietnamese con sâu mondegreen] worm ancestral to con and grub or con worm from Disa, the Leech Planet

säuge: [German Säugetier mondegreen] creature related to mammalians from Germa system

saural: [*Dell Crossword Puzzle Dictionary*] scad fish

sauropodia delta: [Cyclopedia of Worlds] 33-meter sauropod with 3 back-fins from Palul (Lar Don), the Dinosaur Planet

sauropodia eta: [Cyclopedia of Worlds] 36-m sauropod from Palul (Lar Don), the Dinosaur Planet

sauroposeidon: [*The Big Bad Book of Beasts* by Michael Largo] 33-meter herbivorous dinosaur from N. America, Terra (alpha Zodiaci III)

saurornithoid: ["lizard-bird", *Feathered Dinosaurs: The Origin of Birds* by John Long and Peter Schuten] 2.5-meter troodontid with large eyes, relatively large brain, narrow snout and long grasping hands, see ornithosaur

saurornitholestes: ["lizard-bird-thief", *Feathered Dinosaurs: The Origin of Birds* by John Long and Peter Schuten] 1.6-meter theropod from N. America, Terra (alpha Zodiaci III)

savannah walker: [*The Menagerie* by Martin Day] largest creature in Menagerie of Ukkazaal

sawf: [sawfish backformation] sawfish mimicking ichthyoid

sawfish: [*Battles with Giant Fish* by Frederick Albert Mitchell-Hedges] 9.4-meter, 2600-kg fish with saw-like rostrum
sawfly: [Xanth series by Piers Anthony] night construction insect with sharp proboscis from Land of Flies, Xanth
sawjaw: [*Worlds Apart: Nat. Hist. of Furaha and Earth* by Souren Nyoroge] 2.8-meter, black sea creature with short side tusks, white underbelly, 6 flippers and goresacs from Furaha (alpha Phoenicis IV)
sax: [saxophone backformation] ruminant noted for curved bugle-like horn
saxhorner: [trumpeter swan backformation] swan-like ornithoid related to corneteer and tuba swan
saxiphage: rock-eater in many varieties, including little ones like magnetite-fixing bacteria at 6400 meters or 150°C, and big ones like their hosts
saxtubabird: [trumpeter swan backformation] large swan-like ornithoid with saxtuba-like call related to corneteer, saxhorner, and tuba swan
sbi: [sbi ribs palindrome] food vertibrate
sbleal: warmwater seal-like food mammaloid with 2 tails from from Youmisian Homeland (Edonian cluster III), Galaxiki galaxy
scab bee: [scabby mondegreen] bee-like insectoid whose sting and scabs
scalandre: [Continuum] 2-meter beetle steed from Igendal, Belverius Helenis system
scallop: [*Dell Crossword Puzzle Dictionary*] bivalve mollusc
scandaroon: see carrier pigeon
Scanodonian bat: ["Face to Face with Planet Scanodon" by Rocky Strone] 6-meter, 4-winged chiropteran dwelling on crater lake rim from Scanodon, Croft system
scansoriopteryx: [*Feathered Dinosaurs: The Origin of Birds* by John Long and Peter Schuten] epidendrosaur-like coelurosaur
scare-crow: [scarecrow mondegreen] skitt predator
scargan: [*Warrior of Llarn, Theif of Llarn* by Gardner F. Fox] sharp-clawed, half-tonne furry, white spheroid

scarid: [*Dell Crossword Puzzle Dictionary*] parrot-fish, see loro, lauia
scarpia: [*King David's Spaceship* by Jerry Pourelle] deadly warm-blooded scorpion-like sauroid from Makassar
scaup: [*National Geographic Encyclopedia of Animals*] aquatic bird of Americas, Terra (alpha Zodiaci III), [*Dell Crossword Puzzle Dictionary*] sea duck, see ern(e), gull, tern, fulmar, gannet, petrel, scoter
scay: [scold of jays spoonerism, scaup bluejay portmanteau] blue sea duck=like ornithoid
sceli: [scoop of pelicans spoonerismandegreen] garbage can-like creatures which leave malodorous trail
scelidosaur: 3.5-meter dinosaur with 7 rows of backplates and spikes
scelidotaur: [scelidosaur minotaur portmanteau] bovinoid with backplates and spikes
scendent: [transcendent, ascendent mondegreen] flying worm from Tra system
schamir: barleycorn-sized stone-digesting worm, see naggartura
s(c)hish: [school or shoal of fish spoonerism] easily caught dodo-like ichthyoid
schizo carp: [schizocarp mondegreen] carp-like ichthyoid that sometimes behaves like piranha
Schlem eel: [schlemiel mondegreen] eel-like ichthyoid from Schlem noted for its out-of-water clumsiness
schmoo: [*The Life and Times of the Schmoo* by Al Capp] small, pink pear-shaped bipedal invertebrate that gives both eggs and milk, tastes like chicken when fried, steak when broiled, reproduce by 1200% in 4 seconds from Valley of the Schmoon
scho: [kanscho mondegreen] hawk-like ornithoid from Ka system
Schrödinger's bat: [Schrödinger's cat extrapolation] vampire bat that is both dead and undead until observed
Schrödinger's cat: [Erwin Schrödinger] cat that is both alive and dead until observed

scimitar-wolf: [*Star Trek Log 6* by Alan Dean Foster] wolf-like caninoid with scimitar-like horn from Taurea, Taurus
scizzorback: ["The Hunting" by Doris Beetem] lithe, brown herd creature from Rheingeld
scod: [*Dell Crossword Puzzle Dictionary*] horse-mackerel, see merhorse
scoon: [*Throy* by Jack Vance] ichthyoid from Throy
scoonee: [Outernauts] immature, blue-black scrunko
scora: [*Worlds of the Federation* by Shane Johnson] hostile, even though herbivorous, 4-meter bipedal lowland sauroid with six nostrils and four feeding tendrils from Kesir-Tosharra (Vega (alpha Lyrae) IX)
scorpii: [piscium extrapolation] egg-laying scorpion-like creature
scorpion bee: [Avatar #1] bee-like insectoid with scorpion-like stinger
scorpius: [Monster Galaxy] cyberteddybear-like ursinoid
scorpiusaur: dracoid with scorpion tail from Scorpius constellation
scoter: [*Dell Crossword Puzzle Dictionary*] sea duck, see ern(e), gull, skua, scaup, tern, fulmar, gannet, petrel
scotura: ["Knives" by Lawrence G. DiTillio] silent beast from Centauri
scrag: [*Dell Crossword Puzzle Dictionary*] scrawny animal, see ribe
scragator: [scrag alligator portmanteau] alligator-like predator whose bite morphs victim into scrag
scragg: [scraggy backformation] lean, voracious predator
scraggator: [scragg alligator portmanteau] alligator predator whose bite morphs victim into scragg
scramaloupe: [*Space Trap* by Monica Hughes] rare mammoth-like creature with red and gray stripes from Nakhan
scream: see venom
screamer: [*National Geographic Encyclopedia of Animals*] swan relative from S. America, Terra (alpha Zodiaci III)

screaming bird: [Avatar: The Last Airbinder: "The Swamp"] pudgy, lumpy ornithoid with deafening scream
screer: ["The Book of Ptath" by A. E. Van Vogt] voracious 2.4-meter bird with 4.8-meter wingspan used as both steed and weapon from Gonwonlane
screwdriverfly: [Xanth series by Piers Anthony] night construction insect from Land of Flies, Xanth
scrofa: [*The Future Is Wild* by Dougal Dixon] desert boar with long snout for finding cryptile eggs
scrunko: [Outernauts] felinoid with more reddish underside, see scoonee, skoone
scrunt: ["The Lady in the Water" by M. Night Shyamalan] grassy-haired, croc-tailed, red-eyed caninoid nymph-killer
scuda: [Terra Monster] small, shrimp-eating ichthyoid, see predicuda and leviacuda, from Terrarium
scuirrel: [scurry of squirrels spoonerism, scurrier portmanteau] kangaroo-rat-squirrel-like scavenger
scuirrelope: [scuirrel antelope portmanteau] scuirrel with antlers
scup: [*Dell Crossword Puzzle Dictionary*] fish, see porgy
scurrier: ["The Gungan Frontier" by Chris McCubbin] horned kangaroo-rat-like scavenger with forward-curving horns (female) rather than antlers (male) from Tatooine, Jedi galaxy
scutosaur: 2.4-meter sawtoothed herbivorous dinosaur
scutotaur: scutosaur minotaur portmanteau] aka "sawtoothed bull"
scweynwal: boar-whale, see herill
scyk: [*Star Wars Galaxies*] lizard-like reptilian from Tatooine, Jedi galaxy
scyke: [Outernauts] turquoise dracoid with purple pterosaur, also in tawny, shadow (black and red), ivory, scarlet and aqua varieties
scykling: [Outernauts] immature scyke, also in tawny, ivory, scarlet, shadow (black and red) and aqua varieties

scyklingator: [scykling alligator portmanteau] alligator-like predator whose bite morphs victim into scykling

scylla: [*Windhaven* by George R. R. Martin] predatory sea creature from Windhaven

scyphozoa: [Code Lyoko] large, levitating jellyfish-like creature with green crystalline eye with 3 regenerative brain-fluid-sucking tentacles geneered by Xana

sde: [Ekan sde bedsnake palindrome] bedsnake-like amphisbæna from Eka peninsula, Snowi, Nejstea system, Galaxiki galaxy

sdetsi: [tsisdetsi backformation] wren-mouse griffinoid

sdvna: [tsisdvna backformation] wren-crawfish triphibian

se: [wrasse mondegreen] reef ichthyoid from Wra system

sea bladder: ["Echo of the Lost" by Hans Kneifel] blatter-like sea creature

sea dove: [*Medici Tigurini Historiae Animalium Liber IV Paralipomena* by Conrad Gesner] monstrous sea creature with long barbed tail and ray-like body

sea lizard: ["Deja Q" by Richard Danus] sauroid from Markoff

sea neetle: [Xanth series by Piers Anthony] spheroid plant-like creature with toadstool-like gills and large stinging tentacles from Xanth

sea-cat: ["The Ecology of the Sea Lion" by Ed Greenwood] sea-green land shark-like ichthyoid with cougar-like head, clawed forelimbs, whale-like tail, 2 dorsal fins and hairy back, see pe

sea-dog: talbot with webbed feet, scales, dorsal fin and otter-like tail

sea-dogator: [sea-dog alligator portmanteau] alligator-like predator whose bite morphs victim into sea-dog

sea cow: [Xanth series by Piers Anthony] cow-fish used as steed and pet from Xanth or [Xanthian mondegreen] Xa, Thia system

seabee: [C. B. mondegreen] bee-like insectoid that communicates via radiowaves, see baybee

seagle: [sea gull-eagle portmanteau] coastal orinthoid with long wings, webbed feet, hooked beak and sharp eyesight

seahat: [The Legend of Zelda: "The Wind Walker"] large, shark-like flying ichthyoid that shrinks when killed

seamaw: [Outernauts] seahorse-like cat-fish with large "ears", see seamew, seagirr, swamp maw

seamew: [Outernauts] immature seamaw

seargirr: [Outernauts] mature seamaw with large fins, small "ears"

searsnap: [Outernauts] red croc-like singesnap

seasoar: [*Worlds Apart: Nat. Hist. of Furaha and Earth* by Souren Nyoroge] white hermaphroditic ornithoid with long neck, 4 black-tipped wings from Furaha (alpha Phoenicis IV)

seaweed shark: ["Simpsons" series] rare vegetarian shark that eats seaweed

seawolf: creature with wolf's body, fish's tail and webbed feet from Akyby, Rybyka system, Galaxiki galaxy

sec: [Ekan sec ice snake palindrome] ice snake-like amphisbæna from Eka peninsula, Snowi, Nejstea system, Galaxiki galaxy

second mast: [fourth mast backformation] relative of fourth mast from Emeris, Sheel-Sen system

secondhand: [handbird backformation, "Second-hand Rose" by Fanny Brice] rose variety of handbird

sedapa: [*Unexplained!* by Jerome Clark] aka orang-pendek, 1.2-meter, dark red, long-armed pongoid from Sumatra, Terra (alpha Zodiaci III)

sedulous ape: [Robert Louis Stevenson] see homomimus

see: seesee-like nasna

seedis: [Andromeda: "Belly of the Beast"] planet-eater said to return to Savion every 6,270 years

seeker: [hider antonym] fractal-dimensional hider predator

seel: [seething of eels spoonerism, seal-eel portmanteau] long, flipper-less sirenian

seersucker: [*If I Ran the Zoo* by Theodore Seuss Geissel] dog-faced pongoid

seesar: ["Godzilla vs. the Cosmic Monster" by Jun Fukuda] 120-meter anthropoid with long golden fur on head, shoulders and sides, but otherwise blue-scaled, with floppy elephantine ears, blue-tipped forehead horn and red eyes able to shoot destructive beams

seesee: [*Dell Crossword Puzzle Dictionary*] sand partridge

segni: [singesnap ananymondegreen] fire-resistant chelonoid, see slleh

segnosaur: [*Feathered Dinosaurs: The Origin of Birds* by John Long and Peter Schuten] 6-meter primitive therizinosaur

segnotaur: [segnosaur minotaur portmanteau] therizinotaur ancestor

sehc: [chestnut untsehc palindrome antonym] brown unt

seibb: ["seibb at times emit tabbies" palindrome] tabby gestalt

seja: [*Metamorphosis* by Jean Lorrah] herd creature from Elysia

sek: [*Unofficial Questarian Guide*] mite-like insectoid from Tev'Meck, MakTar system

sel-fish: [Xanth series by Piers Anthony] fat-faced pleasure-loving fish from Xanth

seladang: see sladang

seldee: [Ekan seldee needle snake palindrome] needle snake-like amphisbæna from Eka peninsula, Snowi, Nejstea system, Galaxiki galaxy

seldeel: [seldee eel] seldee-like eel

self-lovebird: ["Speed Bump" by Dave Coverly] aka hermaphrodite bird, mutant parenthogenic lovebird that loves only self

selopad: ["selopad at times emit tadpoles" palindrome] batrachian gestalt

semi-freezard: one of two mini-freezards

semiped: mutant with 50% as many legs

sengi: gray-faced elephant shrew from Ndunlulu forest, Tanzania, Terra (alpha Zodiaci III)

senmurv: ["Xoology" by Kittenbaker] metallic orange mammal-bird with silver head, 4 wings, vulture's talons from Persia and Szurane

sepo: [Ekan sepo ropesnake palindrome] ropesnake-like amphisbæna from Eka peninsula, Snowi, Nejstea system, Galaxiki galaxy

seps: [*Dell Crossword Puzzle Dictionary*] serpent from Europe, Terra (alpha Zodiaci III)

septibullus: sprintosaur with seven-knobbed crest

Septicorn: [Lat. seven-horned, Rev. 5:6] aka Heptops, Jesus, the Lamb of God

ser: [merganser mondegreen] black and white duck-like ornithoid from Merga system

seren: [Welch *] 2-D pentapus or hexapus

seriema: [*Dell Crossword Puzzle Dictionary*] carnivorous bird from S. America, see guan, jacu, sylph, turco

serof: [forest serof palindrome] arboreal creature

seron: [sedge or seige of herons spoonerism, serpent-headed heron-like ornithoid

seronster: [seron monster portmanteau] monstrous serpent-headed heron-like ornithoid

serpent-ours: [*Another World* by Jean-Ignace-Isidore Gérard] snake-headed bear from Gérard's world

serpent-tour: snake-headed bull from Gérard's world

Serpent: ["Star Wars" series by Archie Goodwin and Al Williamson] 14-meter mottled serpent controlled via ultrasonics by the Serpent Masters to enslave, among others, Tanith Shire's planet, Jedi galaxy

serpentes: [OviPets] egg-laying serpentine

serpie: [Outernauts] 1-eyed, red-eyed, leg-less, immature serpine

serpine: [Outernauts] 2-headed pterosaur, see serpie, serplex

serplex: [Outernauts] 3-headed mature serpine

serpquin: [serpent-harlequin portmanteau, Terra Monsters] clown-like serpent with collar and red nose, see snozo, from Terrarium

sespia: [*After the Dinosaurs* by Donald R. Prothero] dwarf leptauchenine from Oligocene

sesquinsect: mutant insect with 9, rather than usual 6, legs

sesquiped: [hippopotamonstrosesquipedian backformation] mutant with 50% more legs
sesquovus: [ovis extrapolation] snowman-like trispheroid
seven-eyed giant squid: ["Pearl's Peril"] giant squid with seven vertical-slit eyes, with lash-like tentrils, see Heptops
sevlo: [sevlo wolves palindrome] wolf-like caninoid
sewen: [*Dell Crossword Puzzle Dictionary*] trout from Britain, Terra (alpha Zodiaci III), see sewin
sewer alligator: [Span. el lagarto, "the lizard"] large, sewer-dwelling gator; [Resident Evil] huge, garbage-eating alligator T-Virus victim
sewin: see sewen
sex gas parasite: [Torchwood: "Day One"] gaseous parasite to which air is deadly, in host and ultra-powerful pheromones to attract and suck life from bedmates before host's internal organs explode
sextiped: mutant with one-sixth as many legs
sey: [*Dell Crossword Puzzle Dictionary*] pollack fish
seychellois: white slim furry with wedge-shaped head, other colors, blue eyes
sfear: [qyoob extrapolation] gelatinous sphere that telepathically induces fear in predators and prey alike
sgaoileadh: [Scot. &] 2-D das-like creature
sge: [sge legs palindrome] food batrachoid with regenerating legs
sgoyi: [Cherokee] worm-like creature from Tsalagi system
sha: [*Dell Crossword Puzzle Dictionary*] wild mountain sheep from Tibet, Terra (alpha Zodiaci III), see sha, sna, rasse, urial, bharal, nahoor, oorial
sha'mi: [Star Trek] furry with long curly hair used in textiles from T'Khasi, Nevasa (40 Eridani) system
shaak: ["The Gungan Frontier" by Chris McCubbin] small-legged, small-headed herd, ruminant pachyderm with wiggly snout, large rump from Naboo, Jedi galaxy

shabast: ["Face To Face With Planet Scanodon" by Rocky Strone] amphibious predator from Scandon, Croft system
shabaz: eagle-like giant falcon from Iranian mts., Terra (alpha Zodiaci III)
shabom: [The Legend of Zelda] large, but fragile, bubble from Hyrule, see tornade, marabounta, rover
shachihoko: [shachi (grampus) ideogram] tiger-carp from Japan, Terra (alpha Zodiaci III)
shadokuro: [gashadokuro mondgreen] giant gray-green skeletoid
shadow mastiff: [*Monster Manual* by Skip Williams, etal.] pitch-black mastiff-like caninoid with retractable claws and cat-like tail, ogre/orc-like face, terrifying howl
shadow-crawler: ["The Shadow-Crawler" by Laurie S. Sutton] ravaging space insectoid
shadowmare: [Terra Monster] 3-horned quadruped with backspikes, long sickle-tipped tail from Terrarium
shadowvolt: [Terra Monster] electric deer-like creature, see volteer, from Terrarium
shadytail: [Grk. skiouros "squirrel"] squirrel
shagg: [shagg backformation] long-haired furry
shaggator: [shagg alligator portmanteau] alligator predator whose bite morphs victim into shagg
shagrat: [*The Future Is Wild* by Dougal Dixon] large, shaggy rodent, prey of snowstalkers
shai-hulud: [*Dune* by Frank Herbert] 400-meter long, 100-meter wide silvery-gray sandworm with thousands of carbo-silica teeth from Arrakis (Canopus (alpha Carinae) III)
shake: [*Fantastic Beasts and Where to Find Them* by Newton Artemis Fido Scamander] spiny fish
shakuhachibird: [trumpeter swan backformation] fluter swan-like ornithoid with shakuhachi-like call, related to ti-tzu swan
shalk: [The Elder Scrolls III: "Morrowind"] large, hellfire-breathing beetle-like insectoid, source of shalk resin or from Ahla, Ojikh system, Galaxiki galaxy

shalloth: [*After Man* by Dougal Dixon] sloth-like flightless bat with thumb-claw, mitten-hands

shama: [*Dell Crossword Puzzle Dictionary*] thrush from India, Terra (alpha Zodiaci III)

shambler: [*Monster Manual* by Gary Gygax] 1.8-meter tall, 1.7-tonne creature like rotting vegetable pile

shampoodle: [shampoo poodle portmanteau] poodle-mimic from Godville

shan: [*The Queen of Zamba* by L. Sprague de Camp] 6-legged reptilian from Krishna, tau Ceti system, related to pudamef

shanda: [shyness of pandas spoonerism] fruit-eating ursinoid fond of windowsill pies

shankem: [*The Unofficial Questarian Guide*, Tev'Meckian "four-foot"] quadruped from Tev'meck, Warvan system

shant: [gashant mondegreen] gray-green iguana-like, beaked biped

shantak: ["The Dream-Quest of Unknown Kadath" by Howard Phillips Lovecraft] slimy, horse-headed bat-winged ornithoid larger than elephant, that fears nightgaunts from Inquanok, Dreamworld

shantungosaur: [*The Big Bad Book of Beasts* by Michael Largo] 15-meter herbivorous duck-billed dinosaur

sharabha: [*The Unicorn*] 8-legged deer misidentified as unicorn, see Jersey devil

shark-whale: ["Robot Hugs" by R. Hugs'] shark-headed whale, much more dangerous than whale shark

sharkon: ["Flash Gordon" series] shark-like ichthyoid with long, barbed tail, narwhal-like horn, large flippers from Mongo

sharkonster: [sharkon monster portmanteau] monstrous sharkon

sharkopath: [*The Future Is Wild* by Dougal Dixon] shark that uses bioluminescence to co-ordinate hunts even against rainbow squid

sharktopus: ["Sharktopus" by Mike Maclean] giant shark-headed octopus with spikes on sides and tentacletips

sharkworm: [*A Hero's Guide to Deadly Dragons* by Hiccup Haddock III] black, green and gray amphibious dragon with hammerhead, gator-like legs, fish tail and backfin from Barbarian archipelago

sharlie: [*Monster Spotter's Guide to North America* by Scott Francis] aka "Slimy Slim", 15-meter, mottled brownish-green lake snake with short-snouted, cow-like head from Payette Lake, Idaho, Terra (alpha Zodiaci III)

sharloc: [*City of the Chasch* by Jack Vance] lumpish creature with bristly back and malodorous exudation along dorsal integument from Shattorak

sharsharym: ["Cistern of the Time" by Wim Vandemaan] emerald green snake-like predator with smell of peppermint from Ambur (Vega (alpha Lyrae) X)

shasos: ["Frog in the Mountains" by R. A. Lafferty] eagle-condor hunter from the mountains of Paravata

shass: [shoal of bass spoonerism] food ichthoid

shatarr: [*The Lost Years* by J. M. Dillard] poisonous sauroid from T'Khasi, Nevasa (40 Eridani) system

shaupat: ["The Gungan Frontier" by Chris MoCubbin] small-mouthed nocturnal quadruped with long tail, large pointy ears and poisonous alkyl blood used as bleach

shavokh: [*Vulcan's Forge* by Jack Du Brul] large desert carrion-eating ornithoid from T'Khasi, Nevasa (40 Eridani) system

shawmer: [trumpeter swan backformation] swan-like ornithoid with shawm-like call

sheathfish: [*Last and First Men* by Olaf Stabledon] ichthyoid with 3 fins and 3 tentacles from Venus (alpha Zodiaci II)

sheefla: [*Ghost-Walker* by Barbara Hambly] small, quick predator from Midgwis (Elcidar Beta III)

sheep-man: [sheepman mondegreen] sheep-headed anthropoid

sheep-bear: [sheepberry backformation] aka nannybear, sheep-headed ursinoid

sheepie: [*Tales of the Unexpected* #53] bull-sized herd animals of the Girafon

sheepshifter: [Godville] sheep predator, likely wolfwere, that preys on sheep as handsome ram, munya, pechavy, sheep-dog, battering ram, mimple, or queel

shelath: [*The Howling Stones* by Alan Dean Foster] stinger that nests in yellow-brown vines from Parramat archipelago, Senisran

shelffish: [shellfish mondgreen] fish adapted to being shelved, usually in fishbowl or fishtank

shell blade: [The Legend of Zelda] clam-like creature with vulnerable mouth

shell spider: [*Darth Maul: Shadow Hunter* by Michael Reeves] archnoid with very strong "silk"

shelldrake: [sheldrake mondegreen] black and white duck-like barnacle-goose, see shellduck

shellduck: [shelduck mondegreen] black and white duck-like barnacle-goose, see shelldrake

shellf: [shellfish backformation] shelf-like shellfish mimic

shellfish: [Xanth series by Piers Anthony] creature with dull, broad, serrated pincers from Xanth or [Xanthian mondegreen] Xa, Thia system

shellmouth: [*The Worlds of the Federation* by Shane Johnson] 50-centimeter clam-faced, humpbacked sea creature with 6 short tentacles (2 for feeding), double-pupilled eyes

shellsnap: [Outernauts] immature, small-headed singesnap

shelq: [Irish elk mondegreen] blue elk-like ruminant with large antlers, see blue ox

shemet: [tinshemet mondegreen] snake-bird, amou ancestor

shemhal: [*Cyclopedia of Worlds*] large, long-lived aquatic animal from Messurk

shen lung: multicolored (blue, red, green, gold, orange, yellow) powerful, but lazy, dragon

shenzhouraptor: [*Feathered Dinosaurs: The Origin of Birds* by John Long and Peter Schuten] see jeholornis

shenzhousaur: [*Feathered Dinosaurs: The Origin of Birds* by John Long and Peter Schuten] 2-meter ornithomimosaur with few teeth

shenzhoutaur: [shenzhousaur minotaur portmanteau] ornithomimotaur with few teeth

sheot: [*The Stainless Steel Rat Sings the Blues* by Harry Harrison] ruminant steed like tusked sheep or goat from Liokukae

sher: [*Dell Crossword Puzzle Dictionary*] tiger from Persia, Terra (alpha Zodiaci III), see shir

shermhal: [*Cyclopedia of Worlds*] large sea creature that lives up to 9217 yrs. from Messurk, Oppipus system

Shetland mammoth: ["Robot Hugs" by R. Hugs] small mammoth steed

shichibi: [Jap.] beetle with six wings and seven tails

shikáki: [Japanese shiká-káki portmanteau] deer-oyster amphibian

shillelagh: [Xanth series by Piers Anthony] bipedal walking stick insect, related to silver-headed, Welsh thumbstick, mahogany handled, ivory handled and bamboo-cane walking sticks from Xanth

shinnow: [shoal of minnows spoonerism, shino ow portmanteau] flightless rhinowl-like ornithoid

shino: [Terra Monster] brownish rhinoid with curly orange mane, see rhiyew, from Terrarium

shire: [*Dell Crossword Puzzle Dictionary*] draft horse

shirliken: [*Marune: Alastor 933* by Jack Vance] scaly beast from Marune

shiro: ["The Gungan Frontier" by Chris McCubbin] chelonoid with backridged carapace, eyestalks sometimes symbiotic with tooke trap

shirshu: [Avatar: The Last Airbender: "Bato of the Water Tribe"] large wolf-like caninoid with star-nose

shisa: lion-like dog from Japan, Terra (alpha Zodiaci III)

shish: see schish

shishi: [*Here Be Monsters almanac*] living stone lions

shiwayabird: [trumpet swan backformation] flute swan-like ornithoid with shiwaya-like call

shlorg: [slorg-hlorg portmanteau] pink omnivorous blob with hairless, green-eyed woman's face, retractable fang

shlorgator: [shlorg alligator portmanteau] alligator-like predator whose bite morphs victim into shlorg
shmeagle: ["L'il Abner" by Al Capp] creature that mates FTL
shmink: ["L'il Abner" by Al Capp] rare fur-bearing mammal
shmoo: [pl. shmoo, *Life and Times of Shmoo* by Al Capp] pear-shaped biped that both lays eggs and gives milk, dies of joy when looked at hungrily, reproduces by splitting in a second, feeds from the Valley of the Shmoon
shnú: [i-less ishinú] cave-dwelling herring-dog amphibian
shoat: [*Dell Crossword Puzzle Dictionary*] young wild pig, see shote
shocker lizard: [*Monster Manual* by Skip Williams, etal.] foot-long, blue reptilian with lighter underbelly and black markings, barbed tail, thin antenna-like horns with electric aura
shockworm: [Traversan 3: "The Imperator of Akron" by Peter Terrid] electric worm from Tombstone, Leyden system
shockwraith: [*A Door into Ocean* by Joan Slonczewsky] noted for sinew which is used along the starworms by Sharer wormrunners to secure rafts from Shora the Ocean Moon, Valedon system
shoefly: [Xanth series by Piers Anthony] marching insects from Land of Flies, Xanth
shony: [Shetland pony spoonerism] small equinoid from Petla system
shoo monster: [*The World of Synnabarr* by Raymond C. S. McCracken] harmless relative of intellect devourer from Synnabarr, fka Mars (alpha Zodiaci IV)
shopeyen: [Atbash] see behemoth
shore eel: ["Capt'n Virgil, Sportsman in Space" by David Brooks] shore-dwelling eel-like killer from Arizant
shore muddler: [museumofhoaxes.com by Alex Boese] see strandmuddlare
short-necked giraffe: [Far Side: "The Evolution of the Giraffe" by Gary Larson] giraffe ancestor with shorter neck and longer legs, see neck-less giraffe

short-snout: [*Fantastic Beasts and Where to Find Them* by Newton Artemis Fido Scamander] silvery blue dragon from Sweden, Terra (alpha Zodiaci III)
shote: see shoat
shovel-tusk: see platybelodon
showshoe: furry with white legs, lambda on face
shrape: [shrewdness of apes spoonerism, shrew-ape portmanteau] shrew-headed pongoid, see killer shrew
shravas: [beheaded ishravas] 2-headed wingless pegasoid
shrewe: [shrew-ewe portmanteau] small, wooly-haired rodentoid from Woolarra III, Galaxiki galaxy
shrig: [*The Face* by Jack Vance] phosphorescent bog larva that dance on caudal feet
shrigator: [shrig alligator portmanteau] alligator-like predator whose bite morphs victim into shrig
shrike: [*Dell Crossword Puzzle Dictionary*] see mousebird, coly
shriken: [Terra Monsters] black predatory ornithoid, see jastrike, from Terrarium
shro: [i-less shiro] eyestalked shellfish from Friatica, Friaticalida system, Galaxiki galaxy
shrock: [*After Man* by Dougal Dixon] badger-like burrowing mammal
shroo: [shrew-roo portmanteau] kangaroo-lrat-ike shrew
shrowk: [*A Voyage to Arcturus* by David Lindsay] many-legged creature with serpentine body, spiked head, bat-like wings from Tormance, Arcturus (alpha Boötis) system
shrub ox: [*After the Dinosaurs* by Donald R. Prothero] see eucerathere
shryke: [*Edge Chronicle* by Paul Stewart and Chris Riddell] vicious, toothed ornithoid, females the more colorful
shtaer: [Ekan shtaer wreathsnake palindrome] wreathsnake-like amphisbæna from Eka peninsula, Snowi, Nejstea system, Galaxiki galaxy

shtoonk: ["L'il Abner" by Al Capp] winged shmoo

shtra: [Ekan shtra earthsnake palindrome] earthsnake-like amphisbæna from Eka penisula, Snowi, Nejstea system, Galaxiki galaxy

shu: [Chin. @] 2-D mouse-like at

shug monkey: demondog-monkey from Rendlesham forest, Terra (alpha Zodiaci III)

shunk: [*The Dirdir, The Pnume* by Jack Vance] fat, ugly, yellow creature of Sibol, [Wyst: Alastor 1716 by Jack Vance] vicious creature of Pombal swamp, best ridden by the Zur of island continent of Zumer, Wyst

shunka warakin: ["carries off dogs", *Monster Spotter's Guide to North America* by Scott Francis] 1.2-meter tall, hunchbacked hyena-like caninoid with long snout from Great Plains, Terra (alpha Zodiaci III)

shurrack: [*After Man* by Dougal Dixon] long-legged, snow-leopard-like groat-eating weasel

shush: [Navaho] ursinoid from Diné system

shuttlewren: ["Uncharted Territory" by Connie Willis] perverse creature from Boohte

shuvuuia: [*Feathered Dinosaurs: The Origin of Birds* by John Long and Peter Schuten] 60-cm bird-like theropod with long legs, small head on delicately curved neck, tiny teeth, short, powerful arms with one large clawed finger

shwackee: [bushwackee mondegreen] lavender prey

shyrak: [*Creatures of the Galaxy* by Phil Brucato, Bill Smith, Rick D. Stuart, Chuck Truett] chiropteran pest from Korriban, Jedi galaxy

si: [Haitian sansi mondegreen] leech-like parasite, related to gonera, guessuga, guijuela, guissuga, from Sa, the Leech Planet; [ha-as-tso-si mondegreen] lion and mouse relative

siamang: [*National Geographic Encyclopedia of Animals*] pongoid with throat sac from Indonesia, Terra (alpha Zodiaci III)

siamangator: [siamang alligator portmanteau] alligator-like predator whose bite morphs victim into siamang

sib: [bistre ert sib palindrome] dark brown creature, associated with ert

sibe: ["Bird-watchers' Slang" by Paul Beale] bird from Siberia, Terra (alpha Zodiaci III)

sick sheep: ["Mother Hitton's Littul Kittons" by Cordwainer Smith] beige-brown, kilotonne sheep, source of stroon from Norstrilia

sicken: [salmon-chicken portmanteau, sickening backformation] inedible variety of hen

sickening sleep: [*Monster Manual* by Skip Williams, etal.] sleeping sickness-inducing ooze

sickle weasel: see kamaitachi

sidder: [reddish sidder portmanteau] reddish creature notable for sidding

siddeer: [sidder deer portmantreau] reddish deer-like ruminant

sidehill gouger: [museumofhoaxes.com by Alex Boese] small, burrowing buffalo [Harry S. Knight] in rightward and leftward varieties like rackabore and sidehill hoofer

sidehill hoofer: [Xanth series by Piers Anthony] mountain bovine with short blunt horns and legs of differing lengths, in rightward and leftward varieties, from Xanth

sidewinder: snake that moves sideways like a crab but by waving

sidewindeer: [sidewinder deer oortmanteau] deer-like rumninant that grazes like sidewinder

siegelch: [German Siegel-Elch portmanteau] seal-elk/moose from Germa system, see lelk

sier: [*Dell Crossword Puzzle Dictionary*] pintano-like damselfish

sifaka: [*National Geographic Encyclopedia of Animals*] "dancing lemur" from Madagascar

sificligh: ["In the Walls of Eryx" by Howard Phillips Lovecraft and Kenneth Sterling] wriggling maggot-like insectoid

sifrhippo: [sifrhippus hippo portmanteau] hippoid from Sifr system

sifrhippus: [*After the Dinosaurs* by Donald R. Prothero] horse from Ypresian age (early Eocene)

siggul: [sluggish sigguls palidrome] sloth-like creature

siggull: [siggul gull mondegreen] sloth-gull-like griffinoid

sigh-on: [a sault of lions spoonerism] large felinoid predator with sigh-like cry

sigigi: [Cherokee] katydid-like insectoid from Tsalagi system

siilok: [Estonian siil-loks portmanteau] hedgehog-rattler, burrower with rattle-tipped tail, related to packrattler from Esto system

sika: [*Dell Crossword Puzzle Dictionary*] deer from Japan, Terra (alpha Zodiaci III)

sikap: [Pakistan a-tsikap palindrome] dark green ornithoid from Pakista system

silacopod: ["Duel for a Dracowolf" by Wolf Read] beetle-spider from Epona, Taranis (82 Eridanis)

silefofelis: [mynynym] felinoid from Silefus system

silian: [Barsoom series by Edgar Rice Burroughs] slimy sea serpent from Mars (alpha Zodiaci IV)

silicate: ["Island of Terror" by Edward Andrew Mann and Allan Ramsen] bumpy armored mound with slug-like base, long retractable feeding tentacle, feeding on bones via punctures, reproducing by fission in 6 hours, vulnerable to radiation from Petrie's Island and Japan, Terra (alpha Zodiaci III); any silicon-based creature, see crabdozer, crystal bird, exogorth, Hellguard virus, monolith monster, mucilator, mynock

silivi: [Continuum] 5-meter constrictor sandsnake from Amarillon, Nogullon system

silkat: [Continuum] large catcus from Sotkaard, Galunis system, Firehorse constellation

sillam: [smallish sillams palindrome] small lamb-like creature

silt strider: [The Elder Scrolls III: "Morrowind"] large insectoidal steed ridden in hollowed-out shell from Vvardenfell

silver bug: insectoid-like golem made from silver

silver bugator: [silver bug alligator] alligator-like predator whose bite morphs victim into silver bug

silver coon: [silvercoom mondegreen] raccoon-like golem made from silver

silver fish: [silverfish mondegreen] fish-like golem made from silver

silver goose: [golden goose extrapolation] silver goose that lays silver eggs that resists being plucked

silverbug: [Robert Silverberg malapropism] silver-eating insectoid from Robert's system

silverbugator: [silverbug alligator portmanteau] alligator-like predator whose bite morphs victim into silverbug

silvercoon: seahorse-like creature with club-tipped tail from Bombamania, Phoenix system, Galaxiki galaxy

silverf: [silverfish backformation] multi-legged worm-like scavenger

silverfish: [Xanth series by Piers Anthony] small metallic fish from Xanth or [Xanthia mondegreen] Xa, Thia system

silverspider: [*The Future Is Wild* by Dougal Dixon] eusocial poggle-dependant arachnid able to spin gorge-spanning webs up to 24 km across, whose queen needs poggle blood to stimulate egg productions

silverswimmer: [*The Future Is Wild* by Dougal Dixon] fish-like crustacean including plankton-eaters with many antennae and bristles, bottom-dwellers, parasite varieties

sime: [*Dell Crossword Puzzle Dictionary*] simian, monkey, see marmoset, lar, sai

simkangu: [James Cooke Brown's Loglan simba kangu compound] lion-dog from Logla, Brown's system

simli: [James Cooke Brown's Loglan simba cliku compound] lion-like felinoid from Logla, Brown's system

simurgh: [Persian] aka anqä, huge bird

sinclairomeryx: [*After the Dinosaurs* by Donald R. Prothero] aka Sinclair's deer, dromomeryx with forward-pointing short nose-horns

sinek: ["Frog on the Mountain" by R. A. Lafferty] cat-lion game creature from Paravata mts.

singesnap: [Outernauts] large-headed, heat-resistant chelonian, see shellsnap, searsnap

singing shark: [Godville] shark-like egoboovore (self-esteem-eater) with humanoid teeth

sinha: ["Shadow Lord" by Laurence Yep] sabre-toothed, white "samari panther" from Angira

sinking duck: [Peter MacInnis] aquatic ornithoid whose feathers are eaten nightly by roara prawn from Finnegan's Lake, Ugly Islands

sinocallipteryx: [*Feathered Dinosaurs: The Origin of Birds* by John Long and Peter Schuten] 2.4-meter dromaeosaur-eating compsognathid with long arms and hands from China, Terra (alpha Zodiaci III)

sinorthinosaur: ["Chinese bird-lizard", *A Field Guide to Dinosaurs* by Henry Gee and Luis V. Rey, *Feathered Dinosaurs: The Origin of Birds* by John Long and Peter Schuten] 1-meter bird-like dromaeosaur with very long arms, hollows before eyes and few but large teeth from China, Terra (alpha Zodiaci III)

sinorthotaur: [sinothinotaur: [sinorthosaur minotaur portmanteau] dromaeotaur with long arms and few teeth

sinorthomimus: [*Feathered Dinosaurs: The Origin of Birds* by John Long and Peter Schuten] 2-meter sinorthinosaur mimic from China, Terra (alpha Zodiaci III)

sinosaur: ["Chinese lizard", sinosauropteryx mondegreen] flightless sinosauropteryx

sinosauropteryx: [*Feathered Dinosaurs: The Origin of Birds* by John Long and Peter Schuten] winged, mammal-eating compsognathid with hairy protofeathers from China (alpha Zodiaci III)

sinotauropteryx: [sinotauropteryx]

sinovenator: ["Chinese hunter", *Feathered Dinosaurs: The Origin of Birds* by John Long and Peter Schuten] 1-meter primitive troodontid with long legs from China, Terra (alpha Zodiaci III)

sinraptor: [*Feathered Dinosaurs: The Origin of Birds* by John Long and Peter Schuten] 10-meter predatory dinosaur from Jurassic China, Terra (alpha Zodiaci III)

sinrornis: [mynynym] ornithoid from Sinronia, Sinro system

sinusonasus: ["sinusoidal-nosed", *Feathered Dinosaurs: The Origin of Birds* by John Long and Peter Schuten] troodontid with unserrated front teeth from early Cretaceous

siouqrut: [turquoise siouqrut palindrome] bluish-green ornithoid

siqua: [Cherokee] porcoid from Tsalagi system

sirec: [cerise sirec palindrome] deep to vivid purplish red ornithoid

siren: [*National Geographic Encyclopedia of Animals*] amphibian from S. E. U. S., Terra (alpha Zodiaci III)

siri: [Monster Galaxy] aggressive purple-petaled planimal

sis boom ba: ["The Terror of Sis Boom Ba" by Tom Smith] mutant monster fond of princesses

šiš: [Croatian šišmiš backformation] bat-mouse, ancestral to mouse and bat

sisel: [*Dell Crossword Puzzle Dictionary*] ground squirrel from Europe

siselope: [sisel antelope portmanteau] sisel with antlers

sisi: [*Dell Crossword Puzzle Dictionary*] porkfish; [sisimite mondegreen] small insectoid

sisimite: shaggy chimp-gorilla from Guarunta mts, Terra (alpha Zodiaci III)

sitatunga: [*National Geographic Encyclopedia of Animals*] antelope relative from Africa, Terra (alpha Zodiaci III)

sitatungator: [sitatunga alligator portmanteau] alligator-like predator whose bite morphs victim into sitatunga

sith: [Barsoom series by Edgar Rice Burroughs] Hereford-sized hornet-like insectoid with poisonous stinger from Mars (alpha Zodiaci IV)

sithar: [*Yesterday's Son* by A. C. Crispin] creature like both lion and muskox from Sarpeidon, beta Niobe system

sitora: [Tajik *] 2-D pentapus or hexapus

sittern: [se(d)ge of bitterns, sitting tern portmanteau] flightless, tern-like ornithoid

siulb: [bluish siulb palindrome] bluish ornithoid

sivathere: [*After the Dinosaurs* by Donald R. Prothero] smaller relative of brahamathere with thick neck and more moose-like horns

sivovis: [mynynym] bird from Sivonia, Sivo system

six-ear: [earwing extrapolation] earwalker with 6 long ears adapted for walking from Hy-yi-yi Islands

six-legged air-whale: [airedale malapropism, "As Crazy As Can Be"] variety of air-whale with six legs

skalacervus: [candiacervus extrapolation] deer with ladder-like antlers

skamnicervus: [candiacervus extrapolation] deer with stool-like antlers

skanta: [sky manta portmanteau, spoonerism] flying manta-like creature from My world, see thranta

skaraf: [Fr. Johann Martin Schleyer's Volapük] cockroach-like insectoid from Schleyer's system

skarasen: ["Terror of the Zygons" by Terrance Dicks] sea serpent cyban whose milk is vital to the planet-less Zygons

skarat: [*The Dirdir* by Jack Vance] large, quick black insectoid that exhales foul odor, yet is nevertheless used in recipes of the Carabas, Sibol

skate: [*Dell Crossword Puzzle Dictionary*] ray fish

skatyhr: [Belarussian skaty-tyhr portmanteau] stingray-cheetah amphibian

skeep: [*Frostworld and Dreamfire* by John Morressy] river creature from Hraggellon (Duruos II)

skeese: [skein of geese spoonerism, sky geese portmanteau] leg-less long-necked ichthoid

skeet: see clay pigeon

skegger: [*Dell Crossword Puzzle Dictionary*] see parr

skern: [*After Man* by Dougal Dixon] flightless seal-like seabird

sketto: ["The Gungan Frontier"] flying, blood-sucking reptilian, active at twilight with up to 1-meter wingspan from Tatooine, Jedi galaxy

skidal: [Continuum] 3-meter bird-eating shark-like ichthyoid from Redibillon, Nogullon system

skillywiggler: [*The Twits* by Roald Dahl] batrachian with screwdriver-like teeth, fond of toes

skilok: 15-meter slouching lizard from Betonia (Edonian cluster V), Galaxiki galaxy

skink: [*Dell Crossword Puzzle Dictionary*] lizard, see gila, gecko, guana, varan, iguana

skinnee: [skinny, skinner backformation] thin, furry valued by skinners from Draapaa, Albina system, Galaxiki galaxy

skineel: [skinny eel portmanteau] very thin eel-like ichthyoid

skish: [sky fish portmanteau, Sky Ocean] ichthyopteryx from Sios

skitt: [skittish backformation] meerkat-like prey of scare-crow

skni: [Ekan skni minksnake palindrome] minksnake-like amphisbæna from Eka peninsula, Snowi, Nejstea system, Galaxiki galaxy

skoffin: [Icelandic] vixen-like felinoid with deadly basilisk-like stare

skogkatt: [Norwegian] cat with long hair, ruff, bushy tail, ear tuff

skomb: [Fr. Johann Martin Schleyer's Volapük] mackerel-like ichthyoid from Schleyer's system

skoone: [Outernauts] immature skrunk

skorah: ["In the Walls from Eryx" by Howard Phillips Lovecraft and Kenneth Sterling] carnivore

skovisaur: ["dust-lizard"] large ashi-magari-like lizard, see thed, dust bunny

skovitaur: [skovisaur minotaur portmanteau] aka dust bull, large ashi-magari-like bovinoid

skow: ["Lost Sorceress of the Silent Citadel" by Michael Moorcook] creature with valuable skin from Mars (alpha Zodiaci IV)

skox: [skulk of foxes spoonerism, skunk fox portmanteau] malodorous fox-like caninoid

skrewt: [*Fantastic Beasts and Where to Find Them* by Newton Artemis Fido Scamander] 6-legged fire-crab and manticore cross with stinger that expels fire from rear end

skrill: ["Earth: Final Conflict"] hi-energy bioweapon of Taelons

skrunk: [Outernauts] brown skunk-like creature with white backstripe, see skoone

skua: [*Dell Crossword Puzzle Dictionary*] gull, see jaeger, allan, ern(e), skua, scaup, tern, fulmar, gannet, petrel, scoter

skuid: [sky squid portmanteau] lighter-than-air cephalopodan

skul: ["A Choice of Dooms", "Mourning's End", "Look Homeward, Atom", "Stormy Passage" by Jan Strnad] large ornithoid used as steed from Morlaidh

skulk: ["The Sentinel" by Graeme Morris, Adlerweg series] creature

skullboo: [Outernauts] turquoise-bearded, pink-crested, skull-faced creature, see peekaboo, skullossal

skullf: [skullfish backformation] skullfish micking ichthyoid

skullfish: [The Legend of Zelda] schooling skeletal ichthyoid with vise-like bite from Hyrule

skullion: [*A Hero's Guide to Deadly Dragons* by Hiccup Haddock III] very fast, black and purple flightless, blind and deaf dragon with exceptional sense of smell, forehead horen and tailspikes, from Barbarian archipelago

skullossal: [skull collossal portmanteau, Outernauts] large, bluish-white skullboo with black eyemask, pink crest

skullpecker: see mossbird

skullpelt: [*Edge Chronicles* by Paul Stewart and Chris Riddell] blue, furry, skull-like creature with leathery skin that appears as prey-bait

skulltula: [The Legend of Zelda] large arachnid from Hyrule, possibly related to acromatula

skullworm: ["Astro Quest", "A Space Oddity" by Naren Shankar] green, semi-edible worm from Vellika

skunk ape: [*Monster Spotter's Guide to North America* by Scott Francis] 3-meter, malodorous, reddish-orange, orangutan-like nape from Florida Everglades or Louisiana bijou, Terra (alpha Zodiaci III)

skunk bear: [Avatar: The Last Airbender: "City of Walls and Secrets"] malodorous ursinoid

skunk fish: [Avatar: The Last Airbender: "The Guru"] malodorous ichthyoid

skunka warakin: see ringdocus and thylacine

skurl: ["Squirrel Cage" by Robert Sheckley] arboreal sleg predator from Seer

skuzy: [Monster Galaxy] feral, black creature with pink collar from Cancer constellation

skvader: [Håkan Dahlmark] hare-like griffinoid with with wood grouse wings and tail

skvadeer: [skvader deer portmanteau] deer-like griffinoid with wood grouse wings and tail

skvamaj birdoj: [Thousand Stars] falcon-like ornithoid from Narag III

skwuid: [sky-squid portmanteau, Sky Ocean] flying cephalopod from Sios

sky manta: [Sky Ocean] flying manta from Sios

sky-shark: ["Oil and Water" by Robert T. Jerschonek] flying shark-like ichthyoid from Taur

sky-squid: [*Larklight* by Philip Reeve] from Jupiter (alpha Zodiaci V), see skuid

skybison: [Avatar: The Last Airbender: "The Boy in the Iceberg"] 10-tonne, beaver-like hexapod with rudder-tail, pawed elephant-like legs, arrow-shaped brown patch

skycritter: [*They Live in the Sky* by Trevor James Constable] aerial creature visible only in infrared-ultraviolet

skye: [*Dell Crossword Puzzle Dictionary*] terrier from Scotland, see cairn

skyf: [skyfish backformation] skyfish mimic

skyfish: [José Escamilla, *Monster Spotter's Guide to North America* by Scott Francis] aka rod, multiwinged, headless aerial serpentoid able to move at Mach 1.3, see skycritters

skytoad: [*This Moment of the Storm* by Roger Zelazny] aerial batrachoid from Tierra del Cygnus, 72 Cygni system

skywhale: [Laurence Doyle and Manoj Joshi] airborne cetaceans with echolocation from Blue Moon

sladang: [*Dell Crossword Puzzle Dictionary*] aka s(a/e)ladang, water buffalo from Malaysia, Terra (alpha Zodiaci III), see gaur

sladangator: [sladang alligator portmanteau] alligator-like predator whose bite morphs victim into sladang

slaf: [false slaf palindrome backformation] creature mimicked by pseudoslaf

slamworm: [Ben 10: Omniverse: "It Was Them" by David McDermott] huge, burrowing predator that spits acidballs, only vulnerable in mouth, from Talpaeda

slang: [*Wyst: Alastor 1716* by Jack Vance] long, slender, hairless rodentoid able to make odors at will from Wyst

slangator: [slang alligator portmanteau] alligator-like predator whose bite morphs victim into slang

slarkbug: [barkslug spoonerism] slarktree parasitic insectoid

slarkbugator: [slarkbug alligator portmanteau] alligator-like predator whose bite morphs victim into alligator-like predator whose bite morphs victim into slarkbug

slarth: [slith-larth portmanteau] dangerous cave-dwelling dracoid with lashing tail, claws, fangs

slashback: [*Uhura's Song* by Janet Kagon] sabretooth tiger-like felinoid from Sivao

slashkiller: [*Fantastic Beasts and Where to Find Them* by Newton Artemis Fido Scamander] slashing predator, including unigubular variety

slater: aka pillbug, roly-poly, sowbug, wood louse that moves by curling and rolling

slaughterfish: [The Elder Scrolls III: "Morrowind"] common, aggressive ichthyoid in small, large and legendary giant varieties

slavey: [*Monster Spotter's Guide to North America* by Scott Francis] 18-meter lake snake from Great Slave Lake, North West Territories, Canada, Terra (alpha Zodiaci III)

slayvink: [*Throy* by Jack Vance] arboreal creature from Throy

slean: [*Pawns and Symbols* by Majliss Larson] furred grassland predator from Tahrn

slear: [sleuth or sloth of bears spoonerism, sloth-bear portmanteau] arboreal ursinoids from Skjoob, Bjosko system, Galaxiki galaxy

sleek: [Spelljamer] territorial, aggressive ermine-like creature

sleen: [Gor series by John F. "John Norman" Lange, Jr.] tireless, savage 6-clawed creature used to track runaway slaves; [*Creatures of the Galaxy* by Phil Brucato, Bill Smith, Rick D. Stuart, Chuck Truett] insectovorous lizard from Dagobah, Jedi galaxy; [green slime spoonerism] slug that leaves grimy trail

sleeth: [*Warrior of Llarn* by Gardner Fox] rodentoid from Llarn

sleetroth: [tree sloth spoonerism] arboreal mammalian

sleg: ["Squirrel Cage" by Robert Sheckley] aka omenestee, small rodentoid, occasionally invisible, otherwise prey of hangs, drigs, skurls and omenesters from Seer

slegator: [sleg alligator portmanteau] alligator-like predator whose bite morphs victim into sleg

sless: ["sless at times emit tassels" palindrome] tassel-like gestalt

sli: [Ekan sli oil snake palindrome] oil snake-like amphisbæna from Eka peninsula, Snowi, Nejstea system, Galaxiki galaxy

slia: [slia tails palindrome] food reptilian with regenerating tail

slickribbon: [*The Future Is Wild* by Dougal Dixon] 1-meter gloomworm-eating polychaete (bristleworm) with 2 paddle-like legs per segment and mouthparts on extendable trunk

slider: [*Dell Crossword Puzzle Dictionary*] red-bellied terrapin, see potter

slik't: [*Double, Double* by Michael Jan Friedman] sauroid from T'nufo nr. Romulan Empire

slime devil: ["The Trouble with Tribbles" by David Gerrold, *The World of the Federation* by Shane Johnson, *The Romulan Way* by Terisa Halekala-LoBrotto], aka ahlh, 1.2-meter carnivorous amphibian with 7 horns, 4 segmented limbs, large splayed toes, large blow hole

slime mole: [*Edge Chronicles* by Paul Stewart and Chris Riddell] blind burrower that excretes antigravitational "moleglue"

slime snouter: [*The Snouters* by Harald Stümpke] golden brown, snail-eating snouter with nasarium adapted for crawling from Mairúvili, or armor-tailed variety from Eeza-zofa, Hi-Yi-Yi Islands

slime worm: [Gor series by John Norman] long, eye-less worm-like scavenger companion to the Golden Beetle

slime-lizard: [*Gray Lensmen, Second Lensman* by E. E. Smith] "untouchable" lizard with toxic slime from Borova III

slimebeast: ["The Beasts of Karn" by Ken Koonce and Michael Merton] slimy, beastly creature from Karn

slimebug: ["Shadow Lord" by Laurence Yep] slimy insectoid from Angira

slimebugator: [slimebug alligator portmanteau] alligator-like predator whose bite morphs victim into slimebug

slimehead: [*National Geographic Encyclopedia of Animals*] perch-like fish

slink: [slinky backformation] large, helical inchworm-like creature adapted to descending stairs

slinky dog: ["Toy Story"] dachshund-like toy animal with slinky midsection animated by Love

slitch: [Babylon 5: "Eyes" by Lawrence G. DiTillio] creature native to planet Orion

slith: [*Star Rangers* by Andre Norton] dangerous cave beast from Falthar

slithering tracker: [*Monster Manual* by Skip Williams, etal.] ooze able to slither and track

slithipillar: metalophagous caterpillar from Tincityie (Edonian cluster VII), Galaxiki galaxy

slithis: ["Spawn of the Slithis" by Stephen Traxler] dark green humpbacked predator with large, hairless gumdrop-shaped head, webbed claws, suckerfish-like mouth, dorsal fin, feeding tentacles

slivilith: [*Creatures of the Galaxy* by Phil Brucato, Bill Smith, Rick D. Stuart, Chuck Truett] large, green, space-dweller with red eyes, antennae opposite tentacle cluster with membranous wings between from Jedi galaxy

sllab: [sllabtae meatballs palindrome] food animal related to tae and faol

sleh: [shellsnap ananymondegreen] fire-resistant chelonoid from Pa system, see srae

slobb: [slobber backformation] messy, bee-like insectoidal prey of slobbers

slobber: [*After Man* by Dougal Dixon] marsupial sloth with insect-attracting mucus

Slobbovian king crab: ["L'il Abner" by Al Capp] giant king-eating crab from Slobbovia

slofir: small, slug-like creature from Habitat (Iestonian Spiral IV), Galaxiki galaxy

slok: [i-less siilok] cave-dwelling hedgehog-rattler

slondatra: [Bulgarian slon-ondatra portmanteau] elephant-muskrat, large aquatic rodentoid

slonorka: [Bulgarian slon-norka portmanteau] elephant-mink, shaggy pachyderm

sloog: slug from Lestonian Lushland (Edonian cluster V), Galaxiki galaxy, see bio-sloog

sloogator: [sloog alligator portmanteau] alligator-like predator whose bite morphs victim into sloog

sloord: [*The Sword of Lankor* by Howard L. Cory] swift, stealthy pack creature from Lankor

slorg: [*The Wizard of Lemuria* by Lin Carter] pallid-scaled snake with hairless, green-eyed woman's face, retractable fangs

slorgator: [slorg alligator portmanteau] alligator-like predator whose bite morphs victim into slorg

slowrax: [Outernauts] mature furmo

slowth: [Peter Newby in *The Mammoth Book of Astounding Word Games*] very slow moving arboreal bradypoid with long hook-like claws

sludge slug: [Winx Club] slug-like creature that turns to stone like coral from Black-Mud Swamp

sludge slugator: [sludge slug alligator portmanteau] alligator-like predator whose bite morphs victim into sludge slug

slug: [Piers Anthony] giant hellfire-breathing gastropod from Xanth or [Xanthian mondegreen] Xa, Thia system

slugator: [slug alligator portmanteau] alligator-like predator whose bite morphs victim into slug

slug-snake: [slug snake mondegreen] slug-mimicking serpent

slugg: [sluggish backformation] sloth-like creature

sluggator: [slugg alligator portmanteau] alligator portmanteau] alligator-like predator whose bite morphs victim into slugg

slugoat: [slug-goat portmanteau] coastal bimorph with four legs and omnivorous appetite as adult and slow-moving and gastropod-like as larva

slugow: [slug-cow portmanteau, "Robot Hugs" by R. Hugs'] leg-less bovine

slugull: [slug-gull portmanteau] coastal baracle-gooselike ornithoid with long wings and slightly curved beak

slugulling: [slugull backformation] slow-moving, gastropod-like immature slugull

slugullingator: [slugulling alligator portmanteau] alligator-like predator whose bite morphs victim into slugulling

slukat: [Afrikaans sluk-kat portmanteau] swallow-cat, swallow-like felinopteryx

slummber: [slumber backformation] alley-cat-like predator that slummbs (cat-naps in slum)

slurp: [Peter MacInnes] mostly insectivorous gliding lizard with large orange tongue from Ugly Islands

smag: ["Milk Run" by Robert Sheckley] friendly, herbivorous mammalian that shrink in gravity, lose consciousness and may die if not also frozen, from Vermoline II

smagator: [smag alligator portmanteau] alligator-like predator whose bite morphs victim into smag

smartergake: [snartergake backformation] smarter variety of snartergake able to change its stripes

smee: [*Dell Crossword Puzzle Dictionary*] sea pheasant

smellyfish: [smack of jellyfish spoonerism] malodorous ichthyoid from Akyby, Rybyka system, Galaxiki galaxy

smeerp: ["Call a rabbit a smeerp" by James Blish] rabbit-like lapoid

smew: [*National Geographic Encyclopedia of Animals*] white with black stripes (male) or gray with brown crest (female) duck from Eurasia, Terra (alpha Zodiaci III), [*Dell Crossword Puzzle Dictionary*] merganser or sawbill duck, see garbill

smiku: [James Crooke Brown's Loglan smina kurma] mindworm from Logla, Brown's system

smiletor: [Bart Simpson's Treehouse of Horror Spine-tingling Spooktacular] plasma beast from Galliron

smilodon: sabre-toothed tiger from Pleistocene

smilodonster: [smilodon monster portmanteau] monstrous smilodon

smima: [James Cooke Brown's Logla smima] maker from Logla, Brown's system

smipri: [James Cooke Brown's Loglan smici prire] hidebehind from Logla, Brown's system

smok: [Monster Galaxy] small, black dracoid with batwings and white horns from Virgo constellation

smoker. [Xanth series by Piers Anthony] dragon that breathes smoke to blind, suffocate and smoke victims from Xanth

smolt: [*Dell Crossword Puzzle Dictionary*] 2-year-old salmon, see sprod, mort

smoof: [Outernauts] immature furmo

smorowep: ["smorowep at times emit tapeworms" palindrome] tapeworm gestalt

smulc: [clumsy smulc palindrome] rarely amphibious sea creature

smur: [The Dirdir by Jack Vance] fearsome, sinuous semi-reptilian from Boundary Wood, the Carabas, Sibol

sna: [*Dell Crossword Puzzle Dictionary*] wild mountain sheep from Tibet, see sha, rasse, urial, bharal, nahoor, oorial

snaggle: [snaggletooth backformation] creature noted for its irregular teeth

snagon: [snag-on mondegreen, snow dragon spoonerism] small, porcupine-like dracoid with burr-like bristles from Dro system

snagriff: [Superman mythos] pterosaur from Krypton, Rao system

snah: [Hansa snah palindrome] yellow ornithoid

snake rat: [Winx Club] venomous swamp rodent whose bite causes projectile vomiting

snake-fly: [Xanth series by Piers Anthony] long, narrow flying insect with fangs from Xanth

snakehead: [*National Geographic Encyclopedia of Animals*] perch-like fish from Australiasia, [*River Monsters* by Jeremy Wade, "Snakehead Terror"] 1.2-meter Arctic fish with suprabrachia invading Florida, Terra (alpha Zodiaci III)

snallygaster: [schnelle Geischter, *Valley Register, Hagerstown Mail*] monstrous egg-laying flying creature with elastic giraffe-like neck, very long sharp serrated beak, tusks, snout, hide used by Umbopelanders to polish punkleshells

snamsil: ["snamsil at times emit talismans" palindrome] golem of nails, hair, shrunken heads, hearts, teeth or some other ritualistically significant object

snapdragon fly: [*Through the Looking-glass and What Alice Found There* by Lewis Carroll] insect with plum-pudding-like body, holly-leaf-like wings, swollen raisin-like head from Looking-glass world

snape: [*Earth in Twilight* by Doris Piserchia] one-eyed, soft and furry jungle-dwelling mutant

snapjaw: ["Planet of Storms" by Michelle Stern] basilisk-like predatory lizard from Thersunt

snapper: [*This Moment of the Storm* by Roger Zelazny] green feathered reptilian with armored head, 3 horns under 3 eyes, nose-horn, 50-cm legs, 3.5-meter tail, long sharp sword-like teeth, able to run as fast as a greyhound, swing tail like a sandbag from Tierra del Cygnus, 72 Cygni system; ["Grandpa" by James Schmitz] flat, crayfish-like crustacean colored chocolate-brown with green and red spots on a carapace from Sutang

snarb: [*Creatures of the Galaxy* by Phil Brucato, Bill Smith, Rick D. Stuart, Chuck

Truett] bipedal, gray lizard from Mimban, Jedi galaxy

snark cat: [*Unofficial Questarian Guide*, "Galaxy Busters" by Sheila Paulson, "Attack of the Kreemorians"]] 2.4-meter felinoid from 3rd moon of Arctinus

snark: [snake-shark portmanteau, *The Hunting of the Snark* by Charles Ludridge "Lewis Carroll" Dodgeson] tasty, nocturnal food animal in biting and feathered, unwhiskered, unfeathered and scratching, varieties both charmed by smiles and soap from Snark Island, Looking-glass world or [Peter MacInnis] blue variety that eats both live and dead prey from Ugly Islands, see boojum

snarl: [*The Barber of Aldebaran* by William Moy Russell] exotic life-form

snarp: [*The Perfect Planet* by Edward Packard] primate-like anthropoid from Utopa (Achnar V), Gallatin quadrant

snartergake: [garter snake spoonerism] longitudinally striped snake, not as smart as the smartergake

snat: [snake bat portmanteau] long, leg-less food chiropteroid

snattle: [rattle snake spoonerism] antlered serpentinoid that captures prey by wrapping itself around a straight stick and waiting for its prey to hit itself in the head

sneedle: [*On Beyond Zebra* by Theodore Seuss Geissel] four-winged, four-legged, crested insectoid with harpoon-like proboscis

sneeze bee: [Xanth series by Piers Anthony] laterally breath-taking insect from Xanth

sneirus: [Sneirus esuriens palindrome] always-hungry predator

snek: [Fr. Johann Martin Schleyer's Volapük] snake-like creature from Schleyer's system

sneopar: [Outernauts] blue and white felinoid with black spots, see sneow

sneow: [Outernauts] immature sneopar

snevil: [snow devil portmanteau] see snow devil

snicket: [*Edge Chronicles* by Paul Stewart and Chris Riddell] ratbird kin

snidget: [*Fantastic Beasts and Where to Find Them* by Newton Artemis Fido Scamander] small, red-eyed, yellow bird

sniffer dragon: [*A Hero's Guide to Deadly Dragons* by Hiccup Haddock III] large, pale aquamarine dragon with large nose from Barbarian archipelago

snipe: [*Monster Spotter's Guide to North America* by Scott Francis] 15-cm, nocturnal bird with luminous eyes, shimmering blue and gold feathers

snird: [bird snake spoonerism, snake bird portmanteau] ornithoid with long neck and small beak

snitterjipe: nocturnal apple-eater with luminous eyes, tickling whiskers

snizzer: ["Lost Sorceress of the Silent Citadel" by Michael Moorcock] small, thin lizard with prehensile tail from Mars (alpha Zodiaci IV)

sno: [Monster Galaxy] white and gray creature with forehead star, black eyes from Scorpio

snobb: [snobbish backformation] cetacean with nosestalk

snogg: [Outernauts] rock-like creature with teeth and snout, dull back spikes, see snoggle, snogtaur

snoggator: [snogg alligator portmanteau] alligator-like predator whose bite morphs victim into snogg

snoggle: [Outernauts] immature snogg

snogtaur: [Outernauts] mature snogg with sharper back spikes

snook: [*Dell Crossword Puzzle Dictionary*] sargeant fish

snoom: [notsnoom antonymondegreen] unblue ornithoid

snorg: [snork-org portmanteau] 3-meter long, soft-furred, blue-eyed, hibernating creature with segmented body, wide head, pale little legs, razor-sharp teeth and able to change color with emotions, see mood dragon

snorgator: [snorg alligator portmanteau] alligator-like predator whose bite morphs victim into snorg

snork: [*Moumeikko ja pyrstötähti* by Tove Jansson] small, soft-furred, blue-eyed, short-snouted, short-tailed hibernating biped able to change color with emotions from Moomin Valley, Finland, Terra (alpha Zodiaci III)

snorkack: [*Fantastic Beasts and Where to Find Them* by Newton Artemis Fido Scamander] creature with crumplehorns, able to regenerate whole body phoenix-like

snorke: [*After Man* by Dougal Dixon] long-faced grazing antelope

snorkeling snouter: [*The Snouters* by Harald Stümpke] mud snouter with nasarium adaped as inhaling and exhaling snorkels from Hi-Yi-Yi Islands

snout leaper: [*The Snouters* by Harald Stümpke] shrew-like mammal with nasarium adapted for leaping from Hi-Yi-Yi Islands, in leaf leaper, two-way, toothed and suctorial varieties

snouter: [*The Snouters* by Harald Stümpke] shrew-like mammal with nasarium (snout adapted for standing while devouring prey) from Hi-Yi-Yi Islands, ancestral to snoutwalkers, snout leapers and earwing; [Cloudstone] long-nosed, long-tailed canine

snoutwalker: [*The Snouters* by Harald Stümpke] shrew-like mammal with nasaria adapted for walking from Hi-Yi-Yi Islands, including small and predacious varieties

snow devil: [*The Courtship of Princess Leia* by Dave Wolverton] winged predator adapted to cold from Toola, Kaelta, Hapes cluster, Jedi galaxy

snow dragon: ["Flash Gordon" series] bear-like dracoid with long neck, beaver-like tail, serpentine head from Mongo

snow lizard: [*Hitchhiker's Guide to the Galaxy* by Doug Adams] cold-adapted sauroid from Vega (alpha Lyrae) system

snowball loon: [snowball balloon portmanteau] white loon-like ornithoid that can puff up like a pufferfish

snowbird: [Xanth series by Piers Anthony] white, cold-loving bird with powdery, white hallucinogenic droppings from Xanth or [Xanthian] Xa, Thia system

snowflake ooze: [*Monster Manual* by Skip Williams, etal.] cold-adapted ooze

snowghost: [Motie series by Larry Niven] rare, furry cobra-like serpentinoid from Maxroy's Purchase

snowl: [snow owl portmaneau] white ornithoid from polar regions

snowsheep: [*The Covenant of the Crown* by Howard Weinstein] ruminant of Kinarr Mts., Zenna IV

snowsnake: albino, venomous, warm-blooded serpentoid with pink eyes, [Xanth series by Piers Anthony] variety that melts when exposed to heat from Xanth

snowstalker: [*The Future Is Wild* by Dougal Dixon] white sabre-toothed mustelid that mates every 21 days carrying young until spring

snowyrm: [Terra Monster] white wyrm with black face and cilia, see ragewyrm, from Terrarium

snozo: [Terra Monster] colorful but poisonous wyrm, see serpquin, from Terrarium

snozzwanger: [*Charlie and the Chocolate Factory* by Ronald Dahl] creature noted for wanging its snozz (nose) from Loompaland, Africa, Terra (alpha Zodiaci III)

snuffling sniffler: [*The Snouters* by Harald Stümpke] slime snouter with sticky nosehairs to catch prey, poisonous tail from Hy-dud-dye-fee, Hi-Yi-Yi Islands

sny: [snake-fly portmanteau] snake-like insectoid

snyer: [flying snake spoonerism] long, leg-less murre-like dracoid

snyke: 40-legged creature with harsh wiry hair from Jam-Kaïk's jungle

soar: [sky boar portmanteau, sounder of boars] wild porcopteryx

sobol: [*Dell Crossword Puzzle Dictionary*] marten

sobos: [mynynym] cow- or yak-like bovinoid from rogue planet So

soc: ["soc at times emit tacos" palindrome] creature secrete tacos

sock monkey: [Godville] apparently harmless simian with impenetrable skin

sockness monster: ["Jump Start" by Robb Armstrong] lake snake-like toy animal from the bathtub animated by Love

socktopus: [sock monkey backformation] cephalopod with rounded sucker-less tentacles

socktopuss: [socktopus puss portmanteau] 8-legged, socktopus-like felinoid

soddo: [Sodomite mondegreen] parthenogenic mite-like insectoid

sodih: [bi-sodih backformation] cockerel-like pigasus

soeos: [mynynym] lory-like ornithoid from rogue planet So

soergilia: [*After the Dinosaurs* by Donald R. Prothero] primitive musk ox from Pleistocene

sofor: [Arthur Porges] creature with very powerful malordorous defense from Tartaglia

softim: [hardim antonym] unstarred lizard

sogg: [soggy backformation] amphibian

soggator: [sogg alligator portmanteau] alligator predator whose bite morphs victim into sogg

sognomongos: [mynynym] mongoose-like creature from Sogno system

solacow: ["BraveStarr"] large bovine from New Texas

solar bear: [Godville] 4.2-meter, 12-tonne bear with glowing red eyes and acidic saliva that feeds both on meat and sunlight

solimare: [Continuum] 7-meter mutant carp from Igendal, Belverius Helenis system

sölit: [Fr. Johann Martin Schleyer's Volapük] sole-like ichthyoid from Schleyer's system

solphon: domesticated, furry, bulky quadrupedal rhinoids from Hogoii penal colony Nedub III, Galaxikik galaxy

solphonster: [solphon monster portmanteau] monstrous, furry rhinoid

something-more-dangerous: ["Tremors 2: Aftershocks" by Brent Maddock, S. S. Wilson] bipedal, heat-sensing graboid metamorph, see somoda, somethingie

somethingie: [*A Reader's Guide to Science Fiction* by Baird Searles, Martin Last, Beth Meacham and Michael Franklin] indescribable creature

sommer: [Danish sommerfugl backformation] butterfly-bird, small, brightly-colored ornithoid, ancestral to bird and butterfly
somoda: [acronym] see something-more-dangerous
somouga: [*Histoire des Sevarambes* by Denis Veiras] white-furred bear from Australe
somougator: [somouga alligator portmanteau] alligator-like predator whose bite morphs victim into somouga
son ca: [Vietnamese chim son ca backformation] ornithoid ancestral to chim and songbird from Disa system
sonak: [Outernauts] immature sonark
sonark: [Outernauts] one-eyed quadruped with one antenna, see sonak, sonarkane
sonarkane: [Outernauts] mature sonark with two antennae
sonax: [Terra Monsters] purple chiropteran with gold markings, see swinx, from terrarium
song-lizard: ["Exploration Team" by Murry Leinster] saurian that sound like organ notes from Loren II
songombee: [songomby mondegreen] sweat bee-like insectoid associated with songomics
songomby: [Madagascar] man-eating antelope like hornless, fat bull with uncloven hooves, acidic urine
soog: [Afrikaans soogdier backformation] beastly mammal
soogator: [soog alligator portmanteau] alligator-like predator whose bite morphs victim into soog
sootacl: [*Space Rangers* by Andre Norton] dangerous creature with pointed, fanged jaws from Zacan
sootaclope: [sootacl antelope portmanteau] sootacl with antlers
sootimander: [Terra Monster] volcanic ash-eating, small, quadrupedal pyrosaur with flaming tail, see sootiraptor and sootragon, from Terrarium
sootiraptor: [Terra Monster] bipedal pyrosaur with flaming tail and crest, see sootimander and sootragon, from Terrarium
sootragon: [Terra Monster] large bipedal pyrosaur with flaming tail, backridge and crest, see sootiraptor and sootimander, from Terrarium
sophter: [lowder antonym] large, red beetle-like insectoid
sóquili: [Cherokee] horse-like creature from Tsalagi system
sor: [China rose sor anihc, rosso corsa Sroco's sor palindrome] rose or red anihc from Sroco system
sora: [*Dell Crossword Puzzle Dictionary*] rail bird
sorba: [*Conscience Interplanetary* by Joseph Green] beastly mammaloid whose milk is addictive to Shamblers, merely spicy to Humans, from Misery
sordzoru: [James Cooke Brown's Loglan sorlu dzoru compound] earwalker from Logla, Brown's system
sorecoceros: [mynynym] horned shrew
sorf: [frost sorf palindrome] white furry with gray, pink and cream
sorlopteryx: [scansoriopteryx mondegreen] dinosaur from Sca system
sorozil: purple, furless deer-like rumniant with antlers from Relegooturnia (Phoenix IV), Galaxiki galaxy
sorr: [copper rose sorr eppoc palindrome] rosy-colored eppoc
soulmarauder: [*Planar Handbook* by Bruce Cordell, etal.] Energon predator
soulsipper: [*Planar Handbook* by Bruce Cordel, etal.] fish-like Energon that feeds mostly on psychic energy of pre-incarnate souls
sourpuss: [*Rainbeau's Riddles and Rhymes*] lemon-like felinoid
sovelkapo: ["shovelhead", Thousand Stars] 50-kg bottomfeeder with shovel-like head, immune to poisons, from Oshan
sowbug: aka pillbug, roly-poly, slater, wood louse that moves by curling and rolling; ["Mother's Day" by Astrid Julian] lutscher larva up to 1.2-meter from Sheelar
sowbugator: [sowbug alligator portmanteau] alligator-like predator whose bite morphs victim into sowbug

space amoeba: ["Immunity Syndrome" by Robert Sabaroff] 18 by 3 megameter single-celled creature that destroyed all life in Gamma 7A system from outside of Milky Way galaxy

space bats: [Godvile] ghostly-green chiropterans with translucent wings, and slit eyes (red detects strength, yellow, weakness, male's 3rd green inventor)

space bee: [Dan Dare: "The Red Moon Mystery"] bee-like insectoid from outer space

space bird: ["Space Bird" by James White] giant bird paralyzed and powered by bombeetles by migrating Spacebirdriders from Sector 9

space cephalopoid: [Boris Karloff's Tales of Mystery #56: "A Jagged Orbit"] one-eyed, purple cephalopoid from outer space, see space octopus

space dragon: ["Dragons of Space" by by Aladra Septama] large jellyfish-like creature that abducts cattle, etc., from outer space

space eater: ["The Space Eaters" by Frank Belnap Long] interstellar brain-sucker like shimmering, twisting shaft of light, able to form pseudopod for boring into prey's skull, may cause chilly mist in hunting ground, moves by "eating through space"

space flea: ["The Lights in the Sky" by Phaedra M. Weldon] flea-like creature from Selurian space

space goat: [onlyfatrabbit.com] transdimensional space-dwelling ruminant

space herpes: ["Ice Pirates" by Stewart Raffill and Stanford Sherman] deadly space-dwelling pest

space moth: ["Doctor's Orders" by Chris Black] creature noted for its half-light-year migration from Pychan space

space octopus: [*The Infernal Nexus* by David Stone] small variety of ESO, see space cephalopod

space octopuss: [space octopus puss portmanteau] 8-legged, space-dwelling felinoid

space slug: ["The Empire Strikes Back" by Donald F. Glut] 900-meter silicon-based, worm-like asteroid-dweller that reproduces by splitting

space slugator: [space slug alligator portmanteau] alligator-like predator whose bite morphs victim into space slug

space spider: [Space Patrol: "Lair of the Space Spider"] giant arachnoid from outer space, see Bell spider

space turkey: ["Star Trap" by the Congress of Wonder, "Star Drek" by Bobby Pickett and Peter Ferrara] dangerous turkey-like ornithoid from outer space

space turtle: [*Mothstorm* by Philip Reeve] turtle-like space-dwelling creature from Saturn (alpha Zodiaci VI)'s rings, see gamera

space worm: ["Attack of the Flesh Devouring Space Worms" by Mike A. Martinez and George N. Thompson] giant worms from outer space that reanimate dead in Arkansas, Terra (alpha Zodiaci III)

space-brain: ["The Secret of Superboy's Sister" by Leo Dorfman] symbiotic space creature

space-cow: ["Country Doctor" by William Morrison] 90-meter, 6-eyed, red amorph with 9-meter mouth, tadpole-like young from Ganymede (alpha Zodiaci Vc)

spaceling: [*The Reefs of Space* by Frederik Pohl and Jack Williamson] seal-like with jet-less propulsion

spacelingator: [spaceling alligator portmanteau] alligator-like predator whose bite morphs victim into spaceling

spacemanatee: [*Starcross* by Philip Reeve] space-dwelling, manatee-like creature

spaghetti weevil: [Charles de Jaeger] insect pest of spaghetti trees

spagon: [space dragon portmanteau] space-faring dracoid

spahlen-tier: [Basle "cut-animal"] dracoid

spamalope: ["Far Side" by Gary Larson] antelope-like creature with secondary shoulder and hip corners

spanieel: [spaniel-eel portmanteau] caninoid with droopy ears, silky hair, short legs and. long serpentinoid tongue

spapig: [Cyclopedia of Worlds] 15-meter pelagic animal with prehensile proboscis, 6 fins, 3 broad tails from Shuttleworth, Amon Alpha system

spapigator: [sapig alligator portmanteau] alligator-like predator whose bite morphs victim into spapig

spapo: [James Cooke Brown's Loglan spasi porju (space hog/pig/swine) compound] spacehog from Logla, Brown's system

sparrow-hawk: [sparrow hawk mondegreen] ornithoid with sparrow-like head and hawk-like body

sparrowfish: [*Stations of the Tide* by Michael Swanwick] hightide form of dimorph from Miranda, Prospero system whose low-tide form is rainbird

sparrowkeet: [sparrow-parakeet portmanteau, Avatar: The Last Airbender: "City of Walls and Secrets"] sparrow-headed parakeet

sparrowl: [sparrow-owl portmanteau] nocturnal brownish-gray ornithoid with large head and eyes

spathuala: [Cyclopedia of Worlds] 20-meter vent-dweller with flexible sphincter-tipped mouth lined with extremely hard and sharp scraping teeth from Conus, Arcturus (gamma Boötis) system

spatoptera: ["Face To Face With Planet Scanodon" by Rocky Strone] flying predator from Scandon

spawn beetle: ["Elogium" by Kenneth Biller and Jerri Taylor] insectoid pest from Delta Quadrant

spazz: [*On Beyond Zebra* by Theodore Seuss Geissel] 4-meter flat-footed, antelope-like creature with camel-like hump and large antlers from Bazzim

spearfly: [Xanth series by Piers Anthony] variety of guardfly from Land of Flies, Xanth

spectrox bat: ["Caves of Androzani" by Robert Holme] methane-breathing chiropteroid, source of spectrox, the life extending drug, its milk is only known antidote to raw guano poisoning from Androzani Minor, Sirius (alpha Canis Majoris) system

speed sloth: [Godville] omnivorous sloth with fast-acting digestive system prompting fast foodhunting

spelling b: [Xanth series by Piers Anthony] insect with furry checkerboard jacket-like markings that arranges letterplant letters from Xanth

sphagnum: [*Mothstorm* by Philip Reeve] aka nibbling sporran from Uranus (alpha Zodiaci VI), see leaping and tuffed spagnum

sphexe: ["Exploration Team" by Murray Leinster] 350-kg migratory pack tan-and-blue sauroid that spits like cobra, howls like wildcat, attracted by blood like shark, spiny fringes and horns, vulnerable belly from Loren II

sphinxling: ["Imprisoned with the Pharaohs" by Howard Phillips Lovecraft and Harry Houdini] aka child of the Sphinx, see asakku, dominoboar, dominonim, dominosaur, dominotaur, esha, hall minotaur, maulotaur, minitaur, manshark, minoboar, minonim, minosaur, minotaur, pamola

sphinxlingator: [sphinxling alligator portmanteau] alligator-like predator whose bite morphs victim into sphinxling

sphynx: hairless, heat-adapted furry

spice spider: [*Creatures of the Galaxy* by Phil Brucato, Bill Smith, Rick D. Stuart, Chuck Truett] burrowing arachnoid whose excrement is source of glitterstim from Kessel and glitteryll from Ryloth, Jedi galaxy

spiceweasel: ["Futurama" series] small weasel-like mammalian that blows spice from its snout

spiceweaselope: [spiceweasel antelope portmanteau] spiceweasel with antlers

spickle: [*After Man* by Dougal Dixon] nectar-eating spiny mammal

spiddle: [*Nick and Glimmung* by Philip K. Dick] many-legged, many-tailed insectoid from Plowman's planet

spideer: [spider deer portmanteau] 8-legged spider-like deer

spider snake: [Avatar: The Last Airbender: "Zuko Alone"] long-tailed, spider-like dracoid

spider-cat: [Odd Squad: Sector 21] cute, yet scary, 8-legged, spider-like felinoid

spider-crab: [spider crab mondegreen] many-eyed, spider-headed crab
spider-snake: [spider snake mondegreen] spider-headed serpentoid
spider-monkey: [Spy Kids 2: "Island of Lost Dreams" by Robert Rodriguez] eight-legged spider-like simian
spiderclam: [*Throy* by Jack Vance] black, edible amphibian believed to induce sterility
spidereater: [*Monster Manual* by Skip Williams, etal.] 3-meter bipedal inbsectoid with red head, legs and stinger with black hook, short hairy yellow torso, bluish-black leathery wings, 8 eyes, mandibles, pincers, abdominal spikes, sometimes used as steeds
spidoz: robot-like arachnoid from Tincityie (Edonian cluster VII), Galaxiki galaxy
spidrid: [*Worlds Apart: Nat. Hist. of Furaha and Earth* by Souren Nyoroge] creature from Furaha (alpha Phoenicis IV)
spieltier: [Germ. game-animal, "The Lady Who Sailed the Soul" by Cordwainer Smith] shapeshifting pet able to take the form, for example, of a chicken or furry, long-eared furry or a yellow-haired, blue-eyed girl doll
spift: [spine-tailed swift spoonerism] flightless bird with pig-like corkscrew tail
spigas: ["Son of Godzilla" by Shin'ichi Sekizawa and Kazue Shiba] 1.2-meter tall arachnoid with poisonous spear-like tongue, able to spin white webbing very fast
spiguin: [spider-penguin portmanteau, "Robot Hugs" by R. Hugs'] penguin-like ornithoid with spider-like legs
spike: [The Legend of Zelda] small, metallic sea urchin with retractable spikes, [Monster Galaxy] fiery felinoid with 2 tails from Ares constellation; [*Dell Crossword Puzzle Dictionary*] young mackerel
spiked beetle: [The Legend of Zelda] beetle with spiny carapace
spiller: [Protector II: "The Aftermath"] fuzzy herd arachnoid from Thermia
spink: [*The Future Is Wild* by Dougal Dixon] burrowing ornithoid with shovel-like horny-scaled wings noted for its high-pitched song

spinner: [Pern series by Ann McCaffrey] arachnoid from Pern (Rukbat (alpha Sagittarii) III), see crawler
spinneret: ["The Jesus Incident" by Frank Herbert and Bill Ransom] slow, gray-black mole-like burrower that excretes sticky paralyzing fog from its tail-like appendage from Pandora
spinosaur: [*The Big Bad Book of Beasts* by Michael Largo] 7-tonne sail-backed carnivorous dinosaur from Africa, Terra (alpha Zodiaci III)
spinotaur: [spinosaur minotaur portmanteau] carnivorous bovine with backsail
spiny cucumber: ["The Worm Turns" by Gregory Benford] space creature with spikes and warts, from HD209458 system
spiny gnateater: [spiny anteater backformation] spiny insectivore that eats gnats
spiralpox virus: ["Space Patrol"] measles-like virus that causes spiral spots from Mars (alpha Zodiaci IV)
spirigum: ["Secret Formula"] Venerian arachnoid noted for nearly indestructible webbing, used as truth drug when powdered
spit-spider: [Mad Magazine: "Woodlore"] spider that spits poisonous saliva, indentifiable by orange belly
spitfire beetle: [*The Future Is Wild* by Dougal Dixon] flutterbird-eating beetle adapted to mimic spitfire tree blossoms when in quartet
spitfire: [*The Future Is Wild* by Dougal Dixon] variety of insectivorous flutterbird that gathers chemicals from male and female spitfire tree blossoms and combines them to make acid
spittlebug: insect whose larva produce spittle-like bubbles, aka froghopper
spittlebugator: [spittlebug alligator portmanteau] alligator-like predator whose bite morphs victim into spittlebug
spitz: [Germ. Spitzmaus backformation] shrew-mouse rodentoid
splacknuck: [*Travels into Several Remote Nations of the World* by Lemuel Gulliver] graceful, elegant human-sized mammal

splinter cat: [Xanth series by Piers Anthony] porcupine-like cat able to deposit splinters with touch from Xanth

spog: [Fr. Johann Martin Schleyer's Volapük] sponge-like sea creature from Schleyer's system

spogator: [spog alligator portmanteau] alligator-like predator whose bite morphs victim into spog

spoh: [spoh chops palindrome] food animal related to spoo

sponycynops: [mynynym] newt-like creature from Spony system

spoo: ["Midnight on the Firing Line", "The Geometry of Shadows" by J. Michael Straczynski] worm-like food creature from Narn, [Ekan spoo hoop snake palindrome] hoop snake-like amphisbæna from Eka peninsula, Snowi, Nejstea system, Galaxiki galaxy

spoon fish: [knife fish extrapolation] spoon-shaped ichthyoid

spop: [popstar at-spop palindrome] red-violet ornithoid, see at

sporcupine: [Terra Monsters] quadruped with "electrostatic sence", short beak, see electripine and torqupine, from Terrarium

spore: [Galaxy of Fear: "Spore"] parasitic monster geneered by Ithorians, Jedi galaxy

sporemerops: [mynynym] bee-eater-like insectoid that reproduces by spores

sporilla: [Terrahawks: "Space Giant"] flying monster from Callisto (alpha Zodiaci Vd)

spork: [Spy Kids 2: "Island of Lost Dreams" by Robert Rodriguez] pig with feathery wings

spork fish: [knife fish extrapolation] spork-shaped ichthyoid

spork-fish: pig-like ichthyopteryx

sporkupine: [Terra Monster] porcupine-like creature from Terrarium

sprat: [*Dell Crossword Puzzle Dictionary*] pilchard-like fish

spreal: [spring of teals spoonerism, spring teal portmanteau] bluish green or greenish blue, short-necked, duck-like ornithoid

spriggan: [The Elder Scrolls III: "Morrowind"] territorial walking tree, able to revive from dead twice from Solstheim forests [*Here Be Monsters almanac*, Paracelsus] proto-dryad

spring: [Pern series by Ann McCaffrey] parasite from Pern (Rukbat (alpha Sagittarii) III)

spring lizard: ["The Black Time" by Wim Vandermann] reptilian from Jonathon, Jonah system, Charon nebula

spring-lizard: [spring lizard mondegreen] parasitic lizard

springator: [spring alligator portmanteau] alligator-like predator whose bite morphs victim into spring

springtail: [snouter extrapolation] snout leaper with coiled tail adapted for springing

sprink: [Dutch sprinkhaan backformation] grasshopper-chicken, hopping ornithoid with long legs from Stiria, Airit system, Galaxiki system

sprintosaur: [*The New Dinosaurs* by Dougal Dixon] including knobby-crested quadribullus and broad-bladed dolabratops varieties, related to hook-crested ancorachephalus

sprintotaur: [sprintosaur minotaur portmanteau] bovinoid in knobby-crested, broad-bladed and hook-crested varieties

sprod: [*Dell Crossword Puzzle Dictionary*] 2-year-old salmon, see smolt, mort

spule: [span of mules spoonerism, spark mule portmanteau] electric mule-like equinoid

spulver worm: [*Coldheart* by Trevor Baxendale] mutagenic worm from Aayavex, that turned Eskonese into degenerate "slimers" and mute slave girls

spurgeon: [*Blue World* by Jack Vance] fearless creature from the Blue World

spurgeonster: [spurgeon monster portmanteau] monstrous spurgeon

spwinder: [Monster Galaxy] creature evolved from electrotter from Gemini constellation

sqairdi: [scaredy cat mondegreen] reclusive felinoid, see skitt

squad snake: [*Last Man Running* by Chris Boucher] gestalt snake that attacks with crippling sound from Lentic empire

squalisda: [tsisqualisda backformation] wren-blackbird-like ornithoid

squar: [squarish backformation] nearly-square 2-D creature

squashbug: [squash bug mondegreen] large, juggergnat-like insectoid

squathare: almost immobile predator from Thermistica system, Galaxiki galaxy

squeaky: [squeaky, squeaker backformation] aka squeaker snake, rattler-like serpentoid with tail that squeaks

squealer: [*A Hero's Guide to Deadly Dragons* by Hiccup Haddock III] black slug-like, pack-hunting dracoid with piranha-like jaws, stunning shriek from Barbarian archipelago

squelchy: ["Non Sequito" by Wiley] parasitic insect that destroys environment as well as reason

squibat: [squid-bat portmanteau, Outernauts] pointy-headed pterocephalopod with fangs, see oji, tentafang

squibbon: [squid-gibbon portmanteau, *The Future Is Wild* by Dougal Dixon] arboreal eyestalked cephalopodan

squilla: [*Dell Crossword Puzzle Dictionary*] mantis crab

squirlon: ["Flash Gordon" series] flying squirrel-like creature with maddening bite from Mongo

squirlonster: [squirlon monster portmanteau] monstrous squirlon

squirm: [*A Hero's Guide to Deadly Dragons* by Hiccup Haddock III] transparent, very small dragon with non-fatal electric shock, related to glowworm, from Barbarian archipelago

squirmisher: [Godville] giant worm with 254 hearts

squirrel-cat: ["A Dark and Stormy Night" by Larry Blamire] wild arboreal mammal like both squirrel and cat, particularly knock-kneed variety

squirrelipede: [squirrel-centipede portmanteau, "Robot Hugs" by R. Hugs'] squirrel-like rodentoid with many tiny legs

squirrelope: [squerrel antelope portmanteau] squirrel with antlers

squirrelserpent: [*A Hero's Guide to Deadly Dragons* by Hiccup Haddock III] small, arboreal green, and brown or gray and white stripped dragon with spotted underbelly, may accidentally start forest fires from Barbarian archipelago

squirrel-serpent: [squirrelserpent mondegreen] squirrel-headed snake

squishy: ["Non Sequito" by Wiley] pony-like hyperdimensional colony creature that feeds on redundancies and paradoxes

squomito: [mosquito spoonerism] blood-sucking insectoid

squonk: [*Monster Spotter's Guide to North America* by Scott Francis] worty, loose-skinned creature noted for its weeping cry, leaves puddle behind, from Pennsylvanian hemlock forests, Terra (alpha Zodiaci III)

squonkey: [squirrel monkey portmanteau] squirrel-like arboreal simian

squonzo bonzo: [Odd Squad: Sector 21] hovering blob that cries strawberry yogurt

srae: [searsnap ananymondegreen] red crocodillian from Pa system

srag: ["The Sweeper of Loray" by Robert Sheckley] only non-taboo hunted animal on Loray, with claws, teeth and horns

sragator: [srag alligator portmanteau] alligator-like predator whose bite morphs victim into srag

srang: ["The Menace of Supergirl's Mother" by Leo Dorfman] beast whose venom induces hatred from Kandor, Krypton, Rao system

srangator: [srang alligator portmanteau] alligator-like predator whose bite morphs victim into srang

srar: see balat srar

sregit: [tiger's eye sregit palindrome] brownish orange ornithoid

srel: [srel-like killers palindrome] harmless creature, like nothing else except the srel-mimicking killer

srelope: [srel antelope portmanteau] srel with antlers

sret: ["sret at times emit taters" palindrome] goose-like ornithoid that lays potatoes

sretni: [interstellar allet sretni palindrome] migratory allet

srett: [bittersweet eew srett ib palindrome] pinkish orange eew with red nape (back of neck)

srolra: [Ekan srolra parlor snake palindrome] parlor snake-like amphisbæna from Eka peninsula, Snowi, Nejstea system, Galaxiki galaxy

sroop: arboreal felinoid with sloth-like hind legs from Betonia (Edonian cluster V), Galaxiki galaxy

sru: [ekan sru fursnake palindrome] fursnake-like amphisbæna from Eka peninsula, Snowi, Nejstea system, Galaxiki galaxy

sseikea: [*The Romulan Way* by Terisa Halekala-LoBrotto] aka ßeikea, hyena-like creature from ch'Rihan, Eisn (128 Trianguli) system

ssow: [currassow mondegreen]aka ßow, flying pig from Curra system

ssu ling: [Chinese] aka ßu ling, generic term for either ch'i-lin, fêng-huang, tortoise or dragon (lung, kiu-lung, yü-lung)

ssum: [*River Monsters* by Jeremy Wade] aka ßum, 300-kg catfish from Russia, Terra (alpha Zodiaci III)

ssvaklor: [*Serpent Kingdoms* by Ed greenwood, etal.] aka ßvaklor, poison gas-breathing, green and black serpent-like dracoid created by Yuan-ti

ssyela: [Ekan ssyela Daley's snake palindrome] aka ßyela, Daley's snake-like amphisbæna from Eka peninsula, Snowi, Nejstea system, Galaxiki galaxy

sta: [Ekan sta fatsnake palindrome] fatsnake-like amphisbæna from Eka peninsula, Snowi, Nejstea system, Galaxiki galaxy

stäee: [stäer backformation] prey of stäer

stäer: [stäerchen backformation] large 2-D pentapus or hexapus

stäerchen: [Lux. *] 2-D pentapus or hexapus

stag beetle: [Xanth series by Piers Anthony] antlered insect from Xanth or [Xantian mondegreen] Xa, Thia system

stäg: [Fr. Johann Martin Schleyer's Volapük] deer-like ruminant from Schleyer's system

staga: [*Creatures of the Galaxy* by Phil Brucato, Bill Smith, Rick D. Stuart, Chuck Truett] herd animal with shoulder tufts, scales, horns, flat tail from Ambria, Jedi galaxy

stagator: [staga alligator portmanteau] alligator-like predator whose bite morphs victim into staga

stägator: [stäg alligator portmanteau] alligator-like predator whose bite morphs victim into stäg

stal: [stallion backformation] lion-horse ancestor

stalag: [stalagmite mondegreen, stalag] cave-dwelling mite-like insectoid that traps prey in cave

stalagator: [stalag alligator portmanteau] alligator-like predator whose bite morphs victim into stalag

stalker: [Laurence Doyle and Manoj Joshi] three-eyed, bulbous-headed skywhale predator, in scout and sharp-beaked worker varieties, from Blue Moon

stalope: [stal antelope portmanteau] stal with antlers

stamingo: [stand of flamingo spoonerism, stantor-flamingo portmanteau] pink ornithoid

stantor. ["Feud of the Super-Femmes" by Leo Dorfman] ornithoid from Krypton, Rao system

star fish: [starfish mondegreen] star-dwelling ichthyoid, see star worm

star worm: [starworm mondegreen] star-dwelling worm-like immature star fish

star-sucker: huge serpent-like star-eating creature with 3 radio-sensing antennae from Sirius (alpha Canis Majoris) sector

starfish: [Piers Anthony] brilliantly gleaming ichthyoid feared by the shellfish from Xanth or [Xanthian mondegreen] Xa, Thia system

starfish of David: [star of David starfish portmanteau] starfish with six points from David's system

stargazer: fish with 4 half-eyes (2 for air, 2 for water) and 4 sexes (with right and left sex organs)

stargoat: [*Hitchhiker's Guide to the Galaxy* by Doug Adams] planet-eater said to have threatened Galgafrincham

starf: [starfish backformation] starfish mimic

staria: [Terra Monsters] felinoid with star-shaped tail, see celestail, from Terrarium
starling: [Xanth Piers Anthony] midnight-black bird with brilliant star-like speckling from Xanth or [Xanthian] Xa, Thia system
starlingator: [starling alligator portmanteau] alligator-like predator whose bite morphs victim into starling
starnose: [*Dell Crossword Puzzle Dictionary*] mole with star-like snout
starworm: [*A Door into Ocean* by Joan Slonczewsky] noted for use with shockwraith sinew by Sharer wormrunners to secure raft from Shora the Ocean Moon of Valedon
staryak: [Monster Galaxy] shaggy, purple-haired bovinoid with u-shaped horns, dangerous when un-belled from Taurus constellation
staubhase: [Germ.] dustbunny
stayaway: [*Worlds Apart: Nat. Hist. of Furaha and Earth* by Souren Nyoroge] stinging insectoid from Furaha (alpha Phoenicis IV)
stealth dragon: [*A Hero's Guide to Deadly Dragons* by Hiccup Haddock III] camoflauging dragon with finger lightning, explosive burn streams from Barbarian archipelago
steam frog: [Jets*Rockets*Spacemen trading cards] giant, high-temperature adapted batrachian with long-clawed flippers
steam frogator: [steam frog alligator portmanteau] alligator-like predator whose bite morphs victim into steam
steamer: [Xanth series by Piers Anthony] dragon that breathes steam rather than smoke from Xanth, [steamer trunk] including variety with elephant-like trunk
steato: [steatopygus backformation] food porcoid with large buttocks
steelwooly mammoth: [steel wool wooly mammoth portmanteau] mammoth with steel wire-like hair
steelwooly worm: [steel wool wooly worm portmanteau] worm with steel wire-like hairs
stegocentipede: [*Monster Manual II* by Gary Gygas] many-legged arthropod with double backplates

stegosaur: ["roof-lizard"] 9-meter herbivorous dinosaur with double backplates, 4-spiked tail from Jurassic
stegotaur: [Far Side: "When Cows Ruled" by Gary Larson, stegosaur minotaur portmanteau] bovinoid with backplates and tail spikes
stegoget: [mynynym] cave-dwelling ape-ray with back plates
stella matutina: [*The Snouters* by Harald Stümpke] aka little Morgenstern's nasobame, like hónatata but with shorter tail and diet of low-to-ground berries
stēkok: [Kurd. *] 2-D pentapus or hexapus
stelzaffe: ["The Space Detective" by H. G. Ewers] simian from Drahl
stench kow: [*Monster Manual II* by Gary Gygas] malodorous buffaloid
stench-puffer: [Xanth series by Piers Anthony] small creature that gives off stinking clouds from Xanth
stenomyl: [*After the Dinosaurs* by Donald R. Prothero] gazelle-like camel
stenomylope: [stenomyl antelope portmanteau] stenomyl with antlers
stephanorhinus: [*After the Dinosaurs* by Donald R. Prothero] aka Etruscan rhino from Pleistocene
sterlet: [*Dell Crossword Puzzle Dictionary*] small sturgeon
sterke: [Fris. *] 2-D pentapus or hexapus
sterna: [*Dell Crossword Puzzle Dictionary*] tern
stern: [sternchen backformation] large sternchen
sternchen: [Germ. *] 2-D pentapus or hexapus
stett: [*The Longest Voyage* by Poul Anderson] firefly-like insectoid from Tambur
stib: [*Dell Crossword Puzzle Dictionary*] sandpiper, see ree(ve), stint, ruff
stickback: ["Capt'n Virgil, Sportsman in Space" by David Brooks] 2-headed ichthyoid from Arizant
stick-man: [stickman mondegreen] walkingstick-like anthropoid

sting-fly: [Mad Magazine: "Woodlore"] fly with paralyzing sting, though much easier to catch than common housefly
stingbat: [*This Moment of the Storm* by Roger Zelazny] chiropteroid with stinger from Tierra del Cygnus, 72 Cygni system
stinger fan: ["Alien Animal Planet" by Sean Cooper] tree-like planimal with ambulatory roots, 5 hearts, prey of mudpod
stinger: [Resident Evil 0] giant mutant scorpion; [The Legend of Zelda: "Ocanna of Time"] sting ray-like underground-dweller with dorsal fin
stingfly: [Xanth series by Piers Anthony] sting-fly from Land of Flies, Xanth
stinglice: [Xanth series by Piers Anthony] insectoid noted for inducing painful welts from Xanth
stink bug: [Xanth series by Piers Anthony] stinking insect from Xanth
stink bugator: [stink bug alligator portmanteau] alligator-like predator whose bite morphs victim into stink bug
stink dragon: [*A Hero's Guide to Deadly Dragons* by Hiccup Haddock III] malodorous, orange dragon with black stripes and stinking, misty breath from Barbarian archipelago
stink worm: [Xanth series by Piers Anthony] worm that tastes absolutely awful from Xanth
stinking smut: [The Tick: "Man-eating Cow"] giant, malodorous, parasitic fungus
stinking trumpet snouter: [The Snouters by Harald Stümpke] malodorous, gnat-eating trumpet snouter from Hi-Yi-Yi Islands
stint: [*Dell Crossword Puzzle Dictionary*] small sandpiper, see ree(ve), stib, ruff
stirge: ["The Ecology of the Stirge" by Ed Greenwood] 30-cm brown-to-rust-red mosquitoid with pale pink proboscis, pincers, 4 leathery wings, barbed legs
stirianaa: [*A Call to Darkness* by Michael Jan Friedman] gene-translocating bacteria from Chaquafar
stizard: [starred lizard spoonerism] fatty reptilian
stjerne: [Dan. *] 2-D pentapus or hexapus
stjörnu: [Icel. *] 2-D pentapus or hexapus

stockoceros: [*After the Dinosaurs* by Donald R. Prothero] aka Quintin's pronghorn, with four short horns from Miocene
stoksosaur: [William Lee Stoksos] dinosaur
stoksotaur: [stoksosaur minotaur portmanteau] bovinoid from Stok's system
stone dove: [Xanth series by Piers Anthony] bird able to camouflage as rock from Xanth
stone mite: scorpion-like metallovore able to form electrolytically-bonded shelled triont
stone-monster: see rarnsuk
stormhornet: [*Edge Chronicles* by Paul Stewart and Chris Riddell] underground-dweller wasp-like harbinger of storm
storse: [string or stud of horses spoonerism, storsie backformation] seahorse-like sea monster
storsie: [*Here Be Monsters almanac*] lake monster in Lake Storsjor, Sweden, Terra (alpha Zodiaci III)
stot: [*Dell Crossword Puzzle Dictionary*] young ox from England, Terra (alpha Zodiaci III)
stover: [stand of plover spoonerism, standing plover portmanteau] flightless plover-like ornithoid
strace horse: [string of racehorses spoonerism] pack-hunting predatory equinoid
strandmuddlare: [museumofhoaxes.com by Alex Boese] aka shore mudder, creature with pig's head, squirrel's tail, bird's legs from Sweden, Terra (alpha Zodiaci III)
strank: [*After Man* by Dougal Dixon] rabbuck variant
stratosaur: [stratostrike -saur portmanteau] high-flying pterosaur
stratotaur: [stratosaur minotaur] high-flying bull-like pegasoid
stratoshrike: ["The Beasts of Karn" by Ken Koonce and Michael Merton] high-flying predatory ornithoid from Karn
stratt: [*Creatures of the Galaxy* by Phil Brucato, Bill Smith, Rick D. Stuart, Chuck Truett] large reptilian from Coruscant, Jedi galaxy
stratus: [Outernauts] mature cirrius

strawbear: [strawberry, strawman backformations] top-heavy ursinoid easily knocked down

strawberry jelly: reddish jelly-thick ooze

strawberry blonde jelly: reddish yellow jelly-thick ooze

streeler: [*Fantastic Beasts and Where to Find Them* by Newton Artemis Fido Scamander] snail with poisonous color-shifting (streel) shell

strick: [*After Man* by Dougal Dixon] large-eared kangaroo-like rodent

striger: [streak of tigers spoonerism, *After Man* by Dougal Dixon] monkey-like cat predator that pounces from trees (striges)

strix: [*Ornithologia* by Boios] man-eating, blood-sucking nocturnal bird of ill omen

strom: [maelstrom mondegreen] dinoid sea monster, rarely if ever female, see himicane, hericane

strongfish: [weakfish antonym] strong ichthyoid

strornis: [gastronis mondegreen] gray-green flightless ornithoid

struthio: [OviPets] ostrich-like ornithoid

struthiomimus: ["tall ostrich mimic", *Feathered Dinosaurs: The Origin of Birds* by John Long and Peter Schuten] 4-meter ornithomimosaur with 3 long fingered hands

strutwind: [Terra Monster] large-headed, long-necked flightless ornithoid with lightningbolt tail, two-toed feet from Terrarium

struul: [*Galactic Gourmet* by James Blish] ichthyoid from Corellia

stubbee: [stubby backformation] short, stubby bee-like insectoid

stuff: ["Stuff" by Larry Cohen] addictively sweet, white, amorphous parasite that eats host ("stuffie") from inside out or smother resistant hosts with pseudopods from underground

stunjelly: [*Monster Manual* by Skip Williams, etal.] jelly-thick ooze able to stun

stupendemys: [*After the Dinosaurs* by Donald R. Prothero] gigantic turtle from Zanoclean age (early Pliocene)

sturmopt: mammoth winged creature from Dalinzia, Locomoto system, Galaxiki galaxy

stylax: ["The Gift of Gab" by Jack Vance] food worm for dekabrachs ("deks")

stylemys: [*After the Dinosaurs* by Donald R. Prothero] land tortoise from Oligocene

Styphalian bird: bird with brass beak, wings, talons, able to fire feathers like arrows from Lake Stympalis, Arcadia, Terra (alpha Zodiaci III)

su: [sumimus backformation] creature mimicked by sumimus

sub-vole: [Xanth series by Piers Anthony] see diggle, wiggle

subhu: [subhuman mondegreen] dehumanized Human, monster of the sixth kind; see beast-were

succococcus: [mynynym] disease bacterium from Succia, Succ system

sucehtipopithecus: [mynynym] ape from Sucehtip system

sucker-sap: [Xanth series by Piers Anthony] sweat gnat eating bird from Xanth

suctorial snout leaper: [*The Snouters* by Harald Stümpke] snouter in symbiosis with pillar snouter from Hi-Yi-Yi Islands

sud: [dusk sud] variety of hgiliwt

sugahphagus: [mynynym] sugah-eater

sugarmouse: [*The Snouters* by Harald Stümpke] slime snouter with sweet secretion for attracting prey from Hi-Yi-Yi Islands

sugaragus: [mynynym] sweet variety of agus

suhur mas: [Sumerian] "goat-fish" ichthyoid from Akyby, Rybyka system, Galaxiki galaxy, see mas

suierma: surreal seriema portmantea] fantastic, carnivorous ornithoid

suk: [Durdekors] monstrous creature, see rarnsuk

sul: [lust sul palindrome] red ornithoid

sulb: [blush sulb palindrome] blush pinkish ornithoid

sulī: [Cherokee] buzzard-like ornithoid from Tsalagi system

sulphuric aphid: [Godville] aphid-like insectoid that sucks life fluids leaving a sulphrous odor

sulvo: [Outernauts] mature, red, fiery moltovo, in venomous and non-venomous varieties
sumip: ["sumip at times emit tapimus" palindrome] tusked rodentoid gestalt
summer pudding: [pudding extrapolation] pudding-thick ooze that only hunts in summer
summoning ooze: [*Monster Manual* by Skip Williams, etal.] ooze able to lure victims
sumpter: [*Dell Crossword Puzzle Dictionary*] packhorse that sumpts
sun bear: [*The Big Bad Book of Beasts* by Michael Largo] small bear with yellow or white bib from Indo-China, Terra (alpha Zodiaci III)
sundog: see twook
sundogator: [sundog alligator portmanteau] alligator-like predator whose bite morphs victim into twook
sunfish: [Xanth series by Piers Anthony] fish with hemicircular, bioluminescent backfin from Xanth
sungwas: ["Droids" series] large wolf-weasel-like caninoid from Bodgen bogs, Jedi galaxy
sunk: [surfeit of skunks spoonerism] malodorous bottom-dwelling seacreature from Snobaal, Laabon system, Galaxiki galaxy
suntiger: [Hitchhiker's Guide to the Galaxy series by Douglas Adams] felinoid from Algol (beta Persei) system whose venomous fangs are used in PanGalactic Gargle Blaster
suodnerroh: [horrendous uodnerroh palindrome] monstrous creature, see irroh
super bird: [Col. Bleep: "Scratch and His Feathered Friend" by Robert D. Buchanan] large, black space-faring ornithoid from Anake (alpha Zodiaci Vm)
supercow: [*A Planet for Texans* by H. Beam Piper and John J. McGuire] 12-meter tall, 15-tonne bovine from New Texas (Capella (alpha Aurigae) IV)
supergator: ["Dinocroc vs. Supergator" by Jim Wynorski, Mike MacLean] small megalligator
suplaz: [Czech sup-plaz portmanteau] vulture-reptile, scavenger pterosaur from Snowi, Nejstea system, Galaxiki galaxy
suppihippus: [mynynym] equinoid from Suppi system

supták: [Czech sup-pták portmanteau] vulture-bird, carrion-eating ornithoid
sur: [rust sur palindrome] reddish brown ornithoid
surfbat: [*After Man* by Dougal Dixon] seal-like bat with pointed snout, prominent eyes, penguin-like flipper-wings
surma: large dog with snake-tail and petrifying gaze from Finland, Terra (alpha Zodiaci III)
surpentes: [surreal serpentes portmanteau] extradimensional egg-laying serpentoid
surpie: [surreal serpie pormanteau] extradimensional serpie
surpine: [surreal serpine portmanteau] extradimensional serpine
surplex: [surreal serplus portmanteau] extradimensional serplex
surpquin: [surreal serpquin portmanteau] extradimensional serpquin
sursnake: see duitra
sus: [*Dell Crossword Puzzle Dictionary*] boar
susanasus: [mynynym] nose-shaped porcoid from Susa system, see asus
sussõnn: [Estonian suss-sõnn portmanteau] mule-bull, horned bovine beast of burden
sutecark: ["sutecark at times emit takracetus" palindrome] landwhale gestalt
sutecocetus: [mynynym] cetacean from Sutec system
sutnimla: [James Cooke Brown's Loglan sutme podju nimla (odoriferous animal) compound] skunk-like ornithoid from Logla, Brown's system
suubatar: [*Creatures of the Galaxy* by Phil Brucato, Bill Smith, Rick D. Stuart, Chuck Truett] 6-meter, 6-legged, omnivorous steed from Ansion, Jedi galaxy
suzaku: [Jap.] see vermillion bird
svin: [Fr. Johann Martin Schleyer's Volapük] hog-like porcoid from Schleyer's system
svinki: [Belarussian marskoj svinki backformation] Guinea pig-like creature ancestral to marskoj and Guinea pig
svinpind: [Danish pindsvin backformation] pig-pind ancestral to pind and pig
svinsekt: [Danish svin-insekt portmanteau] pig-insect, porcoid parasite

svirfnebli: [Icelandic "spiral nebula" Adlerweg series by Graeme Morris] bionebula
svya: [at-sv'ya mondegreen] rooster-like ornithoid, see at

 **swallowtail**: [Xanth series by Piers Anthony] bird that disappears when threatened by biting tail like ouroboros or hoop snake from Xanth

swamola: [The Legend of Zelda: "A Link to the Past"] swamp-dwelling amphibious centipede
swamp bantha: ["The Gungan Frontier"] smaller, less hairy than desert bantha
swamp maw: [swamp maws palindrome] swamp-dwelling seamaw
swampbug: [swampbuggy backformation, "Grandpa" by James Schmitz] insectoid with 3-meter wingspan used as steed from Sutang
swampbugator: [swampbug alligator portmanteau] alligator-like predator whose bite morphs victim into swampbug
swampcat: [Space: 1889] felinoid predator from swamps of Venus (alpha Zodiaci II)
swampus: [*The Future Is Wild* by Dougal Dixon] 20-kg amphibious cephalopodan with 4 foot-like tentacles and 2 for pulling that hunts and mates on land using venom from carnivorous swampus lily
swampuss: [swampus puss pormanteau] swamp-dwelling, venomous, carnivorous felinoid
Swan bee: ["The Birds and Bees Affair" by Mark Weingart] Dr. Elias Swan's practically invisible, tiny killer bees dependent on special high-energy honey or [Swan bee mondegreen] from Swa system
swan-bee: [Swan bee mondegreen] long-necked bee-like insectoid
swant: [swarm of ants spoonerism, swan-ant portmanteau] long-necked, flying insectoid
swantel: [swantelope backformation] swantelope without antlers
swantelope: [swan-antelope portmanteau] long-necked antelope-like griffinoid with antlers

sweat gnat: [Xanth series by Piers Anthony] small insect able to induce and feed off sweat, eaten by sucker-saps from Land of Flies, Xanth
swee: [swarm of bees spoonerism, sweetish bee portmanteau] conical bee-like insectoid
sweet: [sweetish backformation] sweetish mimic
sweetish: [Monster Galaxy] icecream cone-like creature from Gemini constellation
swift grazer: [*The Jesus Incident* by Frank Herbert and Bill Ransom] dangerous ground-dweller from Pandora
swin: [swinish backformation] porcoid, see pigg, hogg
swince: ["Seed of Reason" by Daniel Hatch] arboreal woofer from Chamal
swinosaur: ["Bender's Game" by Eric Horsted, etal.] pig-lizard from Vergon VI
swinotaur: [swinosaur minotaur portmanteau] pig-headed bovinoid
swinsect: [swarm of insects spoonerism] swimming insectoid
swinx: [Terra Monster] small, purple chiropteran with gold markings and red eyes from Terrarium, see sonax
switchback: [Xanth series by Piers Anthony] porcoid with sharp retractable side blades and ability to instantly reverse direction from Xanth
switcheroo: kangaroo-were bimorph
swoogle: [hornswoggle backformation] harmless, horn-less hornswoggle
swooper: [*The Worlds of the Federation* by Shane Johnson] 4.5-meter long flying predatory planimal from Merari (Phylos II)
swordbird: [*The Integral Trees* by Larry Niven] dangerous predator from Smoke Ring, LeVoy's star system
swordwing: see khukai
swordwingator: [swordwing alligator portmanteau] alligator-like predator whose bite morphs victim into khukai
swutterfly: [swarm of butterflies spoonerism] fly-like insectoid that swuts
syagush: [*Dell Crossword Puzzle Dictionary*] lynx from Africa, Terra (alpha Zodiaci III)

sycof: [syncophant mondegreen] toady ant-like insectoid from Sycof system

syhtema: [amethyst syhtema palindrome] purplish ornithoid

syllid: [*Dell Crossword Puzzle Dictionary*] marine worm

sylph: [*Dell Crossword Puzzle Dictionary*] bird from S. America, Terra (alpha Zodiaci III), see guan, jacu, turco, seriema

symbiot: two creatures interdependent on each other, like lichen (algae-fungus)

symtriot: [symbiot extrapolation] three creatures interdependent on each other, like chimera

syndyoceras: [*After the Dinosaurs* by Donald R. Prothero] protoceratid with V-shaped nose-horns and long, curved forehead horns

synechococcus: extremophilic cynobacterium resistant to extreme cold

syntaril: [*Creatures of the Galaxy* by Phil Brucato, Bill Smith, Rick D. Stuart, Chuck Truett] woolamander predator from Yavin IV, Jedi galaxy

syntarilope: [syntaril antelope portmanteau] syntaril with antlers

synthetoceras: [*After the Dinosaurs* by Donald R. Prothero] protoceratid with Y-shaped nose-horn and curved forehead horns

syrinxer: [trumpeter swan backformation] swan-like ornithoid with panpipe–like call

systemodon: [*After the Dinosaurs* by Donald R. Prothero] horse from Ypserian age (early Eocene)

sz: [Malayan "sword-ox"] unicorn

t'narama: [amaranth t'narama palindrome] deep reddish purple to grayish purplish red ornithoid

t'stayan: ["Suddenly Human" by Ralph Phillips] 6-legged steed from Talar

ta: bogie beast nasna; [chuchuligata mondegreen] lark-like ornithoid from Chuchuliga system; [danta mondegreen] tapir-like mammal from Da system; [chattamaranta mondegreen] large creature from Chattamara system; [sky manta, thranta mondegreens] flying ray from Skyma or Thra systems

ta-ta: [Sidney H. Sine] aka bogie beast

ta!a'an: ["A !tangled Web" by Joe Haldeman] bone-hungry predator from !ka'al (Morocho III)

taa: [kantaa mondegreen] ursinoid from Ka system

taaraankan: [Hind. *] 2-D pentapus or hexapus

tabbee: [tabby-bee portmanteau] winged furry with insectoid wings and tabby markings

tabbeel: [tabbee eel portmanteau] tabbe-like dracoid with eel-like tail

taborg: [Noon Universe of Boris and Arkady Strugatsky] crayfish-spider from Pandora

taborgator: [taborg alligator portmanteau] alligator-like predator whose bite morphs victim into taborg

tach: [*Creatures of the Galaxy* by Phil Brucato, Bill Smith, Rick D. Stuart, Chuck Truett] harmless simian from Shadowlands on Kashÿyÿk, Jedi galaxy

tachygrade: [tardigrade antonym] FTL waterbear-like creature

tachyhcat: [mynynym] FTL felinoid

tado: [encantado mondegreen] snake-like parasite from Enca system

tae: [tae meat palindrome] food animal related to faol and sllab

taenia: [*Dell Crossword Puzzle Dictionary*] tapeworm

taeniid: dream-infesting parasite (*Dreamwalker: Role playing in the Land of Dreams* ed. by Peter C. Spahn, Michael Patton, David Griffin)

taeniolabis: [*After the Dinosaurs* by Donald R. Prothero] beaver-sized, eeg-laying ground squirrel-like mammal with hooves from Mesozoic and Paleocene

tag: [*Dell Crossword Puzzle Dictionary*] young sheep, lamb, teg

tagator: [tag alligator portmanteau] alligator-like predator whose bite morphs victim into lamb

tāga: [tsitāga backformation] wren-chicken ornithoid

tāgator: [tāga alligator portmanteau] alligator-like predator whose bite morphs victim into tāga

taha: [*Dell Crossword Puzzle Dictionary*] weaverbird from S. Africa, Terra (alpha Zodiaci III), see baya, maha

taho: [Pellucidar series by Edgar Rice Burroughs] cave lion domesticated by Tandar Islanders

tahti neml: [*Planiverse* by Alexander Dewdney] 2-D land animal from Arde, Shems system

tähtimerkki: [Finn. *] 2-D pentapus or hexapus

tai: [*Dell Crossword Puzzle Dictionary*] fish from Japan, see fugu, porgy

tailgraspers: proboscipede variant that uses tail for grasping prey

tailjumper: proboscipede variant that uses tail for jumping

tailleaper: [snouter extrapolation] missing link between two-way snout leaper and tailwalker

tailpasaran: [The Legend of Zelda] underground-dweller with 3-mandibled head, electric blue spherically-segmented body from Jabu-Jabu, see graboid

tailwalker: [snouter extrapolation] multiple-tailed tailleaper adapted for walking on tails

tailypo: [*The Book Hive* by Jackie Torrence] nocturnal, dog-sized black creature with yellow eyes, pointy ears, long tail so-called from its cry

taip: [Fr. Johann Martin Schleyer's Volapük] mole-like burrower from Schleyer's system

taipan: [*National Geographic Encyclopedia of Animals*] small, mammal-eating lizard from S. Pacific, Terra (alpha Zodiaci III)

taipede: [taip centipede portmanteau] mole-like burrower with many legs

tak: [shantak mondegreen] horse-headed bat-winged mimornis from Sha system

takkuri: [The Legend of Zelda: "A Link to the Past"] male vulture-like buzzard or female ["The Minish Cup"] maroon-colored crow-like ornithoid

tala: [gantala mondegreen] cave macropod from from Ga system

taladu: [Cherokee] cricket-like insectoid from Tsalagi system

talchok: ["Random Thoughts"] two-tailed creature noted for musk from Delta Quadrant

talinkabird: [trumpet swan backformation] flute swan-like ornithoid with talinka-like call

talocohc: [Crayola chocolate talocohc palindrome] brown furry, see rep

talp: [plata talp palindrome] silver creature from Spain, Terra (alpha Zodiaci III)

talukab ng: [Filipino talukab ng kalapati backformation] turtle dove-pigeon ornithoid ancestral to pigeon and turtle dove

tama: [Monster Galaxy] bipedal, maskless raccoon-like scavenger from Virgo constellation

tamarin: [*National Geographic Encyclopedia of Animals*] monkey from Columbia, Terra (alpha Zodiaci III), including lion tamarin

tamarou: see dahu, rou

tambor: [Dell Crossword Puzzle Dictionary] puffer fish or rockfish, rasher

tamot: [tomato tamot palindrome] reddish-orange ornithoid

tamure: [*Dell Crossword Puzzle Dictionary*] snapper fish from New Zeeland, Terra (alpha Zodiaci III)

tan: [Azerbaijani qutan backformation] pelican-swan, aquatic ornithoid ancestral to swan and pelican

tanager: [*National Geographic Encyclopedia of Animals*] forest bird from N. W. America, Terra (alpha Zodiaci III)

tanam: [Crayola manatee tanam palindrome] gray ornithoid from Crayol A system

tanamee: [manatee spoonerism] large sea creature fond of sunning itself above water

tanate: [*Dell Crossword Puzzle Dictionary*] wild dog from Japan, Terra (alpha Zodiaci III)

tanchinaro: [Trullion: Alastor 2262 by Jack Vance] black-and-silver ichthyoid from Far South Ocean of Trullion

tandor: [*Tanar of Pellucidar* by Edgar Rice Burroughs] mammoth from Amiocap Island, Pellucidar

tandoor: [tandor door portmanteau] mammath-like creature able to travel through portals

tandozare: [Pellucidar series by EdgarRice Burroughs] 3-meter long-necked sirenian with fanged, snake-like head

taneen: [pl. taninim] reptile, including giant variety (taninim gedolim, Gen. 1:21) dinosaurs, dragons

taniwha: [Maori] deep-water monster

tannin: many-headed dracoid

tannot worm: ["Farscape" by David Wilks] worm that eats toxic tannot root used for Peacekeeper pulse rifle from Sykar, Farscape galaxy

tanoor: [beheaded and curtailed atanooroc] 4-headed, 4-tailed, very large dracoid with red eyes and mossy, forested back

tantony: runt pig

tanuki: [Jap.] aka racoon-dog or ichibi

tanycolagreus: ["elongated limbs", *Feathered Dinosaurs: The Origin of Birds* by John Long and Peter Schuten] 4-meter tyrannosaur ancestor from late Jurassic

Tanzian flu virus: ["Partition" by Tom Szollosi] virus that causes Tanzian influenza from Delta quadrant

taotie: [*Here Be Monsters almanac*] gui-animated cooking pot

taowu: [Chin.] boar-like creature with dog-like hair, 2 long tusks and tiger-like long tail

taozin: [*Darth Maul: Shadow Hunter* by Michael Reeves] huge, transparent insectoid with hardening, adhesive secretion

tapaculos: [*National Geographic Encyclopedia of Animals*] antbird relative from S. America, Terra (alpha Zodiaci III)

tapeti: [*Dell Crossword Puzzle Dictionary*] small swamp rabbit from S. America, Terra (alpha Zodiaci III)

tapetoid: ["carpet-like"] see carpet-thing

tapimimus: [tapimus backformation] small, tusked felinoid

tapimus: [*After Man* by Dougal Dixon] tusked rodent

tapper caillie: [tok of capercaillies spoonerism] wood grouse-like ornithoid that taps like a woodpecker

tar: [tartar backformation] tartar-like nasna

tarag: [*Tanar of Pellucidar* by Edgar Rice Burroughs] sabre-tooth tiger from Amiocap Island, tamed by Tandar Islanders

taragator: [tarag alligator portmanteau] alligator-like predator whose bite morphs victim into tarag

taranter: [*The New Dinosaurs* by Dougal Dixon] anklyosaur with hairy underbelly, mace-like tail, side-spikes

tarasque: [Xanth series by Piers Anthony] cat-like dracoid with 6 ursinoid legs, mane, tusks, bright orange eyes, spiked carapace, reptilian tail with scorpion-like stinger from Xanth; [*The Legend of Tarascan, Here Be Monsters almanac*] from France, Terra (alpha Zodiaci III)

tarb: [FthinraKathi by Dale Murphy] ox-like bovinoid from T'Khasi, Nevasa (40 Eridani) system

tarbosaur: [*Feathered Dinosaurs: The Origin of Birds* by John Long and Peter Schuten] 14-meter, 5-tonne tyrannosaurid from late Cretaceous

tarbotaur: [tarbosaur minotaur portmanteau] bovinoid from Tarb system

tarchee: felinoid from Delta Quadrant, see chee, catchee

tarcheel: [tarchee eel mondegreen] tarchee-like felinoid with eel-like tail

tardigrade: ["slow walker"] see water bear, tachygrade

targ: ["Where No One Has Gone Before" by Diane Duane and Michael Reaves] furry porcinoid with forehead-horn and 3 back spikes

targath: [*The Goddess of Ganymede* and *Pursuit on Ganymede* by Michael D. Resnick and Donald M. Grant] carnivorous 2.4-meter ornithoid sighted only in radar wavelengths from Thane's moon

targator: [targ alligator portmanteau] alligator-like predator whose bite morphs victim into targ

targhee: ["The Perfect Mate" by Gary Perconte and Michael Pillar] creature noted for loud braying

targo: [*The Pirates of Venus* by Edgar Rice Burroughs] 8-legged arachnoid with long black hair, yellow spots over eyes, that spins tarel, vulnerable only in small brain variety from Amtor (alpha Zodiaci II)

tarka: [James Cooke Brown's Loglan tarku kapma] hardhat from Logla, Brown's system

tarku: James Cooke Brown's Loglan tarfu kurma] grimworm-like creature from Logla, Brown's system

tarlow: [*Memoires De Sir George Wallop* by Pierre Chevalier Duplessis, Hannah Hewitt by Charles Dibdin] pheasant-sized black and white bird from Aprilis, New Britain Islands

tarm: [Fr. Johann Martin Schleyer's Volapük] clothes moth-like insectoid from Schleyer's system

tarn: [*Tarnsmen of Gor* by John F. Lange, Jr., as John Norman] 2.1-meter ornithoid with 8.5-meter wingspan, fierce curved beak in black night, white winter, multicolored war and greenish-brown wild varieties from Gor

tärniga: [Eston. *] 2-D pentapus or hexapus

tärnigator: [tärniga alligator portmanteau] alligator-like predator whose bite morphs victim into tärniga

tarpan: [*Dell Crossword Puzzle Dictionary*] wild horse from Tartary, Terra (alpha Zodiaci III)

tarpon: [*Dell Crossword Puzzle Dictionary*] silverfish, see tarpun

tarponster: [tarpon monster portmanteau] monstrous silverfish

tarpun: see tarpon

tartar: [*Dell Crossword Puzzle Dictionary*] shrew, see erd

tartutic: ["The Woman in the Water" by M. Night Shyamalan] tree-camouflaged monkey-like scrunt predator

tasar: [*Dell Crossword Puzzle Dictionary*] silkworm from China, Terra (alpha Zodiaci III)

tass: [Jean Berko] "imaginary" creature, see wug

tasselsnouter: [*The Snouters* by Harald Stümpke] snouter over 2 meters long with 19 pairs of nasuli and 2 tentacle-like nasaria from Hi-Yi-Yi

tasta: [ulgarstasta mondegreen] yellowish maggot from Ulgar system

tatterdemalion: [Xanth series by Piers Anthony] large, raggedy feline addicted to ragweed from Xanth

tattle: tattletail backformation] parrot-like ornithoid with peacock-like tail

tatzlwurm: [*Unexplained!* by Jerome Clark] hellfire-breathing pterosaur from Germany, Terra (alpha Zodiaci III)

taucheria: [leptauchia backformation] semi-aquatic pongoid

taun: tauntaun nasna

tauntaun: [*The Empire Strikes Back* by Donald F. Glut] 2.5-meter swift, surefooted pack creature and steed with thick gray fur, down-turning horns, 4 nostrils, from Hoth, Jedi galaxy

tauron: [Monster Galaxy] black bovine with omega-shaped horns that revives phoenix-like from Taurus constellation

tauronster: [tauron monster portmanteau] monstrous tauron

taurusaur: ["Mortal Nature" by Stephen Dedman] bull-like dinosaur from Northbergen; dinosaur from Taurus constellation

tautog: [*Dell Crossword Puzzle Dictionary*] oysterfish

tautogator: [tautog alligator portmanteau] alligator-like predator whose bite morphs victim into tautog

tayra: [*National Geographic Encyclopedia of Animals*] weasel-like omnivore from S. and Meso-America, Terra (alpha Zodiaci III)

tcedzoru: [James Cooke Brown's Loglan trela dzoru compound] wingwalker from Logla, Brown's system

tcefitpi: [James Cooke Brown's Loglan tsela fitpi (wing foot) compound] aliped from Logla, Brown's system

tchester: [grantchester mondegreen] fish mimic from Gra system

tcini: [James Cooke Brown's Loglan tcidi nirda (food bird) compound] fowl from Logla, Brown's system

te hokoi: [*Here Be Monsters almanac*] huge, though fast, bird from New Zealand, Terra (alpha Zodiaci III)

teakettler: short-legged dog with cat-like ears, walks backward sounds like teakettle

tebbit: [*Starcross* by Philip Reeve] cave-dwelling wool-eater from Thelfall

tebo: [*Fantastic Beasts and Where to Find Them* by Newton Artemis Fido Scamander] invisible warthog

Tecoluta sea monster: [*Monster Spotter's Guide to North America* by Scott Francis] 35-tonne creature with jointed armor sited off Tecoluta, Mex., Terra (alpha Zodiaci III)

teeble: [*The Christmas Adventure of Space Elf Sam* by Audrey Wood] purring treelike creature used as Christmas tree on Zog

teechah: [cheetah spoonerism] crafty felinoid

teg(g): [*Dell Crossword Puzzle Dictionary*] 2-year-old sheep, see bident, tag

tegn: [og-tegn mondegreen] 2-D og relative

tegu: [*National Geographic Encyclopedia of Animals*] lizard from S. America, Terra (alpha Zodiaci III)

teh!ga: [Cherokee] toad or tadpole-like batrachoid from Tsalagi system

teh!gator: [teh!ga alligator portmanteau] alligator-like predator whose bite morphs victim into teh!ga

teich: [German Teichhuhn backformation] moorhen-chicken-like ornithoid

teju: [*Dell Crossword Puzzle Dictionary*] lizard from S. America, Terra (alpha Zodiaci III)

teksir: [teksir brisket palindrome] food animal

tektite: [The Legend of Zelda] red or blue quadrupedal arachnoid from Hyrule

tel: [Estonian tarantel German Tarantel mondegreen] large arachnoid, related to lapók, tola, tul, tule, twla, from Tara system

teleoceras: [*After the Dinosaurs* by Donald R. Prothero] hippo-like rhino with one small nose-horn, barrel-shaped body, stumpy legs from Miocene

tella: [mantella mondegreen] insectivorous batrachoid from Ma system

tellapók: [Hungarian tarantellapók mondegreen] large arachnoid, related to lapók, tel, tola, tul, tule, twla, from Tara system

telli: [telli fillet palindrome] food animal

telp: [telp ir triplet, etc. palindromes] mammaloid with three to eight breasts, see niw, ir, utniu, urdau, utxe, utpe, utco

teltu: [teltu cutlet portmanteau] food animal

tena: [úgan'tēna mondegreen] water mocassin-like snake from Uga system

tenderhook: [*Worlds Apart: Nat. Hist. of Furaha and Earth* by Souren Nyoroge] flyg predator from Furaha (alpha Phoenicis IV)

teng: [banteng mondegreen] bison-like ruminant, related to ateng, from Ba system

tengator: [teng alligator portmanteau] alligator-like predator whose bite morphs victim into teng

tenguin: [tuxedo of penguins spoonerism, tenkoot-penquin portmanteau] black and white tenkoot

tenkoot: [Thousand Stars] tan to brown, with white underbelly, 2-meter hexapodal herd ornithoid with prehensile tail from Impririi

tentacles: [Half-Life] large, green segmented stalk with blade-like "head" with eye-like "ear" and 3 retractable tentacles per pit

tentafang: [Outernauts] mature squibat

tentafangator: [tentafang alligator portmanteau] alligator-like predator whose bite morphs victim into tentafang

tenturka: [kostenurka mondegreen] tortoise-bird, black, carapaced triphibian ancestral to blackbird and tortoise

tepesuo: [tepesuo housepet palindrome] furry companion

ter: [lobster mondegreen] amphibious crustacean from Lob system; [bushmaster mondegreen] small mammal-eating lizard from Bushma system; [taranter mondegreen] spiked anklyosaur from Tara system

ter mite: [termite mondegreen] small parasite insectoid that infests ter

ter(r)apin: [*Dell Crossword Puzzle Dictionary*] edible turtle

terabyte: [*The Future Is Wild* by Dougal Dixon] termite predator of gardenworm noted for leg-less builder, nurse, queen, warrior, and watercarrier castes

terakuk: ["Desert Passage"] one-horned goat-like food creature from Teroth desert

teratomorph: [Monster Manual by Skip Williams, etal.] ooze able to shapeshift into slime, jelly, pudding or blob

teratorn: ["monster-bird"] bird with 3.6-meter wingspan from Pleistocene; [*The Ultimate Monster Guide* by Jaymond] hellfire-breathing winged insectoid

terecon: [*Planets of the Galaxy* by Greg Farshtey, Bill Smith, Ed Stark] burrowing 8-meter long, reptilian predator from Essowyn, Jedi galaxy

tereconster: [terecon monster portmanteau] monstrous terecon

terek: [*Dell Crossword Puzzle Dictionary*] sandpiper from Europe, Terra (alpha Zodiaci III)

terentatek: [*Star War Knights of the Old Republic*] slow, powerful with large claws geneered as weapon against Jedi knights

tereon: [megantereon mondegreen] sabre-toothed cat from Mega

tereonster: [tereon monster portmanteau] monstrous sabre-tooth cat

tergal: [Danish nattergal elision, mondegreen] nightingale-like ornithoid, see at

teri: [mantert mondegreen] quadruped with pincer-tipped tail from Ma system

terio: [Italian batterio backformation] bat germ

terju: [Maltese batterju backformation] bat germ

termiteater: [anteater backformation] insectivore that eats ants like anteater eats termites

tern bird: [lantern bird mondegreen] tern-like ornithoid from La system

tern-fish: [lantern fish mondegreen] tern-like flying ichthyoid from La system

tern-shark: [lantern shark mondegreen] tern-like predator ichthyoid from La system

tern: [*Dell Crossword Puzzle Dictionary*] sea swallow, see ern(e), gull, skua, scaup, fulmar, gannet, petrel, scoter

ternstone: [turnstone mondegreen] tern-sandpiper with petrifying stare

terratail: [*After Man* by Dougal Dixon] rodent with bird snake-like tail from Paucas Islands

terrible termite: [Col. Bleep: "Squeak and the Terrible Termite" by Robert D. Buchanan] giant mutant termite

terror crane: [*After the Dinosaurs* by Donald R. Prothero] see diatryma and gastornis, large flightless birds of Paleocene

terror toad: ["Power Ranger Punks"] monstrous toad from Sorcery VII

terror virus: ["100 years -- lost, strayed or stolen" by Cary Bates] deadly virus from Sonn's world

terroranchula: [Ben 10: Omniverse: "Of Predator and Prey" by Kevin Rubio] predatory arachnoid able to spin forcefield-like web, with sharp legtips, able to squeeze through narrow openings

terrordactyl: [terror pterodactyl portmanteau, "Terrordactyl" by Don Bitters III] space-faring dracoid whose eggs hatch after meteoric planetfall

terrorworm: [Perry Rhodan] larval hornterror

terti-freezard: one of three mini-freezards

tertiped: mutant with one-third as many legs

tesa: [*Dell Crossword Puzzle Dictionary*] buzzard from India, Terra (alpha Zodiaci III)

tescat: [Outernauts] electrical, black felinoid with red markings, see tesleow

esfi: [*Planets of the Galaxy* by Greg Farshtey, Bill Smith, Ed Stark] tiny, swamping insectoid with piercing proboscis, carrier of gangene-like "rotting disease" from Gorsh, Jedi galaxy

tesleow: [Outernauts] tescat with fangs

tessie: [*Monster Spotter's Guide to North America* by Scott Francis] dark, humped lake snake from Lake Tahoe, CA, Terra (alpha Zodiaci III)

testadon: [*After Man* by Dougal Dixon] insectivorous mammal with hinged armadillo-like shell

testadonster: [testadon monster portmanteau[carnivorous, armored mammalois

testar: [*Dell Crossword Puzzle Dictionary*] fish from W. India, Terra (alpha Zodiaci III), see boga, cero

tetee: [*Dell Crossword Puzzle Dictionary*] monkey from S. America, Terra (alpha Zodiaci III), see titi

teteel: [tetee eel montegreen] simian with eel-like tail

tetonius: [*After the Dinosaurs* by Donald R. Prothero] arboreal, tarsier-like omomyid from Ypserian age (early Eocene)

tetrameryx: [*After the Dinosaurs* by Donald R. Prothero] 4-horned pronghorn from Zanclean age (early Pliocene)

pentameryx: [tetrameryx extrapolation] pronghorn with 4 antlers and nosehorn

tetroptee: [tetropter backformation] prey of tetropting (flying with 4 wings) predators

tetropter: ["The Trap" by Finn Donovan] 4-winged ornithoid from Asidia's world

tetroskylos: [triskylos extrapolation] 4-headed hellhound

tetter: [*Dell Crossword Puzzle Dictionary*] ringworm that tetts

tewa: [Cherokee] flying squirrel-like rodentoid from Tsalagi system

Texas turkey: armadillo

tha: [bantha mondegreen] furry quadruped from Ba system

thack: [black thing spoonerism] black packrat-like rodentoid

thai: [pl. thraiin, *The Romulan Way* by Terisa Halekala-LoBrotto] wolverine-like creature from ch'Rihan, Eisn (128 Trianguli) system

than-zie: [Navaho] turkey-like ornithoid from Diné system

thanator: ["Avatar" by James Cameron] predator from Pandora, moon of Polyphemus, Alpha Centauri system

thandner: [*If I Ran the Zoo* by Theodore Seuss Geissel] tall, flightless bird with short beak, two-toed feet

thang: ["Aliens Ate My Pickup" by Mercedes Lackey] hexapod with little squinty white-less eyes, both scaly and furry, putrid green, with 2 ratty and 1 club tail, eats metal, plastic, waste

thangator: [thang alligator portmanteau] alligator-like predator whose bite morphs victim into thang

thanh long: [Viet.] see azure dragon

thanper: [panther spoonerism] felinoid predator that thanps (pounces teleportationally)

thaptor: [Callisto series by Lin Carter] wingless, 4-legged orthinoid steed, but unruly like camel from Callisto (alpha Zodiaci Vd)

tharban: [Amtor series by Edgar Rice Burroughs] puma-sized, hyena-like caninoid with lengthwise red and yellow stripes from Amtor (alpha Zodiaci II)

tharg: [Pellucidar series by Edgar Rice Burroughs] giant elk from Pellucidar

thargator: [tharg alligator portmanteau] alligator-like predator whose bite morphs victim into tharg

tharlarion: [Gor series by John F. "John Norman" Lange, Jr.] saddle-lizard used in swamps and deserts

tharmadillo: [thump of armadillos spoonerism] small armored creature that huddles in gravel pile-like groups

thed: [thoroughbred spoonerism] dust mite gestalt, see ashi-magari, skovisaur

theocodont: crocodilian archosaur, ancestor to both dinosaurs and pterosaurs

ther: see kai-wip

therbee: [*Creatures of the Galaxy* by Phil Brucato, Bill Smith, Rick D. Stuart, Chuck Truett] mammaloid with large claws and teeth used as pets, watchdogs from Almania, Jedi galaxy

therid: [coelantherid mondegreen] beastly creature from Coela system, see kai-wip

therizinosaur: [*Feathered Dinosaurs: The Origin of Birds* by John Long and Peter Schuten] 12-meter giant, turtle-like dinosaur with beak, 3 giant claws per foot

therizinotaur: [therizinosaur minotaur portmanteau] giant turtle-headed bull

Thermian mosquito: [Quasi-Scientific Ponderings: "Greatest Failure" by David Sagus] interplanetary mosquito-like insectoid from Archemelar III, Horsehead nebula

thermophile: extremophile resistant to extreme heat

theropod: [*The Mistaken Extinction* by Lowell Dingus and Timothy Rowe] ancestor of both tyrannosaurs and birds

thesaurus: [treasure-lizard] treasure-guarding lizard, see bogorm, bookworm

thesodon: [*After the Dinosaurs* by Donald R. Prothero] llama-like litoptern from Miocene

thesodonster: [thesodon monster portmanteau] monstrous, carnivorous llama-like creature

thessalgorgon: [*Monstrous Compendium: Forgotten Realms* by William Conners, etal.] thessalmonster with bull-like head, coppery-green scales, bull-like head and paralyzing gas breath

thessalhydra: [*Monstrous Compendium: Forgotten Realms* by William Conners, etal.] reptilian thessalmonster with 8 heads around a central mouth, tail-pinchers

thessalmera: [*Monstrous Compendium: Forgotten Realms* by William Conners, etal.] thessalhydra-like thessalmonster with leonine head and red dracoid head on back

thessalmonster: [*Monstrous Compendium: Forgotten Realms* by William Conners, etal.] any hybrid monster from Thessalar, the undead sorcerer of Greyhawk including thessalhydra, thessalmera, thessalgorgon, thessaltrice

thessaltrice: [*Monstrous Compendium: Forgotten Realms* by William Conners, etal.] thessalmonster with cockatrice heads, petrifying bite

Thetis Lake monster: [*Monster Spotter's Guide to North America* by Scott Francis] 1.5-meter silvery-green ichthropoid with fish-like mouth with razor-sharp teeth, black eyes, facefins, webbed hands and feet from Thetis Lake, BC, Terra (alpha Zodiaci III), see pugwis

Thian shapeshifter: [Xanthian mondegreen backformation] shapeshifting mimicking Xanthian creatures from Thia, Xa system

thidpar: [Pellucidar series by Edgar Rice Burroughs] treacherous pterodactyl from Pellucidar

thiên nga: [Viet. chim thiên nga mondegreen] ornithoid ancestral to chim and swan from Disa system

thimblebear: [thimbleberry backformation] very small ursinoid

third mast: [fourth mast backformation] relative of fourth mast from Emeris, Sheel-Sen system

thirped: ["Prince of Peril" by Otis Adelbert Kline] 2.4-meter, 5-tonne, hairless pachyderm with long pointed ears, relatively thin, long neck from Zarovia (alpha Zodiaci II)

thirsty vortex: ["City of the Forgotten" by Hans Kneifel] 9-meter moisture-seeking dustdevil from Osath (Mousetrap VII), Myrsantrop galaxy

thoat: [Barsoom series by Edgar Rice Burroughs] octopodal steed, 3-meters at shoulder, steered telepathically from Barzoom (alpha Zodiaci IV)

thoathere: [*After the Dinosaurs* by Donald R. Prothero] horse-like, one-toed lipoptern from Miocene

thocyne: [xanthocyne mondegreen] yellow caninoid from Xa system

thoolagal: [*The Yowie: In Seach of Australian Bigfoot* by Tony Healy and Paul Cropper] see yowie

thoqqua: [*Monster Manual* by Skip Williams, etal.] 30-cm brown, steamy armored, segmented worm with glowing orange conical head, magma core

thorn buffalo: ["The End of the Crib" by H. G. Francis] 1-meter bison-like ruminant from Uruch, Alkordoom galaxy, Perseus cluster

thorn-snake: [Showcase #91: "The Planet of Death"] serpentoid with thorny spikes from Pheidos

thornrunner: [*Worlds Apart: Nat. Hist. of Furaha and Earth* by Souren Nyoroge] lizard-like herbivore from Furaha (alpha Phoenicis IV)

thoron: [*The Hobbit* by J. R. R. Tolkien] aka great eagle, large, long-lived eagle of Middle Earth

thoronster: [thoron monster portmanteau] monstrous eagle-like ornithoid

thos: [*Dell Crossword Puzzle Dictionary*] jackal from Africa, Terra (alpha Zodiaci III)
thought-beast: ["The Heroine in the Haunted House" by Bob Kanigher] telepathic beast from Krypton, Rao system
thra: [gathra mondegreen] gray-green, horned and tusked bovinoid
thrai: [pl. traiin, Romulan] wolf or wolverine-like animal from ch'Rihan
thranta: [*Creatures of the Galaxy* by Phil Brucato, Bill Smith, Rick D. Stuart, Chuck Truett] flying, manta-like creature in variety of breeds from Jedi galaxy, see sky manta
thrasher: [*National Geographic Encyclopedia of Animals*] insect and berry-eating songbird from N. America, Terra (alpha Zodiaci III)
thrashtail: [Terra Monster] brown sabertoothed predator with red tail and mane, several tails, see vextail, from Terrarium
thread: [Pern series by Ann McCaffrey] long, thin, mycorrhizoidal spore from Oort cloud that in fifty of every two hundred fifty years plagues Pern (Rukbat (alpha Sagittarii) III)
thread devil: ["The Stranger" by H. G. Ewers] serpentine symbiot in chelao gestalt, see ims and membrillas
threadworm: ["Flight on Titan"] thread-like worm from Nivia colony, Titan (alpha Zodiaci VIa)
three-horn: ["Planet of the Superfluous" by Kurt Mahr] creature with 3 horns from Lycra, see triceratops, triceras
three-tusks: [Dan. 7:5, Media symbol] carnivorous ursinoid with three tusks
threekfish: [knife fish extrapolation] threek-shaped swordfish-like ichthyoid
thrinaxodont: [*The Mistaken Extinction* by Lowell Dingus and Timothy Rowe] cynodont descendant from Triassic
thrintbane: [*World of Ptavvs* by Larry Niven] geneering semi-sentient animal immune to Thrint mindcontrol
throck: ["Persistance of Vision" by Jeri Taylor] food animal from Delta Quadrant, see wood throck
throg: [*The Planiverse* by A. K. Dewdney] 2-D food creature from Astrians, Planiverse

throgator: [throg aligator portmanteau] alligator-like predator whose bite morphs victim into throg
thú: [con thú backformation] creature ancestral to con and panther, beastly con from Disa system
thumbstick: [Xanth series by Piers Anthony] bipedal walkingstick from Xanth
thumper: [*Creatures of the Galaxy* by Phil Brucato, Bill Smith, Rick D. Stuart, Chuck Truett] very quiet, bipedal runner from Cracia, Jedi galaxy
thunder bird: [*After the Dinosaurs* by Donald R. Prothero] dinornis, flightless, 3-meter dromornithine
thunder eagle: [Monster Legends] monstrous electric eagle-like ornithoid, related to thundernix
thunderbird: [*Monster Spotter's Guide to North America* by Scott Francis] black-and-white bird with 10-meter wingspan said to make thunderclaps as it flies
thunderlizard: 10-tonne dinosaur with 4 legs and long tail from Upith (Gergonell III)
thunderlork: ["The Astronautical Revolution" by Leo Lukas] lork with neuro-transmuter venom from Yezzikan Rimba (Rimba III), Dommrath galaxy
thundernix: [Monster Legends] monstrous phoenix-like ornithoid, related to thunder eagle
thwerl: [*If I Ran the Zoo* by Theodore Seuss Geissel] 3.6-meter dog-faced quadruped with long, flexible legs, furry blue feet, long striped neck and torso, antennae
thwerlope: [thwerl antelope portmanteau] twerl with antlers
thylacine: [*After the Dinosaurs* by Donald R. Prothero] tiger-like marsupial, see boraphage and ringdocus
thylacosmilus: leopard-sized marsupial with retractable sabre-teeth
thyreophoran: [*The Mistaken Extinction* by Lowell Dingus and Timothy Rowe] armored dinosaur, including stegosaur, ankylosaur and scelidosaur
ti: [blamanti, mondegreen] white or blue ant-like insectoid from Blama system; [manti

mondegreen] ant-like insectoid from Ma system; [panti mondegreen] planimal from Pa (eta Serpentis) system, titi nasna

ti-tzubird: [trumpet swan backformation] swan-like ornithoid with ti-tzu-like call, related to shakuhaibird

tiano: [Monster Galaxy] armored, black dracoid with gold wings and 4 legs

tibera: [tibera rarebit portmanteau] food animal

Tiberian bat: ["The Undiscovered Country" by Nicholas Meyer and Denny Martin Flinn] chiropteran noted for sticking together from Tiberia

tich: [ticorhinus mondegreen] rhinoid relative of orhinus from Stefa

tichorhinus: [*La Citadelle des glaces* by Paul Alperine] 2-horned rhinoceros ancestor found in salty marshes from Erikraudebyg

ticid: [lepticid backformation] pongoid with elephant-like trunk and kangaroo-like legs

tick-bird: [tickbird mondegreen] tick-like ornithoid, so-called because of their cry, prey of tock-birds

tick-tack-toe: [If I Ran the Zoo by Theodore Seuss Geissel] pongoid with short legs, long sideburns and characteristic markings

tickback: [beheaded stickback] ruminant pestered by tick-birds

tid: [xicantid mondegreen] egg-laying hexapod from Xica system

tidlawnniz: [zinnwaldite tidlawnniz palindrome] dark gray or brown ornithoid

tiffanie: long-haired, blue eyed, golden-fawn, blue-black furry with white feet (socks and gloves)

tiganthropoid virus: [*Eye of the Tyger* by Paul McAuley] geneered mutagenic virus that morphs victim into tigranthropoid

tiger beetle: [Xanth series by Piers Anthony] fierce striped insect from Xanth

tiger moth: [Xanth series by Piers Anthony] carnivorous insect with striped wings from Xanth

tiger shark: [Xanth series by Piers Anthony] large fish with striped sail-fin and tiger-like head from Xanth

tiger-carp: see shachihoko

tiger-crab: [*The Maracot Deep* by Arthur Conan Doyle] black and white, Newfoundland dog-sized crustacean with tiger-like stripes

tiger-shark: [Spy Kids 2: "Island of Lost Dreams" by Robert Rodriguez] shark-headed tiger with backfin

tigerdillo: [Avatar: The Last Airbender: "Tales of Ba Sing Se"] tiger-like felinoid with armadillo-like armor

tigerfish: [*River Monsters* by Jeremy Wade, Game Fish of the World by Henry Gillet] hydrocynus, 80-kg goliath variety from Congo

tigerilla: [tiger-gorilla portmanteau] centaur-like creature with head and arms of gorilla and stripes, legs and tail from tiger

tigermander: [tiger salamander portmanteau] large, tiger-striped amphibian

tigermine: [tiger-ermine portmanteau] slender black-and-yellow striped carnivore with short legs and long, black-tipped tail

tigkatma: [James Cooke Brown's Loglan tigra katma (tiger cat) compound] tabby from Logla, Brown's system

tignirda: [James Cooke Brown's Loglan tigra nirda (tiger bird) compound] tiger-headed ornithoid from Logla, Brown's system

tigrelis: [*La Découverte de L'Empire de Cantahar* by De Varennes de Mondasse] deer-like equinoid with striped coat and white crest between ears used for drawing carriage from Canthahar

tigrid: [Fr. Johann Martin Schleyer's Volapük] tiger-like felinoid from Schleyer's system

tigron: [tiger-lion cross, "Flash Gordon" by Frederick Stephani, George Plympton, Basil Dickey, Ella O'Neill, based on Alex Raymond's strip] tiger-like felinoid with large fangs and curved forehead horn from Mongo

tigrue: [mantigrue mondegreen] dracoid from Ma system

tihcalam: [malachite tihcalam palindrome] greenish ornithoid

tihw: [white tihw palindrome] white ornithoid

tikbalang: [*The Big Bad Book of Beasts* by Michael Largo] horse-headed anthropoid with hoof-like feet, bristly mane

tikbalangator: [tikbalang alligator portmanteau] alligator-like predator whose bite morphs victim into tikbalang
tilapia: [*National Geographic Encyclopedia of Animals*] perch-like fish
tilder: [*Edge Chronicles* by Paul Stewart and Chris Riddell] deer-sized, speckled herd herbivore with curling horns that tilds
tile worm: [The Legend of Zelda: "Twilight Princess"] hideous, purple worm guiding tiles of Forest Temple, City in the Sky, Hyrule
tilla: [pysantilla mondegreen] predator from Pysa system
timartik: [Eskimo] large, male walrus
time shark: [Odd Squad] chronoporting shark-like predator of time sheep
time sheep: [Odd Squad] chronopoting sheep-like prey of time sharks
timentia: red-and-green leonine from Gizmonian Steepes (Edonian cluster II), Galaxiki galaxy
timingila: [*Mahabharata*] whale-swallowing sea monster, see megalodon
tína: [Cherokee] louse-like insectoid from Tsalagi system
tin amou: [tinamou mondegreen] amou-like golem made from tin
tin shemet: [tinshemet mondegreen] shemet-like golem made from tin
tinamou: [*After Man* by Dougal Dixon] large flightless bird (female) or small, bloodsucking female-backrider (male); [*Dell Crossword Puzzle Dictionary*] game bird from S. America, [*National Geographic Encyclopedia of Animals*] rarite ornithoid from Meso-America, Terra (alpha Zodiaci III)
tinea: [*Dell Crossword Puzzle Dictionary*] clothes moth or ringworm
tingler: ["The Tingler" by Robb White] centipede-like creature with 18 legs, pinchers, that feeds on fear via spinal cord, dissolved by scream
tinkler: [*The World of Synnabarr* by Raymond C. S. McCracken] furball with eyes that pees unholy water from Synnabarr, fka Mars (alpha Zodiaci IV)

tinshemet: [Lev. 11:18, 30] reptile-bird, aka archaeopteryx
tinten: [German Tintenfisch backformation] squid-fish, ichthyoid with feeding tentacles from Akyby, Rybyka system, Galaxiki galaxy
tion: [tiger lion portmanteau] tiger-headed lion-like felinoid
tiornis: [enantiornis mondegreen] ornithoid from Ena system
tipous: [tortipous backformation] horned mock turtle
tirisuk: [*Monster Spotter's Guide to North America* by Scott Francis] large reptilian with snapping turtle-like jaws, long prehensile antennae
tirtilki: [Turkish tirtil-tilki portmanteau] caterpillar-fox which has a worm-like larval stage and caninoid adult stage
tirtle: one-i turtle] one-eyed chelonoid
tis: [yantis mondegreen] blue quadruped from Ya system; [volantis mondegreen] ornithoid from Vola system; [mantis mondegreen] insectoid from Ma system; [doberman mondegreen] caninoid from Doberma system
tislash: [mantislash mondegreen] plant-mimicking insectoid from Ma system
tit-mouse: [titmouse mondegreen] monkey-like rodentoid
titanoboa: giant constrictor snake from Paleocene
titanonatit: [mynynym] giant variety of natit
titanosaur: ["The Terror of Mecha-godzilla" by Yuhiko Takayama] 150-meter tall amphibious biped with long neck, slender horse-like head with duckbill, headfin, fin-like ears, antennae, dorsal fin, long fish-like tail; 18-meter dinosaur from late Cretaceous
titanotaur: [titanosaur minotaur portmanteau] large bovinoid
titanothere: ["Avatar" by James Cameron] rhinoid with colorful frill from Pandora, moon of Polyphemus, alpha Centauri system
titanotylopus: [*After the Dinosaurs* by Donald R. Prothero] camel ancestor with 4-meter shoulder height from Zanclean age (early Pliocene)

titanotylopuss: [titanotylopus puss portmanteau] large, camel-like felinoid from Clea, Za system

titci: [mantitci mondegreen] anteater-like creature from Ma system

titi: [*National Geographic Encyclopedia of Animals*] monkey from Bolivia; [*Dell Crossword Puzzle Dictionary*] widow monkey from S. America, Terra (alpha Zodiaci III), see tetee

tiu: [uitnazyb ananymondegreen] red-violetnornithoid from Byzan system+

tiyóhalí: [Cherokee] sauroid from Tsalagi system

tizheruk: aka pal-rai-yûk, seaserpent with 2-meter head, flipper-tail

tjangara: [*The Yowie: In Seach of Australian Bigfoot* by Tony Healy and Paul Cropper] see yowie

tje: [Dutch konintje backformation] bunny-rabbit, lapoid

tkele-cho-g: [Navaho] jackass-like equinoid from Diné system

tkele-cho-gator: [tkele-cho-g alligator portmanteau] alligator portmanteau] alligator-like predator whose bite morphs victim into tkele-cho-g

tlai!ga: [Cherokee] bluejay-like ornithoid from Tsalagi system

tlai!gator: [tlai!ga alligator portmanteau] alligator-like predator whose bite morphs victim into tlai!ga

tlam: [smalt tlams palindrome] dark blue ornithoid

tlaméha: [Cherokee] cheiropteroid from Tsalagi system

tle: [cacomistle mondegreen] raccoonoid from Cacomi system

tleh: [shelty tlehs palindrome] short-legged, stocky equinoid

tler: [rattler mondegreen] rat-headed snake

tlillning: [Mushroom Planet series by Eleanor Cameron] cat-sized, silvery-haired, long-eared equine from Basidium (alpha Zodiaci IIIb)

tlillningator: [tlillning alligator portmanteau] alligator portmanteau] alligator-like predator whose bite morphs victim into tlillning

Tlînian tiger: [*A First Encyclopedia of Tlîn*: "Tlîn, Uqbar, Orbis Tertius" by Jorge Luis Borges] transparent tiger-like felinoid from Tlîn

tlvd: [tlvdatsi, tlvdega mondegreen] panther-like, amphibious felinoid with eel-like tail

tlvdatsí: [Cherokee] panther-like felinoid from Tsalagi system

tlvdega: [Cherokee] eel-like ichthyoid from Tsalagi system

tlvdegator: [tlvdega alligator portmanteau] alligator-like predator whose bite morphs victim into tlvdega

tnagig: [gigantotnagig palindrome] insignificant creature, except giant variety, see naig, tomam, natit

tnagigator: [tnagig alligator portmanteau] alligator portmanteau] alligator-like predator whose bite morphs victim into tnagig

to: [allicanto mondegreen] metallic desert lizard from Allica system; [nigjanto mondegreen] triphibian predator from Nigja system; [basto mondegreen] blue boar-like porcoid from Ba system; [gusto mondegreen] mongoose-like furry from Gu system

toadfish: [troubling of goldfish spoonerism] amphibian with popeyes, large mouth, leg-like fins from Akyby, Rybyka system, Galaxiki galaxy

toadlet: [*National Geographic Encyclopedia of Animals*] small arthropod-eating toad from Australia, Terra (alpha Zodiaci III)

toadpoli: [The Legend of Zelda: "Twilight Princess"] toad-like creature that spits rocks like octorock

toca: see ocama, lieto

tocarret: [terra cotta at-tocarret palindrome, mondegreen] brownish pink ornithoid, see at

tock-bird: [tick-bird backformation] predator of tick-bird and so protector of tickbacks

toco: [*Dell Crossword Puzzle Dictionary*] toucan

tody: [*Dell Crossword Puzzle Dictionary*] tiny bird from W. Indies, [*National Geographic Encyclopedia of Animals*] insect and spider-eating bird from Jamaica, Terra (alpha Zodiaci III)

toe nayo: [Burmese] horse-bodied unicorn, see licorne

toegi: ["Morkheros Prophet" by Ernst Vlcek] mountain-dweller creature from Morbienne [Kraverk's Yuna-cum] III

toewalker: [snouter extrapolation] snouter adapted to walking on toes with atrophied legs and nasarium

tohu: [Maori *] 2-D pentapus or hexapus

toilet snail: ["Bender's Game" by Eric Horsted, etal.] snail noted for infesting toilets

tokolosha: [*Here Be Monsters almanac*] strong, carnivorous pongoid that head-butts oxen from Africa, Terra (alpha Zodiaci III)

tola: [Italian tarantola backformation] large arachnoid related to lapók, tel, tul, tule, twla, from Tara system

tolib: [*Creatures of the Galaxy* by Phil Brucato, Bill Smith, Rick D. Stuart, Chuck Truett] large swamp ornithoid from Mimban, Jedi galaxy

Tollipian mould: [*The Tree of Life* by Mark Michalowski] mold geneered as weapon that eats out from inside out from Tollip's world, see Stuff

Tollipian virus: [*The Tree of Life* by Mark Michalowski] multi-trunk tree virus that exterminated all animal life on Tollip's world except Hammies who merged with Tree of Life

tôm: [con tôm backformation] crustacean ancestral to con and crayfish from Disa system

tomahawk: [Terra Monster] hawk-like ornithoid from Terrarium, see tomaling

tomaling: [Terra Monster] gray and white hawk-like ornithoid with red crest, see tomahawk from Terrarium

tomalingator: [tomaling alligator portmanteau] alligator-like predator whose bite morphs victim into tomaling

tomb-herd: horrid, white, gelatinous and ghoulish extra-dimensionals able to animate crustanthrpoid statues prepared by Yog-Sothoth worshippers and warp near-by space to prevent victim's escape

tomcatfish: [phantom catfish mondegreen] catfish-like ichthyoid, egg-bearing like seahorse, from Pha system

tomeryx: [leptomeryx backformation] ape-deer centauroid

tommam: [mammoth tommam palindrome] insignificant creature, except for mammoth variety, see naig, tnagig, natit

tomoun: [*Alien Encounters* by Jen Seiden] animal hunted on Askaj, Jedi galaxy

tomy: [atomy mondegreen] light brown mite-like insectoid

tonetter: [trumpeter swan backformation] small flute swan-like ornithoid with tonette-like call

tonīqua: [Cherokee] mole-liike burrower from Tsalagi System

too: [phantoo mondegreen] small dom from Pha system; [sooty toos palindrome] gray ornithoid

Tooke dragon: [Paul Tooke, Game of Life] space-faring dracoid capable of c/6

tooke: ["The Gungan Frontier" by Chris McCubbin] small, large-headed, large-footed hopping rodentoid

toothed chicken: [Rich "(Son of) Svengoolie" Koz] ancestor of rubber chicken, see mammoth chicken

topaz: [*Dell Crossword Puzzle Dictionary*] blue, yellow, brown or pink hummingbird, see ava, colibri

tope: [*Dell Crossword Puzzle Dictionary*] small, soupfin shark from Europe, Terra (alpha Zodiaci III)

tophoca: [leptophoca backformation] seal-like sea-ape

topi: [*National Geographic Encyclopedia of Animals*] antelope relative from Africa, Terra (alpha Zodiaci III)

topknot nester: [*If I Ran the Zoo* by Theodore Seuss Giessel] bird with large, nest-like crest

tor: [Fr. Johann Martin Schleyer's Volapük] bovinoid from Schleyer's system; [stantor mondegreen] ornithoid from Sta system

toraton: 120-tonne, long-lived chelonian with vestigial shell, beak and gizzard

torch slug: [The Legend of Zelda: "Ocarina of Time"] hellfire-breathing, man-sized slug

torch slugator: [torch slug alligator portmanteau] alligator-like predator whose bite morphs victim into torch slug

torep: [*Vulcan's Glory* by D. C. Fontana] hunting bird from Areta (beta Circini III)

torfi: [James Cooke Brown's Loglan to fitpi (two feet) compound] biped from Logla, Brown's system

toricle: ["The Substandard Sardines" by Jack Vance] creature from Cordova

tormagon: [*Frostworld and Dreamfire* by John Morressy] one of creatures talked to by Onhla from Starside on Hraggellon (Dunuos II)

tormagonster: [tormagon monster portmanteau] monstrous tormagon

tornade: [Code Lyoko] large, orange isolation sphere geneered by Xana, see marabounta, shabom, rover

tornok: ["Seed of Reason" by Daniel Hatch] swamp-dwelling swimmer from Chamal

toro: [*Dell Crossword Puzzle Dictionary*] bull from Spain, Terra (alpha Zodiaci III)

torok: ["Avatar" by James Cameron] large flying dracoid rarely used as steed from Pandora, moon of Polyphemus, alpha Centauri system

Torothkan virus: ["Men in Black" series] virus from Torothka

torqupine: [Terra Monsters] flightless, blue, black and yellow ornithoid with wingclaws and "electrostatic radar", see sporkupine, from Terrarium

torse: [team of horses spoonerism, torok horse portmanteau] torok used as steed

torta: [Outernauts] virtually headless torteel

torteau panther: [heraldry] monstrous felinoid with red spots, flaming mouth and ears

torteel: [tortoise-eel portmanteau, Outernauts] short-legged chelonian with wide-set hammerhead-like eyes, see torta, tortusk

tortipous: [Terra Monster] armored chelonian with beaver-like tail, cheekspikes, see tortitank, from Terrarium

tortitank: [Terra Monster] large, armored chelonian with beaver-like tail, cheekspikes, see tortipous, from Terrarium

torton: [*Creatures of the Galaxy* by Phil Brucato, Bill Smith, Rick D. Stuart, Chuck Truett] red and green, long-legged cheronian from Roni, moon of Naboo, Jedi galaxy

tortonster: [torton monster portmanteau] monstrous tornon-like chelonian

tortug: [Fr. Johann Martin Schleyer's Volapük] chelonoid from Schleyer's system

tortugator: [tortug alligator portmanteau] alligator portmanteau] alligator-like predator whose bite morphs victim into tortug

tortusk: [Outernauts] chelonoid with spiked carapace, wide neck and head, large upward-pointing tusks and frog-like eyes

torueme: ["Face To Face With Planet Scanodon" by Rocky Strone] worm-like creature from Scandon

tos: [retantos mondegreen] food rodentoid from Reta system

tosfitpi: [James Cooke Brown's Loglan tosku fitpi] cephalopod from Logla, Brown's system

tosmosus: [*After the Dinosaurs* by Donald R. Prothero] large flightless bird from Miocene

toter: [*Dell Crossword Puzzle Dictionary*] stone roller fish

totsúhwa: [Cherokee] cardinal-like ornithoid from Tsalagi system

toucanary: [toucan-canary portmanteau] small ornithoid with brightly green or yellow-colored plumage, very large beak

toucanet: [*National Geographic Encyclopedia of Animals*] fruit-eating toucan relative from S. America, Terra (alpha Zodiaci III)

touka: [mela ntouka mondegreen] rhinoid from Mela system

touniao: [beheaded utouniao] 6-headed bird of ill omen

tove: [*Through the Looking-Glass* by Charles Ludwidge "Lewis Carroll" Dodgeson] lithe, slimy badger-like sauroid that burrows corkscrew-like

towhee: [*National Geographic Encyclopedia of Animals*] seed, insect and fruit-eating songbird from Mexico, Terra (alpha Zodiaci III)

toy animal: [Oz series by L. Frank Baum, etc.] animated animal toy, such as bagpuss, dino, pooh, rubber duckie, slinky dog, sockness monster, velveteen rabbit from Valley of Toy Animals, Merryland
toxen: [team of oxen spoonerism, toxen mondegreen] poisonous droxen
toxin: [Spiderman mythos] strong spawn of carnage symbiot
toxodon: [*After the Dinosaurs* by Donald R. Prothero] hippo-like notoungulate from Pliocene
toxodonster: [toxodon monster portmanteau] monstrous hippoid
tra'cor: [*Creatures of the Galaxy* by Phil Brucato, Bill Smith, Rick D. Stuart, Chuck Truett] mutriok predator from Socorro, smaller, omnivorous, amphibious relative of rancor, Jedi galaxy
trabbit: [trace of rabbits spoonerism] jackrabbit-like herd lapoid
traboon: [troop of baboons spoonerism, trabbit-baboon portmanteau] burrowing pongoid with long ears
tracehound: ["The Forsaken" by Jim Trombetta] enthusiastic Wanoni predator
trackdaw: [train of jackdaws spoonerism, tracking jackdaw portmanteau] variety of jackdaw used as trackers]
Trachon beast: ["Hunters" by Jeri Taylor] beastly creature from Trachon, Delta Quadrant
tractorbeam turkey: [Odd Squad: Sector 21] turkey with tractorbeam-eyes
trad: [Dartmouth tuom trad palindrome] greenish tuom
trae: [trae heart palindrome] food animal
tragelaph: goat-stag cross
tragopan: [*National Geographic Encyclopedia of Animals*] chicken relative from Indo-Asia, Terra (alpha Zodiaci III)
tragor: [*The Goddess of Ganymede* and *Pursuit on Ganymede* by Michael Resnick and Donald M. Grant] giant carnivorous ornithoid from Thane's moon
tragulus: mouse-deer; mouse-headed deer-like ruminant

tran: [con tran backformation] creature ancestral to con and boa from Disa system
trangaroo: [troop of kangaroos spoonerism, tran kangaroo portmanteau] megapod with long constricting tail
transendent: [Perry Rhodan] pig-sized, blood red, slow-moving worm from Negasphere
trapdoor squid: [Alien Pet: "Box of Doom" by Dan Zettel] six-tentacled cephalopodan that lives in shell or other container, trapping prey like trapdoor spider, after hypnotizing it with pyrotechnics rather than ink
trape: [troop of apes spoonerism, trap ape portmanteau] carnivorous pongoid that uses boobytrap to catch prey
trash-rat: ["Feast Your Minds"] social rodent living in and on trash
trebil: [liberty trebil palindrome] blue ornithoid with tinkling call
Tree elephant: ["The Storm Planet" by Paul "Cordwainer Smith" Linebarger] 2-headed elephant discovered by Go-Captain John Jay Tree
tree elephant: [Tree elephant mondegreen, "Crazy As Can Be"] elephant adapted to living in trees, see tree mammoth
tree fish: ["Crazy as Can Be"] ichthyopteryx that nest in trees
tree goose: see barnacle goose
tree hopper: [*The New Dinosaurs* by Dougal Dixon] furry, beaked arbrosaur with long, stiff, striped tail, long arms; [Xanth series by Piers Anthony] Bonzai tree-mimic from Xanth; giant hopper-like golem made from trees
tree jellyfish: ["Combat Ship of the Old" by Ernst Vlcek] umbrella-like invertebrate that falls on prey from tree from Phistral, Pronot system
tree lobster: [Xanth series by Piers Anthony] land adapted lobster with leaf-green claws and brown bark-like body from Xanth
tree mammoth: ["Ice Age: The Meltdown"] mammoth maladapted to living in trees like an opossum, see tree elephant
tree octopus: [Save the Pacific Northwest Tree Octopus organization, museumofhoaxes.com by Alex Boese]

arboreal cephalopod from Pacific Northwest, Terra (alpha Zodiaci III)

tree shark: ["Robot Hugs" by R. Hugs'] arboreal land shark

tree slider: ["The Steel Horde" by Peter Terrid] huge, winged, yellow-brown predator with sharp claws, dagger-like teeth from Cordage, Janzobarr system, Alkordoom galaxy

tree squeak: [museumofhoaxes.com by Alex Boese] black squirrel, seldom seen, but with often heard squeak

tree-ape: ["Seed of Reason" by Daniel Hatch] arboreal pongoid from Chamal

tree-frog: [tree frog mondegreen] barnacle-like batrachoid in symbiosis with tree

tree-frogator: [tree-frog alligator portmanteau] alligator portmanteau] alligator-like predator whose bite morphs victim into free-frog

tree-lizard: see arbrosaur

treel: [tree eel"portmanteau, "TKO" by Lawrence G. DiTillio] arboreal eel-like ichthyoid from Centauri

treesnort: see trylic treesnort

treezard: [Monster Legends] tree-lizard planimal

trel: [kestrel mondegreen] predatory bird from Ke system

Trellan croc: ["Crossfire" by Rene Echevarria] crocodilian from Trella

tremarctos: [*After the Dinosaurs* by Donald R. Prothero] speckled bear ancestor from Pleistocene

treppok: [*Planets of the Galaxy* by Greg Farshtey, Bill Smith, Ed Stark] 30-meter, herd ichthyoid from Baralou, Jedi galaxy

tressym: [*Lost Empires of Faerün*] felinoid with 1-meter feathery-leathery wings, owl-like face, fluffy-ball-tipped tail

trevel: [*After Man* by Dougal Dixon] monkey-like rodent with slender fingers, prehensile tail

trevelope: [trevel antelope portmanteau] trevel with antlers

trianguli: [piscium extrapolation] 2-D triangular creature

tribble: ["The Trouble with Tribbles" by David Gerrold] herbivorous, parthenogenic furball, reproducing when fed at 1200%/hr

tribullus: sprintosaur with three-knotted crest

triceratops: three-horned, herbivorous dinosaur with bony collar

triceromeryx: [*After the Dinosaurs* by Donald R. Prothero] deer with two antlers and nosehorn

trigeon: [trip of widgeons, trimorph c/k/wigeon portmanteau] trimorph in three of cigeon, kigeon, pigeon and wigeon forms

trimorph: creature with three different stages of metamorphosis

tripod: ["Beasts of the Underworld" by Kurt Mahr] geneered water-dwelling prey of twelve-eyes with three legs from Afzot (Frua III)

tripodero: [museumofhoaxes.com by Alex Boese] bipedal creature with extendable legs and blowgun-like snout and long tail or quadrupedal tail-ess ("Manx") variety

triton: [*Dell Crossword Puzzle Dictionary*] newt, see eft, evet

tritonster: [triton monster portmanteau] monstrous newt-like creature from Triton (alpha Zodiaci VIIIa)

trivto: [divto extrapolation] 3-headed, noctural, venomous snake

trizebra: [N. M. Gibbons] aka hexacamel, 6-legged zebra-like cameloid

trochophore: ["wheel-bearer", *The Mathematics of Oz* by Clifford A. Pickover] creature with wheels from Zyph, Betelgeuze (alpha Orionis) system

troctopus: [tree octopus portmanteau] arboreal, egg-laying cephalopodan from Troctopia, Qujhtba system, Galaxiki galaxy

troctopuss: [tree octopus puss portmanteau] arboreal octopuss

trof: [fortnight hgin trof] hgin predator

troglosaur: ["Ratchet and Clank"] burrowing lizard, ["hole-lizard", "Cowboys vs. Dinosaurs" by Anthony Fankanser and Rafael Jordan] underground-dwelling dinosaur adapted to breathing methane

troglotaur: [troglosaur minotaur portmanteau] underground-dwelling bovinoid

trogon: [*National Geographic Encyclopedia of Animals*] bird with 1-meter tail from Central America, Terra (alpha Zodiaci III)

trogonster: [trogon monster portmanteau] monstrous trogon

tromble: [*The New Dinosaurs* by Dougal Dixon] aka gravornis, 3-meter flightless bird with elephantine legs, black, hairy feathers

trompa: [*Game Chambers of Questal* by Robert Kern] 3-meter tall, massive, ferocious, deadly, long-armed biped with sharp claws from Jedi galaxy

tronkey: [troop of monkeys spoonerism, trompa monkey portmanteau] massive, ferocious, deadly, long-armed simian with sharp claws paws, thick fur, 2 spiral horns

troodon: ["wounding tooth", *Feathered Dinosaurs: The Origin of Birds* by John Long and Peter Schuten] 2-meter bird-like theropod with stereoscopic eyes, teeth with coarsely serrated edges, retractable sickle-like toe, U-shaped iguana-like jaw

troodonster: [troodon monster portmanteau] monstrous troodon

trorti: [James Cooke Brown's Loglan troku titci (rock eater) compound] rock-eater from Logla, Brown's system

troth: [tree sloth spoonerism] slow-moving arboreal creature from Slee system

trovamp: [*After Man* by Dougal Dixon] parasitic mammal with barb-like fangs and claws

trugo: [trugo yogurt palindrome] milk animal

trumpet snouter: [*The Snouters* by Harald Stümpke] plankton-eating mud snouter from Hi-Yi-Yi Islands

trumpet swan: [Xanth series by Piers Anthony] small ornithoid with large horn, brassy feathers and raucous call from Xanth

trundlebug: [Pern series by Ann McCaffrey] insectoid from Pern (Rukbat (alpha Sagittarii) III)

trundlebugator: [trundlebug alligator portmanteau] alligator portmanteau] alligator-like predator whose bite morphs victim into trundlebug

trunkfish: [trunk fish mondegreen] ichthypoid with elephant-like trunk

truteal: [*After Man* by Dougal Dixon] blind, rabbit-like shrew with beak-like teeth, large ears

trutealope: [truteal antelope portmanteau] truteal with antlers

truztop: [*Unofficial Questarian Guide*, Tez'Meckian "half-animal"] nasna from Tev'meck, Warvan system

trylic treesnort: [Quasi-Scientific Ponderings: "Greatest Failure" by David Sagus] treesnort peculiar to Archemelar III, Horsehead nebula

tryp: [*Dell Crossword Puzzle Dictionary*] blood parasite

ts'ul: [tsovats'ul backformation] flying walrus-like triphibian

tsa: [dah-nes-tsa, tsa-e-donin-ee mondegreen] ram-fly, related to dah-nes and e-donin-ee

tsa-e-donin-ee: [Navaho] fly-like insectoid from Diné system

tsaagan: ["white monster", *Feathered Dinosaurs: The Origin of Birds* by John Long and Peter Schuten] primitive dromaeosaurid, possibly pack, predator

tsaer: [tsaer breast palindrome] food animal

tsak: ["Flash Gordon" series] 2-headed bovinoid from Mongo

tsaorto: [tsaorto pot roast palindrome] food ornithoid related to saor

tsaquólade: [Cherokee] bluebird-like ornithoid from Tsalagi system

tsark: [tsak-sark portmanteau] 2-headed bovinoid steed

tsasgaya: [Cherokee] yellowjacket-like insectoid from Tsalagi system

tsehc: [chestnut untsehc palindrome backformation] parasite that turns host dark reddish brown

tselec: [celeste tselec palindrome] sky blue ornithoid

tsení: [Cherokee] wren-like ornithoid from Tsalagi system

tse: tsetse nasna

tsetse: 2-winged bloodsucking fly from Africa, Terra (alpha Zodiaci III)

tsgwalegwala: [Cherokee] whippoorwill-like ornithoid from Ysalagi system
tshark: [tsak-shark portmanteau, "2-headed Shark Attack" by H. Perry Horton] 2-headed shark-like ichthyoid
tsharli: [charley horse mondegreen] kneeless wild equinoid
tsi: tsitsi nasna
tsigalīli: [Cherokee] chickadee-like ornithoid from Tsalagi system
tsísadu: [Cherokee Tsalagi] lapoid from Tsalagi system
tsisdetsi: [Cherokee] mouse-like rodentoid from Tsalagi system
tsīsdvna: [Cherokee] crawfish-like crustacean from Tsalagi system
tsisqua: [Cherokee] ornithoid from Tsalagi system
tsisqualisda: [Cherokee] blackbird-like ornithoid from Tsalagi system
tsitāga: [Cherokee] chicken-like ornithoid from Tsalagi system
tsitāgator: [tsitāga alligator portmanteau] alligator-like predator whose bite morphs victim into tsitāga
tsitsi: [Cherokee] winter wren-like ornithoid from Tsalagi system
tsiya: [Cherokee] otter-like amphibian from Tsalagi system
tskunk: [tsak-skunk portmanteau] 2-headed malodorous furry with bushy striped tail
tso: [hash-dore-tso, ha-as-tso-si mondegreen] lion-mouse related to dore, hash and si
tsounkranacervus: [candiacervus extrapolation] deer with rake-like antlers
tsova: [tsovakhozuk backformation] Guinea pig-pig, see ginea, gini, mar, meri, uk
tsuganotsi: [Cherokee] centipede-like creature from Tsalagi system
tsukanvsdena: [Cherokee] bovinoid from Tsalagi system
tsulasgi: [Cherokee] alligator-like predator from Tsalagi system
tsulisdanāli: [Cherokee] catfish-like ichthyoid from Tsalagi system
tsútlá: [Cherokee] fox-like caninoid from Tsalagi system

tteri: [pantteri backformation] leopard-like felinoid from Pa system
tu-long: ["Tremors" and "Tremors: The Legend Begins"] aka dirt-dragon, graboid
tu-longator: [tu-long alligator portmanteau] alligator portmanteau] alligator-like predator whose bite morphs victim into tu-long
tuatara: [*National Geographic Encyclopedia of Animals*] gator relative from New Guinea, Terra (alpha Zodiaci III)
tubabird: [trumpeter swan backformation] swan-like ornithoid with tuba-like call
tubbee: [tubby backformation] bathtub-loving sweatbee-like waterbug
tubeshark: [*Worlds Apart: Nat. Hist. of Furaha and Earth* by Souren Nyoroge] shark-like tubular ichthyoid from Furaha (alpha Phoenicis IV)
tubetucker: [*The Jesus Incident* by Frank Herbert and Bill Ransom] dangerous ground-dweller from Pandora
tubeworm-snouted snouter: [*The Snouters* by Harald Stümpke] burrowing snouter on Mairúvili, Hi-Yi-Yi Islands
tubeworm: [*The Big Bad Book of Beasts* by Michael Largo] 2-meter tubular worm able to live 250 years in hydrothermal vent of superhot, toxic water because of chemosynthesic bacteria
tuborg: [Noon Universe of Boris and Arkady Strugatsky] aka crayfish-spider from Pandora
tuborgator: [tuborg alligator portmanteau] alligator portmanteau] alligator-like predator whose bite morphs victim into tuborg
tucan: [*Dell Crossword Puzzle Dictionary*] rodent from Mexico, Terra (alpha Zodiaci)
tucanae: [piscium extrapolation] toucan-like ornithoid
tue: [*Dell Crossword Puzzle Dictionary*] parson bird, see poe, koko, tui
tuffed sphagnum: [*Mothstorm* by Philip Reeve] aka nibbling sporran, variety of sphagnuma with tuffs from Georgium Sidus (Uranus (alpha Zodiaci VI))
tugboat crab: [*The Cruise of the Kawa* by Walter E. Traprock (George Sheperd Crappel), museumofhoaxes.com by Alex

Boese] crab large enough to pull a ship from Filbert Islands

tui: [*Dell Crossword Puzzle Dictionary*] parson bird, see poe, tue, koko

tukah: ["In the Walls of Eryx" by Howard Phillips Lovecraft and Kenneth Sterling] flying creature

tul: [Bulgarian/Haitian tarantul backformation] large arachnoid, related to lapók, tel, tule, twla, from Tara

tula: ["The Human Fish"] ichthyoid with tentacle-like fins from Magda Ocean, Venus (alpha Zodiaci II); [Lyoko tarantula mondegreen] spider from Lyokotara system; [alutmar ananymondegreen] tarantula gestalt from Ra system

tule: [Czech tanantule backformation] large arachnoid related to lapók, tel, tul, twla, from Tara system

tulk: [*Frostworld and Dreamfire* by John Morressy] creature bristling with sharp horns

tullimonstrum: [The Big Bad Book of Beasts by Michael Largo] aka Tully monster, segmented slug with pincher-snout with 8 teeth, rigid eyestalks and flat, pointed tail

tumnor: [*Star Wars: Dark Empire* by Tom Veith and Cam Kennedy] flying IxII predator of upper atmosphere from Da Soocha and its moons, Jedi galaxy

tungosaur: [shantungosaur mondegreen] duck-billed dinosaur from Sha system

tungotaur: [tungosaur minotaur portmanteau] duck-billed bovinoid

tunnelsnake: [Pern series by Ann McCaffrey] six-legged burrowing serpentoid, some with legs adapted as fins for swimming from Pern (Rukbat (alpha Sagittarii) III)

tuoga: [agouti tuoga palindrome] furry with black, brown, yellow-ticked hair

tuogator: [tuoga alligator portmanteau] alligator-like predator whose bite morphs victim into tuoga

tuom: [Dartmouth tuom trad, Plymouth tuom ylp palindromes] green or grayish mauve ornithoid, see trad and ylp

tup: [*Dell Crossword Puzzle Dictionary*] male sheep, ram

tur: [*Dell Crossword Puzzle Dictionary*] ibex, see kyl, kail; [Swedish turtur duva backformation] turtle-like nasna

turaco: [*National Geographic Encyclopedia of Animals*] long-tailed arboreal bird with gripping feet from Africa, Terra (alpha Zodiaci III)

turanon: [Terra Monster] flightless ornithoid with wings adapted for icedrilling, see pendrill, from Terrarium

turby: [*Wizard of Earthsea* by Ursula K. Le Guin] small ichthyoid noted for its oil from Serd, Ninety Isles, Inmost Sea, Earthsea

turco: [*Dell Crossword Puzzle Dictionary*] rock-wren from S. America, Terra (alpha Zodiaci III), see guan, jacu, sylph, seriema

turf owl: [waterfowl mondegreen] owl-like ornithoid from turf from Wa system

turi: [Finnish turturi backformation] dove-like ornithoid ancestral to kyyhky and pigeon

turkey duck: [Avatar: The Last Airbender: "The Foruneteller"] ornithoid with downy feathers, duckbill, chicken's feet and tail, turkey's snood

turkey-fish: [turkeyfish mondegreen] triphibian with turkey-like wattle

turkey-vulture: [turkey vulture mondegreen] turkey-headed vulture-like ornithoid

turmi: [*After Man* by Dougal Dixon] anteater-like pig

turnip termite: ["L'il Abner" by Al Capp] turnip-eating insect pest

turnstone: [*National Geographic Encyclopedia of Animals*] sandpiper that turns stones to hunt insects from Arctic, Terra (alpha Zodiaci III)

turtle duck: [Avatar: The Last Airbender: "Zuko Alone"] wingless, white-billed, tan and brown duck-like ornithoid with carapace

turtle seal: [Avatar: The Last Airbender: "The Siege of the North"] seal-headed seaturtle

turtle-dove: [turtle dove mondegreen] triphibian with turtle-like carapace

turtle-frog: [turtle frog mondegreen] frog with turtle-like carapace

turtle-frogator: [turtle-frog alligator portmanteau] alligator portmanteau] alligator-like predator whose bite morphs victim into turtle-frog

turtle-ray: [Lester Delray mondegreen] ray-like sea creature with turtle-like carapace from Les system

turtle-snake: aka [Chin.] xuánwǔ, [Jap.] genbu, [Kor.] hyeonmu, [Viet.] huyê vũ, black turtle with snake

turtleroo: [Spy Kids 2: "Island of Lost Dreams" by Robert Rodriguez] megapod with turtle head and carapace

turtodon: ["Flash Gordon" series] huge, fanged chelonoid from Mongo

tuskcat: ["The Gungan Frontier" by Chris McCubbin] tiger- or panther-like felinoid with segmented and flattened tail, sabre-like fangs, tamed as steed and shaakherder from Naboo, Jedi galaxy

tutul: [Indonesian/Malay macantutul backformation] leopard-like felinoid from Maca system

tutulope: [tutul antelope portmanteau] tutul with antlers

tvh!ga: [Cherokee] fly-like insectoid from Tsalagi system

tvh!gator: [tvh!ga alligator portmanteau] alligator-like predator whose bite morphs victim into tvh!ga

tweek: [Encyclopedia Galactica] creature so geneered as to be unrecognizable

tweets: boatlike creature from Tincityie (Edonian cluster VII), Galaxiki galaxy

twelve-eyes: ["Beasts of the Underworld" by Kurt Mahr] sea predator with 12 eyes from Afzot (Frua III)

twigg: [twiggy backformation] thin, boney creature, see scragg

twiggator: [twigg alligator portmanteau] alligator predator whose bite morphs victim into twigg

twilight sea siren: ["Encounter in the Black Galaxy" by H. G. Ewers] siren-like sea creature from Pthor

twla: [Welsh tarantwla backformation] large arachnoid related to lapók, tel, tul, tule, from Tara system

two-headed bird: ["The Planet of Storms" by Michelle Stern] predatory ratite, prey of faltechse from Thersunt

two-way snout leaper: [*The Snouters* by Harald Stümpke] snout leaper with limb-like tail and nasarium composed of nasur and nasibia able to leap forward or backward from Hi-Yi-Yi Islands

twon-ha: [Outcast] large ostrich-like steed from Adelpha

twook: [*Mothstorm* by Philip Reeve] aka sun dog, large transparent space dracoid with glassy exoskeleton

txia: [Basque untxia backformation] non-lapoid burrower with long ears

txirlardi: [Basque txirla-ardi portmanteau] clam-sheep, leg-less sheep-like, shell-dwelling creature

txistulari: [Basque ahate txistulari backformation] widgeon-duck ornithoid

tyhren: [Belarussian tyhr-ren portmanteau] cheetah-wren griffinoid

tyrannonasus: [*The Snouters* by Harald Stümpke] aka predacious snoutwalker with poison-claw-tipped tail from Hi-Yi-Yi Islands

tyrannopede: [Ben 10: Omniverse: "Of Predator and Prey" by Kevin Rubio] 10-legged spinosaur-like predator that shoots web from forehead from Vaxasauria

tyrannosaur: large predatory dinosaur with large legs, jaw, small clawed arms

tyrannotaur: [tyrannosaur minotaur portmnteau] large, predatory bovinoid

tyrg: [*Greyhawk Monstrous Compendium Appendix* by Mike Breault, etal.] tiger-like caninoid with raspy howl from Greyhawk

tyrgator: [tyrg alligator portmanteau] alligator portmanteau] alligator-like predator whose bite morphs victim into tyrg

tytistu: ["Passage" by Joe Haldeman] pale, horse-sized, egg-laying sauroid herded by colonists from Obelobel

tzari: [kallikantzari mondegreen] long-tailed mammaloids from Kallika system

tzuchinoko: pudgy snake with hypnotic stare, able to leap up two meters and roll like hoopsnake

u: [Samoan] lard land snail
u-kwa: [nu-kwa elision] ox-headed snake
uahc: [Schauss uahcs palindrome] pink creature, aka ellimrekab
ualueria: [Hildegard of Bingen's Lingua Ignota] cheiropteroid from Ignota, Hildegard's system
uang: [*Dell Crossword Puzzle Dictionary*] rhinoceras beetle
uangator: [uong alligator portmanteau] alligator portmanteau] alligator-like predator whose bite morphs victim into uong
uao: [manuao mondegreen] honeybee-like insectoid from Ma system
Uaramese marauder: [red Uaramese marauder palindrome] red marauder-like creature from Uaram system
ub: [buff ub palindrome] pale reddish ornithoid
ubeba: [*Creatures of the Galaxy* by Phil Brucato, Bill Smith, Rick D. Stuart, Chuck Truett] simian from Cholganna, Jedi galaxy
ubgnilt: [nightling bug ubgnilt hgin palindrome] nocturnal insectoid
ubmok: [kombu ubmok palindrome] dark green kombu kelp-colored creature
ucha: [*Vulcan's Glory* by D. C. Fontana] gazelle-like herd creature from Areta (beta Circini III)
uchaishravas: [*Dictionary of Hindu Lore and Legend* by Anna Dallapiccola] 7-headed wingless pegasoid
uchuulon: ["The Ecology of the Chuul" by Mike Mearls] aka slime chuul, chuul-illithid symbiot
ucodon: [morganucodon mondegreen] proto-mammal from Morga system
ucodonster: [ucodon monster portmanteau] monstrous ucodon
ud: [dunalielia salt-resistant extremophile from Aileila system
udad: [*Dell Crossword Puzzle Dictionary*] wild sheep with large horns from Africa, Terra (alpha Zodiaci III), see arui, argali, aoudad
udal: ["udal at times emit taladu" palindrome] cricket-like insectoid gestalt
ue: [nue elision] monkey-headed tanuki (raccoon dog) with tiger's legs, snake's tail

ueme: [torueme backformation] bull-infesting worm
ueruprup: [purpureus ueruprup palindrome] purplish ornithoid
uf: [funazz ananymondegreen] pet from Zza rogue planet
ufdaerd: [dreadful ufdaerd palindrome] monstrous creature
ufiti: see sisimite
úgan'tēna: [Cherokee] water mocassin-like serpentoid from Tsalagi system
ugarapsa: [asparagus ugarapsa palindrome] green, plant-mimicking ornithoid
ugaris: [kupranugaris backformation] camel-like desert mammaloid from Kupra system
ugelb: [Crayola bubble gum ugelb bub palindrome] pink relative of bub, elb, from Crayol A system
ughlie: ubiquitous slug-like creature with humanoid "face" from Hypnot, Shine system, Galaxiki galaxy
ughtyndz: [Armenian yndzught backformation] camel-yndz, desert quadruped ancestral to yndz and camel
ugja. [*Creatures of the Galaxy* by Phil Brucato, Bill Smith, Rick D. Stuart, Chuck Truett] solitary creature from Cholganna, Jedi galaxy
uh: [hunanothere ananymondegreen] camelopardoid from Erehtona system
uillo: [Catalan/Spanish doguillo backformation] pug-like caninoid
uimdac: [cadmium uimdac palindrome] green, orange, yellow, or green ornithoid
uinatit: [titanium uinatit palindrome] tit-like yellow ornithoid from Uina system
uintathere: [*After the Dinosaurs* by Donald R. Prothero] elephant-sized anagalid with hooves with six bony head knobs that crossed Bering Landbridge in Paleocene, [*Life History of Our Planet* by William Gunning] and antlers
uitnazyb: [Byzantium uitnazyb palindrome] reddish violet ornithoid
uja: [nuja elision] chiropteran
ujkorb: [Albanian ujk-korb portmanteau] wolf-raven, pack-hunting, predatory black ornithoid

uk: [Armenian tsovakhozuk backformation] Guinea pig-pig, see ginea, gini, mar, meri, tsova
uki: [tanuki mondegreen] raccoon-dog from Ta system; [beheaded yuki] red-and-gray ornithoid
ukkangu: [nukkangu elision] desert caninoid
ül: [gokül backformation] cat-chicken-like griffinoid; [krik, krikül backformation] grasshopper-cricket insectoid
ulb: [blue ulb palindrome] bluebird-like ornithoid
ulgurstasta: [*Greyhawk Monstrous Compendium Appendix* by Mike Breault, etal.] massive, pale-yellow maggot from Greyhawk
uller: [*Creatures of the Galaxy* by Phil Brucato, Bill Smith, Rick D. Stuart, Chuck Truett] horned creature from Kashÿyÿk, Jedi galaxy
ülope: [ül antelope portmanteau] ül with antlers
ulp: [plum ulp palindrome] deep purplish ornithoid between russet and olive, see nurp
ulsio: [Barsoom series by Edgar Rice Burroughs] fierce, unlovely Airedale-sized rodentoid from Barsoom (alpha Zodiaci IV)
ulth: [Thongor series by Lin Carter] white-furred 3-meter ursinoid from Lemuria
ultra-energy beast: [Superboy #98] creature from Rimbor
uluritei: [*The Howling Stones* by Alan Dean Foster] glider from Parramat archepelago, Senisran
um: [munacure ananymondegreen] small water buffalo-like ruminant from Eruca system
umb: [numbfish elision] electric eel-like ichthyoid from Akyby, Rybyka system, Galaxiki galaxy
umbranine: [Monster Galaxy] black equinoid with hairy feet from Leo constellation
umbus: [*If I Ran the Zoo* by Theodore Seuss Geissel] omnivorous, bicentipede bovine with hundreds of stomachs
umbusaur: umbus-like bicentipede dinosaur

umgub: [*Fantastic Beasts and Where to Find Them* by Newton Artemis Fido Scamander] slashkiller-shaped creature
umibouzu: [Jap. "green turtle"] turtle with three tails aka sanbi
un: [Croatian rakun backformation] raccoon-crab or seacoon, masked crustacean ancestral to crab
una: [nuna elision] flightless, neck-less scaly-backed ornithoid with barbels from Zan Mts., Za archipelago, Peggassus, Hippocranea system, Galaxiki galaxy
unagi: [Avatar: The Last Airbender: "The Warriors of Kyoshi"] 75-meter, scale-less sea serpent with headfin, barbels that eats elephant koi
unark: [*Creatures of the Galaxy* by Phil Brucato, Bill Smith, Rick D. Stuart, Chuck Truett] small, acid-spitting worm from Coruscant, Jedi galaxy
unau: [*Dell Crossword Puzzle Dictionary*] two-toed sloth
unch: [gaunch mondegreen] gray-green forest monster
underboss: [Blaster Master] putrid green-yellow and red blob with feelers, used by Plutonium Boss
ung: [Viet. di san chim ung backformation] chim-falcon ornithoid ancestral to chim and falcon from Disa system
ungator: [ung alligator portmanteau] alligator portmanteau] unalligator-like predator whose bite morphs victim into ung
unhcegila: [Lakota] man-eating dragon
uni: [Outernauts] horseshoe-shaped extra-dimensional creature with 3 light blue circular side sensoria that feeds on moon blossoms, most purplish kuni in shocker variety
unicoral: ["Robot Hugs" by R. Hugs] coral that forms narwhal horn-like projection
unicorn: any horned creature whose usual multiple horns are naturally or artificially braided together into one, see braidedhorn
unicorn pig: [*After the Dinosaurs* by Donald R. Prothero] see kubanochoerus

unicorn pigator: [unicorn pig alligator portmanteau] alligator-like predator whose bite morphs victim into kubanochoerus

unicorn: [Num. 23:22, 24:8, Dt. 33:71, Job 39:9, Ps. 22:2, 24:6, Isa. 34:7] one-horned auroch (re'em) or other one-horned animals like horse-boded licorne or toe nayo, with buck legs, lion tail, horse head, [*Monstrorum Historiae* by Ulisse Aldrovandi] with lion's mane, bird hindlegs, hooved forelegs and short tail

unicorndeer: ["The Winged Dreamers" by Jennifer Guttridge] one-horned deer-like ruminant from Durban's world

unigen: ["Winner Lose All" by Jack Vance] non-mattergy spacefaring creature, like feeble, mobile luminous nodes that feed on energy, able to sense changes in electrostatic fields, concentrate energy for defense

uniao: [beheaded ouniao] 4-headed bird of ill omen

unirda: [blanu nirda mondegreen] blue ornithoid from Bla system

unisis: [unicorn-coelophysis?, *The World of Synnabarr* by Raymond C. S. McCracken] creature from Olains of Gleniea, Synnibarr (alpha Zodiaci IV), see shan

unitalp: [platinum unitalp palindrome] one-horned, pale silvery gray mole-like creature with fawn (pale reddish/yellow-orangish) underbelly

unk: [nunk elision] nunk-like creature, see ibling

unnerbeast: [beheaded runnerbeast] messenger gan ceann

unny: [Easter bunny spoonerism] very beastly predator

unodēna: [Cherokee] sheep-like ruminant from Tsalagi system

unrak: crab-raccoon, 6-legged aquatic furry ancestral to raccoon, see un

unt: grey-green river creature, see sehc

untling: [gauntling mondegreen] immature unt

untlingator: [untling alligator-like predator whose bite morphs victim into untling

uo: [rufous uo fur palindrome] brownish red furry

uodnerroh: [horrendous uodnerroh palindrome] uo predator

uoe: [cinereous uoe renic, outrageous uoe gartuo palindromes] brownish gray female (renic) or orange (gartuo) male ornithoid from Crayol A system

uolc: [cloud uolc portmanteau backformation] grounded fog-like cloud viper

uole: [mauvelous uole vuam palindrome] pinkish vuam

uomuf: [fumous uomuf palindrome] smoke-colored ornithoid

upboard: [nupboard ellision] drone board, see board, overboard

uph: [peach puff uph caep palindrome] puffy, immature caep

uph ant: [uphant mondegreen] ant-like food insectoid of uphs

uphant: [valuphant mondegreen] red ungulate with two horns, backridge

upland baluga: [museumofhoaxes.com by Alex Boese] whale adapted to cold from Canada, Terra (alpha Zodiaci III)

upland shark: [museumofhoaxes.com by Alex Boese] shark adapted to cold from Canada, Terra (alpha Zodiaci III), see ice shark

upland trout: [museumofhoaxes.com by Alex Boese] furry arboreal trout adapted to to cold water from Canada, Terra (alpha Zodiaci III)

uqa: [aqua uqa palindrom] sea blue ornithoid, see nirama

uqsib: [bisque uqsib palindrome] off-white ornithoid

ur: [Icelandic svanur back-formation] swan-like ornithoid from Sva; [gaur mondegreen] gray-green ox-like bovinoid, see yal

uran: [*Dell Crossword Puzzle Dictionary*] monitor lizard

urayuli: shaggy 3-meter anthropoid with long arms, luminous eyes, loon-like cry from S. W. Africa, Terra (alpha Zodiaci III)

Urbankan frog: ["Four to Doomsday" by Terrence Dudley] small batrachian with toxin able to contract victim to "size of a grain of salt" (1‰) from Urbanka

urca: [Romanian nurca elision] mink-like furry

urchio: [Hildegard of Bingen's Lingua Ignota] stork-like ornithoid from Lingua, Hildegard's system

urcu: [ucru urcu palindrome] tan ornithoid

urdau: [telp urdau quadruplet palindrome] telp-like mammaloid with four breasts

urdur: [*Monster in the Maze* by Jeffrey Lord] 7.5-meter, cold-blooded serpent-like dragoid bred by Casta the sorcerer with tyrannosaur-like head, scythe-shaped claws on short powerful legs, armor plating from dimension X

ureau: [nureau ellision] bipedal lapoid

urgho falat: ["guardian of love"] see ado idaigh

uri: [Indonesian/Malay nuri elision] parrot-like ornithoid

uria: [air uria palindrome] leg-less murre-like ornithoid

urial: [Dell Crossword Puzzle Dictionary] wild mountain sheep from Tibet, Terra (alpha Zodiaci III), see sha, sna, rasse, bharal, nahoor, oorial

urialope: [urial antelope portmanteau] urial with antlers

urikabe: [nurikabe elision] whompoid able to project blocking or misdirecting "wall"

Urodelean flu virus: ["Genesis" by Brannon Braga] virus that causes Urodelean influenza

Urquat virus: ["Extinction" by André Bormanis] mutagenic virus that causes Loque'equization and urge to return to devastated Urquat

urreep: [*The Sword of Lankor* by Howard L. Cory] swamp-dwelling carnivore with 2 fierce-jawed heads, bulging eyes, crab-like pinchers, tough leather hide from Lankor

ursapteryx: [Perry Rhodan] aka flying bear, small, flying ursinoid from Aptulat (Aptut III)

ursavus: [*After the Dinosaurs* by Donald R. Prothero] long-legged running bear from early Miocene

ursicle: [Terra Monster] large variety of ursnobal from Terrarium

ursinopongoid: aka wuzzy, bear-headed pongoid

ursnobal: [Terra Monster] bluish-white polar bear-like ursinoid, see ursicle, from Terrarium

ursnobalope: [ursnobal antelope portmanteau] ursnobal with antlers

ursodile: [bear-crocodile, "Flash Gordon" series] amphibian with serpentine torso and head, powerful claws from Mongo

urson: [*Dell Crossword Puzzle Dictionary*] porcupine from Canada, Terra (alpha Zodiaci III)

ursonster: [urson monster portmanteau] monstrous, porcupine-like creature

urstorm: [Terra Monster] ursinoid from Terrarium

urtumi: ["Urtumi the Image Eater" by Cary Bates] ectoplasm-eating monster of Honru Indians

uruabird: [trumpeter swan back-formation] clarinet swan-like ornithoid with urua-like call

urubu: [*Dell Crossword Puzzle Dictionary*] vulture, see aura, condor

urus: [Dell Crossword Puzzle Dictionary] extinct wild ox, see unicorn, re'em

urusai: ["The Gungan Frontier" by Chris McCubbin] saprophagous (bone-eating) reptilian from Tatooine, Jedi galaxy

uryti: [Lithuanian nuryti elision] swallow-like ornithoid

ushi-oni: [Jap. "ox-ogre"] horned biped with huge tusks, spurred wrists, webbing for gliding from Negoroji, Japan, Terra (alpha Zodiaci III)

ustilagor: [*Monster Manual* by Skip Williams, etal.] larval stage of intellect devourer bred by Illithid for both food and as guards

ut: [Catalan cucut back-formation] barnacle-goose-like cuckoo-worm, larval ornithoid

utahraptor: [*A Field Guide to Dinosaurs* by Henry Gee and Luis V. Rey] 7-meter, 700-kg dromaeosaur from early Cretaceous

utch: [nutch elision] green, furry, neckless, biped

utco: [telp utco octuplet palindrome] telp-like mammaloid with eight breasts

utniu: [telp utniu quintuplet palindrome] telp-like mammaloid with five breasts

utouniao: [beheaded iutouniao] 7-headed bird of ill omen

utpe: [telp utpe septuplet palindrome] telp-like mammaloid with seven breasts

utpylacue: [Crayola eucalyptus utpylacue palindrome] bluish green ornithoid from Crayol A system

utsetsdi: [Cherokee] possum-like creature from Tsalagi system

utsīya: [Cherokee] earthworm-like creature from Tsalagi system

utum: [*Dell Crossword Puzzle Dictionary*] owl from S. Asia, Terra (alpha Zodiaci III)

utxe: [telp utxe sextuplet palindrome] telp-like mammaloid with sex breasts

uyanka: [beheaded luyanka] 4-headed hydra-like dracoid

uyasgali: [Cherokee Tsalagi] armadilloid from Tsalagi system

uza: [azul uza palindrome] purplish blue ornithoid

uzamaiti: [Miwok] grizzly-like ursinoid

v'sgigi: [Cherokee] deer-like ruminant from Tsalagi system

vaardark: [aardvark spoonerism] dark, nocturnal armored mammalian

vaatch: ["The Survivor" by Donald Kingsley] Kzin odorovore "hung out for fresh air"

vac: [cave vac palindrome] cave-dwelling scavenger, see regne

vacabra: [Catalan vaca-cabra portmanteau] cow-goat, milk ruminant between cow-and goat-sized

vad: [Hung. vadgalamb backformation] turtle-dove-like ornithoid ancestral to pigeon

vadga: [Hung. vadgalamb mondegreen] lamb-dove griffinoid

vadgator: [vadga alligator portmanteau] alligator-like predator whose bite morphs victim into vadga

vai-sehlat: [Star Trek] sehlat-mimic from T'Kasi, Nevasa (40 Eridani) system

vakhen: [*Spock's World* by Diane Duane] fierce flying predator from lesser mountains of T'Khasi, Nevasa (40 Eridani) system

val: [lava val palindrome] thermophilic ornithoid, see edne

Valesic spore: ["Caught in the Act" by Robert Forsyth] parasite that induces lust and then digests partner

valkatma: [James Cooke Brown's Loglan valna katma (wild cat) compound] wildcat from Logla, Brown's system

valkip: [Dutch valk-kip portmanteau] falcon-chicken, wild ornithoid

valkipede: [valkip centipede portmanteau] falcon-chicken worm-like larva with many legs

vallala: [Sinhala &] 2-D das-like creature

valnimla: [James Cooke Brown's Loglan valna nimla (violent animal) compound] beast from Logla, Brown's system

valuphant: [*After Man* by Dougal Dixon] 4.6-meter ungulate with two 1-meter horns and backridge

vampire bat: bat adapted to just ingesting blood

vampire dragon: [*A Hero's Guide to Deadly Dragons* by Hiccup Haddock III] small, blood-sucking, black, dark gray, midnight blue dragon that hunts in packs (vexes, sing. vex) from Barbarian archipelago

vampire squid: [*The Big Bad Book of Beasts* by Michael Largo] small, non-vampiric squid with 8 webbed tentacles, red eyes

vampire virus: ["Horror of the Blood Monsters" by Sue McNair] virus that induces hemophagy from Spectrum galaxy, Spectrum constellation between Eridanus and Lepus

van: swimming, white furry with auburn head and tail rings, amber and blue eyes

vandar: [Thongor series by Lin Carter] 3-meter long, black, jungle lion-like felinoid from Lemuria

vanger: [Afrikaans visvanger backformation] cormorant-like triphibian from Stiria, Airit system, Galaxiki galaxy

vanilla moose: [Xanth series by Piers Anthony] tasty ruminant, related to chocolate moose, from Xanth

vanilla pudding: [pudding extrapolation] pudding-thick ooze, see white pudding

vannāgali: [Kannada &] 2-D das-like creature

vaporizing bacillium: ["River of Stone" by Michael Green] flesh-eating bacillium used by Sowers that vaporizes in an hour

varactyl: [*Revenge of the Sith*] scaly, green geckoid steed with bird-like head and colored neck plumage from Utapau, Jedi galaxy
varactylope: [varactyl antelope portmantea] varactyl with antlers
varan: ["Varan the Unbelievable" by Shinichi Sekizawa] 90-meter tall amphibian, usually bipedal, with long thick neck, small head, white spiral horns, large arms, thin back carapace; [*Dell Crossword Puzzle Dictionary*] lizard, see gila, gecko, guana, skink, iguana
vare: [*Dell Crossword Puzzle Dictionary*] weasel, see ermine, ferret
vari: [*Dell Crossword Puzzle Dictionary*] ruffed lemur
varkat: [Afrikaans vark-kat portmanteau] pig-cat, pig-headed felinoid
varskvlavi: [Georgian *] 2-D pentapus or hexapus
vasa: bacterium from Drecon, Nexonith system, Galaxiki galaxy; [*Dell Crossword Puzzle Dictionary*] parrot, see kea, vaza, lory
vastodon: [Callisto series by Lin Carter] huge boar-elephant from Thantor
vayri: [Albanian vayri bad backformation] duck-like ornithoid
vaza: [*Dell Crossword Puzzle Dictionary*] parrot, see kea, lory, yasa
vážkanec: [Czech vážka-kanec portmanteau] dragonfly-boar, 4-winged, pig-snouted dracoid
vcelabut: [Czech vcela-labut portmanteau] bee-swan, small, white, long-necked, nectar-eating ornithoid
vedbird: [grue-bleen extrapolation] violet bird that turns red, not to be confused with bledbird, blioletbird, gebird, gredbird, grioletbird, redbird, reenbird, rellowbird, rindigobird, rioletbird, ruebird, vedbird, vellowbird, vindigobird, violetbird, vuebird, yedbird, yioletbird from Ora system
veenbird: [grue-bleen extrapolation] violet bird that turns green, not to be confused with bleenbird, blioletbird, gebird, gredbird, greenbird, grellowbird, grindigobird, grioletbird, gruebird, reenbird, rioletbird, vedbird, vellowbird, vindigobird, violetbird, vuebird, yeenbird, yioletbird from Ora system
veermok: ["The Gungan Frontier" by Chris McCubbin] fast-breeding, hunchbacked, lanky, bearded gorilla-like pongoid from Naboo or Mimban, Jedi galaxy
veery: [*Dell Crossword Puzzle Dictionary*] Wilson's thrush, see missel
veganimal: [vegitarian animal portmanteau] animal geneered from omnivore or carnivore to herbivore
Vegan rhino: [*Hitchhiker's Guide to the Galaxy* by Doug Adams] rhinoid from Vega (alpha Lyrae) system
vegdu: [James Cooke Brown's Loglan vegro dunmu (enormous ape) compound] gigantopithicus from Logla, Brown's system
vegmortu: [James Cooke Brown's Loglan vegri mortu compound] green death from Logla, Brown's system
velcrow: [velco crow portmanteau] crow-like ornithoid with burr-fur-like feathers
veld: [Dutch veldleeuwerik back-formation] lark-like ornithoid
velkee: [velker backformation] space-dwelling velker prey
velker: [*Creatures of the Galaxy* by Phil Brucato, Bill Smith, Rick D. Stuart, Chuck Truett] starfighter mimic from Bespin, Jedi galaxy
vellowbird: [grue-bleen extrapolation] violet bird that turns yellow, not to be confused with blellowbird, blioletbird, gebird, grellowbird, grioletbird, rellowbird, rindigobird, rioletbird, vedbird, veenbird, vindigobird, violetbird, vuebird, yedbird, yeenbird, yellowbird, yindigobird, yioletbird or yuebird from Ora system
velociraptor: ["speedy thief"] see deinonychus, 1.8-m pack dromaeosaur with large claws
velveteen rabbit: The Velventeen Rabbit by Margaret Williams] rabbit-like toy animal animated by Love

velvetworm: [*The Big Bad Book of Beasts* by Michael Largo] slimy invertebrate with small eyes, small flat thin antennae, 84 legs
venom: [Spiderman mythos] aka krobaa, scream, phage, riot, lasher, agony, symbiont that binds with host as "living suit" able to feed off cancer, but vulnerable to sound and heat, dependent on phenethylamine, spawned carnage
venoplatyx: [Outernauts] venomous, purple, crocodilian with tail spike, see venopus
venopus: [Outernauts] immature venoplatyx
venopuss: [venopus puss portmanteau] venomous felinoid
venosaber: [Outernauts] mature venoplatyx with hunchback
vensa: [James Cooke Brown's Loglan vendu sarpi (poisonous serpent) compound] poisonous snake from Logla, Brown's system
Venusian saber-tooth: ["Lost Sorceress of the Silent Citadel" by Michael Moorcock] creature noted for curiosity and reflexes from Venus (alpha Zodiaci II)
Venusian shrew: [*Mothstorm* by Philip Reeve] shrew-like mammaloid from Venus (alpha Zodiaci II)
veplys: [Lithuanian juru veplys back-formation] juru-walrus sirenian ancestral to juru and walrus
verme: [*River Monsters* by Jeremy Wade] giant river eel from Ganges River, Terra (alpha Zodiaci III)
vermi-lion: [vermilion mondegreen] lion-like felinoid with worm-like larva
vermicula: ["Manhunt" by Tracy "Terry Devereaux" Tormé] ichthyoid from Antedia
vermilion bird: aka [Chin.] zhū què, [Jap.] suzaku, [Kor.] jujak, [Viet.] chutuó'c, flaming pheasant-like bird, not to be confused with fenghuang
vermisaur: [*The New Dinosaurs* by Dougal Dixon] worm-like dinosaur, like arm-less wyrm
vermitaur: [vermisaur minotaur portmanteau] worm-like leg-less bovinoid
vesp: [*Creatures of the Galaxy* by Phil Brucato, Bill Smith, Rick D. Stuart, Chuck Truett] poisonous lizard-like reptilian from Lok, Jedi galaxy
vespa: [*Dell Crossword Puzzle Dictionary*] wasp
vestaceratops: [Cyclopedia of Worlds] herbivorous ceratopsian dinosaur on Palul (Lar Don), the Dinosaur Planet
vexillosaur: ["flag-lizard", *The New Dinosaurs* by Dougal Dixon] herd hadrosaur with feather-like tail on males that varies by species
vexillotaur: [vexillosaur minotaur portmanteau] bovinoid with flag-like tail
vextail: [Terra Monster] red, 3-tailed, fanged fox, see moxtail and thrashtail from Terrarium
vibio: extremophilic bacterium resistant to extreme alkaline, see psychrobacter, arthrobacter
vibrus: ["Home, Home on the Waves" by Bob Rozakis] sea creature that gives off vibration energy from Vortuma
vicetopus: [Ben 10: Omniverse: "Showdown" by Marty Isenberg] long-bodied cephaopodan predator from Cerebrocrustacea
vicetopuss: [vicetopus puss portmanteau] long-bodied felinoid predator
vicuña: [*National Geographic Encyclopedia of Animals*] small mountain ruminant from Andes
vilewing: [Terra Monster] flying creature from Terrarium
vilewingator: [vilewing alligator-like predator whose bite morphs victim into vilewing
vilo: [olive vilo palindrome] dark yellow-green ornithoid
vilser: [vilserfish backformation] prey of vilserfish
vilserfish: [silverfish spoonerism] small, multi-legged, aquatic insectoid
vilupis: [Continuum] giant, one-eyed kangaroo rat from Vilupixis, Ilisris system
vinagaroon: [*National Geographic Encyclopedia of Animals*] scorpion with vinegar-spraying whip rather than stinger S. N. America, Terra (alpha Zodiaci III)
vindaloo: ["Red Dwarf: D. N. A." by Rob Grant and Doug Naylor] monster that transmogrifier turned curry into

vindigobird: [grue-bleen extrapolation] violet bird that turns to indigo, not to be confused with blindigobird, blioletbird, gebird, grindigobird, grioletbird, rindigobird, rioletbird, vedbird, veenbird, vellowbird, vindigobird, violetbird, vuebird, yindigobird, yioletbird from Ora system

vintha: [The Kalarba Adventures: "Battle of the B'rknaa" by Dan Thorsland] grillable food animal from Indobok, Kalarba system, Jedi galaxy

violetbird: [grue-bleen extrapolation] violet bird that remains violet, not to be confised with blioletbird, grioletbird, rioletbird, vedbird, veenbird, vellowbird, vindigobird, vuebird or yioletbird from Ora system

vioness: [venomous lioness portmanteau, Terra Monster] felinoid with poisonous thorny tail, see purrpetal and dandylion, from Terrarium

viper-fish: [viperfish mondegreen] poisonous eel

vipermine: [viper-ermine portmanteau] burrowing, nocturnal, 1.1-meter caninoid predator with black-tipped tail, brown fur, venomous fangs from Brom, Kivrozog system, Galaxiki galaxy

vipertooth: [*Fantastic Beasts and Where to Find Them* by Newton Artemis Fido Scamander] 4.5-meter, smooth-skinned, omnivorous, copper dragon with short horn from Peru, terra (alpha Zodiaci III)

viperwolf: ["Avatar" by James Cameron] pack-hunting predator from Pandora, moon of Polyphemus, alpha Centauri system

vippee: [Outernauts] immature viprillo with small "ears"

vipper: [vipee backformation] viper-like vippee predator

viprillo: [Outernauts] cobra-like purple serpentoid with yellow spots, pale blue underbelly

virenz: [Hildegard of Bingen's Lingua Ignota] fly-like insectoid from Ignota, Hildegard's system

vireo: [*National Geographic Encyclopedia of Animals*] song bird from America, Terra (alpha Zodiaci III)

virgultasaur: ["thicket-lizard", *The New Dinosaurs* by Dougal Dixon] aka dwarf titanosaur, about a third the size of a normal titanosaur

virgultataur: [virfultasaur minotaur portmanteau] dwarf titanotaur

viscacha: [*National Geographic Encyclopedia of Animals*] large rodent from Andes, Terra (alpha Zodiaci III)

visinkt: [Dutch inktvis backformation] fish-inkt ancestral to inkt

vissimbu: [submissive vissimbus palindrome] domesticated food animal

viterce: [secretive viterces palindrome] rarely seen creature

vitha: [*Yesterday's Son* by A. C. Crispin] large-chested, shy creature like otter and goat, 2.4 meters when on hind legs from Sarpeidon, beta Niobe system

vizzia: [Hildegard of Bingen's Lingua Ignota] swallow-like ornithoid from Ignota, Hildegard's system

vlakasni: [James Cooke Brown's Loglan vlako kasni] lake cow from Logla, Brown's system

vlase: [James Cooke Brown Loglan vlako serpi] lake snake from Logla, Brown's system

vle(e)r: [Afrikaans vlermuis, Dutch vleermuis backformation] bat-mouse ancestral to mouse and bat

vliegans: [Afrikaans vlieg-gans portmanteau] housefly-goose, small goose-like ornithoid with compound eyes, antennae and mandibles

vliegier: [Dutch vlieg-gier portmanteau] housefly-vulture, housefly-goose, small vulture-like ornithoid with compound eyes, antennae and mandibles

vlilseena: [Mushroom Planet series by Eleanor Cameron] fungus-like creature from Basidium, Terra (alpha Zodiaci IIIc)

vluf: [fulvous uo vluf palindrome] dull reddish-yellow, brownish-yellow or tawny furry

vod: [Tev'Meckian] hart-like ruminant from Tev'Meck, MakTar system

vogelch: [German Vogel-Elch portmanteau] bird-elk, griffinoid with antlers

voi cá: [Vietnamese cá voi antonym] elephant-fish, not be be confused with cá voi (whale) from Disa system

voidbeast: ["A Beast of the Void" by Raymond Z. Gallun] hemispherical spacefaring steed with many eyes, several edge-claws at the end of spoke-like ridges

volantis: [piscium extrapolation] egg-laying flying ichthyoid

volcano mutant: [*Hawkman* #23] 15-meter long dracoid with snake-like body, 4 claws, wings, able to shoot lightning from fingers, exhale hellfire

volcoro: [Outernauts] 6-legged crustacean with crest

vole: [*Dell Crossword Puzzle Dictionary*] meadow or field or snow mouse

volkangu: [James Crooke Brown's Loglan volti kangu] leap dog from Logla, Brown's system

volma: [James Crooke Brown's Loglan volti madzo (leap maker) compound] leaper from Logla, Brown's system

volper: [volpertinger mondegreen] creature that volps

volpertinger: [museumofhoaxes.cometer by Alex Boese] wolpertinger from Austria, Terra (alpha Zodiaci III)

volteer: [Terra Monster] small electric buzzgrass grazer, see gazolt and shadowvolt, from Terrarium

volter mite: [voltermite mondegreen] small, electric insectoid, see jolter mite

voltermite: [Terra Monster] large, electric beetle-like insectoid with blue spots, see joltermite, from Terrarium

voltifly: [Outernauts] yellow, electrical insectoid with pink underbelly

volvox: ["Mathematical Zoo" by Martin Gardner] creature whose young turn themselves inside out when they mature enough to use flagellae

volvoxling: [volvox backformation] immature, flagella-less inside-out volvox

voomot: [Afrikaans voom-mot portmanteau] roach-moth, cockroach-like insectoid that matures into moth-like adult

voorpak: [*Creatures of the Galaxy* by Phil Brucato, Bill Smith, Rick D. Stuart, Chuck Truett] carnivorous furball with stick-like legs from Jedi galaxy

vorfi: [James Cooke Brown's Loglan vo fitpi (eight feet) compound] octopus-like sea creature from Logla, Brown's system

vorkl: ["The Swordsmen of Varnis" by Clive Jackson] scaly, hexapodal steed

vorklope: [vorkl antelope portmanteau] vorkl with antlers

vornskr: [*Heir to the Empire* by Timothy Zahn] long-legged, nocturnal quadruped with vaguely dog-like muzzle, sharp teeth, poisonous whip-like tail, semi-tamed by tail-cutting from Myrkr, Jedi galaxy

vorpent: [*A Hero's Guide to Deadly Dragons* by Hiccup Haddock III] bright yellow, very small but with venomous bite and stinging tail from Barbarian archipelago

vortex: [*After Man* by Dougal Dixon] 12-meter whale-like penguin with sieve-like beak

vouivre: one-eyed dragon from French Switzerland, Terra (alpha Zodiaci III)

vram: ["The Canine That Outclassed Krypto" by Cary Bates] zkon predator

Vrenomese squid: [Power Rangers: "The Fall of the Phantom"] giant man-eating squid from Vrenom

vsdena: [tsukanvsdena backformation] bovinoid from Tsuka system

vuam: [mauve vuam, mauvelous uole vuam palindromes] purple creature from Mau system, see nedom, airyt, uole

vuebird: [grue-bleen extrapolation] violetbird that turns blue, not to be confused with bledbird, bleenbird, bellowbird, blindigobird, blioletbird, bluebird, gebird, grioletbird, gruebird, rioletbird, ruebird, vedbird, veenbird, vellowbird, vindigobird, violetbird, vuebird, yioletbird or yuebird from Ora system

vukonj: [Croatian vuk-konj portmanteau] wolf-horse, small, pack-hunting predatory equine, not easily broken

vulko: [Bulgarian vulk-kos portmanteau] wolf-blackbird, black, pack-hunting griffinoid
vulpes: [OviPets] egg-laying fox-like furry
vulpoon: [*Edge Chronicles* by Paul Stewart and Chris Riddell] scraggy, sharp-beaked ornithoid
vulpoteryx: ["fox-wing"] aka flying-fox, aka vulpteryx, fox with bat-like wings but without echo location
vulturchin: [vulture-urchin portmanteau] carrion-eating triphibian with hooked beak, clacareous shell covered in long spikes
vulturmine: [vulture-ermine portmanteau] weasel-like carrion-eater with black-tipped tail, powerful beak and brown fur except on neck and head
vum: [Fr. Johann Martin Schleyer's Volapük] worm-like creature from Schleyer's system
vuohi: [Finnish taivaanvuohi back-formation] snipe-like ornithoid from Taivaa system
vurtur: [Fr. Johann Martin Schleyer's Volapük] vulture-like ornithoid from Schleyer's system
vu: vuvu nasna
vuvu: [Monster Galaxy] skull-headed, purple, biped with horns from Aries constellation
vykar: [*Yesterday's Son* by A. C. Crispin] equinoid with nose-horn and camel-like locomotion from Sarpeidon, beta Niobe system
vynock: [The Kalarba Adventures: "Battle of the B'rknaa" by Dan Thorsland] flying relative of mynock with batwings, thick tail tip, "head" with sensoria from Indobok or Kalarba, Jedi galaxy
vyp: [viper backformation, *Creatures of the Galaxy* by Phil Brucato, Bill Smith, Rick D. Stuart, Chuck Truett] poisonous lizard-like reptilian from Cholganna, Jedi galaxy
w(h)elk: [*Dell Crossword Puzzle Dictionary*] large marine snail, see wilk, abalone
waag: [*Dell Crossword Puzzle Dictionary*] monkey from Africa, Terra (alpha Zodiaci III), see grivet, mona
waagator: [waag alligator portmanteau] alligator-like predator whose bite morphs victim into waag

wab: [*Unofficial Questarian Guide*] prey animal from Tev'Meck, MakTar system
wabbit: [wab rabbit portmanteau] lapoid prey of the polve
wachtelch: [German Wachtel-Elch portmanteau] quail-elk/moose, mottled brown griffinoid with antlers
wad: [dawn wad] variety of hgiliwt
wadaduga: [Cherokee] dragonfly-like insectoid from Tsalagi system
wadadugator: [wadaduga alligator portmanteau] alligator-like predator whose bite morphs victim into wadaduga
wadulīsi: [Cherokee] bee-like insectoid from Tsalagi system
waf: [fawn waf palindrome] yellowish tan furry
waga: [Cherokee] cow-like bovinoid from Tsalagi system
wagator: [waga alligator portmanteau] alligator-like predator whose bite morphs victim into waga
wagtail: [*Dell Crossword Puzzle Dictionary*] lark
wah: [*Dell Crossword Puzzle Dictionary*] panda
waheela: [*Monster Spotter's Guide to North America* by Scott Francis] aka bear-dog, 1.2-meter warg-like caninoid from N. E. Pacific coast, Terra (alpha Zodiaci III) [*Here Be Monsters almanac*] with short legs, lone hunters
wahoo: [*Dell Crossword Puzzle Dictionary*] fish, see peto
wahya: [Cherokee] wolf-like caninoid from Tsalagi system
waif: [*Edge Chronicles* by Paul Stewart and Chris Riddell] cheiropteroid with bulbous head, large ears, with amnesia-inducing ultrasonics, includes greywaif, ghost waif, flitterwaif, knightwaif, nightwaif and waterwaif variants
wail: [whale mondegreen, Xanth series by Piers Anthony] large lake creature like a gray cloud with many tiny feet with which it walks on water leaving lingering footprints and wailing call from Xanth
wajano: see what-do-you-know

wakka: [*After Man* by Dougal Dixon] ostrich-like bipedal rodent with elongated face

wal: [lawn wal mondegreen] green or brown ornithoid

walaus: [German Wal-Laus portmanteau] large aquatic insectoid

waleli: [Cherokee] hummingbird-like ornithoid from Tsalagi system

waler: [*Dell Crossword Puzzle Dictionary*] horse from Australia, Terra (alpha Zodiaci III)

Walgren Lake monster: [*Monster Spotter's Guide to North America* by Scott Francis] aka Alkali Lake monster, 18-meter, malodorous, gray or brown alligator with horn from Lake Walgren, Neb., Terra (alpha Zodiaci III)

wality: [*The Perfect Planet* by Edward Packard] giant gopher-like rodentoid from Utopa (Achnar V), Gallatin quadrant

wall gopher: ["Bender's Game" by Eric Horsted, etal.] gopher fond of burrowing rat-like in apartment walls

walla: [wallaby back-formation] griffinoid with wallaby-like legs and tail and bee-like wings from Ahla, Ojikh system, Galaxiki galaxy

wallrus: [wall walrus portmanteau] small, crevice-dwelling walrus adapted to living in walls

wally: [*Monster Spotter's Guide to North America* by Scott Francis] 30-meter, humped amphibian with hog-like snout, buffalo and/or rhinoceros horns from Wallowa Lake, Ore., Terra (alpha Zodiaci III)

walopus: [Cloudstone] short-tentacled cephalopodan used as hat

walopuss: [walopus puss portmanteau] short-legged felinoid used as hat

wamaz: [Hildegard of Bingen's Lingua Ignota] heron-like ornithoid from Ignota, Hildegard's system

wamba: [*Creatures of the Galaxy* by Phil Brucato, Bill Smith, Rick D. Stuart, Chuck Truett] hooved creature from Cholganna, Jedi galaxy

wampa: [*The Empire Strikes Back* by Donald F. Glut, *Prophets of the Dark Side* by Paul and Hollace Davids] tundra cave-dwelling, white-furred, 2-meter tall biped with yellow eyes, sharp claws and teeth that capture prey alive for larder from Hoth, Jedi galaxy

wampus: [*Monster Spotter's Guide to North America* by Scott Francis] 1.8-meter, panther-like felinoid from Appalachia, in right and left-sidewinding varieties

wampus cat: aka wampuss, bipedal felinoid with glowing red eyes, large fangs from Appalachia, Terra (alpha Zodiaci III)

wan: ["Conflence" by Brian Aldiss] race tortoise from Myrin; [wedge of swans spoonerism, wanderer mondegreen] derer relative

wanderer: [*National Geographic Encyclopedia of Animals*] seeds, leaves and invertebrate-eating bird from Australia

wanderoo: large kangeroo

wandrella: [*Splinter of the Mind's Eye* by Alan Dean Foster] huge, phosphorescent brown-streaked cream-colored worm-like omnivore with-brown-slashes, eye-spot clusters, sharp black teeth, armored underside locomotion suckers from Jedi galaxy, see wan and drella

warble fly: [*The New Dinosaurs* by Dougal Dixon] tromble pest, whiffle prey

warg: [*The Hobbit* by J. R. R. Tolkien] demonic and/or dire wolf from Middle Earth

wargator: [warg alligator portmanteau] alligator-like predator whose bite morphs victim into warg

wari: ["Turning Point" by Josepha Sherman] red ornithoid from Thallon, Thallonian empire

warke: [*Voiage de Sir John Maundevile*] elephant-like pachyderm from Calonack

warni: ["Battle of Ferrol" by Michael Marcus Thurner] algae-eating hippoid from Ferrol (Vega (alpha Lyrae) VIII)

warsop: ["Wing Commander" by Kevin Droney] egg-laying reptile from Frase

warun: ["The Web" by Michelle Stern] blue ornithoid

warun: ["The Web" by Michelle Stern] blue ornithoid

wasabee: [Monster Galaxy] insectoid moga with superspicy-hot poison from Gemini constellation

wasch: [Germ. Waschbär back-formation] raccoon-bear, ursoid with mask and ringed tail, ancestral to bear and raccoon
washiká: [Jap. washi-shiká portmanteau] eagle-deer griffinoid
wasket: [*There's a Wocket in My Pocket* by Seuss] 50-cm, pink doll-like biped
wasohla: [Cherokee] moth-like insectoid from Tsalagi system
waspeater: [*The New Dinosaurs* by Dougal Dixon] green and yellow, scaly, wasp-eating arbrosaur
waspider: [wasp spider portmanteau] wasp-like arachnoid
waste: [Special Unit 2: "The Waste" by Joel Surnow] fat golem
watac: [catawa watac palindrome] purple grape-colored ornithoid
watch-wher: [Pern series by Ann McCaffrey] geneered omnivorous, lizard beast-of-burden and tracker in gold, brown, blue, green and bronze varieties from Pern (Rukbat (alpha Sagittaurii) III)

water bear: [*The Big Bad Book of Beasts* by Michael Largo] aka tardigrade, moss piglet, extremophile with 8 clawed legs, 4-segmented body able to survive extreme cold, vacuum, heat and radiation, in tun (dormant) state
water cow: [water-cow mondegreen] cow-likw golem made from water
water dog: [water-dog mondegreen] dog-like golem made from water
water dragon: [*A Hero's Guide to Deadly Dragons* by Hiccup Haddock III] desert sandy or mustard yellow dragon with water-storing hump and powerful waterjet from Barbarian archipelago
water echidna: [water-echidna mondegreen] echidna-like golem made from water
water elephant: [water-elephant mondegreen] elephant-like golem made from water
water leaper: [*An Encyclopedia of Fairies, Hobgoblins, Brownies and Other Supernatural Creatures* by Katherine Briggs] giant, bipedal frog with wings, long lizard-like tail from Wales, Terra (alpha Zodiaci III)
water monkey: lake-dwelling simian from China, Terra (alpha Zodiaci III)
water panther: see mishibizhiw
water serpent: [*Mothstorm* by Philip Reeve] large aquatic serpentoid from Ganymede (alpha Zodiaci Vc)
water worm: [Xanth series by Piers Anthony] worm that turns creature it touches into water from Water Isle, Isles of Joey, Xanth
water-bear: [water bear mondegreen] bear-like golem made from wood
water-cow: manatee-like sea creature from St. Mary's Loch, Scotland, Terra (alpha Zodiaci III)
water-dog: [*River Monsters* by Jeremy Wade] hydrocynus or tigerfish
water-dogator: [water-dog alligator portmanteau] alligator-like predator whose bite morphs victim into tigerfish
water-dragon: [water dragon mondegreen] dracoid golem made from water
water-echidna: ["A Fact Sheet for the *Marco Polo*" and "The City and the Spaceship" by Hans Kneifel] 20-cm fish-like echnidna with both gills and weak lungs from Leffa, Mayselan system, Sombrero galaxy
water-elephant: elephant as small as a mouse, but strong enough to threaten elephants upon whose brains it feeds, source of elephant's mouse-phobia, from Burma, Terra (alpha Zodiaci III)
water-horse: see kelpie
water-monkey: [water monkey mondegreen] simian golem made from water
water-panther: [water panther mondegreen] panther-like golem made from water
water-serpent: [water serpent mondegreen] serpent-like golem made from water
water-waif: [water waif mondegreen] waif-like golem made from water
water-wyrm: [water wyrm mondegreen] wyem-like golem made from water
waterhog: aquatic porcoid, minihippoid

waterhogator: [waterhog alligator portmanteau] alligator-like predator whose bite morphs victim into waterhog
waterhogg: aquatic hogg
waterhoggator: [waterhogg alligator portmanteau] alligator-like predator whose bite morphs victim into waterhogg
waterwaif: [*Edge Chronicles* by Paul Stewart and Chris Riddell] waif variant living near water
waterwyrm: [*The New Dinosaurs* by Dougal Dixon] wyrm adapted for water
watoo: [*After Man* by Dougal Dixon] rabbuck variant
watt: [Outernauts] immature dekawatt
wawee: [*The Yowie: In Seach of Australian Bigfoot* by Tony Healy and Paul Cropper] see yowie
wax golem: golem made from wax
weakfish: [*Dell Crossword Puzzle Dictionary*] acupa
wease: felinoid predator of small squeaking rodentoids in turn preyed upon by greels
weatar: [Monster Galaxy] blue squirrel-like rodentoid
web worm: [webworm mondegreen] worm-like golem made from webbing
webweaver: [*Han Solo and the Lost Legacy* by Brian Daley] large, deadly, lower-level forest arachnoid from Kashÿyÿk, Jedi galaxy
weebil: [boll weevil spoonerism] small, vole-like rodentoid
weebilope: [weebil antelope portmanteau] weebil with antlers
weep: [weeplet backformation] large, weeplet-like jelly
weeplet: [Monster Galaxy] squishy gelatinous but with spikes from Pisces constellation
weezit: [*Edge Chronicles* by Paul Stweart and Chris Riddell] long-armed, fanged arboreal predator of wind-welks and cray-spinners
wek: [skewbald lab weks palindrome] spotted laboratory animals
weka: [*Dell Crossword Puzzle Dictionary*] wood hen or rail bird from New Zeeland, Terra (alpha Zodiaci III)

welcome-homer: [*Uhura's Song* by Janet Kagon] arboreal throwers from Sivao
wellington: [Cyclopedia of Worlds] hermaphroditic hexapodal carnivore up to 30 meters tall on Palul (Lar Don), the Dinosaur Planet
wels: [*River Monsters* by Jeremy Wade] 3-meter, 230-kg giant catfish from Danube river, Terra (alpha Zodiaci III)
welter-wing: ["The Long Midwinter" by Philip Purser-Hallard] flying creature from Yesod, Tiphereth-Kether system
welter-wingator: [welter-wing alligator portmanteau] alligator-like predator whose bite morphs victim into welter-wing
wendingo: [Algonquin] aka windingo, large, furry, skinny man-eater with big eyes
wenguin: [weeble of penguins spoonerism] white polar ornithoid with flipper-like wings and black underbelly
wentelteefje: ['Dut. 'curl-up", M. C. Escher] 6-legged, eyestalked, segmented creature able to curl up like a wheel
werik: [Afrikaans leeuwerik back-formation] lark-lion griffinoid ancestral to lion and lark
werje: [*Nick and the Glimmung* by Philip K. Dick] wrinkled umbrella-like leathery glider with claws and hollow eye sockets from Plowman's planet
wermine: [worm-ermine portmanteau] wooly caterpillar-like furry
werp: [Antwerp mondegreen] ant parasite from Belgium, Terra (alpha Zodiaci III)
wesa: [Cherokee] felinoid from Tsalagi system
wespect: [Afrikaans wesp-spect portmanteau] wasp-woodpecker, small wasp-like ornithoid living in hollowed tree
wespin: [Dutch wesp-spin portmanteau] wasp-spider, insect-like arachnoid
weta: [*Dell Crossword Puzzle Dictionary*] locust from New Zealand, Terra (alpha Zodiaci III)
wetsh: [wetsh stew palindrome] food animal
whackin' blight: [black'n'white spoonerism] white amphibious cephalopod with black stripes and whip-like and paddle-like tentacles

whale: [Xanth series by Piers Anthony] land cetacean with 4 lion-like legs, boar-like head with tusks and spike-lined body from Xanth or [Xanthian mondegreen] Xa, Thia system
whale-fish: [whalefish mondegreen] whale-mimicking ichthyoid
whangdoodle: [Ronald Dahl] forest-dwelling centipede
Wharton's Swamp monster: ["Slime" by Joseph Payne Brennan] gray-black voracious amorph from ocean floor able to move at nightmarish that eats frogs, snakes, mammals, Humans
what-do-you-know: [*If I Ran the Zoo* by Seuss] aka wajano, 3-meter walrus-like sea creature with upward-turned tusks, flipper-thumbs
what-was-it: ["The Hitchhiker's Guide to the Galaxy" movie] rooted, rust-brown pole-like creature with top rectangle that smacks anyone with an idea
wheelie: [Robert G. Rogers] quadruped with ball-and-socket hip joints that moves by alternately rolling on and rewinding large circular padded feet-wheels
wherrie: [Pern series by Ann McCaffrey] large, carnivorous griffinoid from Pern (Rukbat (alpha Sagitaurii) III)
whiffle: [*The New Dinosaurs* by Dougal Dixon] small, flightless insectivorous companion to tromble
whinebear: [wineberry backformation] ursinoid that whines
whip phage: [Resident Evil 4] whip-like phage
whipe: [whisp of snipes spoonerism, whiptail snipe portmanteau] snipe-like ornithoid with whip-like tail
whiptail: [*National Geographic Encyclopedia of Animals*] herbivorous lizard from W. U. S., Terra alpha Zodiaci III)
whistlepig: see woodchuck
whistlepigator: [whistlepig alligator portmanteau] alligator-like predator whose bite morphs victim into whistlepig
whistler: [*After Man* by Dougal Dixon] ornithoid in massive-beaked nut-eater, pointed-beaked insectivore, hook-beaked

flesh-tearing and golden varieties from Pacaus Islands
white hunter: ["Grandpa" by James Schmitz] large, white, herding shark-like ichthyoid from Sutang
white mercy: black mercy fungus-eater
white pudding: [*Monster Manual* by Skip Williams, etal.] pudding-thick ooze adapted to arctic
white non-raven: [Carl Gustav "Peter" Hempel] white creatures not ravens
white pudding: [pudding extrapolation] pudding-thick ooze, see vanilla puddling
white raven: [Carl Gustav "Peter" Hempel] non-black raven associated with every white non-raven
white tiger: aka [Chin.] báitŭ, [Jap.] byakko, [Kor.] baekho
white-white: [Continuum] large seabird from Lemur (aka Korina)
whitefish: [*Dell Crossword Puzzle Dictionary*] cisco; [Pern series by Ann McCaffrey] food ichthyoid from Pern (Rukbat (alpha Sagittarii) III)
whitengale: [watch of nightingales spoonerism] cliff-dwelling ornithoid which whitens cliffs with droppings
whitey: [*Monster Spotter's Guide to North America* by Scott Francis] legally protected, 9-meter, mottled (NOT white) serpentine with spiny backbone from White River, Ark., Terra (alpha Zodiaci III)
wholesnouter: [*The Snouters* by Harald Stümpke] allsnouter including Holorrhinus variegatus with buckle-shaped brain and H. rhinenterus aka Pinnochio's wholesnouter
whomp: [SuperMario 64] see nurikabe
whoopee: [whooper backformation] mocking bird-like prey of whooping predators
whorilla: [whoop of gorillas spoonerism] large predatory pongoids
whortlebear: [whortleberry backformation] usinoid from Bil, Whortle system
whown: [white-brown portmanteau] white beast that turns brown in the spring, see brite beast

whuffa: [*The Courtship of Princess Leia* by Dave Wolverton] long, tough worm used as rope from Dathomir, Jedi galaxy
whydah: [*National Geographic Encyclopedia of Animals*] seed-eating songbird from Africa
widdlefly: ["Protective Mimicry" by Alguis Bulgess] large biting insectoid from Deneb XI
wide-mouth frog: [*Genius Loci* by Ben Aaronovitch] geneered as translator/datapad from Jaiwan, see chuba
widehead: ["The Empress of Therm" by William Voltz] food ichthyoid from Drackrioch (Yoxa-Sant III), Nypasor-Xon galaxy
widgiebird: ["Placet Is A Crazy Place" by Frederick Brown] superdense ornithoid that flies through Placet, Argyle system
wigeon: [*National Geographic Encyclopedia of Animals*] duck from Europe, Terra (alpha Zodiaci III)
wiggle-worm: ["The Chosen People" by Robert Randall] larval hugl, not affected by edris powder, [Xanth series by Piers Anthony] larval wiggle; [Odd Squad] spiral, photonic creature allergic to Humans, with egg very similar to kraken's
wiggle: [Xanth series by Piers Anthony] sub-vole one-tenth the size of a diggle, dangerous when in worm-like larval swarm able to zap through anything, but harmless once they find the kind of rock they need from under Xanth
wilderburr: [Cloudstone] clawed monster
wildkin: [Warcraft III] see owlbear
wilk: [*Dell Crossword Puzzle Dictionary*] marine snail, see w(h)elk
willo: [Monster Galaxy] nocturnal, blue ichthyoid with curly crest from Libra constellation
Wimplemeyer toad: [*The Deadly Experiments of Dr. Eeek* by R. L. Stine] giant, singing toad geneered by Herbert "Dr. Eeek" Wimplemeyer
wind-whale: [*Larklight* by Philip Reeve] from Jupiter (alpha Zodiaci V), see air-whale
windalgo: [*Zorgamzoo* by Robert Paul Weston] large pongoid with long, thin arms;
windingo: arboreal wendingo that sounds like wind

windrunner: [The Future Is Wild by Dougal Dixon] blue crane-like ornithoid with long, narrow gliding-wings and feathered wing-like legs for maneuvering, canards (feathery eyebrows) for stability, males more "colorful" in uv
wing slug: ["Menage a Troi" by Fred Bronson and Susan Sackett] winged slug-like creature from Orion constellation
wing-tail: see caudipteryx
wingcow: [Xanth series by Piers Anthony] aka pegataur from Xanth
winged behemoth: [Xanth series by Piers Anthony] large flying beast used for mass transportation from Xanth
winged buffalo: [Buffalo wings back-formation] buffalo-like pegataur
winged cat: [Superman] aka flitty, feline pegasoid from Krypton, Rao system,
winged croc: [Showcase #91: "The Planet of Death"] crocodile-like pterosaur in purple, quadrupedal and reptilian-headed with 3 headfins and backspikes varieties from Pheidos
winged wolf: ["The Monster Master" by Jerry Siegel] see flolf, lupopteryx
winipogo: [Monster Spotter's Guide to North America by Scott Francis] manipogo from Lake Winnipeg, Terra (alpha Zodiaci III)
winnip: cold-adapted serpentoid noted for its eggs
winnipede: [winnip centipede portmanteau] winnip mimic with many legs
wintail: [Terra Monster] pale blue and white fox with forehead horn, long mane, bushy tail, see flofox and cyclonine from Terrarium
wip: [kai-wip back-formation] creature ancestral to kai and kai-wip or zatcher
wire-haired cow: [Xanth series by Piers Anthony] small, shaggy bovine that gives shaving cream from Xanth
wisent: [*National Geographic Encyclopedia of Animals*] bison from Europe, Terra (alpha Zodiaci III)
witiku: [*The Price of Paradise* by Colin Brake] red-eyed wolf-like caninoid with thick, black hair from Laylora

wock: [wocket backformation] larger variety of wocket (gopher-mouse)

wocket: [*There's a Wocket in my Pocket* by Theodore Seuss Geissel, pocket gopher-pocket mouse] pocket mouse-gopher, see mrehpo

wodah: [shadowy wodah palindrome] black elusive forest-dweller

woerdief: [Afrikaans woerd-dief palindrome] mallard-ferret, burrowing and aquatic griffinoid

wogneer: ["Allegience" by Richard Manning and Hans Beimer] life-form from Ordek nebula

woh: [red woh chowder palindrome] red food animal

woháli: [Cherokee] eagle-like ornithoid from Tsalagi system

wol-la-chee: [Navaho] ant-like insectoid from Diné system

wolf-bear: [wolfberry backformation] wolf-headed ursinoid, see cub

wolf-fish: [wolfish mondegreen] wolf-headed ichthyoid

wolf-liobear: chimera like wolf, lion and bear, see cub

wolf-lion: wolf-headed lion-like felinoid, see cub

wolf-spider: [wolf spider mondegreen] wolf-headed arachnoid

wolferine: [wolf-wolverine portmanteau] burrowing caninoid with gray fur and bushy tail

wolfra: [wolframite backformation] small insectoid that infests wolves

woll: ["woll at times emit tallow" palindrome] bee-like insectoid that produces tallow

wolpertinger: [museumofhoaxes.com by Alex Boese] furry, webfooted triphibian with antlers, fangs, feathered wings [*Here Be Monsters almanac*] from Bavaria, Terra (alpha Zodiaci III), see dilldapp, rauracki, rosselbock, volpertinger

wolvus: [Terra Monster] blue-and-gold striped, electric ratcatcher with bushy tail, wide jaws, see maulverine, from Terrarium

womp rat: ["A New Hope" by George Lucas] vicious 3-meter rodentian with mane and hairy back from Tatooine, Jedi galaxy

wompat: ["Chain of Command" by Frank Abatemarco] pet from Cardassia

wonkey: [wilderness of monkeys spoonerism] most mild-mannered monkey

wood cock: [woodcock mondegreen] cock-like golem made from wood

wood lark: [woodlark mondegreen] lark-like golem made from wood

wood louse: aka pillbug, roly-poly, slater, sowbug that moves by curling and rolling

wood throck: ["Persistence of Vision" by Jeri Taylor] forest-dwelling food creature from Delta Quadrant, see throck; throck-like golem made from wood

wood worm: [woodworm mondegreen] worm-like golem made from wood

wood woose: [woodwoose mondegreen] woose-like golem made from wood

wood-duck: [wood duck mondegreen] decoy duck-like golem made from wood

wood-frog: [wood frog mondegreen] frog-like golem made from wood

wood-frogator: wood frog alligator portmanteau] alligator-like predator whose bite morphs victim into wood frog

wood-grouse: [wood grouse mondegreen] grouse-like golem made from wood

wood-hen: [wood hen mondegreen] hen-like golem made from wood

wood-louse: [wood louse mondegreen] louse-like golem made from wood

wood-mouse: [wood mouse mondegreen] mouse-like golem made from wood

wood-robin: [wood robin mondegreen] robin-like golem made from wood

wood-thrush: [wood thrush mondegreen] thrush-like golem made from wood

wood-warbler: [wood warbler mondegreen] warbler-like golem made from wood

woodchucker: [woodchuck extrapolation] arboreal creature that chucks bark and branches on passersby

woodoo: [*Creatures of the Galaxy* by Phil Brucato, Bill Smith, Rick D. Stuart, Chuck Truett] carnivorous, ground-dwelling ornithoid from Tatooine, Jedi galaxy

woodwoose: ["Dear Mom" by Stephen C. Fisher] man-sized blue-black lagardbird from La Paz

woofen-poof: [Augustus C. Fotheringham, museumofhoaxes.com by Alex Boese] 17-cm short-winged pelican-like bird from Gobi desert, Terra (alpha Zodiaci III)

woogle: [woogle-bug backformation] creature that the woogle-bug bugs

woogle-bug: [*The Woogle-bug Book* by L. Frank Baum] pea-sized, 6-legged insectoid with brown and white stripes from Oz

woogle-bugator: [woogle-bug alligator portmanteau] alligator-like predator whose bite morphs victim into woggle-bug

wooker: [*The Cry of the Onlies* by Judy Klass] large, furry, rank-smelling, arboreal rodentian with that wooks with its clammy, spongy, clingy toes from Boaco IV

woolamander: [*Creatures of the Galaxy* by Phil Brucato, Bill Smith, Rick D. Stuart, Chuck Truett] blue-furred pongoid with long multi-colored face and tail, prominent belly, prey of syntaril from Yavin IV, Jedi galaxy

woolf: [Monster Galaxy] wooly, neckless, large-mouthed creature with ram's horn from Aries constellation

wooly hen: [Xanth series by Piers Anthony] fast flying bird with curly fleece from Xanth

wooly newt: [Flonk News: "A 'Rotini Worm' Fossil on Mars?"] wooly newt from Aldebar

woon: [worry of loons spoonerism] ornithoid that nests on trucks

woose: [woodwoose backformation] large flightless ornithoid

worb: [brown worb palindrome] brown (dark yellow-red) furry

worker fly: [Xanth series by Piers Anthony] insectoid from Land of Flies, Xanth

world-destroyer: ["The World-Destroyer Beast" by Jerry Siegel] space beast that destroys worlds

wormzer: [*The Ultimate Monster Guide* by Jaymond] purple, burrowing omnivore

worrt: aka frog-dog, omnivorous, orange, rock-dwelling insectoid that injects poisonous neurotoxin into host for larva

worththerm: [earthworm spoonerism] large furry iceworm hunted for its pelt from Draapaa, Albina system, Galaxiki galaxy

woset: [*There's a Wocket in My Pocket* by Seuss] 2-meter, yellow, long-eared, long-necked web-footed, dogfaced bird

wover: [wing of plovers, winging plover portmanteau] leg-less murre-plover-like ornithoid

wowlf: [wolf-owl portmanteau] nocturnal wolf-headed owl-like griffinoid with large head and eyes

wōya: [Cherokee] dove-like ornithoid from Tsalagi system

wraid: [*Creatures of the Galaxy* by Phil Brucato, Bill Smith, Rick D. Stuart, Chuck Truett] large, lizard-like creature hunted for armored head plates from Tatooine or Korriban, Jedi galaxy

wraith: ["Queen of Air and Darkness" by Poul Anderson] cell swarm from Roland

wrasse: [*National Geographic Encyclopedia of Animals*] reef fish of Indo-Pacific, Terra (alpha Zodiaci III)

wrasse: [*Dell Crossword Puzzle Dictionary*] peacock fish

wreathsnake: [*People from the Retort* by H. G. Ewers] ectoparasite of that lays eggs in skin of host from Refuge (Ubigeir VIII)

wrongwhale: [rightwhale antonym] anglewhale not a rightwhale, an obtuse whale or a cute whale

wrongworm: [rightworm antonym] angleworm not a rightworm, obtuse worm or a cute worm

wu: [xuánwŭ mondegreen] turtle-snake from Xua system

wuffalo: [water buffalo portmanteau] web-footed buffaloid amphibian

wug: ["The Child's Learning of English Morphology" by Jean Berko] cute "imaginary" creature

wugator: [wug alligator portmanteau] alligator-like predator whose bite morphs victim into wug

wulkarsh: [*Creatures of the Galaxy* by Phil Brucato, Bill Smith, Rick D. Stuart, Chuck

Truett] solitary hexapod jungle predator from Joralla, Jedi galaxy

wulture: [wake of vultures, wulkarsh vulture portmanteau] 6-legged, vulture-like pegasoid

wumbus: [*If I Ran the Zoo* by Theodore Seuss Geissel] pink, bipedal, mountain cetacean from Tibet, Terra (alpha Zodiaci III)

wurmaus: [German Wurm-Maus portmanteau] worm-mouse, leg-less rodentoid

wuzzard: [wake of buzzards spoonerism] food ornithoid

wuzzy: ["Fuzzy Wuzzy"] ursinopongoid, bear-headed gorilla-like pongoid, see naked bear

wyrm: [*The New Dinosaurs* by Dougal Dixon] orange desert vermisaur with black stripes, red, armored head, belly and rump, 2 legs, long neck, see treewyrm, waterwyrm

wystryscwrystrys: [Welsh] oyster-cwystrys ancestral to oyster and cwystrys

xac: [xac-gel, xac-yij mondegreens] Energon sphere with one eyespot and swimming tentacles, ancestor of xac-gel, xac-yij

xac-gel: [*Planar Handbook* by Bruce Cordell, etal.] fire-energy Energon sphere with 2 eyespots and swimming tentacles

xac-yij: [*Planar Handbook* by Bruce Cordell, etal.] acid Energon sphere with 2 eyespots and swimming tentacles

xag: [xag-az, xag-ya mondegreens] Energon sphere with one eyespot, ancestor to xag-az and xag-ya

xagator: [xag alligator portmanteau] alligator-like predator whose bite morphs victim into xag

xag-az: [*Planar Handbook* by Bruce Cordell, etal.] psychic-energy Energon sphere with 2 eyespots

xag-ya: [*Planar Handbook* by Bruce Cordell, etal.] positive-energy Energon sphere with 2 eyespots and swimming tentacles

xangelfish: [Xanthian angelfish portmanteau] angelfish from Xa, Thia system

xamilimax: [mynynym] slug-like creature from Xami system

xanthocyne: [Continuum] 1-tonne, 4-meter yellow canine from Igendal, Belverius Helenis system, see cyanocyne

xap: [xap-yaup mondegreen] Energon sphere with one eyespot and swimming tentacles, ancestor of xap-yaup

xap-yaup: [*Planar Handbook* by Bruce Cordell, etal.] electrical-energy Energon sphere with 2 eyespots and swimming tentacles

xartatrax: [mynynym] funnel-web spider-like arachnoid from Xarta system

xat: [*The Sword of Lankor* by Howard L. Cory] soft-padding creature from Lankor

xeg: [xeg-yi mondegreen] Energon sphere with one eyespot, ancestor to xeg-yi

xeg-yi: [*Planar Handbook* by Bruce Cordell, etal.] negative-energy Energon sphere with 2 eyespots and swimming tentacles

xegator: [xeg alligator portmanteau] alligator-like predator whose bite morphs victim into xeg

xeluculex: [mynynym] mosquitoid from Xelu system

xelxa: ["To Him Who Waits" by H. G. Stratmann] coprophagous parasite used as laxative on Lactomagnyzia V

xeme: fork-tailed arctic gull

xemicimex: [mynynym] bedbug-like insectoid from Xemi system

xenicohippo: [xenicohippus hippo portmanteau] hippoid from Xenico system

xenicohippus: [*After the Dinosaurs* by Donald R. Prothero] horse from Ypresian age (early Eocene)

xenosaur: strange lizard from Calypso

xenotaur: [xerosaur minotaur portmanteau] strange bovinoid

xerophile: extremophile resistant to extreme dryness

Xian aix: [mynynym] wood duck-like ornithoid from Xia, Xi system

xiaoxia: [Chin. new internet user] small lobster-like crustacean

xicantid: [Cyclopedia of Worlds] hermaphroditic egg-laying hexapod on Palul (Lar Don), the Dinosaur Planet

xilehelix: [mynynym] snail-like creature from Xile system

ximbopithecus: ["Planet of the Knob-Heads" by Stanton A. Coblentz] nearly brainless pongoid from Ximbo

xinrutocoturnix: [mynynym] quail-like ornithoid from Xinrut system

xirdor: ["Planet pof Storms" by Michelle Stern] white anti-grav carpet-like flyer in pack of 9 from Thersunt

xirdoor: [xirdor door portmanteau] magic carpet-like creature able to travel through portals

xiulador: [Catalan ànec xiulador back-formation] widgeon-like ornithoid ancestral to duck and widgeon

xiuladoor: [xiulador door portmanteau] duck-widgeon-like ornithoid able to travel through portals

xnylolynx: [mynynym] lynx-like felinoid from Xnyl system

xol: [Fr. Johann Martin Schleyer's Volapük] ox-like bovinoid from Schleyer's system

xong: [xong-yong mondegreen] Energon sphere with one eyespot and swimming tentacles, ancestor to xong-yong

xong-yong: [*Planar Handbook* by Bruce Cordell, etal.] sonic-energy Energon sphere with 2 eyespots and swimming tentacles

xongator: [xong alligator portmanteau] alligator-like predator whose bite morphs victim into xong

xooplankton: exotic zooplankton

xor: [xor-yost mondegreen] Energon sphere with one eyespot and swimming tentacles

xor-yost: [*Planar Handbook* by Bruce Codell, etal.] heat-energy Energon sphere with 2 eyespots and swimming tentacles

Xoxian virus: [Marvel: "Telepathy War"] anti-telepathic virus from Xox

xuaedrob: [bordeaux xuaedrob palindrome] red or white ornithoid

xuánwǔ: [Chin.] see turtle-snake

xuth: [Thongor series by Lin Carter] "unthinkably huge" slimy, gelatinous, pain-insensitive worm from Lemuria

xybmobombyx: [mynynym] silkworm-like creature from Xybmo system

xyccoccyx: [mynynym] creature with tail at both ends, see anæbsihpma

xyecoceyx: mynynym] kingfisher-like ornithoid from Xyec system

xyremomeryx: [mynynym] deer-like ruminant from Xyrem system

xyretpopteryx: [mynynym] flying creature from Xyretpo system

xyroryx: [mynynym] oryx-like ornithoid from Xyr system

xyxyl: [*The Dirdir, The Pnume* by Jack Vance] sacred ornithoid from Sibol

xyzor: [Outernauts] "skeletal chameleon", see xyzyzaur

xyzyzaur: [Outernauts] blue xyzor with purple spots, red eyes, pink underbelly

ya: [Catalan aranya backformation] arachnoid, related to ha, from Ara constellation; [gaya mondegreen] gray-green goat-like herd creature; [xag-ya mondegreen] Energon sphere with one eyespot and swimming tentacles, xag-ya ancestor; [tsiya backformation] wren-otter grifflnold

yacket: [yellowjacket spoonerism] insectoid jello predator

yaf: [fayaan ananymondegreen] carnivorous lute-shaped ichthyoid from Aa rogue planet

yaffle: green woodpecker

yagrum: [Superman mythos] rare, dangerous monster from Krypton, Rao system

yahoo: [*The Yowie: In Seach of Australian Bigfoot* by Tony Healy and Paul Cropper] see yowie

yani: [Swahili nyani elision] baboon-like pongoid

yank: ["Bird-watchers' Slang" by Paul Beale] bird from America, Terra (alpha Zodiaci III)

yanka: [beheaded uyanka] 3-headed hydra-like dracoid

yantis: [Terra Monster] levitating, blue quadruped with white markings, large beak and ears and small wings, see buntis, from Terrarium

yara: [Monster Galaxy] legless crab-like moga with heart-shaped ears and feet, humanoid face from Cancer constellation
yarcan: ["The Day Super-Horse Went Wild" by Leo Dorfman] mutant beast from Krypton, Rao system
yardworm: larger variety of footworm
yarg: see yerg
yargator: [yarg alligator portmanteau] alligator-like predator whose bite morphs victim into yarg
yarlap: [*Throy* by Jack Vance] wild beast from Throy
yat: [Fr. Johann Martin Schleyer's Volapük] squirrel-like rodentoid from Schleyer's system
yatagarasu: 3-legged raven from Japan, Terra (alpha Zodiaci III), see samjogo
yathrib: [Callisto series by Lin Carter] fierce tiger-like dracoid with emerald scales fading to tawny yellow on underside, back spikes, lashing, snake-like tail, bird-like claws from Thanator
yati: [Swahili nyati elision] buffaloid
yaup: [xap-yaup mondegreen] Energon sphere with one eye and swimming tentacles, ancestor of xap-yaup
yawm: [Resident Evil] huge snake infected with T-virus
yayax: ["Ewoks" series] fierce panther-like felinoid from Endor's moon, Jedi galaxy
ybbuh: [shabby ybbuhs palindrome] rather ugly beast-of-burden
ycamel: [aepycamel mondegreen] chartreuse yellow giraffe-like camel
ycamelope: [ycamel antelope portmanteau] ycamel with antlers
ycolagre: [tanycolagreus mondegreen] long-armed tyrannosauroid from Ta system
yd: [dynafly ananymondegreen] electric insectoid from Ylfa system
yddur: [ruddy yddur portmanteau] ruddy (reddish-brown with tickings of dark brown or black or reddish-rosy crimson) furry
ydeep: [speedy ydeeps palindrome] cheetah-like rodentoid
ydnac: [candyapple elppa ydnac palindrome] orangish red ornithoid, see elppa, nottoc

ydnu: [burgundy ydnu grub palindrome] insectoid with reddish brown larvae
yean: [*Dell Crossword Puzzle Dictionary*] lamb, ewe, ean
yedbird: [grue-bleen extrapolation] yellow bird that turns red, not to be confused with blellowbird, bledbird, gebird, gredbird, grellowbird, redbird, reenbird, rellowbird, rindigobird, rioletbird, ruebird, vedbird, vellowbird, yedbird, yeenbird, yellowbird, yindigobird, yioletbird and yuebird from Ora system
yeenbird: [grue-bleen extrapolation] yellow bird that turns green, not to be confused with bleenbird, blellowbird, gebird, gredbird, greenbird, grellowbird, grindigobird, grioletbird, gruebird, reenbird, rellowbird, veenbird, vellowbird, yedbird, yeenbird, yellowbird, yindigobird, yioletbird or yuebird from Ora system
yeki: [The Queen of Zamba by L. Sprague de Camp] tiger-sized, 6-legged mink-like creature from Krishna, tau Ceti system
yekko: [*On Beyond Zebra* by Theodore Seuss Geissel] furry-crested biped with horizontal stripes and flat feet from Gekko
yelk: [Helliconia trilogy by Brian Aldiss, see biyelk] creature from Helliconia, Batalix-Freyr system
yellow dog: [*Old Yeller* by Fred Gibson] see xanthocyne
yellow dogator: [yellow dog alligator portmanteau] alligator-like predator whose bite morphs victim into xanthocyne
yellow pterodactyl: ["Summons from Space"] pterodactyl-like creature from Venus (alpha Zodiaci III)
yellow top: [*Monster Spotter's Guide to North America* by Scott Francis] 2.1-meter, black nape with yellow top hair from nr. Cobalt, Ontario, Terra (alpha Zodiaci III)
yellowbird: [grue-bleen extrapolation] yellow bird that remains yellow, not to be confused with blellowbird, gebird, grellowbird, rellowbird, vellowbird, yedbird, yeenbird, yindigobird, yioletbird or yuebird from Ora system

yellowhead: ["Grandpa" by James Schmitz] swift and vicious, though flabby-looking, man-sized batrachoid with vertical toothed mouth from Sutang

yellowl: [yellow-owl portmanteau] ornithoid with hooked and feathered talons, large heads with short beaks, large forward-looking eyes and fluffy yellow plumage

yelsimi: ["Face To Face With Planet Scanodon" by Rocky Strone] small sponge-like amphibious filter-feeder up to 15 cm from Scandon

yeltz: [*Creatures of the Galaxy* by Phil Brucato, Bill Smith, Rick D. Stuart, Chuck Truett] amphibian, transparent and predatory in water, from Lupania ring, Jedi galaxy

yembla: [Thongor series by Lin Carter] large, purple, flying arachnoid from Lemuria

yendi: [yendi kidney palindrome] food dracoid from Gaa system, see etha

yeomet: [*Creatures of the Galaxy* by Phil Brucato, Bill Smith, Rick D. Stuart, Chuck Truett] omnivorous scavenger quadruped

yep: [*If I Ran the Zoo* by Theodore Seuss Geissel] 2.5-meter horned, green biped with long snout, yellow toe-tuffs

yer: [yer prey palindrome] omnivorous predator

yérc: [Hung. nyérc elision] mink-like mammaloid

yeren: 2-meter red-haired pongoid from China, Terra (alpha Zodiaci III)

yerg: [grey yerg palindrome] aka yarg, gray furry

yergator: [yerg alligator portmanteau] alligator-like predator whose bite morphs victim into yerg

yeth: [yeth-hound backformation] corpse-animating symbiot with 2 yellow "eyes", see reth

yeth-hound: [*The Denham Tracts* by Michael Aislabie Denham, etal.] headless, black, photophobic dog yet with yellow eyes

yeti: [Tib. "rock bear"] large, white ursinoid from Himayalas, Terra (alpha Zodiaci III), see himamanāv, dzu-teh

yeticlaw: [Terra Monster] long-armed, white-furred, blue-faced pongoid with curved horns, upward fangs, 3-toed feet from Terrarium

yeticrab: [Terra Monster] small relative of yeticlaw from Terrarium

yetiking: [Terra Monster] large pongid with large orange and black lobster-like claws not limited to arctic, see yeticrab and yeticlaw, from Terrarium

yetikingator: [yetiking alligator portmanteau] alligator-like predator whose bite morphs victim into yetiking

yff: ["yff at times emit taffy" palindrome] creature that secretes taffy-like substance

ygg: [scraggy ygg racs palindrome] lean, boney rac

yggah: [shaggy yggahs palindrome] long-haired furry

yggip: [piggy yggip palindrome] pink pigasus

yggipede: [yggip centipede portmanteau] pink porcoid with many legs

yggo: [soggy yggos palindrome] marsh-dwelling creature

yh: [shy yhs mynynym] rarely seen creature

yhal: [Hung. arahyal backformation] goldfish-like ichthyoid from Ara constellation

yi: [xeg-yi mondegreen] Energon sphere with one eyespot and swimming tentacles, ancestor of xeg-yi

yie: fat, little and sweet non-sauroid burrower, some of which are black-furred from T'Khasi, Nevasa (40 Eridani) system

yihauhau: [yap of chichuahuas spoonerism] small, pesty chigger-like caninoid fond of legs

yindigobird: [gru-bleen extrapolation] yellow bird that turns indigo, not to be confused with blellowbird, blindigobird, gebird, grindigobird, indigobird, rellowbird, rindigobird, vellowbird, vindigobird, yedbird, yeenbird, yellowbird, yindigobird, yioletbird, yuebird from Ora system

yij: [xac-yij mondegreen] Energon sphere with one eyespot and swimming tentacles, ancestor of xac-yij

yioletbird: [grue-bleen extrapolation] yellow bird that turns violet, not to be confused with blellowbird, blioletbird, gebird, grellowbird, grioletbird, rellowbird, rioletbird, vellowbird, violetbird, yedbird, yeenbird, yellowbird, yindigobird, yioletbird or yuebird from Ora system

yip: yipyip nasna

yippa: [*After Man* by Dougal Dixon] long-necked antelope

yipyip: [Outernauts] legless, immature yupyak

yipyipede: [yipyip centipede portmanteau] mutant yipyip with many legs

yknit: [stinky yknits palindrome] malodorous creature

yksud: [dusky yksud palindrome] dusky-colored ornithoid

yl: [sly yls mynynym] fox-like predator; [lynar ananymondegreen] cheiropteroid from Ra system

ylf: [i-less iylf] chiropteroid

ylith: ["Cure for a Ylith" by Murray Leinster] unlikely pet from Loren III

ylkci: [sickly ykcis palindrome] plague-carrying insectoid

yll: [Alb. *] 2-D pentapus or hexapus

ylor: [gaylor mondegreen] gray-green wolf-quail pegasoid

ylp: [Plymouth tuom ylp palindrome] grayish mauve tuom, see ettabtnuom

yltsahg: [ghastly yltsahg palindrome] monstrous creature

yltsahgator: [yltsahg alligator portmanteau] alligator-like predator whose bite morphs victim into yltsahg

yma: [Star Control] herd animal of Gaia, Betelguese (alpha Orionis) system

ymph: [nymph elision] wingless grasshopper-like larval insectoids

ynaur: [Welsh pysgodyn aur mondegreen] ichthyoid ancestral to goldfish

yndz: [Armenian yndzught mondegreen] pard-camel, desert quadruped ancestral to camel, leopard and giraffe

ynnep: [copper penny ynnep eppoc palindrome] bright to brownish orange eppoc

yno: [Crayola onyx yno palindrome] black creature from Crayol A system

ynx: [i-less iynx] cave-dwelling woodpecker-like ornithoid

yoake: [Monster Galaxy] 7-tailed fox-like caninoid from Libra constellation, see kyuubi

yobstrimp: ["The Gungan Frontier" by Chris McCubbin] crab-like crustacean from Jedi galaxy

yog: ["Babylon 5: TKO" by Lawrence G DiTillio] treeworm usually eaten fried; [*Creatures of the Galaxy* by Phil Brucato, Bill Smith, Rick D. Stuart, Chuck Truett] swamp ornithoid from Mimban, Jedi galaxy

yogator: [yog alligator portmanteau] alligator-like predator whose bite morphs victim into yog

yoka: [Swahili nyoka elision] serpentoid from Snowi, Nejstea system, Galaxiki galaxy

yolianpore: [Cyclopedia of Worlds] dust-like omnivores that reproduce upon eating by DNA-swapping from Conus, Arcturus (gamma Boötis) system

yona: [Cherokee] ursinoid from Tsalagi system

yong: [xong-yong mondegreen] Energon sphere with one eyespot and swimming tentacles, ancestor of xong-yong

yongary: ["Yongary, Monster of the Deep"] underground-dwelling, bipedal saurian with nosehorn, backplates that attacked Korea, Terra (alpha Zodiaci III)

yongator: [yong alligator portmanteau] alligator-like predator whose bit morphs victim into yong

yongbi: [Jap.] 4-tailed monkey

yorik: [*Creatures of the Galaxy* by Phil Brucato, Bill Smith, Rick D. Stuart, Chuck Truett] sea creature whose coral-like shell was cultivated as hull of Yuuzhan Volg ships, Jedi galaxy

york: [nyork elision] jumping mollusk

yornis: [aepyornis, genyornis mondegreens] chartreuse yellow flightless, goose-like ornithoid

yoshi: [Mario series] small bipedal dinosauroid steed with large head, short tail

yost: [xor-yost mondegreen] Energon sphere with one eyespot and swimming, ancestor of xor-yost

yot: [*There's a Wocket in My Pocket* by Theodore Seuss Geissel] 1-meter orange and magenta biped, see yottle

yottle: [*If I Ran the Zoo* by Theodore Seuss Geissel] 40-cm orange and black striped biped with tubular snout, see yot

yowie: [*Here Be Monsters almanac*] pongoid from Australia, Terra (alpha Zodiaci III)

yox: [yokes of oxen spoonerism, yak ox portmanteau] yak-headed ox-like bovinoid

yoxen: [yoke of oxen spoonerism, yak droxen portmanteau] yak-headed droxen

ypeel: [sleepy ypeels palindrome] cat-napper

yppotryll: ["Xoology" by Kittenbaker] chimera with boar's head, camel's hump, ox's legs and hooves, serpent's tail from Szurane

yraala: [nyraala elision] flailing, slimy multi-tentacled creature

yrev: [very hairy riah yrev palindrome] long-haired riah

yrgnuh: [hungry yrgnuh palindrome] voracious predator

yrreb: [-berry yrreb palindromes] purple ornithoid, see lum, psar, cimzzar

yrrebe: [Crayola blueberry yrrebe ulb palindrome] variety of ulb from Crayol A system

yrrehc: [Crayola cherry yrrehc palindrome] red ornithoid from Crayol A system, see ossolb

yrthak: [*Monster Manual* by Skip Williams, etal.] 6-m green, legless, eyeless pterodactyl-like creature with dorsal fin, short head spikes that "sees" with tongue, attacks with "sonic lance" on head

ysalamiri: [*Heir to the Empire* by Timothy Zahn] 50-centimeter, salamander-like, arboreal furry with sessile claws that grows into branches, noted for 10-meter Force-immunity from Myrkr, Jedi galaxy

ysengrinia: [*After the Dinosaurs* by Donald R. Prothero] amphicyon or beardog that in Miocene migrated to America, Terra (alpha Zodiaci III)

yt: [airyt backformation] large flightless ornithoid, see airyt

ytta: [ytta patty palindrome] food animal

yü-lung: [Chinese] half-fish dracoid

yü-lungator: [yü-lung alligator portmanteau] alligator-like predator whose bite morphs victim into yü-lung

yuckyduck: ["Darkwing Duck"] duck with photosynthetic green and sliminess of algae because of Bushroot's IQ2U

yuebird: [grue-bleen extrapolation] yellow bird that turns blue, not to be confused with bledbird, bleenbird, blellowbird, blindigobird, blioletbird, bluebird, gebird, gruebird, ruebird, vuebird, yedbird, yeenbird, yellowbird, yindigobird, or yioletbird from Ora system

yuffle: [*Ultra Klutz* by Jeff Nicholson] mutant worm-like creature with 2 arms and handlebar mustache

yugg: [Ponape Scripture] large, pale gray slug-like servants of Ythogtha and Zoth-Ommog with sucker-mouth and 6 feeding tentacles from Xoth in Taurus

yuggator: [yugg alligator portmanteau] alligator-like predator whose bite morphs victim into yugg

yûk: [pal-rai-yûk mondegreen] seaserpent-like tizheruk ancestor

yukari: [The Adventures of Buzz Lightyear: "The Yukari Imprint"] small, but very prolific, pod-laying shapeshifter that assumes the form of its "mother" (the first creature it sees upon hatching)

yuki: [Swahili nyuki elision] bee-like insectoid from Ahla, Ojikh system, Galaxiki galaxy; [Monster Galaxy] 2-headed red-and-gray ornithoid

yúl: [Hung. nyúl elision] lapoid

yulduzcha: [Uzbek. *] 2-D pentapus or hexapus

yuliböd: [Fr. Johann Martin Schleyer's Volapük] bluebird-like ornithoid from Schleyer's system

yupyak: [Outernauts] neckless, biped with large head, see yipyip

yuszi: [Hung. nyuszi elision] yúl-like lapoid

yutyrannus: [Sino-Grk. "feathered tyrant"] 10-meter tyrannosaur with feathers

yvar: [yvar gravy palindrome] long-eared, burrowing food griffinoid with both insectoidal and ornithoidal wings, related to ar and bee-eagle

ywon: [snowy ywons portmanteau] cold-adapted creature

ywonster: [ywon monster portmanteau] monstrous ywon

yzzuwyzzuf: [Crayola fuzzywuzzy yzzuwyzzuf palindrome] brownish pink ornithoid from Crayol A system

z'zzy: buzzing insect

za: [an onza, nyanza mondegreens] off-white wolf-like felinoid from Nya system

za-aat: ["The First" by Peg Robinson] little silver fish from Shadrasi's world

zaagbok: [Dut. sawhorse] animated wooden horse from Oz

zabathu: ["Pen Pals" by Hannah Louise Shearer] steed from Andor (epsilon Indi VIII)

zable: [*There's a Wocket in My Pocket* by Theodore Seuss Geissel] 60-cm short-legged, yellow and white biped

zaekon: [Bulgarian zaek-kon portmanteau] rabbit-horse, large lapoid steed

zafretti: [The Ultimate Monster Guide by Jaymond] flying, desert healer

zah: ["Liline, the Moon Girl" by Edmond Hamilton] low-gee dracoid with black scaly wings with 12-meter wingspan, barrel-shaped body, long neck, turtle-like head, red eyes, short thick legs, webbed feet

zai be: [bai ze spoonerism] shaggy quadruped

zakdir: ["Friday's Child" by D. C. Fontana] herd animal from Capella (alpha Aurigae) IV

zakkeg: [*Creatures of the Galaxy* by Phil Brucato, Bill Smith, Rick D. Stuart, Chuck Truett] large, solitary pachyderm with spikes and horns from Dxun, Jedi galaxy

zakkegator: [zakkeg alligator portmanteau] alligator-like predator whose bite morphs victim into zakkeg

zamp: [*There's a Wocket in My Pocket* by Theodore Seuss Geissel] 1-meter orange, arboreal weasel-like creature with pink crest

zamph: [Thongor series by Lin Carter] yellow-fanged, 3-tonne voracious boar-like porcoid with forehead horn, bony neck shield from Lemuria

zamzit: [Hildegard of Bingen's Lingua Ignota] peacock-like ornithoid from Lingua, Hildegard's system

zang: [Dutch zangvogel back-formation] symbiot that sings through a host ornithoid

zangator: [zang alligator portmanteau] alligator-like predator whose bite morphs victim into zang

zanggh: [gazanggh mondegreen] gray-green beastly vulture-like ornithoid

zanig: [zaniget mondegreen] predatory mountain variety of et from Pia or Touca systems

zanigator: [zanig alligator portmanteau] alligator-like predator whose bite morphs victim into zanig

zanigret: [*The Covenant of the Crown* by Howard Weinstein] predator from Kinarr mts., Zenna IV

zapod: [*After the Dinosaurs* by Donald R. Prothero] jumping mouse from Miocene

zara: [Italian zanzara back-formation] mosquitoid from Za system

zarander: [After Man by Dougal Dixon] large elephant-like pig

zard: [i-less izard] cave-dwelling reptilian

zaska: [James Cooke Brown's Loglan zaspi kangu] demondog from Logla, Brown's system

zatcher: see kai-wip

zatz-it: [*On Beyond Zebra* by Theodore Seuss Geissel] long-legged, long-necked quadruped with flat feet

zavinac: [Czech @] rolled-herring

zawyi: ["They Live Forever" by Lloyd Biggle, Jr.] milk creature of the Rualis

zazaxa: yellow-and-indigo pongoid with 25-cm retractable claws from Gizmonian Steepes (Edonian cluster II), Galaxiki galaxy

zebra seal: [Avatar: The Last Airbender: "The Boy in the Iceberg"] black-and-white zebra-striped seal

zebra squirrel: [Cloudstone] black-and-white zebra-striped squirrel

zebrhino: [zebra-rhinoceros portmanteau] rhinoceros-like equinoid with nose horn and black-and-white zebra stripes

zebrouk: [Czech zebr-brouk portmanteau] zebra-beetle, black-and-white striped insectoid

zebu: [*Dell Crossword Puzzle Dictionary*] ox from India

zech: [eikzech mondegreen] eikzech ancestor

zedonk: [zebra-donkey portmanteau] equine with both zebra and donkey characteristics

zee: [zeer backformation, chimpanzee mondegreen] small pongoid prey of zeeing (tree-felling) predators from Chimpa

zeelbra: [zebra-eel portmanteau] black-and-white striped equinoid with long, wet serpentine tail

zeer: ["The Gungan Frontier" by Chris McCubbin] camelopard that zees (fells trees) from Jedi galaxy

zeit: [Monster Galaxy] "sentient energy" like white hand with purple vapor from Leo constellation

zell: [Callisto series by Lin Carter] variant lajazell, small winged sauroid from Thanator desert

zellope: [zell antelope portmanteau] zell with antlers

zenomoglin: [Tokyo MewMew] bug-like creature that spits poison

zenu: [*Dell Crossword Puzzle Dictionary*] domesticated sheep from Africa, Terra (alpha Zodiaci III)

zeppelin: [Count Ferdinand von Zeppelin, Monster Galaxy] ornithoid with curly, green crest and blue eyes from Virgo constellation

zeppeloon: [zeppelin-balloon portmanteau, Worlds Apart: Nat. Hist. of Furaha and Earth by Souren Nyoroge] "loony" 15-meter, 200-kg, tentacled, color-changing sky-cephalopod from Furaha (alpha Phoenicis IV)

zer: [-zer mondegreens] egg-layer from Ga system in do (burrowing), friz (electric), sniz (lizard) and starga (fish) varieties

zerkee: [*Making Plans* by Cheryl Rice] ambulatory poached-eggs with vestigial wings from Vendril

zerpagon: [dranzer pagon mondegreen] egg-laying pagon-like dracoid from Dra system

zetkgee: [*The Perfect Planet* by Edward Packard] 3-horned, prolific deer-like ruminant, including mutant resistant to bitter-skinned slaif plant toxin, from Utopa (Achnar V), Gallatin quadrant

zeton: [*The Goddess of Ganymede* and Pursuit on Ganymede by Michael D. Resnick and Donald M. Grant] 7.5-meter tall brontosaur-like red-orange creature with 6 forelegs, 2 hindlegs, thin prehensile 6-meter tail from Thane's moon

Zeus eagle: ["Superman under the Red Sun"] giant eagle able to project lightning bolts from eyes

zhar: [zhar-ptitza mondegreen] zhar-ptitza ancestor

zhar-ptitza: [*Figures of Earth* by James Branch Cabell] purple bird with golden neck, red and blue tail from Acaire forest, Poictesme

zhoumy: ["When In the Course" by H. Beam Piper] yak-like ruminant from Freya

zhū què: [Chin.] see vermillion bird

zhukot: see žukot

zhy: see žy

zi: [Swahili panzi back-formation] grasshopper-like insectoid from Pa system

ziam: [maize ziam palindrome] multicolored ornithoid

ziddah: [*After Man* by Dougal Dixon] long-armed, slender-legged primate

zie: [than-zie mondegreen] turkey-like ornithoid from Tha system

ziegeier: [German Ziege-Geier portmanteau] goat-vulture with horns and goatee, carcass-eating (ziegeying) griffinoid

zilchtron: [Mad Magazine: "Flesh Garden"] horrible, palpitating, limb-ripping monster from Mong's world

ziliton: [Continuum] small, multicolored snake from Sotkaard, Galunis system, Firehorse constellation

zilitonster: [ziliton monster portmanteau] monstrous ziliton-like snake

zillo: [The Clone Wars series] large, quadruped predator with fifth "leg" between shoulder blades from Malastare, Jedi galaxy

zintal: ["A Ticket to Tranai" by Robert Sheckley] aka "desert croc", source of belt and shoe leather from Almagordo III, Southern Ridge Belt
ziporüt: [Fr. Johann Martin Schleyer's Volapük] goldfish-like ichthyoid from Schleyer's system
zir: [Maltese hazir back-formation] boar-like porcoid from Ha system
zirdzinš: [Latvian juras zirdzinš backformation] sea creature ancestral to juras and seahorse
zitidar: [Barsoom series by Edgar Rice Burroughs] large, mastodon-like herbivorous beast of burden from Mars (Sol IV)
ziuka: [Belarussian hadziuka back-formation] skunk-viper, malodorous and poisonous serpentoid from Snowi, Nejstea system, Galaxiki galaxy
ziz: [ziza (red/orange/yellow) ziz palindrome] aka "flying behemoth" red, orange and/or yellow giant ornithoid
zkon: ["The Canine That Outclassed Krypto" by Cary Bates] dog-like space creature
zkonster: [zkon monster portmanteau] monstrous space caninoid
zlard: [i-less izlard] cave-dwelling, fatty reptilian
zlock: [*There's a Wocket in My Pocket* by Theodore Seuss Geissel] 20-cm, thin, pencil-like biped with large, flame-like crest, pink and white striped neck, long nose and collar
zmajež: [Croatian zmej-jež portmanteau] dragon-hedgehog, hellfire-breathing hedgehog-like burrower
zo: [hanzo mondegreen] chiropteran from Ha system, see zo(h), zobo
zo(h): [*Dell Crossword Puzzle Dictionary*] aka zobo, zebu-yak hybrid
zobo: see zo(h)
zod: ["Secret of the Space Capsule"] alien beast
zodiolestes: [*After the Dinosaurs* by Donald R. Prothero] weasel-like carnivore that migrated in Miocene to America, Terra (alpha Zodiaci III)
zog: [*The Christmas Adventure of Space Elf Sam* by Audrey Wood] colorful, teardrop shaped creatures, used as ornaments, that hang bat-like in canyons on Zog
zogator: [zog alligator portmanteau] alligator-like predator whose bite morphs victim into zog
zoilto: ["Incompatible" by Rog Phillips] food animal of vampiric Fwoumies
zol: [The Legend of Zelda] large, red gel from Hyrule
zola: [The Legend of Zelda] fireball-spitting river creature
zolt: [gazolt mondegreen] gray-green ruminant
zólw: [Polish zólw golab back-formation] ancestor to pigeon and turtle dove
zom-bee: ["Zom-bees" by John Hafernik] not-quite-dead bee infested with unhatched zombie fly larvae
zombie fly: ["Zom-bees" by John Hafernik] fruitfly that lays its eggs in bees and paper wasps
zombie wasp: ["Zom-bees" by John Hafernik] not-quite-dead wasp infested with unhatched zombie fly larvae
zombie dog: [The Infinite War] caninoid from Adum
zomoo: [Monster Galaxy] bovinoid with L-shaped horns, blue hair infected with deadly infectious insects from Taurus constellation
zooch: greyhound-like caninoid from Betonia (Edonian cluster V), Galaxiki galaxy
zooey: [Treks Not Taken: "The Crusher in the Rye" by Steven R. Boydett] ornithoid adapted to superhurricane winds from Caulfield VII
zook: ["The Invaders from the Space Warp" by Jack Miller] short, orange, mischievous, little extradimensional creature with antennae
zool: ["See Spot Run" by Kathy Oltion] 15-cm, light blue many-tentacled creature from Gorson
zooplankton: ["animal-drifter", *The Big Bad Book of Beasts* by Michael Largo] small sea

creatures including krill, ctenophore, dinoflagellate

zorat: [Amtor series by Edgar Rice Burroughs] zebra-like steed with bovine head from Amtor (alpha Zodiaci II)

zorchton: [Mad Magazine: "Flesh Garden"] hairy, many-clawed monster from Mong's world

zorse: [zebra horse portmanteau] zebra-headed horse-like equinoid, see hebra

zoril(la): [*Dell Crossword Puzzle Dictionary*, *National Geographic Encyclopedia of Animals*] "stripped polecat" from Cape of Good Hope, S. Africa, Terra (alpha Zodiaci III)

zotuane: [*Mémoires De Sir George Wallop* by Pierre Chevalier Duplessis] fox-like creature from Aprilis, New Britain Islands

zower: [*There's a Wocket in My Pocket* by Theodor Seuss Geissel] 1.5-meter red-brown, long-eared canine

zubrouk: [Czech zubr-brouk portmanteau] bison-beetle, large, horned, maned insectoid, related to bugalo

žukot: [Belarussian žuk-kot portmanteau] beetle-cat, carapaced felinoid

zuxu: [*Creatures of the Galaxy* by Phil Brucato, Bill Smith, Rick D. Stuart, Chuck Truett] carnivorous lungfish-like ichthyoid with large, padded, prehensile fins from Ganlihk, Jedi galaxy

zvaignīte: [Latv. *] 2-D pentapus or hexapus

zvezdico: [Sloven. *] 2-D pentapus or hexapus

zvezdochka: Rus. *] 2-D pentapus or hexapus

zvjezdica: [Croat. *] 2-D pentapus or hexapus

zwim: [*The New Dinosaurs* by Dougal Dixon] aka naremys, 30-cm, insectovorous amphibian with webbed feet, long, flat tail

žy: [Belarussian žyrat mondegreen] giraffe-like rodentoid

zyglophodon: [*After the Dinosaurs* by Donald R. Prothero] mastodont

zygor: ["Supergirl's Choice of Doom" by Leo Dorfman] dangerous animal, last died in Kandorian zoo, from Krypton, Rao system

zylo: ["11001001" by Maurice Hurley and Robert Lewin] egglayer

zyzzyva: cicada-like weevil from S. America, Terra (alpha Zodiaci III)

Zzinbriizi jackal: [*Prime Time* by Mike Tucker] jackal-like caninoid augmented into cyban weapons by Fleshsmiths from Zzinbriizi